# THE COMPLETE GUIDE TO CREATING ENDURING FESTIVALS

# The Wiley Event Management Series

Series Editor: Dr. Joe Goldblatt, CSEP

*The Complete Guide to Creating Enduring Festivals*
by Dr. Ros Derrett, OAM

*Special Events: Creating and Sustaining a New World for Celebration, Seventh Edition*
by Dr. Joe Goldblatt, FRSA

*The Sports Event Management and Marketing Playbook, Second Edition*
by Frank Supovitz and Bobby Goldwater

*Event Marketing: How to Successfully Promote Events, Festivals, Conventions, and Expositions, Second Edition*
by C.A. Preston and Leonard H. Hoyle

*Ethics and Corporate Social Responsibility in the Meetings and Events Industry*
by Elizabeth Henderson, CMP, CMM, M.E. Des. and Mariela McIlwraith, CMP, CMM, MBA

*Professional Event Coordination, Second Edition*
by Julia Rutherford Silvers, CSEP

*The Complete Guide to Greener Meetings and Events*
by Samuel deBlanc Goldblatt

*The Complete Guide to Careers in Special Events: Steps Towards Success!*
by Gene Columbus

*The Complete Guide to Event Entertainment and Production*
by Mark Sonder, MM, CSEP

*Dictionary of Event Management, Second Edition*
by Dr. Joe Goldblatt, CSEP and Kathleen S. Nelson, CSEP

*Corporate Event Project Management*
by William O'Toole and Phyllis Mikolaitis

*Event Risk Management and Safety*
by Peter E. Tarlow, Ph.D.

*Event Sponsorship*
by Bruce E. Skinner and Vladimir Rukavina

*The Guide to Successful Destination Management*
by Pat Schaumann, CMP, CSEP

*Art of the Event: Complete Guide to Designing and Decorating Special Events*
by James C. Monroe, CMP, CSEP

*Global Meetings and Exhibitions*
by Carol Krugman, CMP, CMM, and Rudy R. Wright, CMP

# THE COMPLETE GUIDE TO CREATING ENDURING FESTIVALS

Dr. Ros Derrett, OAM

WILEY

This book is printed on acid-free paper. ∞

Copyright © 2016 by John Wiley & Sons, Inc. All rights reserved.

Published by John Wiley & Sons, Inc., Hoboken, New Jersey
Published simultaneously in Canada

No part of this publication may be reproduced, stored in a retrieval system, or transmitted in any form or by any means, electronic, mechanical, photocopying, recording, scanning, or otherwise, except as permitted under Section 107 or 108 of the 1976 United States Copyright Act, without either the prior written permission of the Publisher, or authorization through payment of the appropriate per-copy fee to the Copyright Clearance Center, Inc., 222 Rosewood Drive, Danvers, MA 01923, 978-750-8400, fax 978-646-8600, or on the web at www.copyright.com. Requests to the Publisher for permission should be addressed to the Permissions Department, John Wiley & Sons, Inc., 111 River Street, Hoboken, NJ 07030, 201-748-6011, fax 201-748-6008, or online at www.wiley.com/go/permissions.

Evaluation copies are provided to qualified academics and professionals for review purposes only, for use in their courses during the next academic year. These copies are licensed and may not be sold or transferred to a third party. Upon completion of the review period, please return the evaluation copy to Wiley. Return instructions and a free of charge shipping label are available at www.wiley.com/go/returnlabel. Outside of the United States, please contact your local representative.

Limit of Liability/Disclaimer of Warranty: While the publisher and author have used their best efforts in preparing this book, they make no representations or warranties with respect to the accuracy or completeness of the contents of this book and specifically disclaim any implied warranties of merchantability or fitness for a particular purpose. No warranty may be created or extended by sales representatives or written sales materials. The advice and strategies contained herein may not be suitable for your situation. You should consult with a professional where appropriate. Neither the publisher nor author shall be liable for any loss of profit or any other commercial damages, including but not limited to special, incidental, consequential, or other damages.

For general information on our other products and services, or technical support, please contact our Customer Care Department within the United States at 800-762-2974, outside the United States at 317-572-3993 or fax 317-572-4002.

Wiley publishes in a variety of print and electronic formats. Some content that appears in print may not be available in electronic books. For more information about Wiley products, visit our website at www.wiley.com.

*Library of Congress Cataloging-in-Publication Data:*

Derrett, Rosalyn M.
 The complete guide to creating enduring festivals / Rosalyn M. Derrett.
— 1
   pages cm. — (The Wiley event management series)
 Includes index.
 ISBN 978-1-118-29931-9 (hardback)
 1. Festivals—Planning. 2. Festivals—Management. 3. Festivals—Social aspects. I. Title.
 GT3930.D44 2015
 394.26068—dc23
                         2014049368

Printed in the United States of America
10  9  8  7  6  5  4  3  2  1

Vision of festival, revisiting and refreshing (*cont.*)
   positive, accentuating, 320–21
   refreshment, preparing for, 305–7
   revitalized festivals, designing, 303–4
   staff commitment, leveraging, 305
Visiting friends and relatives (VFRs), 108, 112
Visitors. *See* Patrons
VisitScotland, 234
Visual equipment, 311t
Vivid Sydney, 6t
Volunteer nonprofit (or for-profit) community-based festival committees, 74
Volunteers, 85–87, 148–49
   community festivals and, 86–87
   mementoes, 208t
   resource requirements and, 148–49
   volunteer program, managing, 85–86
Vox Pop, 133t

Walker, B., 32
Wang, D., 345
Wastewise event, 164
Water, M., 297
WaterFire, 261
Waterfront Festival, 166

Watt, D. C., 143
Watts-Jones, M., 346
Weather, 161
Website, 245
   interaction, 283t
   marketing plan and, 232–33
We Did This, 155
Weiss, J., 218
Welcome
   delivery of traditional, 210
   service quality and, 203
Well-being, 41, 42, 60–61
*What Works: Success in Stressful Times* (McRae), 27–28
Whyte, W. H., 345, 350
Winterlude, 254
Womadelaide Festival, 175, 293
WOMAD (World of Music, Arts, and Dance), 4t, 187t, 264
Woodford Folk Festival, 87–88, 114, 297, 352
Word Alliance, 136
WordPress, 238
*World Cities Culture Report* (BOP Consulting), 212, 250
World Conservation Union of the United Nations Commission on Sustainable Development, 166

World Cup, 10
World Festival, 141
World Festival Network, 264–65
World Fringe Congress 2012, 271
World Grits Festival, 189t
World Tourism Cities Federation (WTCF), 256
Worldviews, shared, 50t
Worthy Farm, 166
WOW factor, 204–5
Writers' Festival, Sydney, 142
Writers' festivals, global, 135, 136–37
WTCF. *See* World Tourism Cities Federation (WTCF)

Yahoo!, 239
Yeoman, I., 254, 331
Yield, increasing, 111
Young, S. F., 279
YouTube, 19, 25, 132, 135, 192, 204, 234, 236, 239, 240, 242, 263, 283t, 321, 342, 345

Zeithaml, V. A., 202
Zhaolin Garden, 264
Zukin, S., 254

*Stretch Your Horizons, Stay Curious*, 201
Subculture, buying behavior and, 130, 130f
Success, secrets of enduring, 24–45
    how festival organizations function, 28–30
    resilient and successful festivals, 25–28
    resilient festival practices, 31–39
Success factors
    attributes of leading festival city and, 35–37
    evaluating, 38, 39t
    lessons on, 27–28
    links with festival industry, maintaining, 38
    recognizing, 26–27
Summer Sundae, 166
Sundance Film Festival, 92–93
Sung, H. K., 348
Sunrise Celebration, 166
Suppliers, needs of, 147
Survey
    definition of, 283t
    sample of, 284–85t
Survival, 30
    chances of, 332–33
Sustainability, 30, 163
    creativity and, 354
    of cultural sector, 287–88t
    definition of, 30
    in environmental context, 163
    festival management implications, 128t
    in future festivals' mosaic, 330f
    in globally competitive festival mosaic, 250f
    policy, 148
    Road to Sustainability, 324–25
Swell Sculpture Festival, 180, 183, 204
SWOT analysis, 177, 306, 306t
Sydney Biennale signage, 137
Sydney Festival, 141–42, 342
Sydney Festival First Night, 141–42
Sydney Fringe, 266t
Sydney Gay and Lesbian Mardi Gras, 61
Sydney Harbour Foreshore Authority, 142
Sydney Opera House, 201

Tagging, 240
Tallinn Song Festival, 339
Tangibles, service quality and, 202, 203, 278
Taxation, 75
Taylor, L., 143

Teams, 73–95. *See also* Volunteers
    building, 82–83
    innovative, characteristics of, 175
    internal and external team mosaic, 74f
    organization frameworks, 74–77
    popular festivals, origins of, 77–88
    resilience in, 82–83
    teamwork in, 342
Technology
    creativity and, 181–82, 182t
    FIST Model, 345–47
    in PESTEL framework, 332
    trends in, 128t, 310–12, 311t
TED program, 313
Templates, 314
    risk analysis, 159–60t
    schedule and action plan, 160t
Ten Days on the Island, 187t
Tennessee Williams/New Orleans Literary Festival, 136
Tension, 125, 125f
Tension fabrics, 182t
Terracini, L., 352–54
Tet Nguyen Dan Festival of the First Day of the Lunar New Year, 4t
Thanksgiving, 4t
Theoretical frameworks for sharing messages, 231t
This Is Not Art Festival (TiNA), 191
Thorne, S., 258
*Thundering Hooves* report (AEA Consulting), 35
Thunder Over Louisville, 289
Ticketing, 162–63
Tilley, S., 234
Time, in FIST Model, 340, 340t
Timing, appropriate, 35
TiNA. *See* This Is Not Art Festival (TiNA)
T in the Park (TITP), 77t, 109t, 211
TITP. *See* T in the Park (TITP)
Tobin, C., 223
Toffler, A., 303
Tourism, 347–49
    boosterism and, 290–91
    component, 43
    creativity and innovation, 348
    destination image, 347–48
    FIST Model, 347–49
    food for thought, 348–49
    outreach, 348
Tourism and Community Event Funding program, 69
Traditions of light: Hanukkah, 6t

Traffic, pressure from, 57
Transformational creativity, 176, 177f
Transience, 2
Transparency, 276
Transport, 162
Travel blogs, 347
Trends, 188
Triple J Unearthed Splendour in the Grass Program, 192
Tropfest, 93
Tsai, S., 141–42
Tuan, Y.-F., 351
Tumblr, 237
Turner, V., 351
Twigiff, 235
Twitter, 186, 234, 235, 236, 238, 239, 240, 241, 246, 283t

Ubud Writers' and Readers' Festival, 136
UEFA European Championships, 288
UFO Festival, 189t
UGC. *See* User-generated content (UGC)
UK Manchester Jazz Festival, 351
Unique selling proposition (USP), 38, 133, 177
United States Association of Fringe Festivals, 266t
Urban regeneration, 64
User-generated content (UGC), 240
USP. *See* Unique selling proposition (USP)

Vance, L., 297–99
Vancouver International Writers' and Readers' Festival, 136
Van Zon, C., 323
Variable costs, 154
VEIC. *See* Victoria Events Industry Council (VEIC)
Venice Biennale, 138t
V Festival, 211
VFRs. *See* Visiting friends and relatives (VFRs)
Victoria Events Industry Council (VEIC), 34t
Vimeo, 234
VIPs, mementoes for, 208t
Vision of festival, revisiting and refreshing, 302–27
    change, managing, 304–5
    external environments, reacting to, 307–17
    failure, avoiding, 317–20
    festival review mosaic, 303f

Rowling, J. K., 190
Royal Opera House at Covent Garden, 316
RSS. *See* Really Simple Syndication (RSS)
Russell, M., 323

Safe environment, creating, 341–42
St. James Ethics Centre, 201
St. Lucia's Day, Sweden, 6t
SALA Festival, 293
Sales, securing, 230t
Salt, D., 32
Salzburg Festival, 109t
Sambadrome, 9
Sankey, E., 338
Sante Fe Opera Festival, 261
Sao Paulo Biennial, 138t
Sapporo Snow Festival, 264
Sarasota for Free, 175
Satisfaction, 126–29, 276
 arts attendance journey, 129
 consumer orientation, 128
 consumption analysis, 129
 decision making, 129
 environmental scans, 127–28, 128t
Saturnalia, 2–3
Sawyer, K., 175, 176
Schedule and action plan templates, 160t
Schmader, S., 219–20, 291
Schmitt, B., 201
*Science of Human Innovation: Explaining Creativity, The* (Sawyer), 176
Scrupulous financial acquittal, 276
Search engine optimization (SEO), 240
*Secret River, The,* 353
Security, service quality and, 203
Seifert, S. C., 320
Self-appraisal, defined, 280t
Self-concept, buying behavior and, 130f, 131
Seligman, M., 208, 209
Sense of place, 63–65, 64f, 66, 214
SEO. *See* Search engine optimization (SEO)
Service delivery aspect of festival-making, 199
Service factors, 202–3
Service provision, creativity and, 178t
Service quality, 278
SERVQUAL, 203, 278
Settings, creativity and, 178t
Shakespeare, W., 51
Shambala Festival, 166
Shared experience, 125, 125f, 126

Shared good-practice objectives for, 111–12
Sharjah Biennial, 138t
Sheehy, B., 323
Shenandoah Valley Music Festival, 39t
Shepherd, Liz, 244–46
Shwedagon Pagoda in Yangon, 7
SIG. *See* Special interest group (SIG)
Signage, 65, 122, 124, 126, 132, 137
Silvers, J., 81–82, 91, 198
Singapore Writers' Festival Biannual, 137
Sites
 creativity and, 180–81
 selection of, 64
Ski Festival, 264
Skyscanner, 234
SMART objectives, 35, 227
SMO. *See* Social media optimization (SMO)
Social capital
 bonding and bridging, 262
 cultural indicators of, 286, 286f, 287t
Social class, buying behavior and, 130, 130f
Social community, 59–60
Social factors
 influencing buying behavior, 130, 130f, 131
 in PESTEL framework, 332
Social implications of festivals, 62, 62t
Social media, 75, 132, 233–39
 challenges of, 236
 Coachella Music and Arts Festival and, 240–43
 dynamic online presence, establishing, 235
 for festivals, 236
 marketing through, 234–35
 rules for using, 235
 uptake of new approaches, 237
Social media optimization (SMO), 240
Social networking, 132, 133, 336
Social responsibility, community, 56–57
Sociopsychological motivational domains, 11–13, 12f
Software packages, 314
Sónar, International Festival of Advanced Music and New Media Art, 78t
Son et Lumiere and digital light projections, 6t
Songkran festival, 17–18
 contemporary activities in, 18
 traditional activities in, 17–18
South by Southwest (SXSW), 233

Space, in FIST Model, 340, 340t
Special interest festivals, 74
Special interest group (SIG), 168
Splendour Arts program, 192
Splendour Forum, 192
Splendour in the Grass, 114, 192–93
 Buskers Stage, 192
 environmental commitment, 193
 giving program, 193
 Global Village, 192–93
 jobs and other income-generating activities, 193
 music, 192
 Splendour Arts program, 192
 Splendour Forum, 192
 Splendour Kidz Club, 192
 Triple J Unearthed Splendour in the Grass Program, 192
 vision of, 193
Splendour Kidz Club, 192
Spoleto Festival USA, 310
Sponsors, ceremony/ritual and, 210, 211
Sponsorship, 108, 110, 245
Spotify, 238
Spowart, J., 91
Staff, 83, 84, 148–49
 commitment, leveraging, 305
 responsibilities, 79t
Staging, 311t
Stakeholders, 1–2, 2f, 13, 14, 15, 36, 103, 103f, 105–7t, 205–9
 communication with, 111–12
 elements of festival experience and, 206t
 global scenarios, 335–36
 mementoes and, 207, 208t
 quality of life and, 208–9
 roles of, 105–7t
Standon Calling, 166
Starlight Parade, 291
StartSomeGood, 155
State Library of Queensland, 139
State-managed festivals, role of civic authorities and, 290
State-type tie, 337
Statuses, buying behavior and, 130f, 131
Stebbins, R., 200
Steinbeck Festival, 136
Stern, M., 320
Strategic planning, 147–48
 marketing, 229f
Strategy
 long-term, 35
 setting, 250–51
Stress, 82

# INDEX

Promise, delivering on, 246
Promotion, 230t
Promotional marketing, 134
Prosperity, elements of, 30
Psychological factors influencing buying behavior, 130f, 131
Public engagement, 36
Public sectors' role in success, 37
Pukkelpop Music Festival, 161
Pulizzi, J., 232
Purification, rites of, 209
Purple Forge, 186
Putnam, R. D., 59

QFF. See Queensland Folk Federation's (QFF)
QPAC. See Queensland Performing Arts Centre (QPAC)
Qualitative research methods, defined, 281t
Quality
 of festival, 257, 333, 333–34t
 investing in, 36
 of life, 208–9
 service, 278
Quantitative research methods, defined, 281t
Quebec City Winter Carnival, 264
Queen Margaret University's International Center for the Study of Planned Events (ICSPE), 316
Queen's Day (Amsterdam, Netherlands), 3, 4t
Queensland Art Gallery, 139
Queensland Cultural Centre, 139
Queensland Folk Federation's (QFF), 297
Queensland Museum, 139
Queensland Music Festival, 353–54
Queensland Performing Arts Centre (QPAC), 139–40
Questions
 asking, 283–85
 in risk management, 160
Queuing theory, 122
Quinn, B., 55, 348
Quinn, J. B., 75
Quirky festival options, 188, 189t

Radio frequency identification (RFID), 237, 241
Radiohead concert, 161
*Raison d'etre*, 35
Ralston, L., 203
Raymond, C., 258

Readers' festivals, 135
Really Simple Syndication (RSS), 239, 240
Record management, 279–80
Recover equilibrium, 12
Recycle, 163–64
Redden, N., 323
Redford, R., 91–93
Reenvisioning, approach to, 309
Reference group, buying behavior and, 130, 130f
Refreshment, in festival model, 343t
Refreshment, preparing for, 305–7
 ideas and issues, 306, 307
 pace of change, 307
 SWOT analysis, 306, 306t
Regional festivals as lens for resilience, 40–43
 cultural resilience, reflecting on, 43
 festival tourism component, 43
 governance, 41, 42f
 participation, 41
 resilience component, 42–43
 well-being component, 41, 42
Reis, D., 191
Relationship marketing, 134–35
Relationships, reassessing, 310
Relationship trajectory, 102f
Reliability, service quality and, 202, 203, 278
Remembered life, 2
Reporting, defined, 280t
Research, 152–53
Resilience
 challenges, commitment and collaboration, 26, 27f
 community and, 31–32, 60t
 component, 42–43
 cultural, reflecting on, 43
 defined, 30
 evidence for, gathering, 35–38
 implementation tasks, 26
 resilient festivals' mosaic, 25f
 strategy for, 32–35, 33–34t
 in teams, building, 82–83
*Resilience Thinking* (Walker and Salt), 32
Resonance, personal, 125f, 126
Resourcefulness, 145–71
 defined, 146
 environmental festival plan, 163–66
 external partners, 150–53
 festival resource mosaic, 145f
 financing the festival, 153–55
 operational considerations, 161–63
 project management, 156–58

resource requirements, assessing, 146–49
risk management, 158–61
Resource requirements, assessing, 146–49
 customer loyalty, 148
 practice principles and strategic planning, 147–48
 staff and volunteers, 148–49
 sustainability policy, 148
Resources, 36, 75
Responsibilities of boards and committees of management, 79t
Responsiveness, service quality and, 202, 203, 278
Return on investment (ROI), 232
Reuse, 163–64
Reversal, rites of, 209
Revitalized festivals, designing, 303–4
RFID. See Radio frequency identification (RFID)
Richards, G., 254, 258, 351
Riddle, P., 307
Rigging, 311t
Rio de Janeiro (Carnival), 9
*Rise of the Creative Class Revisited, The* (Florida), 176, 177
Risk analysis templates, 159–60t
Risk management, 158–61
 major issues, examples of, 160–61
 questions, 160
 risk analysis templates, 159t
 schedule and action plan templates, 160t
 weather, 161
Ritchie, B. J. R., 251
Ritual and ceremony. See Ceremony and ritual
Ritual and spectacle, 260–66
 globalization, 263–65
 international recognition, 265
 open-source festival content, 265–66, 266t
"Road to Sustainability," 324–25
Robinson, M., 24, 75
Rock 'n' Roll Portland Half Marathon, 291–92
Rocks Aroma Festival, 142
ROI. See Return on investment (ROI)
Roles, buying behavior and, 130f, 131
Roosevelt, T., 103
Roper, T., 166
Rose Cup Races, 291
Rose Festival Foundation, 291
Roskilde, 148

# INDEX

Marketing plan, 143, 228–33
　benefits of, 228
　community events, 245
　effective, 36
　Internet, 232–33
　objectives, 228
　print, 231–32
　sharing, 229–31t
　strategic, 229f
Market research, monitoring, 111–12
Market saturation, 318
Mary Arden's Farm, 51
Mashup, 240
Maslow, A. H., 30
Mathew, V., 251
McBride, T., 293
McIntyre, M. H., 132
McIver, R., 2
McKay, S. L., 11–13, 12f
McMaster, B., 323
McRae, H., 27–28, 255
Meaningfulness, in festival model, 343t
Media, Entertainment and Arts
　　Alliance, 338
Media connection, 231t
Media coverage, 283t
Media platforms, 223–47
　audiences, reaching, 224–25
　communication, 225–28
　content management systems,
　　237–40
　marketing plan, 228–33
　meaningful media relationship
　　mosaic, 224f
　social media, 233–37
Media support, 37
Meek, G., 244–46
Meetings, 83
Mega events, 10, 68, 168
Melbourne Fringe Festival, 266t
Melbourne International Comedy
　　Festival, 141
Melbourne Writers Festival, 136
Membership, sense of, 50t
Meme, 240
Mementoes, 207, 208t
Memorable festival experiences,
　　elements of, 206t
Memory, ceremony/ritual and, 214
Mendip District Council, 289
Message boards, 234
Metropolitan Planning Council of
　　Chicago, 350
Microblogging, 240
Middleton, V. T. C., 231t
Middleton, W., 339

Miles, S., 336
Mintzberg, H., 75
Mobile staging, 182t
M1 Singapore Fringe Festival, 266t
Monitoring
　coordinated processes of, 37–38
　defined, 280t
　evaluation and, 280 (See also
　　Evaluation)
Monterey Jazz Festival, 39t
Montreal Just For Laughs Comedy
　　Festival, 33t
Morrison, A., 231t
Morrow, C., 43
Mossop, A., 201
Motivation
　buying behavior and, 130f, 131
　of current and potential audience,
　　assessment of, 132–33, 133t
Mud Men at the Goroka Festival, 351
Mumford and Sons, 260
Museum Mile Festival, 139

Naming festivals, 64
Narratives, ritual, 209
National Young Writers' Festival, 191
Nelson, K., 91
Networking, 50t, 55, 56–57, 118,
　　238–39
　community social responsibility,
　　56–57
　inclusion and exclusion, 57
　internal and external relationships,
　　55, 56f
　locals, respect for, 57
　partners in projects, 57
　program design and development, 57
　traffic, people, noise, and
　　overindulgence, pressure
　　from, 57
Networks, 238–39, 336–37
　affiliations, shared
　　memberships, 337
　formal, 336
　informal, 337
　social, 336
Network theory, 337
New Italy Anniversary Celebrations, 69
New York City's Metropolitan
　　Opera, 316
Nimbin Aquarius Festival, 14
Nimbin Cannabis Law Reform Rally,
　　61–62
Nimbin Mardi Grass, 61–62
Noble, P., 43–44, 323
Noise, pressure from, 57

Northern Ireland Tourist Board, 257
Novak-Leonard, J. L., 127
Novelty, in festival model, 343t
Novelty inflatables, 182t
Novelty/regression, 12

Observation and participation, 312–13
Occupation, buying behavior and, 131
Ogilvy, D., 231t
Oktoberfest (Munich, Germany), 4t
Olympic and Paralympic Games, 148
Olympic Games, 10, 184, 185, 194
Online media marketing, 231t
Opening Ceremony of the Olympic
　　Games, 184, 185, 194
Open-source festival content,
　　265–66, 266t
Opera Australia, 215, 352–54
Opera on the Lake festival, 215
Operational considerations, 161–63
　communication, 162
　destination marketing, 162
　health services, 162
　individual care, 161
　ticketing, 162–63
　transport, 162
Organization
　environments that influence, 28
　experience, ceremony/ritual
　　and, 212
　external and internal organizational
　　pressures, 28, 29f
　function of, 28–30
　mementoes for, 208t
　organizational survival, features of,
　　29, 29–30t
　structures, 76f
　visions, missions, and objectives of,
　　33–34t
Organization frameworks, 74–77
　adaptive skills, 75
　founders of festival, 76–77
　models for, 74
　participants inside festival
　　organization, 76f
　resources, 75
Organizer, festival, 84
O'Toole, B., 214
O'Toole, W., 91, 167–68
Ottawa Bluesfest, 254
Ottawa Fringe Festival, 266t
Our Lady of Mount Carmel
　　Society, 39t
Outcomes, defined, 281t
Out of the Box Festival, 139–40
Outputs, defined, 281t

Outsourcing, 317
  in-house *vs.*, 289
Overindulgence, pressure from, 57
OzAsia Festival, 293

Packaging, 231t
Palio in the Piazza del Campo, 262, 263
Palmer, R., 254, 351
Parasuraman, A., 202, 278
Participant observation, 283t
Participants inside festival organization, 76f
Participatory evaluation, 276–77
Partnerships, 96–118. *See also* Networking
  arrangements, scoping, 118
  assessment of, 104–8, 104t
  ceremony/ritual and, 210
  components of, 98–104
    collaboration and cooperation, 99
    commitment, 98
    communication, 99
    community engagement, 101
    competitors, 100
    conflict resolution, 100
    consequences, 102
    consultation, 98
    content, 98–99
    context, 98
    contracts and controls, 100
    contribution, 101
    corporate social responsibility, 102
    creativity and innovation, 99–100
    customers, 100–101
    economy, 101
  destination drivers and, 255–56
  establishing, 97
  examples of, 109f
  external, 150–53
  festivals as, in cultural tourism, 110–13
  global scenarios, 337
  monitoring, 108
  partnership mosaic, 97f
  relationship trajectory, 102f
  sponsors as, 108, 110
  stakeholders as, 103, 103f, 105–7t
Passage, rites of, 209
Patrons, 19–20
  distribution of visitors, increasing, 111
  encouraging year-round, 111
  mementoes for, 208t
  needs of, 147

  pressure from, 57
  repeat, increasing, 111
  too many, 339
Peat's Ridge Sustainable Arts and Music Festival, 338
Peerfunding, 155
Pegasus Parade, 289
PEN World Voices Festival of International Literature, 136
People. *See* Patrons
Perception, buying behavior and, 130f, 131
"The Perfect Stage," 33t
Performance management of festivals, assessing, 295–96
PERMA, 208
Personal factors influencing buying behavior, 130f, 131
Personal feedback, 283t
Personality, buying behavior and, 130f, 131
PESTEL framework, 331–32
  economic factors in, 332
  environmental factors in, 332
  legal factors in, 332
  political factors in, 331–32
  social factors in, 332
  technological factors in, 332
Pew Partnership for Civic Change, 58
Phii Ta Khon, 209
Photobooth festival, 191
Photo booths, 182t
Pilgrimages, 7
Pine, B., 126, 142, 200, 203
Pinterest, 238, 239
Place
  community legacies, 65
  festivals and, 64–65
  host community landmarks, 65
  implications for, 65t
  livability features, 65
  logos and brands in destinations, 65
  naming festivals, 64
  sense of, 63–65, 64f, 66, 214
  signage, 65
  site selection, 64
  urban regeneration, 64
Placeless festivals, 259–60
Place-making, 258–59, 350–51
  importance of, 350
  needs provided by, 350
  principles of, 350–51
  temporary and transient, 351
Planning. *See also* Marketing plan
  long-term, 35
  preparing, 253, 254–55

Planting Festival, 297
Policy, preparing, 253, 254–55
Political factors in PESTEL framework, 331–32
Political situation, 128t
Political will and independence, 36
Polson, John, 91–93
Popular festivals, origins of, 77–88
  boards, 79–80, 79t
  CEO, 80–82
  community festivals and volunteers, 86–87
  examples of, 77–78t
  festival organizer, 84
  job satisfaction, concept of, 87, 88
  meetings, 83
  staff, 83, 84
  teams, building, 82–83
  volunteers, 85–86
Porter, M., 231t
Portfolio approach, 335
Portland Rose Festival, 77t, 109t, 291–92, 324–25
Positioning, 256
Positive, accentuating, 320–21
Postcard from edge of, 349
Poster competition, 135
Post-evaluation, 293–94
  results, reporting, 294
Post-event issues, 182
Powerful Thinking, 166
Pozible in Australia, 155
Practice principles, 147–48
Practitioners dealing with festival resilience. *See* From Inside the Mosaic
Print, marketing plan in, 231–32
Print collateral, 246
Private investment in festival programs, 74
PR/media, 245–46
Product demonstrations, 98
Product development, monitoring, 111–12
Profile of festival, 31, 279, 281, 289, 299, 315, 320, 346
Programming, focused and innovative, 36
Programs, 342
  creativity and, 178–79
  design and development, 57
Project management, 156–58
  actual *vs.* planned recording and reporting form, 158t
  project definition form, 157t
  templates, 157, 157–58t

# DEDICATION

*To the memory of my mother
Anne Marie Hayden, OAM,
and to my husband,
Peter Derrett, OAM*

# CONTENTS

Foreword, Dr. Donald Getz — ix
Series Editor Foreword, Dr. Joe Goldblatt — xi
Preface — xiii
Acknowledgments — xxi

**CHAPTER 1** The Nature and Role of Festivals — 1

    The Nature and Role of Festivals — 2
    Historic Perspective on Communal Creativity and Celebration — 7
    The Roles for Festivals — 13
    Summary of Festival Essentials — 14
    Festival Ideas and Issues — 21
    Festival Focus Activities — 22
    Suggested Reading — 23

**CHAPTER 2** Secrets of Enduring Festival Success — 24

    Resilient and Successful Festivals — 25
    How Festival Organizations Function — 28
    Resilient Festival Practices — 31
    Festival Ideas and Issues — 45
    Festival Focus Activities — 45
    Suggested Reading — 46

**CHAPTER 3** Festivals Connect to Community and Place — 47

    Festivals Working with Communities — 48
    What Is Community? — 49
    Festival Focus: Community Consultation and Communication — 54
    Community Capital and Sense of Community — 59
    Festival Contribution to Well-Being — 60
    Building Community Culture — 61
    What Are the Social Implications of Festivals? — 62
    Festival Ideas and Issues — 69
    Festival Focus Activities — 71
    Suggested Reading — 72

**CHAPTER 4** Building and Nourishing the Festival Team — 73

    Festival Organization Frameworks — 74
    Origins of Popular Festivals — 77
    Festival Ideas and Issues — 94
    Festival Focus Activities — 94
    Suggested Reading — 95

**CHAPTER 5** Building Partnerships That Work — 96

    Establishing Festival Partnerships — 97
    Partnership Components — 98
    Festival Partnerships — 104
    Festival Ideas and Issues — 116
    Festival Focus Activities — 117
    Suggested Reading — 119

**CHAPTER 6** Alignment with the Target Audience — 120

    Audience Relationships — 121
    The Festival Experience — 121
    Festival Satisfaction — 126

## CONTENTS

|   |   |   |
|---|---|---|
| | Major Factors Influencing Buying Behavior | 130 |
| | Establishing the Best Fit | 131 |
| | Marketing Mechanisms and Reach | 134 |
| | Festival Ideas and Issues | 142 |
| | Festival Focus Activities | 142 |
| | Suggested Reading | 143 |
| **CHAPTER 7** | **Festival Resourcefulness** | **145** |
| | Assessing Festival Resource Requirements | 146 |
| | External Partners | 150 |
| | Financing the Festival | 153 |
| | Project Management | 156 |
| | Risk Management | 158 |
| | Operational Considerations | 161 |
| | Environmental Festival Plan | 163 |
| | Festival Ideas and Issues | 169 |
| | Festival Focus Activities | 169 |
| | Suggested Reading | 171 |
| **CHAPTER 8** | **Ensuring Creativity at All Levels of Festival-Making** | **173** |
| | Start with the Heart | 174 |
| | Explaining Creativity | 175 |
| | The Business of Creativity | 184 |
| | Festival Creativity Trajectory | 186 |
| | Festival Ideas and Issues | 195 |
| | Festival Focus Activities | 195 |
| | Suggested Reading | 196 |
| **CHAPTER 9** | **Delivering Memorable Festival Experiences** | **198** |
| | Memorable Festival Experiences | 199 |
| | Service Factors | 202 |
| | Experience Factors | 203 |
| | The WOW Factor | 204 |
| | Stakeholder Factors | 205 |
| | The Role of Ceremony and Ritual | 209 |
| | Challenges | 215 |
| | Festival Ideas and Issues | 220 |
| | Festival Focus Activities | 221 |
| | Suggested Reading | 221 |
| **CHAPTER 10** | **Festival Media Platforms** | **223** |
| | Reaching Festival Audiences | 224 |
| | Communication | 225 |
| | Marketing Plan | 228 |
| | Introduction to Social Media for Festival Engagement | 233 |
| | Content Management Systems | 237 |
| | Festival Ideas and Issues | 246 |
| | Festival Focus Activities | 247 |
| | Suggested Reading | 248 |
| **CHAPTER 11** | **Maintaining a Global Competitive Edge** | **249** |
| | Setting Festival Strategy | 250 |
| | Destination Competitiveness | 251 |
| | Festivals as Destination Drivers | 252 |
| | Ritual and Spectacle | 260 |
| | Challenges for Globally Competitive Destinations Hosting Festivals | 266 |
| | Festival Ideas and Issues | 272 |
| | Festival Focus Activities | 272 |
| | Suggested Reading | 274 |
| **CHAPTER 12** | **Documenting, Monitoring, and Evaluating Festivals** | **275** |
| | Evaluating Festival Endurance | 276 |
| | Evaluation Plans | 282 |
| | Cultural Indicators | 286 |
| | Economic Impacts | 289 |
| | After the Evaluation, What Then? | 293 |
| | Understanding a Festival Legacy | 294 |
| | Festival Ideas and Issues | 299 |
| | Festival Focus Activities | 299 |
| | Suggested Reading | 300 |
| **CHAPTER 13** | **Revisiting and Refreshing the Festival Vision** | **302** |
| | Designing Revitalized Festivals | 303 |
| | Managing Change | 304 |
| | Preparing for Refreshment | 305 |
| | React to External Environments | 307 |
| | Avoiding Festival Failure | 317 |
| | Accentuate the Positive | 320 |
| | Festival Ideas and Issues | 326 |
| | Festival Focus Activities | 327 |
| | Suggested Reading | 328 |
| **CHAPTER 14** | **The Future of Festivals** | **329** |
| | Addressing the Future of Festivals | 330 |
| | Global Scenarios | 331 |
| | Too Many … Choices | 338 |
| | The FIST Model | 340 |
| | Postcard from the Edge of the Future | 349 |
| | Festival Ideas and Issues | 354 |
| | Festival Focus Activities | 354 |
| | Suggested Reading | 355 |
| | Abbreviations | 357 |
| | Glossary | 359 |
| | Index | 365 |

# FOREWORD: A PERSONAL PERSPECTIVE

*The Complete Guide to Creating Enduring Festivals* deals with an extremely important issue in the field of event management: Can festivals and events be created or managed to endure? First, I do not think "enduring" means permanent. It does imply longevity, because the word itself means lasting, having patience, being resilient, resisting threats, and meeting challenges. But forever? When I sing the praises of hallmark events as permanent institutions in a community, I am coming close to saying that some events do last forever. But being a hallmark event is really about its function, and the function of any given event to meet goals and solve problems can indeed be replaced by another event or another program.

Enduring does not equate with "sustainability," especially if we only see it as an issue of going green or practicing social responsibility—attributes that do not ensure an event will be successful or long-lasting. If we view sustainability more as a process of becoming, then the two concepts are similar. It is not a state of being, but a mindset and an evolving process.

I do not believe anyone can "create" an enduring or sustainable event; it has to be a permanent effort. New events should be established with all the green and sustainability criteria expressed as goals, and the processes should be institutionalized to ensure compliance. But this will not protect an event from external forces or internal management problems. All organizations face crises from within and without, ranging from cultural clashes about goals and strategies to competition and policy or funding changes. Adaptability is therefore a major part of enduring. Being a learning organization is important, which means a permanent emphasis on research and evaluation.

There are at least five general dimensions of sustainability that must be considered. The first is connected to ecology and the natural resource base, which includes the environment as impacted by events and environmental forces acting on events, such as climate and weather. This is the domain of "green" practices and the growing necessity for certification. But sustainability is also going to be dependent on broad, uncontrollable forces like climate change and the attractiveness of the area. Also important is using events as tools for environmental learning and conservation.

Community and political support constitutes the second dimension, with enduring events being the ones that find a (permanent?) place in their community. This relates to the process of becoming a permanent institution. Institutions solve important problems and their permanence is taken for granted. Politicians and other stakeholders will support those events that best meet multiple goals. But this context might also apply to events that are well established within particular communities of interest, in which case we talk about social worlds.

There are two economic dimensions to consider. Enduring or sustainable events will be those that find a competitive niche, are adaptable and continue to attract paying customers or the external funds needed for survival. These are life-cycle and competitive considerations that require strategic thinking. Adaptable organizations are also learning organizations and they foster quality and innovation within. At a micro-economic level, it is necessary to balance costs with revenues and avoid debt. Probably most event failures can be attributed specifically to financial problems, so it is always important it know the value of events to corporations, the tourism industry, or various government policies that determine if support will continue.

The fifth dimension can be called sound organization and competent management. Professionalism is part of the equation, but also continuous improvement through evaluation and learning. A central question for every event is whether or not its organizing body, its owners, will actually want to continue with the event. A case can be made for planning the life cycle and determining in advance when and how an event is to be terminated.

I believe that practitioners, theorists, and policymakers must shift their attention from a focus on single events to portfolios and populations. Within a managed portfolio, or a whole population of events, it probably does not matter much that events are coming and going all the time—it is the health of the portfolio or population that matters. This might not be good news to the struggling, nonprofit festival manager, but it should make perfect sense to policymakers who fund events.

A healthy and sustainable festival portfolio or population has not really been described anywhere, but some guiding principles can be suggested, starting with the premise that "healthy" is a relative term, so a multistakeholder approach will be needed. Just what type of agency or mechanism can accomplish this is hard to say. It is easier to contemplate a tourism agency or event development board taking control of a specific portfolio of events than it is for a public authority to oversee a diverse event population.

Another premise is that resources will be a key to ensuring health, and to encouraging growth in the events sector. Cities that support festivals financially will have more of them, and they will generally be more effective. As well, bringing events together for collaboration and sharing knowledge is bound to have a positive impact overall. While events compete within an environment, for resources and support, some might have to be subsidized or protected if they are both vulnerable and of high value.

Measures of value are needed for single events and the entire population. Residents and specific stakeholder groups will have to help determine the worth of events, which suggests that new methods are needed. Valuation in this sense is different from standard ROI calculations, which make more sense in the for-profit segment and for a portfolio that is structured explicitly to boost economic development or tourism.

While the viability and effectiveness of a festival or event is of utmost importance to its owners and managers, there can never be a guarantee of permanence. To endure is to face challenges, to get stronger after a crisis, and to constantly try to be more sustainable, it is clearly a process, not a state of being. Policymakers should be more concerned about a healthy population of festivals and events than the comings and goings of individual events. This will require a paradigm shift, linked to planning, evaluation, and funding.

—*Donald Getz, PhD*
*Emeritus Professor of Tourism, University of Calgary, Canada*

# SERIES EDITOR FOREWORD

The terms *endurance* and *resilience* imply a sense of permanence such as when you listen to Stravinsky's *Rite of Spring* or another piece of classical music or a master work of visual art such as George Suerat's pointillist painting *La Grande Jatte*. All great works of classical art not only stand the test of time but also provide each reader, listener, or viewer with a highly personal experience that is reflected through the lens of their own life history. This is just one of many reasons why *The Complete Guide to Creating Enduring Festivals:* represents a major literary and academic achievement in the canon of festivals and events literature.

Roslyn Derrett has carefully researched and thoughtfully transmitted the very best practices of many of the world's leading festivals and their artistic directors to provide you with a beautiful mosaic of ideas and information to help you create your own future classic works of art. In fact, the first time I met Professor Derrett I knew that I was in the presence of a fantastically talented festival and event artist.

I traveled in 2000 to Sydney, Australia, to give a speech at the Australian Centre for Event Management conference on the subject of the *Events Beyond 2000: Setting the Agenda*. This was a time when the world appeared gentler and travel was somewhat easier due to the minimal security inconveniences in the era before widespread international terrorism. Despite my jet lag from the long flight, I looked forward to meeting my fellow academics from the Southern Hemisphere and clearly remember seeing Dr. Derrett enter the room and simultaneously change my view of festivals and events in many wonderful ways.

Roslyn was wearing a dress that can only be described as a kaleidoscope of gorgeous colors and her wide smile reached out to me from far across the room. Immediately I was drawn to her and was impressed with the way she, like no others I had met before, seamlessly blended art and events into a new and exciting vocabulary. Years later, I served as a member of her doctoral dissertation committee and began to better understand the depth and breadth of her great mind as she further explored the concept of resilience through festivals and events.

Therefore, one of the easiest decisions I have made as the long-time editor of the Wiley Event Management series was to invite Dr. Derrett to write this book. Her professional and academic experience in the field of cultural festivals and community events constitute a wide and deep background, bringing a new, eloquent, and powerful voice to this expanding field of study.

In my adopted city of Edinburgh, Scotland, festivals have become so commonplace that it appears sometimes that every event, regardless of size or type, is now defined as a festival. In addition to our massive Edinburgh International Festival and Edinburgh Festival Fringe we also annually present the much smaller Festival of Politics and the Festival of Television. I often wonder what actually defines a enduring festival experience and now, for the first time through the pages of this book, Roslyn Derrett provides the answer.

Dr. Derrett's clever and effective use of the mosaic model to help you arrange and rearrange the critical elements that will help you produce beautiful and enduring festivals are revealed for the first time through the chapters of this book. She has interviewed the key leaders of festival management from throughout the world and their voices further confirm that every festival must include the individual and collective methods, ideas, and inspirational factors defined by the resilience mosaic.

This process is best exemplified by the award-winning American Broadway composer Stephen Sondheim who wrote a popular song titled "Putting it Together." One of the verses to this song includes these words:

> *Bit by bit, putting it together*
> *Piece by piece, only way to make a work of art*
> *Every moment makes a contribution*
> *Every little detail plays a part*
> *Having just a vision's no solution*
> *Everything depends on execution*
> *Putting it together, that's what counts!*

This book is destined to become a valuable reference for aspiring as well as experienced festival and event artists. Dr. Derrett generously provides you with the canvas and paint as well as the blank musical sheets and instruments you need to create your next festival and event artistic triumph. One day, your work may be similarly referred to as classical, because bit by bit, you have created, with the help of Dr. Derrett, a masterpiece of artistic achievement exemplified by a seamless mosaic of great beauty destined for enduring appreciation by future connoisseurs of great festival and event art. May your festival and event masterpiece endure and grow to inspire future generations, as will this priceless book by Roslyn Derrett.

—*Joe Goldblatt, FRSA*
*Edinburgh, Scotland*

# PREFACE

## Welcome To
## The Complete Guide to Creating Enduring Festivals

### The Resilience Mosaic

*This book will benefit experienced festival planners as well as those who aspire to enter or develop their skills in the dynamic field of festival-making.*

Here we address contemporary festival-making practice through a mosaic approach. We particularly examine organizational resilience and the human factors that allow festivals to flourish. How do you measure success factors that ensure festival continuity and endurance? The book tests the complexity of culture through a festival lens. It recognizes the combination of diverse elements that comprise the uniqueness of small and large festivals and the legacies they leave.

Some practitioners suggest two vital characteristics of enduring festivals are vision and leadership. Sometimes these come in the same package! As you work through this book, you will note how the rest of the festival infrastructure is bound to these two important elements. How you aggregate all of these will help you develop your own set of mosaic tiles to build a sustainable and unique celebration.

It seems to me that the mosaic metaphor is eminently appropriate for an exploration of the creative processes, innovation, and resilience of festivals. A mosaic is comprised of artistic passion and endeavor manifesting in a public display of engagement through symbol, meaning, and long-lasting aspirations that represent cultural exchange. Historically, majestic

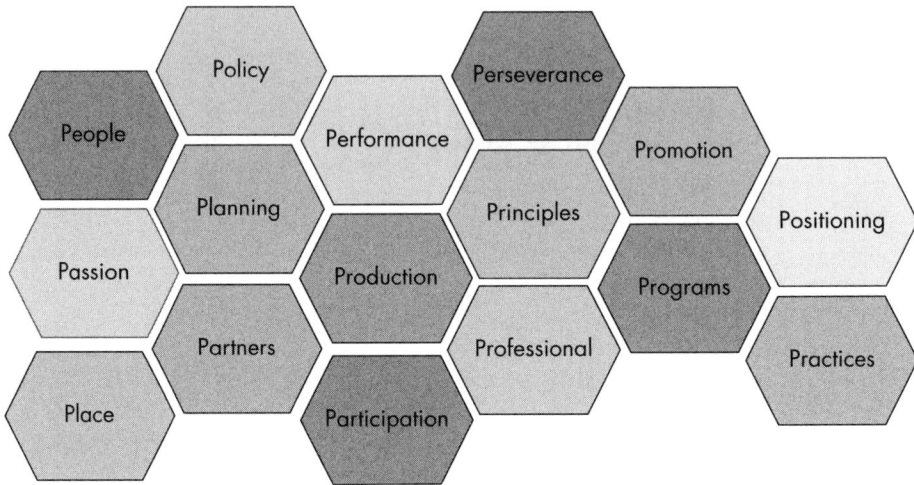

mosaics of scale, as well as domestic renderings of personal expression for intimate spaces, have demonstrated the value of enhancing the quality of life for those interacting with the output. The mosaic's colored pieces of inlaid stone, pottery, or glass tiles (or tessarae) deliver a spectacle that captures an idea, a theme, a vision of importance to the artist, maybe to a mentor or benefactor, and then shared with a broader audience over time.

This book uses the big picture, as well at the intricate details that comprise the delivery of a festival. You will find each chapter makes a contribution through the synergy evident in a mosaic building a whole. Emphases change, contributions by individuals, organizations, communities, and governments vary over time and as resources are available, and when a preparedness to adapt to change is accepted by stakeholders. Thus the resilience of festivals is dependent on marshalling the appropriate human capital, economic drivers, and contextual influences that you will note differ for each festival.

In the mosaic presented above you will notice key elements that are consistently critical parts of the design, development, and delivery of enduring festivals. They can be applied to the broad dimensions of festival-making. I suggest that **people**, **passion**, and **place** are significant elements. They are dependent on sound **policy**, **planning**, and **partners** that affect the **performance** and **production** that will stand the test of time. The active **participation** of all parties and their **perseverance** to generate solid governance and **principles** will impact the festival's public, local, national, and global reach. The **professional promotion** of festival **programs** through **positioning** the celebrations top of mind for host communities and visitors is based on considered management **practices** and understanding of the environments in which festivals are situated.

There are major challenges to the longevity of festivals. An individual's multiple cultural identities provide a complex picture of how they may choose to spend their discretionary leisure time and income. As festival-makers design, develop, and deliver memorable festive experiences, they need to be alert to trends in the local and global marketplace. As students of festival management it is crucial you seek to identify patterns of effective management that have emerged in festivals. Welcome to the grand adventure!

## A Mosaic Approach to Festival Management Knowledge

A mosaic approach is taken in the organization of the material in this book. You will be able to access relevant prior knowledge gleaned from practitioners. You will recognize good practice by exploring further the themes, ideas, and issues identified in the text. You will be able to respond to questions you raise yourself or are contained in case studies, discussion questions, or through their interpretation of digital leads in each chapter. Each chapter is seen as a tile in the mosaic of knowledge production. There are many visual and sensory images to stimulate further understanding of the festival experience for all partners. It is important that inferences are drawn from the text to ensure that the systems that need to be in place for festival and community resilience can be defined and measured.

In a speech at the annual awards ceremony of the International Festivals and Events Association *World Festival & Event City Award* in 2011, CEO Steven Wood Schmader highlighted the value of peer review for festival organizers and host destinations. This prestigious industry acknowledgment provides a useful template for our thinking about designing and delivering quality festival experiences. Many of the case study events included in this book are alumni of these and other global awards programs that festival organizers enter to demonstrate their commitment to best practice.

## Building Festival Endurance

Festivals help communities understand who they are and what makes them tick. Festivals help us understand where residents are, determine where they want to be, how they can bring together the resources they require that will ensure what is known as cultural capital will add to the quality of life of residents and visitors, enhance opportunities for creativity, prosperity, and livability for all stakeholders, and demonstrate resilience when the challenges arise.

The creativity festivals provide in their design and delivery builds on the intangible value of the imagination and the inclusiveness that can be generated in communities where a festival provides an umbrella. The diverse interests and practices that are represented through the clustering of economic and social activity can be readily exposed and later exploited to benefit the community more broadly. What emerge are processes that strengthen collaborative governance, acknowledgment of distinctive place-making, and promotion of a community's identity and generally urban/local sustainability and well-being.

Making inclusive celebrations unleashes relationships between many stakeholders. Each participant contributes to the program, traditions, cultural practices, impact, and reach of events with differing voices and emphases. You can see how celebrations demonstrate belonging and community resilience through inclusive and effective participation, governance, and clear understanding of the nature and context of events. It builds on the notion that resilient people with healthy coping skills through clear self-knowledge, optimism, and comfort with strong community relationships are better equipped to lead organizations through the challenges that are thrown up when festivals are developed. This model suggests that by keeping

| Domain | Implications |
|---|---|
| **1. Participation** | |
| Collaboration and cooperation | Partnerships provide intrinsic and extrinsic synergies for positive social action to increase individual and collective capacity to develop and share practical, respectful, and spiritual goals |
| Creativity, adaptability, innovation | Growth of personal and community capacity to accommodate change and generate festivities with unique creative characteristics that satisfy participants and address artform/cultural bodies of knowledge |
| Proactivity and engagement | Offering opportunity for volunteerism, social entrepreneurship, storytelling, and trusting networks for open dialogue |
| **2. Governance** | |
| Prudence, preparation, and planning | Growth of the understanding of ethical design and delivery of festivals for the "common good" reflecting the "way things are done around here" to the best extent |
| Leadership and advocacy | Encourage community champions with strong commitment to participative decision making and thinking and ethical practice and human resource management |
| Responsibility and learning | Stimulate ownership of festivities through provision of life-long learning options for joining in and interacting with |
| **3. Nature and Context of Event** | |
| Awareness of environments | Develop alertness to the dynamic social, political, technological, economic, environmental, and global influences on local activity |
| Infrastructure and capacity-building | Ensure timely investment from broad stakeholders into hard and soft infrastructure to enhance capacity of residents to reflect and determine their values, interests and aspirations through effective, well-resourced management systems and festival assets |
| Research and evaluation, reviewing and refreshing festival vision | Monitor ongoing activity within community and festivals to ensure responsiveness, durability, and best practice to revive and refresh and to replicate success |

Indicators of Nourishing Resilience through Community Cultural Festivals
Derrett (2007).

the objectives of the organizational team in perspective and through practice in problem solving, a robust organization will emerge. Participants will be better placed to deal with challenges that occur when multiple partners are involved in future collaborative decision making in the wider community. Meanwhile, below, the porous borders of festival engagement are revealed through a simple Venn diagram.

## Enduring Festival Rationale

How do festivals thrive? We examine what festival-makers need to do to attract a target audience, nurture their loyalty, and present attractive programs that stimulate positive word of mouth. We acknowledge the key success factors for the longevity and survival of cultural and

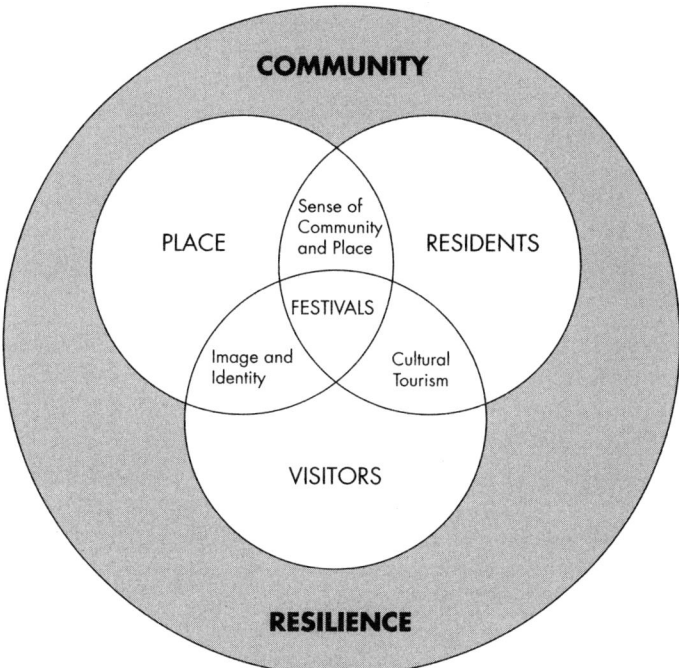

Enduring festival basic research model.
Derrett (2005).

community festivals. Those wishing to better understand how to design, develop, and deliver memorable planned public celebrations will find the mosaic-style case study approach offers solid anecdotal evidence for choices that can be made to build efficient management teams, generate adequate resources, collaborate with partners innovatively to allow for programs that address consumer trends and legislative obligations, and support distinctive destination marketing and management in the growing international festival marketplace.

## Survival of the Fittest?

There are discrete elements of each festival that provide evidence in our search for the characteristics and the practices that allow festivals to survive. It may be through their origins, development, and management, or how each demonstrates what occurs when residents and visitors become involved with creating their own culture. An examination of sustainability and resilience factors of each festival provides a better understanding of its potential longevity.

What emerges is that the longer established festivals demonstrate a better chance of survival because of their consistent delivery of an event that encourages others to partner, share resources, or invest in its management. The history of many festivals demonstrates the abilities of human communities to withstand external stresses to their vision, the festival infrastructure, and their human resources and then to recover momentum. Researchers are finding that festival organizers who recognize the significance of interaction of numerous disciplines and the importance of networking and functioning with direct knowledge of local cultures enhances the capacity of the festival to survive and thrive. The mosaic of this human ecological approach works to stabilize all the components required to maintain quality experiences for all parties involved.

## Mosaic Approach to the Text

The book identifies not only the success factors but confronts why some festivals fail. All this is done through an investigation of festivals and interviews with experts from the field. This is distilled through an **Instructors' Manual** into workable templates that assist lecturers and students to maximize learnings for future application.

The companion **Instructors' Manual** is provided to supplement the pedagogical development of the text. The manual provides instructors with additional teaching and learning suggestions and resources. The **Instructor's Manual,** Test Bank, Respondus Test Bank, and Lecture PowerPoint Slides can be found on the book companion website: www.wiley/com/college/derrett.

## Conclusion

Throughout your reading about successful festivals you can canvass the major characteristics each chooses to emphasize. You will recognize the wonder, the mystery, and the spirit of time and place reflected through ritual, revelry, ceremony, and feasting. The ambience each aims for will be revealed through the service provided by staff (either paid and/or volunteer). Festivals are labor-intensive, so you can assess whether there has been adequate distribution of human resources with buy-in from residents and emergency services personnel and other support groups. The intangibility and perishability of festivals means that hosts and guests are working at the experience level. They recast their attendance in terms of memories, telling stories of their engagement to others, exciting interest in further festivals, and building their motivation for repeat visitation. So, what works and what are the unique elements of the program and its promotion? What is the connection to the host destination, its traditions and cultural heritage? Are expectations met through personal interactions, exposure to outstanding content, new ways of delivering knowledge with a residual overwhelming feeling of well-being and satisfaction?

There is an old maxim that goes, "The chain is only as strong as its weakest link." Explore the links to dozens of **Internet and academic resources** referenced in the Suggested Reading sections. You should visit these links to further expand your thinking and help ensure the future endurance of your festivals and events. Analyze the **case studies** and explore the **festival ideas, issues, and activities** at the end of each chapter. The contribution by each of the **subjects from Inside the Mosaic** will help you better understand how practitioners deal with festival resilience.

Over the years I have participated in hundreds of festivals around the world as audience, organizer, and researcher and I have observed that the conditions for preparing, producing, and presenting festivals are not static. I am continually stimulated by the decisions taken by festival directors to tweak the fundamental performance elements to generate memorable mosaics. At the core are the spectrums of sound–silence, stillness–movement, and darkness–light. Markers along each continuum can be massaged to create extraordinary spectacle and artistic feats that make the hairs on the back of my neck stand on end and that special shiver that indicates I am in the company of high-voltage creativity. This fascinates me. Why is this so? Some of my favorite festival experiences have allowed me to:

> Dance as though no one is watching me
> Sing as though no one can hear me
> Live as though heaven is on earth
> Eat as though fresh local food is sacred
> Sit still and people watch as though I am invisible
> Learn something new and meet wonderful people as though by osmosis
> Imagine a likeness of another world through wit
> Wonder at some built and natural spaces as though by magic.

*—Ros Derrett, OAM*
*Lismore, NSW, Australia*

# ACKNOWLEDGMENTS

My thanks to colleagues from around the globe for their perspectives on festival-making. I am indebted to them for their observations, conversations, and deliberations. This peer support is a measure of the importance they place on the value of education for the next generation of festival directors, designers, leaders and managers, and audiences.

The input of Neil Cameron, Steve Connelly, Jeff Curtis, Carol Davidson, Kay Dimmock, Graeme Dunstan, Vanessa Eden, Don Getz, Joe Goldblatt, Jessica Golding, Damien Grant, Jyllie Jackson, Leo Jago, Faith Liddell, Jo Mackellar, Vicky Majajas, Donna McIntyre, Greg Meek, Baden Offord, William (Bill) J. O'Toole, Pantawan Phummuang, Nigel Redden, Zoe Robinson-Kennedy, Jeanti St. Clair, Justin St. Vincent Welch, Steven Wood Schmader, Liz Shepherd, Lyndon Terracini, Sonia Tsai, and Lenny Vance is much appreciated.

I am obliged for the ongoing belief in my capacity to emerge from the academy, from the practice of making community cultural festivals and from a passion for observing and participating in festivals and celebrations around the world demonstrated by the Series Editor, Joe Goldblatt, from Queen Margaret University, Edinburgh. His commitment to this project has been extremely valuable. His encouragement of students pursuing higher-education event management studies and his engagement with the international tourism and festival industry is to be commended.

Support from the staff at Wiley has been appreciated as I navigated the journey to publication.

The majority of photographs included in this book are the work of my husband and key supporter, Peter Derrett. Together we have been fortunate to participate in numerous festivals around the world. Peter's images capture not only the spaces and places for community cultural celebrations but the mood experienced by audiences. I have welcomed his perspectives on the teaching and learning processes underpinning this textbook.

# CHAPTER 1

# The Nature and Role of Festivals

"Wonder," the first of the passions, is at play at festivals and events. It couples surprise with a wish to know more, the pleasurable promise that what is novel or rare may become familiar.

—*Descartes (1596–1650), French philosopher*

This chapter provides an opportunity for you to better understand:
- The key principles of communal creativity and celebrations
- The essence of the festival meaning and practice
- The shape and scale of traditional and contemporary festivals and events
- The arts and community cultural festival experience

As you trawl through your social media connections or look through family photograph albums from yesteryear, you will no doubt come across visual representations of memories of how people you have known have celebrated a wide variety of relationships, happy and sad moments, and special locations. Your own memories of times when you have enjoyed engaging moments with family and friends are no doubt comprised of some particular features. What are they? What are the features that remain with you from those personal or public celebrations? In this chapter we explore the major characteristics of festivals. This underpins the content of the whole book. You will come to recognize the value of a mosaic to describe the diverse elements that satisfy those who create and nurture the events, those who participate or spectate, and those who reflect on their value and importance over time, as identified in Figure 1.1. We investigate traditions in private and public celebrations that continue to resonate across the globe and through time. Why is this important to us? How do we see and feel about arts and cultural experiences in a festival context—personally and professionally? It might be timely for you to reflect upon what is important in life through the lens of a festival.

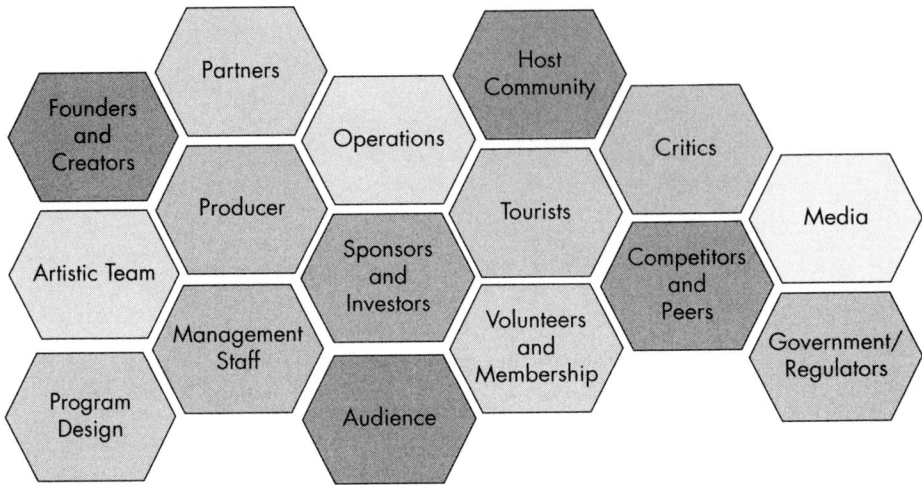

**Figure 1.1** Festival Stakeholder Mosaic.

> A creative life. An expressive life. A connected life. A remembered life.
>
> It seems to me that a diverse, rich, and vital cultural ecology in any city, state, or country fosters opportunity for every citizen to inform these elements of their existence. **A creative life**—The opportunity to make something from nothing, or transform fragments of objects or thoughts into a cohesive whole, is an ennobling and empowering thing. Everyone should have the option to do so, no matter what his or her stage of life, circumstance, technical ability, or training. **An expressive life**—Finding your voice and having an opportunity to be heard is an essential quality of being alive and aware in the world. **A connected life**—The interpersonal and social sharing of meaning is the connective tissue between loved ones, community members, and civilizations. While the arts are not the only means to this sharing, they are among the most powerful and enduring. **A remembered life**—The accumulated actions and artifacts of our expressive lives are our most vital threads to who we were, who we are, and who we might become. Beyond our children, they are the most compelling evidence that we ever existed at all. —*Andrew Taylor*

# The Nature and Role of Festivals

A defining characteristic of a special event or festival is its *transience*, whether spontaneous or planned. Therefore we investigate how difficult it might be to induce and sustain the same sense of occasion and excitement if such an event was to be held more frequently. Robert McIver suggests that healthy human beings crave an occasional wildness, a jolt from normality, a sharpening of the edge of appetite; his own little festival of Saturnalia is a brief excursion from his way of life. Has that been your experience? How best do we satisfy our need for unique exposure to ritual and ceremony that stands one experience apart from others?

The word festival derives from *feast* and implies *a time of celebration*. Originally a pagan rite, the festival evolved as small- and large-scale celebrations to mark high points on the secular as well as religious calendar. Festivals commemorate foundation elements of particular societies and become part of their cultural heritage. Festivals link landscape to lifestyle in simple and complex ways. Falassi (1987) suggests that both the social function and symbolic meaning of the festival are closely related to a series of overt values that the community recognizes as essential to its ideology and worldview, to its social identity, its historical continuity, and its physical survival, which is ultimately what festivals celebrate.

The work of Getz (2007) collects together contemporary thinking on the social and cultural phenomena that are festivals, which have long occupied sociologists and anthropologists. He summarizes these as:

1. A sacred or profane time of celebration, marked by special observances
2. An annual celebration of a notable person or event, or the harvest of an important product
3. A cultural event consisting of performances of works in the fine arts, often devoted to a single artist or genre
4. A fair
5. Generic gaiety, conviviality, and cheerfulness

Street festivities in Amsterdam, the Netherlands, for the Queen's Birthday celebrations involve residents and visitors, many wearing the symbolic orange-colored clothing.

What do you think comprises a festival's essential elements? Who owns the festival? Who decides what elements of a festival are crucial for its survival? How are these nurtured so as to ensure the festival endures and satisfies the various partners in the stakeholder mosaic? What aspects of their hindsight provide the insights required to determine a festival's best features? The influence and aspirations of those represented in Table 1.1 are examined throughout the book. Each has a role in determining the future of a festival.

Essentially the event organizers' physical palette comprises place/people/passion through a spectrum of *darkness and light, stillness and movement, sound and silence*. The degrees of separation between each and the rhythms used to explore each space can

| Festival | Location | Description |
|---|---|---|
| Tet Nguyen Dan Festival of the First Day of the Lunar New Year (between January 19 and February 20) | Vietnam | National New Year holiday with official and religious celebrations with offerings, street, and quiet family activities. Personal spiritual reflections combine with noisy public displays and light for good luck. |
| Carnival (annually) | Rio de Janiero, Brazil | Cultural mix of Portuguese, Indian, and African heritage comprising street parties, drummers and singers, samba parades, and colorful costumes. Activities are described as glitzy, glamorous, outlandish, competitive, erotic, and energetic. |
| Oktoberfest (16 days, starting late September/early October) | Munich, Germany | Large party event with beer and food in marquees after Brewer's parade and street entertainment. |
| WOMAD, World of Music, Arts, and Dance (annually) | Charlton Park, Malmesbury, Wiltshire, England; WOMAdelaide, Australia; WOMAD, New Zealand; WOMAD, Sicily | Days of concentrated, diverse performances representing global cultures from artists with a wide range of appeal. Musician Peter Gabriel a co-founder. Family-oriented, highlighting various musical styles of both recorded and emerging artists. |
| Thanksgiving (fourth Thursday in November) | United States | Thanksgiving Day is a time for communal and family thanksgiving with feasting, reunions, and gifting to remember the pilgrims who celebrated an autumn harvest initially in 1621. |
| Queen's Day (April 30) | Amsterdam, Netherlands | Celebration of previous Queen Juliana as city explodes into markets, street entertainment, and music; it is tradition to wear the color orange. |
| Carnaval de Quebec (late January–mid-February) | Winter Carnival, Old Town Quebec City, Canada | Established in 1894, now has night parades, street ice and dog-sled races, outdoor cinema, a snow sculpture competition; and canoeing across the frozen St. Lawrence River. |

**Table 1.1** Diverse Global Festivals

provide just the right amount of wonderment. What are the characteristics you have noticed at the memorable festivals with which you have been associated? You could follow up on the global festivals in Table 1.1 and investigate the distinctive features that attract participation.

Festivals have provided a meeting point for cultures and faiths to demonstrate tolerance, understanding, and interaction and to share knowledge and celebrate life with merrymaking, fun, and frivolity. They have provided occasions to be enjoyed; have set a mood, tone, or spirit; responded to a sense of place, time of year, or season; symbolized fertility; been dedicated to fears and images, good and evil, and light and darkness; and reminded us of structures, traditions, and superstitions through masks, dancing, singing, costumes, food, elaborate processions, or simple rituals. Can you connect the key

Profusion of lanterns light up the night sky at the Brisbane Festival, 2012.

Light and laser display on the river at Brisbane Festival, 2012.

elements identified above with long-standing community or arts-based festivals that you have experienced?

What can you find out about the origins of particular festivals? Circumstances that inspire the establishment and ongoing nourishment of festivals include a whole portfolio of celebratory tools; they can come out of commemoration of war, peace, harvest of plenty, or reminders of scarcity; they can build on cultural and heritage strengths and communal memory; and they can respond to specific environments such as the seasons, weather, and productivity of the land.

One such element might be how festivals have used light over time to engage observers and participants in rites of passage that encourage social relationships, generate cultural innovation, and consolidate the human need for comradeship and ritual (see Table 1.2).

| Festival | Description |
| --- | --- |
| St. Lucia's Day, Sweden (December 13) | Folk tradition that follows the longest night of the year in winter Sweden, with family and community wreaths of candles. |
| Traditions of light: Hanukkah (annually) | Hanukkah is the Jewish Festival of Lights celebrating a 165 B.C. event when oil lamps miraculously lasted eight days and became a symbol for resilience. Lighting candles for eight nights continues in families and Jewish communities. |
| Loi Krathong (loy-kruh-thong) Festival, Thailand (November) | Celebrated in Thailand, Laos, and Cambodia on a full moon in November annually. *Loy* means "to float" and a *krathong* is a lotus-shaped vessel made of banana leaves. The krathong usually contains a candle, three joss (or incense) sticks, some flowers, and coins. Community festivities last for days. |
| Diwali, India (annually) | Diwali, meaning "array of lights," is a Hindu light festival. It symbolizes the triumph of light over darkness. |
| Beltane Fire Festival, Calton Hill, Edinburgh, Scotland (annually) | Community festival with spectacular fire displays marking the change of the seasons, each with special traditional Celtic and modern rituals with symbolic significance. |
| Kwanzaa, United States (December 26) | Cretaed in 1966, Kwanzaa honors African harvest traditions. Candles representing the seven principles of Kwanzaa are lit each night for a week. |
| Son et Lumiere and digital light projections on building facades as part of festival programs (e.g., Vivid Sydney, Australia; Lyon, France; Kharkov, Ukraine; Prague, Czech Republic (annually) | Creative applications now using laser, 3D, video, animation, transformations, installations, virtual spaces, and outdoor trompe l'oeil; an ambient component of numerous global urban festivals |
| Vivid Sydney | Vivid Sydney is a forum for the creative industries to collaborate. As part of the lighting collaboration, members of the public are able to "play the building" via a purpose-built interface that interacts with music and vibrant, cutting-edge projections. Integrates film, music, digital, media, animation, fashion, design, and architecture. |

**Table 1.2** Examples of Enduring Themed Global Festivals of Light

# Historic Perspective on Communal Creativity and Celebration

Historically cultural patterns of behaviors and beliefs have been adapted. This dynamic informs the sort of celebrations with which individuals, communities, and nation-states now engage. Private and planned public festivals have been formed and transformed over time. Generally, if successful, these activities can be validated in the community consciousness and be taught to and absorbed by following generations. We might recognize this invention, discovery, rediscovery, and development within the festival organizational experience, as well as that of festival attendees.

Significant antecedents of modern festivals are the elements of traditional pilgrimage, as experiences of participants, spectators, and host communities attest. Primarily of religious and spiritual origins, individuals and special interest groups undertook a journey. The destinations were sacred places or shrines. Secular pilgrimages allow pilgrims an opportunity to commit to seeking out locations where they can explore "the other," reflect on beliefs held and knowledge gained from accessing natural and built phenomena that add meaning to their lives. In contemporary society many religious sites attract large groups of pilgrims who arrive independently or travel in groups. The experience provides belonging and exposure to shared rituals of eating, music, contemplation, mystery, and wonder—characteristics of many large gatherings hosted in communities today through planned festivities. There are people worshipping at the altar of favored music, writing, theater, science, thinking, and so on, in the company of like-minded pilgrims, often from far away.

As we examine the function of popular festivals historically, we find that the role of authorities, whether civic or ecclesiastical, contributed to the control or suppression of community festive practice. There is evidence in Europe and Asia of such interventions. In recent times, the Shwedagon Pagoda in Yangon in Myanmar resumed its role of accommodating a festival formally banned by the military government for over 20 years. This sacred Buddhist shrine once again hosted thousands of people in ceremonial costumes and event organizers expect massive numbers of pilgrims to take advantage of the revival of this traditional festival into the future.

In Italy, the Carnevale di Venezia (Carnival of Venice) is said to have originated as a celebration of military victories. It was first recorded in 1268. The intermittent conduct of the masked and costumed festivities led to its heyday in the 18th century. Venice's decline in power was accompanied by a conspicuous consumption of pleasure. Rich young nobles doing the European "Grand Tour" made sure these pleasures were theirs as well as those of the residents. Mussolini banned the Carnevale in the 1930s. However, in 1979 the Carnival was revived and now over 3 million people participate in a range of activities on the canals and the side streets of the city. It features feasting, masked balls, outdoor spectacles like the Flight of the Angel across San Marco Piazza, water processions, music, and games. The event occurs during the 12 days prior to Ash Wednesday, so is consistent with the worldwide Christian celebration of Mardi Gras. Mardi Gras means "Fat Tuesday." Mardi Gras is always during the 40 days of Lent plus seven Sundays. A Carnevale festival that is more spectator-oriented at this time of the year is in Viareggio in Italy. While it

Designer masks displayed for the Carnevale di Venezia celebrations.

offers fireworks, performances, and seasonal regional food, the outstanding feature is a parade of extraordinarily massive floats over four consecutive Sundays. The floats satirically exploit contemporary and traditional local political leaders, clowns, skeletons, and celebrities.

In summary, already we can confirm the inclusion of numerous features that through the ages have become incorporated in contemporary festivals (e.g., accessible outdoor venues, spectacles, parades, religious influences, government authorities, arts practice, and natural elements such as water, light, and food).

## Enduring Festival Focus

Carnival is a strong element of the European heritage transmitted through colonization into the New World. It has strong links to Christianity. As a living celebration its focus is on providing a change from everyday life, and is based on religious and secular rituals through shared songs and stories. The connection with seasons offers a mix of popular and ecclesiastical culture. These themes were represented in plays on stages in the streets and in marketplaces delivered by actors and spectators alike. The holiday offers games, freedom, indulgence, and abundance through harvests. Extremes were presented through farce and mock battles. Costumes revealed gender reversals and a chance to pay off old grudges and conflicts of status. There was sometimes fasting and abstinence as well as feasting and ecstasy. Early English poet Geoffrey Chaucer clearly captures the imagery of carnival and pilgrimage in his *Canterbury Tales*.

During mid-February Ancient Romans observed what they called the *Lupercalia*, a circus-type festival that was, in many respects, quite similar to the present-day Mardi Gras celebrations. Christianity appropriated numerous ancient celebratory customs at the Lenten time that commences on Ash Wednesday and ends at Easter. There was feasting as participants indulged in voluntary madness by donning masks and dressing up. Public celebrations absorbed local pagan habits. The Middle Ages established festivities for all classes of society in this season. Remnants of such activity still feature in German, English, and French festivals. These were precursors for the Mardi Gras we know of today.

Some suggest Mardi Gras came to America as early as 1699 with French explorer Sieur d'Iberville after he arrived near present-day New Orleans. Others record that the Mardi Gras of New Orleans began in 1827 when a group of students who had recently returned from school in Paris donned strange costumes and danced their way through the streets. What emerge are the legends of origin that play an important role in sustaining public festivities. The shared story documents how the celebrations became more elaborate, culminating in an annual Mardi Gras Ball.

Communities that now host carnivals (literally "farewell to the flesh") and Mardi Gras festival seasons are diverse. Some are invested in by individual community members, others are a result of yearlong fundraising drives by individuals and special interest groups. Their attractiveness to tourists now means that governments invest in destination promotions based on such cultural heritage. Louisiana's Mardi Gras is celebrated not only in New Orleans, but also in numerous smaller cities and towns around the state and in the neighboring Gulf Coast region.

## Rio's Carnival

Similar celebrations are also held in the Brazilian city of Rio de Janeiro, arguably the world's most elaborate Carnival location. Rio's Carnival's spectacular samba street parades end at the open-air Sambadrome. They are the result of yearlong intense and secretive creativity. There is stiff competition between seven top samba schools as they prepare allegorical floats and hundreds of lavishly costumed singers, dancers, and musicians. Hundreds of thousands of spectators (locals and tourists) revel in the holiday mood, line the streets, and secure special event tickets in order to observe the artistic talent and creative genius of the designers, artistic directors and musicians and the general zest for life demonstrated by all those involved in the preparation and presentation of spectacle.

As suggested earlier, Carnival is played out with equal enthusiasm in other Brazilian cities such as Sao Paulo and Salvador. Each year there is an overarching theme that can be drawn from the city's rich cultural heritage. Celebrities are engaged as well as city, town, and village residents who generate parades and street parties of their own. Brazil now recognizes the economic impact of such events, which in Rio generates 250,000 jobs and revenues of $640 million for the food and beverage sector.

## The Essence of Festivals Today

Festivals as we know them today have emerged in response to a number of factors. From a festival-making perspective, we can recognize:

- Increased affluence of some sections of society
- Increased resources available to events
- Growth of the serious leisure concept
- Expectation audiences have of a quality, authentic experience
- Stimulation of the market for entertainment and events

- Acceptance of events as part of the tourism destination's "marketing mix"
- Expanded corporate involvement in events to enhance brand loyalty
- Growth in sponsorship that has led to increased corporate support for events
- Growth of tourism
- Awareness of the ability of events to attract tourists and extend their length of stay
- Awareness of the ability of events to enhance the image, identity, and profile of destinations
- Awareness of the ability of events to generate economic benefits and create jobs
- Increased government support for and involvement in events, as demonstrated by the formation of government-based event corporations in many jurisdictions
- Increased media interest in and coverage of events

There has been a distinctive increase of mega events with wide public appeal such as national anniversary celebrations, sporting events like the Olympic Games and World Cup, Art Biennales, and music concerts.

## Serious Leisure Spectrum

We need to understand what triggers the curiosity of those who pursue serious leisure. They have been called dabblers, enthusiasts, experts, and fanatics along a spectrum that explains their involvement with special interests. Their festival experience has implications for those determining local assets and management choices (built, natural, heritage, contemporary, animated, participatory, spectator based). For those who have identified their festival target market, they need to ensure the festival:

- Lets the experience reflect the existing wealth of creative cultural production that resides in particular environments;
- Encourages active participation and interaction between visitors and creative individuals and groups;
- Ensures audiences are offered excellent programs;
- Celebrates things that are valued by the locals;
- Captures the heritage of residents past and present;
- Reveals any links to Indigenous settlement and cultural practice;
- Accesses multicultural communities; and
- Offers a destination that is open for business when visitors come to town and delivers links organizers have forged with others in the business, government and health, education, recreation, and tourism sectors.

The implications of this holistic approach to designing, developing, and distributing experiences to visitors that meet (or exceed) their expectations comprises a mosaic worthy of analysis.

## What Do Festival Attendees Want?

So what do participants or spectators want from a festival? Like consumers of many experiences, individuals participating as the audience at a festival or special event wish to satisfy their curiosity about place and people, learn more, understand customs better, and appreciate the intricacies of landscape and lifestyles. They may come to appreciate beauty, collecting things endemic to the place and its people and that particularly remind them of the celebratory experience. They can improve themselves in terms of accessing knowledge and expertise new to them through workshops, master classes, and demonstrations; and opportunities to express their personalities through dress, food, and beverage through the company of like-minded people and to be respected and even receive approval from others.

Participants enjoy being the first in their social group to undertake an activity. They may join their social group through the sharing of a festival. Having had the festival experience they want to be recognized as authorities and be influential. They wish to emerge from contact with the event with stories to tell and experiences that can satisfy some inner needs they may not have readily identified. Events provide a context for such needs. This is why tourism marketers, too, research individual satisfiers to better present a product that respects these attributes, attracts increasing numbers to events, and secures ongoing commitment by organizers, sponsors and host communities to particular events.

The sorts of benefits sought by event attendees include filling their increased leisure time, value for money expended, new experiences, a high standard of service, increased enjoyment, better health and well-being, personal prestige, security, and personal recognition. Festivals and special events provide vehicles for the "self," which is the center of modern consumer society, to tie together issues of choice, identity, status, alienation, and culture. So, these people want to avoid unsafe situations, discomfort, doubts, worries, embarrassment, making too many complex decisions, being treated as just a number, and being made to feel a nuisance. This is a huge "ask" of festival-makers, which is why we explore what works to satisfy these needs in Chapter 2.

An individual's motive for attending an event is an internal factor that arouses, directs, and integrates a person's behaviour. Identifying and prioritizing motives is a key ingredient in understanding decisions to attend events. It is a marketing truism that people do not buy products or services, they buy the expectation of benefits that satisfy a need. Identification of needs is often the basis for developing a successful events program. So how do festival-makers craft the mosaic of best fit for patron and festival through choice and layout of site; the program of appropriate, engaging entertainment; personal safety through the use of technology for communication; design and delivery of ambience; and comfort and efficiency throughout the whole interaction from beginning to end?

The key to understanding motives is their close relation to satisfaction. Motives and expectations occur before the experience and satisfaction after it. For individuals to return to a repeat experience (and be a willing conduit of positive word of mouth), they must be satisfied with their previous experience. If needs are fulfilled (or surpassed) then satisfaction will result. It makes little sense to study satisfaction in isolation from motives. In order to monitor satisfaction, there should be knowledge of the needs that audiences are seeking to satisfy. Therefore identifying and prioritizing motives is a key ingredient in audience development. Building audiences is dependent on satisfying existing patrons and attracting new ones.

Crompton and McKay (1997) investigated visitors to festivals in the United States. As part of their study they attempted to identify the set of motives that stimulated visitors to attend festivals and to assess the extent the perceived relevance of motives changed across different types of events. Their framework for studying motivation of festival visitors embraced five sociopsychological motivational domains:

- *Cultural exploration* (also education value/intellectual enrichment), a desire to gain knowledge and expand intellectual horizons.
- *Novelty/regression* (seek), a desire to seek out new and different experiences through pleasure motivated by a need to experience thrill, adventure, and surprise, and a desire to engage in behavior reminiscent of an adolescent or child.
- *Recover equilibrium* (escape), a desire to refresh oneself mentally and physically from day-to-day stresses and to alleviate boredom.
- *Known group socialization*, a desire to interact with a group and its members, and to enhance family relationships and friendships, and a desire to strengthen or establish cultural identity.
- *External interactions/socialization*, a desire to be with, observe and meet new like-minded people.

Crompton and McKay's (1997) study outlined in Figure 1.2 found that although differences emerged in the relative relevance of the motives to different types of events, and these appear to have useful management implications, there is a pervasive similarity of motives across different events. The results suggested the importance of considering multiple motives in the attendance decision-making process. It emerged that attendance at an event is rarely the result of a single motive. An individual may have several different needs that he or she desires to satisfy through event attendance. For example, a need to interact with family, often inhibited by the independent actions of individual members in the home environment, may be accompanied by a desire for cultural enrichment. These may be facilitated by different elements in the package of offerings that constitute the event. Different individuals may engage in the same package of elements and derive different benefits from the experience. Thus for some, listening to particular

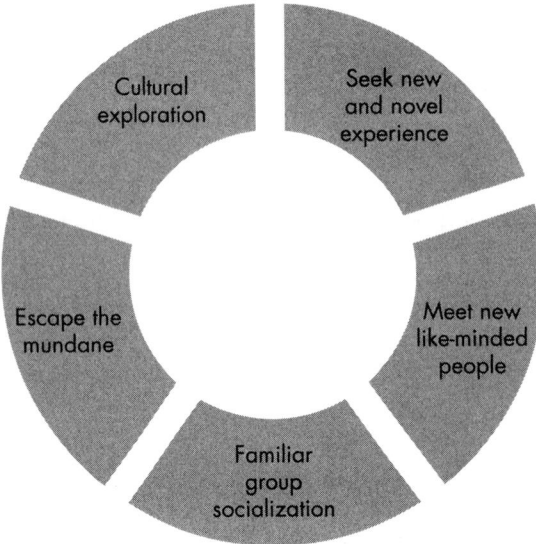

**Figure 1.2** Sociopsychological Motivational Domains. *Based on Crompton and McKay (1997).*

music may be a means of experiencing a cultural tradition, for another it may be a new and novel experience, while for others it may be a means of facilitating inter- or intra-group socialization.

## The Roles for Festivals

The scope and scale of a festival affects its place in the consciousness of host communities and other festival partners. Festivals play a number of significant roles in a town or region. Getz (2007) identifies these as attractions, image-makers, animators of static attractions, and catalysts for further development. They can be seen to minimize negative impacts of mass visitation and foster better host–guest relations. Festivals can lengthen tourist seasons, extend the peak season, or introduce a "new season" into the life of a community.

So it appears that arts and cultural tourism can enhance the whole creative ecosystem, especially through arts-based celebrations. The legacies are increasingly being recognized by all stakeholders, including the creative industries, encouraging excellence in arts practice those qualities that add value to life.

Festivals can:

- Raise spirits of host communities; engender civic pride as hospitality and assets are shared by custodians of the community's capital with visitors.
- Act as a catalyst for the support and promotion of strong, vibrant communities that highlight a distinctive sense of place for residents and visitors.
- Celebrate cultural diversity.
- Minimize isolation and diminish silos among residents and festival arts practitioners and provide networks and build communitas.
- Celebrate and protect a region's culture, heritage, and natural environment and the residents' lifestyles.
- Attract visitors for longer stays and encourage greater visitor spending.
- Add value to existing travel experiences available in the region.
- Recognize arts and cultural development in the broader context of people's ordinary lives.
- Facilitate and promote partnerships between arts and non-arts industries and government at all levels.
- Stimulate arts infrastructure as legacies for ongoing public and private investments (e.g., cultural precincts, galleries, theaters, indoor and outdoor venues).
- Encourage arts and cultural entrepreneurship, offering educational opportunities for social/cultural entrepreneurs through incubator workspaces building on a labor-intensive sector.
- Stimulate distinctive place-making for festival-hosting destinations through purpose-designed signage, ephemera, public art, responding to seasonality, and encouraging clusters within and between creative industries.
- Promote and communicate excellence through partnerships and product development, encouraging imagination and innovation that provides tools to bring about acceptable change.

Graeme Dunstan has been a cultural development worker and festival maker for over 40 years. As an officer of the Australian Union of Students he directed the significant 1973 Nimbin Aquarius Festival in Australia. He subsequently served and advised various government agencies on community art, festival design, events and cultural tourism, and crowd management. In 1994 Graeme wrote of the nature of celebration. What do you think?

### FIRST LAW OF CELEBRATION: To celebrate is to be human and possibly divine.

This law states that the need to celebrate is as much a part of being human as is breathing. Humans are herd animals and they like clustering. If a UFO beamed up a bunch of humans at random and put them down and left them on a desert island with adequate food, water, and shelter, it would only be a matter of time before they would make a party with singing, dancing, storytelling, feasting, carousing, and so create meaning of the mystery they share being alive, together in that time and that place.

### SECOND LAW OF CELEBRATION: Celebration creates community.

This law says that you can have a bunch of people sharing the same time and geography but they won't experience themselves as being part of community until they take the time and make the effort to celebrate. Celebration is the way we humans affirm our connectedness to each other in meaning, time, and place. It is the ritual by which we make and renew our sense of community, whatever and wherever that might be.

- Establish international links across festival programs and post festival networks to drive professionalism in festival design and delivery (e.g., WOMAD, Biennales, IFEA [International Festival and Event Association], and EFA [European Festivals Association] Atelier program).
- Acknowledge and stimulate strategic regional/urban solutions by celebrating innovation and building public policy and effective advocacy and community confidence building.
- Grow the funding pie.
- Create career pathways, skills development, and mentoring opportunities in both the arts and tourism sectors.

Communities hosting festivals use them to feature the talents, experience or skills of locals or an opportunity for creative exchange by inviting others to join in through competitions, performances, displays, and free interaction.

## Summary of Festival Essentials

This chapter introduced the fact that different stakeholders will expect different features and memories from their festival experience. While the focus has been on cultural celebrations, through arts-based practice or community-based festivals, it is evident that there is

The converse is also true. A community without a signifying celebration is no "community" at all. "Community" used in this context is just a word signifying nothing, an abstract idea, a yearning in the hearts of the socially isolated, or a lie to camouflage manipulations of self-interest.

### THIRD LAW OF CELEBRATION: *The more profound the sharing of meaning in the celebration and the more beautiful the art, the more intimately bonded is that community.*

This law suggests that celebrations are a measure of the spiritual health of a community and the more a celebration can join people in sharing the core concerns and mysteries of the human condition such as birth, death, and connectedness, the more intimately they will realize their shared humanity as a universal brother and sisterhood of all people, a fundamental unity of love, justice, and peaceful coexistence.

## MORE CREATIVITY AND CHANGE COMPETENCE

Festivals make a tangible statement about the prevailing "state of the art" in the community and festivals stimulate and inspire evolutions. The arts might be the arts of organization and promotion, music, making of spectacle, dance, theater, pageantry, costumery, or storytelling about the time and the place. It is as if a big mirror is held up and the community of people who care sees itself reflected there, they see what's good and what's not so good and they start planning changes. Festivals also create temporary community where new values and art can be explored as joyful community practice.

a broad spectrum of program options for planned public events. Traditional activities and their contemporary interpretations satisfy an audience's interest in the cultural heritage, especially from the perspective of sharing authentic values and a sense of place. Exposure to the sites, performances, interaction and learning all contribute to a framework that goes beyond pure entertainment value.

Researchers have observed over time the evolution to embrace industrial aspects of the design and delivery of festivals. There is greater understanding of the levels of importance to individuals and communities of the roles festivals can play in the lives and livelihoods of diverse stakeholders. The proliferation of social media ensures the increase of sharing images and personal responses to the interaction instantly. This digital documentation of the sights, sounds, locations, and festival programs allows the memories to endure. This new technological dimension enhances the investment in social, economic, political, and environmental aspirations of festival organizations and host communities particularly. Each impacts on the legacy felt at the conclusion of annual festivals and feeds into the longevity and sustainability of each event. The motives, functions, and contributions of each stakeholder varies and informs the strengths and sustainability of the mosaic.

At the core of the individual's satisfaction experience are such festival attributes outlined in Figure 1.3 as:

- Feeling validated, respected, and accepted
- Exposure to something creative, innovative, risky, stimulating, and memorable

- Interaction with like-minded patrons and host community, sense of sharing and belonging
- Exposure to fun, humor, mystery, wonder, spirituality, and magic
- Capacity to engage in episodes of conscious excess and be free from daily constraints
- Safety and security through efficient and effective, aesthetically comfortable personal and crowd management
- Opportunity to learn and appreciate new skills
- Value for money
- Clear, compelling, targeted marketing messages
- Contact with friendly, knowledgeable, accessible, and hospitable staff and volunteers

Those responsible for organizing modern festivals need to understand the porous boundaries that festivals engender as the mosaic of life engulfs those who wish to celebrate in public. The portfolio of skills, tools and personnel available to share the journey makes the result ever more memorable.

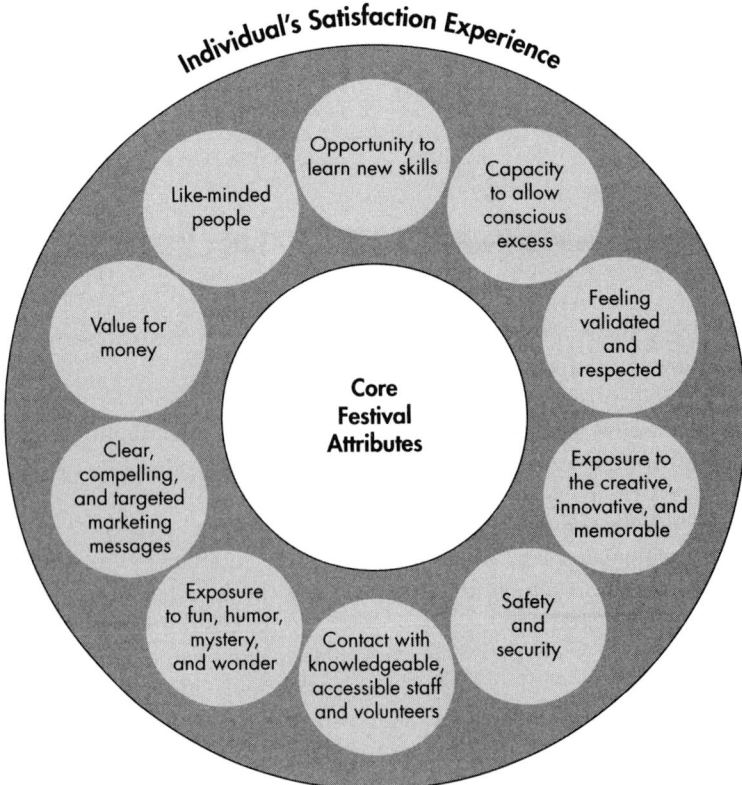

**Figure 1.3** Core Festival Attributes.

## CASE STUDY

### Songkran Bangkok, Thailand

Songkran holidays have been significant for a long time in Thailand. It used to be celebrated officially as New Year's Day until 1941 before the international New Year's Day was adopted. The word *Songkran* is from the Sanskrit language. It means "to pass," which implies the moving of the sun and other planets into one of the zodiacal orbits. The festival date was primarily set by astrological calculation between April 13 and 15. Like its Indian origins, the festival was celebrated during springtime, as it was a moment that agriculturists were freed from their regular work in order to pay respect to their ancestors. In Thailand, it represented respect for the family. Family members traditionally used this opportunity to go back home, gathering in order to express respect to their elders and to make merit together for their ancestors. This social collaboration in order to clean houses, temples, and other public places enhanced the value of the shared religion.

### Traditional Activities in Songkran Festival

Typical activities included doing good things for good luck into the New Year. The activities began early in the morning; people dressed up in their best attire and went to the temple with their family. They prepared a variety of food and made merit

Specific merit-making by building sand pagodas at Bangkok temple during Thailand's annual Songkran celebrations.

Streets are packed with locals and visitors celebrating the annual Songkran festival in Bangkok, Thailand, using water pistols, buying food, and through temple offerings and mementoes.

by offering those foods to monks. After that, they released animals such as birds, turtles, and fish because long ago, before the period of Songkran, fish were too small to eat due to the weather so people kept animals caught at home until there was more water during Songkran, and then released them to nature. Traditionally, Thais didn't bring ashes of dead people back home but buried them under a tree in the monastery and monks were asked to perform rites over them.

The significant part of the celebration was spent paying respect to elders by pouring Nam Ob (scented water) over their hands and in return they wished young people good luck, prosperity and happiness. Young people brought sets of new clothes and personal belongings that they gave to their elders. This was accompanied with the traditional candles, joss sticks, and flowers.

The bathing ceremony for Buddha images was the traditional honor to pay homage to the Buddha for blessings for the New Year. People made an offering of flowers, candles, and incense sticks to the Buddha images, then poured a little quantity of the scented water on the hands of the Buddha image. The ceremonial bath was also for monks, particularly the chief monk who was a leading personage in the community as a teacher and adviser with wide knowledge and experience. Furthermore, he combined the role of doctor and astrologer. After the bathing rite, the abbot gave a sermon to people and blessed them for good luck.

Splashing of water implied the washing-away of bad luck. People used the water that had been poured over the Buddha images as "blessed" water, poured gently on their shoulder in order to give good luck to them and their family. Another tradition involved people bringing sand into the monastery's premises in order to compensate for sand that they had carried away on their feet before. The sand was built into a pagoda shape and decorated with colorful flags. People gathered to look after their holy places by cleaning the buildings and the area around the temple, making merit and demonstrating the unity of the community as well.

Each community prepared its own entertainment such as folk performances and traditional games for enjoyment, including a Miss Songkran Contest in which young women presented themselves through their beauty and special talents for judgment by a community audience. Songkran was also the opportunity to stop bad behavior and do good things as New Year resolutions.

## Contemporary Activities During Songkran Festivals

Thais today are more likely to spend this holiday individually, particularly people in the sprawling capital of Bangkok, because of the change of family structures. Thai families have changed in character from extended families to nuclear families. Many families spend the gazetted holiday without involvement in family reunions. Single people are likely to be alone or with friends instead of their families. Some people spend time at home watching TV, reading, or sometimes going shopping and seeing a movie. Some spend the holidays traveling with their friends domestically or internationally instead of with their families.

Traditional activities of the festival have been modified. New generations emphasize fun and public water splashing. The throwing of water in public places is now popular, as people wander the streets with water guns or stand at the side of the street with water containers, splashing one another and people riding by in vehicles. There are more alcohol-related road accidents as well as injuries ascribed to extreme behavior such as splashing water into the faces of travelling motorcyclists.

International tourists have found a place in such activities. On Khao San Road in Bangkok, foreigners outnumber locals and expect to spend their time outdoors. Some arm themselves with water pistols or buckets of water to actively engage with the colorful street life and markets, away from the temples. There is a government campaign to promote this festival (celebrated throughout the Kingdom), creating a party for foreigners and also a further reason of many visitors coming to Thailand during the festival. There's tension as other cultural campaigns attempt to encourage people to keep the traditional way of the festival via media campaigns.

# FROM INSIDE THE MOSAIC

## Three Festival Patrons

Donna, Kay, and Peter were among the over 80,000 people who attended the 23rd Byron Bay Bluesfest (in Australia) in 2012.

Each felt well supported throughout their time in festival venues because there were five enormous state-of-the-art performance stages, four licensed bars including a VIP bar and a beer garden with a big screen, many diverse fresh food stalls, market/merchandise stalls of local products, a CD shop, opportunities for artist signings, undercover food courts with seating (given the precarious weather experiences that can become a feature of Easter in the subtropics), an undercover coffee tent with seating, a children's activities/play area, music workshops, banking facilities, first-aid amenities, disability access, a coat room, information stalls, on-site camping, shuttle bus services from local towns, and free car parking (though a donation is invited for a local charity).

Peter Derrett OAM

Dr. Kay Dimmock

Each was reluctant to identify any major negative aspects of the conduct of the festival or their participation in it. There were no concerns for long queues, for example, or poor personal amenities, no comments regarding the use of drugs by individuals. There was no mention of rowdy or risky behaviors or violence, although there was mention of the sponsorship by a well-known alcohol distributor. There was acknowledgment that there were a lot of people. There was also comment that some items for sale had inflated prices. Each had attended other large public events but they were impressed by the professionalism of the staff in all festival locations. They all observed people having a good time.

Donna attended the festival for the full five days with her husband Craig and their two children. She and Craig have not missed this annual festival since 1995. As the children grew up, they have also become regular festival-goers. Craig and Donna love music. Craig plays guitar. They attend performances from domestic and international musicians who deliver their favorite brands of entertainment. They travel distances to enjoy the company of other fans and to be in the same space as their idols. So, the annual Bluesfest in Byron Bay, just a half-hour drive from their home, is a part of their annual cultural and social calendar. The Byron Shire sites for the festival have changed over the years, but all have helped established Byron Bay as the go-to destination for quality music experiences. Donna and Craig haven't taken up the camping option, as thousands of other patrons often do, but drive home at the end of a long but totally absorbing day.

They love the big-name international and domestic artists that have always been on the bill. They arrive with their portable chairs and park themselves in a central location, having determined which particular acts they will seek out by scouring the program prior to coming. They use the festival website and YouTube to investigate styles of performers. A comprehensive program is published in *Rhythms* magazine and other media promotions identify who they will listen to. The programming at the festival has never disappointed them. They like to seek out new talent, as well as joining thousands to sing along with famous contributors to the line-up. Donna works at the local university and knows that students are part of the volunteer and staff workforce. Through a partnership between the Bluesfest and the university, artists come on campus to conduct special workshops and performances.

Donna believes the current venue offers safety and security and a clean and welcoming ambience. Over the years the weather has been unpredictable in April, but festival management has worked hard to solve problems exacerbated by rain. The 2012 Bluesfest was a sun-filled time and that generated a spirited response from the wide demographic range of patrons.

Kay had not attended the festival before, though a long-term resident of the region. She had relied on the media coverage and personal contact with friends who were regular attendees to learn of the experiences the festival offered. She camped out for three days. Kay took her own tent and met interesting fellow travellers in what she saw as a social atmosphere that was extremely engaging. She didn't stay in the more salubrious purpose built tents that were based in an adjacent area for hire at a greater expense than she was prepared to spend in her first foray. Kay found those people staying in the campground to be an eclectic mix and all had come for the music. A village-like atmosphere emerged with a friendly exchange of chit-chat, food, and program suggestions. It was a most comfortable way to immerse herself in what the festival had to offer more broadly than just being a spectator at a concert. Kay noticed lots of international visitors among the campers, and while many of the people didn't come with cars, they had tents and hammocks in which to settle. Each morning there was interaction while the performance spaces were being prepared; sound checks could be heard in preparation for an action-packed musical program well into the night.

Kay found a distinctive flavor of the region shared with the patrons. She thought people were there for the music. She found the music extraordinary and wondered at the value of having access to a world-class line-up on her doorstep. She went to most performance spaces and was impressed by the technology and the punctuality of each set of performers. She tried many food stalls, caught up with friends, listened to performances on the thoroughfares, and was impressed with the amenities that were associated with her accommodation and the festival at large. She thought staying overnight provided an extra dimension for social interaction, as programmed performances started late in the morning and "residents" had time to mingle, eat, and purchase merchandise. Kay learned a great deal about the etiquette expected of attending such events. She linked arms with other people of a certain age to stand up front and sing loudly with Cold Chisel, Crosby, Stills and Nash, and John Fogarty through the nostalgia of their sets.

Both Donna and Kay bought their tickets for next year's Bluesfest before they left the site! They were both totally positive and trusting of the organizers' capacity to deliver a memorable experience with a world-class program (sight unseen). They wonder about the threshold of numbers for such an event and whether organizers are considering the future. The site is a destination that could handle the volume, but what about the patron's experience, getting up close and personal with their favorite artists (on stage or from the pit) and exposure to new talent?

Peter attended the festival for one day. His musical interests were satisfied. He bought CDs and had them autographed by artists. He was intrigued by the demographic changes that occurred during the day of the audience in response to the changes in the program. After 4:00 p.m. the youthful set arrived. Peter saw the atmosphere amongst the audience akin to a pilgrimage in terms of the celebrity nature of some artists. A principal interest for him was to visually document how the festival was managed and the responses of patrons to staff, volunteers, and artists. His photographs have been included in this book. Peter has been to many festivals around the world and he was impressed by the attention to detail demonstrated by the organizers. He had some concerns about his own experience in trying to purchase tickets online, parking a long way from the center of the action, and the sale of cheaper one-day tickets onsite. He will return to an intrinsic experience of the festival in the future without the obligation of a mission!

# Festival Ideas and Issues

1. The sorts of benefits sought by festival attendees include filling their increased leisure time sensitively, value for money expended, new cultural authentic experiences, a high standard of personal service, increased enjoyment from socializing, a learning environment, better health, personal prestige, social/cultural advancement, security, and recognition. Festivals provide vehicles for the "self," which is the center of modern consumer society, to tie together issues of choice, identity, status, alienation and culture. People want to avoid:
   o Unsafe situations
   o Discomfort, doubts, and worries
   o Embarrassment
   o Making too many complex decisions
   o Being treated as just a number
   o Being made to feel a nuisance
   o Antisocial behaviour (ASB) such as drunken, rowdy, and potentially life- and property-threatening behavior
   
   How can festival organizers maximize the positive impacts and minimize the negative to ensure greater appeal of their festival?

2. The way in which the media portrays the images of celebration is interesting. What role can the media play in highlighting the benefits and challenges that may emerge? How can local leaders manage the community pride that festivals often generate?

3. Let's examine the position of participants and spectators at festivals. What does each term suggest to you? What could be the individual's perspective of involvement in events and festivals? Individuals may be drawn to the company of family or friends, a sense of community and place, access to artists, and collaboration offered by particular festivals. Others may be attracted by the opportunity to become an attraction themselves within the specific confines of a celebration (e.g., dancing at an outdoor rock concert). So, the spectator becomes part of the spectacle.

4. Many festivals are modeled on what is done elsewhere. The cultural exchanges within and between countries and the influence of technological advances have all affected how we celebrate publicly. How can festival organizers establish uniqueness for their event?

5. With a growing concern for *authentic* experiences, festival-goers are demanding greater access to the everyday rituals occupying the lives of host communities. How can this be achieved?

6. Discuss how audiences become scenery at large-scale events; how huge amounts of money are committed to sharing events globally; how substantial capital is invested by governments to satisfy society's desire to have purpose-built public spaces.

7. What does a festival of the future look like? What do you consider the most enduring feature of popular festivals?

8. How would you introduce the contemporary arts and festive practice into what can be often quite traditional programs?

9. If festivals offer opportunities for artists to take risks in their practice, how can festivals go about encouraging audiences to dare too?

# Festival Focus Activities

1. Take a moment to contemplate the festive ceremonies that populate our personal lifelong cultural calendars:

| | | |
|---|---|---|
| naming ceremonies | national festivals | crafts |
| births | flags | demonstrations |
| a time for reflection | songs | protests |
| initiations | holidays | pilgrimages |
| coming of age | pageants | holy places |
| investitures | fireworks | shrines |
| awards | patriotism ceremonials | worship |
| family festivals | coronation | use of vestments |
| reunions | military tattoos | liturgy |
| Mothers'/ Fathers' Days | (gun) salutes | ritual |
| weddings | proclamations | silence |
| vows | parliamentary procedures | sermon |
| tokens | beginnings | vigils |
| feasting | laying foundation stones | days of obligation |
| betrothal or engagement | launchings | passion plays |
| funerals and remembrances | sports | new-year celebrations |
| death and mourning | competition | fireworks |
| lying in state | exhibition | fire |
| praise and thanksgiving | acclamation | purification |
| burial or cremation | chanting | bonfire |
| full military honors | music | fertility and harvest festivals |
| music gatherings and assemblies | dancing | fairs |
| crusades | specific arts-based festivals | thanksgiving |
| conferences | drama | mystery |
| | visual arts | sacrifice |

What others can you think of?

If you generate a timeline of specific periods of your life, you may observe numerous celebratory occasions.

2. How highly developed is your festive vocabulary?

   What do the following words suggest to you?

   Can you attribute a name or a location of an event suggested by the following words?

| | | |
|---|---|---|
| festival | commemoration | harvest |
| feast | fete | fiesta |
| holiday | holy day | carnival |
| celebration | entertainment | gala |
| happening | competition | tournament |
| contest | milestone | occasion |
| games | mega event | parade |
| pilgrimage | exposition | convention |
| natural phenomenon | displays | pageant |
| rally | reception | street party |
| fair | agricultural show | |

## Suggested Reading

Crompton, J. L., and S. L. McKay. "Motives of Visitors Attending Festival Events." *Annals of Tourism Research* 24, no. 2 (1997): 425–439.

Dunstan, G. *Becoming Coastwise, the Path of Festivals and Cultural Tourism, Landscape and Lifestyle Choices for the Northern Rivers of NSW*. Lismore, Australia: Southern Cross University, 1994.

Falassi, A. *Time out of Time: Essays on the Festival*. Albuquerque, NM: University of New Mexico Press, 1987.

Getz, D. *Event Studies: Theory, Research and Policy for Planned Events*. Oxford, UK: Butterworth-Heinemann, 2007.

Gilbert, D., and M. Lizotte. "Tourism and the Performing Arts." *Travel and Tourism Analyst* (1998): 73.

Jordan, J. "The Buxton Festival Lifecycle: Towards an Organizational Development Model for Festivals," in *Discussion Papers in Arts and Festival Management* (DPAFM 13/1) (Leicester, UK: de Montfort University, 2013).

Iso-Ahola, S. *The Social Psychology of Leisure and Recreation*. Dubuque, IA: Brown, 1980.

Phummuang, P. *Investigation of the Influences on the Decision Making of Thais for Their SongKran Holidays*. Master's thesis, Naresuan University, Bangkok Campus, Thailand, 2012.

Pine, B., and J. Gilmore. *The Experience Economy: Work as Theatre and Every Business a Stage*. Boston: Harvard Business School Press, 1999.

Salamone, F. A. (ed.). *Routledge Encyclopedia of Religious Rites, Rituals and Festivals*. New York: Routledge, 2004.

Schechner, R. *The Future of Ritual, Writings on Culture, and Performance*. London: Routledge, 1995.

Stebbins, R. "Cultural Tourism as Serious Leisure." *Annals of Tourism Research* 23, no. 4 (1996): 948–950.

Taylor, A. *The Artful Manager*. Arts Management Program, American University, Washington, DC: 2007.

Turner, V. *Celebration: Studies in Festivity and Ritual*. Washington, DC: Smithsonian Institution Press, 1982.

# CHAPTER 2

# Secrets of Enduring Festival Success

> Adaptive resilience is the capacity to remain productive and true to core purpose and identity whilst absorbing disturbance and adapting with integrity in response to changing circumstances.
>
> —*Mark Robinson, Making Adaptive Resilience Real (2011)*

---

This chapter provides an opportunity for you to better understand:

- The concepts of survival, sustainability, resilience, longevity, and prosperity in festivals
- The business of successful arts and community cultural festival-making
- Maintaining momentum and relevance
- Why some festivals fail and how the challenges, commitment, and collaboration can help festivals thrive

---

There are numerous components of the festival mosaic that need to be mastered as festival organizations and their leaders commit to ensuring their festival is in for the long haul. This chapter examines the major human, organizational, leadership, and process elements that determine the success of effective preparation, production, and presentation necessary for enduring festivals. These are represented in Figure 2.1.

At the core of our investigation is finding what works as well as what works best for specific situations. It will be dependent on the tools employed to ensure that decisions made through the creative and administrative processes are tested, are appropriate, are timely, and are based on sound intelligence. This knowledge management is key to delivering an integrated approach to making a memorable and well-positioned festival in the contemporary marketplace.

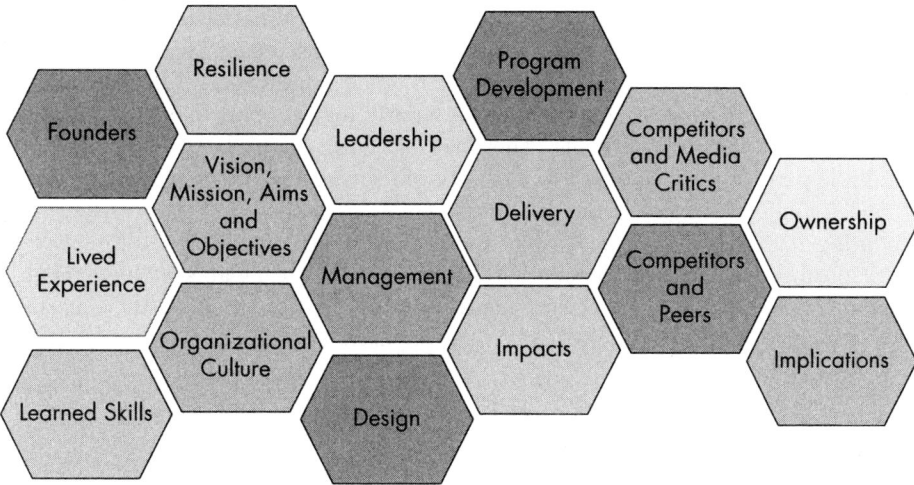

**Figure 2.1** Resilient Festivals' Mosaic.

# Resilient and Successful Festivals

The creativity festivals provide in their design and delivery builds on the intangible value of the imagination and the inclusiveness that can be generated in communities where a festival provides a stimulating incubator for further capacity-building. Diverse interests and practices that involve clusters of economic and social activity can be readily exposed and later exploited to benefit the community more broadly. What emerge are processes that strengthen collaborative governance, acknowledgment of distinctive place-making initiatives, promotion of a community's identity and its general urban/local sustainability and well-being.

You will notice that successful festival organizations consistently look to accumulate current data on their performance as well as that of any competitors and any trends in the industry, by sharing this with internal and external stakeholders. The information they gather as they monitor their progress helps generate effective actions by the staff and volunteers, festival audiences, and partners. It assists in determining innovative choices in programming, logistics, and relationship-building to deliver a lasting festival identity and worthwhile experience for all participants. Festivals look to incorporate new ideas. How are ideas generated and how do they catch on (maybe like a YouTube clip gone viral) and how can resources be released to ensure they are applied in the best interests of each festival? Timing and trust are important, as change by management to festival programs, for example, can be unpredictable and so risk has to be calculated.

The combination of personal and professional talent within productive festival teams and a balanced approach to managing explicit and tacit knowledge makes them learning organizations. So, where does the resilience reside? Is festival longevity a resilience marker? A community's capacity to sustain a connection to its community festival or other civic occasions beyond the festival period (represented in local, regional, and national environments) may be a guide. This network approach to festival success and resilience suggests that some connections lay dormant until required. While there is no clear indication of how connectivity is related to resilience, it appears to provide a mechanism for attending to activity in the public interest in communities of any scale. These social systems can't be managed in isolation. The multiple partnerships that exist in each of the festival communities appear to embrace governance practices that are adapted to their own circumstances.

Enduring festivals emerge from dynamic organizations where the culture is learned rather than inherited and is understood and embraced by participants. It requires ongoing nourishment (which is investigated in Chapter 4) as the culture controls the way staff and volunteers behave among themselves and with people external to the organization.

## Underpinning Enduring Festivals

There are several important questions that need to be addressed as festival teams prepare for their resilience practices. These implementation tasks include building the team; getting parties energized and interested in projects within the festival; breaking down the work to be undertaken into manageable units; estimating the resources required to minimize costs; assisting in scheduling so that crises can be minimized and less time wasted; and identifying who and when partners will become involved in the journey through negotiation and training programs. Throughout this preparation all activities need to be well monitored, recorded, and documented for future reference and refreshment to address the festival's long-term vision. All assets need to be well maintained and operational with clear procedures for use and application to the designated tasks in logistics, programs, marketing, and site management. Finally, in this mosaic activity it behooves the organization to regularly check the systems in place are working in the best interests of the overall mission and carrying out any adjustments that can be identified.

By comparing actual progress against the festival plans, the integrity of the whole is sustained. Festivals are complex entities, so it is important to introduce a series of controls that can ensure longitudinal coordination over time. This helps document the festival's history. Establishing a system of coordination, reporting, and control can reveal a current situation analysis through ensuring any boundaries established for project units within the total organization are defended and function in line with the organization's resource allocation and staffing in a timely way.

Another aspect of preparing for the long haul involves anticipating adversity (in any shape) and preparing contingency plans for all elements of the festival design. In attempting to minimize the negatives that can come from any quarter and threaten the capacity of the festival organization to deliver on its promise, leaders and managers need to anticipate the effects that may emerge of resistance to change. This requires internal improvements being made to incentivize and reward success in an attempt to maintain momentum within the team. Any change, gradual or otherwise, is one of the ways a festival evolves and endures, as we shall see in Chapter 13. This whole exercise can be summed up through sensitively dealing with the challenges incurred as the festival is prepared, the commitment by all individuals involved, and the collaboration required of each partner as identified in Figure 2.2.

## Recognizing Success Factors

There are simple ways to recognize a festival's success. If the festival reaches its goals, the organization can claim it has effectively achieved success. If it has met the needs and aspirations of its

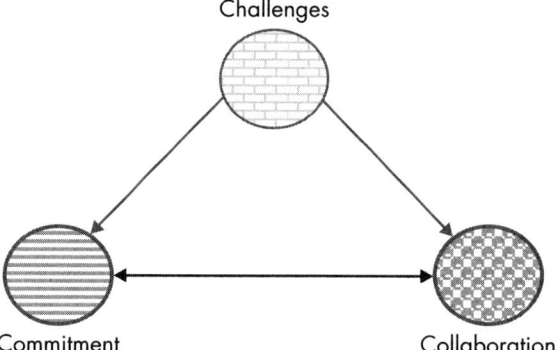

**Figure 2.2** Festival Evolution and Endurance.

core partners, it has been successful. The processes of design, development, and delivery as well as the productive outcomes shape a festival's success. The legacy of a successful festival needs to address the social, cultural, economic, and environmental needs of the host community.

So, how do the organization and its partners value a festival? Economic impact is often a driver, with new money coming into play, jobs being created, with implications for further investment in infrastructure to ensure amenities for use by residents and visitors. Many festival organizations make a profit, or at least break even. Many for-profit festival organizations reinvest in their ongoing commitment to providing festival activities that have wide appeal with specific social and cultural outcomes through community well-being and quality of life experiences at their base.

There is considerable value gained from media coverage, destination image, and identity branding through sponsorship, donations, links to charities, and individual investors. Host community perceptions are important to consider as well, so the recognition of a sense of place and community reflects the willingness of residents to offer ongoing support for the festival. If the planning, the program, and the audience mix are the best fit for local values, then there is a good case for the festival to endure and prosper. Local scrutiny of how well festival management deals with challenges like natural disasters, adverse weather events, or operational or technical malfunctions can all build confidence and long-term endorsement. That would be a success. An overarching factor is whether the festival offers optimum satisfaction to the targeted audience. If their expectations are met and their experience is positive, word-of-mouth promotion ensues that will demonstrate resilience and facilitate the potential for ongoing success.

## Lessons on Festival Success Factors

In Hamish McRae's (2010) analysis of international organizations and communities, *What Works: Success in Stressful Times*, he observes some critical principles that comprise the mosaic proposed by the current investigation. He recognizes that each enterprise is different and takes from the mix elements that fundamentally assist those involved to transform their vision into practical platforms that can be shared with others over time. In fact, he uses Edinburgh's festivals as one of his case studies. In Chapter 11 we explore further the opportunities that the city of Edinburgh has generated to sustain an international competitive advantage.

McRae identifies lessons from how organizations deal with times of economic stress and pressures that impact on actions inside the organization and in diverse external environments. He suggests the organization's optimism is vital, as is engagement with host communities and governments at all levels. The organization needs to recognize the value of being accessible to the quality of talent the festival wishes to share. Being able to recognize success factors and being alert to actions and outcomes that are not advancing the organization's vision must be confronted honestly. The capacity to adapt quickly once critical market, administrative, and artistic challenges arise is a measure of a festival's resilience.

These themes will be reaffirmed as we examine the creativity and innovation that has been accrued by festival-makers around the world as they seek to demonstrate their commitment to quality and longevity.

## How Festival Organizations Function

Festival organizations do not operate in a vacuum. They operate in economic, social, physical, political, and cultural contexts that determine what they can do and the costs associated with doing it. The principal environments that influence strategic and operational festival management choices, and in turn generate a "culture" within each organization, include a substantial list in which all play a role:

- (Inter)national practice trends
- (Inter)national economic trends
- Legal/political environment
- Demographics/composition of society by subcultures
- Labor market forces
- The media
- Geographical location
- Physical resources of the organization
- Cultural sector competition
- Advances in technology
- Consumer behaviors and motivations
- Personal qualities of founders and leaders
- Cultural sector education and training

During any given period in an organization's history, it will be growing, stable, or declining. During each stage of an organization's life cycle the forces that cause management adjustments influence the culture and vice versa. Goals are not always met, for reasons beyond the control of the board, committees, and the membership. How the individual organization deals with the crises that arise from time to time—the skill, the luck, the planning, the leadership, and the corporate experience that come into play—clearly reflects and influences the culture of the organization.

External influences vary too. They can be episodic or regular, general or focused, detached or personal, initiative or obstructive, formal or informal. The impact, for example, of the interaction of government agencies (at all levels) and funding opportunities for organizations is affected directly by these variables. Many community-based organizations are resource-poor—whether financial or in relation to technology and amenities. The sorts of relationships these organizations establish with other groups in their communities are identified in Figure 2.3 demonstrating a measure of their management savvy, experience, and resilience.

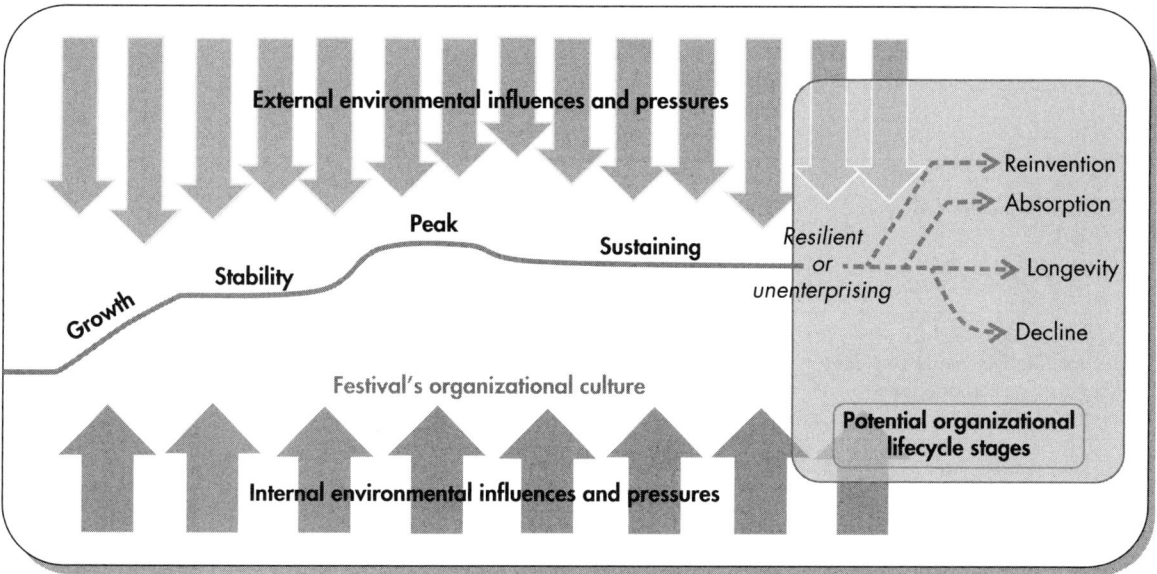

**Figure 2.3** External and Internal Organizational Pressures.

## Features of Festival Organization Survival

A characteristic of a festival organization's survival is the capacity of the team to deal with intertwining and simultaneous challenges that can emerge from the internal and external environments in which it operates. There needs to be a shared response that is based on the festival organization's mission, its aims and objectives and how these are measured and what procedures can best be applied to any action required. This is based on a documented philosophy accepted by all parties. There is generally a shared vocabulary for the systems in place to clearly explain the organization's authority procedures, peer-review mechanisms, and incentives and rewards.

An understanding by all internal personnel, particularly of what the product is, what the festival looks and feels like, and what the likely impact of it will be when all the planning, design, and development is completed is critical. Have all the team actually attended a festival? Have they compared their outputs to those of their competitors? What are the features of an enduring festival? See Table 2.1.

| Independent/Community | Festival Organization | Partnerships |
|---|---|---|
| An initial good idea that finds resonance with the host community and a potential market sector. | Consistent delivery of a creative program that allows residents and visitors to provide positive word-of-mouth promotion. | Satisfaction by stakeholders who believe they receive a sound return on their investment of finance, market access, time, energy, social outcomes, and brand connections. |
| Volunteerism is appreciated and nurtured. | Local infrastructure satisfactorily delivers accessible comfort/security/fun for participants and organizers. | A demonstration that the image and identity of the target market is one the existing audience wishes to perpetuate; new subsets allow for diversification. |

**Table 2.1** Features of Festival Survival

| Independent/Community | Festival Organization | Partnerships |
|---|---|---|
| People with passion involved at all levels. | Organizational structure accommodates new members and develops succession management strategies. | Few barriers exist in terms of regular, informed community communication. |
| Individuals' experience and influence as resources are offered and tested. | Consolidation of organizers' experience through documented corporate history, garnering of community respect and understanding of values held by residents. | Substantial partnership with local government through effective communication, offers to leverage external funds, management, and promotional support. |
| Clear connection of festival with landscape, lifestyle, sense of place and community, heritage, and economy. | Willingness to take risks, respond to new ideas, sustain popular core elements, unlock access to community assets to build program. | Provision of effective links with regional media for editorial, corporate goodwill, sponsorship opportunities, and advertising. |
| Shared knowledge and leadership skills of some individuals. | Provision of an umbrella forum for special interest groups. | Provision of fundraising opportunities. |
| Communal memory generated and consolidated. | Interest of organizers to up-skill themselves through training in business and event organizing. | Encourage greater visitation and prolong stays in region. |
| Memorable generated experiences. | Organization's objectives met annually. | Stimulation of local economy, generates employment, introduces investment, builds brand with tourism implications. |

**Table 2.1** Features of Festival Survival *(continued)*

## DEFINITIONS

A festival's longevity and prosperity emerges from the following three elements:

**Survival:** Maslow's hierarchy of needs and aspirational pyramid representing biological and physiological, safety and security, belongingness, esteem and self-actualization needs.

**Sustainability:** The nourishment that arises from the appreciation and application of a triple bottom-line approach to planning and development based on social, economic, and environmental factors.

**Resilience:** Regarded as a complex mosaic of interrelated factors, it is the organizational capability to anticipate key events from emerging trends, constantly learning and adapting to change and rapidly bouncing back from disaster. It demands leadership and management.

Key mechanisms that organizations can develop to respond positively to change and to recover faster from adversity include.

- How the organization can better foresee its future by using scenario planning
- How it can become adaptive and enhance partnerships
- How it scans internal and external environments to better understand context over time
- How it should address crises and adversity

# Resilient Festival Practices

You might have already registered that there is a community cultural ecosystem that includes a variety of agents that operate under the radar. The nature and role of festivals demonstrably encourages those hidden human and cultural resources in communities to be revealed in formal and informal ways. These adaptive processes include ensuring the widest possible reach is secured across a community's interest groups, and this is where the engagement of festival partners becomes important.

Most festivals take advantage of trusting relationships between multiple enterprises that generally exist independently of one another yet for the festival become mutually interdependent. This places substantial responsibility on each of the players involved in the collaboration. The process of evolution and change is observed in each festival. These are driven by individuals and agencies looking to exploit new opportunities.

Openness to collaborate is seen as a positive trait in organizations' leaders. In the host communities this leadership can come from within or outside the festival organization. Some festivals adopt a program of festival 'ambassadors' to assist in raising the festival profile, linking to targeted audiences, and supporting host communities in their endeavors. What leaders can recognize is the value of connections with partners who can extend the organization's reach, enhance its program and networks, and energize its processes and practice. Some leaders, though not all, have personal skills and relationships that take the organization forward through their understanding of connections with strategic partners. Some festival organizations enlist the support of 'community champions' from beyond their specific sector who advocate on the festival's behalf in relevant environments such as media, government, and special interest groups. All festivals have over time confronted change inside and outside their organizations. Some react defensively and ineffectually and fail to endure as a result. By building coalitions from among festival partners, the resources, knowledge, and political clout can be mobilized to make things happen in the best interests of the festival.

When communities experience stress, it is the courageous and creative leaders who are called upon to address the challenges and help their partners rebuild. Communities around the world are keen to identify the best strategy to ensure their community finds appropriate and timely solutions. Some see two pathways: one that focuses on a community's needs, deficiencies, and problems and another that begins with a commitment to discovering a community's capacities and assets. Therefore festivals can provide a lens for what is known as resilience inside and outside the organization.

## Community and Festival Resilience

A truly mosaic process, resilience refers to the ability to "bounce back" from negative experiences that may reflect the innate qualities of individuals or be the result of learning and experience. Regardless of the origin of resilience, there is evidence to suggest that it can be developed and enhanced to promote greater well-being. This is important for enduring festivals. Resilience is not regarded as a quality that is either present or absent in a person or group, but rather a process that may vary across circumstances and time. These degrees of resilience are dependent on the situational challenges being faced. Individuals and teams may demonstrate increased capacity and confidence to tackle extreme pressure to varying levels and assume roles of quick creative responses and flexibility in comparison with others by drawing on personalities and previous experience.

Some festivals demonstrate resilience and longevity simply because they have been staged for a long time and solutions to problems that have arisen over time have become embedded in the organization's culture. Festivals face very public scrutiny, before, during, and after their staging. They are often dependent on external sources of funding, so there is considerable interest in transparency and accountability. Festivals not only depend on financial investment, but on public goodwill through relationships with volunteers, charities and the business community. These organizations consistently monitor how their efforts are received and as they work through the life cycle, leaders and managers can anticipate how to prepare for any challenges or changes that may emerge.

## Festival Resilience Strategy

To ensure festivals endure, it can be argued that it comes down to strategy and structure. It is difficult to know what should come first. Whether a festival organization emerges from a community self-help group, a private enterprise, a limited company, or collaboration between public, private, and community entities, each will have statutory obligations that influence the way that organization can conduct its business legally.

The influence of structure on strategy generates the policies that inform the process that makes the festival tick, such as administration, human resource management, finance, and procurement of suppliers—from artists through to logistics, communication, and marketing. Strategy provides the roadmap for future decisions. The influence of resilience thinking through a systemic approach, as suggested by the work of Brian Walker and David Salt in their 2008 book *Resilience Thinking*, recognizes the dynamic world in which festivals operate. They suggest that resilience is "the capacity of a system to absorb disturbance and still retain its basic function and structure." Our mosaic framework suggests there are options. Look at the strategies outlined in Table 2.2 prepared by organizations committed to

Festival organizations recognize the diversity of audience ability to ensure access for all as at the Opera on the Beach performances with the Bleach Festival at Coolangatta, Gold Coast, Australia.

# Resilient Festival Practices

## National Focus

**EventScotland**

Scotland 'The Perfect Stage'

A Strategy for the Events Industry in Scotland 2009–2020

"The Perfect Stage" builds on EventScotland's established reputation and strong track record of delivery by presenting a clear strategic direction for the future of events in Scotland.

Our 2020 vision for Scotland established as the perfect stage for events.

**Mission:**
To develop a portfolio of events that delivers impact and international profile for Scotland.

To envisage that partner organizations and those involved in staging, organizing, developing, and funding events will use this strategy as an underpinning principle to their own strategies, plans, and activities.

The strategy builds on:
- Our cultural identity and heritage
- Our people
- Our natural environment
- Our built facilities
- Our signature events

## State Focus

Eventscorp
Tourism Western Australia

Eventscorp's areas of expertise include event management, television broadcast, marketing, research, media, government relations, and venue identification.

**Mission:**
To identify, develop, and deliver world-class events that promote and enrich Western Australia.

Eventscorp is Western Australia's Government Event Agency and a division of Tourism Western Australia.

It achieves its goals by implementing a number of strategies, including:
- Identifying and attracting a diverse range of world-class events to Western Australia.
- Providing funding for both major events as well as regional events through the Regional Events Scheme.
- Supporting and developing events from concept to successful implementation.
- Managing and growing events, where appropriate, particularly in regional areas.
- Leveraging tourism, business, and media opportunities through events.

The appeal of world or national sporting championships and other world-class events to potential travelers and investors should not be underestimated. Eventscorp sets world benchmarks in organization and professionalism. Post-event research consistently reports high satisfaction among stakeholders with Eventscorp's organization, management, and support before, during, and after an event.

## Specialist Festival

Montreal Just For Laughs Comedy Festival, Canada

Known the world over as being one of the most exciting cities to visit in the summer, Montréal also enjoys renown for the diversity of its neighborhoods, its *joie de vivre*, and its cultural mix.

The Collectif de Festivals Montréalais is a nonprofit organization.

The Collectif de Festivals Montréalais, from mid-July to mid-August, offers four weeks of festivals. Montréal Festimania is the establishment of a long tradition of festivities. The program has 11 festivals with outdoor concerts, electronic music, fashion, comedy, stage arts, world music, cinema, and shows of all descriptions. With Montréal Festimania, the Collective wants to contribute to making Montréal a world-class tourist destination and North America's festival hub offering visitors an authentic experience.

**Table 2.2** Examples of Organizations' Visions, Missions, and Objectives

## Industry Network

Victoria Events Industry Council (VEIC) Australia

VEIC is a peak industry council of associations, corporations, and government agencies representing event organizers, venues, suppliers, and service providers for Melbourne and regional Victoria.

VEIC provides leadership for Victoria's events industry through advocacy and representation supported by industry and business development services.

Victoria's Events Industry Development Plan (2010)

**Mission:**
- To provide leadership, representation, and focus for Victoria's events industry.
- To undertake activities that serve to develop the capacity of the Victorian events industry.
- To seek to create a united events industry that speaks with one voice.

- To seek to enhance professional networks within the Victorian events industry.

## Community Festival

CenterFest Arts Festival, Durham, North Carolina

CentreFest is the longest-running street arts festival in North Carolina and Durham's largest arts and community festival. This annual event features more than 150 juried visual and performing artists from across the nation, music and entertainment, food, and fun, family-friendly, educational activities. The festival site is located in the vibrant Durham Central Park District, surrounded by galleries, restaurants, and the Farmers' Market.

**Mission:**
Durham Arts Council, Inc. promotes excellence in and access to the creation, experience, and active support of the arts for all the people in the community. It makes all of its programs, facilities, and services available without regard to race, color, sex, creed, religion, ancestry, national origin, age, disability, gender preference, marital status, or political affiliation.

How Durham Arts Council supports the arts. It:
- Helps professional and amateur artists and arts organizations produce music, theater, dance, visual, media, and literary art.
- Helps residents and visitors find, enjoy, and participate in the artistic and cultural events available in the community.
- Manages the Durham Arts Council Building, a city-owned, multipurpose community arts center in downtown Durham.
- Produces CenterFest, Durham's annual street arts festival each September.
- Produces the Edible Arts Festival of Food & Art each June.

Durham Arts Council, (DAC) producer and presenter of CenterFest Arts Festival for 37 years, announced its plans to dramatically expand and re-envision CenterFest, the longest-running outdoor arts festival in North Carolina. DAC and its key partners launched a one-year visioning/production process for the 2012 expanded arts and entertainment festival format.

**Table 2.2** Examples of Organizations' Visions, Missions, and Objectives *(continued)*

effective leadership and management of festivals and identify the key components of their aspirations. You'll notice they wish to make clear to all the participants, inside and outside their organization:

- Their experience of the sector, the shared purpose, and the robust contexts and links they maintain
- how the strategy offers a framework for them to coordinate their action when SMART objectives emerge, providing useful and realistic expectations (SMART objectives are generally defined as **S**pecific, **M**easureable, **A**chievable, **R**ealistic, and **T**ime bound)
- The language they use is not complex so all can grasp the implications of the choices made by festival management.
- It represents as feasible, realistic, and helpful so each partner can own the proposition and collaborate to better tolerate any changes
- It clearly identifies any obvious practical constraints, fears, and intellectual, human, and practical assets to adapt to opportunities

Such strategies (incorporating visions, missions, and aims/goals) help define the *raison d'etre* of festivals and guide the leadership, management, and relationships going forward. All internal and external festival partners need to know where they are going and what they are aspiring to achieve. The vertical (top-down or bottom-up) links are vital for individual festivals, as are the horizontal partners represented in our mosaic.

## Gathering Evidence for Resilience

The strategies and the subsequent festival action or implementation plans need to be underpinned by robust analysis of research such as that undertaken in the 2006 AEA Consulting *Thundering Hooves* report, *Maintaining the Global Competitive Edge of Edinburgh's Festivals*, which identified the key elements of success for festivals more broadly.

There are a number of apparent critical success factors and our research suggests that a leading festival city should be able to demonstrate the following attributes:

- Long-term planning and strategy: Festivals development should be considered in minimum blocks of five years and set within a strategic context of a city's long-term development and competitiveness.
- Importance of context: The historical, physical, social, and cultural context of a city is a major source of the uniqueness of each festival.
- Distinctiveness of location: The location must be "attractive" in terms of beauty, geology, or distinctiveness.
- Appropriate timing: The dates of key festivals must be set to enable both strong programming and to attract a required and expanding number of visitors (both local and tourists).
- Diversity of cultural ecology: The city should offer a wide range and variety of year-round cultural activities, and the festivals should be well integrated into this ecology through networks, relationships, and projects at local, regional, and national levels.

The festivals should be an integral part of their host cities' cultural life, with deep relationships to their local communities, and not have the feel of being grafted onto them.
- Coordinated action: Opportunities for collaborative initiatives should be explored and maximized, making linkages with and across different facets of the cultural systems at play.
- Invading and interacting with the city: Events should be "audience friendly" and "safe," but at the same time energizing and continually surprising, creating a "spirit of excitement" or "buzz" (p. 20).
- Investing in quality over quantity: Success depends on achieving and sustaining a consistent international quality threshold for all festivals and not on the number of festivals. Careful impact assessment of each new festival to be added to an existing mix should be a requirement. This is more a question of understanding the implications (both positive and negative) of new entrants rather than creating a cartel of existing players.
- Talented and experienced direction: Visionary artistic and managerial leadership are essential, and conditions for recruitment, selection, retention, and succession need to be carefully considered to attract the best talent and to offer platforms and solid operational frameworks that can support the creativity that such leadership inspires.
- Focused and innovative programming: The cultural programs must be curatorially focused and be continually innovating; investment in innovation is a prerequisite of sustainability.
- Effective marketing and branding: Marketing and branding should operate within a coordinated strategy on several integrated dimensions, with clear responsibilities agreed between partners and adequate resourcing taking into account the competitive environment.
- Political will matched by strong leadership and political independence: Sustained policy-driven support by funders should be linked to strong leadership offered by the governing structures. Members of governing bodies should have appropriate expertise and balance of skills, interests, and contacts to support a festival's objectives. Political interests should not influence the program and the operational structures should be autonomous, characterized by strong governance. Political and operational alliances must work toward agreed-upon goals.
- Wide public engagement: There is a balance between the involvement and engagement of resident and visiting publics, with the former being the dominant sector.
- Adequate resources: The combined sources of finance must be sufficient to enable appropriate levels of quality, volume, and breadth of festival activity in a city, with sufficient opportunity for new development and risk-taking.
- Many financial stakeholders: There needs to be an appropriate balance of resources offered by different stakeholders from both public and private sectors, and a means of "brokering" the particular interests and needs of each. It is often the public sector that must take the responsibility to coordinate and facilitate discussions, which need to involve players at all levels (local, regional, national, and international).

- The public sector has a key role to play: Investment by the public sector should offer a measure of confidence in each festival and to the festivals' system as a whole, to help lever other forms of support and partnership development. The public sector has a prime responsibility for supporting the development of festival infrastructure, in the delivery of publicly managed or public–private partnership projects, and in the setting of priorities and offering incentives to the private sector. In addition, the public sector should take the major responsibility for ensuring longer-term impacts of festivals and their sustainable benefits, based on end-user research and engagement, are monitored and understood.
- Developed festival infrastructure for all visitors: This includes high-quality information, accommodation, transport, and visitor services when compared to competitors.
- Excellent facilities: Provision of "world-class" venues, outdoor event spaces, and other festival infrastructure to accommodate 'world-class' programs, including the need for continuous innovative use of existing and new indoor and outdoor spaces.
- Wide media support: Worldwide press and media must be attractive because of the quality and stature of the events and be sufficiently motivated to ensure that the coverage is extensive and prominent. Indeed, the ability to attract national and international press coverage is critical to success. The prospect of press coverage enables a festival to secure performers at lower rates than would otherwise be the case, affecting benignly the underlying business model. Press coverage tends, given scarce resources (and inertia), to focus disproportionately on the top one of two events. A failure to secure press coverage has a correspondingly adverse impact on both the ability to attract and retain performers at competitive rates and, because of the obvious benefits of free publicity, the level of effective demand.
- Coordinated processes of monitoring and evaluation: All interested parties should agree on the criteria, priorities, and processes for monitoring and evaluation of each festival and festivals as a whole. A "toolkit" should be devised that balances economic, social, and cultural factors with innovation and management effectiveness. The primary aim of monitoring and evaluation should be to promote a learning environment that encourages continuous improvement, with the acknowledgment of successes and achievements as well as problems and mistakes of the festivals and the funders. Financial control systems should be in place to help negate adverse cost variances, as well as business planning that uses options appraisals, scenario planning, and financial modeling techniques.

In gathering evidence for the choices on strategy and organizational structure and ongoing prosperity, festival-makers can locate useful data from documenting all stages of their festival's design and development by gathering feedback from all partners (audiences through to sponsors, funders, media, artists, and suppliers); monitoring activity and processes on a variety of technology platforms to take partners on the journey by keeping them informed; analyzing the festival's customer profile by monitoring social media for impact and logistics match of program content with commentary and reach; monitoring the efficiency of festival suppliers; being alert to research being undertaken in sectors associated with the festival like tourism, demographic change, and arts practice; monitoring internal administration, finance, human resources, training of all staff including volunteers, and gathering intelligence from their experience during a festival.

Another framework that is vital for creating enduring festivals is maintaining links with the festival industry. The growing number of networks, professional associations, academic programs, and research provide important information to underpin creative and management decisions to satisfy the agreed-upon festival objectives. Festival management needs to maintain links to local, national, and international agencies that can enhance learning, provide competitor perspectives, and assess trends in technology, management and design.

Communication allows the organization to keep abreast of changes that can impact the festival's social, political, environmental, and economic environments. Staff can attend relevant conferences and seminars, the festival could host such information forums exploring good practice. Membership of international festival networks such as the International Festivals and Events Association (IFEA), Arts Hub, or the European Festivals Association (EFA) provide cutting-edge leads in current practice. Industry award programs allow for festivals to reflect on their efforts and learn from peer review. For those wishing to maintain a festival employment trajectory it is helpful to be linked to employment opportunities, internships, and staff exchanges. Publications of a practical or academic nature also provide useful underpinning for choices organizational can make about sustaining a healthy organizations culture.

So, in keeping with how strategy informs future directions and allows festivals to thrive, consider these important features as you evaluate festivals with which you are familiar or those outlined briefly in Table 2.2. You'll observe in a mosaic sense there will be overlapping or juxtapositioning of diverse needs along the way.

- How have they dealt with research appropriate to their needs?
- How have they scanned the competitive environment in which they operate?
- Do they regularly assess their assets and test the feasibility of their plans?
- Are they alert to industry trends and good practice?
- Have they identified the USP (unique selling proposition) that will make their festival distinctive in the marketplace? Have they found a niche through identifying substantial ideas and their practical application?
- Have they nurtured long-term relationships that are both stable and intermittent (as required) that are logical or causal, inclusive and require memberships, or are personal and contractual to everyone's satisfaction?
- How is the human-resource mix revealed in the best interests of the festival?
- How have they dealt with timely and effective internal and external communication?
- How robust is the marketing plan and what capacity has it to adapt to changing technological platforms to best match the customers' demands with the festival's capacity to deliver a satisfying experience?
- How have they gone about getting the financial and investment mix right?
- How have they recorded the challenges and solutions they have experienced over time and fed them into the evaluation and strategy-building cycle?

Find out what you can about the origins, the mission, and the mechanisms applied by management to create the enduring festivals listed in Table 2.3. What are the distinctive features of their success?

| Festival | Success Factors |
|---|---|
| Our Lady of Mount Carmel Society Hammonton, New Jersey, 1875 | The festival is an independent nonprofit Catholic organization formed in 1875 by Italian immigrants new to Hammonton, who took time to celebrate their safe journey to America and a successful harvest by giving praise and thanks to the blessed Virgin Mary. The main function of the Our Lady of Mt. Carmel Society is the preparation and presentation of the feast each July 16. The Society is also involved in a variety of community activities and charitable endeavors, regularly supporting school, community, and church fundraising efforts. |
| Columbus International Film and Video Festival, Film Council of Greater Columbus, Ohio, 1950<br>    Longest-running film festival in the United States | Aware of the power of cinema to educate and transform, the Film Council of Greater Columbus' mission is to encourage the creation of film, video, and electronic images of vision in both form and content by publicly screening these productions and awarding recognition to both the productions and the makers of the productions.<br>Founded by a group of progressive educators, the Film Council, through the Columbus International Film and Video Festival (a six-day event in downtown Columbus), continues their legacy, honoring and screening the work of makers whose creations of vision, beauty, and power help us understand the complexities of our world by using their committed artistry to touch our minds and hearts. |
| Monterey Jazz Festival Monterey, California, 1958<br>    Longest-running jazz festival in the world | Held every September on the 20-acre Monterey Fairgrounds site where the Festival was first presented in 1958.<br>The Monterey Jazz Festival presents the best jazz performers in the world for a three-day celebration. It features jazz conversations, panel discussions, workshops, exhibitions, clinics, and an international array of food, shopping, and festivities.<br>The festival is a nonprofit organization and has donated its proceeds to musical education since its inception. |
| Jacob's Pillow Dance Festival, Berkshires, Massachusetts, 1933<br>    America's longest-running dance festival | This festival is a National Historic Landmark and a National Medal of Arts honoree. Founded in 1933 by modern dance pioneer Ted Shawn in the beautiful Berkshire Hills of western Massachusetts. It is an international celebration of dance, music, the visual arts, and culture and includes an impressive blend of world premieres, U.S. premieres, live music, company debuts, legendary dance companies, emerging choreographers, and more than 300 ticketed and free events, talks, performances, classes, exhibits, and tours hosted at the Pillow's 163-acre site. Year-round creative development residencies support artists as they create new work. |
| Shenandoah Valley Music Festival, Orkney Springs, Virginia, 1963 | In 1963 outside of the region's county fairs, there was a decided lack of professional music presented in the Shenandoah Valley. A small group of people found this hard to accept and formed the Shenandoah Valley Music Festival. The music menu and the setting have changed but the Shenandoah Valley Music Festival remains instrumental in presenting great music. The festival's grown and thrived by keeping one simple point in mind: it's all about the music. Present high-quality music in an intimate, up-close, pastoral setting and people from all around will come. The festival has remained true to its beginnings as a presenter of symphonic music and to its role in music education. |

**Table 2.3** Five Enduring U.S. Festivals: Assessing Festival Success Factors

# CASE STUDY

## *Regional Festivals Provide a Useful Lens for Resilience*

Research undertaken in four regional community cultural festivals over a number of years provided a lens of the resilience that was nurtured internally and within host communities. The universal themes that the research highlighted are relevant as we try to explain how festivals can survive, sustain themselves, thrive, and maintain resilience. A series of indicators from the study were presented in the Preface of this book.

It is evident that for festivals to survive, attention needs to be paid to the collective political and public will to ensure appropriate resources are mobilized, that risk-taking is credible, and the partners stay the course. The host community's vision needs to resonate with its particular circumstances and possibilities, including local assets and constraints, while connections among appropriate individuals and organizations are nurtured and consolidated. This can be achieved through the deployment of adequate resources including money; people with available time, expertise, skills, and knowledge/information; and social relationships and spaces for networking. For festivals to survive they need time to demonstrate that they are addressing issues over long periods, which may mean speeding up processes as opportunities arise, or delaying to a more acceptable timeframe.

Regardless of the transient nature of such experiences, their value is that they induce and sustain a shared sense of occasion and excitement. This connectivity helps build resilience. This glue is demonstrated in three major ways. These celebrations demonstrate belonging and community resilience through participation, governance, and the nature and context of event.

It suggested that by ensuring each domain is attended to effectively and inclusively, the resulting social/cultural well-being, environmental sustainability, and economic prosperity, the host community aspires to contribute to resilient festivals and communities.

Active participation by festival security and ancillary support services builds confidence in community cultural events.

## Participation

Partnerships are seen to be a valuable aspect of festival-making. The active collaboration and cooperation that can be brought to bear enhances the creative and innovative options available to the festival. They are seen as positive aspects of community development. By taking initiatives in the public domain for a common good, individuals and groups can demonstrate personal and professional skills that can be translated into other aspects of community life. The communication that takes place and the mutual support offered through teamwork are valuable characteristics of resilience.

## Governance

Leadership can provide guidance and management to individuals and groups set on a negotiated course. Successful festival management offers a litmus test for organizers' skills. Strategic and tactical planning, management, and marketing decisions influence not only festival outcomes, but also direct application of the learnings into other parts of community life. By engaging with people committed to planning worthwhile celebrations with care and attention to detail, organizations are able to handle the responsibility of developing festivals that encourage relationships that are able to deal with challenges both internal and external to the task at hand. The responsibility taken up by leaders, managers, and partners in line with legal statutory obligations as well as nurturing good corporate practices are further characteristics of resilience.

Good governance can come about through prudent investment in existing creative practice in communities that will enhance the end product—the festival. This can relate to marketing strategies, communication techniques, social networks, technology assets, and residual public art that may be attractive during the event but sustains a mood or tone long after. This creates tradition, which is a useful resilience building block. Encouraging arts practice as part of a community festival offers opportunities to fill the gaps that social well-being seeks to satisfy and also consolidates resilience capacity. Broader engagement by festival-goers in artistic pursuits, demonstrations, workshops, meet-the-artist programs, and established participatory experiences also contribute to the resilience bank for communities.

Stakeholder groups demonstrate the best and worst of the interaction that occurs when a festival is made. Some demonstrated levels of exclusivity and hierarchical management that limited capacity to generate social capital and well-being. They also provide evidence of significant benefits accrued from cooperation and collaboration, leadership and advocacy, research, encouragement of participation and partnerships, innovative approaches to funding, technology, and increasing infrastructure and capacity-building.

Follow the arrows in Figure 2.4 to better understand the interconnectedness of relationships and their implications between festival stakeholders. The critical factors to ensure festivals contribute to their own resilience and that of their broader community are an engagement with active participation, sound governance, and an understanding and appreciation of the nature and context of each event. The robustness of these elements will inform the capacity of the festival organization and its partners to use both positive and negative experiences to demonstrate resilience in a broader context.

## Well-Being Component

How community-based festivals celebrate "belonging" for residents and visitors is demonstrated with high levels of participation, festivals give a voice to locals who are brought together by a common interest. Festivals are seen to improve the quality of life and well-being of residents through their shared interactions and by providing a place for people to participate and take some responsibility for celebrations. Festivals thus contribute substantially to the liveability of communities through support of the locally held image and identity and creatively engaging large numbers of people over a long period. Locals want to hold onto festivals they value.

Historically the concept of resilience emerged as a quality aspired to and demonstrated by the participants in festival organizations. Organizations' members believe that their festival had implications for broader community development. A sense of place and community helps construct resilient communities and networks of people despite evidence of stresses within communities, represented

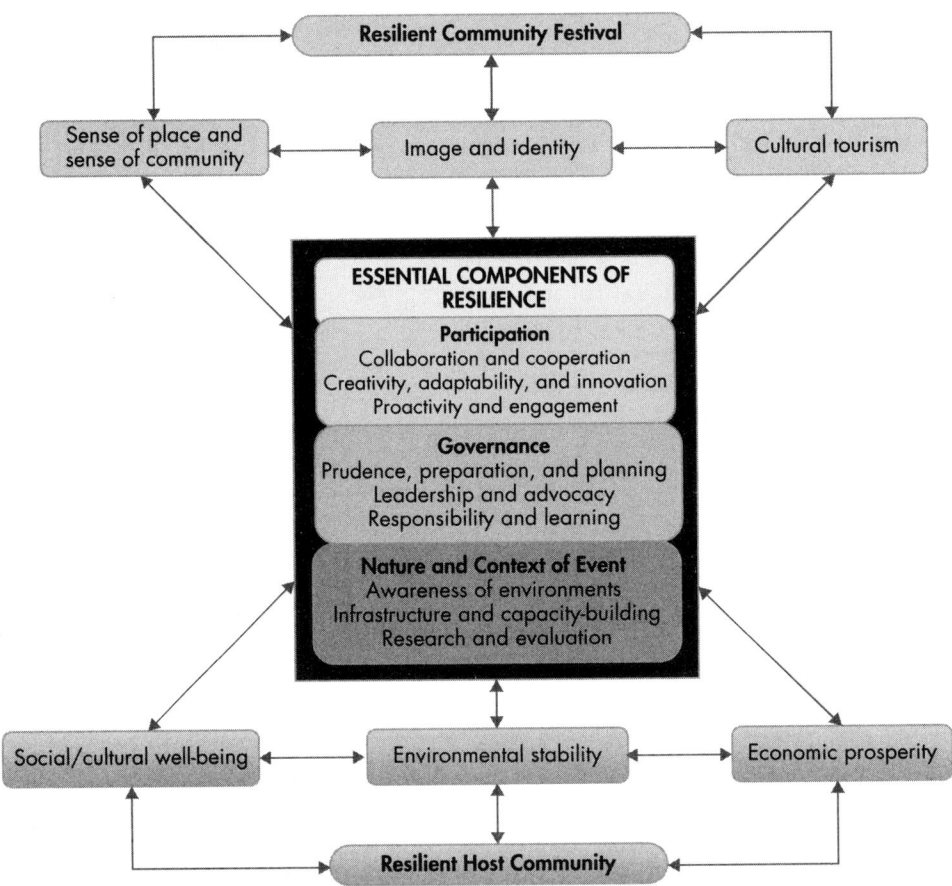

**Figure 2.4** Festivals and communities demonstrate resilience. Derrett (2007).

by specific interests, power struggles, differences in aspirations and levels of participation, and economic pressures. Festivals provide a level of confidence to function within the internal and external environments. Festivals demonstrate a degree of harmonious partnership *and* cohesiveness, offering meaning to residents' lives. They provide interaction or reciprocal relationships between all the determining factors. Festivals show how some things can be worked out through openness and collaboration.

## Resilience Component

The strength of the ties between festival stakeholders affects the durability of the networks beyond the festival-making. A number of internal variables from these relationships, such as trust and reciprocity, influence not only the durability but also the meaningfulness stimulated by the festival-making. This can extend the trust and the loyalty within the festival organization and between festival partnerships beyond the delivery of the festival.

Festivals as collaborative entities protect against risk inherent in day-to-day interactions between people. They provide participants with an opportunity to show what they can do rather than feeling restricted as to their options as active residents. This resilience feeds into the well-being framework mentioned above. These frameworks promote the building and nurturing required by communities to address sustainability and productivity from a position of strength and innovation. Festivals offer participants at all levels opportunities to know what resilience feels like and encourage others in the community to build on it.

## Festival Tourism Component

Community well-being is important when addressing how residents share their destination with visitors. It is evident that networks can have boundaries that are, in a temporal and spatial sense, open and closed, vertical or horizontal within the community or across the region. Cultural tourism is taken to be the art of participating in another culture, of relating to people and places that demonstrate a strong sense of their own identity. It is concerned with the ways of life of a place. It is doing what the locals do. The destination's economy in which these festivals reside seems amorphous, complex, and dynamic, challenging the conventional paradigm of the market economy.

## Reflecting on Cultural Resilience

Festivals are open to personal interpretation. The resilience sought by festival organizations in regional communities comes from the interaction between three key aspirations: social/cultural well-being, environmental sustainability, and economic prosperity. Individuals and groups involved with community cultural festivals demonstrate strengthened civic pride, social activism, and a sense of community. The festival content they manage enriches local understanding and helps the community focus on future development. Festivals become tourism attractors by introducing locals and visitors to traditional and emerging local cultural heritage. In turn this enhances the image of the host community in the perception of the wider world. The implications for cultural tourism include visitor interest in longer stays in the region, repeat visitation, increased expenditure, and word-of-mouth promotion of both the destination and the event.

# FROM INSIDE THE MOSAIC

## Peter Noble, Bluesfest Festival Director

In 2011 the Bluesfest (East Coast Blues and Roots Festival) was recognized with the state Award for Business Excellence at the NSW Tourism Awards. This is quite an achievement for a rural event that started out in a local nightclub. "We may be a bunch of hippies but we can still go out there and do it with the best of them!" laughs festival director Peter Noble. In 2008 Noble, through his record label AIM, was the first ever Australian independent record label to win a Grammy Award. In 2005 and 2006 Bluesfest won the Helpmann Award for "Australia's Best Contemporary Music Festival." Between 1994 and 2010 Bluesfest has consistently been awarded "Australia's Best Music Festival" by *Rhythms* magazine's readers' poll.

In 2011 the festival had a personal attendance of 53,577. Of that total, 29,055 traveled from interstate. That means that 52.47 percent of total visitors had traveled there. As a result of Bluesfest, 317.6 full-time jobs occur in the Byron Shire, 427.8 in the Northern Rivers, and 562 in Australia. The number of attendees for the five-day 2012 Bluesfest was over 80,000.

Figures released after the 2013 festival by Morrow (2013) indicated that Bluesfest contributed AU$64 million into the local economy, more broadly the region injection was AU$84 million, while AU$150 million feed into the state of NSW. Bluesfest created almost 400 full-time jobs. A record-breaking AU$120,000 was raised by festival charity stalls. Significant money was spent in the local economy.

Bluesfest was awarded the best contemporary music festival in Australia at the prestigious 2013 and 2014 Helpmann Awards that recognizes distinguished artistic achievement and excellence across major disciplines of Australia's live performance industry. At the awards ceremony Noble acknowledged the contribution of the 500-plus staff and volunteers who make the event what it is.

## Maintaining the Passion

Peter believes Bluesfest has always been less about bucks and more about maintaining a passionate commitment to fulfilling a dream. It's perhaps why the event has created a unique niche in the national cultural events calendar at a time when festivals around the country are struggling for numbers. "We never viewed Bluesfest as anything but a crusade. It's all about the music," he says.

An important factor in the success of Bluesfest, is the event's capacity to stay connected to its roots. "People forget where we came from, from a little event in a nightclub. Around here we all started with something small. We have stuck to our guns, we have never sold out and never stopped recognizing our counterculture roots." Bluesfest is proud of the work they do with charities. The aim is to bring awareness to local and international good causes through fundraising activities. The charity work is an important element of Bluesfest's social responsibility.

So 25 years on, what is Byron Bay's Bluesfest's secret to success?

The envy of festivals, Bluesfest enjoys not only a powerful and established brand, but it does so on its own permanent purpose-built site in the heart of Byron Bay. Tyagarah Tea Tree Farm is nestled on 296 acres, just 6.8 miles north of Byron Bay and 5 miles south of Brunswick Heads. It is a fully operational tea tree farm for most of the year and turns into a Bluesfest site for a few weeks before, during, and after the Easter Festival weekend. It's taken 24 years of working with and alongside artists, the local community, and the government to reach this enviable position.

"You might say learning to run a great festival is a little like learning to play the blues. It takes time and experience. Even heartbreak. We're so uncool we're cool," laughs Noble, "We put on artists who are in their 80s—and then again we put on artists who are 12 or 14 years old. We treat every band equally—there are no levels or distinctions."

"I think if a lot of people knew how long and hard and even disappointing and heartbreaking it can be to book a festival, they'd never do it. For every artist that plays Bluesfest, chances are, unless they are playing exclusively, a whole tour (to attend other national events) has been put together. I look at that as ploughing the ground and sowing the seed."

"Bluesfest features musicians who have something to say on the planet. This may be by being the finest players of their respective instruments, or it may be by sharing their culture and particularly social-justice issues in the content of their music, of which I am proud to present. Bluesfest is a peaceful gathering of people from around the world. A marriage of diverse cultures, religions and beliefs is the unifying factor of the positive nature in the artists that I book."

"I believe there is a message that is universal and that is why I book an event that is meant to be seen and heard by all ages and backgrounds. It is about bringing everyone together. Doing the right thing is what should be done anyway and I have up until now not publicized our ongoing commitment to social and environmental responsibility. However, I see the importance of increasing public awareness of all the environmental issues and to lead by demonstration."

Over time, three separate companies have been developed within Bluesfest: the festival itself, the festival site and Bluesfest Touring. The latter has grown substantially by necessity. "You've only got to look at our website and count how many acts we are touring—we're up there with the big boys in this country now. It was never part of the original plan, but it's become part of the necessity to continue to deliver the level of talent."

Compiled from an interview by M. Nolan (December 30, 2011—Echonetdaily, Edition 72) and from Martin Jones's interview with Peter Noble in *Rhythms*, March, 2012, p. 4.

## Festival Ideas and Issues

1. What definition of organizational culture best reflects what you have observed in festival organizations with which you are familiar?
2. Can you change organizational culture to ensure ongoing strength and success? What specific strategies have you noted that have been embraced to fundamentally change the organizational culture of a festival organization and what impact has it had on the design and delivery of a festival?
3. How do you account for festivals causing social, cultural, and political outcomes? Give some examples.
4. Festivals experience significant public scrutiny during their preparation and presentation. How can organizers best deal with calls for accountability and transparency, especially when the organization is in receipt of public funding?
5. How can festival-goers' personal positive or negative experiences of a festival be captured? How can their satisfaction be used to enhance a festival's longevity?
6. Identify three key festival partners and explore the potential each would place on being involved with a successful festival. What sort of challenges might destabilize the relationship into the future?

## Festival Focus Activities

1. If you identified a need for a festival, what type of organizational culture would you aim to create as its founder and why?
   How would you set about trying to achieve your aim?
   What difficulties do you anticipate and how would you overcome them?
2. If you were a festival manager, what might be a major change your organization has to deal with? What could you learn from this change? It may come from the external environment of the festival, from using alliances and partnerships.
3. What tools can festival management use to identify emerging trends that could positively impact a festival? Draw up a list and link to specific festival examples you research.
4. Design a meeting with key festival stakeholders to address a specific challenge (funding, site selection, media campaign, tourism packaging). Role-play a meeting with festival management on canvassing solutions through shared responsibility.

## Suggested Reading

AEA Consulting. Thundering Hooves, Maintaining the Global Competitive Edge of Edinburgh's Festivals, Scottish Arts Council and Festivals Edinburgh, 2006.

Archer, R. *Detritus, Addressing Culture and the Arts*. Perth, Australia: UWA, 2010.

Getz, D. *Event Studies: Theory, Research and Policy for Planned Events*. Oxford, UK: Butterworth Heinemann, 2007.

Goldblatt, J. J. Special Events: Best Practices in Event Management (2nd ed.), New York: Wiley, 1997.

Goldblatt, J. J. Special Events: A New Generation and the Next Frontier (6th ed.). Hoboken, NJ: Wiley, 2011.

Handy, C. *Understanding Organisations*. London, UK: Penguin, 1993.

Hegney, D., H. Ross, P. Baker, C. Rogers-Clark, C. King, E. Buikstra, A. Watson-Luke, K. McLachlan, and L. Stallard. *Building Resilience in Rural Communities Toolkit*. Toowoomba, Queensland: University of Queensland and University of Southern Queensland, 2008.

Hewison, R., and J. Holden, J. *The Cultural Leadership Handbook: How to Run a Creative Organization*. Farnham, Surrey, UK: Gower, 2011.

Jones, M. "Interview with Peter Noble, Festival Director Bluesfest Program." *Rhythms* (2012): 4.

Maslow, A. H. "A Theory of Human Motivation." *Psychological Review* 50 (1943): 370–396.

McRae, H. *What Works: Success in Stressful Times*. Hammersmith, UK: Harper Press, 2010.

Morrow, C. "Bluesfest's $64m boost to economy." *The Northern Star* (June 1, 2013): 4.

Robinson, M. *Making Adaptive Resilience Real*. London, UK: Arts Council England, 2010.

Walker, B., and D. Salt, D. *Resilience Thinking: Sustaining Ecosystems and People in a Changing World*. Seattle, WA: Island Press, 2006.

Willcoxson, L., and B. Millett. "Management of Organisational Culture." *Australian Journal of Management and Organisational Behaviour* 3, no. 2 (2000): 91–99.

# CHAPTER 3

# Festivals Connect to Community and Place

"…an arts festival goes to the heart of things. It's a chance to focus on an area of human activity which, in my view, is the most important expression of our humanity, and that is our imagination. For me a festival is about celebrating a place and the people who live there by reminding them that we are all essentially creative people, and by encouraging people to feel that the festival belongs to them and is about them."
—*Paul Gabowsky, Former Director, Adelaide Festival, Australia*

---

### This chapter provides an opportunity for you to better understand:

- How festivals contribute to the concepts of a sense of place, sense of community, social and cultural capital, place attachment, and community well-being
- How festivals can provide identity and positive images for host communities
- The appeal of authenticity, historical continuity, and *communitas* for stakeholders
- How festivals can be linked to the values, interests, and aspirations held by host communities and subcultures
- How festivals provide a lens for the development of community resilience
- The social and cultural implications of festival interaction with communities and place
- Festivals in the built and natural environment

**Figure 3.1** Festivals of Community and Place Mosaic.

Festival organizers have recognized the importance of connecting well with host communities. They have noticed how cultural festivals that involve the local population in a shared experience works for their mutual benefit. They know that celebrations that have been sustained through collaborative effort over long periods have seen the strengthening of communities and festivals alike. The above quote from a festival director indicates recognition of the important link of arts and cultural celebrations with place. It introduces the notion of a portfolio of considerations required when designing a festival as represented in the mosaic in Figure 3.1. It is consistent with the overarching mosaic approach to festival-making underpinning this book.

## Festivals Working with Communities

Communities around the world are keen to identify the best strategy to ensure their festival-making begins with the capacities and assets of residents and their location. As you investigate what helps festivals survive and thrive you will notice that a clear match of the needs, aspirations, and values held by the hosts and those being planned for the arts and cultural festival is crucial.

A significant factor in ensuring a festival's resilience is its connectivity to community and place. Communities, whether geographical, of specific arts or of historic interest are the custodians of the cultural content of the events they host and share with visitors. As such, diverse stakeholders feel a responsibility to nurture, sustain, and grow the cultural capacity of their host community. They work to ensure mechanisms are in place to encourage effective communication and relationship-building by growing social and cultural capital.

Festival organizers need to be not only alert to trends and demands made by the growing event industry but the challenges facing individual communities and locations chosen to host particular festivals. Demographic changes impact on potential audiences and those actively committed to designing and delivering the festival. The exposure and access to dynamic technology through use of social media platforms informs some choices. The heritage of the destinations, stories of evolving growth and prosperity, diverse characters and community champions, traditional leisure pursuits and exposure to and experience with formal cultural production, and lifestyle and employment choices of residents influence the festival's interaction with locals. Then there is the biophysical environment; its location, idiosyncratic landscape features, and land-use options, distance from other centers, climate, seasons, and contribution to the image and identity of the place. The built environment too affects how the place is shared.

All of these elements profoundly interact with a decision to create a festival of enduring meaning and appeal to locals and potential visitors.

## What Is Community?

Sociologists generally use the term "community" in a combined social and spatial sense, referring to people who occupy a common and bounded territory within which they establish and participate in common institutions. But just because people feel they are a community doesn't necessarily mean they are in terms of a willingness to collaborate and cooperate. A community comprises people who identify themselves as a group because of their shared cultural heritage, spirituality, geographic location, special interest, or gender. Usually a community is defined as a group of people living near one another, in a social relationship in which intent, belief, resources, preferences, needs, and risks are present and common. These inform the identity of the participants and their degree of commitment to the community.

An essential ingredient in achieving community appears to be a commitment by the group to meaningful communication. It is now commonplace to talk of creating or building community. Survival needs don't seem to be sufficient to satisfy the human spirit. People

Children in costume are an integral part of heritage celebrations in Kenilworth, UK.

| Indicator | Strong Sense of Community | Weak Sense of Community |
|---|---|---|
| Sense of membership | The active participants proudly display symbols of membership in the community. | The active participants do not view themselves as a community. |
| Mutual importance | The active participants recognize, cherish, and support the contributions of each other. | Participants are active only because one or a few powerful persons are involved. |
| Shared worldviews | The active participants hold common beliefs and promote shared values important to them. | The active participants hold fundamentally different beliefs and values and cannot reconcile their differences. |
| Bonding/networking | The active participants enjoy one another and look forward to time spent together. | The active participants have no affinity for each other and relationships are formal. |
| Mutual responsibility for the community | The survival and health of the community is a primary concern of all its active participants. | One or only a few persons struggle to keep the group together. |

**Table 3.1** Sense of Community Indicators
*Based on Community Planning Task Force (2002).*

are complex beings. They seem to have an instinct for community. They are sustained by social interaction and emotional support garnered from a sense of collective action. Local governance on a voluntary level and through government authorities encourages public participation in decision making, problem solving, sustainable practices, and appropriate actions aligned to values expressed by the host community.

Sound, current knowledge of each part of the mosaic influences how a festival is staged. It affects the social and cultural impact, often understood in terms of community well-being. Arts activity, including cultural festivals, stimulates job creation, tourism, attracts visitors and investment, and diversifies the local traditional focuses. The arts and culture contribute to community well-being, cohesion, and quality of life. The sense of community indicators in Table 3.1 identify a sense of membership, mutual importance and dependence, shared worldviews, bonding/networking, and mutual responsibility for the community.

## Lifestyle and Livelihoods: Influence on Festivals

You may have noticed how festivals that are predicated on how the local people earn a living have proved attractive to residents and visitors alike. Local land use, heritage and the local agricultural economy along with contemporary recreation pursuits became the catalyst for the festivals identified here. The festivals are integral to the identity of the host community. They become a draw for residents and their visiting friends and relatives whose memories of their connection with these elements also help sustain the celebration.

- **Gilroy Garlic Festival, California.** Since 1979, this festival, based on the local prosperity from the growing of garlic, has distributed over $9 million to local participating nonprofit organizations. The Gilroy Garlic Festival Association is operated by over 4,000 volunteers and is internationally renowned. At inception, the festival founders created the Volunteer Equity Program, whereby profits are allocated to

Traditional dancers from the local community perform during Apple Days at Mary Arden's Farm, Stratford, UK.

non-profit organizations as well as invested in Gilroy capital improvements that are shared among the community year round. The annual food and entertainment extravaganza has live music, nationally prominent cooking competitions, and renowned cuisine enhanced with more than two tons of fresh local garlic. As a responsible festival it encourages sustainable products and local vendors especially in its Gourmet Alley, the heart and soul of the festival with that special aroma! The Friends of the Gilroy Garlic Festival are dedicated people from all walks of life. The festival brings people together. It has bolstered a community that needed pride and a sense of identity. The celebration consolidates the city's global garlic credentials.

- **Mary Arden's Farm, Shakespeare Birthplace Trust, Stratford upon Avon, UK.** At apple harvest time in August each year a Tudor-style celebration of the apple takes place, with juice and cider-making, crafts, plays, music, and dance. Called *Apple Days*, the celebrations are hosted at the farm where William Shakespeare's mother grew up. Local farmers, performers, and schoolchildren provide the human dimension to entertainments for thousands of visitors keen to get into the mood of a bygone era. Volunteers in costume assist with the management of the celebrations, facilitate entertainments, share historical details, and sell food and drink surrounded by all aspects of a working farm. There are demonstrations of traditional skills like basket-weaving, writing words of wisdom like William with a quill, and learning cures for ailments using herbs from the garden are all part of familiarizing visitors with the local (and global) heritage. A contemporary ecological concern for the endangered nature of heritage apple species has meant the inclusion in the program of education programs and the distribution of plants to festival participants.
- **Casino Beef Week, NSW, Australia.** The first festival in 1982 was small but introduced the concept that has made Casino Beef Week unique: having cattle in the main street! The beef industry is a major local economic driver and flavors each annual celebration.

It satisfies the need to accommodate locals at leisure and ultimately attract visitors. A Miss Casino Beef Week competition features young women sponsored by the various beef breeder associations. The winner represents the town and the festival throughout the year. A Mr. Beef Week festival segment is now part of the program to ensure gender equity. The main parade day attracts over 20,000 visitors. On this day the country comes to town, with a steer and stud heifer competition followed by a live auction taking place in the town's center. The main streets are closed and filled with food stalls, entertainment stages, whip-cracking, wood-chopping, junior stock competitions, street entertainers, and arts and craft exhibitions. It provides residents with opportunities to meet one another. After the grand parade there's a rodeo. The Festival is regarded as a Signature Event by the local Richmond Valley Council, one of the many local sponsors. The festival is valued for its support for the local identity and cultural diversity of the Council's constituency.

## Nature and Context of a Festival or Event

Festival creation demands planning approaches that are strategic (long term), tactical (short and medium term), and opportunistic (requiring constant vigilance) to ensure the festival organization is alert to current host community values, interests, and aspirations. A mosaic approach is helpful in fitting together existing resources, potential partners, skills, and experience of the internal and external stakeholders into the planning, production, and presentation of a festival. An appreciation and an understanding of the circumstances in which festivals are accommodated provide valuable knowledge for festival organizers and explain the need for sensitivity to partners' needs. It has implications for the resources required to ensure the festival can be delivered systematically in a timely fashion with characteristics that can be replicated as required and that satisfy the host community and visitors. The demographics and lifestyle characteristics of each festival's host community help interpret the forms of popular cultural, recreational, and leisure pursuits that are positively accepted.

Over time festivals need to demonstrate a strong connection to what is the *essence* of the local value chain. As you examine examples of small and large festivals you will notice that the culture of the host community becomes the raw material of the location and offers the creative means to exploit local and imported resources. The host culture is not necessarily consensual. Often communities are thought to be homogenous, traditional entities that are reluctant to address change. Festivals are a useful vehicle to appreciate the level and capacity of communities to recognize how they can best represent their circumstances and share them with visitors. There can be tensions between long-term residents and newcomers, between subcultural groups, and between public discourses on issues of local importance. Festival organizers need to satisfy any host community concerns through regular effective communication and honest engagement that allows diverse perspectives to be heard.

Festivals provide specific contact opportunities when visitors and hosts share resources and facilities available to both such as recreation precincts, public transport, shopping areas, public buildings, and restaurants. Sometimes festival-goers will go beyond these moving into living, working, and playing places of residents. Both hosts and guests are tested for their responses to cultural differences, tolerances for behaviors and social attitudes, differing languages, and familiar lifestyle choices. There are positive and negative impacts of the interaction and festival managers need to negotiate with authorities regarding practices that are acceptable, or places that are not accessible. There needs to be recognition of the porous boundaries that exist in the festival–host community interface. It can provide major challenges to festival administration, programming and marketing, as contact may be direct or indirect.

A festival can help conserve traditions of the host community; it can provide opportunities for local people to actively participate collaboratively in civic activities with confidence and pride. It can offer employment, volunteer experience, and support innovation through merchandising and souvenir development. It may demonstrate sustainable environmental practices that can be picked up by the hosts for application after the festival ends. Shared access to public spaces may encourage stimulating learning exchanges between individuals.

A balance can emerge through effective communication that ensures negative impacts are minimized if the community has accepted the delivery of a long-standing festival. Organizers of enduring festivals will have determined how to best deal with such diverse issues as different moral conduct, illicit drug use, access to safety and health facilities, and problems such as crime and accidents. Intrusion into the locals' quality of life, loss of privacy, and a sense of crowding, traditions, identities, habits, beliefs, and values can have both positive and negative consequences ranging from crime, social conflicts, traffic, traditions, materialism, community service and cultural activities. Fears are held at times that festival-goers' behaviors may be copied by local residents in what is known as the demonstration effect and have negative residual implications for the host community. Many impacts of a sociocultural nature that need to be addressed are the outcome of a lack of information, false impressions, misinformation, poor communication, and poor knowledge of festival content and reach. Understanding ill feelings that can arise from an influx of visitors has been tracked through the tourism experience by Doxey's Irridex Model in Figure 3.2.

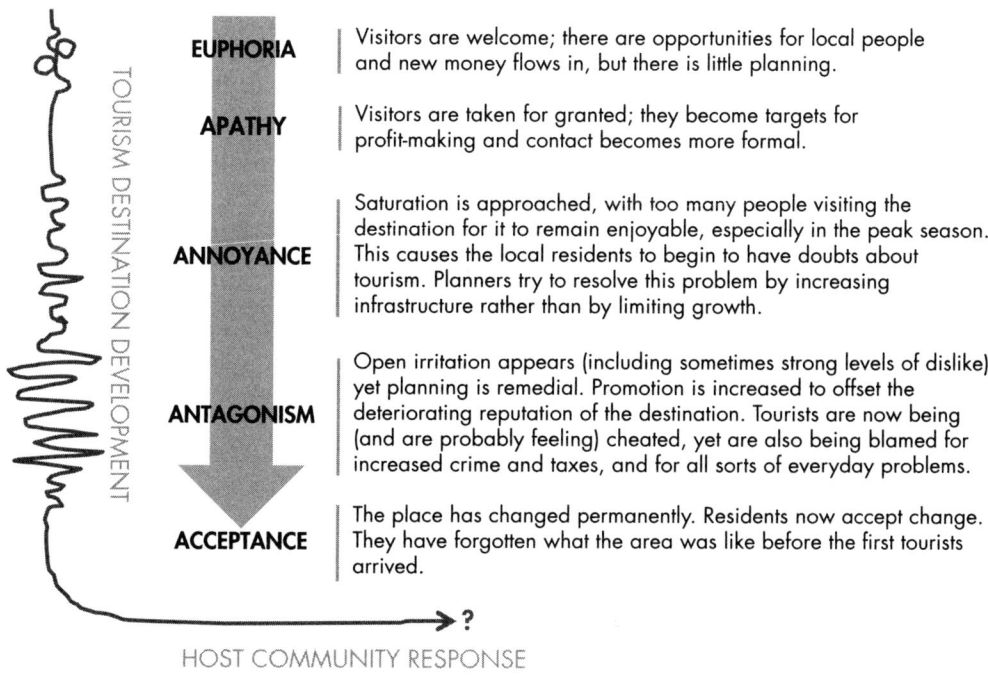

**Figure 3.2** Doxey's Irridex Model.
*Based on Doxey (1975).*

## Festival Focus: Community Consultation and Communication

Festival organizers require discrete strategies for community engagement, communication, and marketing that ensure there are opportunities for mutual benefit from relationships that are established with individuals and groups based in the host community. Continuity of the connections over extended periods and not just at festival time among leaders, between leaders and followers, and among followers is vital to the strength of a community. Members individually hold the collective personality of the whole, but through sustained connections and continued conversations, participants in communities develop emotional bonds, intellectual pathways, enhanced linguistic abilities, and even a higher capacity for critical thinking and problem solving. Their perspective on administrative, operational and artistic can often provide a tactical lift for festival organizers

- **Active participation.** Organizers need to keep members and residents involved and supported. This can be achieved through the use of social networking technology, friendly phone contact, emails, hosting regular meetings at convenient times, congenial lead-up social events, distributing newsletters through the press or personally, and celebrating input by individuals and groups with awards. A comprehensive database of membership, sponsors, funding partners, suppliers, and community champions with details of their skills, experience, and interests provides useful underpinning for ongoing engagement.
- **Community information.** Similarly, it is crucial that organizers maintain open communication with the host community through the distribution of updates, ideas, and issues in press releases, newspaper columns, display boards, online surveys, websites, digital networking outlets, mainstream print media, TV, radio, and through availability of staff or artists for public-speaking opportunities. There is value in regular community consultation and resident feedback sessions. These can be auspiced by other agencies

The daily ritual of alms-giving to Buddhist monks in the streets of Luang, Prabang, Laos.

in the community, business, local government, or local community champions in conjunction with partners of the festival organization. Links to sponsors' publications, partnering different community organizations, or local tourism promotions ensures the festival's vision and activities become top of mind for residents (who often host visitors personally during festival time) who then become part of a word-of-mouth distribution channel. It is consistent with encouraging local ownership of the festival.

- **Connections to wider communities of interest.** It is important to ensure that not only local but also broader links to individuals of influence are maintained. These champions are connected to networks in the broader milieu. They can assist in promoting the intentions and scope of the festival. They may be people of influence, like celebrities, former residents, politicians, officials in government at all levels, and professional networks related to the content of the festival. They need to be briefed regularly (personally or professionally) with regular updates, newsworthy initiatives, and user-friendly reports. They need to be invited to launches and social and festival functions. This group of contacts also involves regular contact with media to ensure greater exposure. These people need to be on specific databases for the distribution of appropriate information. Attending national and international conferences, seminars, and training sessions allows a public face to the festival organization to be sustained.

  It is particularly important for event organizers not to lose sight of their local relationships as they experience increasing success with attracting international visitation. They may be tempted to concentrate on growing the festival reach at the expense of maintaining a quality relationship with residents. The work of Irish researcher Bernadette Quinn (2006) provides us with relevant observations on the tensions that can ensue when a festival grows rapidly with external interest through audience and sponsorship, but neglects to reflect on the original intent of the festival.

- **Festival Relationships.** The complex relationships that festivals provide for individual members of a community when each exchanges information and energy offers the stability and protection that community can provide and what isolation cannot. Festivals can offer the heart to a community, and even though they are transient occasions, they provide conditions of freedom and connectedness, as outlined below.

- **Structure.** A strong influence on the development and delivery of long-lasting festivals is the attention initially paid to the structure of the organization. It can be argued that strategy follows structure. It offers a framework to engage with others who wish to be involved with the making of the festival. Its design, development, and delivery will be facilitated by the roles and structures put in place to accommodate the key internal and external relationships listed in Figure 3.3.

Getz, Andersson, and Larson (2007) highlight the importance of networking with festival partners and acknowledge the roles each can play in enduring festival management. They categorized such stakeholder roles as

- Regulator
- Facilitator
- Co-producer
- Supplier
- Collaborator
- Audience

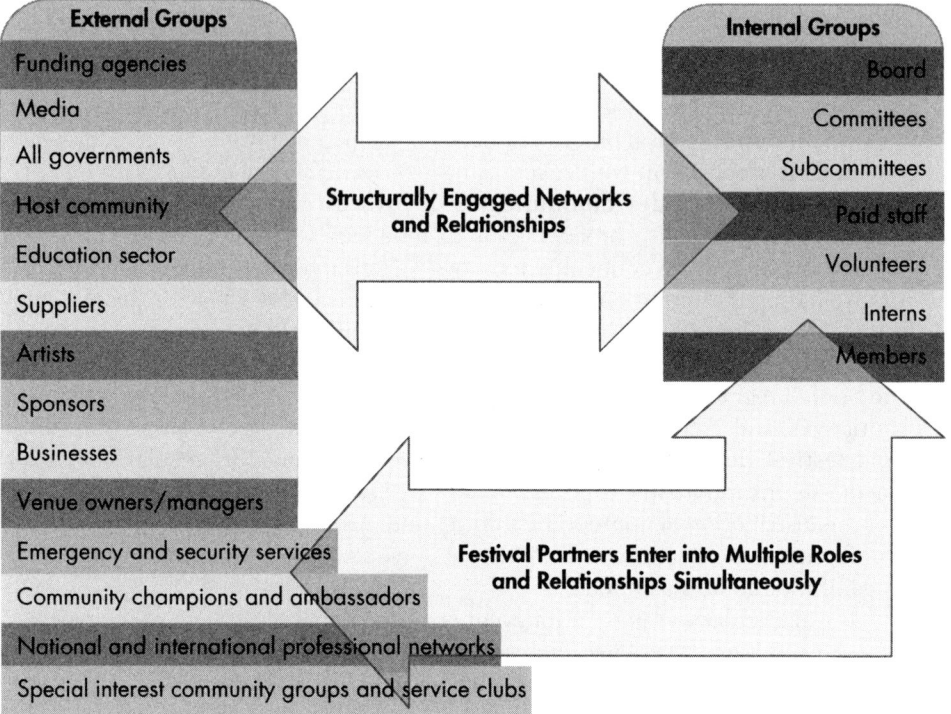

**Figure 3.3** Key Internal and External Relationships. *Derrett (2013)*.

Often partners demonstrate a number of roles simultaneously in effectively delivering a festival. As the social, economic, and political contexts are modified, the longevity of the relationships accounted for and the changes in internal and external organizational contexts examined, the practical implications of the partnerships become clearer.

These partners, mentioned in Figure 3.3, sustain local networks after the festival experience. The networks activated can break down other community infrastructure, bureaucracy, or negotiation for the common good. They can promote local solutions to local problems by supporting the establishment of social activism, self-help mechanisms and community leadership. It also has implications for intercommunity or regional collaboration. Partnerships that support the host community's sense of itself and its place through festival investment, whether in-kind, by sponsorship deals, by sharing resources, or by offering media promotion help build confidence in the life of the festival and ultimately the community.

The interaction between each at various levels and at distinctive junctures of a festival's development needs to be understood by festival organizers. So, for example, local government can be a regulator, a facilitator, and a collaborator or partner simultaneously. How would you characterize the roles of the others listed?

- **Community social responsibility** is manifested with commitments to festivals by commercial and government agencies. Festival organizers can build relationships by matching festival needs through specific interaction businesses, partners in the same

or diverse practice, or existing projects to grow the cultural capacity of each partner. Businesses are increasingly drawn to ethical investment in human capital and festivals offer a valuable option for shared practical and philosophical practices.
- **Partners in projects** Individual, public, and private partners can recognize opportunities to work collaboratively for mutual benefit that may involve marketing, fundraising, community education, shared resources, investment in infrastructure, destination image, and consolidation.
- **Inclusion and exclusion** Community participation is a known catalyst for a healthy and vibrant community. There are some sections of a host community that may feel marginalized, so it is important that efforts are made to ensure those who wish to engage with a festival are offered effective, accessible pathways. A full and exciting portfolio/calendar of events and festivals generates a range of opportunities for individuals or groups to participate in collaborative community-based activities. In particular it has been shown that participation in events can lead to:
  o Increased community interaction and project collaboration
  o Enhanced community focus and innovation
  o Diverse learning and skills development
  o Engaging recreation and entertainment
  o Satisfying and durable social inclusion and community resilience
- **Program design and development** can respond to features of the community vision for itself. Sister-city arrangements, international connections, heritage and traditions can be incorporated over time to enhance the audience experience. The use of diverse venues of local importance can enliven more static elements. There is increasing attention to street parties, parades through accessible neighborhoods and cross-pollination with other festivals hosted in the region. Seasonality impacts the choices for festival programs when indoor versus outdoor venues are being considered for entertainments and demonstrations by local and imported artists.
- **Respect for locals** The development of strong community networks of organizations and individuals is an important outcome of event development. Throughout the planning, implementation, and evaluation of events, networks of community groups come together to meet a common goal. By working together they strengthen the ties between the group and/or nodes of the network. These strengthened ties allow for better platforms for future communications, and the development over time of trust, reciprocity, and reliable communication.
- **Pressure from traffic, people, noise, and overindulgence** provides challenges for festival organizers and host communities. It is imperative that roles and responsibilities are clearly defined and implemented, festival-goers receive appropriate information to minimize harm to all parties, and risk management strategies have been shared with statutory and community agencies. When enduring festivals have successfully negotiated the management of these challenges, confidence grows within the host community for long-term relationships.

## What Does a Healthy Community Look Like?

Festivals provide an opportunity for community cultural development, which is nearly an invisible phenomenon. People know when it is not there. Festivals and events can provide direction for communities. Engaging festival programs can draw out views through symposia, workshops, skills development workshops, dreaming places, graffiti walls, and postcards from the particular place. Community events can use place to demonstrate confidence in how they have kept order and developed interpretation so that others can do likewise when they visit.

Bruce Adams of the Pew Partnership for Civic Change suggests that communities can be healthy or not. The domains outlined in Table 3.2 will be familiar to anyone or any organization facing the challenges of change. These can be applied to festival-making as well. Through regular auditing, all parties can monitor the existing festival (portfolio) and

| Healthy | Unhealthy |
| --- | --- |
| optimism | cynicism |
| focus on unification | focus on division |
| "We're in this together" | "Not in my backyard" |
| solving problems | solution wars |
| reconciliation | hold grudges |
| consensus-building | polarization |
| broad public interests, interdependence | narrow interests |
| collaboration | parochialism |
| win–win solutions | win–lose solutions |
| tolerance and respect | confrontation |
| trust | mean-spiritedness |
| patience | frustration |
| politics of substance | politics of personality |
| empowered citizens | apathetic citizens |
| diversity | exclusion |
| citizenship | selfishness |
| challenge ideas | challenge people |
| problem-solvers | blockers and blamers |
| individual responsibility | me-first |
| listening | attacking dividers |
| focus on future | redebate the past |
| sharing power | hoarding power |
| renewal | gridlock |
| "We can do it" | "Nothing works" |

**Table 3.2** Healthy Community Indicators
*Based on Adams, Pew Partnership for Civic Change USA.*

determine if there needs to be any modifications to the roles and responsibilities taken by the internal and external festival stakeholders. This mosaic approach encourages community vibrancy that is shared through smarter ways to embrace change, experiment, welcome alternative thinking, take risks, and invest in the future. How can these be applied to a festival and host community with which you are familiar? How are conflicts resolved?

# Community Capital and Sense of Community

What is termed "community capital" can emerge from the self-knowledge accrued from a reflection on the framework mentioned above. Community capital is an aggregate of natural, human, social, and built capital from which a community receives benefits and on which the community relies for continued existence. To ensure sustainability, all four types of capital need to be actively pursued so communities can function successfully. The interaction between the four types of capital empowers festival organizers to share their vision for the festival with the wider community.

Elements of community capital such as an appreciation of unique geography, remembered and celebrated history, and how that is carried forward into contemporary society with a cast of familiar characters provides solidarity, security, and confidence for residents. Individual and collective connections with festivals as leisure experiences can demonstrate what is described as one way in which people *practice* space.

## Communities and Social Capital

Putnam's (1993) influential definition "social capital refers to connections among individuals—social networks and the norms of reciprocity and trustworthiness that arise from them," which may facilitate coordination and cooperation for mutual benefit, is relevant to festival-making. Festivals and events can boost individuals' ability and motivation to be engaged with their host community, as well as build resilience through organizational capacity for ongoing effective action.

There are benefits for numerous festival partners as they invest in each festival. These include:

- Create a venue and set of experiences that draw people together who would otherwise not be engaged in constructive social activity.
- Foster trust between participants/spectators and thereby increase their generalized trust of others.
- Provide an experience of collective engagement that encourages further collaborations across the community.
- Enhance a sense of pride in community and place and increase the scope of social networks.

Social capital can emerge from community-based, collaborative festival and event projects by:

- Improving communication of ideas and information between interested parties.
- Improving the skills in planning, managing, and marketing activities.
- Encouraging understanding of different cultures or lifestyles.

| Key Drivers | Components |
|---|---|
| (1) People | Residents' beliefs, attitudes, and behavior in matters of leadership, initiative, education, pride, cooperation, self-reliance, and participation |
| (2) Organizations | Scope, nature and level of collaboration within local organizations, institutions, and groups |
| (3) Resources | Extent to which the community builds on local resources to achieve its goals, while drawing on external resources strategically |
| (4) Community process | Nature and extent of community economic development planning, participation, and action |

**Table 3.3** Community Resilience
*Based on Community Resilience Canada (2000).*

- Encouraging effective consultation between government and community.
- Generating attractive programs for residents and visitors in safe and friendly environments.

## Community Well-Being

Enduring festivals have been recognized as making a valuable contribution to the quality of life of the host community. Festivals have been found to contribute to the social fabric of the community, strengthening existing relationships and introducing new networks to one another. They can reach into sections of the community, to people who may be at risk of social isolation, and provide them with a purpose, shared with others. The types of positive outcomes for enhanced well-being include improved community livability, sustainability, viability, and vitality. Festivals stimulate well-being outcomes such conviviality, equity, prosperity by preparing and presenting programs through activity, participation, and interaction. These responses to the human and physical environments are at the very least aspirational. The development of social capital and community well-being through festivals brings a new understanding of resilience as it is applied to communities (see Table 3.3).

## Festival Contribution to Well-Being

Enduring festivals work on ensuring that the program, logistics, marketing, and legacy of its production address specific issues in the well-being portfolio. Areas given attention are the health of attendees and communities; education programs to up-skill, co-produce, and share knowledge among stakeholders including universities and schools; particular sectors of the population (e.g., disability access); celebrations that reflect anniversaries of local importance;

and highlights documented for the building of a long-term archive (e.g., on websites, stored in public libraries, and represented in artwork remaining after the festival) to provide enjoyment for residents and visitors.

## Community Cultures

One of the problems encountered in dealing with culture is that there are so many different meanings and definitions attached to the term. Conventionally, culture can be considered in two ways: in terms of aesthetic matters (relative to the arts) and as a concept used by anthropologists to describe the way people live. It can be a collective name for all behavior patterns socially acquired and transmitted by means of symbols.

Culture is the unique signature of being human. We are all producers and consumers of culture; we all experience culture in diverse forms. This becomes apparent when examining festival relationships, as it appears that a community can influence its members by strengthening interpersonal connectedness and simultaneously residents may believe they have an influence on community.

## Building Community Culture

- **Sydney Gay and Lesbian Mardi Gras–Australia (now known as Sydney Mardi Gras)** This festival began in 1978 as a celebration of gay and lesbian identity and rights. Annually over a million people are engaged in some way with a diverse cultural program. Mardi Gras offers a focus on education as well as a season of celebrations that include a festival of approximately 100 different arts events, a 70,000-person daytime picnic called Fair Day, a parade (up to 10,000 colorful participants), and a post-parade party. Clearly Mardi Gras has been crucial for building community, forming identity, providing social support, and changing prejudicial public attitudes. Festival management works to represent the diverse subsets of community groups by listening to, involving, and regularly consulting on issues and ideas that ensure the festivities deliver artistic and production excellence. Links to destination management and tourism generally has increased over the years.
- **Nimbin Mardi Grass, Nimbin, NSW, Australia—(known as Nimbin Cannabis Law Reform Rally)**
  The Nimbin Mardi Grass bills itself as the biggest hemp harvest festival in the Western world. It regularly attracts over 10,000 people to the village of Nimbin (population 600) over the first weekend in May to celebrate all things hemp, from medicine, fiber, and fuel, to food. The political event is conceived as a drug law reform protest. There is a street parade, public seminars, markets, and an education program alongside the use of whimsy through the Hemp Olympix to highlight some of the serious and contentious issues associated with hemp use. Powerful emotional and oftentimes conflicting views are held within the rural host community and expressed through a unique forum mechanism. The volunteer management by the Help End Marijuana Prohibition (HEMP) organization conducts a retail information service in the main

street of the village as well as delivers Mardi Grass. The police, local government, the Chamber of Commerce, tourism agencies, and regional media are all significant players in how the image of the village is projected beyond the festival. Over the years, a closer collaboration has taken place to minimize tensions that arise from the pressure of visitation, the logistics of parking, noise, overnight camping, toilets, litter, and drugs.

## What Are the Social Implications of Festivals?

As you reflect on the diverse social impacts of festivals, consider some of the implications for the host community, the festival places and spaces, the festival organization, and its partners in Table 3.4. What would you add to the list?

| Outcome Areas | Indicators |
|---|---|
| Building and developing communities | • Stronger sense of community identity<br>• A decrease in people experiencing social isolation<br>• Improved recreational options for community<br>• Development of local or community enterprises<br>• Improvements to, and increased use of, public facilities |
| Increasing social capital | • Improved levels of communication in community<br>• Improved levels of community planning and organization<br>• Greater tolerance of different cultures or lifestyles<br>• Improved standards of consultation between government and community<br>• Increased appreciation of community culture |
| Activating social change | • Increased community awareness of an issue<br>• Community action to resolve a social issue<br>• Greater tolerance of different cultures or lifestyles<br>• Increase in local or community employment options<br>• Increased levels of public safety |
| Developing human capital | • Improved communication skills<br>• Improved ability to plan and organize<br>• Improved problem-solving abilities<br>• Improved ability to collect, sort and analyze information<br>• Improved creative ability |
| Improving economic performance | • Cost savings in public services or programs<br>• Increase in local or community employment options<br>• Improved standards of consultation between government and community<br>• Development of local or community enterprises<br>• Increased business investment in community cultural development<br>• Increased resources attracted into community and spent locally |

**Table 3.4** Social Implications of Festivals
*From Williams (1995).*

# Festivals and a Sense of Place

Festivals provide a useful lens to explore where space becomes place and where culture declares its presence. The hosting of arts and cultural celebrations provides another function that acknowledges how residents convert physical boundaries to satisfy social and cultural needs. For places to achieve distinctiveness and status as places to go, or to be seen in, they have to be created. Organizers of festivals can offer tangible and intangible experiences to connect people to places, which is why some popular events are sited in spectacular locations, such as riverbanks, mountain tops, sites of heritage importance, city malls, and indoor stadiums.

## ■ What Is a Sense of Place?

The same place, the same piece of land is looked upon with different eyes by different generations. Culture is connected to the landscape in differing ways for different people. Each person makes sense independently or in groups about the landscape. This implies that the environment is being collectively molded in an ongoing way. So the landscape, the place in which residents and visitors find themselves for celebrations, comes to reflect the prevailing beliefs, practices, and technologies of culture and community at any given time as suggested in Figure 3.4. The demographics are changing in many locations and this is leading to greater complexity and heterogeneity in suburbia, inner-city environments, and rural areas.

What makes a place memorable? How do we perceive the places in which we live on a daily basis? Why do places look the way they do? These questions are all related to the abstract notion of sense of place, a notion that is often difficult to define. It is the combination of the built and natural environment and the sum of the human interaction with it. It reflects the history of each place and how it has evolved into what residents and visitors can experience. It also concerns the influence sites/places bring to bear on activities like festivals.

Many former residents return regularly to festival sites for nostalgic reasons or to introduce following generations to their personal heritage. Festivals with strong international participation provide opportunities for attendees to get to know the host community by

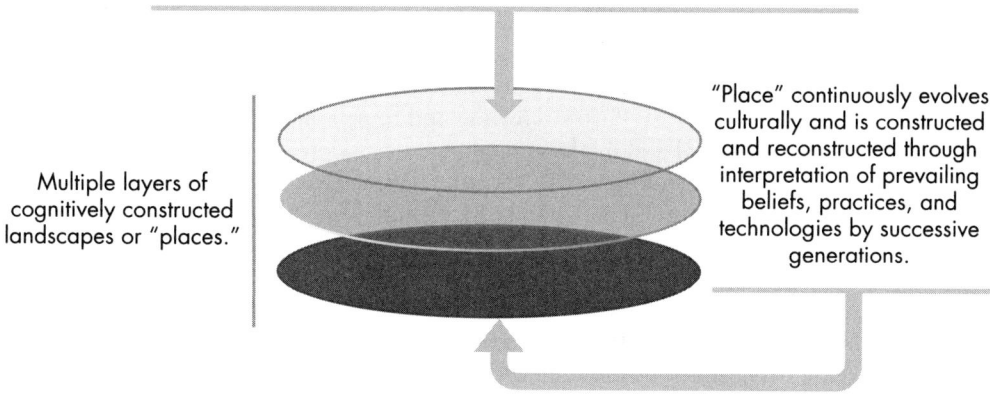

**Figure 3.4** A Sense of Place. Derrett (2013).

situating the program in accessible venues where there can be interaction. Taxi drivers are conduits for introducing visitors to popular local amenities and festival managers have recognized the importance of maintaining good relationships with destination transport sources to ensure a positive experience for both hosts and guests.

Individual residents' relationship with the landscape or material festival environments may vary in intensity, discretion, and manner of expression. Community involvement in a festival is an important factor in predicting the strength of a person's attachment to a community or place. Recognizing peoples' attachment to a place influences their sense of stewardship with that place. This would suggest that the locals themselves during an event would take on issues of security for people and property.

The emotional attachment to the natural landscape and the built environments, climatic changes, and shared memories of communal heritage allow individuals to come together for formal or spontaneous interactions such as festivals and community cultural events. Place is said to have spirit or personality. It seems that a sense of place can vary from person to person and time to time. There can be a distinction between the characteristics of place for residents and of those of visitors. Can visitors ever develop an appreciation and commitment to the same extent as locals? Does the contact with festival places and spaces allow visitors to go beyond just appreciation and understanding to conservation of sites or experiences based on access to particular location and natural forms?

## Festivals and Place

- **Site selection.** The Top Half Festival in Australia is a shared event, rotated each year through a number of places in the Top Half of Australia—Darwin, Mt. Isa, Katherine, Alice Springs and Jabiru (situated in Kakadu National Park). Rotating the venue of this festival in this way could be seen as a disruption to the connections between a place and its community, but after talking to festival participants and reflecting on the festival's music performances, it appears that this dislocation provides the impetus for community formation (Duffy, 2000).
- **Urban regeneration.** Toronto's (Canada) film festival is the world's largest, having eclipsed the iconic Cannes Festival. Its Pride Week also is the world's largest. Toronto ranks third in live theatre in North America. Toronto boasts more parkland per capita than most North American cities and is kilometers ahead of congested European capitals in that respect. Toronto has regional and international tourism draws year-round. *The Economist* quality of life survey has Toronto in the top 10 of the world's most liveable cities. As the fastest-growing and fourth-largest city on the continent, Toronto is the financial and media capital of a G8 nation—a status recognized by its host-city role for a G20 summit. It leads among Canada's corporate head-office cities. All of that makes the city richly endowed with active and prospective philanthropists along with ambitious expansions of the Art Gallery of Ontario and the Royal Ontario Museum. What contribution can festivals make to urban place-making?
- **Naming festivals.** The names for festivals are often linked to the place in which they are held. Can you list some that are linked to location? They may be linked to traditions or original host community languages to lend authenticity to origins and heritage, be linked to artform practice, named for personages, and in recent times linked to the naming rights negotiated with sponsors. Domestic and international visitor participation is a feature of the traditional and contemporary artform mix in Table 3.5. Consider community and place relationships the organizers need to negotiate.

| Name of Festival | Location | Description |
|---|---|---|
| Notting Hill Carnival | West London, United Kingdom | Europe's largest outdoor street festival based on Caribbean heritage—music, food, entertainment |
| Oktoberfest | Munich, Germany | Two-week festival of beer houses, entertainment, amusement park rides, and food |
| Singapore Lantern Festival | Singapore | Held under a full moon in the fall each year. The venue is the Chinese Gardens where lanterns of all shapes and sizes float on a huge lake. |
| Glastonbury Festival of Contemporary Performing Arts | United Kingdom | Glastonbury Festival is the largest greenfield music and performing arts festival in the world. It's a huge tented city in 900 acres in the Vale of Avalon, an area steeped in symbolism, mythology, and religious traditions dating back many hundreds of years. |
| South by Southwest (SXSW) | Austin, Texas | Annual 10-day indoor festival in March focused on technology, film, and music. |
| Roskilde Festival | Denmark | Roskilde Festival is the largest North European culture and music festival and has existed outdoors since 1971. A nonprofit organization consisting of 25 full-time employees and thousands of volunteers, the Roskilde Festival Charity Society ensures that the profits from the festival are donated directly to humanitarian and cultural purposes. |

**Table 3.5** Festival Links: Implications for Community and Place

- **Livability features** of host communities impact on festivals that include camping components. Landscape; health and sanitary amenities; built cultural precincts that offer comfort, safety, and shade; food and beverage outlets; and adequate parking and transport options all have implications for the festival period and beyond.
- **Specific host community landmarks** in the built and natural environment become features of the image and identity of a festival and host community. Isolated rural venues or metropolitan locations can become identifiers and unique selling propositions for festivals.
- **Signage** is an important element of presenting both the destination and the festival. Site selection for bold, effective, timely signs replicated at gateways, on highways, and in towns provide long-term links between the community and the festivals. A destination may choose to be named as "the home of" a specific event or portfolio of festivals—"a festival city." Appropriate aesthetics need to satisfy all parties through use of color, scale, style, and clarity.
- **Logos and brands in destinations.** There needs to be synergy between visual representation of both community vision and festival brands and logos. Prominent electronic signage has been successfully utilized to offer passersby information on a countdown to festival dates. The same image can be included on digital platform promotions.
- **Community legacies** that reference the needs and aspirations of most parties instill confidence in ongoing relationships with festival organizations. The experience of festivals to deliver successful celebrations can inspire investment in infrastructure and amenities valued by hosts and guests and these sustain environmental, social, cultural, and economic programs that will in turn satisfy residents, visitors, and partners.

## CASE STUDY

### *BorderFest, Hidalgo, Texas*

For four days in the first weekend every March, a city on the banks of the Rio Grande, 5 miles from Mexico, hosts an award-winning festival that demonstrates a deliberate commitment to its sense of community and sense of place. Local strengths are at play on various levels through entertainment, the audience, and how the festival is organized.

### Sense of Community and Place

BorderFest was initiated in 1976 by the local Chamber of Commerce. They wished to celebrate the community's unique border culture. Hidalgo's setting on an international border, along with the spirit of the host community, spurred them on to establish an event that started with 500 participants. It has grown to attract over 85,000 attendees annually, while 1,000 local volunteers contribute to its preparation and staging through the BorderFest Association. Its endurance is clearly represented in the capacity-building in developing the Festival of Lights as another significant annual event in December each year.

The City of Hidalgo has a population of 14,000 in a county with a population of approximately 800,000. The arrival of the "Winter Texans" or retirees swells the Rio Grande Valley population to 150,000. Its local government is sympathetic to the efforts of the festival committee and along with local business support each reflects the values held by the local community who are proud of the success of the festival. A significant entertainment venue, the 6,800-seat State Farm Arena has hosted a variety of globally known artists that satisfies the 2 million people that reside in the Valley. The site is integral to the celebration of border music, heritage, and culture of BorderFest.

At the southern tip of Texas, the oldest city in Hidalgo County, a city with a long and rich influential history in the Rio Grande Valley, Hidalgo's proximity to Reynosa Mexico, a city of over 1 million residents, provides the fourth-largest point of entry on the country's southern border. The Hidalgo/Reynosa International Bridge annually accommodates over 3 million pedestrians and over 10 million cars, making it one of the busiest ports of entry into the United States. The bridge is the site for the *Abrazo*, when mayors from both cities come together for the symbolic embrace of friendship between the two countries and communities. Each year the program includes Ambassadors of Goodwill from both sides of the border.

The demographic diversity of the residents, including its substantial Hispanic community and their history and culture, influences the festival program. Students and residents function in a binational, bicultural, and bilingual world and the international connections sit well with participants with a broader worldview. The low socioeconomic status, youthful population, and strong arts and sporting commitments in local education connect with the planning for each year's festival offerings. Curriculum is developed linked to the chosen international partner. This outreach aspect of festival programming supports other activities such as school participation through designing and building parade floats and bands for performances.

### Creating an Enduring Festival

What attracts domestic and international visitors to BorderFest is a program of entertainments for all ages. It celebrates the diversity of the local population through performances, exhibitions, demonstrations, parades, carnival activities, and food.

The BorderFest highlights international perspectives—thus borders are expanded—when the annual program addresses the iconic entertainments from selected nations that contribute to performing groups. In recent years these have included Australia, Jamaica, China, and the United Kingdom. There is educative as well as entertainment value in such connections.

This aspect of the festivities influences *Pepper*, the festival mascot, who each year takes on a persona symbolic of the dedicated guest country (e.g., Crocodile Dundee for Australia or as a Jamaican pirate, of a Chinese- or Irish-costumed character) used in promoting the festival. This mascot appears in public places, on marketing materials, education programs, and within festival events and civic celebrations.

The program appears to offer something for everyone—from nominating a Border Texan of the Year that honors the contribution made by an individual to the Lower Rio Grande Valley to a BorderFest Queen/Miss Hidalgo Pageant, to a Square Dance Jubilee, a Leaders' Dinner, a Bike Fest, a Car Show, an Outdoor Mainstage with major entertainers representing the guest country's entertainment, and offering prizes for attendees to subsequently visit those places. Other stages draw on bands that celebrate country and western, Tejano, and world music genres. Strolling buskers and performance artists mingle with festival-goers. Food features in cookoffs, demonstrations, and booths focus on local cuisine.

The festival has received acknowledgment from its peers locally and nationally. International accolades like those from the International Festival and Events Association (IFEA) in successive years recognize the scope and scale of attention to satisfying the locals' needs and aspirations. The festival and the city punch above its weight in terms of how to understand and deliver to its local and visiting markets.

Fundraising by the central festival organization contributes scholarships to the region's youth and community groups are able to use their involvement in the event to generate funds for their causes.

Festival organizers appear to have created a cultural celebration that offers the best fit between the heritage and contemporary culture of the host community. The willingness of residents to come together to design and deliver an inclusive festival that offers locally sourced entertainment, as well as positioning this relatively small community into a global framework through support from individuals, businesses, and local authorities, provides an exemplar for enduring festivals.

Festivals emerge from the local lived culture and allow residents and visitors to be involved with their creation. By participating in festivals we find a particular sense of life, a particular community of experience that hardly needs explanation. Festivals, as planned social phenomena, permit encounters with authentic expressions of culture like those exposed in BorderFest.

# FROM INSIDE THE MOSAIC

## Festival Researcher
## Dr. Jo Mackellar, Australia

Dr. Jo Mackellar's extensive experience in tourism and hospitality management and marketing and as an academic has informed her work as a researcher in the field of event management. A particular interest of hers is the examination of the arts and cultural legacies emerging from mega events. While she looks at the policies, programs, and funding that support the cultural programs attached to such events, she's interested in listening to the stories of those involved and the types of outcomes (positive and negative) that may have resulted from participation in, or coordination of, such cultural programs.

Dr. Jo Mackellar

© Peter Derrett

She has also been working with communities in regional Australia to establish a clearer idea of the impact that festivals have on residents and other stakeholders. She has initiated hundreds of surveys undertaken by event organizers, local government, and Chambers of Commerce seeking to better understand the economic, social, and cultural implications of their festival's resilience.

Two significant research projects involved the investment by local government working with community event organizers keen to (1) strategically plan for inclusive festivals that satisfy local aspirations and attract visitors to a festival that had been growing over 20 years; and (2) articulate the benefits and challenges of social and cultural indicators for an annual portfolio festivals held within a district.

1. The purpose of the strategic plan was to establish an agreed-upon direction for the *Australian Celtic Festival* and define improvements to ensure visitor satisfaction and financial sustainability for a 10-year period. The adopted plan was the result of stakeholder consultation, comparable festival research, discussion with participants and visitors to the event about their vision and expectations, and the use of survey and interview data. Key features of the process examined future sustainability and economic growth; evolving the event to continue to meet customer expectations; building community partnerships; and succession planning.

    The core values that assisted in devising the vision for the event included sustaining Celtic heritage; embracing the Celtic community; celebrating and having fun; and showing pride in Celtic heritage. The vision 2010–2020 was to become an iconic event of Celtic culture and ceremony at the Australian Standing Stones. The festival objectives were:
    - To be a Signature Celtic experience for Australia
    - To ensure event sustainability and economic growth
    - To build on partnerships
    - To meet visitor expectations
    - To build strong business engagement
    - To ensure operational succession planning

2. Jo's research project for the Richmond Valley Council in northern NSW, Australia, focused on the benefits accrued by the community of a portfolio of events. Her initial research assessed the economic and tourist value of events to the Richmond Valley community and to Council. It was recognized that the events

drew visitors from other areas and those visitors provided substantial economic benefits. Furthermore, the events contributed to the image of the destination as a vibrant dynamic area for a wide range of recreational pursuits, as well as providing opportunities and venues for engaging events to occur.

When developing policy and delivering strategies that make a positive impact on the prosperity and quality of life of its constituency, Councils need to recognize the anticipated and actual success factors of the projects in which it invests. This Council conducts a Tourism and Community Event Funding program that attracts great interest from festival organizers. Included in Council investments are the Casino Beef Week Festival, Casino Flower and Garden Show, Crankfest Extreme Youth Fest, New Italy Anniversary Celebrations, and numerous sporting events.

Jo suggests that the following principles are worthy of consideration:

- that the communities address stated and accepted needs or aspirations control projects;
- that the organization's aims and objectives are clear to all parties;
- that there is a connection to local needs and opportunities, while not simply transplanting things that work in one place in the expectation they'll work anywhere;
- that responses identified fit with what people want to do, and support their voluntary commitment;
- that diversity is genuinely valued because diversity is both fundamental to a healthy society and because it is vital to a living and developing cultural tradition through informed consent;
- that effective partnerships are encouraged and pursued; and
- that best-practice management is promoted to ensure event visions are achieved for all parties.

Council cannot assume responsibility for all outcomes from events as a result of their investment, but it can be mindful of the potential positive impacts that accrue. They can reflect on community interaction, focus, and participation; network development; and social capital.

Jo's research is making an important contribution to ensuring festival and events are understood by numerous stakeholders, particularly local government, which is increasingly committed to ensuring its constituency's values and vision coalesce in the conduct of satisfying and successful community cultural events.

# Festival Ideas and Issues

1. Discuss who owns a festival.
   Who are the major stakeholders and how might they react in a public forum to specific questions like:
   o A media campaign using a celebrity for festival promotion
   o Construction of city gateway signage utilizing a significant, disputed heritage design
   o The choice of a particular leader of the festival parade
   o Siting of an outdoor stage in a busy thoroughfare in the central business district
   o Hosting a festival event on a day of traditional religious observance
      Develop a public forum role-play exercise where particular stakeholders put their arguments in relation to the topics chosen for discussion and feedback. What are the issues raised from either side?

Alternatively work in pairs. Partner 1 pitches a parade for the upcoming agricultural festival while Partner 2 argues from the point of respect for local concerns for content, traffic disruption, crowd control, and noise.

2. How does local government determine its policy for the distribution of funds for local festival-making? What arguments might be used to justify their investment?

Councils need to understand the delicate balance of an event's life cycle, applicants' organizational capacity, the financial impacts of any Council investment, and the engagement of residents and visitors with each event. Social impact perspectives generally include individuals, enterprises, host organizations, and the broader community/society. This can focus on growth, the quality of attendees' experience, and leverage for each sector. It is difficult to standardize, measure, and align with changing priorities offered by each party. It is evident that clear and consistent policy and communication between funders and recipients is the key. What else?

The following principles are worthy of consideration in your discussion.
- Projects are controlled by the communities to address stated and accepted needs or aspirations.
- The organization's aims and objectives are clear to all parties.
- There is a connection to local needs and opportunities, while not simply transplanting things that work in one place in the expectation they'll work anywhere.
- Responses identified fit with what people want to do, and support their voluntary commitment.
- Diversity is genuinely valued because diversity is both fundamental to a healthy society and because it is vital to a living and developing cultural tradition through informed consent.
- Effective partnerships are encouraged and pursued.
- Best-practice management is promoted to ensure event visions are achieved for all parties.

Council cannot assume responsibility for all outcomes from particular events as a result of their investment, but it can be mindful of the potential positive impacts that accrue.

3. What contribution can festivals make to a discussion of the discipline of place-making?
    - The essence of place-making is the creation of economically vibrant, aesthetically attractive, lively and engaging, pedestrian-friendly places.
    - Should place-making address a mix of emotional, intellectual, and physical needs?
    - How best can it involve people, attract and respond to their needs, create pleasure, and be interesting?

4. How can festival organizers and community leaders use responses to the following questions to better inform their long-term relationship and ensure effective collaboration?
    - How involved are residents in their communities?
    - What are the current key issues that concern them?
    - How satisfied have residents been with their public involvement experiences?
    - What parts of the engagement process are they most and least satisfied with?
    - What is the residents' most favored approach to community engagement?
    - How do residents view the role of public input into festival projects and subsequent impacts of festivals on them?

Construct a community consultation prior to a proposed festival. What is innovative about the planned event? What would sell the idea to the host community (e.g., stages, street parties, online streaming, parades, traffic management, local involvement)?

Make a list of ways organizers can keep in touch with the host community and other communities of interest. What will make this connection strong? How can trust be developed?

## Festival Focus Activities

1. Undertake an audit of specific sites in your immediate location that are currently used to host festivals and events. List their features and best attributes to service residents and visitors.
2. From the festivals identified in this chapter or case studies from your own research, list the features of the host destination and community being celebrated and link them to arts and cultural activities included in the program.
3. Examine nontraditional sites in your location, airport terminals, showgrounds, supermarket parking lots, mountaintops, and riverbanks and establish some assessment tool to determine the appropriateness for future use as a festival site. List the advantages and disadvantages.
4. Identify a major festival from your reading and analyze the number, scale, and type of venues utilized in the program for the festival.
5. From the case study festival in this chapter, identify the ways in which festival organizers have linked to the host community. How has this affected the program? Has it contributed to the longevity of the festival?
6. Identify some of the community stakeholders that have collaborated and cooperated to ensure the festival's appeal is sustained over a long period of time. Imagine representatives are gathered for a final evaluation of a recent festival. Role-play the potential feedback highlighting their unique perspectives from their experience. How can this contribute to the festival's resilience?
7. Choose a festival website and analyze it to establish what sorts of relationships the festival organization has established with its host community. Indicate the internal and external stakeholders that may contribute to the annual program and identify (list) key mutual benefits accrued.
8. Design a logo and brand for a hypothetical festival in a destination with which you are familiar. How can you best provide a visual and textual base that reflects a strong sense of community and place? What features can be applied to digital communications most effectively?

## Suggested Reading

Adams, B. Pew Partnership Initiatives for the Development of Enterprising Actions and Strategies.

Chao, G. T., and H. Moon. The "Cultural Mosaic: A Metatheory for Understanding the Complexity of Culture." *Journal of Applied Psychology* 90, no. 6 (2005): 1128–1140.

Community Planning Task Force. *Models of Community Engagement, and Capacity Building for Community Planning,* Scottish Executive, Scotland, 2003.

Community Resilience Project Team. *Community Resilience Manual,* Centre for Community Enterprise, Port Alberni, B.C. *Making Waves,* Vol. 10, Issue 4 (2000): 10–14. http://www.ontario-sea.org/Storage/37/2905_Section_1_-_The_Community_Resilience_Manual.pdf.

Deery, M., and L. Jago, "Social Impacts of Events and the Role of Anti-social Behaviour." *International Journal of Event and Festival Management* 1, no. 1 (2010), 8–28.

Doxey, G.V. "A causation theory of visitor-resident irritants: Methodology and research inferences." Proceedings of the 6th Annual Conference of the Travel Research Association, San Diego, California, pp. 195–198, 1975.

Duffy, M. "Lines of Drift: Festival Participation and Performing a Sense of Place." *Popular Music* 19, no. 1 (2000).

Getz, D., T. Andersson, and J. Carlsen. "Developing a Framework and Priorities for Comparative and Cross-Cultural Research." *International Journal of Event and Festival Management* 1, no. 1 (2010): 29–59.

Getz, D., T. Andersson, and M. Larson. "Festival Stakeholder Roles: Concepts and Case Studies." *Event Management* 10 (2007): 103–122.

Guetzkow, J. *How the Arts Impact Communities: An Introduction to the Literature on Arts Impact Studies.* Paper presented at the Taking the Measure of Culture Conference, Princeton University, June 7–8, 2002.

Higson, R. "Three of the Best." *The Weekend Australian* (December 10–11, 2011): 12–13.

Matarasso, F. *Culture Makes Communities* (VAN Briefing No. 42). Cardiff, UK: Volunteer Arts Network, 1999.

Putnam, R. D. "The Prosperous Community: Social Capital and Public Life." *The American Prospect* 1.4, no. 13 (Spring 1993).

Quinn, B. "Problematising 'Festival Tourism': Arts Festivals and Sustainable Development in Ireland." *Journal of Sustainable Tourism* 14, no. 3 (2006): 288–306.

Williams, D. The Social Impact of Arts Program, How The Arts Measure Up: Australian Research into Social Impact (Working Paper No. 8), Comedia, 1995.

# CHAPTER 4
# Building and Nourishing the Festival Team

Festival directors share some definite qualities. Take your pick from the list: passion, bloody-mindedness, vision, infuriating stubbornness, optimism, sheer stamina, brinkmanship, and a profound belief in the power of culture and literature to transform life. In Edinburgh since 1947, it is the blood, sweat, and tears, the energy, and the drive of individuals that have created our world-leading festival and rich cultural scene.
—Catherine Lockerbie, (former) Director of the
Edinburgh International Book Festival, 2007

### This chapter provides an opportunity for you to better understand:

- How festival organizations determine their human-resource needs
- The impact of organizational origins, culture, policy, and process on motivation of all festival internal stakeholders
- The importance of leadership and management in team-building and maintenance
- Approaches to human resources management of staff and volunteer recruitment, selection, training, and professional development
- The contribution individuals make through the application of their passion, skills, and experience to festival effectiveness

This chapter focuses on the human dynamics of the internal operations of a festival organization. It seeks to explore the importance of sound policy and planning required to ensure all individuals and teams coalesce to address the artistic, administrative, operational, and relational aspects of effective leadership and management in a timely and professional manner. The collaboration needed between all levels of personnel, inputs of expertise, and

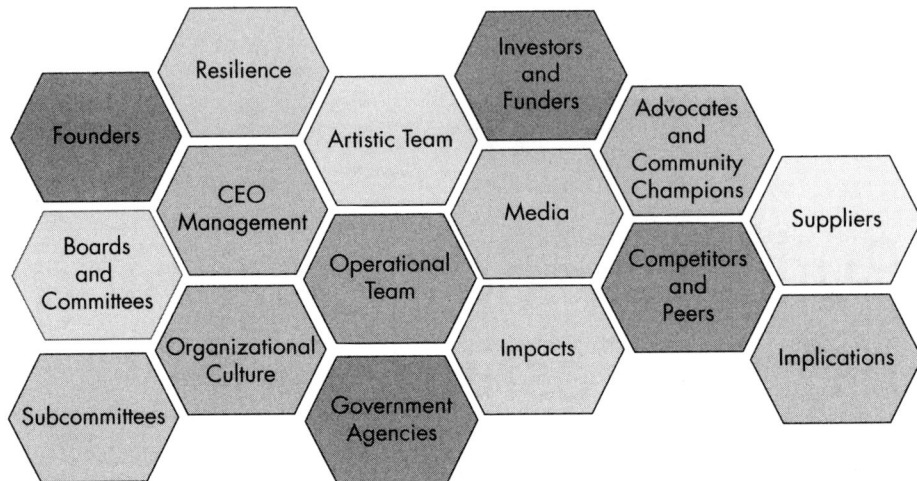

**Figure 4.1** Internal and External Team Mosaic.

intellectual and physical efforts varies but much can be learned from practices in other sectors of the economy, especially business. Community-based volunteer festival organizations face the same checklist of tasks to achieve their goals as corporate or public agencies committed to delivering quality experiences for audiences and other external stakeholders. As you will recognize in Figure 4.1, we examine the organization's human capital through the roles of founders, leaders and managers, committees and boards, paid staff and volunteers, and outsourced specialists and consultants.

## Festival Organization Frameworks

There are four popular models for festival organizations:

1. Initiatives taken by the public sector through financial commitments from government(s)
2. Volunteer nonprofit (or for-profit) community-based festival committees responding to local expressed interest, with or without paid professional staff
3. Special interest festivals specifically convened by statutory or independent public–private bodies generally collaborating for profit. There are professional agencies or individuals available to deliver a festival or event for a public or private client as a consultant or contractor
4. Private investment in festival programs by concert promoters with associate partners

Each is impacted by government agencies whose brief is to monitor and regulate aspects of the sector. Festival organizations have statutory obligations to ensure they have evidence of current legal documentation. These cover such aspects of their operations as development applications to councils for staging festivals in public outdoor places; regulations for safe sale of food; logistics of street, traffic, and noise control; risk and waste management plans; and occupational health and safety conditions for patrons and staff. The publication of business data, an organization's annual report, commercial practices, and disclosure of financial matters are common practice.

A thorough understanding of the law as it applies to the use of social media (personal and professional risks) and the implications of copyright infringements are important to recognize so as to avoid legal action and to protect the individuals' and organization's reputation. There are laws that influence human resources management like employment practices and taxation that ensures a transparent compliance framework is in place for the engagement with skilled (licensed) and professional staff and volunteers.

Management options in the arts and community cultural sectors are now as well informed as anywhere else in business. Mintzberg and Quinn's (1991) explanation of the six parts of an organization include the basic operating core formed by people who perform the basic work; the strategic apex occupied by a manager; middle-line management created as the organization grows; techno-structure for analysts outside the hierarchy of line authority; and support staff. He claims all active organizations have an ideology that is its culture and encompasses the traditions and beliefs that distinguish it from other organizations.

Robinson (2010), in *Making Adaptive Resilience Real* for the Arts Council England, draws on literature in ecological and business thinking that suggests that resilient organizations can be characterized by a combination of the following eight resources and adaptive skills:

## Resources

- Culture of shared purpose and values rooted in organizational memory
- Predictable financial resources derived from a robust business model
- Strong networks (internal/external)
- Intellectual, human, and physical assets

## Adaptive skills

- Leadership, management, and governance
- Adaptive capacity: innovation and experimentation embedded in reflective practice
- Situation awareness of environment and performance
- Management of key vulnerabilities: planning and preparation for disruption

Robinson (2010) suggests that organizations and sectors need *both* resources and adaptive skills to be resilient over time, although they may not necessarily need all of them at all times. Strong leadership skills alone will not deliver resilience, for instance, a lack of financial flexibility or a dominance of people working in specialist silos and lack of networks could undermine them. Equally, an awareness of the situation without a strong culture of shared purpose, made real by organizational memory, might lead to mission-drift and loss of purpose. A blend of change and continuity is essential for resilience. Without change—driven by innovation, networks, and an evolving environment—organizations and sectors risk falling into the "rigidity trap." Simply maximizing the efficiency of an organization or system can lead to inflexibility and vulnerability in the face of change. Without continuity of purpose, there is only persistent activity. Resilient organizations have a mix of change in personnel or approach alongside some stability, including some people who had remained with organizations productively for 25 years and more. An example of organization structures is identified in Figure 4.2.

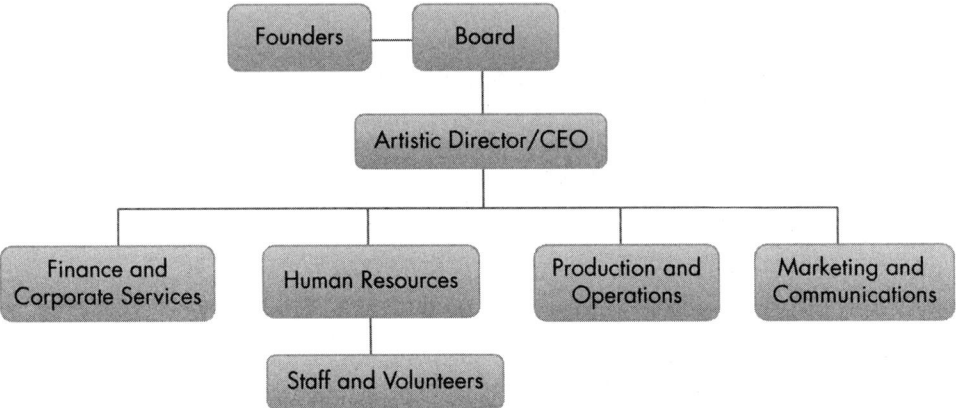

**Figure 4.2** Participants Inside the Festival Organization.

We briefly recognize the contributions of Festival Founders; Board (of Trustees) or Committees of Management; CEOs or GMs (Chief Executive Officers/General Managers); Directors of key portfolios in Finance, Artistic Direction/Programs, Marketing, Technical/Operations, and Human Resource Management; and teams addressing ICT, fundraising, hospitality, external relations, staff, and volunteers. Research using job descriptions and job advertisements has identified specifications and personal and professional attributes across a spectrum of potential employment opportunities for festival workers. We won't be dealing with them all here, but you may find some of the data of over 355 different position titles of interest in Arcodia and Barker (2003).

People management is a challenge for festival leaders, who are managing individuals who are passionately committed to expressing their values, identity and demonstrating their creativity through their professional practice. Leaders must demonstrate the value of teamwork, trust, and commitment to clearly articulated deadlines. These aspects of leadership and management are similar to those facing the corporate sector. Those in the business world seeking creative responses when faced with restricted resources and diverse competition for audiences could appropriate solutions that have been articulated by arts organizations and cultural festival makers.

## Festival Founders

Groups and organizations do not form accidentally or spontaneously. They are usually created because someone takes a leadership role in seeing how the concerted action of a number of people could accomplish something that individual action could not. The process of culture formation in the organization begins with the founding of the group.

You may notice some fundamental steps that have been taken when a festival organization is formed and subsequently sustained. The roles that emerge include:

1. A single person (founder) has an idea for a festival enterprise.
2. A founding group is created on the basis of initial consensus that the idea is a good one, is workable, and is worth running some risks for.

3. The founding group begins to collaborate to create the organization by raising funds, promoting itself and the festival opportunities, may be incorporated, establishing links with existing individuals and groups in the community.
4. As others are brought into the group according to what the founder or founding group considers necessary, the group begins to function by developing its own history. In this process the founder will have a major impact on how the group solves its external survival and internal integration problems. Because the founder had the original idea, he or she will typically have biases on how to get the idea fulfilled, based on prior cultural experiences and personality traits.

## Origins of Popular Festivals

Observe the distinctive origins of the popular enduring festivals in Table 4.1. What might the founders have brought to the initiative and how has their passion and vision endured?

| **T in the Park** (TITP) Scotland | TITP was established when two of the UK and Ireland's leading concert promoters teamed up with Scotland's favorite brewer, Tennent's Lager. They strongly supported the Scottish live music scene in the late 1980s. They had considered the development of Scotland's first large-scale, multistage music event to act as an annual focal point for the music scene, and Tennent's was keen to further increase its support of live music. From its beginnings at Strathclyde Country Park, with 17,000 music fans attending in 1994, to the lush environs of Balado in 1997, TITP has grown in size and influence to become one of the most important and critically acclaimed music events on the international festival circuit. |
|---|---|
| **Portland Rose Festival** Portland, Oregon USA | The Rose Festival has its roots in tradition, while its program is both contemporary and nostalgic. Farsighted city leaders started the festival during the first decade of the 20th century in order to put Portland on the map and brand it the "summer capital of the world." The Rose Festival is now world famous for its amazing, award-winning events, as well as serving as a community leader for celebrating values such as volunteerism, patriotism, and environmentalism. In 2010, the Rose Festival was acknowledged as Portland's Official Festival by proclamation of the Council. |
| **Kentucky Derby Festival** Louisville, Kentucky USA | A Festival for the Kentucky Derby provides a full week of fun for Kentucky Derby visitors. The first try was a quarter of century too soon, referring to the ill-fated and ultimately flooded-out Festival starts of 1935–1937. The Kentucky Derby Festival was born of four men with an idea. Addison McGhee, Earl Ruby, Ray Wimberg, and Basil Caummisar—a public relations man, a journalist, a Chamber of Commerce committee member, and an active civic volunteer—enjoyed lunch often, but one winter day in early 1956, a midday meal made history. |
| **Burning Man Festival** Black Rock, Nevada USA | The Burning Man project grew from a small group of people gathering spontaneously on a small beach in San Francisco in 1986 to an annual community celebration of over 55,000 people. Once a year, participants gather in Nevada's Black Rock Desert to create Black Rock City, dedicated to community, art, self-expression, and self-reliance. They depart one week later, having left no trace whatsoever. Founder Larry Harvey is executive director of the project and serves as its executive committee. He maintains oversight of most of the project's creative endeavors. He has also lectured on subjects as diverse as art, religion, civic planning, and the rise of cyberculture in the era of the Internet. |

**Table 4.1** Festival Origins

| | |
|---|---|
| **Jacaranda Festival**<br>Grafton, NSW, Australia | The Jacaranda Festival came from knowledge of the festivals of other lands in 1935 and from the words of the traditional English folk song *Quaint Old Cornish Town*. Alderman Edward Howard ("Jacaranda Bill") Chataway was the driving force for the event. He enthused others to join him and ignore the skeptics. The role of an archetypal community champion, the Festival drew together a community isolated by distance and emerging from an economic depression. *So was born a tradition of yearly festivity, when the trees shall bloom again—when song, dance and gaiety shall reveal the Australian capacity of real comradeship in Jacaranda Time in Grafton*. The charisma, influence, and strength of personality of the founder achieved the goal of enhancing the quality of local life through celebration. He demonstrated determination, motivation, and coordination. His leadership in this venture and others in the growing town is almost legendary. Much of the initial organizational scaffold is still in place and it may be a measure of the power and simplicity of his vision that much of this continues to resonate with successive leaders within the organization and the broader community. |
| **Sónar, International Festival of Advanced Music and New Media Art**<br>Barcelona and various other cities in the world including Tokyo, Japan, and São Paulo, Brazil, since 2002 São Paulo was also a Sónar venue. The Brazilian version is a co-production by the Spanish company Advanced Music, the creator of Sónar, and Brazil's Dream Factory, the producer of Rock in Rio. | Sergio Caballero, Enric Palau, and Ricard Robles created Sónar in 1994. Unique in its format and content, Sónar is a leading international festival in the field of advanced music and the application of new technologies to artistic creation. Sónar is a combination of entertainment, cutting-edge and experimental modern music, emerging artists, and new media art. More than 80,000 visitors from all over the world attend the sociocultural experience. |

**Table 4.1** Festival Origins *(continued)*

Spectators line the streets for the Grand Floral Parade at the Rose Festival, Portland, Oregon.

# Boards

Governance is a major issue for boards and committees of management. There are numerous resources available to explain the basic tasks that this important tier of a festival organization needs to address (as in Table 4.2). To ensure the organization's success, boards concern themselves with the organization's legal and financial accountability, strategic vision and objectives, fundraising, advocacy and monitoring, and evaluation of the organization's performance. As with all aspects of the organization's relationship-building, there are lots of

| Board Responsibilities | Staff Responsibilities | Joint Responsibilities | Ensuring a Successful Relationship |
|---|---|---|---|
| • Setting long-term goals<br>• Having the final say when determining yearly objectives<br>• Ensuring the mission of the organization is adhered to<br>• Finalizing budgets and allocating funds<br>• Approving any changes or additions outside the budget<br>• Taking responsibility for the company's financial records<br>• Evaluating programs, services, and products<br>• Evaluating board members and their performance<br>• Employing the organization's CEO, setting his/her compensation package, and evaluating his/her performance<br>• Appointing new board members and evaluating the board's performance<br>• Taking ultimate responsibility for all legal matters<br>• Taking ultimate responsibility for compliance with regulatory requirements (e.g., annual general meeting, annual returns, audits)<br>• Appointing auditors and approving the audit of the financial records<br>• Managing committees<br>• Maintaining and building the organization's public profile | • Providing information to the board, including recommendations for action<br>• Supporting the board's planning function<br>• Determining and understanding community needs<br>• Operating programs and reporting on their successes and shortcomings<br>• Evaluating performance<br>• Organizing the organization's events, fundraising activities, etc., once approved by the board<br>• Managing volunteers and staff (other than the CEO)<br>• Implementing board decisions<br>• Conducting day-to-day financial operations<br>• Monitoring and managing daily operations | • Discussing ideas and forming long-term goals<br>• Planning organizational strategies<br>• Designing programs to achieve the group's mission<br>• Proposing fundraising ideas<br>• Ensuring risk management programs are implemented<br>• Ensuring that achievements are recognized and documented<br>• Promoting the organization | • Suitable processes and procedures<br>• Clearly defined management roles<br>• Defined boundaries<br>• Clear limits to the authority of the staff<br>• A CEO whose performance is adequately monitored by the board |

**Table 4.2** Governance Responsibilities
From http://www.ourcommunity.com.au/boards/boards_helpsheet.jsp?articleId=1376

meetings! Members of a festival board or the management committee of a community-based festival will want to ensure management overseen by a CEO through staff and volunteers delivers high-performance work practices to meet the organization's goals. Respectful communication is the key.

All parties within the organization, senior management (including an executive team), staff, volunteers, and external partners over time need to be responsive to changes that impact on the design and delivery of the festival. For example, by using collaborative creative thinking a festival's vision can be enhanced and transformed into virtual and then viral alignment through the organization's information, communication, and ICT practices.

## Festival Chief Executive Officer (CEO)

Effective leadership by CEOs or General Managers (GMs) is derived from the mastery of a range of skills, from implementing and administering processes to inspiring others to achieve excellence. Research into organizational management and leadership has identified the shared characteristics of leaders and followers. This suggests that an effective follower is both active and an independent thinker and wants both their leaders and colleagues to be honest and competent. Followers want to be led, not controlled; they want their peers to be dependable and cooperative. These features help develop a sense of organizational community.

When you examine the diverse definitions of leadership as demonstrated by CEOs, you'll recognize:

**Leadership as the art of inducing compliance:** casting leadership in terms of the will, intentions, and/or wishes of the leader.

**Leadership as the exercise of influence:** employing the concept of influence as separate and distinct from dominance, control, or forcing compliance—leading by example.

**Leadership as a form of persuasion:** reflecting the movement of others through strongly held convictions and/or reason (e.g., leadership is the ability to decide what is to be done and get others to want to do it).

**Leadership as a power relationship:** focusing on the key role played by power in relationships.

CEOs need to reflect on their natural leadership style, identifying what they are good at and assessing what leadership style is the best fit for the organization they lead. Generally their experience, either coming up through the ranks of cultural organizations or business or community management, will provide guidance for a career trajectory. Career trajectories are being refined now as the events sector becomes more formalized through higher education, mentoring and on-the-job training. There is increasing mobility of senior management, as work tends to be contractual. Tertiary studies, mentoring, diverse work experience, and travel and festival attendance all inform the individual's approach as an attractive vacancy arises. Then there is the headhunting style recruitment that has now become part of the sector, where outstanding, capable personnel are located by professional agencies. The "swipe" file that all alert practitioners maintain becomes an integral part of the portfolio such people bring to senior positions.

Some larger, established festivals employ a cooperative leadership model. A CEO/festival director (sometimes called an artistic director) leads an organization with an executive director who has oversight of the administration. The nomenclature varies. You may have seen job titles like Head of Programs, Creative Director, or Festival Producer. Investigate what the distinctive features of each may be. Meanwhile, this binary setup allows leaders to work closely with a senior management team. Each ensures they keep connected to professional networks to keep abreast of opportunities for their festival, recognize trends in the marketplace, and observe good practice in similar enterprises around the world.

The much sought-after leadership attributes include the CEO's capacity to accumulate and implement effective/successful strategies to involve employees in decision making, support employment performance by staff and volunteers so they can demonstrate their professional strengths, negotiate robust relationships with partners, and share information and knowledge in line with the culture of the host festival organization. Of course, over time they become instrumental in embedding positive organizational culture. The CEO, by creating opportunities for engagement within and between teams, festivals themselves become the beneficiaries of the increased skill levels, high morale, staff motivations, and matching ability to tasks required to make the delivery of the festival seamless. There are techniques they employ to build trust, loyalty, and festival identity among the individual staff at all levels of the organization, some formal, others informal such as social and exchange programs.

There is evidence that a cohesive program that encourages semi-autonomous teams, problem solving, staff suggestion mechanisms, ongoing professional development help develop the flexibility CEOs might aspire to. These approaches can address particular challenges as they recognize the varying demands that might arise in any given situation as the critical planning path is followed.

Former Melbourne Writer's Festival Director Steve Grimwade warns against changing directors too frequently: "It usually takes a year to really understand the audience and the role and the work and then you need to be able to play with the job and sometimes you need to be able to make a few mistakes before you find your way, so I'd say changing directors too quickly doesn't enable anyone to get the most out of the position. I think three to five years is a good period of time. Obviously if things aren't working, you need to move on but if things are working I think there's a lot of relationships that are established in these jobs and I think it enables everyone to achieve more than chopping and changing every three years."

Because of the pressures of the job, along with the competitive nature of the festival market, it's no wonder that there seems to be a revolving door when it comes to festival directors and there is definitely a tendency for arts festival boards to want to rotate the director's position—and that is the same across most arts festival boards.

—*Sarah Adams, 2012*

While there has been a trend in recent times for festival organizations to operate a flat management approach to the division of labor, the notion of a senior management team, or an executive team comprised of the directors of the key elements of the festival business, is a useful tool to achieve goals. The Event Management Body of Knowledge (EMBOK), a collaborative initiative developed by event authority Julia Rutherford Silvers, provides a dynamic and practical framework for professional knowledge to be employed by senior management and applied throughout the festival organization. The competence and knowledge experienced personnel bring to the core fields of administration, operations, risk management, and marketing are key to successfully embedding good practice. By arranging clusters of activity, teams of workers can deal with the mosaic that involves research, planning, organizing, and implementation, and the control and the evaluation that builds confidence in the cyclical nature of festival design, development, and delivery.

The notion of a festival lifecycle builds on the marketing techniques adopted in the 1960s identifying the phases of exploration, involvement, development, consolidation, and stagnation potentially followed by rejuvenation, stability, or decline. This can be applied to festivals and their host organizations. An understanding of the flow represented by such an organization or festival alerts leaders to anticipate future demand and prepare adaptive strategies. This is another measure of effective management. As each festival competes for audiences whose expectations are rising and becoming more sophisticated, organizations need to stay fresh (along with the programs they deliver) or each is likely to decline rapidly.

## Building Teams

When you read the literature about how people build teams in organizations to achieve their goals—like an exceptional festival for all parties—you'll recognize an iterative process emerges and it feels like a checklist you come across in a magazine in the dentist's waiting room of what you believe to be important qualities for relationships anywhere. Does one person comprise all these features, or are we looking to ensure teams as a whole can aggregate the sorts of qualities? It seems imperative that the team members know there's a plan and by knowing the industry and working to a set of clear goals, these people will have self-respect and will show respect for others on the team, have good communication skills, and demonstrate courage and persistence.

The team leaders will lead through action and not just by celebrity, charisma, or reputation. They need to demonstrate passion, imagination, authority, trust, integrity, humility, openness, creativity, justice, confidence, enthusiasm, commitment to excellence, motivation, and, above all, sense of humor.

The literature on leadership is extensive and diverse. Outside the business and management literature, leadership is treated as a psychological construct where the leader is a person who possesses certain desirable personality and demographic traits, while others suggest a sociological phenomenon where the leader is a result of the confluence of a person, a group, and the needs arising from a situation faced by each. Are leaders of successful teams born or made?

The strategies festival organizations use to build resilience in teams with staff, volunteers, and external stakeholders include:

**R**elationships: interpersonal communication and social networks

**E**nergy: reenergizing during stress and directing energy fruitfully

**S**tress: coping with stress and knowing your limits

**I**nformation: working effectively with the information available

**L**etting go: allowing yourself to move on to new ways

**E**valuation: reviewing the event and learning from the experience

Teams need to be established with a clear purpose and sufficient resources to achieve it. Skills of participants need to be balanced, with specific roles that consolidate experience, creativity, formal expertise, and willingness to collaborate. Much has been written about nurturing the relationships, placing timeframes on the team's brief, and setting up links to colleagues outside the team to maximize the team's performance. This is as much the responsibility of the organization's culture and its leadership as well as the individuals close to the action.

## Meetings, Meetings, Meetings

Effective communication is an essential element of enduring festivals. Meetings sustain the festival organization's people. They may be small or large scale, round table, bilateral or plenary. All the management tasks are negotiated through interpersonal communication. Whether it is leader to staff member or small teams who are consulting with one another, resolving issues, budgets, analyzing data, supervising volunteers, anticipating risk management, reviewing work to date—all are dependent on openness and effective documentation. Networking with festival partners provides more meeting opportunities whether in the festival's home base or further afield. Meetings take time and need to be planned for. People within meetings need to have authority to respond responsibly to actions determined from the exchange that takes place. They need to listen as well as speak.

Festival organizations will have protocols that ensure that meetings are held when required and involve people who can make a useful contribution and will benefit from sharing the intelligence generated. These meetings need to have agendas with achievable objectives. Recording of inputs and outputs for onward distribution to appropriate personnel in a timely way will allow for productive outcomes for the festival. This does not mean that informal meetings at the water cooler don't make a valuable contribution to the progress of the festival, but all staff need to appreciate the principles that make for conversations that matter professionally!

## Staff

The performance of individuals and teams within the festival mosaic is determined by core competencies through a skills portfolio, knowledge, and qualifications in specific disciplines appropriate to tasks being undertaken and personal attributes that enhance productivity. There are a number of distinctive features in festival life that involve work outside normal business hours, the necessity for high levels of attention to detail, an ability to work to deadlines and within budget, and a capacity at times to work autonomously and sensitively as part of a team and with parties external to the festival organization. There's an expectation that personnel approach their positions creatively with a positive attitude and demonstrate excellent communication skills.

A distinctive feature of current festival workplace recruitment is through internship programs. These introduce students from universities and colleges undertaking academic event management courses with an effective service learning or work experience component. Some festivals have instigated a scholarship process especially for emerging festival workers to ensure they access professional work practice and can learn from experienced mentors from inside the festival organization. There is a growing number of freelance festival workers. They are on short-term contracts as consultants or contractors to pursue specific project-based elements of a festival program. Again their track record in the diverse fields of

## Festival Organizer: Typical Job Description

Organizers are responsible for the production of a festival from conception through to completion. They can work in the public, private, and not-for-profit sectors or for event management companies; in-house for an organization like local government; or freelance.

The role of festival/event organizer is hands-on and often involves working as part of a team. Event organizers must be able to complete a wide range of activities requiring clear communication, excellent organizational skills and attention to detail. They must work well under pressure, ensuring the smooth and efficient running of an event.

## Typical Work Activities

The role varies depending on the type of organization, available human resources and budget, and the scope and scale of the festival. Typical activities include:

- Researching markets to identify opportunities for the festival
- Liaising with clients/artists/suppliers/charities to ascertain their precise event requirements
- Producing detailed proposals for components of the festival and its central program (e.g., timelines, venues, suppliers, legal obligations, staffing, and budgets)
- Agreeing to and managing a budget in conjunction with a finance director or team
- Securing and booking a suitable venue or location
- Ensuring insurance, legal, health, and safety obligations and risk management strategies are adhered to
- Coordinating venue management, caterers, stand designers, contractors, and equipment hire
- Organizing facilities for car parking, traffic control, security, first aid, hospitality, and the media
- Identifying and securing speakers, civic dignitaries, celebrities, or special guests
- Planning room layouts and the entertainment program, scheduling workshops and demonstrations
- Coordinating staffing requirements and staff briefings
- Selling sponsorship/stand/exhibition space to potential exhibitors/partners
- Preparing delegate packs and papers
- Liaising with marketing and Public Relations colleagues to promote the event, especially embracing ICT (Information and Communications Technology)
- Liaising with clients and designers to create a brand for the event and organizing the production of tickets, posters, catalogues, and sales brochures
- Coordinating suppliers, handling client queries, and troubleshooting on the days of the festival to ensure that all runs smoothly
- Overseeing the dismantling and removal of the event and clearing the venue efficiently
- Post-event evaluation (including data entry and analysis and producing reports for event stakeholders)

the arts, construction and design, environmental management, risk management, and legal or financial matters make them attractive to organizations with scarce financial resources to temporarily boost their core complement of staff with targeted expertise.

While jobs in the festival sector are numerous, not all are full-time permanent positions. There are many proponents of the peripatetic nature of festival work that allows them to gain experience at a variety of events to build their portfolio of skills and experience. This is not unlike the phenomenon of seasonal work that occurs in the tourism industries.

## Volunteers

*Volunteers don't get paid, not because they're worthless, but because they're priceless.*
—*Sherry Anderson*

Volunteerism is a potent tool in the festival-making business. The dynamic this group brings to the mosaic is palpable and needs to be nourished. There needs to be recognition of the free or low-cost assistance and valuable skills, contacts, enthusiasm, and commitment they bring to all levels of a festival's success. It is useful to understand what motivates individuals to contribute as they do to festivals. This is formalized in another growing aspect of festival collaboration, that of corporate social responsibility, where businesses particularly commit to growing the festival's reach and prosperity.

People may have observed a festival for some time and believe they can make a worthy contribution because they like to help others and give something back to their community. Some want to get work experience. Others wish to feel needed and grow from a social experience that comes from working with others on a project of shared interest. Some are driven by the status they feel they accrue from their engagement, or the power they feel in situations that come from a festival that is highly regarded by their peers. Knowing what attracts people to become involved helps festival organizers to connect them with appropriate tasks that are meaningful and satisfy both parties.

## Managing a Volunteer Program

The festival organization's commitment to a volunteer program requires resources. Before embarking on a recruitment drive, budgetary considerations must be addressed. These are apportioned for out-of-pocket expenses, financial allocations that may be necessary as paid staff are delegated to supervise volunteers and appropriate insurances. Consideration needs to be given to the spaces and equipment to be utilized by volunteers inside and outside to comply with occupational health and safety obligations. The availability of relevant training for volunteers needs to be thought through. A variety of records need to be kept in a secure and confidential manner for every volunteer engaged with the festival who delivers diverse tasks in administration, maintenance, security, reception, marketing, and hospitality. Such documents could include application forms, any records of interviews, the published job description to which the volunteer is responding, any referee reports, ongoing performance appraisals, and some personal demographic and contact details.

Planning is essential for the success of any volunteer program and involves the whole organization embracing the concept and contributing to the development of appropriate policies and procedures and position descriptions and the creation of application forms. Presumably the organization believes there is value to be added by the engagement with volunteers, that services will be enhanced, that the connectedness to local and broader communities will be strengthened, and that increased participation will augment promotion of the festival. An audit of the tasks requiring attention for this increased workforce needs to be undertaken. This will allow paid continuing staff to concentrate on core activities while other tasks are delegated to volunteers. Position statements need to clearly identify the criteria for selection, the scope of responsibilities, acknowledgment of screening procedures, areas of accountability, and lines of supervision and authority. Given the lead-up, the duration of the festival, and the follow-up that is factored into the management of the festival as a whole, volunteers need to be clear on the time and energy commitments expected in specific workplaces.

> Here's to all volunteers, those dedicated people who believe in all work and no pay.
> —Robert Orben

For satisfaction of all parties, volunteers need to be engaged in meaningful work. Observe a festival with which you are familiar and consider the roles for which volunteers are responsible. What are the characteristics you notice initially? Do they appear to be integrated into the whole festival business regardless of what special service they are delivering? Do they exhibit knowledge of the organization's goals and policies and procedures? Do you expect that they have specialist knowledge that can satisfy the needs of their colleagues and partners? Do you see that there has been attention to the abilities, needs, and background of the volunteer with their assigned tasks? Presumably the underpinning to their performance involved the allocation of a volunteer manual with information outlining expectations and documentation, including past media coverage, organizational charts, and intent to conduct training and orientation activities. An induction program is present in most festivals concerned that individuals will confidently deliver quality services. This is an important aspect of the risk management strategy the organization has in place.

> No one who achieves success does so without acknowledging the help of others.
> The wise and confident acknowledge this help with gratitude.
> —Author Unknown

For all workers there are practices that demonstrate the organization's appreciation of their efforts. You will notice in the links to long-standing festival volunteer programs (Portland's Rose Festival; BorderFest in Hidalgo, Texas; Kentucky Derby Festival) that there are ways in which the efforts of volunteers are acknowledged through public and private praise for their contributions, letters of thanks, awards, complimentary tickets to parts of the festival program and social events, maybe life membership of the organization as recognition of lengthy or outstanding commitment, names registers on halls/walls of fame, or mentions on festival publications. Popular mementos of participation like being given merchandise such as T-shirts, hats, jackets, lanyards, or bags or complimentary food and parking are common practice. Volunteers will return regularly if they are enjoying their exposure to passionate people, bold and exciting programs and positive employment experiences. This donation to the shared cause is as important as the financial investments we discuss in Chapter 5. These people deserve rewards, recognition, and respect.

## Community Festivals and Volunteers

Community festivals are an important crucible for festival learning. Volunteers are the backbone of most community-based festivals that can vary from the simple to the sophisticated. Community-based festivals are valued for the level of investment by the people who prepare them and those who attend them. Often community-based festivals are seen as the poor relation in the planned events sector, when in fact their complexity is well served by the passion, expertise, time, energy, and commitment invested from organizers. Community members recognize that long-standing festivals play an integral part in the social, cultural, and economic lives of those involved and those who attend, whether they are local or have traveled across the globe.

The human capital involved needs to deal with the planning, administration, information sharing, teamwork, creativity and innovation, risk, funding, and documentation that all events require. Generally they source the individuals and groups needed to deliver broad-based "umbrella" celebrations for the host community. They are well placed to know their way around the local infrastructure and the local government agencies, and are connected to business and community service groups experienced through their engagement with a range of other existing community activities. Community champions, social/political/environmental activists, and arts specialists will be experienced in locating resources to ensure the festival can maintain its reputation, understand the local boundaries when an influx of visitation occurs, and recognize what sort of legacy will be appreciated by the host community. In festival destinations there's an adage that suggests that if you want something of worth to be undertaken in the interests of others, ask a busy person!

Some festivals, having identified a niche in their program content, have sited a festival in a spectacular geographic location in a comfortable season. They have established positive relationships with the host community, demonstrated effective management, and gained an international reputation for delivery of distinctive experiences and have gone on to become iconic in specific genres and become part of a global trail. Check out the origins of Notting Hill Festival celebrations in London, Hidalgo's BorderFest, the Bluesfest in Byron Bay, Australia, and the Portland Rose Festival and note how many volunteers have retained an interest in such resilient and prosperous festivals.

## The Concept of Job Satisfaction

Job satisfaction is a topic in the work and organizational literature drawing on sociology, management sciences, and psychology disciplines. Employees' behavior can be explored by the influence of work productivity, the individual's work effort, employee absenteeism, and

### THE WOODFORD FESTIVAL EXPERIENCE

The significance of this long-standing commitment to volunteerism is not lost on the Woodford Folk Festival, in Australia which has a section on the participation link on their website specifically for returning volunteers. The Woodford Folk Festival, an event of international standing, is held annually over six days and six nights from December 27 through January 1. More than 2,000 performers and 580 events feature local, national, and international guests. The event is powered by an army of volunteers whose numbers are now in excess of 2,300. Volunteering is seen as a great way to get involved and experience the spirit of the Festival that is produced by the Queensland Folk Federation, a not-for-profit, community association. The first festival in 1987 attracted 900 people! Despite its current large size, the festival has retained its grassroots, noncommercial feel to satisfy its vision of an inclusive, creative, and inspiring community. It is popular with all ages. During the festival time the festival's Woodfordia site is transformed into a village that hosts over 25,000 patrons, performers, stallholders, volunteers, and organizers daily. During the event, the festival is actually the 67th largest town in Australia!

staff turnover. Management needs to keep an eye on the individual worker's overall well-being by observing the intentions or decisions of employees to leave a job.

Festival management needs to regularly review the care its takes of its staff. Satisfied employees are great to be with, are highly motivated, and are harder working than dissatisfied ones. Job satisfaction is a major determinant that may lead to high staff turnover if needs and aspirations are not understood. The reduction of employee turnover has a significant impact on the festival's bottom line. Moreover, employees' satisfaction is likely to better serve the festivals' internal and external relationships and enhance market share and good service experiences for their festival patrons.

Overall satisfaction focuses on the general internal state of satisfaction or dissatisfaction within the individual. Positive experiences in terms of friendly colleagues, good remuneration, compassionate supervisors, and attractive jobs create a positive internal state. Negative experiences emanating from low pay, less than stimulating jobs, and overt criticism create a negative internal state. Therefore, the feeling of overall satisfaction or dissatisfaction is a holistic feeling that is dependent on the intensity and frequency of positive and negative experiences. There can be a cluster of evaluative feelings about one's job caused by diverse issues such as supervision, coworker relationships, job content, remuneration and extrinsic rewards, promotion, physical conditions in the work environment, and operation procedures. Feedback from staff and volunteers needs to contribute to the ongoing design of the division of labor and its connectedness to the organization's strategic goals.

Hertzberg's (1968) two-factor theory is an important frame of reference for managers who want to gain an understanding of job satisfaction and related job performance issues. He suggested that employees be motivated by challenging work in a climate that allows them to take responsibility for their actions. This observation offers a useful reminder that there are two important aspects of all jobs: what people do in terms of job tasks (job content) and the work setting in which they do it (job context).

## CASE STUDY

### *Educating Festival Leaders*

People are managing events in their personal and professional lives and call on numerous levels of skill, experience, and talent to allow them to fulfill their obligations in the workplace, community, or family arena. The growth of event management programs in tertiary institutions is indicative of the needs felt by organizations and individuals to better prepare to deliver appropriate, safe, and stimulating events with a minimum of stress. There are various transferable management skills.

Project management involves a balance of creativity, administration, financial confidence, and technical know-how. Recognizing the optimum conditions to provide an effective service involves specialist training. The tourism sector has become inextricably linked to the emerging event management profession. People involved with the tourism and hospitality industries already have wide experience at bringing together people to complete projects to satisfy internal and external clients. The customer wants to have fun.

Event managers also appreciate success and satisfaction in the workplace.

The global implications should not be overlooked as those working in the area of event management recognize the transferability of their skills and experiences. The mobility of event participants is reflected in the array of personnel required to deliver festivals. Understanding the host country's culture is an important underpinning to staging successful events. Festival managers need to understand the importance of the host/guest relationships that highlight the collaborative nature of sound event management policy and planning. The context in which any festival operates requires sensitivity, intelligence, and a set of behaviors that will allow for lasting positive impacts of a social, cultural, and environmental nature as well as the more obvious economic spinoffs that communities find attractive about hosting special events.

Goldblatt (2002) acknowledges the growth of the global events industry and offers three characteristics that must inform the training and research into the sector. The profession must have (1) a unique body of knowledge; (2) it typically has voluntary standards that often result in certification; and (3) it has an accepted code of conduct or ethics so that event management meets each of these qualifications, even though as a total package it is yet to have in place government licensing.

## Are Festival Managers Born or Made?

For those seeking a career in event management there are clear alternative strategies to those that accidentally have you known as an event patron or observer. Oftentimes that informal approach involves:

- Accumulating experience in convening successful events
- Demonstrating leadership through "force of personality"
- Being "the right person in the right place at the right time"
- Demonstrating attention to detail or a sound capacity to network at your place of employment or community
- Being perceived as a "party animal" and must know how to forgather like-minded folks
- Being a great self-promoter, so you will know how to market a specific event
- Being critical of functions you've attended and now you've been asked to show how it could be done better

The propensity to organize, practice, share, and deliver has been formalized in management programs worldwide. Professional organizations are emerging that allow practitioners opportunities to translate practice into consolidation of their specialization. Event managers deal with issues of marketing, finance, creative program design, human resources, and technical operations. They are multiskilled but they are also specialists. How do they find out about best practices? Is it through observation, going to other festivals, meeting with managers of similar events, listening to guest speakers, surfing the Internet, reading brochures, or reviewing their own programs?

Getz (1998) explores the nature of the information exchange between professionals, but establishes the relative importance of formal education, professional associations, books and journals, and attendance at others' events. He suggests that benchmarking should occur in the festivals sector. Getz offers some indicators of the learning processes undertaken by nonprofit festival organizations:

- Is there a formal evaluation and planning process?
- Is research valued and adequately supported?
- Are staff and volunteers encouraged to seek knowledge and new skills?
- Are innovations encouraged and rewarded?
- Does the festival have a mission, vision, or strategic plan that stresses learning and adapting, as opposed to protecting the status quo?
- Are professionals utilized for their expertise?
- Does the organization belong to professional associations?
- Does networking take place?

## The First Emerit® International Professional Standard

The event management profession is witnessing the growth of its body of knowledge, codes of practice, and competency systems. "An international body of knowledge sets the stage for global consistency in the scope of duties and capabilities required of industry practitioners and the conditions they could expect to encounter," says Julia Rutherford Silvers (EMBOK).

International networking and partnership is rapidly becoming standard practice and the Canadian Tourism Human Resource Council (CTHRC) predicted that globally recognized standards and credentials would be in high demand. Based on the Council's track record for developing top-quality professional certification, international stakeholders agreed that the CTHRC was the natural choice to spearhead the industry-led *emerit* Event Management–International Competency Standards project (EMICS, formerly known as IEMS).

CTHRC's leadership enabled participants from around the world to combine their experience, perspectives, and multidisciplinary skill sets to compose the EMICS credential. Working in close collaboration with international stakeholder groups, the CTHRC used existing national standards from participating countries, materials from the EMBOK, and cutting-edge research to create a comprehensive summary of the knowledge, skills, and attitudes needed to expertly manage an event anywhere in the world. Once completed, events practitioners from over 20 countries subjected the standards to a rigorous large-scale validation in 2009.

A professional, internationally recognized certification program, the Emerit Event Management certification program consists of an exam, a practical evaluation, and on-the-job experience. An international benchmark, the EMICS credential transcends borders and event disciplines, allowing the mutual recognition of transferable qualifications.

The Queen Margaret University of Scotland is one of the first post-secondary institutions in the world to officially accept and endorse EMICS and educators at the Art Institute of Vancouver, Canada, have successfully integrated the standards into their curriculum. Universities and colleges around the world are addressing competencies compatible with industry expectations.

The new international competency standards should complement existing International Festivals and Events Association CFEE programs. According to the CTHRC, "Our strategic, long-term goal is to support the industry by developing the *emerit* tool and make it available via a free download from our website. We will look at articulating the competency-based certification program, i.e., interpreting it, with other existing programs, such as CFEE, CMP, CSEP, and college and university programs, and eventually, to identifying and working with overseas partners to administer the program." IFEA could be one of those partners. (2009, IFEA Industry Compass, Global Issues, Trends, Challenges and Opportunities Impacting the World of Festivals and Events)

## International Events Qualifications Framework (IEQF)

The common ground for all qualifications is the competency level of individuals who are successful in achieving a qualification **as it relates to industry roles in the events field** (i.e., ability to perform at the support, coordinate, manage, or Direct level as an event practitioner). With this industry practitioner focus, it allows benchmarking of qualifications without comparison between levels of different national qualification frameworks in various countries. This comparison is best left to education authorities. Next steps in the development of an IEQF are identified as piloting the application and placement of some key event qualifications onto the IEQF using the identified criteria for inclusion, and development of governance and administrative structure and business plan for this global venture.

## International Overview through Event Management Body of Knowledge (EMBOK)

The EMBOK is a framework to be used for the development of events. It can be used as the foundation for competency levels in event management and, therefore for the development of curriculum. It can be used by the numerous associations around the world to evaluate their accreditation and develop event-type specific EMBOKs, such as Festival EMBOK.

The EMBOK is international. International leaders in festival design, management, and education—including Glenn Bowdin, Matthew Gonzalez, Janet

Landey, Kathy Nelson, Julia Rutherford Silvers, Joe Goldblatt, William O'Toole, and Jane Spowart—have worked to satisfy the aim *"To create a framework of the knowledge and processes used in event management that may be customized to meet the needs of various cultures, governments, education programs, and organizations."*

They wish to encourage its use to help develop a responsible and sustainable international industry. The EMBOK is open for use—acknowledgment is all that is needed.

Event management is made up of five areas of management:

- Design
- Administration
- Marketing
- Operations
- Risk

The EMBOK term for these areas is knowledge domains (see Table 4.3).

| Administration | Design | Marketing | Operations | Risk |
|---|---|---|---|---|
| Financial | Content | Marketing Plan | Attendees | Compliance |
| Human Resources | Theme | Materials | Communications | Decisions |
| Information | Program | Merchandise | Infrastructure | Emergency |
| Procurement | Environment | Promotion | Logistics | Health and Safety |
| Stakeholders | Production | Public Relations | Participants | Insurance |
| Systems | Entertainment | Sales | Site | Legal |
| Time | Catering | Sponsorship | Technical | Security |

**Table 4.3** Knowledge Domains

## FROM INSIDE THE MOSAIC

### Festival Founders: Robert Redford and John Polson

Much has been written about 'founder's syndrome.' In the field of festival creation it is worth examining the characteristics of some founders that ensure the continuation of their initiative during their leadership tenure and beyond.

Founders have to convince many stakeholders of the value of their initiative to establish firm and respectful partnerships that will allow the festival to thrive. Arts- and community-based festivals have regularly been established on the initiative of an individual who has seen a need as a result of their participation and engagement with a particular arts practice. Their own standing in that sector, the links they have established with their peers and the public, help to position the festival in the marketplace. Many such programs start small and focus on specific outputs that slot neatly into a strategic vision for its longevity and its appeal to growing audiences, private and public investment, and artists willing to commit to the journey.

Such leaders demonstrate an understanding and capacity to strategically position the festival and its organization for continued success. They are able to deliver results to make change happen and to build organizational systems that work. They engage, motivate, and communicate with employees, staff, and volunteers. By delegating, planning, and mentoring individuals for future leadership from inside and outside their organization they can encourage new perspectives on practice, policymaking, and planning that build on their own professionalism. There is speculation regarding the relative importance of personal attributes that demonstrate leadership effectiveness such as charisma, capacity to learn, willingness to take risks, networking skills, confidence, advocacy, fiscal prudence, entrepreneurship and negotiating ability. The experience of two such festival initiators is described below. You may wish to further investigate the progress made since their festivals originated and what the impacts have been on the team gathered to deliver the festivals and the implications for succession management.

## Sundance Film Festival

The annual Sundance Festival is held for 10 days each January in the small town of Park City, Utah. It is widely recognized as the premier showcase for American and international independent film. Inclusive and eclectic in its program, the festival has grown to include film culture events, panel discussions, youth programs, online exhibitions, and live music. Attended by more than 45,000 people from around the world each year and with an online audience exceeding one million users, the Sundance Film Festival creates a vibrant, unique community of artists and audiences.

It was set up by actor Robert Redford in 1981 under the Sundance Institute, Filmmakers and Directors Lab after Redford bought the area with profits from his hit movie, *Butch Cassidy and the Sundance Kid*.

He saw the festival as a mechanism where new voices in film would come. Independent short films were given a chance to develop and exhibit on the world stage. His long-standing commitment to filmmaking as an actor and producer, his passion for sharing a diverse range of quality cinematic experiences, his connection to the global industry, and his charisma have all contributed to the independence and integrity he demonstrates through his leadership of a successful festival. The initiative to build audiences for independent filmmakers attracts people from around the world. The program has grown and international satellite festivals have introduced new practitioners and content. The commitment to new artists and new audiences for all aspects of the festival program is managed by a team of professionals who recognize the importance of collaboration in the creative process.

A creative celebratory atmosphere emerged through the firm leadership of Redford, making sure it doesn't become one huge red carpet event. The location is far removed from the pressures of the marketplace. Emerging artists are encouraged to take creative risks through a program of activities expanded to include:

- Sundance Playwrights Lab
- Feature Film Program
- Documentary Film Program
- Theater Program
- Native American and Indigenous Program
- Film Music Program
- Creative Producing Initiative
- Establishment of an archive, an institute collection, and alumni and community programs

This diversity has created growth, continuity, and activities all year. The first-ever Sundance London film and music festival was held in 2012. It offered four days of film premieres, live music performances, discussions and panels with guest speakers hosted by Robert Redford. As the President and Founder of Sundance Institute, he said: "Sundance London marked our first time hosting an event in the UK, and we are grateful to all our supporters and collaborators for the reception we received. These four days have seen features, documentaries, and live events with insightful filmmakers and musicians, as well as passionate audiences, in attendance."

The festival uses a large volunteer force and a "Festival Insider" network to keep it running.

It has launched many original works that became huge hits (e.g., *Reservoir Dogs*, *An Inconvenient Truth*, *Little Miss Sunshine*, and *The Cove*).

The resilience of this festival is due to the constant launching of exciting new independent films and the year-round support for all aspects of film and theatre, but mostly because of Robert Redford as a respected actor, director, producer, businessman, environmentalist, and philanthropist. Having won two Academy Awards, a lifetime achievement award, many honorary doctorates, and a French Knighthood, Redford has the connections, credentials, and finances to allow this festival to continue.

He is always looking for initiatives. The recent "Being Green at the Festival" and the embracing of new technology (iPhones and iPads for viewing new short films) are highly successful examples.

## *Tropfest*

Tropfest is the largest short film festival in the world. It provides a unique platform for emerging filmmakers and has had a huge impact on the Australian film industry.

Like Sundance it was founded and continues to be driven by one man, award-winning actor/director John Polson.

Polson appeared in many Australian TV series then went on to direct films such as *Siam Sunset*, *Swimfan*, *Hide and Seek*, and *Tenderness*. In recent years he has forged a reputation for small-screen direction with *Fringe*, *The Mentalist*, *The Good Wife*, and *Flash Forward*.

Tropfest started in 1983 when Polson showed his own short films on a TV set at the *Tropicana*, a café in Sydney's Darlinghurst. Two hundred people came to the first screenings.

Now over 150,000 people come to the Sydney's Centennial Park each year with a live satellite broadcast to all Australian capital cities, with 1 million viewers on subscription *Movie Extra*, and a free DVD in *The Sydney Morning Herald* newspaper.

Tropfests have now been started worldwide in New York, Berlin, London, Bangkok, Beijing, and Aspen, with large expansion plans. Now it is the world's largest short-film festival. As it expands its reach to the United States, the competition introduced a uniquely New York touch when Hugh Jackman hosted Tropfest New York. There, entrants were required to include a bagel in their seven-minute film produced especially for Tropfest.

Tropfest stays true to its origins. It is free to attend. Filmmakers are given a limited time and a key word/image to produce their work. It is open to all. Judges are high profile industry people like Cate Blanchett, Nicole Kidman, Geoffrey Rush, Russell Crowe, and John Woo, who contended with over 600 entries nationally in 2012.

Winners now have a ticket to a successful career in film and/or television. From an Australian perspective, Sam Worthington and Joel Edgerton are among the alumni. The festival is based on a competition. Australian filmmaker, Alethea Jones, won the 2012 Tropfest competition. Her success led to her introduction to industry opportunities that can otherwise take decades to achieve. The exposure to a broad audience of film professionals concurrently with the general public is a major benefit for artists' participation in such an event. So audiences play a significant role in a process that generates engaging entertainment, stimulates industry development, and builds a national cultural platform.

The festival's resilience is due to its "grassroots" nature, the enthusiasm of a large volunteer festival workforce, its broad accessible community appeal, the incorporation of digital technology into its design and distribution, and the constant inspiring leadership of John Polson.

## Festival Ideas and Issues

1. What are the key objectives for a festival human resource strategy? How do they inform policies and procedures adopted by a festival organization?
2. How can festival leaders and managers inspire excellence among staff? What strategies can motivate staff (paid and volunteer)?
3. Compare leadership and management. Various roles need to be mastered. Give examples of best practices in each field. Are there distinctive styles? How do such people fulfill their key roles in a festival organization?
4. Identify some practical techniques that show how teams are built up and function effectively by producing results in line with festival objectives. Compile a simple checklist to match types of teams to fit particular tasks.
5. What's the best way to organize a festival's work?
6. How can a best fit be achieved between what employees wish to achieve from their employment experience and those organizational outcomes articulated in strategy and policy? Is it possible to achieve one set of outcomes without the other? Why or why not?
7. "There is a limit to the number of original ideas in any field of human activity, and management is no exception" (Kennedy, 1991, p. ix). How does this affect the way people work within a festival situation? Identify some innovation you have seen implemented in festivals and seek to understand how they may have been determined before their implementation.

## Festival Focus Activities

1. Investigate a familiar festival's organizational structure. Construct a chart and join a team to work through how members of staff might deal with a specific task. Evaluate whether the existing structure is the best fit for the purpose and offer any alternative suggestions.
2. Choose one role from the festival's organizational chart and develop a job description for that position. Scope the processes for locating an appropriate candidate through policies, recruitment, advertising (where? how?), selection (interviews, referees, screening), hiring, and induction.
3. "Your primary stakeholder is the artist; your second is the audience, because you are bringing into reality an artist's vision. On a number of occasions, humorously and seriously, men have said there is a multitasking style in arts and so women are better at it. But some people say the best management style is when a man adopts a female management style" (Leigh Small, Sydney Film Festival, 2012). Do you agree or disagree and why? Nearly half of the CEOs at Australia's top performing arts companies are women (Australia Council for the Arts World Economic Forum, 2012).
4. Review festival volunteer recruitment application forms. What special requirements are identified for particular tasks? What sort of training and induction strategies would you suggest for these tasks?
5. Investigate the statutory or legal obligations that face a festival organization in their preparation and presentation of a festival. How do these impact the shape of the festival and what are the specific implications for staff, volunteers, and interns?

6. In small groups role-play an interview situation for a job at a long-standing popular music festival. First prepare a skeletal job description. See how the scenario evolves based on a few key questions: *Why are you interested in this role? Why should we hire you? What five adjectives best describe you? How well do you work with people? Do you prefer working alone or in teams? How would you measure success?*

## Suggested Reading

Adams, S., 2012, *The Last Writes of a Festival Director,* http://www.artshub.com.au/au/news-article/opinions/arts/the-last-writes-of-a-festival-director-190636, Arts Hub Holdings Australia, Melbourne.

Allen, J., W. O'Toole, I. McDonnell, and R. Harris. *Festival and Special Event Management* (5th ed.). Milton, QLD, Australia: Wiley, 2010.

El Ansari, W. *A Study of the Characteristics, Participant Perceptions and Predictors of Effectiveness in Community Partnerships in Health Personnel Education: The Case of South Africa* University of Wales College Newport, United Kingdom: 1999 (Unpublished Doctoral Thesis).

Arcodia, C. V., and T. & Barker. "The Employability Prospects of Graduates in Event Management: Using Data from Job Advertisements, in *Riding the Wave of Tourism and Hospitality Research, Proceedings of the Council of Australian University Tourism and Hospitality Education Conference,* ed. R. W. Braithwaite (Coffs Harbour, NSW, Australia: CAUTHE, 2003), 1–16.

Boedker C., R. Vidgen, K. Meagher, J. Cogin, J. Mouritsen, and J. M. Runnalls. *Leadership, Culture and Management Practices of High Performing Workplaces in Australia: The High Performing Workplaces Index.* Sydney, Australia: Society for Knowledge Economics, Sydney, Australia, Australian School of Business, 2011.

Drucker, P. *Managing the Non-Profit Organisation.* Oxford, UK: Butterworth Heinemann, 1993.

Getz, Donald. "Information Sharing among Festival Managers." *Festival Management and Event Tourism* 5 (1998): 33–50.

Goldblatt, J. *Special Events—21st Century Global Events Management* (3rd ed.). New York: Wiley, 2002.

Goldblatt, J., and C. M. Matheson. "Volunteer Recruitment and Retention: A US/Australian Comparison," in *People and Work in Events and Conventions: A Research Perspective,* ed. Tom Baum, M. Deery, C. Hanlon, L. Lockstone, and K. Smith (Wallingford, UK: CAB International, 2009).

Hertzberg, F. "One More Time: How Do You Motivate Employees?" *Harvard Business Review* 46, no. 1 (1968): 361–367.

Kennedy, C., *Guide to Management Gurus,* Century, 1991.

Maslow, A. *Motivation and Personality.* New York: Harper and Row, 1954.

Mintzberg, H., and J. B. Quinn. *The Strategy Process: Concepts, Contexts, Cases* (2nd ed.). Englewood Cliffs, NJ: Prentice Hall, Englewood Cliffs, 1991.

Robinson, M. *Making Adaptive Resilience Real.* Arts Council England, 2010.

Schien, E. H. *Organizational Culture and Leadership* (2nd ed.). San Francisco: Jossey-Bass, 1992.

Watt, D. C. *Event Management in Leisure and Tourism.* Harrow, UK: Addison Wesley Longman, 1998.

# CHAPTER 5
# Building Partnerships That Work

*Alliances have become an integral part of contemporary strategic thinking.*
—*Fortune magazine*

### This chapter provides an opportunity for you to better understand:

- The relationships festivals have with stakeholders
- How festival organizations can build relationships, establishing the worthiness of shared ideas, issues, influences, impacts, and implications
- How value means different things to different people
- How by working together, partnerships can grow capacity and meet shared aspirations
- How effective collaborations reap the benefits through the co-creation of innovation and festival success to satisfy festival patrons who are central to delivering worthy partnerships

This chapter examines the powerful role that partnerships provide for festival prosperity and longevity. The pace of change in many aspects of our lives has had a profound impact on the way we calibrate our relationships. The shift in emphasis from festivals solely providing a service to a targeted market to the recognition that it is just one part of a mosaic that satisfies diverse stakeholders is what is under scrutiny here. The vocabulary in Figure 5.1 will inform our discussion. Flexibility is required to position a festival as an opportunity for fun, entertainment, and learning, so associations forged through the formalization of partnerships now nuance socializing and celebration.

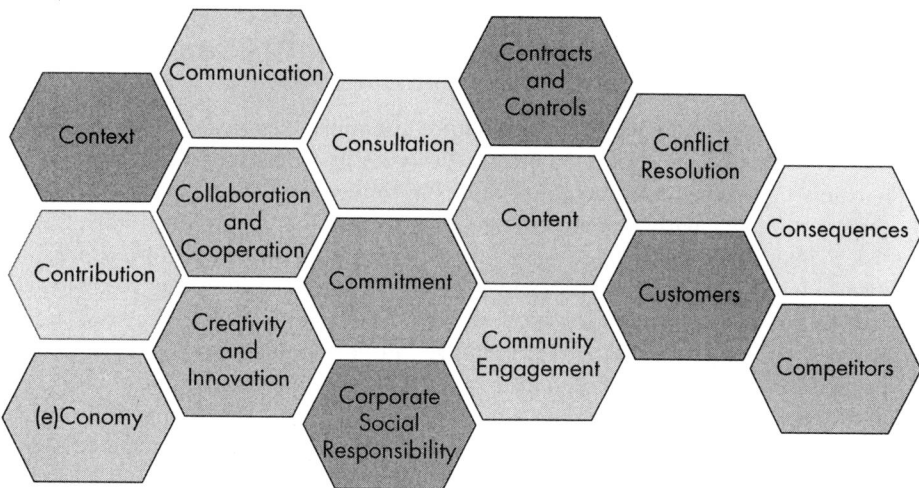

**Figure 5.1** A Partnership Mosaic.

Festival organizations still rely on their own strengths, traditions, and internal confidence to deliver as we saw through our exploration of the festival organization's internal stakeholders. Now we examine the opportunities and challenges that emerge when links to individuals, groups, government agencies, businesses, and institutions ratchet up the reach and the impact the festival can have in building the resilience of all parties.

# Establishing Festival Partnerships

Festivals organizers have realized the opportunities to adapt to the forces at play in the economy at large, advances in technology, individuals' motivations and their demographic spectrum, decision-making behaviors, and the globalization of enterprise. They have learned how to grow their capacity to reach their goals by working beside entities active in these areas. What they have recognized is that for a smooth-running festival ecosystem, customers are now more prone to simultaneously call in the information, services, and products they require when they make a decision to attend a festival and this means that the festival organizers and their partners/suppliers/stakeholders need to respond holistically. This collaboration, whether through web-based facilities or face-to-face contact, will hasten the breakdown of organizational silos and attract greater access from patrons. There is an understanding that the potential customer is the center of the arrangement and this makes them a vital stakeholder.

The mosaic that manifests itself comprises elements that reflect the strategic directions that need to be pursued, the qualities of the relationships nurtured, and the outcomes of mutual benefit that can be nourished.

## Partnership Components

- **Consultation** Through the cyclical nature of enduring festivals, managers will regularly consult existing partners and nurture potential new long-term and short-term partners to ensure their current relationship obligations are being met. They check their compliance with government agencies for development applications, waste and risk management details, and policy protocols are all addressed in a timely way. If terms change due to legislation they need to share the intelligence so that financial commitments are fulfilled for such administrative areas as insurance, taxation, and corporate governance. With rapid changes in communication technology, material design, and service delivery, parties need to keep one another informed to allow adequate preparation of outdoor sites, indoor venues, staff training with new appliances, etc. Such developments will affect the human, financial, and infrastructure resources required, so ongoing contact is important. Specific personnel in each organization needs to be identified as negotiators in particular areas of the relationship and sound documentation to record the decisions made needs to be communicated within each.
- **Commitment** Initial negotiations in a comfortable and professional manner will establish the willingness of parties to collaborate or work commercially for mutual benefit. Some partners exchange documents like a memorandum of understanding to secure the relationship once arrangements have been agreed-upon. Each party needs to prepare their approach to establish the opportunities that can be explored. Each needs to ensure they present one another with a timely and specific package of benefits and a practical action plan and demonstrate an understanding of each other's corporate goals. Signoff can take time, as each party determines how best to deliver on the commitment. Some exchanges will be purely commercial; others may involve in-kind support, barter, sponsorship, charity fundraising, product demonstrations, or co-branding. Comprehensive detailing of the commitment needs to be documented. Contracts need to be signed.
- **Context** All the parties that can have a relationship with a festival-goer exist independently of one another; however, they can combine through mutual interdependence to deliver quality experiences for all involved in the process and product. Festival organizers who appreciate the context in which they operate, understand their host communities, their festival's sectoral interests, the dynamics of internal management, and the cultural distinctiveness inside and external to the festival organization, the economic and political environments are better placed to guide their festival on a sustainable and enduring path. The resources that are required to deliver an attractive festival are complex and variable. Festivals are risky enterprises and links with others will allow the festival to increase its profile; attract adequate financial, material, and emotional resources; and inspire confidence among stakeholders that may more nimbly deal with challenges to stability and longevity.
- **Content** Organizers spend a great deal of time and thought in preparing the look and feel of the festival with design elements deemed to satisfy the target market. They take the opportunity to design the spaces to be occupied and plan the content of the theme chosen for each event. They will be concerned for environmental good practice,

comfort, security, and sound engineering of logistics as well as all the elements of entertainment, learning, hospitality, and services that deliver a quality experience for the festival-goer. They ensure that appropriate venues chosen can accommodate the expected numbers and that performers, workshop leaders, merchandisers, catering amenities, emergency services are provided in an effective manner. It is important that staff and volunteers are able to create an acceptable style of program that can include a mix of engagement opportunities for the audience in terms of scale, personal spaces for socializing, and use of ritual and cultural exchanges that match the expectations of audiences. This could include the inclusion of celebrity, sensory stimulation through light and sound, and culinary options. Customers' satisfaction with the content of the experience influences repeat visitation that is important for festival sustainability.

- **Collaboration and cooperation** offers partners opportunities to deal with complex situations and outputs for mutual benefit through the co-production of solutions informed by the resources, expertise, and shared commitment in terms of festival delivery. This could involve peer technical support, cooperative marketing through an annual festival calendar, staff training, catering amenities, organizational assistance, communication support, or other goods that can better be shared than invested in independently. Local government authorities hold practical resources for the common good and will make these available for community festivals. Other festival managements and professional special interest networks provide advice, support, and conduits to reach compatible audiences. Success through collaboration (in teams or bipartisan activities) isn't necessarily expensive to ensure operational and process improvements. They require inspiration, mentorship, and leadership to encourage partners to take responsibility for aspects of implementation.

- **Communication** between all parties involved in delivering a festival is crucial and demanding. It requires formal and informal interaction, sometimes face-to-face, sometimes broadly based with extensive use of public distribution of messages to ensure all potential customers and partners are up to date with relevant information. Exchanges can take place at festival launches, across all media platforms, in print, through marketing collateral, direct personal contact from databases, via third parties with an interest in the festival and over long periods of time through a managed communication plan. This plan identifies the layers of communications required along a critical path of dissemination. Some of the levels of communication will require disclosure of highly sensitive materials; others will be lively, inspirational, and imaginative approaches to sharing the message of the festival excitement from the imminent staging of the festival. Regular bulletins will ensure that the festival remains in the public gaze and encourage followers to share their enthusiasm peer-to-peer through social networking channels.

- **Creativity and innovation** are as much attitudes as they are guided by sets of principles and processes. These can be incorporated in all aspects of social interaction. When new ideas are called for and links have to be made between habits of thinking and looking at different ways to approach challenges, festival organizers are keen to ensure they address playfulness, curiosity, sensitivity, self-awareness, and independence. Festivals provide opportunities to generate fresh new approaches to ways of celebrating. By bringing partners together for problem solving throughout all the diverse dimensions of festival planning, the co-creation of knowledge offers opportunities to challenge existing patterns and practices. New ideas and concepts can impact on the design of the program's content, on the approach to new technologies, waste management, and environmental practices. Arts and cultural festivals provide a context for enhancing the meaning-making that humans crave. The perspectives of all festival partners can contribute to enriching the festival experience. Creativity is not the gift of a few, it isn't the exclusive domain of the arts, and it can be disciplined, systemic, organized, and even logical when applied by resourceful, inventive, and imaginative people from all walks of life.

- **Contracts and controls** start with policy that emerges from the strategic goals of the festival organization. By periodically reviewing these goals, the nature of each festival partnership can be assessed and the formal, legal relationships established can be successfully maintained. Legal advice is essential. Experience will inform partners of the appropriate way to reach an understanding of their obligations under the law in particular circumstances in a timely way and how settlement of disputes may be dealt with in a professional way. In community festivals local government authorities are often called upon to be the auspicing body when government funding is attracted and parties need to be clear on what items and processes are included in each contractual arrangement and what aspects of their relationship may be outsourced to third parties. There may be a need to identify where the leadership resides in particular arrangements, where limitations may apply, where regulation may supersede informal exchanges, and what specific resource constraints each party may have to preside over.
- **Conflict resolution** Handling difficult conversations and actions between partners and building sustainable and flexible working relationships can be an unwelcome diversion. Resolving conflict isn't always easy but it is necessary to ensure those involved don't leave things unchecked as the festival's outputs may be delayed or lost. It is important that morale remains buoyant and the common goals are not jeopardized. However, there are mechanisms that encourage efficient meetings and open, honest communication through external mediation (maybe another partner with relevant experience in law for example). The conflict needs to be identified, analyzed, and managed with a solution that minimizes any damage to an ongoing working relationship.
- **Competitors** Support for a festival may not be uniform across the community or event industry. As is revealed in this chapter, most businesses recognize the value of some sort of connection with a long-standing, well-organized and attractive celebration. We have seen the growth of industry-based links that are responding to the diminution of some competitive practices; however, a healthy understanding of where the customer is likely to spend their money, time, and energy is important. There could be turbulence in a destination if the portfolio of events is not well calibrated and tension can arise when businesses are approached to offer support for an event. This can affect sponsorship investments, for example. It is beholden on festival organizers to know their own business and identify ways to distinguish their efforts from others in an annual calendar in a specific locality, all the while being cognizant of the fact that people's discretionary expenditure could easily be committed to an online world away to white goods, alternate travel, and entertainment experiences.
- **Customers** are central to the festival's decision to partner with others to ensure their satisfaction through practices that are efficient, attractive, and readily accessible and meet their needs in a timely way. There is a personalization emerging in

the relationship between festivals and their patrons and so mechanisms are put in place to reach these individuals and groups where they are and to respond to their intention to participate in a festival. These are best served through a network of interdependent collaborators who work to embrace the customer and deliver a seamless chain of services that Pollock called a "cycle of need" (i.e., offering alternatives, comparisons, selecting, purchasing, assembling, experiencing, and evaluating possible solutions to their aspiration). It is hard for just one enterprise to deliver on all aspects effectively, but through a shared vision with key partners a collaborative approach can satisfy the target market. This influences the festival organization in their choice of partners.

- **Community engagement** Trying to get others to buy in to a festival takes a mixed bag of skills. There is information-sharing, facilitation of exchange between various parties who may become interested in the role and nature of the festival and how they may become more involved, and extensive listening to hear from particular interest groups or the host community at large to understand their level of acceptance. The notion of public participation is getting traction in many aspects of life and many festival partners are keen to engage with the broader communities whether geographical, geopolitical, social, and cultural and minimize marginalizing sectors unintentionally. All this requires effective communication skills. Messages need to be consistent, clear, and engender enthusiasm from an informed position to create an atmosphere that embraces all that a festival can celebrate.

- **(e)Conomy** The economy is connected to all the players in festival development. There needs to be research, analysis, and forecasts of the local and broader economic dynamics; an understanding of the demands on individuals' discretionary incomes; and employment regimes that exist among the staff and volunteers required for the festival and allied collaborators. Host communities like festivals because they are seen to introduce new money into the local economy and diverse businesses can benefit—from laundromats to service stations to media through advertising. The festival generates new income for the community and the associated enterprises; grant-funding from governmental agencies inject financial resources that assist creativity, experimentation, and innovation that can last beyond the festival. There could be investment in infrastructure that benefits residents long after the festival closes for the year or if it discontinues altogether.

- **Contribution** Partners in the festival enterprise have diverse relationships with one another and thus influence outcomes for a festival in different ways at different times. Their involvement within a network of partners can vary, as can the power they may wield, the resources they commit to the shared vision, the individual leadership they possess, the experience they have had in their own sector, the host community, with government at all levels and their experience with the festival. Each entity will wish to maintain its autonomy. They will judge that there are advantages to cooperation with others and so will maintain their identity and independent governance while contributing products and services that enhance the scope and scale of the festival. They may fulfill multiple roles. Research that has been undertaken into stakeholder, network, and partnership theory explain the roles and contributions partners can make in building trust, delivering festival identity, and maintaining a viable and civil exchange within and between entities tied to a specific goal.

- **Corporate social responsibility** Corporate volunteering is one way in which companies are addressing some interesting demographic trends. In recent years volunteering in the corporate sector has doubled. The idea of encouraging staff to become involved regularly in the arts and cultural community to demonstrate how their professional skills and experience can add value to enterprises like festivals is spreading. Staff members are given an opportunity to share their expertise through contributing governance, marketing, accounting, technology, training, management, and planning support, for example. They can provide targeted services much needed by the not-for-profit sector, particularly through upskilling festival volunteers or paid staff. This engagement allows for higher staff morale, improved productivity, and a better public image for both organizations. In fact, there is evidence that sponsorship is seen to be a more cynical approach to partnering, with money given in exchange for promotional opportunity. Individuals participating in links to festivals laboring in the scarcity paradigm have had positive experiences, learning about the programs and processes that enrich everyday lives through entertainment, education, and logistics. Through active involvement in the delivery of a festival, a number of corporate staff get leadership and project management experience by being on boards and committees. The resultant business and community leaders can have broad influence beyond the festival.
- **Consequences** The coming-together of various forces identified in this chapter can result in a successful festival. The relationships identified by the festival organizers to bring about the desired fruitfulness can be fragile. There are numerous variables that require vigilance. Stakeholders can take on multiple roles that can be voluntary, contractual, resource-laden, and dependent on externalities with no ties to the festival, all with robust goodwill, and all need to be managed. There needs to be a strategic best fit to underpin the relationships to ensure continuity for long-term mutual benefit that goes beyond the festival itself. The social, cultural, economic, and environmental impacts and implications for host communities, tourism brands, and national and international profiles are substantial. Effective partnerships sustain festivals when responsibilities are clearly identified so that over time they can renew themselves as required, maybe self-repair, and be revitalized to meet the challenges and opportunities and avoid premature extinction.

The strength of partnerships may be determined by the festival organization's relationship trajectory as shown in Figure 5.2.

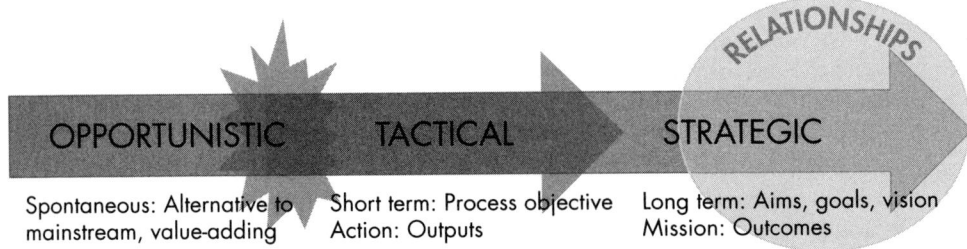

**Figure 5.2** Festival trajectory.
*Derrett (2013).*

## Partnership Components

> The most important single ingredient in the formula of success is knowing how to get along with people.
>
> —*Theodore Roosevelt*

The stakeholders identified in Figure 5.3 influence many of the choices that the festival host organization makes as it prepares and delivers its program. The exchanges that take place between parties can be capitalized upon through the parallel independent and interdependent relationships that may exist between all parties. These relationships can become catalysts for further interaction for short or long periods beyond the interaction that takes place with specific festivals. We look at the roles of each of these stakeholders as they engage with a festival and one another. We see the essence of a successful partnership and the principles and protocols that underpin them. We can, for example, trace who takes the initiative and why; what shape the relationship can take and for how long; what constitutes the best sharing mechanisms to satisfy the "what's in it for me" question; which goods and services can be made available to the public in a celebratory environment; how economic resources can be decentralized and disseminated; provision of education, training, and skills to employees; and act as a mechanism through which minority or marginalized groups can take advantage of opportunities often denied to them by larger organizations. The direction a festival organization might take as it determines the best fit for cementing relationships is shaped by strategic and tactical opportunities.

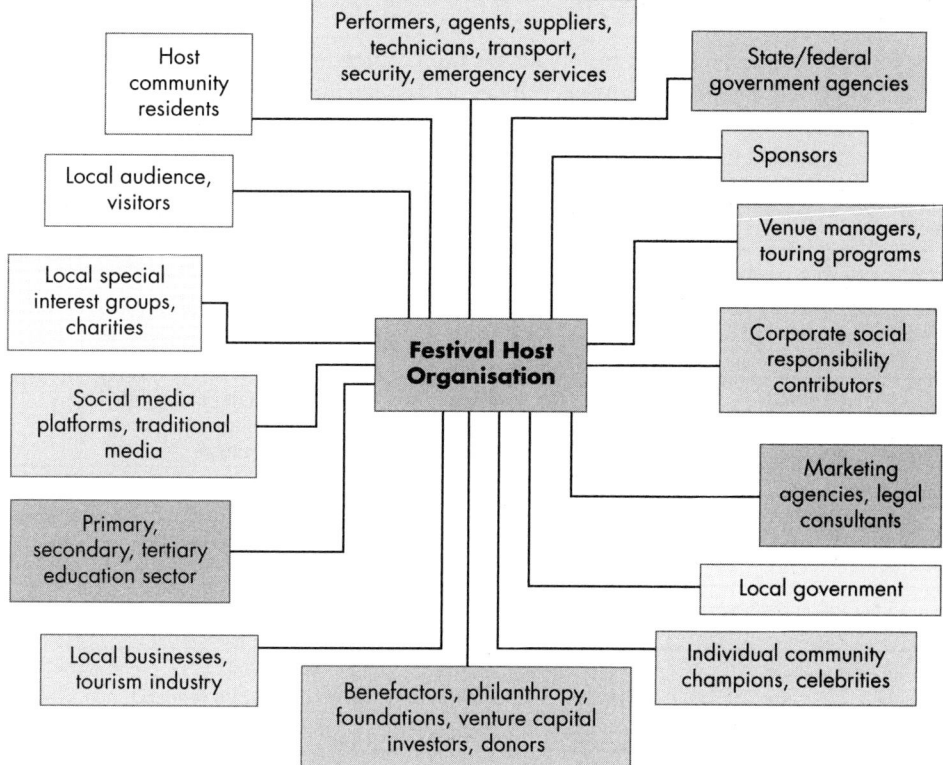

**Figure 5.3** Festival Stakeholders.
Derrett (2013).

So, how do relationships work best? How do you encourage an investment in great ideas to maximize their impact and contribute to a resilient community/organization/project/individual? Who is best placed to facilitate this? You need to know who is on your patch and what their interests, values, and aspirations are. What role can each play in developing a realistic, attractive, timely, and cost-effective activity? What are the mutual benefits for collaboration and cooperation? This may provide a useful framework:

- Co-thinking—working with partners to understand needs and wants
- Co-designing—joint problem solving by better defining issues and potential solutions
- Co-evaluating—testing ideas, building networks, and getting feedback
- Co-developing—garnering input from dabblers, enthusiasts, experts, and fanatics to attract dynamic, diverse inputs
- Co-communicating—cultivating advocates, exchange of ideas, reviews, use of technology
- Co-supporting—broadly sharing timely feedback when challenges arise

"The greatest change in corporate culture—and the way business is being conducted—may be the accelerated growth of relationships based ... on partnership."
—Peter F. Drucker

## Festival Partnerships

Although interest and commitment from your festival partners may be high, it is actually the amount of resources, time, and capacity of each member or organization that can be dedicated to this effort that should determine the magnitude and scope of work. So before defining your goals and objectives, you need to look critically at individual and organizational capacity (Table 5.1).

| Steps | Description |
|---|---|
| Clarify why you want to involve others | Clarify why the participation process is being started, who has the final say, and what your brief is. |
| Understand your role | Identify key community interests, including voluntary, business, and community organizations. |
| Decide where you stand | Consider the level of participation appropriate; make informal contacts to identify local concerns and whether your stance—the level you are adopting—is likely to be acceptable. |
| Prepare for participation | Run a workshop session(s) within your organization to ensure key people are clear about the purpose of the participation process, the roles and responsibilities, and the answers to basic questions that will be asked when you go public. |
| Choose participation methods | Consider the stance (inform, consult, etc.) you are taking in more detail, and in light of that decide on what methods you will use. |
| Develop support with your organization | Review whether your organization will be able to respond to the feedback, and follow through on any decisions reached. |
| Develop your skills as an enabler | Demonstrate confidence and capability. |
| Choose an appropriate structure | Review your timescale and prepare an action plan based on the level of participation. |

**Table 5.1** Festival Partnership Assessment

It is essential that you go through this organizational capacity activity whether you are working with a long-standing or recently created partnership. Even within groups that have worked together for a long period of time, organizational capacity is seldom assessed or communicated to members. Often assumptions are made in this area about participating individuals or organizations that may be incorrect, so articulating group capacity is critical to the planning process.

In order to appraise individual and organizational capacity, you need to be confident of responses to the following about each partners' organizational mission that captures an organization's purpose, clientele orientation, and philosophy; the community or population(s) each serves; the financial and resource capacity they have to commit; any conflicts of interest; staffing, organizational support, and skills they can contribute; the research capacity they bring to the collaboration; the technological support and expertise available; their connections to multi-platform media communication; their existing links, allies, or partners that can be shared; and the level and type of involvement they are willing to commit. Responses from the diverse partners are examined below, firstly through the potential festival stakeholder represented in Figure 5.3 and then in the roles stakeholders play in enduring festivals (Table 5.2).

Below is a brief scan from observations at a series of regional community-based cultural festivals (Derrett, 2007). Partnerships that support the host community's sense of itself and its place through festival investment either in-kind, by sponsorship deals, or by sharing resources or offering media promotion help build confidence in the life of the festival. The diverse inputs identified in the Table 5.2 summary demonstrate the influence of the relationships and how they enrich the efforts of organizers and encourage local support for

| Stakeholder | Roles |
|---|---|
| Host community—the impacted audience, paying customers, and sometimes special guests | • Produce and consume festival<br>• Act as host for visitors<br>• Free access to most of festival as audience<br>• Contribute and celebrate cultural diversity<br>• Traditional and new settler exchange of rituals, volunteer support, and >75% of participants<br>• Interest in creating a legacy<br>• Target market supporting image of festival and identity for its promotion |
| Community champions—facilitators, advocates | • Individuals providing vision and leadership, generating enthusiasm, delivering advocacy, and attracting respect and loyalty from organization members and wider community<br>• Bringing goodwill and external recognition to festival |
| Volunteer coworkers—internal stakeholders | • Demonstrate active participation in community life<br>• Establish and consolidate networks<br>• Local problem solving<br>• Personal skills development and empowerment<br>• Greater understanding of local beliefs, attitudes, and values |
| Festival organization—internal stakeholder, owners, producers, volunteer and paid staff | • Formal structure emphasizes identity and connection to host community<br>• Offers safety and security for participants<br>• Membership comprised of local community<br>• Succession strategies<br>• Community profile |

**Table 5.2** Stakeholder Roles in Enduring Festivals

| Stakeholder | Roles |
|---|---|
| Local government—regulators, sometimes co-producers, facilitators | • Policy and planning frameworks<br>• Events officers and project management personnel and infrastructure support<br>• "In-kind" and financial investment<br>• Improve amenities for residents and visitors<br>• Facilitate regional and government alliances and investment<br>• Support tourism marketing initiatives<br>• Reflect community traditions and interests |
| State and federal government—often regulators, sometimes facilitators as grant givers | • Provide funding to support elements of festival programs and value-add to economic initiatives and harmonization challenges<br>• Ensure regulations (e.g., alcohol in public places) are adhered to<br>• Arts funding for performers |
| Regional alliances (agencies and organizations representing sectoral interests), collaborators, facilitators | • Desire to respond to locally agreed-upon agendas<br>• Offer financial support and advice<br>• Encourage initiatives with regional outcomes (e.g., collaborative tourism promotion, arts development, regional cuisine, entrepreneurial initiatives)<br>• Some e-technology support<br>• Consolidate communication through networks<br>• Provide elements of programs |
| Business community (local and regional), suppliers, vendors | • Be open during festival!<br>• Provide feedback to organizers on economic impacts<br>• Provide sponsorship—"in-kind" or financial<br>• Collaborate in packages and promotion<br>• Active involvement during event highlighting local products and services<br>• Social responsibility |
| Sponsors, co-producers | • Demonstrate local corporate goodwill<br>• Share target markets<br>• Establish links to host destination<br>• Share brand<br>• Naming rights |
| Supplier, performers, merchandisers, transport, logistics | • Provide entertainment reflecting local cultural objectives<br>• Offer educational workshops, knowledge-sharing, and demonstrations<br>• Repeat contributions builds loyalty |
| Special Interest Groups (local, regional, (inter)national), audience, collaborators, facilitators | • Festival acts as umbrella for diverse but themed pursuits<br>• Consistent involvement brings repeat visitation and builds momentum<br>• Encourages engagement in social action<br>• Provide connection to community issues, concerns, and interests<br>• Attracts visitors from further afield<br>• Offers broad network distribution of promotional material |
| Media (local, regional (inter)national—print, audio-visual, Web-based) | • Significant coverage by regional print and a/v media, before, during, and after festivals<br>• Document and editorialize image and identity, generate archive<br>• Promotion of regional lifestyle<br>• International market reached through Web casting, Internet, documentaries<br>• Stimulate debate and controversy<br>• Encourage community responses<br>• Sponsorship |

**Table 5.2** Stakeholder Roles in Enduring Festivals *(continued)*

| Stakeholder | Roles |
|---|---|
| Education sector—audience, participants, researchers | • Provide research and evaluation services to assist with planning and management<br>• Provide an audience for festivals<br>• Provide entertainment for festivals<br>• Provide industry training in event management |
| Visitors—audience, participants | • Interest in doing what the locals do<br>• Curiosity to learn, discover, and interpret local traditions<br>• Repeat visitation substantial because of connection with host community (VFR or reunion) or event<br>• Substantial visitation interstate<br>• Word-of-mouth value |
| Benefactors, funders, investors, co-producers | • Nurture formal and informal relationships, tax deductibility, anonymity, celebration, promotion, look at structures like foundations |

**Table 5.2** Stakeholder Roles in Enduring Festivals *(continued)*
Derrett (2007).

each festival. The formal and informal links become known to the potential audience for each event and help consolidate the impression of widespread awareness, satisfaction, and value derived from the relationship for each contributing partner.

Partnerships that support the host community's sense of itself and its place help build confidence in the life of the festival and ultimately the community. The formal and informal links become known to the potential audience for each event and help consolidate the impression of widespread awareness, satisfaction, and value derived for each contributing partner from the relationship. Key partners demonstrate the principle of active participation, the belief in quality of all cultures and the notion of diversity as a social asset. The density of civic participation can be connected with regional economic development. It suggests that social capital is not only a product of the region's economy through the exchange of good and services, but connected vitally to bureaucracies, special interest networks, and on a communal level through strong, shared identity.

The roles and interactions shown in Table 5.2 reveal that the impacted audience plays a significant role in the success of each festival. The audience can comprise representatives of the various stakeholder groups. The multiplicity of roles some individuals and some agencies hold in the design, management, and delivery of each festival requires sensitive management. The interaction between each at various levels and at distinctive junctures of a festival's development needs to be understood by festival organizers. So, for example, local government can be a regulator, a facilitator, and a collaborator or partner simultaneously.

Each festival can have strong links with its respective communities of interest, but the growing number of visitors brings stress on infrastructure, pressure on internal relationships, and resentment about the influx of outsiders. Issues of community carrying capacity become a concern to organizers, Council planners, and businesses. Organizing a major festival takes a lot of individual and collective effort. To get the job done the organizers have to be able to give a lot of time personally and be able to call in a lot of favors and/or inspire volunteerism. Celebration can bind a community and it can also be the instrument that provides it with fresh and constantly renewing experiences, an elixir that keeps the community relevant and responsive to the needs of the times.

Annual festivals create a community of witness that marks the passage of time, notes the changing of the guard as new power relations arise and old ones change. Kanter suggests in organizational terms that communities need to have both magnets and glue. Magnets broaden community horizons, attract and expand skills, and attract external resources. Leaders, festival spirit, and experience can be the glue that brings people together through social cohesion, with joint plans and agreed-upon strategic goals. Festivals fulfill this role.

Festivals provide service clubs, community special interest groups, local government, and businesses with opportunities to raise funds. Some fundraising involves new money from visitors and offers benefits such as investment in infrastructure for residents. Some investment in the promotion of the destination using the festival themes adds to the image and identity developed in each community. The destination-marketing dollar is increased at times when it is connected to the festivals. This in turn influences greater visitation and increased expenditure by visitors, visiting friends and relatives (VFRs), hosts, and local businesses anticipating the influx.

The feedback from partners involved with festival organizations is instructive too. Festivals marshal such comments as part of their monitoring and evaluation programs to ensure they are meeting the needs of their partners. Building effective relationships with partners requires attention to detail for the best fit of skills, resources, experience, and corporate objectives. Regular monitoring of the relationship might reveal:

- Degree of success of how any one component influences the success of all other components
- Demand for your services is elastic, seasonal, vulnerable to changes in taste and fashion
- No amount of advertising or promotion will successfully sell a poor product or service
- A good idea or product, on its own, is not enough
- Half the money we spend on advertising is wasted, but we never know which half

How these items can be implemented is demonstrated in the partnership examples in Table 5.3.

## Sponsors as Partners

One significant aspect of establishing partners involves event sponsorship. It is a means of spirited communication inspired by the festival but overtly in the interests of specific corporates or institutions. By increasing awareness in significant collaborative terms, companies are likely to engage in sponsorships for festivals through:

- Creating awareness for a new product
- Increasing awareness of an existing product in new target markets
- Bypassing legal prohibition on television advertising imposed on tobacco and alcohol products
- Attracting media attention to differentiate the product or company
- Heightening visibility through a variety of media

Sponsorships may be used to change or enhance the sponsor's image by specifically identifying markets that will build a desirable profile. From a business perspective there is a keenness to avoid any lack of understanding and commitment to what business needs from the relationship, such as any lack of commitment by the sponsored organization to deliver agreed-upon outcomes, promising what they couldn't deliver, or a hand-out mentality with no concept of shared benefit and responsibility.

Sponsorship is a versatile tool in "cause-related marketing" when agreed-upon beneficiaries can utilize the festival for fundraising or profile-raising. Businesses are not unlike individuals

Festival Partnerships 109

| Festival | | |
|---|---|---|
| **Portland Rose Festival, Oregon** Partner testimonial: "The Centennial Rose promotion was brilliant in every respect. The concept, the follow-through, the media support—we have never been involved with a more successful promotion. The Rose Festival team did an extraordinary job of understanding the client's needs and putting together a promotion that built | more than just awareness, it generated store traffic and sales for the client. Thank you, Rose Festival, you made us look great." Richard Petralia, East Bank Communications  There are hundreds of ways for businesses and individuals to participate in the Rose Festival! As a self-sustaining nonprofit organization, | the festival relies heavily on the enthusiasm of its volunteers and corporate sponsors, local business partners, and foundation donors. Programs to be supported include Emerging Artists, Scholarships, SOLV partnership/Cleanest & Greenest Award, Volunteer Program, Recycling Program, Sister City Programs, and Park Restoration. |
| **T in the Park (TITP), Scotland** Partner testimonial: "Playing festivals is a world of difference from playing your own shows. You have people there outside who aren't necessarily there to see you. And they're in the front because they wanted to get the good seats. And they're mingling with people that came to see you. So there's no time for comfort. You got to have energy. You can't expect the | crowd to help you—you can't feed off the crowd. The last time we played T in the Park what I remember most is that the crowd was nuts. The crowd was crazy. I just love Scotland, I love playing Glasgow, I love playing Edinburgh. Edinburgh's gorgeous." The Black Eyed Peas  TITP is Scotland's biggest and most successful outdoor music event, | selling out every year since 1996 despite now being more than four times its original size when it was launched. The festival has developed into a benchmark event, leading to a strong, sustained outdoor live events industry in Scotland with over 200 artists across 11 stages over 3 days. The live music promoters, DF Concerts, with founding partner Tennent's Lager attract international talent. |
| **Bregenz Festival, Austria** Founded in 1946, the Bregenz Festival evolved through a high degree of private initiative. Since the Bregenz Festival adopted the legal form of a limited liability company, the Friends of the Bregenz Festival have carried on the tradition of private involvement by means of donations and patrons' contributions, to ensure that even in | times of limited public subsidy the festival program remains artistically varied.  With the establishment of the Bregenz Festival Foundation, the Friends of the Bregenz Festival were able to transfer their rights of ownership to the Foundation. Thus the Friends have been able to concentrate on the task | of promoting the Bregenz Festival. The Friends has 1,300 members from Austria and abroad. The Friends, Patrons, and Members of the Circle are dedicated to supporting the Bregenz Festival, along with support from main, presenting, co-sponsors, official carriers, and cooperative partners in culture, tourism, and the media. |
| **Salzburg Festival, Austria** "Aren't you afraid that the sponsors will try to influence your program?" is a common question in the arts sections of various newspapers, especially since we have been so successful in acquiring sponsors. And I can always answer both spontaneously and | honestly: No, I am not afraid of that. Our sponsors are far too intelligent not to know that trying to influence the content of our program would have a boomerang effect. On the contrary, I hope our sponsors continue to influence us, in the sense that they make it possible to implement projects that we | could not realize otherwise for lack of money. Therefore, on behalf of the festival, I would very much like to thank our sponsors, donors, supporters and friends as well as the public authorities subsidizing the festival for their generous support. Helga Rabl-Stadler, President of the Salzburg Festival |
| **The Canadian Tulip Festival, Ottawa, Canada** The Canadian Tulip Festival was first held in 1953 as a Board of Trade initiative inspired by internationally renowned photographer Malak Karsh. It is the largest Tulip Festival in the world. This annual ritual of spring welcomes more than 500,000 visitors to admire the 1 million tulips that are in bloom in the National Capital. | Partner testimonial: "We are very pleased to be partnering with the Canadian Tulip Festival on this innovative mobile application. This is a bold technological step forward in festival marketing and attendee engagement, allowing visitors to become ambassadors of the festival and share the experience with their friends." John Craig, VP Sales and Marketing, Purple Forge  The festival partnering initiatives with Purple Forge create a mobile | application for iPhones that allows users to create postcards on-the-fly by selecting their own stamps, themes, and photographs of the festival that can be shared with their friends using email, Twitter, or Facebook. Combined with event schedules, video, a QR code scanner, and weather information, the application is the go-to mobile electronic guide for the Canadian Tulip Festival and the Great Canadian Tulip Treasure Hunt. |

**Table 5.3** Festival Partnership Examples

when committing to a sponsorship arrangement. They recognize the key ingredients of successful cultural sponsorships allow focus on good understanding between the parties through

- Mutual understanding with good, clear, and continuous communication
- Cooperative nature of the sponsorship and the commitment of key individuals
- Partnership approach with a good working relationship that regularly reviews expectations and clearly defined benefits of both parties
- Successful benefits for (1) community, (2) festival organization, and (3) sponsor
- Sincere shared belief in the event's goals and outputs

Companies want to be able to get on with their core business and see sponsorship as an effective tool to broaden their customer base. These arrangements can be seen as sales opportunities and product trials. They can induce incremental sales increases through promotional giveaways, coupon tie-ins, sweepstakes, and point-of-purchase displays. Festivals provide a powerful vehicle to target specific customers and useful links to other sponsors, suppliers, government agencies, and community institutions. This collaboration is regularly seen on the festival audio-visual collateral as each party is represented by a logo or signature. While they have paid for the right to be in this position, they have already identified the best fit for their investment as a promotional tool.

Hosting sponsors at events provides an opportunity to strengthen and personalize a business relationship. The bonding allows for links to be established with key customers, develop in-house incentive opportunities, entertain associates like staff and VIPs, and introduce these people to celebrities generated by the event.

There are risks that can be associated with sponsorship too. These include the intrusive presence of a sponsor at an event in various guises from use of hospitality seating in key locations, and inappropriate placement of brand name (ambush marketing), merchandising, and choice of branded merchandising. This can detract from the event and appears to embrace the corporate focus rather than the art, sport, or community event itself. "Amidst this crowded market, festival promoters and brand owners need to be particularly careful when they are considering sponsorship deals. There will always be a minority of brand-sceptic people who would prefer big corporations to stay out of sight at festivals altogether. The challenge is to get them to appreciate that a credible brand experience can actually add value to a festival, if the right brand/audience fit can be found" (Bruns, 2012, 1).

## CASE STUDY

### Festivals as Partners in Cultural Tourism

*Cultural tourism is based on the mosaic of places, traditions, art forms, celebrations, and experiences that portray a region (or country) and its people, reflecting its diversity and character.*

Tourism is one of the structured economic environments in which a festival culture is embedded. There are a number of benefits that accrue for festivals from engagement with cultural tourism. The arts community is seen to provide the catalyst for the creativity and distinctiveness each festival organization seeks to present, meanwhile redefining the tourist experience. So it appears that arts and cultural tourism can:

- Act as a catalyst for the support and promotion of strong, vibrant communities that highlight a distinctive sense of place for residents and visitors

- Celebrate and protect a region's culture, heritage, and natural environment and the residents' lifestyles
- Attract visitors for longer stays and encourage greater visitor spends
- Value-add to existing travel experiences available in the region
- Recognize arts and cultural development in the broader context
- Facilitate and promote partnerships between partners at all levels of the economy
- Promote and communicate excellence through partnerships and product development
- Acknowledge and stimulate strategic regional solutions by celebrating innovation
- Encourage investment in appropriate and lasting infrastructure
- Create career pathways, skills development, and mentoring opportunities in both arts and tourism sectors.

Tracking the impact of cultural tourism initiatives can be qualitative or quantitative—from dollar value of coverage in the media to anecdotal personal feedback of an experience online after attending a festival. The culture that festivals purvey can be seen as a marketing ploy by some, a fad, or a new social artform. Has it changed tourism practices? Professor Jennifer Craik has examined the partnerships between the arts and cultural sector and tourism and identifies some potential tensions in the connection in terms of commercialization and restructuring of culture, greater government investment, and service-based and consumer-oriented industries. Her observations offer challenging insights into these phenomena (Craik, 1995).

The more entrepreneurial festivals become, the easier it is to slide into practical relationships with operators in the tourism system in transport, accommodation, hospitality, other attractions, tour companies, destination management, and marketing entities. Connections that allow for packaging of the visitor experience wrapped around a festival are very attractive. Notice on festival promotion collateral the number of tourism companies that have allied themselves with the dynamic of a festival. It also connects these companies to the host community.

Shared good-practice objectives for festival organizations and public and private tourism organizations include:

**Increasing yield.** Rather than the metric of volume (number of visitor arrivals), the emphasis can be on the value of receipts each visitor injects into the regional economy. This can be through a set of good experiences in accommodation, transport, food and beverage, and purchasing of artwork and arts services. Festivals and arts trails are recognized as significant contributors to this factor.

**Increasing length of stay.** Cultural experiences are timeframed and intense, allowing for scheduled participation (e.g., festivals and heritage events). They provide visitor motivation in their own right as an extension of a planned journey to a destination. Longer stays can increase yield.

**Encouraging year-round visitation.** Scheduling cultural festival experiences provide opportunities to minimize the seasonal peaks and troughs that are often part of a destination's tourism portfolio. Specific market segments could be targeted (e.g., women, children, families) for particular products and services.

**Increasing distribution of visitors.** Ensuring the visitors are spread across the whole destination/region by showcasing the arts and cultural assets of each subdestination through exposure to diverse peoples, histories and traditions, arts practice, and landscape and natural heritage. Educational arts workshops could be tied to existing community events.

**Increase repeat visitation.** Recognizing that the arts and cultural portfolio can incorporate educational/participatory workshops, exhibitions, performances, festivals, trails, and studio visits that can be linked to other tourism products like farm and nature tourism, wineries, and national parks to encourage repeat visitation and even loyalty programs. Surveys of accommodation and venues and attractions would help build the picture of market opportunities.

**Ongoing monitoring of cultural tourism product development, market research, effective governance through collaborative decision making, and communication with**

**regional and industry stakeholders.** This can be achieved by festivals recognizing the impact that consistent communication and opportunities have for buy-in by diverse enterprises in the host destination. There are ways to attract the connection through shared promotion options like vouchers, discounts, in-kind support, sponsorship relationships or corporate volunteering to the array of businesses that deal with visitors. These include airlines, car hire, taxis, petrol stations, and public transport such as buses and train service. Businesses that want to leverage from the staging of a festival include those in the food and beverage sector like cafés, restaurants, bars, pubs, supermarkets, clubs, and fast-food outlets. There are ways of negotiating a mutually beneficial approach to ensuring visitors to the festival leave the destination with positive experiences and use many media platforms to promote their own repeat visitation and encourage others to visit.

Other cultural enterprises can collaborate with festival management by creating sympathetic programs that may keep visitors longer in the destination. Galleries, theaters, libraries, and museums are particularly well placed to animate the destination for locals and festival-goers to position the community as a must-see travel destination.

The emphasis for visitors needs to be on the entertainment, educational, experiential, and communicative experiences and on the authenticity, transparency, or honesty of their contact with artists, locals, and their lifestyle and landscape. Visitors are increasingly seasoned travelers who are more mature, demanding and discriminating in their travel choices. Cultural tourism highlights the cultural, heritage, or artistic aspects of a destination through experiences and activities for tourists—a kind of cultural immersion. Some people define themselves as cultural tourists because culture is their primary motivation for travel.

## Destination Image and Identity Through Festivals

The universal elements of a festival program can be massaged to ensure that it represents local interests and aspirations. How can a festival take the opportunity to distinguish itself from other events while building a discrete picture for the host destination? The distinctiveness of a local host destination, as well as the wider regional environment, requires vigilance, otherwise both become less attractive to the cultural tourism marketplace.

The repeat visitation and local participation respond to word of mouth. It can generate intelligence that the festival had been going long enough to have sorted out any problems, so each year brings returning visitors as well as new attendees. It provides a form of nostalgia and place attachment for returning former residents, especially through the Visiting Friends and Relatives (VFR) sector.

The parades during festivals provide a showcase of how the locals want to be seen. The parades offer an opportunity for residents to present an annual snapshot of their community at play. Floats became a statement of how the community deals with new residents, new ideas, and issues of local importance. These can be delivered in a satirical or serious manner to best represent how locals feel.

The promotional material of each destination emphasizes the appeal of local hospitality, friendliness, and access to the local amenities contributed by festivals. Images of festivals find their way virally, instantaneously to global audiences. This happens formally and informally. Captured images or compiled text showing the visitor experience go peer to peer. The lack of mediation of this material by event organizers is an interesting dimension to how images and identity of the host communities are seen and shared. Organizers need to consider their own monitoring of social media conversations and commit to supplying their perspective to the commentary.

The relationship between festivals and a destination's prosperity, identity, tourism image, and marketing strategies can be explained through the roles festivals and events play as attractions and markers in the tourism system. A destination is a place that has a story to tell. The expectation of destination planners, managers, and marketers is that satisfied consumers will tell others of their positive experience.

## Cultural Tourism

Over the last two years, 6.5% of adult Americans attended a theater, film, or music festival while on an out-of-town, overnight trip of one or more nights. Attending music festivals (4.8%) was the most common

Locals and visitors documenting their experience through active participation at Lismore Lantern Festival.

activity, followed by attending theater festivals (1.2%), comedy festivals (0.8%), international film festivals (0.7%), and literary festivals or events (0.7%). Almost one-half of those who attended a theater, film, or music festival while on a trip (45.9% of adult Americans) reported that this activity was the main reason for taking at least one trip in the past two years.

Relative to the average U.S. pleasure traveler, those who attended theatre, film, or music festivals while on trips were overrepresented among younger travelers (18 to 24 years old). While most in this segment are married, they are overrepresented among singles and those without dependent children (18 or younger) living at home. They are generally well educated, but reflecting their age, their household incomes ($79,645) are only slightly above average. They are more likely to live in larger cities (Lang Research).

The festivals show off, not only to visitors, but also to other towns in the region that they are adding value to the whole of the region's attractiveness to visitors. Each destination is open to the market potential of cultural tourists. The commercial benefits of this type of visitation vary because of the timing of the festivals, their duration and location, and the attitude of local businesspeople to their staging. Shops need to be open!

The authentic experiences visitors seek through cultural tourism allow tourism businesses to be economic beneficiaries of event tourism, but more are becoming interested in the capacity of community to maintain their identity, integrity, and quality of life. Businesspeople are residents too. Chambers of Commerce in all destinations are keen to contribute to the tourism debate at festival times. There are regular discussions about parking pressures. Initiatives like "park and drive" and street security are raised.

Community cultural tourism offers a model for the future of the industry as a whole. Tourism is vulnerable to change. The tourism resource base, natural and human, can be irreversibly lost through degradation, exploitation, and entrenched practices. The challenge to a region's cultural capital is intimately linked to the needs, expectations, and perceptions of all stakeholders. Festivals can provide a vision for destination planning. They can provide particular meaning for the visitor through exploring what lies behind the image of the tourism brochure.

A community cultural festival converts a host culture into a tourism attraction or marker. What is demonstrated is that it is only after the hosts come to consider their culture as capital, as a source of financial transactions, that they came to regard their culture as worthy of safeguarding. Attractions drive the tourism industry and festivals have become a tool to encourage longer stays in destinations.

There are limits to acceptable cultural growth through tourism. Central to this is whether the collaboration between the festival stakeholders and tourism provides for trivialization and commodification of one and diminution of sustainability in the other. Festival partners attempt to address the balance between responsiveness to the hosts' sense of community and the need for survival in both sectors. With tourism overlapping several different sectors of society and the economy, planning can provide guidance to bypass unexpected and unwanted impacts.

# FROM INSIDE THE MOSAIC

## Jyllie Jackson, Founder, CEO and Artistic Director of LightnUp

Jyllie Jackson, Founder, CEO and Artistic Director of LightnUp

© Peter Derrett

Jyllie came to Australia after a career in fashion and design in the United Kingdom and the United States. She quickly settled into the alternative lifestyle offered during the 1970s. She ventured into the bureaucracy of the public service. At each stage her work experience built on her personal curiosity, willingness to innovate, and capacity to work hard with diverse sectors of society. She is an organizer. She can do what she does because she is resourceful. Like many community artists, she works in a scarcity paradigm but she has finessed her relationships with a wide range of partners to deliver spectacle, ritual, and flare in a range of large and small national arts, business, and community celebrations.

As a social entrepreneur she has developed a business model that allows her to earn funds from the delivery of educational, artistic, and practical services. These include regular gigs at opening and closing ceremonies; lantern, puppetry, and illuminated sculpture workshops; and processions and installations at the Woodford Festival, Splendour in the Grass, and the Bellingen Global Carnival. The organization she leads, *LightnUp*, survives through its artistic vision, its committed volunteer base, its artistic integrity, and its ability to package various services like the hire of completed, complex lanterns of any scale, décor for public and private functions, artists' residencies, commissions, and festival design and leadership. The Board of Management of the *Lightnup* Incorporated Association links her to her host community and comprises a rich source of support and intellectual and professional connectivity.

For the past 20 years she has led a volunteer team of individuals and groups to deliver an annual Lantern Festival with a spectacular parade of lanterns at its core. The Lismore Lantern Parade in regional NSW, Australia, brings up to 25,000 locals and visitors together at the winter solstice outdoor street celebrations. Jyllie's own ethical stance on professional practice, health, and community well-being has influenced the choice of collaborators who have joined in the ancillary programs that have emerged to create a holistic weekend of community cultural engagement.

The Lantern Parade/Festival comprises specific, related activities—workshops in lantern-, prop-, costume-, and mask-making; performances with schools, colleges, and universities; and work experience opportunities for corporate groups, special interest community groups, culturally diverse people, people with varying ability, and senior citizens. The parade has over 2,400 participants, four bands, choirs, dance groups, and lantern carriers. There is a market in the closed-off central business district with over 70 stalls selling locally created merchandise, produce, and fair trade goods. The Laneways Eats Street and WinterWarmers accommodate selected healthy food stalls among shops and offices and decorated walls in the Back Alley Gallery and the Art in the Heart precinct. The Carnival Street Party, likewise, allows three stages to pump out music, cabaret, and choirs to entertain late-night hedonists. The downtown shopkeepers enter into the spirit with Enchanted Windows comprising their own appreciation of lanterns on the different annual theme chosen for the festival. The KidsArtFest is a collaboration with the Lismore Regional Gallery with activities for children to experiment with recycled and upcycled items to

Lismore Lantern Parade—fire and light.

prepare for the parade. The Greening of the Heart includes portable street-level plantings of food and decorative plants looked after by the business owners. There are pop-up galleries, art exhibitions and projections on city buildings.

A wide network of regional, national, and international artists and performers contribute. The reputation of the festival has been garnered through its connectivity with in-kind and financial commitments from local government, other government agencies including employment services, local suppliers, transport services, security and police, education resources, the Chamber of Commerce, and specific business interests. Having articulated a clear vision for the power of such an event, partners are also derived from the tourism sector with hospitality and accommodation packages addressing the needs of travelers who comes especially to experience the skies lit up creatively. Many businesses recognize the economic benefits that accrue and have increased their involvement, as they have prospered as a result of attracting new money into the local economy.

Jyllie values the support she receives from individual community champions and professional peers, whether local or across the world, as she learns more and shares the documentation of her success in generating community ownership for an inspirational public celebration. Participants and spectators alike find their involvement moving and stimulating. Many return to actively participate in the development of succeeding years' programs. Many volunteers have gained skills in design, construction, project management, parade marshaling, security, and customer relations. Volunteers come from different walks of life, each adding perspective, ideas, skills, and richness to the outputs. The impact on the host community is positive and residents are ready to recognize the festival as a worthy signature of the city's cultural diversity, energy, and identity. The word of mouth and social media distribution of feedback assists the organizers in the renewal they use to adopt concepts of the next year. The debrief each year comes from interaction with all stakeholders in written and conversational form. There have been economic and artistic evaluations that have informed ongoing programs and administration. The festival evolves. The route of the parade has changed over time. The finale features have been amended on the suggestions of partners. The media partnerships provide useful input into the ongoing design elements.

A pivotal question for Lightnup is succession planning. While Jyllie is a tour de force, members of the core team, the local Council, and the Board of Management are all working with Jyllie to determine the future operation of this enduring festival. Her skill set and creativity will need to be absorbed in alternative ways to solve the challenges inherent

# CHAPTER 5  BUILDING PARTNERSHIPS THAT WORK

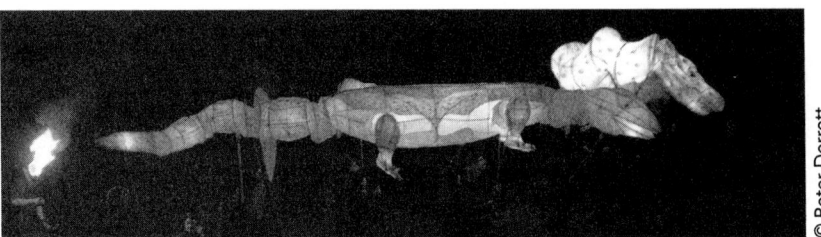

Goanna Lantern carried through the streets at the Lismore Lantern Parade.

in such a densely packed venture currently surviving on the goodwill or the volunteer team and audiences. There are financial underpinnings, partnerships that require constant nourishing, and media and promotion decisions.

Over time Jyllie has become aware of people returning to the parade sites as if for a safe pilgrimage to walk beside friends, neighbors, or perfect strangers in the dark to share beautiful illuminations and watch performances down by the riverside. The finale highlights the simplicity of a moment in time with people, light and trust in a spirit borne of unconditional love by an individual nurturing the engagement. Participants are hardwired to the gentle lights and may not undertake such an experience in any other part of their life. Jyllie considers her contribution has been to encourage others to actively aspire to creativity in diverse ways, her capacity to accommodate difference, her doggedness, her commitment to community collaborations through attention to detail, and her straight talking!

## Festival Ideas and Issues

1. The following quotations reflect diverse perspectives on the **value of partnerships**. How do each relate to your understanding of enduring festivals?

   In an age where community involvement and partnerships with civil society are increasingly being recognized as indispensable, there is clearly a growing potential for cooperative development and renewal worldwide.
   —*Kofi Anan, Diplomat and former Secretary General of the UN*

   It is vain to talk of the interest of the community, without understanding what is the interest of the individual.
   —*Jeremy Bentham, philosopher (1748–1832)*

   Surplus wealth is a sacred trust which its possessor is bound to administer in his lifetime for the good of the community.
   —*Andrew Carnegie, industrialist and philanthropist*

Our mission in this new century is clear. For good or ill, we live in an interdependent world. We can't escape each other. Therefore, we have to spend our lives building a global community of shared responsibilities, shared values, shared benefits.

—Bill Clinton, former President
of the United States

I want to work for a company that contributes to and is part of the community. I want something not just to invest in. I want something to believe in.

—Anita Roddick, founder of the Shop

Relationships are all there is. Everything in the universe only exists because it is in relationship to everything else. Nothing exists in isolation. We have to stop pretending we are individuals that can go it alone.

—Margaret J. Wheatley, writer and
management consultant

2. To **sponsor** something is to support an event, activity, person, or organization financially or through the provision of products or services. What should be included in a sponsorship agreement?
3. What happens when a festival embraces commercial **naming rights**? Generally naming rights are a financial transaction whereby a corporation or other entity purchases the right to name a festival or facility, typically for a defined period of time. The distinctive characteristic for this type of naming rights is that the buyer gets a marketing opportunity to promote products and services and all that entails. What's in it for the festival?

In the United Kingdom, Virgin and Tennent's have structured successful sponsor-naming deals despite dropping their full name from the festivals' titles: T in the Park (Scotland) and especially V Festival (England) are now rivaling Glastonbury and Reading and Leeds in terms of footfall. Subtlety is a key consideration when brands and festivals unite for a naming-rights deal (Bruns, 2012, 1).

# Festival Focus Activities

1. Explore and clarify the purpose of the festival partnership.

    Each participant writes five answers to each of the following questions on a piece of paper and ranks them in order of importance:

    Why is the partnership necessary in this particular festival project?

    What value is it trying to add to the project?

    Compare individual lists by starting with the reasons that are most important and following through to those that are least important. Look for the points of consensus, but also be aware of any differences. Do organizations have a clear understanding of what each can contribute to the partnership?

2. Discuss:
    **Networking** involves the exchange of information for mutual benefit. This requires little time and trust between partners. For example, youth-oriented festivals stakeholders within a local government area may meet monthly to provide an update on their work and discuss issues that affect programs for young people.
    **Coordinating** involves exchanging information and altering activities for a common purpose. For example, partners may meet and plan a coordinated campaign to lobby the council or regional government agencies for specific investments.
    **Cooperating** involves exchanging information, altering activities, and sharing resources. It requires a significant amount of time, a high level of trust between partners, and sharing the turf between agencies. For example, logistical, technological, and operational resources may be assets managed by different partners but could be pooled for use at a festival.
    **Collaborating**. In addition to the other activities described, collaboration includes enhancing the capacity of the other partner for mutual benefit and a common purpose. Collaborating requires the partner to give up a part of their turf to another agency to create a better or more seamless service system in order for the festival to be more successful and reach the target market (Himmelman 2001, 277–284).
3. This **mapping exercise** is designed to place all of the festival partners in relation to one another.
    Use the stakeholders identified earlier in the chapter. Lines are drawn between them to show the strength and nature of the relationship.
    Mapping the relationship is a way of clarifying roles and the level of commitment to the partnership.
    This is important as partners may have different understandings or expectations of what their involvement means. If done collectively, this exercise can help to strengthen a partnership because people are able to raise issues of concern. This provides an opportunity to address areas in which there is a lack of consensus.
    It is interesting to note patterns in the relationships and how these change over time. Many partnerships are strong on networking and coordinating but considerably weaker on collaborating.
    Completing the map provides an opportunity to look at ways in which relationships can be strengthened and made more effective.
4. Plan a one-day workshop to **scope partnership arrangements** between festival stakeholders.
    - Setting up the plan and understanding the basic principles of engagement
    - Knowing who will be affected and tailoring your engagement/partnership plan to them
    - Planning for maximum impact for all parties
    - Effective stakeholder engagement in practice examples
    - Risk management: Know what can go wrong
    - Measuring and evaluating the success of your collaboration

# Suggested Reading

Australian Business Arts Foundation. The Strategic Direction in Corporate Sponsorships: Practical Implications for the Arts. Cultural Ministers Council, Statistics Working Group, Australia, 2002.

Allen, J., W. O'Toole, I. McDonnell, and R. Harris. *Festival and Special Event Management* (5th ed.). Milton, QLD, Australia: Wiley, 2010.

Bruns, J., http://www.utalkmarketing.com/pages/Article.aspx?ArticleID=23177&Title=Tips_on_creating_a_cool_brand_presence_at_music_festivals, 2012.

Byrnes, W. J. *Management and the Arts* (4th ed.). London, UK: Focal Press, 2008.

Craik, J. "Cultural Tourism," in *Special Interest Tourism*, eds. N. Douglas and R. Derrett (Brisbane, Australia: Wiley, 2001).

Craik, J. "The Culture of Tourism," in *Touring Cultures: Transformations of Travel and Theory*, eds. Chris Rojek and John Urry (London, UK: Routledge, 1997).

Craik, J. "Are There Cultural Limits to Tourism?" *Journal of Sustainable Tourism* 3, no. 2 (1995): 87–98.

Crompton, John. "Benefits and Risks Associated with Sponsorship of Major Events." *Festival Management and Event Tourism* 2 (1994): 65–74.

Crompton, John, L. "Factors That Have Stimulated the Growth of Sponsorship of Major Events." *Festival Management and Event Tourism* 3 (1995): 97–101.

Derrett, R. *Community Festivals: Nourishing Resilience: The Nature and Role of Festivals in Regional Australian Communities*. Saarbrucken, Germany: VDM, 2009.

Frew, W. "Exhibiting Talent, Women Run the Shows." *Sydney Morning Herald*, Weekend Edition (2012, April 28–29): 7.

Getz, D., T. Andersson, and M. Larson. "Festival Stakeholder Roles: Concepts and Case Studies." *Event Management* 10 (2007): 103–122.

Himmelman, A. "On Coalitions and the Transformation of Power Relations: Collaborative Betterment and Collaborative Empowerment." American Journal of Community Psychology 29, no. 2 (2001): 277-284.

Kanter, R. M. *World Class, Thriving Locally in the Global Economy*. New York: Touchstone, 1997.

Lang Research Inc. TAMS 2006: U.S. Activity Profile: Attending Theatre, Film and Music Festivals While on Trips. Canadian Tourism Commission.

Pollack, A. Customers: The G-Force That Will Pull Web Services into the Frame. London: Desticorp UK Ltd., 2002.

Rojek, C., and J. Urry, eds. *Touring Cultures: Transformations of Travel and Theory*. London, UK: Routledge, 1997.

UCLA Center for Health Policy Research. Health DATA Program—Data, Advocacy and Technical Assistance.

Watt, David, C. *Event Management in Leisure and Tourism*. Essex, UK: Addison Wesley Longman, 1998.

# CHAPTER 6

# Alignment with the Target Audience

People will forget what you said.
People will forget what you did.
But people will never forget how you made them feel.
—*Maya Angelou (1928–2014), American poet*

---

This chapter provides an opportunity for you to better understand:

- How to know customers' motivations and behaviors to determine a useful profile for effective festival marketing

- How to develop communication mechanisms to reach targeted market segments with distinctive festival attributes

- How to manage a customer focus within festival organizations in terms of festival themes, program content, online marketing, database research and analysis, monitoring, and reporting

- How to recognize relevant global trends that may impact festival communication and reach

---

In this chapter we explore ways in which festival-makers can secure the audience they require to deliver quality experiences over a sustained period of time. Generally they wish to increase participation in established programs they have developed. They wish to enhance their reputation for delivering memorable interaction between audience and specialists. They work to retain the loyalty of people who already recognize the strengths and appeal of the existing festival and to broaden its attractiveness to engage with individuals and groups who have so far not made the important attendance commitment.

**Figure 6.1** A Target Audience Mosaic.

# Audience Relationships

Participation might be sought from those already involved with the festival to intensify their relationship by assisting in capturing a greater share of the market through peer-to-peer contact, bringing on board new partners, and maybe identifying an audience less familiar with the festival's offerings. Loyal audiences and their repeat attendance are regarded as success factors. Approaches to the engagement that builds audiences through reaching diverse and maybe new cohorts is complex. It demands research and consideration of the festival organization's resources and internal culture in addressing the needs and aspirations of those targeted. Once again there can be strategic, tactical, and opportunistic approaches that come into play to satisfy the need for focused and creative alignment.

What are the best ways for the festival organization to maintain the relationships it has nourished over the years as identified in Figure 6.1? What sort of planning is required to ensure the festival maintains its competitive advantage over other pressures potential audiences may succumb to? What is the best way to listen to their patrons and satisfy their desire for a premium experience? This customer orientation is not a new phenomenon, but there is increased attention in the literature to an experience beyond the simple purchase of goods and services. The relationship festival patrons want appears to cover the spectrum from initial attractions through deliberate stimuli, guidance through a process to direct engagement with the festival, and an ongoing post-experience link.

# The Festival Experience

Conifer Research (2002) created a model that benefits from an understanding of anthropological practices associated with the human connection to ritual (Figure 6.2). Inside festivals these rituals are replicated to engage patrons, but as a strategy to chart the customer–festival relationship it is useful to recognize their five major interventions.

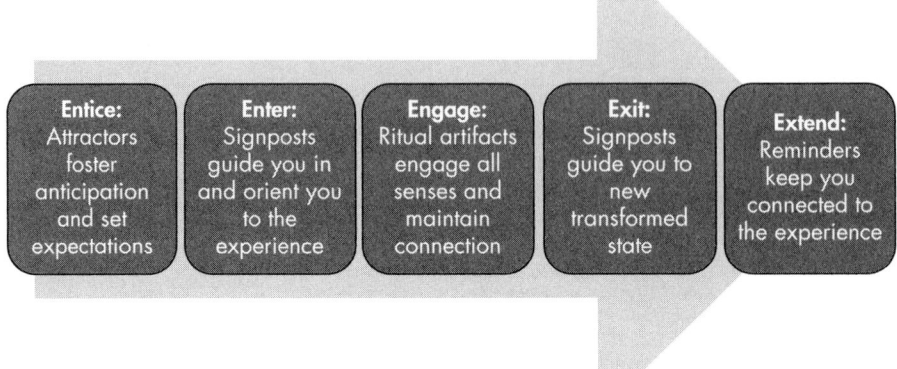

**Figure 6.2** The Festival Experience.
*Based on Conifer Research (2002).*

Mapping the festival patron's experience is an important part of our investigation in this chapter. We need to identify the stages in the decision-making process of prospective festival patrons, the sensations they most favourably respond to as active or passive participants of what is scheduled to be at the core of the experience, and the ancillary elements of the relationship. The tracking of the individual's personal memories has been much enhanced by the embrace of social media that now provides deep and wide engagement. We need to walk in the patron's shoes to break down the journey's touchpoints to minimize any frustration and disappointment as the relationship develops.

## Personal Cultural Interests and Practices

How festival management observes and records the patron's behaviors provides useful data. They may arrive alone, avoid other patrons, and situate themselves in a position to scope the venue, locate key amenities, and orient their route from collateral provided in hardcopy, or on a digital device before heading to a comfortable zone to engage with the program. Others arrive in a social group and have already generated the tone and camaraderie that will infect their interaction with the festival program and opportunities. They connect with other patrons, they move about the site easily, locate a camping area, park a vehicle, pitch a tent, stow their belongings, or find a bar, a stage, a place in the sun, and be quickly enveloped by the tone or mood of the festivities. By noting the initial movement patterns of patrons, organizers can better address issues of layout, signage, and access to amenities in their future logistics and risk management planning. Queuing theory comes into use here, as organizers predict queue lengths and waiting times. This aspect of festival operations needs to be well researched and implemented, as it can compound patron dissatisfaction if not adequately delivered.

Festival engagement is affected by personal and social considerations. Distractions can affect participation, as listening, learning, dancing, and sitting can become risky for individuals and surrounding patrons. Enjoyment is closely connected to how crowds are handled, the levels of customer service, and the quality of the entertainment. Loyalty is connected to

Audience members sit back and relax and settle in readiness for the music program.

longevity and confidence in festival direction and management. Fans can become fanatics and develop an eagerness to contribute beyond festival contact into strong relationships of value to organizers. This buy-in by audiences generally ensures greater acceptance of change when programs are adjusted, festival site locations are shifted, and contingencies of a physical or content basis are undertaken.

Research undertaken in Australia (*Connecting://arts audiences online*) interpreted audiences' online journeys. It followed the trajectory from discovery of an event through to attendance, participation, and talking about it afterward. The role of word of mouth, which increasingly appears online, is of interest to festival organizers. As is discussed elsewhere, harnessing this sidebar communication becomes imperative as festivals look to build a picture of their target audience.

Staff and volunteers need to interpret all they see, feel, and learn to ensure the festival maintains contact with established audiences. Familiarity with such nuanced knowledge of this continued support is valuable. This builds knowledge and capacity from the perspective of both the audience and the organization. It promotes a sense of belonging and community while contributing to a better understanding of the expectations and motivations for future possible interactions within the festival program, ambience, venues, and amenities.

## Walk in Their Shoes: Map the Journey the Festival Patron Might Take

Marketing is so basic that it cannot be considered a separate function.... It is the whole business seen from the point of view of its final result, that is, from the customer's point of view.
—Peter Drucker (1909–2005), *Austrian-born American management consultant, educator, and author*

When staff and volunteers walk in the shoes of the festival audience (before, during, and after the event), they can get an appreciation of the impression festival patrons get, whether

Clear signage, secure uncrowded entry, and welcoming staff appeal to patrons launching into their music festival experience.

individually or part of a group, and what value they place on their exposure to the services provided. There are some who would argue that creating memorable experiences has become more critical now than delivering outstanding service. Some simple exercises in mapping audience experiences to identify where appropriate planning can deliver more value, personal attention, and enhance enjoyment appear in Table 6.1.

# Flow

What is flow and how can organizers incorporate the concept in their planning and presentation of the festival? Mihaly Csikszentmihalyi (2002) defines flow as "the state in which people are so involved in an activity that nothing else seems to matter; the experience itself is so enjoyable that people will do it even at great cost, for the sheer sake of doing it." During his professional life he pursued investigations into what makes people happy. He suggests

| Locating | Connecting |
| --- | --- |
| • Current information about the festival, dates, venues, prices, program, transport<br>• First impressions of style, tone, mood, content, and services provided at festival<br>• Site and amenities accessible and well appointed<br>• Links for an ongoing relationship with the festival organization to be kept informed | • Initial contact to answer queries, make bookings, satisfy curiosity<br>• Be included in communication through social media or press to stay informed of any changes<br>• Speak to organizers if required<br>• Find staff and volunteers at event to be hospitable and well informed<br>• To have services at event to match or exceed your expectations |
| Searching | Attending |
| • Ensuring links are up-to-date with appropriate and timely details through accessible websites<br>• Make social media contact relevant; clear and friendly websites | • Contribute feedback on festival experience in good faith |

**Table 6.1** Mapping the Audience Journey

that happiness doesn't depend on chance or external events but on our perception of them. As such, happiness has to be cultivated. But this does not mean that we should recklessly pursue pleasure. The best moments are not those of passive pleasure but those when we feel exhilarated by achievement—when we are in a state of flow. Festivals offer a structure that can accommodate major aspects of his findings.

Festival organizers need to appreciate how the concept of flow is usually associated with interactive, "doing" tasks and is experienced by people from all walks of life and across many different cultures. So, the end product is less important than the process of doing the work itself. External rewards were less important than intrinsic pleasure. It seems that what people do and why they do it varies immensely, but the quality of the enjoyment produced by investing attention in an activity is remarkably similar and comprises one or more of the following five dimensions of audience experience. This intelligence can inform robust and engaging festival programs.

When determining a festival program it is important to attract new audiences and retain regular supporters through the following, also in Figure 6.3:

1. *Engagement and concentration.* The extent to which the performance consistently captures and maintains the audience's attention, allowing people to become lost in the moment by being totally immersed in the program.
2. *Learning and challenge.* The "challenge" is a key component both in life-learning and intrinsically rewarding experiences. It need not be unpleasant or uncomfortable (although it may be both).
3. *Energy and tension.* Energy, in the context of a festival audience experience, can convey a palpable sense of excitement and demonstrate that people are emotionally engaged with the content of the program.
4. *Shared experience and atmosphere.* The collective experience of festival attendance has been well documented, suggesting the importance of belonging to groups,

**Figure 6.3** Attract and Retain Audiences.

Clear local signage assists with the flow of festival-goers and passersby to the annual Tropical Fruits New Year celebrations.

either through bringing communities together or peer interaction or shared engagement with a mood created by organizers.
5. *Personal resonance and emotional connection.* Individuals and groups often identify with the atmosphere generated, the stories being shared, the location and program content that connect to their lived experience or their aspirations. The memories harvested contribute to artistic and social understandings and personal enrichment.

## Festival Satisfaction

So, while knowing a great deal about the target market, the festival organization needs to ensure that all parties adhere to the shared vision of the festival to avoid compartmentalization. Each needs to recognize and articulate the same message for prospective patrons. This suggests an organizational culture that appreciates that synergy is required to deliver seamless communication, security, emotional appeal, and personal benefits to each customer—existing and potential. This may be approached by adding value by offering a premium experience (at a premium price) for exclusivity, access to artists, and added comfort; offering welcomes as a host should from reception, to front of house, to program delivery, honesty in promotion, ticketing, and signage at on-site amenities; knowing what people are saying about your festival online; not just making the offer of a great entertaining, educational, recreational, aesthetic, and escapist experience but getting others to recommend the opportunity. Trust needs to be consistently developed and delivered in small ways that coalesce these elements.

There has been much debate regarding what festival satisfiers offer. Increasing affluence and changes in work patterns, education, and technology now has festival-makers clearly addressing key drivers such as the need to socialize with friends and family, the need for stimulation and excitement, the need to escape from the daily grind, and a willingness to experiment and engage with novelty. Festivals can provide numerous social, physical, and psychological benefits for festival patrons in formal and informal ways. The diverse personal characteristics pose a challenge for festival-makers as there is an increasing expectation for specially tailored experiences. Retailers (in other parts of the economy) have recognized the revolutionary shift that has the customer at the center of business. Previously, stores and services ruled that world, but now consumers have changed, affecting whole brands and demanding the retailers go on a virtual journey with them!

*The Experience Economy* (1999) by B. Joseph Pine II and James H. Gilmore recognized a further perspective from earlier marketing practices in terms of preparing products and services for distribution and promoting their value to potential customers. Organizations have to differentiate

Elaborate leather masks heighten the festival-goers' experience of multiple art forms.

what they offer from other services and experiences in the marketplace to respond to the content of the on-demand economy. They postulated that the historic movements from commodities and goods to services have now leveraged "experience" as a distinctive fourth economic offering. They claim experiences need to be specifically designed to engage customers and this allows for a fee to be applied. The characteristics they identify for their theory can be readily applied to the interest that festivals have in increasing participation to aid their prosperity and longevity. Pine and Gilmore suggest that when designing and delivering experiences, the aim should be to:

- Theme the experience
- Harmonize impressions with positive cues
- Eliminate negative cues
- Mix in memorabilia
- Engage all five senses

Pine and Gilmore (1998) identify four realms of an experience: entertainment, educational, escapist, and aesthetic. They suggest a spectrum of engagement ranging from passive participation, through absorption to active participation and immersion will address market segmentation trends.

Arts participation can be understood as occurring in multiple modes, sometimes overlapping: arts attendance, personal creation and performance, and arts participation through electronic media.

—*Novak-Leonard and Brown (2011)*

## Environmental Scans

Experienced festival managers will include regular reviews of the environments in which their festival operates. They recognize that any shifts in the major economic, political, sociocultural, and environmental domains requires agility to ensure the mission of the festival organization is not compromised and can be supported coherently while any changes can deftly be communicated to internal and external partners. In fact, the capacity to deal nimbly with the impacts of policy, financial, social, and environmental movements on the internal culture and resources demonstrates that adaptation is a sound measure of the organization's resilience (Table 6.2).

## Consumer Orientation

Festivals of long standing have adopted a customer orientation by learning as much as possible about the current and probable audience behavior to underpin the marketing strategy to be employed. It identifies the best fit for a niche they wish to occupy in the marketplace by matching their product (their program, location, values, and reputation) to the resources they can commit and the spectators and participants they are keen to attract or retain. It is a complex maneuver to research, test, and apply marketing practices that have been developed over recent years to ensure the audiences' expectations are satisfied. Organizers can become too product oriented by ignoring demands of specific markets to have a memorable experience. A balance can be achieved to ensure the quality of the experience satisfies the provider through professional scheduling, while introducing, even educating, audiences to new diverse opportunities. It doesn't have to be either/or. It is a knowledge management issue. It is important that there is an understanding of the decision-making processes demonstrated by the potential consumers of the festival and how these can be influenced by what the festival organizers have in mind.

| Domain | Sustainable Festival Management Implications |
| --- | --- |
| Political situation | Recognizing changes to policy and application, public and professional leadership traits, and change management |
| Economic conditions | Local and global dimensions, foreign exchange rates, changing shape of jobs, distribution of wealth, flexible income levels |
| Demographic dimensions | Aging population, migration, urban and regional divide, educational attainment, cultural diversity |
| Environmental expectations | Rising costs of energy and travel costs, reuse, recycle, green practices, climate change |
| Technological trends | Digitization, access, skills, platforms for social media, pace of data transmission, artistic expression, design, intellectual property |
| Festival competition | Alternative social and artistic pursuits, serious leisure trends, existing commercial and not-for-profit events, creation of new work, globalization of festival content |
| Funding constraints | Revenue sources from governments at all levels, mixed cultural economy, earning capacity, investment, capital reserves |
| Infrastructure | Venues, indoors and outdoors, costs of operation, hire, maintenance |
| Internal resources | Organizational human capital, cultural, and physical resources |
| Corporate support | Shifts in sponsorships, corporate social responsibility, philanthropy, goodwill, trust between partners |
| Employment patterns | Permanent, casual, workforce mobility, independent arts workers, personal skill sets |
| Research into audience engagement | Trends in different societies, experience economy, and cultural shifts |

**Table 6.2** Environmental Scan.
Derrett (2013).

## Consumption Analysis

Festival organizers are clearly concerned to access current data about the individuals, groups, or organizations that comprise the festival's potential patronage. They have experience at interpreting this data to better understand the processes these participants use to select, secure, use, and dispose of leisure products, services, and experiences. They recognize the move from simple consumer behavior or "why people buy." The present emphasis has shifted to consumption analysis, that is, why and how people consume in addition to why and how they buy. Now, in aligning their festival to target markets, there is a need to understand how individuals make decisions to spend their available resources (time, money, and effort). The intelligence required includes what these people buy, why they buy it, where they buy it, how often they buy it, and how often they use it. This process leads to predictions and the capacity to control aspects of the process.

## Decision Making

Festival marketing teams particularly need to understand the decision-making processes—from those that precede the purchase of goods or services to the final experience of using the product or service. There are numerous influences on purchasing decisions. Philip Kotler and colleagues have published extensively on these practices and festival-makers are as much in need of decision-making frameworks as other entrepreneurs in the entertainment, arts, tourism, and leisure market. The conundrum is the nexus between the individual's exposure to marketing stimuli that can include the traditional 4Ps—price, product, place, and promotion—and the actual decision to be made. We have identified some of the external stimuli in the environmental scans above that affect the festival patron's decisions, such as economic, technological, political, and competitive.

---

### THE ARTS ATTENDANCE JOURNEY

Awareness
: First hearing about the event (e.g., from a friend, via an e-newsletter, or on the radio)

Research
: Activities leading up to the decision to attend, such as finding out more about the event, reading reviews, or discussing the idea with others

Booking
: The decision to attend, including the ticket-booking process, if required

Preparation
: Activities after deciding to go, but before the event itself, such as preparing for the experience and discussing logistics with others

At the event
: Activities at the event itself, like interacting with the organizers, telling others that you're there

After the event
: Activities after the event, such as sharing feedback, buying merchandise, telling others of attendance, and reliving the experience

Based on "Arts audiences online: How Australian audiences are connecting with the arts online," Nielson 2011.

## Major Factors Influencing Buying Behavior

Kotler (1991) suggests that consumer purchases are influenced strongly by cultural, social, personal, and psychological characteristics, as shown below and in Figure 6.4.

1. **Cultural Factors**
   Cultural factors exert the broadest and deepest influence on consumer behavior.
   1.1 Culture: Culture is the most fundamental determinant of a person's wants and behavior. A set of values, perceptions, and preferences, are developed through family, heritage, and key institutions.
   1.2 Subculture: Each culture consists of smaller subcultures that provide more specific identification for its members. Subcultures include nationalities, religions, racial groups, and geographical regions.
   1.3 Social class: Virtually all societies exhibit social stratification.

2. **Social Factors**
   In addition to cultural factors, a consumer's behavior is influenced by such social factors as reference groups, family, and roles and statuses.
   2.1 Reference group: A person's reference groups consist of all the groups that have a direct (face-to face) or indirect influence on the person's attitudes or behavior.

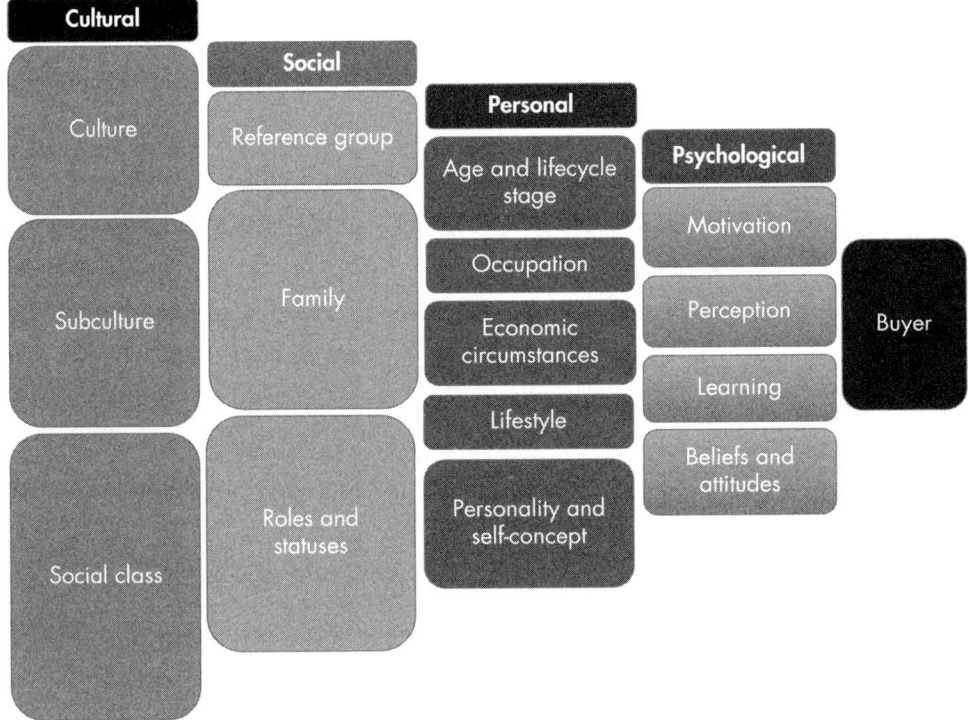

**Figure 6.4** Major Factors Influencing Buying Behavior.
*Based on Kotler (1991, p. 165).*

2.2 Family: The family is the most important consumer-purchasing organization in society.

2.3 Roles and statuses: A person participates in many groups throughout life, family, clubs, and organizations.

3. **Personal Factors**

   A buyer's decision is also influenced by personal characteristics. These include demographic details such as age and stage in the life cycle, occupation, economic circumstances, lifestyle, and personality and self-concept.

   3.1 Age and stage in the life cycle: people buy different goods and services over their lifetime.

   3.2 Occupation: A person's occupation also influences his or her consumption pattern.

   3.3 Economic circumstances: Product choice is greatly affected by one's economic circumstances that includes their spendable income (its level of stability and time pattern), savings and assets, debts, borrowing power, and attitude toward spending versus saving.

   3.4 Lifestyle: People coming from the same subculture, social class, and occupation may lead quite different lifestyles. A person's lifestyle is the pattern of living as expressed in the person's activities, interests, and opinions; it portrays the "whole person" interacting with his or her environment.

   3.5 Personality and self-concept: Each person has a distinct personality that influences his or her purchasing behavior.

4. **Psychological Factors**

   Psychological factors influence buying behavior through motivation, perception, learning experience, and beliefs and attitudes.

   4.1 Motivation: A person has many needs at any given time. They can be biogenic or arise from physiological states of tension such as hunger, thirst, and discomfort. Other needs are psychogenic; they arise from psychological states of tension such as the need for recognition, esteem, or belonging.

   4.2 Perception: A motivated person is ready to act. How the motivated person actually acts is influenced by his or her perception of the situation. Perception is the process by which an individual selects, organizes, and interprets information inputs to create a meaningful picture of the world.

   4.3 Learning experience: learning involves changes in an individual's behavior arising from experience. Most human behavior is learned. Learning theorists believe that learning is produced through the interplay of drives, stimulus, responses, and reinforcement.

   4.4 Beliefs and attitudes: Through doing and learning, people acquire beliefs and attitudes. These in turn influence their purchasing behavior (Kotler, 1991).

# Establishing the Best Fit

Festival organizers assess the motivations they learn of from their audiences and ensure there is a good fit from the supply side. Look at these stated motivations that typically appear in response to festival feedback. How does a festival with which you are familiar deal with satisfying such motivations and consequently enjoy a solid reputation to attract ongoing audiences? Is there evidence that they have accurately segmented their market based on people's views, motivations, and values as well as attitudes and behaviors. This mix is a mosaic in itself and provides marketers with a complex task to interpret the best fit. Marketers in the tourism industry regularly determine how they can package the tourism experience best for specific target markets.

Work done in the United Kingdom by Morris Hargreaves McIntyre (2013) defines a culture segments framework well suited for the arts audience that could be attracted to festivals. Their research identified eight segments within the market for arts, culture, and heritage that resonate with the festival sector:

| Enrichment | Mature, traditional, heritage, nostalgia |
| Entertainment | Consumers, popularist, leisure, mainstream |
| Expression | Receptive, confident, community, expressive |
| Perspective | Settled, self-sufficient, focused, content |
| Stimulation | Active, experimental, discovery, contemporary |
| Affirmation | Self-identity, aspirational, quality time, improvement |
| Release | Busy, ambitious, prioritizing, wistful |
| Essence | Discerning, spontaneous, independent, sophisticated |

*Based on Morris Hargreaves McIntyre (2013, p. 5).*

Festival-makers are keen to formally and informally assess the motivations of current and potential audiences and use such questions to fashion their festival offerings (Table 6.3).

Organizers might consider offering discounts to audiences in advance to sell out to early-bird buyers and groups through social media. Incentives might be offered to the first large groups booking. This could be linked to buy-in from festival sponsors online or through local retailers or sponsors who can on-sell tickets for the festival. Use survey results to determine what aspects of the program were popular and match levels of interest with potential entertainment next time. Provide online event banners and links to all other partners, sponsors, media, volunteers, and local organizations and use online ticketing programs and send regular messages to those on the database to update them on festival preparation and contests, photos of preparation, Facebook, YouTube posts or program content elements, and fundraising events to be held prior.

There are cues included in this feedback that can direct the design and layout of the site hosting the festival to ensure patrons have opportunities to situate their socializing in clean, intimate, comfortable areas close to amenities like food and beverage, that signage is clear, and that there is duty of care demonstrated through availability of shade and shelter with proximity to parking and transport that is accessible and safe. Memorable experiences are not only based on thrills and excitement, they are generally enhanced through knowledge. How can organizers ensure that patrons have sufficient timely information before, during, and after their interaction at the festival?

Qualitative research, listening, asking questions in focus groups, having online feedback loops, and scanning blogs, media, and other sources assist in ascertaining how profound an impact specific festivals had on their audiences. Integrating social networking into the

| |
|---|
| To see and do different things |
| To have fun and be entertained |
| To be free and easygoing |
| To be with friends |
| To be with someone special |
| To get away from the stress of everyday life |
| To observe other people at the festival |
| To rest and relax |
| To enjoy talking about the festival after returning home |
| To change usual surroundings |
| To meet similar people and make new friends |
| To find excitement |
| To be with family |
| To enjoy live music |
| Because I am a fan of the artist(s) |
| For the festival's atmosphere |
| To experience cultural happenings that I don't usually have the chance to attend |
| Because I have been to this festival before and I liked it |
| Because it is well organized |
| To be part of the festival crowd |
| To meet people with the same interests |
| Because I was curious to attend this festival because of who sponsors it |
| To participate in activities that are apart from the festival's main theme |

**Table 6.3** Vox Pop: Why did you choose to attend this festival?

relationship allows for increased useful knowledge. What needs to be identified is what specific elements resonated, from festival promotion through to program content, to site attractiveness that may influence the choice of this festival again. By checking what competitors are offering, organizers can refine and rethink what is distinctive about the whole experience they offer and simply focus attention on delivering their unique selling proposition (USP).

Feedback from all stakeholders can inform the achievement of effective audience alignment. Festival board members, sponsors, on-site vendors, transport providers, and community and industry partners can all supply insights into the appeal of a festival. This can be gleaned from face-to-face contact, during post-festival debriefings and media coverage, and will assist in building focus and allowing the festival to achieve its goals.

## Marketing Mechanisms and Reach

Much has been written about how best to reach the target audience in the services and experience market. It is referred to as a marketing mix, and as we have noted, its complexity is determined by the customer focus the festival wishes to pursue. Kotler and Armstrong suggest the marketing mix is the set of tools that are manipulated to assist in delivering on the festival's objectives. You may be aware of the original product-oriented marketing considerations that included product (that can include objects, services, persons, places, organizations, and ideas), price, place (distribution), and promotion. In the services sector people (within the host organization) were seen to be an important factor as was the capacity to position the company, product, or brand in the marketplace more broadly. Festivals have recognized new market conditions specific to their environment and value the importance of partnerships, like packaging their festival with other things like transport and accommodations.

The product in marketing parlance can also represent the product features, the whole package, the festival brand name, and post-sales service support to the patron. Whatever it is, it is purchased to satisfy personal wants.

The price is generally regarded as the revenue-raising element of the mix. It is also the sum of values that consumers exchange for the benefits accrued from buying into the festival experience. Price can be calibrated to add value for targeted customers. It is important that the revenue is invested into the resources required to deliver the festival program and ancillary marketing expenses. Pricing is thus flexible through incentives and discounts that can be used to attract audiences. Setting the right price is one of the most stressful and pressure-filled tasks. If a price is set too high in consumers' minds, the perceived value will be less than the cost, and sales opportunities will be lost. If the price is set too low, it may be perceived as a great value for the consumer (or valueless as cheapness might reflect poorly on the festival) but may not meet the company's profit goals. Festival prices must contend with broader elements of the economic environment, competition, discretionary income of the target audience, and current global economic conditions. Vigilance is required to set price signals appropriately to the diverse parties targeted.

In the era of digitization, the place or distribution of material and services is determined by where the customer is and what mechanisms provide the best fit for maintaining contact and delivering pre- and post-contact, particularly in a timely and comfortable manner. The particular partnerships the festival has might influence the distribution or ticketing, merchandising, and promotion of some elements of the program.

In Chapter 10 we explore the connection between the all-important promotional marketing and the numerous media platforms available today. There has been a remarkable change in communication technologies, but nevertheless many festivals engage with traditional means of communication to share the messages that promote forthcoming festival attractions. The promotional tools employed need to inform, influence, and affect behaviors and persuade potential patrons. Generally promotional devices such as advertising, public relations, and personal selling reach the target. Now emphasis is being placed on social media that encourages others to sell the festival on the organization's behalf. This requires clear messages, strong visual representation of content, and honest and precise information about place, dates, and location that are available for such circulation.

Relationship marketing is a significant aspect of the marketing mix, particularly where festivals can deliberately consolidate that feeling of attachment that loyal patrons demonstrate and wish to share. It is often undervalued, but with the impact of social media ringing in the ears of festival marketers, it is a vital aspect of increasing festival participation through nurturing loyalty and support for advocacy for the festival through incentives and newsletters and access to specific subscriptions. With increasing noise in the marketplace, festivals are looking to a long-term commitment from their patrons.

Some festival marketers have found a successful strategy to engage their audiences through offering an annual poster competition. Do you know of any that have been sustained over time? The Edinburgh Fringe Festival and the Adelaide Fringe Festival are two festivals that can track stronger relationships through inviting the design of promotional images that have been translated into posters, advertising brands, inspiration for merchandising, and printed documents such as programs, tourism guides, and banners. Such a device is uploaded through digital distribution platforms, acts as a dynamic historical reference, and rewards the designer (young or old, local or external) with exposure, some festival prizes and incentives, and an emboldened sense of belonging.

## Global Writers' Festivals

Book festivals, readers' festivals, writers' festivals, and literary festivals all popularly engage a broad spectrum of the professional and general public. Such festivals provide a useful insight into the application of flow outlined earlier. Festival content may vary, responding to local culture and contemporary trends in writing and emphasis may reflect proclivities and feedback from past audiences. Such festivals provide a regular top-up for those interested in face-to-face exposure with favorite writers, robust debate and controversy, and celebrity.

Many festivals include skills-based workshops with professionals and opportunities to participate in master classes and share works in progress. There is a palpable commitment to vibrant lifelong learning. Many target youth to encourage a greater appreciation of the arts practice. Like most regular (and annual) arts and cultural special interest festivals, a global circuit has evolved and collaborative marketing keeps aficionados informed. The selection of iconic landscapes and hosting destination increases cultural tourism and value-adding to existing arts infrastructure has become a feature of literary festivals. There are participants that range from dabblers, enthusiasts, and experts to fanatics who make it their mission to attend regularly whether close to home or to experience such festivals elsewhere.

As you examine the festivals listed below, you might want to explore the composition of audiences for each and learn how organizers have managed the best fit for their demographic and psychographic characteristics. What are the key age, gender, cultural heritage, income level, and educational dynamics? Have they travelled a distance? Is it attractive to international audiences? Does the audience comprise readers or writers or wannabes? Are most women over age 50 who regularly attend as a result of membership of book clubs? Do people exhibit a preference for specific genres like fiction or nonfiction, writing for stage and screen, biography, applied uses for blogs, games, and travel? Are the issues and ideas represented by speakers an attraction? How are children accommodated? Is the event documented for nonattendees through podcast, video, YouTube, and other broadcast media? Do organizers match venues to particular styles of delivery, intimate venues, studios, plenary in large auditoria, or utilize outdoor spaces?

The annual Byron Bay Writers' Festival, in Australia, includes a popular sculpture exhibition, which organizers say proves the two art forms can connect. Residents and visitors not

| Festival | Description |
|---|---|
| The Word Alliance: bringing together the world's leading literature festivals for a strategic international partnership that supports and showcases the work of writers, facilitates the creation of international literature projects, and provides opportunities to enhance each festival's artistic program. | Collaboration of independent organizations rather than an organization in its own right. Each member festival brings and retains its own distinct brand, organization, aims, and artistic integrity, but the Alliance facilitates these festivals working together on projects of mutual interest. |
| PEN World Voices Festival of International Literature<br>New York, April–May | World's oldest literary and human rights organization so the program has a strong political bent. Many of the events are free and tickets are available online. |
| Jaipur Literature Festival<br>Jaipur, India, January | Offers a range of activities for guests, including camel safaris, yoga and ayurvedic massage, as well as literary delights. |
| The Bookworm International Literary Festival<br>Beijing, March | |
| Tennessee Williams/New Orleans Literary Festival<br>March | Program includes contests, literary panel discussions, theatrical performances, and master classes for intensive individual one-on-one opportunities with notable experts in writing or the arts. |
| Etonnants-Voyageurs<br>St. Malo, France, May | |
| The Guardian Hay Festival of Literature<br>Hay on Wye, Wales, UK, May | With its bucolic setting and wealth of secondhand bookshops—almost 40 in a town of 2,000 people—Hay is a mecca for book lovers and those with a passion for ideas and debate. Bill Clinton described the festival as "the Woodstock of the mind." |
| Byron Bay Writers' Festival<br>NSW, Australia, August | An extensive and popular schedule of workshops precedes the main festival, so if you've ever wanted to write your memoir or learn about the art of travel writing, meeting national and international practitioners, participate. |
| Steinbeck Festival, National Steinbeck Centre<br>Salinas, California, August | |
| Edinburgh International Book Festival<br>Scotland, August | Largest public celebration of the written word in the world. Over 800 writers and thinkers from around the world come together. |
| Melbourne Writers Festival<br>Australia, August/September | |
| Ubud Writers' and Readers' Festival<br>Bali, Indonesia, October | Frangipanis, fine food, and the tropical heat help create an exotic atmosphere and the festival features a strong contingent of Southeast Asian writers as well as the big names in Western literature |
| International Festival of Authors<br>Toronto, Canada, October | |
| Vancouver International Writers' and Readers' Festival Canada, October | Since 1988 on Granville Island, the cultural hub of Vancouver, this festival manages to lure the often-shy literary greats into the spotlight. Granville Island is filled with galleries, boutiques, waterfront restaurants, cafés, and bars, and don't miss the popular seven-day-a-week Public Market. |
| Litquake<br>San Francisco, October | |

| Festival | Description |
|---|---|
| Singapore Writers' Festival Biannual June | Words Go Round school's program celebrates literature in Singapore's official languages—English, Malay, Chinese, and Tamil—with writers generously sharing their ideas, stories, and lives. |
| Dublin Writers Festival Ireland, June | |
| International Literature Festival Berlin, Germany, September | |

participating in the festival as a whole can also access the exhibition. Some UK writers' and readers' festivals include other artistic genres with theater performances, film interpretations of the written word in particular styles (e.g., Crimefest, Bristol, UK), or reflect an alignment to specific writers (e.g., Daphne Du Maurier Festival in Cornwall, UK).

## Biennales

The contemporary art biennale has become a global phenomenon that gathers artists, curators, gallery owners, and directors along with sponsors, celebrities, and politicians. The general public is drawn along through substantial media attention and the outputs determine the careers of participating artists worldwide. The spectacular locations and installations, and the massive promotional and positioning statements they represent have become vital resources for scholars, students, curators, artists, and critics alike.

For a city to host a biennial today has significant implications for destination management and marketing. The scale some biennales have assumed has meant some cities have moved into three- and four-year cycles. The biennales that proliferate address a v with visual arts, architecture, design, fashion, and landscape design and the accompanying spectacle, interaction, stimulation, and creativity.

The major international expositions include those in Table 6.4. Many were established or consolidated from domestic arts events during the 1990s, indicating the growing interest

Sydney Biennale signage on the harbor foreshore, 2012.

| International Biennales | Commentary |
|---|---|
| Venice Biennale | Art Biennale alternates with architecture expositions in the Giardini and the Arsenale; the oldest, since 1895 |
| Sao Paulo Biennial, Brazil | Since 1951, national presentations and international inclusions |
| Documenta, Kassel, Germany | Since 1955 and now held every 5 years |
| Biennale of Sydney, Australia | Australia's largest visual arts event since 1973, celebrating cultural diversity |
| Havana Biennial, Cuba | Established in 1984 with emphasis on Latin America and Caribbean artists |
| Istanbul Biennial, Turkey | Established in 1987 after initial festival in 1973 as a bridge between Europe and Asia |
| Biennale de Lyon, Lyon, France | Each biennale explores specific themes since 1991 |
| Dak' Art Biennial of Contemporary African Art, Dakar, Senegal | Emphasizing contemporary African artists through promotion, encouraging creativity, and integration with international markets since 1992 |
| Sharjah Biennial, United Arab Emirates | Sharjah was UNESCO cultural capital of the Arab World in 1998 and continues to encourage contact between Arab countries and international artists |
| Berlin Biennale, Germany | Contemporary art Biennale offers an open space that experiments, identifies, and critically examines the latest trends in the art world since 1996 |

**Table 6.4** List of Established International Biennales

in the specific agenda that arts practitioners have in sharing their output, networking with peers, and supporting the emergence of the creative industries and the support infrastructure required to encourage cultural tourism in host communities. Art fairs are attractive destinations in their own rights, utilizing the built and natural environments and demanding a high level of festival management.

Active participation with confetti by visitors within the Belgium Pavilion at Venice Biennale, 2009.

## FOR ONE NIGHT ONLY

New York's *Museum Mile Festival* continues to engross visitors from all over the world who are looking to take part for one evening only in a festival that allows attendees to walk the mile between 82nd Street and 105th Street, visiting some of New York's greatest cultural institutions in the process.

All the participating museums, including the Museum for African Art, El Museo Del Barrio, Museum of the City of New York, the Jewish Museum, National Design Museum, National Academy Museum and School of Fine Arts, the Guggenheim Museum, Neue Galerie New York, German Cultural Centre and the Metropolitan Museum of Art, are completely free from 6:00 P.M. to 9:00 P.M. on the day of the festival. Several museums also offer music and outdoor arts activities.

Since 1978, the festival raises public awareness about the many engaging cultural institutions that New York City has to offer and attendance records indicate that over 26 years, no less than 1.5 million people have taken part in the extraordinary event.

## CASE STUDY

### *Alignment Comes* Out of the Box, *Brisbane, Australia*

The **Out of the Box Festival** celebrated its 20th birthday in 2012. It is a biennial festival for a special audience, children 8 years and under held in Brisbane, Australia. It takes pride in its history as a national leader in programming for young children, nurturing creativity and imagination during a week of cultural activity crafted to celebrate and support learning, play, curiosity, and discovery for children and their families as they learn and grow together.

*Out of the Box* takes place in and across the Queensland Cultural Centre precinct from its hub at the Queensland Performing Arts Centre (QPAC) to the State Library of Queensland, Queensland Museum and the Queensland Art Gallery, and the Gallery of Modern Art.

John Kotzas, chief executive officer, QPAC, suggests that "what distinguishes every aspect of Out of the Box—from planning and viewing performances, eating, playing, painting, dancing, the train trips to and from the festival—is a deeply thought-through positioning of the role of children and their relationship within the communities in which they live. The festival's underlying aim is always to enhance children's experience through involvement in the arts by encouraging a sense of wonder, curiosity, discovery, and "serious fun."

Carol Davidson, Executive Producer of the festival, believes the curatorial framework that creates alignment between a program of both ticketed and nonticketed events at sites in and around QPAC with satellite events animating the major institutions inside the adjacent cultural center precinct, and research that underpins the design and content of the program of participatory activities for children, caretakers, and early childhood workers fosters deeper understanding of early childhood learning, attachment, and brain science. The organizing principles that underpin the preparation and presentation of the festival are grounded in contemporary research into children's self-development, interpersonal relationships, and exploration of arts experiences.

Creative development for the week-long event occurs in creative studios, schools, universities, and childcare centers across Brisbane and surrounding areas. The festival is aligned to numerous partners through a personal and professional network of agencies with a commitment to informing and inspiring active participants. The goals and philosophical principles that inform this family festival provide a holistic approach to the enjoyable programs of interactions with professional artists, other children, and exciting transformed spaces.

Thousands of youngsters thoroughly enjoy their exposure to diverse fun and learning that emerges when they watch, make, play, listen, sing, dance, read, and make contact with whimsical, cultural challenges and the essence of darkness and light, stillness and movement, and sound and silence. There seems to be something for everyone! Shadow plays, a petting zoo for dinosaurs, baby chefs hats for food preparation, exposure to an orchestra, sticky mazes, book swaps, meeting media celebrities, connections with puppets, learning stories from the Indigenous Dreamtime, and a chance to create their own masterpiece to take home as a souvenir all energize the children and make for long-lasting memories.

In terms of valued festival associates the organizers have aligned their aspirations to partners in business, education, the arts, and community services. There is a festival launch for teachers and childcare providers offering an opportunity to exchange ideas and issues and allow schools priority bookings before the public release of the program. The festival's opening night showcases the lineup and introduces the themes and family orientation. Sponsors are sought to invest financially and offer in-kind support with items that are employed to engage the children. Cultural center partners and external business partners and supporters are all celebrated on the festival website where each is invited to explain why they chose to support the festival.

Artistic contributors to the program demonstrate enduring commitment to the festival. Repeat participation with new artworks especially curated for inclusion to match festival themes provides some continuity to build the corporate memory with skills. Some work is bought in and other contributions are designed and prepared in-house. Extensive documentation of the outputs are archived and used for promotional purposes. The city's print and audio-visual media are major supporters for broad communication with residents and visitors offering coverage of the attractive event. The major investment is met by QPAC. This is significant as the festival would not be viable commercially, especially with the input from over 400 volunteers who support QPAC's efforts.

Over 25,000 visitors daily come for free or ticketed entertainment, sit on picnic rugs complete with sunscreen, hats, a wristband, a photograph for identification, and a water bottle to access over six distinct shows over any three-hour period. The familiar buildings are transformed along the riverside frontage with chalk walks, huge tunnels, sticky mazes, reading tents, and energetic, rewarding contact with literacy, cultural, artistic, and literary attractions the festival delivers. The feedback from young audiences of their memorable experiences encourage organizers to come out of the box again in two years' time!

## FROM INSIDE THE MOSAIC

### *Sonia Shares Her Passion for Festivals*

Sonia Tsai is typical of festival workers the world over. Her passion for arts management and festival engagement has provided a stimulating workplace during a variety of festival environments in Australia. Her skills and experience have ensured she is employed in responsible positions.

*Sydney Festival and Festival First Night* are among the portfolio of festivals and events that met with success in the IFEA's annual World Festival and Event City Awards in 2010 and 2011.

Sonia Tsai

Sydney is the largest and most populous city in Australia and the state capital of New South Wales. Located on Australia's southeast coast, Sydney is Australia's premier city, a vibrant, cosmopolitan, creative city blessed with the natural beauty of its unique landscape and breathtaking harbor. With a culturally diverse population of 4.6 million and over 200 languages spoken, Sydney is also Australia's business and media capital and home to the nation's thriving creative industries. The *Sydney Festival* attracts over 600,000 local, national, and international visitors.

Each January after New Year's Eve celebrations attracting close to one million spectators to the harborside icons of the Sydney Harbour Bridge and the Sydney Opera House to view fireworks displays and entertainment, the long-running *Sydney Festival* works its magic for residents and global visitors. For three weeks audiences celebrate music, dance, theater, comedy, and visual arts in centrally located and satellite venues to the city's west. In recent years, *Sydney Festival First Night* was a free event drawing audiences to local and international artists performing on open-air stages and spaces in city streets and central parklands, such as Hyde Park and The Domain. It provided an opportunity to launch the festival program and for visitors to linger longer in the metropolitan precinct. It also offers potential audiences a taste of the full festival program and encourages further bookings for ticketed events. Organizers have to deal with the realities of funding such a program with diverse sources from state and local government, sponsors, and philanthropy. Free entertainment has been appealing for audiences, but pruning its availability confronts management as it balances celebrations of artistic excellence with budgetary constraints.

The professional management of this world-class festival includes a staff of skilled and experienced workers and a team of volunteers and interns. While numerous full-time staff are employed by the festival organization, many of the people engaged to deliver the demanding schedule are on short term contracts. They are trusted freelance arts and technical workers who are integral to the setup and execution of myriad elements of such a vast exercise—from programming, logistics, front of house, marketing support, security, and venue management.

Freelance members of festival teams bring a great deal to each gig with which they are associated. They offer accumulated experience in briefing, cross checking, managing, arranging, scheduling, sourcing, and handling materials and equipment that builds the strength of the festival capacity. One such professional administrator and logistics coordinator is Sonia Tsai, who has worked for the Sydney Festival team over the years and has particularly enjoyed her association with Sydney Festival First Night. Sonia has worked on diverse festivals in Sydney and Melbourne. Her portfolio of experience includes such roles as Assistant Venue Manager for the Melbourne International Comedy Festival; a Stage Manager for the International FIFA Fan Festival at Sydney's Darling Harbour; Event Assistant for the Marketing and Events Division of the Sydney Harbour Foreshore Authority that convenes such events as Art on The Rocks, Darling Harbour Fiesta, Hoopla, and the Rocks Aroma Festival; and Front of House Operations Manager for the Sydney Writers' Festival.

Sonia has observed the power of Sydney Festival First Night to introduce artists to audiences, to act as a catalyst for word-of-mouth promotion, and as an animator of public spaces to generate a festive spirit for the duration of the summer festival. Her studies (BA, Media and Cultural Studies at Macquarie University) provided a foundation for her communication skills in dealing with a variety of colleagues. She has developed her logistics skills through working on festivals, in particular coordinating performers, event suppliers, security, police, and crew ensuring compliance with various protocols within the organization and with external agencies. Such positions are extremely competitive and the right person for a particular job requires the right mix of personal and professional traits. The festival organization is keen to ensure there is a good fit for the organizational culture and adequate reward for the freelance worker. Once they are familiar and demonstrate effective and efficient contributions to a festival, regular employment satisfies each party. Understanding of and familiarity with the regular audience to each event allows for staff to satisfy the needs and expectations and deliver memorable festival experiences.

## Festival Ideas and Issues

1. How does the Pine and Gilmore *Experience Economy* (1999) model sit with a festival with which you are familiar? How does this build on the notion of customer-centric marketing?
2. If a particular festival is not for everyone, how do organizers deliberately determine a target market?
3. What is demographic segmentation? How can those marketing a festival use this information to connect with specific audiences?
4. How have the innovations in technology and the proliferation of social media impacted the communication choices of festival organizers to attract greater participation?
5. Is it easier to retain existing festival-goers than attracting new ones? Why? How can a festival organization build loyalty among regular attendees?

## Festival Focus Activities

1. Plot decision-making processes that an individual may undertake to attend a particular festival with which you are familiar. Use your model to identify how the festival organizers might deal with each stage.
2. Walk in the shoes of a prospective festival attendee for a particular festival and note the effectiveness or success of the existing interventions (e.g., website, promotional campaigns, peer-to-peer communication, phone contact, sponsorship partners, location

of festival, price of tickets, quality of program, transportation, security, etc.). Were there any major challenges? How could these be addressed?
3. Develop a marketing strategy for a hypothetical festival focusing on the product and program, the festival's position in the marketplace, the price for attendees, the people involved, potential packaging of the festival with other events or attractions, appropriate partnerships, and promotion. Watt (1998, p. 60) offers Lyndsey Taylor's framework to underpin a conventional marketing plan:

**M**eeting customer needs

**A**ttracting new customers

**R**eacting to market trends

**K**eeping up with competitors

**E**ncouraging customer loyalty

**T**argeting specific customers

**I**dentifying market opportunities

**N**oting customer feedback

**G**etting it right every time

4. Look at the program of the Out of the Box Festival and evaluate the connection made between the target audience and the content on offer. What do you think would comprise the underlying principles organizers would consider in developing an appropriate alignment?

# Suggested Reading

AEA Consulting. *Anticipating Change in the Major Performing Arts*. Sydney: Australia Council for the Arts, 2008.

Arts Audiences (Una Carmody). Arts Attendance in Ireland, Target Group Index, 2011.

Australia Council for the Arts. *Arts Audiences Online: How Australian Audiences are Connecting with the Arts Online*. Sydney: Nielson Online Division, 2011.

Australia Council for the Arts. *More than Bums on Seats: Australian Participation in the Arts*. Sydney: Author, 2010.

Brown, A. S., and R. Ratzkin. *Making Sense of Audience Engagement* (Vol. 1). San Francisco, CA: San Francisco Foundation, 2011.

Bunting, C., T. W. Chan, and J. Goldthorpe. *From Indifference to Enthusiasm: Patterns of Arts Attendance in England*. London, UK: Arts Council England, 2008.

Cary, J. *What Good Are The Arts?* London, UK: Faber & Faber, 2005.

Conifer Research. *How to Find Buried Treasure Using Experience Maps*. Chicago, Illinois: 2002. www.coniferresearch.com.

Crutchfield, L., and H. McLeod-Grant. *Forces for Good: The Six Practices of High Impact Nonprofits*. San Francisco, CA: Jossey-Bass/Wiley, 2012.

Csikszentmihalyi, M. *Flow: The Classic Work on How to Achieve Happiness*. London, UK: Rider, 2002.

Hewison, R., and J. Holden. *The Cultural Leadership Handbook: How to Run a Creative Organization*. Farnham, UK: Gower Publishing, 2011.

Kotler P. *Marketing Management, Analysis, Planning, Implementation and Control* (7th ed.). Englewood Cliffs, NJ: Prentice Hall, 1991.

Kreidler, J., and P. J. Trounstine. *Creative Community Index: Measuring Progress Toward a Vibrant Silicon Valley*. San Jose, CA: Cultural Initiatives Silicon Valley, 2005.

McCarthy K. F., and K. Jinnett. *A New Framework for Building Participation in the Arts*. San Diego, CA: RAND Corporation, 2001.

McDowell, S. "A comparison between Thai residents and non-residents in their motivations, performance evaluations and overall satisfaction with a domestic festival" *Journal of Vacation Marketing* 16, no. 3 (2012): 217–233.

Morris Hargreaves McIntyre, Cultural Strategy and Research, Culture Segments, Manchester 2013.

New Economics Foundation. Capturing the Audience Experience: A Handbook for the Theatre. London, UK: Independent Theatre Council, The Society of London Theatre, Theatrical Management Association. Available at www.itc-arts.org/uploaded/documents/Theatre%20handbook.pdf.

Novak-Leonard J. L., and A. S. Brown, A.S. *Beyond Attendance: A Multi-modal Understanding of Arts Participation*. National Endowment for the Arts, 2011.

Pine B. J., and J. H. Gilmore. *The Experience Economy: Work is Theatre and Every Business a Stage*. Boston, MA: Harvard Business School Press, 1999.

Pitts, S. E., and C. P. Spencer. "Loyalty and Longevity in Audience Listening: Investigating Experiences of Attendance at a Chamber Music Festival." *Music and Letters* 89 (2008): 227–238.

Pitts, S. E., and C. P. Spencer. *Welcome to the Experience Economy*. Boston, MA: Harvard Business Review, 1998.

Radbourne, J., K. Johanson, H. Glow, and T. White. "The Audience Experience: Measuring Quality in the Performing Arts." *International Journal of Arts Management* 11, no. 3 (2009): 16–29.

Saget, A. *The Event Marketing Handbook*. Chicago, IL: Kaplan Publishing, 2006.

Tomlinson, R., and T. Roberts. *Full House: Turning Data into Audiences*. Surry Hills, Australia: Australia Council for the Arts, 2006.

Watt, D. C., *Event management in leisure and tourism*. London: Addison Wesley Longman Ltd. (1998).

# CHAPTER 7
# Festival Resourcefulness

"There are no secrets to success. It is the result of preparation, hard work, learning from failure."

—*Colin Powell, an American statesman and retired four-star general*

## This chapter provides an opportunity for you to better understand:

- The resources required to deliver a responsible festival based on the organization's human, financial, social, natural, and physical capital
- Good practices deployed by successful festivals demonstrating innovation, ingenuity, and inventiveness using owned, shared, or borrowed assets
- How festivals are strengthened and sustained through appropriate systemic policy, planning, and presentation

**Figure 7.1** A Festival Resource Mosaic.

# CHAPTER 7  FESTIVAL RESOURCEFULNESS

This chapter deals with the realization of the "great big festival idea." It builds on creative festival design and ensures implementation strategies deliver quality experiences. A significant measure of festival success can be its organizational resourcefulness as represented in the mosaic of Figure 7.1. How does the festival organization marshal the resources it requires and deploy them in a meaningful way for environmental sustainability, economic efficiency and effectiveness and align an energized program to satisfy patrons over the long term? It needs to cultivate loyalty among key stakeholders, ensure it is well capitalized, attracts ongoing investment and grows sufficient revenue to promote an engaging festival. It needs to meet its vision by the application of workable, legal, and appropriate policies and practices. The realistic assessment of resources required in the areas of logistics, administration, and risk can deliver a long-term enterprise.

## Assessing Festival Resource Requirements

It requires a convergence of the major forms of capital—human, physical (the materials, stocks and stores, technical assets, equipment and property), financial, environmental (natural), and social. The festival's strength and success is based on the organization's capacity to integrate, in a seamless manner, all these elements. It needs to assemble strategic (long-term) plans and tactical plans for security, risk, and project management and coordinate partnership arrangements that allow for mutual benefits from the investment of each into marketing, environmental, and capability outcomes. Media, suppliers, the host community, government agencies, visitors, and the tourism sector are not only partners but markets that need to be creatively harnessed in the interests of a dynamic festival.

> Resourcefulness is the ability to act effectively or imaginatively, especially in regard to difficult situations and unusual problems.

Organizers seek to grow their organization's capacity to achieve the festival's set goals through a positive and systematic approach to create order out of potential chaos, comfort through appropriate decision making, positive outcomes out of challenges that inevitably arise as resources are marshalled for such a substantial enterprise as a festival. The ethical dilemmas, audits of existing assets, and internal knowledge management help determine the distribution of responsibilities among staff and partners. From experience within the culture of the host organization, or through the disciplines of education and on-the-job training elsewhere, festival organizers prepare templates and timelines and allocate tasks and through leadership invested in their position, encourage their teams to assess any vulnerability. They can moderate the equilibrium required to pace themselves through the planning and presentation of the festival to minimize unwelcome peaks and valleys. Otherwise the nuances that make each festival distinctive become lost.

Festival leaders recognize the need for managed flexibility as they connect with all aspects of the mosaic. They have in place mechanisms to monitor performance. They meet regularly with all participants to appraise performances that can demonstrate individual

# Assessing Festival Resource Requirements

The festival site layout allowing unfettered access to performance venues, amenities, merchandising, and food outlets is critical to ensure safety and security.

and team independence of thinking, observation, creativity, logic, and energy. Each leader needs to assess underutilized resources that may exist in communities and businesses that may be co-opted to enhance the delivery of a quality festival by having local knowledge. They can identify innovative ways out of any imminent complexity and chaos. These skills and experience become the essence of a resourceful festival team and need to be embedded and transmitted through all tasks to boost capacity, minimize silos, and assist with communication. The festival leader's tool kit that includes engagement with technology, especially with customized scheduling and division of labor, has improved outcomes for contemporary festivals. All these aspects of festival management are covered in this chapter through increasing your understanding of

- Performance required of festival teams
- Benchmarks, milestones, and administrative controls required
- Standard financial practices employed
- Effective communication links
- Logistics on- and off-site

When taking a systematic approach to festival operations, organizers seek to ensure that significant thought has been given to good practice principles and strategic planning (for at least three-to-five-year perspectives) as they determine how they address the needs of:

- Patrons by identifying practical actions applied to such needs as transport, traffic, maintenance of essential amenities especially with positive environmental outcomes, waste, cleanliness, safety, emergency and security, ticketing, queuing, information services and staff management, location of food, beverage, and merchandising outlets, seating, crowd control, toilets, vagaries of weather
- Festival suppliers including liaison and compliance with statutory authorities such as police, ambulance, security service providers, and technical, energy, and water services efficiently and effectively, with infrastructure maintenance and utilities and relationships with host communities to source quality goods locally at competitive prices
- Internal and external communication involving equipment, media, documentation, licenses, hosting of artists and celebrities, and accreditation

Responses in these areas will be informed by earlier strategic, administrative, and design decisions made by management.

## Sustainability Policy

Whether festivals are urban, community, indoor, or outdoor, all require attention to detail. Many established festivals have recognized the importance of preparing comprehensive policies, strategies, and action plans including *Bluesfest*, in Byron Bay, Australia; *Roskilde* in Denmark; the 2012 *Olympic and Paralympic Games* in London; and *Burning Man* in Nevada. Such tools provide a framework to demonstrate a commitment to mapping the festival ecosystem and to develop indicators of sustainability consistent with the world's best practice. They help to bring balance to the heightened human activity that festivals stimulate, the resource usage applied to deliver the festival, and explanation of how negative environmental impacts can be minimized. Large outdoor festivals that are keen to be in business for the long haul recognize that they need to care for the natural environment in which they operate as well as attend to the sustainable practices associated with the business, cultural and social environments as well.

The ISO 20121 is set to transform the events sector. Event Sustainability Management Systems is the new international management system standard that has been designed to help organizations in the events industry improve the sustainability of their event-related activities, products, and services (Parry, 2012).

## Customer Loyalty

Building on the relationship marketing discussed in Chapter 6, it is important that festival patrons are recognized as a resource to cultivate a strong and viable festival. It can be through merchandising that a connection can be made and sustained. Satisfied patrons will happily purchase items such as T-shirts, hats, scarves, reusable bags with logos of partners, stickers, drink containers, and jewelry that might have a connection with a favored festival through striking design, use of logos, color, and other identifying features that link the individual to the source of a satisfying experience. It becomes another communication and promotional tool.

Loyalty needs to be rewarded and festival organizations have looked to commercial and retail practices for inspiration and innovation. Schemes that build on people's interest through the accrual of points or to leverage cash are popular and can be redeemed through registration and ticketing, the purchase of merchandising or through offering membership or subscriptions to festival associates on- or offline. The publication of regular (e)newsletters or redeemable print items at intermittent functions has become attractive. Redeemable benefits can include ticket discounts, packages of experiences through tourism and hospitality partners, or in-house through festival fundraisers during an annual program of events.

## Staff and Volunteers

Many festival organizations have designated specific teams that become significant bearers of diverse festival messages. It appears to be essential that the organizational climate and culture mentioned in earlier chapters informs the quality of the people in these teams. Management needs to have confidence that these people will provide the spine for the important big-picture aspirations and the detailed delivery of operations outlined in this chapter. These can support the festival's environmentally sustainable credentials, educate patrons about issues and ideas that the festival supports, and raise awareness about the activities of designated charities that may be beneficiaries of festival partnerships. These people are seen on-site throughout the duration of the festival, maintaining personal contact and building relationships with festival patrons.

They are generally recruited and trained for their personal skills and experience, local knowledge, and connection with the content of the festival program and can be of assistance as an information hub for safety and emergency situations. This extends the formal communication festival marketers engage with by having personal contact with potential repeat patrons. In marketing terms, the festival needs to behave like a friend, and while the Internet has provided a pivotal turning point in the relationship dynamic, face-to-face exchanges build the reputation of the festival to be a customer-focused event. While these teams can't control people per se, they can help mitigate any fallout that might develop from an inconsistent service while at the festival and helps foster festival likeability.

Members of such teams are often repeat contributors to the festival. The volunteers especially may be scheduled in such a way as to have access to sessions at the festival during their free time. They provide another layer of research for debriefing sessions with feedback and observations of customer satisfaction. It builds word-of-mouth campaigns and generally provides a positive shift in relationships with festival traders, technical staff, camping and parking personnel and visitors and helps build a sense of belonging and community. The human capital that staff, traders, suppliers and volunteers bring to a festival is substantial. The human resources underpin the success of the festival.

Festival volunteers and staff are crucial to maintaining cleanliness and order on-site.

## External Partners

There are a number of festival partners that require ongoing formal and informal communication and compliance contact. Nurturing productive relationships with the following agencies will ensure the festival can plan rigorously and enjoy professional support and advice. These areas of expertise involve collaboration to consolidate the resourcefulness of festival management initiatives and include:

- Community liaison collaborating on strategic plans to prevent antisocial behavior
- Hoteliers, the responsible service of alcohol legislation, promotion of safe drinking campaigns
- Neighborhood property owners, including venue owners
- Police and community relationships, emergency services, fire department
- Legal partners, familiarity with compliance, legislation, statutory obligations
- Education and training of staff, volunteers, and community
- Hospitality and tourism training programs for interns and volunteers as staff
- Health agencies, ambulances and hospitals, medical practitioners
- Waste management consultants, environmental groups
- Local government specialist liaison workers (e.g., in youth, indigenous, aged) and arts development and recreation officers

## Harm Minimization

An overarching principle of festival management resourcefulness is harm minimization. The inclusions in any operational plan need to address potential harms and the means needed to diminish risk. This will impact the approaches taken to satisfying festival patrons' needs

The provision of secure money exchange at festivals satisfies attendees and demonstrates connections to the business community.

for a safe environment, the supply of products and services to the festival, and the event site logistics. Some possible considerations are outlined in Table 7.1.

Festival management can determine that a harm minimization strategy be incorporated across all festival domains, especially in the area of logistics and operations. The following benefits can accrue:

- Decrease in accidents and injuries
- Control of public space

| Domain | Potential Harms | Minimization Strategies | Actions |
|---|---|---|---|
| Assaults | Minor physical contacts<br>Fights—large- and small-scale violence<br>Sexual harassment | Precautionary measures | Parking restrictions, licensee restrictions, liquor restrictions, police walk-throughs, street marshals, extra security |
| Injuries | Road accidents<br>Falls, cuts, fractures, lacerations, heat exhaustion | Compliance (simplify but comply) | Occupational Health and Safety guidelines, insurance, noise ordinances, fire codes |
| Death | Substance overdose<br>Vehicle accidents<br>Suicide<br>Assaults | Restrictions | Control over sale of prohibited items like elicit substances, knives, firearms, improvised weapons, and damaged foodstuff at event or venue |
| Theft/burglary/property damage | Graffiti<br>Littering<br>Property damage | Increasing safety | Improving design of public facilities, portable toilets, street lighting, signage, information sharing |
| Public order | Abusive language<br>Resisting arrest<br>Drunk and disorderly conduct<br>Noise disruption | Surveillance | Security, marshals, police patrols, negotiated management |
| Environmental | Damage to grounds and infrastructure<br>Air/water/waste pollution<br>Tree damage | Facilitation | Provision of food and entertainment, accords, provide nonalcoholic beverages, encourage mixed-gender groups, street performance, care with carrying capacity of site, fence off fragile areas |
| Economic costs | Policing and security costs<br>Clean up operations<br>Emergency services<br>Negative tourism impacts | Rewards | Reduced police control, removal of antisocial behavior, control of drinking behaviour, a more peaceful event |
| Social disruption | Irritation of host community<br>Overcrowding<br>Traffic congestion<br>Social segregation | Access | Barriers, car checks, belongings checks, scheduling |

**Table 7.1** Festival Harm Minimization
Derrett (2013).

- Lower associated costs
- Prevention rather than control approach
- Safer events
- Enhanced community participation
- Spread of benefits to the host community
- Improved police and community relationships
- Reduction in problem behavior
- Ownership of community space and events

Organizers, though, need to be mindful of some unintended consequences from such strategies. For example:

- Displacement—where crowds are diverted to other locations with less stringent controls
- Driving people away—where control strategies may deter potential audience attendance
- Deterring young people by creating a family-oriented event; young adults may be alienated, so audience alignment is critical
- Decrease in sales—if the event is too restrictive, it may lower retail sales or tourist activities
- Civil rights—community members have rights that may be affected by event strategies and ongoing information-sharing alleviates most tensions
- Resource implications—Be budget aware! Know where the costs lie and use most effective measures to stage the event
- Limitation of recreational opportunities—allow for alternative recreational activities for a diverse crowd, not all groups want to do, see, hear, or participate in the same celebration
- Order versus freedom—the event needs to be designed to support freedom of expression in an orderly and peaceful manner; use the event as an opportunity as a learning experience for the whole community.

## Research

Festival managements have noted the improvement in their capacity to deliver effective events based on stored and shared information and knowledge from their previous festival-making experiences. This intelligence needs to be disseminated across all sections of the organization. Key decision-makers need to integrate earlier research, feedback from stakeholders, competitive practices, global good practice and industry trends, legislation, and statutory obligations into the knowledge mix. There is a great deal of material to be held, integrated, and leveraged in the interest of making the best use of resources the festival organization can access. This will ensure that standardized knowledge can be translated into technology-driven actions to serve the control and management of operations for each festival activity. It can assist in improving the internal assignment of operational tasks from bump-in, through staging to shutdown. It also informs the way the organization does business, including budgetary controls.

There is a growing body of literature dealing with legal obligations in the use of technology and multimedia and festivals. Management needs to be clear about its obligations through any sponsorship arrangement, recording of events, dispersal of images from events, documenting of proceedings, etc., in terms of copyright infringements. Performers are vulnerable, with their work exploited for use in a wider (global) arena without their knowledge through their involvement in an event. Signage at festival sites beamed around the world has huge marketing implications. Technology can be used to document and distribute festival images and text is owned by someone—and someone is always going to have to pay!

## Financing the Festival

Festival organizations recognize the need to finance their endeavors through a mix of earned and contributed income. See Table 7.2 for some examples of festival expenditures. The responsibility to ensure prudent investment strategies requires an understanding of available options to provide appropriate and timely capital injections to back the strategic directions for the long-term goals set for the organization and for each specific festival activity. Numerous partners have a stake in financing, underwriting, guaranteeing, bankrolling, subsidizing, sponsoring, and endowing aspects of the desired strategic direction. Over time festivals can accumulate assets such as financial reserves, property, and goods, and sometimes they have amassed liabilities that will influence choices made going forward.

| Items of Festival Expenditure | Budget Guidelines |
|---|---|
| • Administration<br>• Staff, consultant salaries<br>• Artist, performer, agent payment<br>• Security<br>• Cleaning<br>• Royalties<br>• Exchange rates<br>• Venue hire, site preparation, maintenance<br>• Promotion<br>• Documentation and printing<br>• Insurance (public liability, weather, workers' compensation)<br>• Compliance, legal fees, permits, Council, food and beverage<br>• Equipment (purchase or hire, sound, lights, toilets, signage, barriers)<br>• Materials<br>• Transport, travel costs<br>• Accommodations<br>• Hospitality<br>• Volunteers<br>• Distribution to charities and community groups<br>• Contingency | • Be familiar with current fees and charges in each sector; seek best prices for services rendered; negotiate; document; consider barter, lease, or hire rather than purchase of some items<br>• Have cash flow mechanisms in place to ensure prompt payment to minimize relationship difficulties later<br>• Fit purchasing and procurement with ethical practice and sustainability plan<br>• Assess unit costs of each item to create historical record and value for money, know exactly what comprises each item in terms of quantity and quality<br>• Ensure payment terms known at the outset of arrangements<br>• Ensure contracts stipulate process, including upfront deposit and payment at end of festival, delivery of goods and services are timely with caveats for noncompliance<br>• Limit the number of people within the organization who can incur festival expenditures<br>• Look to leverage from partnerships to reduce expenditures through shared promotion, in-kind supplies, borrowed equipment, contributions from volunteers |

**Table 7.2** Items of Festival Expenditure

Costs of staging a festival and the predicted sources of income comprise a budget. The budget acts as a master plan for control of financial resources for the festival. The process of developing a budget in the first instance focuses on estimating the costs and projected income in line with the overarching plan and design. When costing the enterprise it will be noted that there are what are known as fixed costs and variable costs. Depending on scale and tradition some festival organizations have a treasurer, a finance committee, an accountant, and a finance director working for senior management.

Someone must have responsibility for preparing as accurate a picture as possible of the precise activities to be carried out, the cost associated with each, priorities for expenditure in line with benefits sought from their inclusion. The proposed income streams that have been established by any feasibility study, professional advice received, and experience of staff and board should be clearly declared and incorporated.

Financial controls for each festival vary but essential elements include transparent monitoring by authorized personnel, clarity in explanation to staff, inbuilt flexibility, immediate recognition of unscheduled deviations, and direct remedial action. Templates exist in the industry literature that formalize alignment with festival aims and objectives that inform strategic plans for each section of the festival business, feed into festival planning, delivery timetable, and budgetary process based on a cash flow represented in a profit-and-loss account, and finally residing in the reconciliation of accounts and a statement of a financial situation going forward. This flow can readily be accommodated by computer technology and working relationships with financial institutions that understand the festival's practices and needs.

While the budget is established through various iterations, it is important that the festival is effectively supported financially from the beginning. Depending on the scale of the festival, organizers need to know that appropriate available financial resources prior to their undertaking the enterprise. In the early stages there will be forecasting, but the budget will also be informed by historical data collected from previous festivals. This might influence choices for ticketing, for example, through offering group discounts, season tickets, promotional pricing dependent on the broader economic environment, the location of the festival, and cultural demographics.

## Methods of Generating Income for a Festival

Festival organizations have numerous options as they prepare a portfolio of income sources to invest in the festival (Table 7.3).

## Crowdfunding

Crowdfunding platforms are increasingly attractive to community-based festivals, performance projects for artists to participate in festivals, and collaborations for new social, cultural, and environmental initiatives. These often peer-supported projects are attractive to those in specific sectors, to friends and family, and to those with a commitment to investing in creativity and innovation. Popular sites explain how individuals and groups can raise money to kick-start their projects or careers using a tried and tested concept. This approach offers fewer financial connections to formal financial institutions and access to cash injections

| Options for Revenue Generation | Principles of Revenue Generation |
|---|---|
| • Fundraising<br>• Government grants<br>• Donations, bequests<br>• Philanthropy (foundations, trusts, individuals)<br>• Merchandising<br>• Licenses, franchising<br>• Food and beverage sales<br>• Admission charges<br>• Parking and camping<br>• Interest<br>• Sponsorship<br>• Advertising, broadcast rights<br>• Corporate hospitality<br>• Online "crowdfunding" campaigns<br>• Corporate social responsibility<br>• "In-kind" monetary value<br>• Barter | • Use a variety of methods to generate resources<br>• Adopt ethical standards for fundraising and resource development methods<br>• To make profit on sales, attention must be given to fixed and variable costs<br>• Food and beverage sales—ensure health and safety standards are met; money handling is controlled; alcohol is wisely managed<br>• Sometimes it is better to let professional traders do the selling of merchandising. Use licensing agreements to ensure fair returns<br>• When setting admission prices consider the event's goals and marketing strategy. Prepare a breakeven analysis to calculate the minimum revenue required to recover costs<br>• Design and manage control programs like a capital replacement fund and working capital reserves<br>• Prepare and manage a sponsorship plan<br>• Negotiate philanthropic investment attracting assistance beyond the grant |

**Table 7.3** Revenue Generation Options

from the community that may already know of artists' skills and experience. The buy-in from diverse parties helps build an audience and take people on a creative journey. Often a marketing-style campaign can prolong and deepen the relationship through the offer of on going contact, rewards, and incentives to stay the course as excitement builds for the target to be reached.

Such fundraising projects have been utilized to great effect in the United States through initiatives such as Kickstarter and more recently in the United Kingdom through We Did This, as well as Pozible in Australia. StartSomeGood is a crowdfunding platform for socially aware initiatives globally; this form of social entrepreneurship is sometimes called peerfunding. It supports the nonprofit sector, governments, festivals and arts organizations to better engage communities. Although each program differs slightly in their setup and administration, the basic premise is consistent. It is all about creative individuals (or groups and organizations) promoting their projects to a global online community, and ordinary people pledging money to see creative ideas realized.

The online pages are filled with project ideas—across visual art, performance art, music, film, journalism, design, publishing, and more—easily accessible for potential investors' perusal, along with the relevant funding targets and deadlines and indicators to keep the audience informed on the funds already raised. Most programs utilize an "all-or-nothing" funding model. Either the project achieves its funding target by its deadlines, or no money changes hands. Generally you have to be invited, followed by a straightforward process that involves submitting a project brief and agreeing to comply with agreed guidelines.

## Project Management

The festival project management framework accommodates the skills, tools, and professional processes required to design and deliver a successful project within a specific timeframe. Within the festival organization, teams of staff and volunteers are often authorized to pursue specific tasks to deliver aspects of the final event. Senior management determines whether the required series of tasks actually constitutes a discrete project and establishes a team to set objectives, plan, and monitor relationships, resources, and results.

Project management comprises a coalition of appropriate human resources that set priorities and compliance protocols; plans the allocation of tasks, roles, and responsibilities; communicates clearly; develops teamwork; overcomes challenges; maximizes reach; identifies milestones, tracks progress through the project's life cycle; ensures appropriate investment and allocation of resources, manages scheduling and documentation; monitors outputs and outcomes; and evaluates key inputs. The endeavor undertaken needs to fit with the organization's overall aims and objectives and as such satisfy the festival's core vision and strategic direction.

There are challenges facing teams within organizations tasked to take responsibility to control the completion of logistical and technical activities, communication, administration, relationship compliance, context, and festival content. Some people find themselves in multiple teams. There are leadership issues such as personal and professional styles to fit the mix of personnel involved; their levels of commitment, time, and energy; organizing meetings; streamlining internal communication; and addressing the nature of resourcing levels, contingency plans, and risk management. It is all about direction, details, decisions, and delivery.

Like any cyclical action approach, a useful starting point is the evaluation of team members and previous projects within the organization. This feedback can inform the stages of team-building and project management. Effective dynamics include:

- Understanding of the key dimensions of the project team's brief
- Appointing team members with appropriate functional skills and expertise
- The importance of people management skills
- Communication mechanisms within and between the team and the broader organization
- Exploiting the competencies of members of the project team
- Ensuring authority and responsibility issues are understood
- Ensuring appropriate resourcing for the project from the outset that supports success
- Inspiring leadership from within and outside the team

The organization's financial plan, risk management plan, communication plan, partnership liaison plan, marketing plan, procurement plan, compliance obligations, quality program and operational plans all provide guidance for the number of project teams required to deliver the festival. Targets for festival deliverables from each branch of the organization's portfolio of tasks need to be set by leaders of relevant teams and senior management. Monitoring of developments in each strand of the festival's business is important to ensure items are controlled. Templates can be developed to register and share progress and task status in a timely way. At the conclusion of each project, success can be judged against defined objectives and from feedback on the festival's performance by participants. Evaluation of the benefits accrued from established protocols and any shortcomings that may have arisen need to be assessed and documented.

# Project Management Templates

Templates can also be specifically developed to itemize the following elements of a project management action plan either electronically or in hard copy and be maintained over time to record and compare processes used year on year:

- Project Board/Steering Group Members: List names and contacts
- Project Team Members: List names and contacts
- Budget for total project to include:
    - Resource Costs:
    - Other Costs:
    - Total Costs, including a breakdown of the overall budget:
- Project Start Date:
- Project Completion Date:
- Signature of Project Manager: Date:
- Approval from Sponsor: Date:

An example of a project management template is outlined in Table 7.4.

| | |
|---|---|
| **Project Title:** | Brief title for the project |
| **Sponsor/Partner:** | Name and title of the sponsor/partner |
| **State Link with Corporate Agenda** | Actual words in the festival corporate agenda, showing the link with this project |
| **Project Background:** | Background of the project with enough information to inform the reader |
| **Project Benefits:** | Outline of what the benefits are to the organization, individuals, or stakeholders in delivering the project |
| **Project Objectives:** | Specific objectives for the project. *Note:* The objectives can be one line or more detailed text. |
| **Project Deliverables:** | What you will be delivering at the end of the project. *Note:* These are what you will have at the end of the project (e.g., a report, a building, improved service levels, etc.) |
| **This project will include:** | This section defines the boundaries of the project |
| **This project will not include:** | Planning details should not be included at this stage |
| **Success criteria:** | How you will measure the success of the project. *Note:* The success criteria must be measurable. |
| **Constraints:** | Examples here can be specific (a skill that the project team must have) resources or a legal deadline. *Note:* Only include time and money if you can quantify them. |
| **Key Assumptions:** | Assumptions you are making in putting this document together |
| **Project Manager:** | Who fulfills this role and what they do |
| **Project Sponsor:** | Who fulfills this role and what they do |

**Table 7.4** Project Definition Form

| Activity | Planned Time | Actual Time | Difference | Planned Cost | Actual Cost | Difference |
|---|---|---|---|---|---|---|
|  |  |  |  |  |  |  |

**Table 7.5** Actual versus Planned Recording and Reporting Form
Based on www.projectagency.com.

A template represented by Table 7.5 can record planned and actual activity providing a useful resource for festival organizers and can be shared amongst staff.

## Risk Management

Festival organizers are familiar with the notion of developing a risk management plan along with all other elements of compliance and preparedness. A characteristic of risk analysis and control requires ongoing monitoring. There are competencies required in the installation of equipment, setting up a site, organizing people, assessing dimensions from the weather to Council regulations to artists' needs, and audience expectations and satisfaction. So, it is a process that involves individuals as part of an organization, identifying potential risks and minimizing the unpredictable. There are templates that provide frameworks to manage any threat through avoidance, reduction, transfer, retention, or total elimination. This all still requires conscientious attention.

- Establish the context—undertake an audit.
    It is important that all relevant corporate documents are reviewed to ensure any learnings from previous years' experience can be taken into account. This will include a review of such things as the festival's business plans, project plans, financial commitments, overall strategic aims and objectives, SWOT analyses, and external environmental scans.
- Identify and define the risks—document well from data collected.
    When searching for points of uncertainty it is useful to find the gaps in areas that cast doubt on how the festival can best achieve its goals by determining when, how, where, and why risks are likely to occur. Having identified the festival priorities in each domain, what might hamper their achievement? Who are the internal and external partners that would be called on to mitigate any threats?
    Those responsible can employ various tools in identifying examples of possible risks from a business or operational standpoint; recognizing opportunities for inconsistency through procurement protocols and implementation, use scenario-building to assess particular incidents that could arise, employ process mapping, and regularly return to earlier organizational audits, program and project evaluations, or external research reports.
- Analyze the likelihood of occurrence from internal, external, and random sources.
    Through the risk assessment process it is important to understand why the festival may be confronted with particular risks. To minimize suspect eventualities it is critical that current controls and their levels of effectiveness are tested and assessed for the long term. To eliminate doubt and speculation, it is critical to systematically acknowledge

potential impacts on festival objectives and outcomes. Templates need to be employed so all implications can be documented and shared with relevant personnel.

- Estimate potential impacts—extreme, high, moderate, and low severity of consequences.

    In evaluating the prospect of risks it is useful to each item in a matrix such as below by recognizing factors that affect the human resources, the festival's reputation, and any business and stakeholder processes against historical data. Each consequence and likelihood measure needs to be charted against these elements.

| High probability<br>Low impact | High probability<br>High impact |
|---|---|
| Low probability<br>Low impact | Low probability<br>High impact |

- Determine the strategy to minimize risk.

    The organization can avoid the risk and not undertake the activity that might trigger misadventure. There is a cost associated with this choice. This will be informed if the risk is sufficiently low or an external compliance issue arises or an opportunity exists that outweighs the perceived level of threat. It is crucial the reasons for accepting a risk as acceptable needs to be documented by the person making the decision.

- Manage the risk and implement action plan—avoid, control, transfer, retain.

    The plan should scope the options to avoid, control, transfer, and retain any risk. At each stage there are questions of cost/benefit analysis, consequences for all aspects of the festival organization and its business units, minimizing exposure through maintenance, quality assurance, and contingency planning.

- Monitor and review event for risks.

    Risks and their priorities do not remain constant. The currency of identified risks needs to be regularly monitored. New risks and their impact on festival preparation and plan implementation need to be established. How will the success of outcomes be measured? Milestones or benchmarks for success and "warning signs" for failure need to be identified and matched against previous practice to ensure valuable data is not lost and can be utilized in future plans. Responsible personnel need to evaluate treatments for future applications.

## Risk Analysis Templates

Table 7.6 represents an example of a risk analysis template to assist festival preparation and management.

Score as follows for likelihood and impact: High = 3, Medium = 2, Low = 1

| Nature of Risk or Uncertainty | Likelihood | Impact | Likelihood × Impact [Score] | Actions Required and Who Manages Risk |
|---|---|---|---|---|
|  |  |  |  |  |

**Table 7.6** Risk Analysis

| Risk Reference | Potential Action Options | Costs and Benefits | Action to Be Implemented (Y/N)? | Target Risk Level | Responsible Person | Timetable for Implementation | Monitoring to Measure Effectiveness of Risk Action Plan |
|---|---|---|---|---|---|---|---|
| | | | | Likelihood<br>Consequence<br>Target Level | | | |

**Table 7.7** Risk Management Schedule and Action Plan Templates

Table 7.7 allows all festival staff to be alert to potential risks and to deliver best management strategies in a timely and responsible manner.

## Questions, Questions

Public commentary abounds when a public festival experiences a trauma. Who is to blame for site destruction from an adverse weather incident? Who should take responsibility when tragedy besets a well-established, popular festival? The vocabulary becomes as emotive in the media as with the experiences, as the interface with the disaster unfolds, a stage collapses, an unexplained change to programming or venue, a freak storm affects equipment and amenities, people are injured and lives are lost. Politicians, police and security service providers, festival administrators, and festival audiences are in an inextricable situation and under heightened scrutiny. All have questions to answer.

Were mistakes made through sloppy planning, construction and maintenance on-site by taking shortcuts in compliance obligations, unrealistic expectations within marketing and promotion campaigns, choices made predicated on unsubstantiated economic and tourism benefits? Was safety compromised, ineffective internal communication choices conducted, agreed roles and responsibilities poorly documented, undue influence by persons in positions of power demonstrated, on-site shortcomings with dispersal of audiences and evacuation strategies evident. Maybe there was unprecedented pressure, as a free event, that conspired to allow unknown numbers of patrons to become distressed victims of ineffectual management.

Challenges exist for festival organizers whether intended audiences are to be hosted indoors or outdoors. The latter domain is particularly vulnerable to external threats and significant resources need to be mobilized at short notice. Significant among harms that affect the experience are fear, panic, physical impacts, major transport inconveniences as people flee stressful, uncomfortable and unsafe venues. Instructive observations can be made from the major issues that emerged from the experience at three extraordinary festivals in recent years:

> **Love Parade in Duisburg, Germany, in 2010**
>
> Berlin's Love Parade grew from a huge outdoor peace party in 1989 to a peak of 1.5 million people in 1999. It moved from Berlin because of noise and overcrowding and found a home in Duisburg, a Ruhr region city of 500,000. In 2010 the free event became a panic-filled tragedy at the music festival venue, an old freight railway station with an estimated 1.4 million attendees. Twenty-one people died and over 350 people were injured when access to and from the site was blocked by the mass of patrons. Subsequently, attention has been drawn to the festival organization's planning, site and security management, and marketing strategies.

| **Pukkelpop Music Festival in Hasselt, Belgium, in 2011** |
|---|
| Two stages (+ equipment) collapsed leading to five deaths and many injuries after a huge storm swept into Belgium's popular festival. Emergency and transport services were mobilized to assist the movement of patrons from the site as patrons and organizers prepared to deal with unforeseen savage weather. |
| **Indiana State Fair in Indianapolis in 2011** |
| Weather again challenged the safety of patrons at an outdoor event resulting in death and material devastation. Close by, another venue evacuated its audience and artists. |
| **Radiohead concert in Toronto, Canada, in 2012** |
| Safety concerns were raised and industry equipment standards questioned when a stage collapsed before a concert where a performer was killed. Stricter guidelines for staging, engineer signoff, weather monitoring, security, and emergency plans were called for. |

## Weather

In communities around the world the imminent arrival of the festival season introduces heightened concern over the vagaries of weather. Locals speculate on scenarios of sunshine, storms, deluges, or extreme or subtle impacts that can affect the festival experience. It behooves organizers to seriously address weather conditions as they prepare their risk or crisis management plans. Wayne Mahar, a weather forecaster and researcher, suggests early identification of risks can ensure a deliberate approach to planning, making considered adjustments, monitoring, and delegation that ensures known calculated responses to potential threats from meteorological disturbances. Have a severe weather plan; determine dedicated personnel to provide the go-to resources, delegate the decision-maker and make sure people know who it is, where they are located, and what authority they command; have precise communication protocols in place for timely responses for staff, audiences, and service providers; use substantial technology (loudspeakers, lights, signals, SMS messaging) to warn of safe evacuations, movement of resources, or delays in programs or transportation; and animate alternative building and site amenities in a timely manner. While historical data may provide guidance for organizers it is essential that official meteorological agencies or professional personnel are connected and can provide advice and inform the action plan. A severe weather plan can take into account wind, tornadoes, lightning, and hail.

The City of Chicago and the concert promoter's 2012 Lollapalooza Severe Weather Plan made emergency decisions a joint process, declaring that "the internal decision to suspend festival activities and move patrons to a safe area rests with the (promoter) C3 Presents partners, in conjunction with City of Chicago Public Safety Officials." It became operational when the music festival was suspended and tens of thousands of fans were evacuated to shelters as the city braced for dangerous storms with high winds in 2012. Many of the fans were told to go to one of three underground parking garages designated as "emergency evacuation shelters."

## Operational Considerations

- **Individual Care.** Amenities and staff to deal with providing services to satisfy health and ethical and safe activities for young people. Facilities to deal with lost and found and those with disabilities require attention.

**162** CHAPTER 7 FESTIVAL RESOURCEFULNESS

- **Communication.** On-site, off-site, international, emergency—all aspects of a communication system that satisfies a multitude of needs for staff and participants and external sources. Technology needs to be top grade and key personnel need skills and experience in dealing with stress. Volunteers can be trained, computers in place, and partnerships with mobile telecommunications and Internet providers are now part of the mosaic.
- **Transport.** Access for staff and participants to all parts of the event site are required for a variety of modes of transport. Marshals are required to ensure the smooth flow for participant parking (bikes, buses, trucks, and cars), adequate space and assistance for unloading at points for dispersal of goods and personnel, and emergency entrances and exits well patrolled and with adequate lighting and signage are all part of a transport strategy.
- **Destination Marketing.** Dealt with within the parameters of the marketing brief, it is important that adequate, interesting, and timely information about the host community and tourism amenities are close to the event. Partner programs may be in place for participants of the event, but material that enhances the image of the destination in which the festival is hosted is a valuable tool for ongoing promotion.
- **Health Services.** Provision of medical care and attention for participants can be maintained at a sound level by the engagement of such services as volunteer ambulance services, sports medicine specialists, or local Red Cross personnel.
- **Ticketing.** Potential clients need to have accurate detailed information to allow them to participate in the event. Tickets may be purchased prior to the event as part of a subscription season, through the Internet, through syndicated box offices, via direct mail, in bulk, or as individual tickets purchased at the door or gate just prior to opening. All ticketing must inform, document, and allow access for the ticketholder. Streamlined access to venues, the use of electronic databases for ongoing promotion of the event, plastic wristbands for ease of entry and exit, stamping, and laminated

Tickets on sale for future events.

cards on lanyards worn around the neck all require attention to detail. Tickets become a memento and part of the souvenir collection process. Tickets/programs are a preshow promotional tool. Ticketing provides the substantial income an event can generate. It requires immense attention to detail in terms of collection and monitoring. It is most often used as a performance indicator of the event's success to all stakeholders.

## Environmental Festival Plan

The natural capital (assets such as land, soil, water, flora and fauna, air) that enterprises have to deal with are diverse and the emphasis specific, but more and more festivals are committing to good practice strategies in an attempt to avoid negative impacts from human exploitation of the environment. Sustainability in an environmental context is front-of-mind when green events are mooted. Considerations to minimize negative impacts are incorporated in policies and practices. We examine a number of initiatives taken up by global festivals to be socially responsible in this chapter's case study. Checklists are developed that position each festival in the best way to address the inevitable tons of waste, damage to landscape, use of electricity and fuel, and $CO_2$ emissions.

What are known as "green events" satisfy increasing numbers of patrons who identify with the global concern for limiting carbon footprints and maintaining a balance of humans within natural and built environments. They save resources through recycling, reusing, and reducing materials used. Most initiatives contribute to the bottom line financially, saving expenditure if partnerships with other "green services" can be negotiated. They satisfy regulatory obligations that are increasingly enforced by statutory authorities and can minimize risk to patrons through unhealthy activity, occupational hazards and liability of organizers. There are also benefits that accrue to the festival in the long term in terms of customer and supplier loyalty and motivation to participate. There is also a growth in formal recognition within the festival and event industry for festivals that are doing the right thing and working to increase awareness by moving away from the novelty value of a "green event" and toward mainstream good practice. Winning an award is also a dynamic promotional tool.

There are expenses associated with good practice. Professional agencies have developed worthy checklists that festivals can use as guidelines for specific plans. Inclusions will reflect on organizational choice of indoor and outdoor venues, equipment ownership or hire, partner policies and priorities, travel and transport arrangements for staff, stores, equipment, patrons, suppliers, entertainment, links to carbon-neutral agencies, promotion of water and water-efficiency techniques, communication of festival aspirations and efforts to all stakeholders prior to the event through some sort of environmental manifesto.

Why do festival managements choose to reuse and recycle?

- Creates a positive image for their event
- Provides savings in disposal and production costs
- Conserves resources and the environment for present and future generations
- Reduces environmental impacts

Providing adequate amenities for festival-goers is critical.

- Changes purchasing and consumption patterns
- Creates employment and supports the growth of the recycling industry and the market for recycled content products.

A wastewise event is one that takes responsibility for waste management by adopting sound purchasing and packaging policies, waste and recycling collection services, and cleanup practices. Special events are particular in their temporary nature, which generates a high volume of disposable materials. A wastewise event will aim to divert the maximum amount of material from being sent to landfills by implementing recycling. Waste reduction is also achieved through early communication with stallholders to ensure they minimize packaging used and that it is either biodegradable or recyclable. Such advice is now well dispersed through agencies in each jurisdiction and festival management needs to work closely with such external partners, like the northeast waste forum in Australia, A Greener Festival, and Yourope.

How can a festival deal with renewable power? Use renewable energy from solar, wind, and biofuel and minimize energy use as much as possible. Organizers can feature some examples of alternative energy at smaller stages around the festival, such as a solar-powered stage, a bicycle-powered dance tent, or a dance floor that generates energy from vibrations when people dance on it. At the Woodford Folk Festival there is a program of tree-planting.

## CASE STUDY

### Maximizing Natural Capital for Festivals

Increasingly organizers recognize the value and importance of a green agenda in their preparation and promotion of their festivals. The concern for the biophysical environment (natural capital) and the impact of massive aggregations of humans on it has encouraged creative and practical responses. Environmental-friendly practices have become a feature of contemporary festivals.

Festivals have provided a forum to cultivate a clearer expression of the public commitment to sustain the environment. There is an educative function to what festivals are increasingly sharing with festival patrons. Outdoor events whether large or small take place on sites that may have little or no appropriate infrastructure, requiring the importation of toilets, fencing, pathways, and parking areas. Community festivals are reliant on teams of volunteers on limited budgets, so making a difference can be problematic, but a few simple things can satisfy the public's expectation that greener events are achievable, protect the environment, and enhance the reputation of the festival. The strategies organizers can employ can mitigate against increasing costs of fuel and transport and achieve a more efficient and economically viable event.

The areas that are attracting responses among organizers to beneficial effect include:

- Having an environmental policy and implementation plan that includes a comprehensive checklist of pre- and post-festival practices as well as actions to be undertaken by teams of staff and volunteers who understand how the festival can best live within the festival's commitment to accepted sustainability principles.
- $CO_2$ emissions derived from power use and transport components impacting the carbon footprint and delivering a carbon-neutral festival by reducing energy use, replacing fossil fuel by avoiding waste, and using renewable sources of energy and neutralizing other emissions by carbon offsetting schemes.
- Choice of venue, construction materials, and equipment used for program and amenities.
- Waste, water, and noise pollution mitigation.
- Recycling bins for bottles, cans, glass, plastic, food containers, and packaging to minimize rubbish accumulation, use of bins for compostable waste.
- Service of food and drink considering food miles, fair trade products, local produce, organic foods, biodegradable containers, cutlery out of recycled materials.
- Partnerships with organizations that demonstrate eco-friendly practices
- Teams of staff and volunteers that encourage audiences to mind how they use the site, amenities, merchandise, and waste management strategies in place; this is part of the partnership with audience, so can be announced on promotional material for the event and be known ahead of time.
- Energy conservation, such as use of energy-efficient bulbs for lighting.
- Use of biodegradable recycled paper with soy ink.
- Camping issues from waste management, soil preparation, sanitary devices, and access to drinking water.

In the United States many festivals demonstrate care and attention to environmental good practice:

- Manchester, Tennessee's Bonnaroo Music and Arts Festival (e.g., Bonnaroo's solar-powered stage presents an eclectic schedule of music, dance, environmental speakers and interactive entertainment)
- California's Coachella Valley Music and Arts Festival (e.g., at random times, random cars with four or more people with a CARPOOLCHELLA on their dash or writ-

ten on their car will be approached for questioning and might possibly win a VIP ticket/pass for life starting in 2013 or one of the other prizes drawn randomly)
- Chicago's Lollapalooza (e.g., Green Street is the face of the Festival's greening initiatives and home of eco-friendly art vendors, nonprofit organizations, and food producers)
- Waterfront Festival in Rockford, Illinois (e.g., implemented a recycling program that has diverted more than 12 tons of recyclables from landfills).

In the United Kingdom a variety of initiatives highlight festival commitments to securing an environmentally sustainable future for itself, including:

- Camp Bestival, Festival Republic, Shambala Festival, Summer Sundae, and Sunrise Celebration are among the first festivals and promoters to join Powerful Thinking, the Green Festival Alliance's first campaign, which aims to reduce energy costs and carbon emissions through increased efficiency and drive the market for renewable energy supply at festivals.
- Standon Calling (e.g., festival is run 100 percent on biodiesel and has composting bathrooms and full waste recycling). It's 100 percent carbon neutral and 98 percent powered by wind, sun, and vegetable oil. As well it features a dog show. Is it the only UK festival to allow dogs on-site. The annual dog show is becoming a firm favorite with festival-goers, although it's probably one of the more chaotic spectacles at the event.
- Shambala Festival is completely free from any kind of sponsorship branding and also emphasizes that they subsidize coach travel as part of their sustainable transport strategy for the family-friendly event.
- Glastonbury Festival. Since 2004 the first load of compost made from organic food waste was spread at Worthy Farm by Michael Eavis. This significant new venture by the festival was the first time a large outdoor event diverted tons of waste, which would otherwise have gone to landfill, and has addressed environmental concerns about the impact of the event.

In summary, the basic principles of "greening" festivals that should be incorporated by the host organization, suggested by Roper (2006) from the document *Leaving a Greening Legacy: Guidelines for Event Greening* prepared by the World Conservation Union of the United Nations Commission on Sustainable Development include:

- Environmental best practices—reduce negative environmental effects by employing technologies and behavioral practices that minimize waste, energy usage, and air and water pollution by utilizing resources sustainably and conserving biological diversity.
- Social and economic development—select options that raise public awareness of environmental issues, involve communities in all levels of decision making, create local jobs, and stimulate urban economies.
- Education and awareness—communicate and explain greening plans and their benefits with the aim of changing public attitudes and future actions.
- Monitoring, evaluation, and reporting—assess the effectiveness of greening activities before, during, and after the major event.
- Leave a positive legacy—ensure that both the short- and long-term impacts of decisions and actions in producing a major event lead to a substantial improvement in environmental sustainability.

Environmental Festival Plan 167

# FROM INSIDE THE MOSAIC

## Observations from the Frontline in Events Development
### William J. O'Toole, CFEE, MEng
### (Project Management) Events Development Specialist

William (Bill) O'Toole is a Founding Director of Event Management Body of Knowledge (EMBOK), advisor to the Event Management International Competency Standard, and a member of the World Board of the International Festivals and Events Association (IFEA).

Bill has worked on the development of events and festival strategies for governments, educational institutions, the events industry, and communities around the world. Among others, he has worked with the Kingdom of Saudi Arabia, the European Union, Dubai Tourism Commerce, Islamic Development Bank, and the Johannesburg Development Corporation. He has trained event staff for the UN in Entebbe and Khartoum and developed the national event forums in Uganda and Kenya. He has been a keynote speaker for the International Festival and Events Association conference in 2010 and national events conferences in Australia, South Africa, Singapore, Dubai, and New Zealand.

As a presenter and teacher in event management, he also consults for public and private organizations for events, including numerous tourism and regional authorities on their event support mechanisms. Bill is not only versed in theory but currently organizes concerts, festivals, and other events around Australia and throughout Asia.

He has coauthored two internationally renowned texts on event management, festival and special event management, and corporate event project management. These textbooks are used for courses around the world and have been translated into Chinese, Korean, Indonesian, and Portuguese. His adaptation of project management to event and festival management as published on his CD-ROM, EPMS.Net, is used for events in the United States, Europe, Australia, and China. Bill's textbook *Events Feasibility and Development* was released in 2011.

One of the major problems in the development of any sector or industry is the lag in information and

William J. O'Toole, CFEE, MEng (Project Management)

hence the lack of data collation and analysis. This is a particular problem with the events sector as it has grown so rapidly and it is such an integral part of the growing economies of the Gulf and China. My role in this has been to assist the development of events. Hence my observations are from the perspective of participant and an "engaged" analyst. In this role, I was fortunate to be at the beginning of the rapid event growth in Dubai and the other Gulf states. I used this experience to inform and assist the growth of events in the Kingdom of Saudi Arabia, Uganda, Jordan, Kenya, and many other cities, companies, government entities, regions, and countries.

My first observation from the frontline is that many events are hidden from the senior officials who make the decisions concerning events. There are events scattered around a country that are unknown to the Government. Every special interest group (SIG) has events. Local antique car owners, for example, already have "meets" where they show off their cars. The local bridge card-playing club has many events. These can be used as the basis of events and festivals. The advantage is that the members of the SIG have a keen interest in the event and will work tirelessly to ensure it is a success. One of the problems in the sustainability of an event or festival is that the organizing team must overcome huge disappointments. To establish a sustainable event may need a few years of disappointment and monetary loss. Individuals quickly burn out if they do not "love" the subject. On the frontline, I have seen too many artificial events (i.e., those that are imposed on the population).

The second observation is that a festival should have income based on the people who benefit from the event. The economy of the event is rarely examined and festival management spends far too much time looking for sponsors or going "cap in hand" to the Government. The result is that the events need constant and increasing funding.

In Saudi Arabia we created events based on the new development in agriculture around the country, hence the Baha Honey Festival, the Al Jouf Olive Festival, and the Khalayja (a biscuit) Festival. These events worked well as they had their industries supporting them. The festival provided a place for the growers and sellers to demonstrate their products. The olive festival developed in seven years to have over half a million visitors. The events were based on two fundamental principles. The olive growers loved their industry and they know how to control the event's economy.

The third observation is the four big mistakes I have seen around the world. These are:

1. Focusing on mega events and forgetting they are built upon micro events
2. Outsourcing events with no cost/benefit or risk analysis
3. Not using event experts to assess the feasibility of major events
4. Assuming that everyone is an expert in events and festivals

Mega events, such as the well-known car races, are often sold on the basis of huge benefits to the host country. The host country is too often unaware of the costs of these mega events and, in the excitement of the sales pitch, they forget their financial duties and procurement and risk management policies. Of course the event seller will not correctly assess the cost of the event. In all other areas of procurement, the host country, city, or company will have experts and guidelines for the assessment of a proposal. The concept of the contract gatekeeper is essential in the procurement process. Too often it is forgotten with the events and festivals. One of the reasons I found is that everyone seems to be an expert in events! Events and festivals are high risk with huge costs and benefits. It needs professionals to assess this.

This situation is frighteningly common around the world and the solution is to treat the events as assets. Most organizations and government departments have an asset management policy. The event, as an asset, has a return on investment. Like any asset, this return is commercial, social capital, and goodwill (also called brand). The asset may not have a positive return for years. It may have to be devolved or improved as the years go by. It may be outsourced or developed in-house. It must have project and risk management as support for the innovation and creativity that ultimately gives the greatest return on the investment.

## Festival Ideas and Issues

1. What loyalty marketing programs could be assembled to ensure the festival organization builds its customer base and increases festival attendances?
2. What should be included in a festival environmental policy?
3. What are the key characteristics of a project manager?
4. There should be worldwide standardized regulations for safety, particularly at outdoor venues for public entertainment. Discuss the implications of industry changes to ensure avoidance of tragic accidents.
5. What is the media's role in ensuring responsibility and accountability for event misadventure in the public domain?
6. Examine the experiences of audiences during and after tragic festival incidents. How can festival organizations and partners mitigate negative impacts and deal with fallout from audience responses? A negative reputation can be bad for business. How do festival organizers avoid controversies, protect their reputation, and build their social license to operate in a way that doesn't tarnish their stature? If they choose to maintain their position in the marketplace, what must they do to regain any lost esteem?

## Festival Focus Activities

1. Analyze attendance data collected at a festival with which you are familiar and identify opportunities to assist the organization to attract and retain the loyalty of festival patrons. What sort of incentives could be offered?
2. Design and document a communication schedule to build relationships with existing patrons and reach out to attract potential festival patrons. How can you collect useful data for ongoing marketing purposes ensuring permission and privacy guidelines are met? How can you achieve this in an informative, convenient, and timely manner?
3. Research the *Greener Festival Awards* and review the criteria used to assess each category. Investigate practices at the festivals successful in 2011 and appraise their initiatives.

    Forty-six festivals across the UK, Europe, Australia, and North America have been awarded the prestigious Greener Festival Award for their green efforts in reducing their environmental impact in 2011. To achieve the award, each festival must complete a detailed 53-part questionnaire; submit relevant information such as a carbon footprint, traffic plans, and waste and recycling management schemes; and undergo an independent environmental audit.

The winners of the Greener Festival Award 2011 are:

| Outstanding | Highly commended |
|---|---|
| Croissant Neuf Summer Party (England) | Bestival (England) |
| Falls Festival, Lorne, Victoria (Australia) | Bonnaroo (U.S.) |
| Falls Festival, Marion Bay, Tasmania (Australia) | Co-operative Cambridge Folk Festival (England) |
| Isle of Wight Festival (England) | Glastonbury Festival (England) |
| Lightning in a Bottle (U.S.) | Grassroots (Jersey) |
| Oya Festival (Norway) | Lollapalooza (U.S.) |
| Peats Ridge (Australia) | Malmo Festival (Sweden) |
| Shambala (England) | Island Vibe (Australia) |
| Sunrise Celebration (England) | SOS 4:8 (Spain) |
| We Love Green (France) | |
| **Commended** | **Improving** |
| Austin City Limits (U.S.) | Camp Bestival (England) |
| Calgary Folk Music Festival (Canada) | Download (England) |
| East Coast Bluesfest (Australia) | Greenbelt Festival (England) |
| Festibelly (England) | Hard Rock Calling (England) |
| Heineken Dia de la Musica (Spain) | Lounge on the Farm (England) |
| Ilosaaririock (Finland) | Radio 1 Big Weekend (England) |
| Hadra Trance Festival (France) | Wireless (England) |
| The Open Air Festival (Czech Republic) | |
| Rock for People (Czech Republic) | |
| San Sebastián Quincena Musical (Spain) | |
| Sonisphere (England) | |
| Splendour Festival (England) | |
| Splendour in the Grass (Australia) | |
| Summer Sundae Weekender (England) | |
| T-in-the-Park (Scotland) | |
| Waveform (England) | |
| Welcome to the Future (Netherlands) | |
| WomAdelaide (Australia) | |

4. Reflect on the outdoor sites of festivals with which you are familiar. What are the key topographical features and how are they incorporated into the activities planned by a specific festival? Has the site been utilized for planned public events for a long period of time and have there been any infrastructure modifications during the period? If it is a historic site, can it be linked to local stories, community experts, and cultural heritage? What harm minimization strategies have festival organizers employed?
5. Conduct a survey at a local festival, utilizing the indicators listed below, and any others you could consider from your reading and experience. From the checklist, what do you observe about the take-up of green credentialing?

- Recyclable/biodegradable plates, cutlery, and cups
- Local/organic foods recycling
- Glass recycling
- Paper and cardboard use
- Monitoring of recycling
- Promotion of public transit, bicycling, or carpooling
- Carbon offsets for performer travel
- Bike lock-up area
- Green electricity
- Building materials reused/donated
- Green measures publicized
- Promotion of local green initiatives
- Donation to local environmental initiatives
- Other initiatives

6. Examine a balance sheet from a festival's annual report and analyze the income and expenditure against common practice to ensure ongoing solvency and investment in future festivals. What are the key features you notice?

# Suggested Reading

Asia-Pacific Centre for Philanthropy and Social Investment. *How the Wealthy Give: Comparisons between Australia and Comparable Countries (USA, Britain and Canada).* Petre Foundation, Melbourne, Australia: Swinburne University of Technology. www.swinburnephilanthropy.web. 2004.

Australia Business Arts Foundation (AbaF) and Australia Council for the Arts. Arts and Business: Partnerships that Work. Sydney http://2014.australiacouncil.gov.au/__data/assets/pdf_file/0006/77730/AbaF_AusCouncil_researchreport_22Jul_draft10FINAL.pdf, 2010.

Dodds, R., and S. Graci. *Greening of the Pride Toronto Festival: Lessons Learned*, Tourism Culture and Communication, Vol. 12, no. 1, Cognizant, 9–38, 2012.

Dredge, D., and M. Whitford. "Policy for sustainable and responsible festivals and events: Institutionalisation of a new paradigm—a response." *Journal of Policy Research in Tourism, Leisure and Events* 2, no. 1 (2010): 1–13.

Goldblatt, S. *Greener Events*, in *Special Events: A New Generation and the Next Frontier* (6th ed.), ed. J. Goldblatt (Hoboken, NJ: Wiley, 2011).

Jones, M. *Sustainable Event Management: A Practical Guide*. London, UK: Earthscan, 2010.

Mahar, W., "Weather, the Most Important Thing,… But…," IFEA's ie: the business of international events, (International Festivals and Events magazine), 30–31, Summer 2012.

McCarthy, K. F., and K. Jinnett. *A New Framework for Building Participation in the Arts*. San Diego, CA: RAND Corporation, 2001.

Musgrave, J., and R. Raj. *Event Management and Sustainability: Introduction to a Conceptual Framework for Sustainable Events*. Wallingford, UK: CAB International, 2009.

O'Toole, W. J. *Events Feasibility and Development*. London, UK: Routledge, 2011.

O'Toole, W. J. *Event Project Management System*. London, UK: Routledge, 2012.

Parry, A. ISO 20121 Set to Transform the Events Industry. 2012. http://www.eventindustrynews.co.uk/festivals-outdoor-event-news/iso-20121-set-to-transform-the-events-industry/.

Positive Solutions. *Arts Plus: New Models, New Money*. International Research, 2009.

Roper, T. "Producing environmentally sustainable Olympic Games and 'Greening' major public events." Global Urban Development 2, no. 1 (2006). http://www.globalurban.org/GUDMag06Vol2Iss1/Roper.htm.

Tomlinson, R., and T. Roberts. *Full House: Turning Data into Audiences*. Australian Council for the Arts, 2006.

Trapnell, S. *Capitalising Your Organisation to Achieve Artistic Vision and Impact*. Los Angeles, USA: Arts Consulting Group, Inc., 2012.

Wright, K. *Generosity versus Altruism: Philanthropy and Charity in the US and UK*. Civil Society Working Paper 17, Centre for Civil Society, London, 2002.

# CHAPTER 8

# Ensuring Creativity at All Levels of Festival-Making

Creativity and innovation are normally complementary activities, since creativity generates the basis of innovation, which, in its development, raises difficulties that must be solved once again, with creativity. ... It is not possible to conceive innovation without creative ideas, as these are the starting point.

—*European Commission (1998)*

---

This chapter provides an opportunity for you to better understand:

- How festival stakeholders actively engage with creativity in all aspects of festival preparation and presentation, especially focusing on imaginative, original, inventive, and resourceful approaches

- The application of innovation through highlighting exemplars that distinctively represent new and traditional ways to think, problem-solve, inspire, entertain, and educate by drawing together human, natural, and financial capital to excite interest from audiences over time

- The roles of meaning and design in festival-making

---

This chapter explores the creativity and innovation that is demonstrated by enduring festivals. It recognizes the mosaic dimensions of the personal and professional passion of festival partners and the interface of invention, resourcefulness, imagination, intuition, ideas, and curiosity and how each contributes to distinctive design and delivery of satisfying festivals. Chapter 9 deals with implications of creativity on tangible and intangible elements for memorable experiences for all partners. By exploring creative problem-solving techniques employed by festival organizers, we can assess the interdisciplinary nature of specific aspects of festival vision, program design and content, service provision, site management, and relationships with partners. The elements of the mosaic presented in Figure 8.1 offer a framework for our investigation.

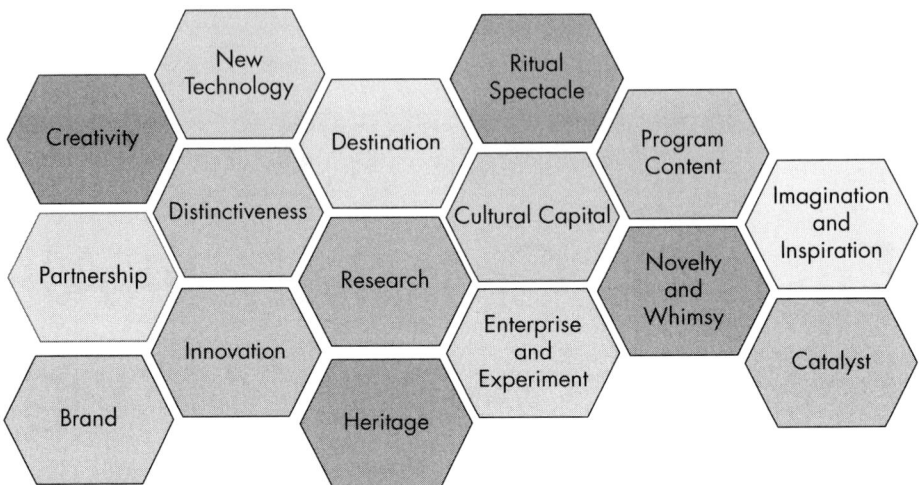

**Figure 8.1** A Creative Festival Mosaic.

In much commentary, the terms *creativity* and *innovation* are used interchangeably. Creativity is a fundamental core to innovation. Creativity doesn't operate independently, it requires application and that's where innovation steps in. The very nature of enduring festivals is the capacity of each to demonstrate relevance to existing patrons and to satisfy and attract new ones. The process of review and refreshment allows knowledge to inform and accommodate change to meet the needs of festival partners, so the festival not only survives, but also thrives. To best deal with internal and external circumstances a creative and innovative approach is required.

## Start with the Heart

There is a view that each festival is the specific creation of an organization's artistic director or festival producer. Individual passion, intuition, skills, and professional experience influences the director's own artistic vision. According to Brett Sheehy (Adams, 2012), a veteran festival director, this separates each festival from, say, just being another international festival in a city. This mitigates any homogenization of festivals, the fact that each artistic director has a very distinct and unique voice. Sheehy suggests that the quirks and foibles of each pertain directly to the taste and judgment of the festival director and aren't necessarily part of any specific groundswell of change in contemporary festival culture. With contractual arrangements in place for festival CEOs or Artistic Directors, the turnover of direct input ensures adaption and change.

Festivals need to be representative *of* their host destination and it is important that festival directors recognize how best to match a program to the cultural identity of their community and its cultural practitioners. You have observed that there is not a one-size-fits-all approach taken by successful festival leaders, as they seek to provide a meaningful and distinctive. With the proliferation of festivals globally, the mobility of audiences and artists, it behooves festival directors to design bold and attractive features for their festival.

Festivals themselves are, by their very nature, about change. Art reflects and comments on social and cultural issues of the time, but as well as collections and gatherings of creative types, arts festivals are also enormous commercial enterprises. Even the location of the festival makes an impact on its direction. [In Australia] Sydney Festival is a more outdoorsy, summery, holiday atmosphere enterprise, while the Melbourne Festival is focused indoors—outside entertainment in Melbourne in October is rarely feasible, because of the weather. (Adams, 2012)

Creative leaders in the cultural festival sector, as we discussed earlier, successfully demonstrate a capacity to take risks in a fragile environment, have self-assurance and self-respect, have current industry knowledge (though they don't need to be practicing artists), are able to synthesize data from diverse sources and are able to nourish the contributions that can be made by communities of practice with which their festival is associated. What each has observed is that their commitment and the focus they bring to bear over long periods of time is hard work. They come as individuals with dreams, curiosity, potent ideas, experience, stories, and feelings that infuse the direction each festival takes each time a planning cycle is engaged.

## Explaining Creativity

The work of Keith Sawyer in *Group Genius: The Creative Power of Collaboration* (2007) demonstrates the creative power of collaboration evident in making successful festivals. Often innovation is ascribed to a broader organizational situation. Sawyer has identified seven key characteristics of effective creative teams determined to be innovative:

- Innovation emerges over time
- Successful collaborative teams practice deep listening
- Team members build on their collaborators' ideas
- Only over a period of time do the meaning and significance of each idea become clear
- Surprising (i.e., unforeseen) ideas emerge
- Innovation is inefficient (trial and error, frequent false starts and detours, dry wells)
- Innovation emerges from the bottom up

An initiative undertaken in Adelaide, the capital of the state of South Australia that brands itself as The Festival State (a tagline on all state vehicle registration plates), involves the collaboration between the city's biggest festivals. The director of the Womadelaide music event leads the city's 10 major festivals that have joined forces under the banner of a new organization called Festivals Adelaide. The coalition includes the Adelaide Festival, the Fringe, Comeout and the Cabaret, Film, and Guitar Festivals. The expected benefits of such a collaboration in terms of marketing, economies of scale, resource-sharing, staff training, shared research and knowledge exchange and brand awareness are similar to the Festivals Edinburgh initiative in Scotland and the clusters of community festivals in Florida such as Sarasota for Free.

Sawyer's review of the research into creativity developed in *The Science of Human Innovation: Explaining Creativity* (2012) offers two definitions. The first is an individualistic definition where creativity is a new mental combination that is expressed in the world. He suggests (p. 7) its basic requirement is that *a creative thought or action is novel or original; it is a combination*, as all thoughts and concepts are combinations of existing thoughts and concepts; and that creativity must be *expressed in the world* because if they can't be or understood they remain unknowable. It would be like blinking in the dark!

The second definition is of a sociocultural nature, as creativity is the generation of a product that is judged to be novel and also to be appropriate, useful, or valuable by a suitably knowledgeable social group. He further explores the features of Western cultural models of creativity and notes 10 beliefs that you may wish to evaluate in light of festival ideas, products, and services you have investigated. What evidence can you identify to support any of these points? They are:

1. The essence of creativity is the moment of insight.
2. Creative ideas emerge mysteriously from the unconscious.
3. Creativity is more likely when you reject convention.
4. Creative contributions are more likely to come from an outsider than an expert.
5. People are more creative when they are alone.
6. Creative ideas are ahead of their time.
7. Creativity is a personal trait.
8. Creativity is based in the right brain.
9. Creativity and mental illness are connected.
10. Creativity is a healing, life-affirming activity.

## Creativity and Innovation

It can be argued that creativity involves the generation of new ideas or the recombination of known elements into something new. While they come from the same place, creativity serves an idea-production purpose while innovation is about translating ideas into action. In the commentary among enterprises now committed to delivering on both creativity and innovation to address their vision, the interlinking of the inspiration that comes from brainstorming, for example, with a process that encourages alternative possibilities to a third area that looks for solutions that are tied to specific festival objectives. This iterative process allows for the changes we have already observed that festival organizers need to address.

You may wish to follow the research of Margaret Boden (1998) who discusses three types of creativity through known elements making something new, providing valuable solutions to identified problems and involving motivations and emotions (Figure 8.2). All apply to festival-making. She suggests three main types of creativity, involving different ways of generating the novel ideas:

- The *combinational* creativity that involves new combinations of familiar ideas.
- The *exploratory* creativity that involves the generation of new ideas by the exploration of structured concepts.
- The *transformational* creativity that involves the transformation of some dimension of the structure, so that new structures can be generated.

Richard Florida in *The Rise of the Creative Class Revisited* (2012) examines the multifaceted processes involved with individual and social creativity. Festivals can represent a creative

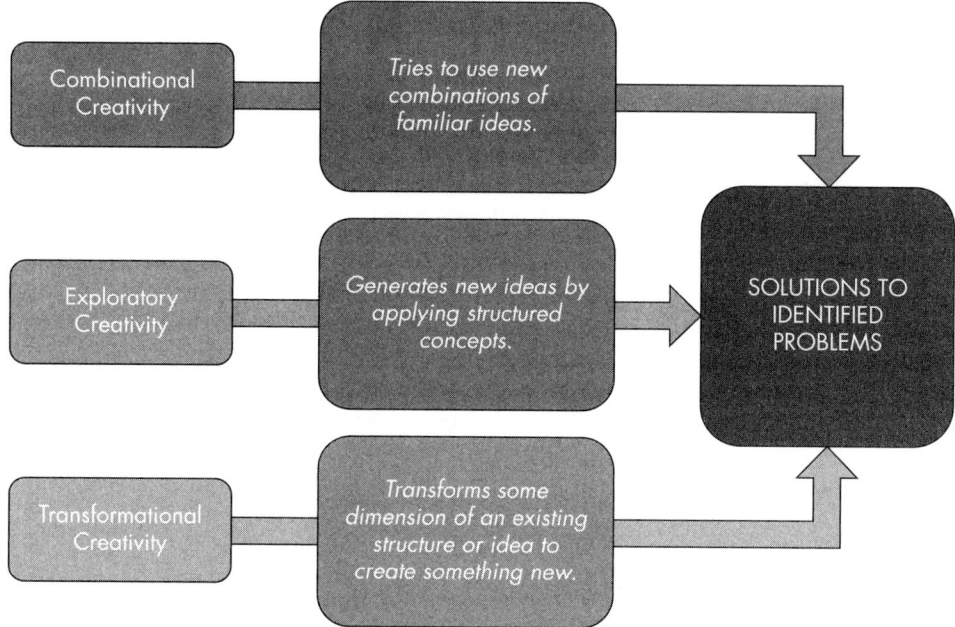

**Figure 8.2** Types of Creativity. Based on Boden (1998).

ethos through organizational workplace culture built on shared values, by meeting community expectations, and by reinforcing the power of celebration as a medium of education, entertainment, cultural development, and economic stimulus. Risk-taking is inherent in innovation. Much is written about how success regularly emerges from failures along the way. In making festivals there can be incremental steps taken over time to apply sophisticated creative solutions by ordinary people. There are extraordinary people in the festival sector too and the creative thinking festivals sustain is generally ascribed to four festival design elements.

Professor Don Getz draws together recent research in *Event Studies: Theory, Research and Policy for Planned Events* (2007) into the four areas of:

- Festival setting—site and venues
- Festival theme and program design
- Service provision
- Consumables

These provide a central scaffold upon which the practical tools hang for organizers to demonstrate their capacity to be creative and innovative (Table 8.1). Each festival program director considers a portfolio of choices to satisfy audiences dependent on connections with past festivals, having conducted a SWOT (strengths, weaknesses, opportunities, threats) analysis of existing resources, experiences, and potential appeal of the key themes underpinning the whole festival. Program design, for example, is both a technical and creative exercise. It takes into consideration the lifecycle of festival-making that impacts choices in each domain. Documentation of past festival feedback and experiences informs decisions made in preparation of the stimulating sense of celebration. It builds on the unique selling proposition (USP) delivered over previous festivals.

| General Categories | Examples | General Categories | Examples |
|---|---|---|---|
| **Festival setting,** site and venues, layout and décor, ambience, access, crowd management, signage, information, technical expression of themes, budgetary considerations, host community response | Accessible indoor/outdoor sites, purpose built, improvised, heritage, contemporary, sensory stimulation through lighting, sound, color, movement, aesthetic, taste, touch, mapping, intimate and open spaces, crowd density | **Festival theme and program design,** core theme made manifest, active and passive engagements through content, entertainment, interpretation, learning, humor | Schedule distributed prior and during festival, based on concept accepted by all partners, offers meaning to audience, culturally acceptable, stimulating program offering wonder, mystery, distinctiveness, ritual, the wow factor, continuity with past festivals, authenticity |
| **Service provision,** sequencing tasks, design associated with safety and security, artists involved, hospitality, staff and volunteer support, camping, technology, communications | Planning to ensure quality exposure to amenities, program, links to external support agencies, ensuring quality experiences with safe materials and practices to secure audience engagement, contingencies | **Consumables,** food and beverage preparation and distribution, merchandising, general commerce, gifts, souvenirs, exhibitions, not just commodities, but support connections to partner inputs | Best fit with planned experience for audiences to ensure on-site satisfaction of host/guest relationship through items that can be exchanged |

**Table 8.1** Festival Framework
*Based on Getz (2007).*

These choices may influence how human and technical resources are to be employed. Audiences can be controlled through the content of the program. Experienced festival directors bear in mind the perspectives of others. For those who may be attending a festival (regardless of type, location, theme, etc.) for the first time, the experience may have an enormous impact on their personal and professional lives. The spectator or the participant (performer, patron, supplier, host community) may regard their involvement as a great opportunity. If the program is delivered well, the impact will be positive for all concerned, otherwise it can become an unpleasant experience.

## Festival Programs

Festival organizers want to create an event that is different, special, or better than any other, local or distantly located. They will ensure there is adequate time available to plan effectively for a dynamic program with each component attended to comfortably within the whole festival schedule. The program will be designed so that interest is maintained throughout for staff and participants and the program is not so tight as to cause anxiety, breeches of safety, or lack of audience satisfaction. Program components that could be regarded as socially unacceptable or that contravene legislation need to be addressed.

All festivals are themed in some way, as they celebrate things that are valued, of interest, or are aspired to by the target market. The program content provides a unifier for the participants and underpins all aspects of the experience. Creating a theme is hard work and has its own creative journey. There are many distractions for festival audiences, and directors need to derive a coherent, accessible festival theme from commonly held views and bodies of

Lanterns, costumes, and masks attract participants as part of the Lismore Lantern Parade.

knowledge that will maintain the patrons' interest. The theme can be overtly expressed in a number of ways through logos, signage, parades, and mascots; in the setting and site design; with uniforms and distinctive outfits worn by staff and volunteers: through activities and attractions and entertainments and celebrities; in specific local food and beverages; through merchandise for sale; in consistent advertising formats on multiple media platforms, and by highlighting benefits for targeted partners.

The success and complexity of a festival is not judged solely by its level (local or international), scale, scope, or longevity, or simply from the number of attendees. Those preparing the festival need to demonstrate capacities for the minutiae in such domains as creative problem solving, planning, organizing, motivating, communicating, and controlling to deliver comprehensive and memorable experiences. There can be tensions between professional,

An example of themes from a Danish cultural festival based on the idea of integrating the coastal environment in the presentation of contemporary art, specifically, unique tidal differences are utilized to stage a range of performances. (Manifest of the Wadden Sea Festival Denmark, 2008)

- You will see nature, you did not know existed
- You will experience something unforgettable
- You will find simplicity in what you thought to be complicated
- You will perceive connections, you did not know existed
- You will feel compelled to discover your inner Spring Tide again

Liburd and Derkzen (2009, p. 133)

Promotional banner for Swell Sculpture Festival, Gold Coast, Queensland, Australia.

The Swell Sculpture Festival, in Currumbin Beach, Queensland, Australia, is a free exhibition, open all hours with a selection of sculptures. At night they are lit up under the southern sky. It inspires, amuses, uplifts, and captures the hearts and minds of all who visit. Over 10 days, visitors can experience the sculptures, enjoy twilight walks and informative artist talks, discover new perspectives at the Public Art Forum, wander through the Swell Smalls Gallery; and participate in artist master classes and children's' workshops. It is staying true to its mantra "getting art out there."

amateur, and recreational partners; competitive versus noncompetitive models; indoor versus outdoor setting; degree of involvement by participants or spectators; price structures to be implemented, whether the event is offered free versus paid admission or whether there are tangible and intangible products and services being sold and consumed by visitors. Each decision must provide the patron with an opportunity for seamless engagement with the festival's overall vision.

## Festival Sites

Festival organizers have particular locations in their sights that they believe will match the psychographic needs of their audience with the festival program. The proximity of venues to amenities, transport, and infrastructure contributes to appropriate site selection. Traditional, purpose-built sites that have sufficient capacity to deal with anticipated audiences may be selected, or improvised alternative venues may be considered, so long as all the technical, safety, and crowd-control issues can be dealt with. Many festival sites are street based (for parades, markets, multiple-stage entertainments) and revitalize quiet downtown urban areas.

Camping is an integral part of the audience experience at popular festivals.

Each venue site has its own idiosyncrasies to be addressed. Access, placement of amenities, entrances to festival sites, parking for cars and buses, walking paths, and disability access are important considerations. The human scale of the event in terms of the size of venue, relevance to goals and vision, and distance between attractions and amenities is important. Principles and processes used in urban planning, heritage management, and traditional land use may also be issues in the choice of a site and effective management of it.

This includes the provision of appropriate shade, shelter, and seating for attendees. Parades are an attractive feature of festivals, but spectators need to be relaxed and comfortable. There needs to be good sight lines, access for performers, toilets, first-aid facilities, childcare, food and beverage outlets, and places for stalls and concessions that may be merchandising items for the duration. Detailed plans need to be available in a timely fashion to staff, media, and the community clearly outlining the location of activity, layout of amenities, and routes for processions and street performance to guide the flow of traffic efficiently. Comprehensive planning by organizers addresses crowd control, evacuation strategies, and emergency procedures.

Adequate facilities need to be available for storage and loading for material required during the run of the event. Items need to be secured, particularly if the event is in an open space, subject to pressure from people, or vulnerable to weather changes. Security may involve lighting, human resources, dogs, or other techniques.

Many festivals provide camping. This can necessitate satellite sites for aspects of the program and service provision. A clean, healthy environment with substantial pathways, ablution blocks, well-lit night access, and effective waste management need to be in place. Satellite sites require the replication of information-sharing through clear signage, notice boards, ticketing, gatekeepers, and security personnel.

## Festival Technologies

The technology palette available to festival design and content expands daily. It is important that the technology applied to materials, machinery and equipment, communication, hygiene, media requirements, buildings, fabrications, stages, security, and open spaces are matched with the style and purpose of festival. Technology attracts attention and patrons and improves communication. Communication systems utilized within the festival

| Mobile staging | Laser light shows | Customized festival management software for volunteer, finance, planning, and scheduling |
|---|---|---|
| Tension fabrics | Flat screens | Specific apps for smartphones |
| Hydraulic stages | Pyrotechnic and special effects, LED lighting, digital lighting, projectors | Interactive media for internal and external communication |
| Photo booths | Digital signage | Crowd simulators as "what if" logistics for normal and emergency situations |
| Novelty inflatables | Seating, tents, folding furniture, torches, parade barriers, shade makers | Data capture and archival documentation |

**Table 8.2** Technology and Logistical Options

organization and available to patrons through, for example, Wifi, allows the distribution of images and content globally and instantaneously. New technologies help minimize pollution, encourage efficiencies that enhance natural light and acoustics, boost existing equipment, and encourage employment for available local technical labor. The advances in audiovisual, lighting, and sound technologies, special effects like fireworks, projections, lasers, and LED for use of music and entertainment demand efficient secure power sources, well distributed and controlled by professional and licensed personnel.

The new materials that now inhabit the technological and logistical arena for festival organizations make for some challenging choices for organizers. Keeping abreast of appropriate new products and services, prices of purchase or hire, and resource-sharing options' availability is important with specialist knowledge held either within the organization or from consultants who advise on all aspects of festival management. Table 8.2 is a list of recent additions to the palette of technology and logistic options employed in indoor and outdoor festival sites.

## Post-Event Issues

Then there's the cleanup! The post-event task of cleaning up the site, returning hired or borrowed equipment, and restoring the site to a reasonable condition takes as much creative planning as other elements of the event's production. It is how the host community will remember the event. The disposal of waste, the lack of litter, the repair of damage to existing equipment, and the removal of signage all need to be addressed. It is essential to tie up the exercise with a careful acquittal of all contractual obligations relating to the site, the provision of services, and the use of equipment. If the festival was recorded the documentation can be shared with the host community for promotion, or legal purposes or online for future merchandising.

## Festival Design

There are technical, aesthetic, and creative aspects to designing a successful festival. Often festivals endure simply because creativity and innovation are front and center in

Explaining Creativity   **183**

Beach sculpture as part of Swell Sculpture Festival, Gold Coast, Queensland, Australia.

the design process. Irrespective of a festival's core platform, its scale, theme, location, duration, and partners, there needs to be attention to maximizing distinctiveness for targeted audiences. By generating a blueprint that engages audiences with clear embedded motifs and a sound matching style, the festival patrons' experience will be enhanced. The intention of the festival must be clearly represented in all aspects of program development, marketing, and on-site build to ensure the audience expectation is met.

## Creative Choice Spectrum

There is a spectrum of choices and decisions organizers embrace as they determine the themes that deliver their vision for the festival (Table 8.3). They need to understand the local circumstances and generate a good match that can offer a catalyst over the long term for community engagement, building a destination brand, positioning the festival top of mind for repeat visitation, and accommodate the creativity expected from within the organization and between the festival partners.

## 2012 LONDON OLYMPICS

The Opening Ceremony of the 2012 Olympic Games in London was a phenomenon of mega proportions and demonstrated clearly the dynamic elements of festival creativity, design, and innovation. At each stage audiences inside the stadium, others in outdoor locations across the city, and global spectators on diverse media platforms could gain an appreciation of the vision of the ceremony director, film and theater director Danny Boyle, but also the aspiration of the athletes, the host nation, and the Olympic organization. The complexity of the brief obviously dealt with all aspects of the creative problem-solving paradigm, engagement with diverse human resources, the technical and design components and their installation and activation, the physical setting, the audience safety and security, and the virtual distribution of an experience. The sensory engagements resonated for all—participants and spectators—just "being there" and through the use of ritual, narrative, novelty, humor, cultural awareness, spectacle, and engagement with the arts and ingenious groundbreaking technologies.

Commentators around the world seemed swept up with the festival spirit introduced by the ceremony. There was recognition that

| | |
|---|---|
| Stillness < > Movement | Indoor < > Outdoor |
| Light < > Darkness | Free access < > Ticketed access |
| Sound < > Silence | Niche segmented target market < > Open to anyone |
| Low tech < > High tech | Spectator < > Active participation |
| Curated festival program content < > Free-flowing input on theme | Daytime < > Nighttime |
| Sacred < > Profane | Large-scale environment < > Small-scale intimate environment |
| Narrative < > Dispersed | Elite < > General public |
| Ritual < > Unconventional | Traditional content < > Risky experimental new works |
| Symbol < > Brand | Local artists < > Imported renowned entertainment |
| Innovation < > Imitation | Humor, whimsy, comedy < > Serious, drama |
| Costume < > Informal/contemporary dress | Real < > Virtual |
| Competition < > Cooperation | Outside broadcast < > Podcast |
| Specific theme < > Carte blanche input | |

**Table 8.3** Examples of Creative Spectrums

## The Business of Creativity

In an attempt to glean the most promising ideas from within the festival organization, management can be innovative in its approach. These ideas might solve problems that are encountered each time the festival's strategic and tactical plans are mobilized. There are a

preparations over the previous seven years had been painstaking, that the theme of "Inspire a Generation" was effectively represented, the soundtrack was inextricably linked to the storytelling and the energy of the volunteer and professional performers, and the epic nature of the athletic aspiration could be appropriated to the director's slyly subversive rendering of heritage, cultural alertness, contemporary technologies, and communal delight of the host community.

The celebration comprised massive amounts of new technology that transformed the stadium, with LED lights as the river of molten steel and colored patches in the stands that allowed the audience to become an integral part in the staging below. The Olympic cauldron's massive, intricate design was inclusive of the 204 separate nations participating and provided a strong symbol for the formal elements of the ceremony of flag-carrying and -hoisting. The Queen's cameo role in the proceedings took celebrity to new heights and focused the dimensions of elevation on display from pyrotechnics, balloons released with cameras attached to beam back images from the stratosphere, to aerial performers to give texture to the tapestry of color, movement, sound, and silence. There were pinpoint intimate moments in the vast space and rousing all-in singing with living iconic musicians. The Isles of Wonder theme resoundingly represented through Caliban's speech from Shakespeare's "The Tempest"—"*be not afeared: the isle is full of noises*"! And then there was the march of the athletes!

number ways to approach creative problem solving within organizations, especially with a focus on transforming the most promising ideas into effective solutions. A random selection of strategies could include:

- Openness to new, blue-sky thinking among employees
- Igniting creative sparks within your organization through celebrations, a field trip, events, brainstorming and think tanks
- Building a vibrant research and development strategy in your organization without spending a fortune
- Incentivizing and rewarding great ideas through diverse teams within and between festival partners
- Creative people clustering through curiosity that reveals current situations and proposes alternatives
- Encouraging rituals as a set of actions, performed mainly for their symbolic value that emerges from the positive organizational culture
- Documenting ideas for implementation now and later through an accessible and sustainable communication management system

To achieve a successful festival the organization needs to predict what this success looks like. Once this is determined, systems can be prepared to ensure it is carefully documented (online, on a notice board, celebrated and reported to senior management). It can then inform the ongoing references to the indicators. Festival teams can learn from any misadventures encountered and the creative thinking employed can be fine-tuned along the way as challenges arise. Of course there are marked differences in contexts for community cultural festivals, compared to large-scale commercial specialist arts festivals, but by enhancing the creativity of the team's aspirations, their thinking, experiences, resilience under pressure, confidence in their intuition, and collaboration, a clear trajectory can emerge.

## Festival Creativity Trajectory

To accommodate the creativity trajectory, many festival organizations are building customized business and operational systems. A planning framework is outlined in Figure 8.3 indicating the strategic and tactical approaches that can be taken. Digital platforms offer the technology now for management to streamline their communication, scheduling, and workforce management through specifically tailored software, designed either from inside the organization or through off-the-shelf commercial products. Data can be better managed across all the teams within and between the festival staff and volunteers. They feel empowered when they have access to all the information required to ensure their contribution matches the set goals and they can deliver set performance predictors. Many commercial products can be massaged to ensure specific needs within each festival enterprise are satisfied.

Some festivals use digital communication tools—apps, for example, for personal tablets and smartphones—so that audiences can also keep abreast of festival development before, during, and after the event. Patrons can create their personal festival planner to schedule access to their favored program elements, make bookings, and watch videos of artists. They can download their own schedule and maps and keep their social circle informed of their activities and become virtual ambassadors for the festival. The Canadian Tulip Festival has partnered with Purple Forge to create a mobile application for the iPhone that allows users to create postcards on-the-fly by selecting their own stamps, themes, and photographs of the festival that can be shared with their friends using email, Twitter, or Facebook. It can combine with event schedules, video, a QR code scanner, and weather information.

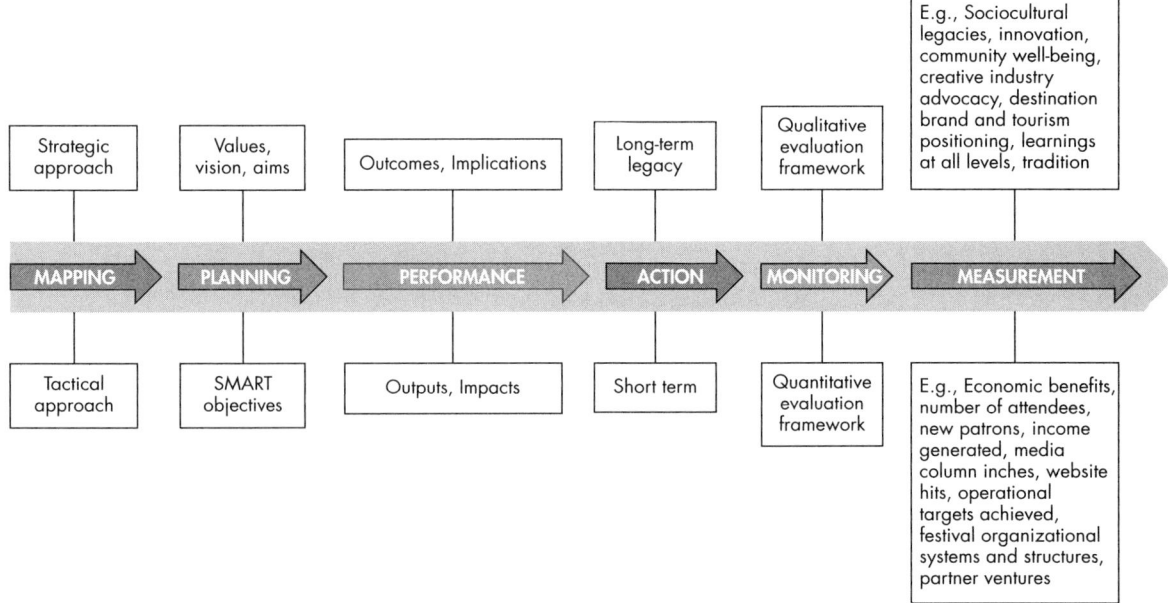

**Figure 8.3** Planning for Creativity.
*Derrett (2013).*

## Interrogate Trends for Inspiration

By being linked to domestic and international organizations like the International Festival and Events Association (IFEA), the European Festivals Association (EFA), the British Arts Festivals Association (BAFA), and local destinations' collaborations like Edinburgh Festivals (Scotland), ideas can be exchanged. You will observe that festival organizers that are responding to the distributed digital forms of intelligence have recognized the globalization of the festival sector. Festival directors attend one another's festivals and collaborate with their international peers, while promoters of entertainment develop tours for artists among their colleagues in diverse locations. We live in a networked age. Networks encourage like-minded people to experiment with boundaries, whereas conventional and long-standing practices can retard the application of good ideas. Innovation generally means doing things differently and while many festival organizations despair as their energies focus on financial capital, innovation works well when the focus moves to the social capital inherent within the organization and across the network of practitioners across the globe (Table 8.4).

As has been discussed earlier, ongoing professional development by festival employees through internships, exchanges, and site visits provide opportunities to seek inspiration and test possibilities prior to introducing them into the mainstream culture of the home festival. This can range from experience with experts who share knowledge of staging technicians, technical managers, designers, project managers, art installers, and special effects designers. Their knowledge is based on principles of science, engineering, construction, and communications management. It will also encompass live performance environments such as those found in theaters and outdoor and improvised venues. Research indicates that Gen-Y-ers appear to have a natural disposition to be creative thinkers and are willing to be bold and take responsibility for making change happen within organizations, so exposure to alternatives elsewhere can ultimately benefit the festival of origin in delivery of distinctive programs, settings, administration, and legacy.

Change has been evident in many festivals over time and some festival organizers have retrofitted some program elements as new generations seek to explore their heritage. In 1935

| **Lollapalooza** |
|---|
| One of the United States' leading music festivals, Lollapalooza has in recent years broadened its geographical horizons. The original festival hosted by Chicago now shares its vision and content with festivals in Brazil, Chile, and Tel Aviv. |
| **WOMAD** |
| WOMAD is the World of Music, Arts & Dance founded by Peter Gabriel. In 2012 WOMAD celebrated 30 years in the UK at Bristol Zoo and Chatterton Park; 20 years of WOMADelaide, Australia; 21 years in Caceres, Extremadura, Spain; WOMAD Fiesta Las Palmas de Gran Canaria in New Plymouth, New Zealand. |
| **Ten Days on the Island, Tasmania** |
| This biannual festival hosts a program of creativity from host island residents and those from around the world. The critical and commercial success of the program has attracted innovative approaches to sharing cultural heritage and artistic excellence in diverse venues over 10 days across the island state of Australia. |

**Table 8.4** Global Festivals

at the inaugural community-based Jacaranda Festival in Grafton (NSW, Australia), maypole dancing was a popular participatory inclusion. It disappeared from view later, but in the early 2000s it was reintroduced to excited acclaim. By reflecting on design elements that have worked in the past, contemporary tweaking can garner a whole new audience. There is now greater recognition of the interdisciplinary approach to festival design with play options joining the spectator portfolio and active participation encouraged in response to the greater understanding of the contribution the creative industries make to local economies. Thus the employment of artists involved with movies, TV, popular music, technology, games, advertising, and marketing design all become features of a creative and innovative approach to festival-making.

Diversity in its many manifestations has been embraced in successful festival design as a precursor to creativity and innovation. By responding to cultural heritage, immigration, transient populations, visitors, global links, demographic change, new ways of organizing information, and sharing experiences, a festival can build resilience, build belief in what it stands for, and be confident and tolerant, which attracts specific audiences.

By utilizing the most promising ideas contributed by festival internal and external partners, innovation can generate uniqueness, create impact, and ensure memorable experiences for all. The buy-in from partners committed to the festival helps clarify any identified challenges, can assist with research, evaluate options, and help organizers draw up a design action plan. Valuable knowledge resides in different parts of the festival network and a specific knowledge management system can create, organize, share, and use those intangibles like memory, mood, judgment, and experience. The new ideas can stimulate defining moments for patrons' quality of life because they involve people's habits of mind and influence patterns of behavior. It is by recognizing the palette of patterns in festival markets and their social behaviors that festival organizers can address what Peter Fisk in his book, *Creative Genius* (2011, p. 126), identifies as distinctive influencers:

- Trends—ideas that evolve and endure
- Fashion—ideas that have a place in time and are usually part of a trend, but are associated with a certain moment and a particular style
- Fads—ideas embraced by a small audience, followed with extreme interest, and rarely part of a longer-term trend
- Crazes—ideas that catch on incredibly quickly, spreading through groups, and then go as quickly as they came, not part of a trend

It is interesting to look through the lens of new communication technologies to see how organizers deal with a trend for quirky festival options (Table 8.5). People like to dress up, eat a lot, get dirty, laugh a great deal, and celebrate heroes of the past and present in literature, music, movies, and movement.

## The Dispersed Model

Indoors or outdoors there are venues that fit the themes and design aspirations of festival organizers. These can be trigger responses from other stakeholders like residents, business premises, and statutory authorities to satisfy the celebratory requirements for each specific event. Festival programs can produce a stimulating balance to meet the expectations of the targeted festival audience. There can be street parties and neighborhood gatherings that allow visitors and residents to pick up on the theme of the festival in a personalized way and introduce local food and drinks. The "long lunch" provides an opportunity for local

| Cheese Rolling At Cooper's Hill, Gloucestershire, UK |
| --- |
| The annual Cheese-Rolling Festival at Cooper's Hill takes place in front of crowds of 2000 who arrive early for the anticipated spectacle. The ground conditions on the hill are generally softened by recent rain. Hilarity ensues as participants who begin in an upright posture end up tumbling down the hill within seconds to chase large wheels of cheese that hurtle down the hill. |
| **World Grits Festival, St. George, South Carolina** |
| The three-day grits celebration has put this small town on the map. Festival-goers can expect eating and cooking contests, corn tossing and shelling, crowning of Miss Grits, carnivals, and live music. The festival draws more than 45,000 attendees. The people of St. George actually ate more grits per capita than any other place in the world! It is dedicated to community improvement through wholesome family fun. It attracts a lot of visitors. |
| **Battle of the Oranges, Ivrea, Italy** |
| The orange-throwing Carnevale di Ivrea (near Turin) origins are uncertain but a popular account says that the festival commemorates the city's defiance against a ruling tyrant. Every year for the battle, residents dressed in medieval costumes are divided into nine teams and take turns attacking each other with thousands of oranges. Tips for surviving the fight range from wearing a helmet to having shoes with good traction to avoid slipping. Wearing a red hat identifies a person as a spectator and allows them to watch the event untouched. |
| **Darwin Lions Beer Can Regatta, Darwin, Northern Territory, Australia** |
| An annual family day. There are beach events for all ages and the water events are spectacular! Entrance is by a gold coin donation, with proceeds to community projects. There are also food and craft stalls. |
| **Calgary Stampede, Calgary, Alberta, Canada** |
| An annual event celebrating Alberta and its western heritage. The Calgary Stampede includes a 10-day rodeo, agriculture, parade, music events and fireworks, merchandise, and musical icons. |
| **UFO Festival, Roswell, New Mexico, USA** |
| Roswell is the capital of extraterrestrial culture and invites UFO enthusiasts and skeptics alike to join in the celebration of one of the most debated incidents in history. The three-day event features guest speakers, authors, live entertainment, a costume contest, a pet costume contest, parade, and family-friendly activities. Whether or not you believe that a spacecraft crashed in the desert 65 years ago, you are welcome at alien-themed events. |

**Table 8.5** Quirky Celebrations

produce to be showcased; in addition, progressive or moving feasts will allow a chance for festival-goers to engage with cellar doors at wineries or farmers to highlight the journey of food from the farm to the restaurant table for local delicacies. In urban festivals, organizers have involved retailers and commercial enterprises to host artists-in-residence within their premises that connect to the wider festival, have window decoration competitions using the agreed-upon theme, or link to the festivities through "adopting" some aspect of the environmental, artistic, or administrative regime of the festival.

The Festival Fringes in Edinburgh, Scotland, and Adelaide, Australia, accommodate festival performances over days, around the clock, in a diverse array of buildings. This provides an effective way to share the metropolitan or natural landscape with festival-goers. They can walk the streets, meet locals, engage with local businesses, and exploit access to artists in nontraditional performance spaces such as churches, pub backrooms, staircases, small city squares, parklands, skateboard parks, galleries, libraries, rooftops, or bank foyers in intimate or massive settings.

A popular long-running children's festival in a rural community in New South Wales, Australia, holds a festival where *all* activities are dispersed. There is no central meeting place and young festival-goers are encouraged to actively participate in a portfolio of cultural activities in bakeries, offices, parklands, and swimming pools all day long for the duration of the celebrations that introduce arts practices, access for disabled youngsters, and encourage marginalized groups to have contact with professional local and imported artists.

## Write It Down

Professional organizers look to maintain a "swipe" file, an accumulation of ideas and inspirations sourced from everyday life and their professional experiences. This becomes an astute approach to co-creation of knowledge, to add value when you apply ideas to your new circumstances. This is an important part of the portfolio each brings to new positions. Some keep a journal, extensively curated computer files, and notes from meetings, and others are compulsive list makers who reference good practice from reading, talking, observing, and reviewing related material.

This makes a valuable contribution to problem solving by not only utilizing promising ideas they generate themselves but more importantly, in festival design and successful experience generation, working together with others. This is the basis of innovation. Embracing mistakes made or observed from the efforts of others makes a useful alternative to training. People are often motivated by things they notice don't work so effectively and they can then visualize models and behaviors that may address challenges in the preparation of aspects of a festival. This sort of "what if" scenario building can lead to some creative solutions.

Such formal documentation can harness the dreams, intuitions, feelings, and ideas that come to festival directors as they prepare the scope and scale of their next festival. It can help ground the audacity they embark on in their program design and the perseverance they need to maintain to see the planning through from core values held to deliver the intended outcomes.

## Creative Festival Challenges

J.K. Rowling, author of the best-selling *Harry Potter* book series, in her commencement address, "The Fringe Benefits of Failure and the Importance of Imagination" to Harvard alumni in 2008, provides a telling introduction to the notion of failure and how individuals can use challenges to become inspired to pursue with passion the projects they value. It is worth a read in the context of the many people who commit themselves to work hard in festival-making and take a constructive approach to failure. Personal and organizational learning is the capital of the future.

Festival Director Robyn Archer's message to the next generation of festival-makers identifies the challenges that any artistic director committed to the future of festivals face. We have examined the features of creative enterprises and the valuable contributions individuals bring to each aspect of festival design, action, and impact. For festivals to be sustained all personnel involved need to persevere, feel their efforts satisfy themselves and their partners, and remain true to the core vision. Archer goes on to invoke an imperative for the future of festival-making:

> If we commission and support the kind of art which is genuinely creative, not just copying, not just recycling and this goes for genuinely fresh versions of old work, or the creative placement of traditional work in a surprising context, or the commissioning of

brand new work bristling with new challenging ideas, then we are doing the greatest service we can to our audiences, our community, our society. We are presenting them with the means to stimulate the creative muscle and awareness they need to go out and do all their respective jobs in a way that works towards a more engaged society, a clever society, and one receptive to new ideas.

—*Robyn Archer, 2011 Keynote Address at EFA Atelier for Young Festival Managers, Turkey*

As a festival organiser you cultivate all types of courage but primarily intellectual courage, moral courage and the courage to be great. Courage is essential to creativity and innovation.

—*Detlef Reis (2012)*

## Innovation in Festival Thinking and Delivery

A photobooth festival was held in London in 2012 to accommodate the growing interest from such venues as clubs, private parties, and weddings. Celebrating the humble photobooth, everyone's favorite automaton, it showcased a collection of unique, hand-built booths. They included a one-of-a-kind converted camper van (The Dinky Dub) to the Discobooth and vintage Airstream-inspired Photostream. Patrons got snapped in the most amazing and imaginative photobooths ever with unlimited mementoes!

Another initiative undertaken in 2012 was the Los Angeles mobile art festival that celebrated the pioneers of iPhonography and the underground mobile arts movement. It encouraged iPhone art as well as interactive digital, sculptural, film/video, and performance-based iPhonic installations. It allowed art and technology to unite. It provided a forum for creators of print techniques, mixed-media installations, sound and video projects, sculptural installations, and performance art.

Newcastle, Australia, has hosted the free, independent This Is Not Art Festival (TiNA) since 1998. It is dedicated to the exploration of experimental and emerging arts media and concepts, providing a platform for innovative and passionate culture-makers to conceive, collaborate, and critique through an aggregation of participating festivals including the Crack Theatre Festival, a national festival and forum devoted to experimental, fringe, cross-artform theater and performance. It's a launching pad for emerging artists who wish to journey into the festival scene. Critical Animals is a creative research symposium held annually as a part of the TiNA festival. It's a forum for students, researchers, writers, artists, thinkers, and curious individuals who are critically engaged with creative and experimental art practices. The National Young Writers' Festival is a gathering place for young and innovative writers working in both new and traditional forms including zines, comics, blogging, screenwriting, poetry, spoken word, hip-hop music, journalism, autobiography, comedy, songwriting, and prose.

## CASE STUDY

### The Splendor of Splendour

#### Splendour in the Grass, Byron Bay, NSW, Australia

The regional cultural development agency (Arts Northern Rivers) that hosts regular forums for festival organizers is acutely aware of the depth of the diverse arts and cultural festivals that populate the New South Wales region annually. They promote events through their website and social media networks. The following is a précis from one such a promotion of the popular internationally known festival Splendour in the Grass staged in Byron Bay, a part of their regional constituency. The three days of music, arts, discussion, and discovery, with a supersonic line-up of over 90 acts from around Australia and across the globe, played to a soldout crowd each day in 2012. In 2013 the festival moved to its own newly purpose-built site.

ARTS NORTHERN RIVERS

#### Creative and Innovative Program Highlights Included:

1. **Splendour Arts.** The Splendour Arts program showcases new works by established Australian and international artists alongside installations by emerging artists through the Splendid Project. While an increasing number of festivals are embracing the display of public art at their venues, Splendour continues to lead the way by investing in the commissioning of new works that they hope will engage their audiences and bridge the gap between art and popular culture.

2. **The Splendour Forum.** Splendour's live discussion program explores some of the most fascinating issues of the moment, with local, national, and international guests including an eclectic array of musicians, comedians, filmmakers, writers, artists, actors, tech geeks, politicians, and scientists. Previous year's highlights are uploaded on YouTube.

3. **Triple J Unearthed Splendour in the Grass Program.** Every year, in conjunction with national radio station Triple J Unearthed, Splendour offers one unknown Australian band the once-in-a-lifetime opportunity to play the opening set of the Festival, on the main stage. Bands just upload their music tracks to the Triple J Unearthed website, where they might also benefit from the added bonus of getting their work in front of staff at one Australia's most popular music/youth culture radio networks.

4. **The Buskers Stage.** Splendour has its own dedicated Buskers Stage, where they showcase a handpicked selection of the best acoustic talent, every day.

5. **The Music!** Where else do you get this caliber of artists at your doorstep! Splendour presents over 90 acts on its main stages over three days. No wonder tickets always sell out in half an hour!

6. **Splendour Kidz Club.** The Splendour Kidz Club is a special bit of paradise for anyone age under 12 and their parents.

    The Kids Club operates as a mini-festival in a dedicated fully fenced area and offers arts and crafts, face painting, clown school, dress-up theater, storytelling, music, and performance. Parents/guardians supervise their own children during daytime Kidz Club sessions while a creche facility is available for festival patrons in the evenings.

7. **The Global Village.** The Global Village celebrates local community. There are workshops, dance performances, craft stalls, bamboo art, lanterns, a late-night fire extravaganza, rainbow flags, massage and the Chai Tent. It's home for

the Gyuto Monks of Tibet, who always attract a crowd with their chanting, sand mandala creations, and personal puja blessings.

8. **Commitment to the Environment.** From its beginning Splendour has been committed to putting in place environmental programs that reduce the festival's impact, acknowledged with a Commended Award from the prestigious international Greener Festival Awards. On Splendour's website, for anyone to download, are copies of their policies and procedures. They're intended for festival patrons, so everyone who attends can get involved in achieving the festival's enviro targets. They're a resource for any other festival who's thinking of putting similar policies in place.

9. **Jobs and Other Income-Generating Activities.** There are jobs for local artists, musicians, fashion designers, food gurus and healers, people running programs and organizing different aspects of the event, or popping out from behind the sound desk. In a difficult economy Splendour provides an opportunity for hundreds of local people to work close to home. It also provides students at regional universities work placements in a world-class event setting.

10. **Giving program**. Splendour has provided grants and donations to various not-for-profit community groups and causes. Consistent with their own organizational values, the majority of donations have been made to environmental or youth groups. The program is their way of giving something back to the host community. Splendour tickets go to various community groups for fundraising, they have even sponsored other local events.

## The Big Picture

Undoubtedly pulling together an event of this scale requires a clear vision. We asked Splendour in the Grass Director, Jessica Ducrou, what's the big picture she has in mind when she puts the program together each year. "We have always tried to put together an event that was more than just bands on a stage in a field. We're more than just a straight up-and-down music festival. While the bands are undeniably an integral and important part of the show, we feel that the additional features of the event are equally attractive.

"As the years go by we want to see Splendour grow, mature, and become broader in its appeal. That can be done as much through broadening the musical genres as it can through refining and expanding the 'experiences' that people enjoy at the event. This is especially effective when those experiences are unexpected. We get lots of feedback from our punters about the surprise elements of the festival that end up being some of their favorite, enduring memories.

"We've been working for a long time getting an appropriate venue where we have the room to try things and improve from one year to the next. We're looking forward to the future."

Permission from Peter Wood, CEO/Regional Arts Development Officer, Arts Northern Rivers, 2012.

# FROM INSIDE THE MOSAIC

## Neil Cameron

Neil Cameron

Neil Cameron is a theater director, teacher, author, and consultant. For over 34 years he has run successful festivals, arts events and celebrations in Germany, Belgium, Holland, Canada, the United States, Japan, New Zealand, and Australia. His award-winning productions are well known for their creative community involvement and their exciting use of large-scale imagery, fire, and music. Neil shares his extensive practical knowledge and cultural insight through teaching, writing, and consultancy. He is a passionate advocate of the importance of festivals and celebrations in achieving social cohesion, cultural development in community, and personal enrichment. His following musings capture his commitment to festival-making. He writes:

"I have been to many events in different parts of the world and, while some have been more than satisfying, some have been absolutely outstanding and memories have remained with me to this very day. So what has been the magic ingredient that has imbued certain events with that extra "something," the lift that remains in the memory as something special? Some of those events have been spectacular with thousands of people involved; the Opening of an Olympic Games is an example but some have been simple gatherings, such as the morning I sat on a hillside watching the sun come up on millennium day with Buddhist monks chanting in the background.

"As a director of arts events in festivals I have given this question a great deal of thought. Sometimes the events I have brought together have remained flat and lifeless while other gathered emotional momentum and reached for the stars. In the end I think it is the transfer of *meaning* from us to the audience that is the difference between good and wonderful.

"So what do I mean by this?

"Maybe an example will help. I remember being in a small Australian town when the Olympic flame was being carried around the country in 2000. The people lined the street cheering and clapping, obviously emotionally moved, some crying and some hugging each other when a single person came running down the street carrying a flaming touch. The event couldn't have been simpler yet it stirred emotions in the people watching, many of which reported it was a sight they would never forget. Now why was it so powerful? There was no spectacle, no firework display, there were no costumes or music or marketing campaigns that told everyone what to feel, yet the magic was there: a simple flame, that would be unremarkable in any other context, somehow touched the crowds watching throughout the country. The answer of course is meaning. The flame was a vibrant message, a symbolic energy, carried by ordinary people that expressed the idea that the world could be united, that the human race could live in peace and prosper: the flame represented the human spirit held within all of us.

"So what meaning does your event hold? This question lies at the heart of every worthwhile event and if you get the design right it can mean the difference between the ordinary and the wonderful. It starts with the team itself whose enthusiasm and clarity of propose will be at the heart of the event; there is no room for cynicism or shallow aims in designing a wonderful event. It is vital that the team really believe in what they are doing and take the design seriously and understand what their event is for and why they are doing it.

"So many events are designed to manipulate the audiences into a good time, selling fun as a product. Here's what Larry Harvey, the producer of the extraordinary *Burning Man Festival* held in September in Nevada, points out: "There is plenty of 'spectacle' around us, but it doesn't produce human interactions. It's merely consumed. It doesn't have the power to generate new experience" (cited in Rockwell, 2006, p. 126). To produce magical events one has to really connect with people's inner feelings in a genuine way, which is the only way that sustainability will be maintained and fresh energy generated.

"So producers should not be afraid to dig deep into the meaning of their event and use their skills and ideas to express these important messages to the participants and audiences. This does not mean a boring, serious gathering where everything is weighted down with deep ideas but rather an event that carries these valuable and important messages to the world with lightness and feelings of exuberance. When we touch audiences in this way they will truly feel the spirit of celebration and that's what they remember for years to come."

## Festival Ideas and Issues

1. What is creativity? Discuss the differences between the individualist definition and the sociocultural approach as they apply to making enduring festivals.
2. Think about the points made by Robyn Archer in her presentation to young festival directors. What are the challenges that face the new generation of arts and cultural festival creators? How can they be met to successfully deliver enduring festivals?
3. *Imitation is not just the sincerest form of flattery. It is one of the shrewdest ways to become a successful entrepreneur.* When developing a festival program how do organizers ensure distinctiveness that separates their festival from others, or is it okay to simply appropriate others' ideas?
4. Author Richard Florida (2012) suggests that the arts contribute to the economy in ways that may not be fully understood. Clearly, investing in arts and culture over the long run makes our economy stronger, but we do not know the exact mechanism through which that works. Do you? Discuss in groups. What can arts and community cultural festivals contribute to the age of creative capitalism, premised on the city as the social and economic unit?

## Festival Focus Activities

1. Design a specific program for a two-day community-based cultural festival. List at least 10 elements that a festival program director would consider for inclusion.
2. Examine familiar festivals and analyze evidence of connections to the conventions of theater.
3. Develop a plan for a specific event to address the needs of crowd management and crowd control.

4. In a group devise a map of a festival site indicating the factors that may have appeal to organizers. What facilities may be required for a specific style of festival? What are the constraints? The focus could be on an outdoor music festival, a street party to introduce a city festival, or an indoor/outdoor multivenue heritage celebration.
5. Analyze websites of companies offering new technologies that can assist with event management. Compare and contrast the relative merits of event management software for particular festivals with which you are familiar.

# Suggested Reading

Adams, S. "The Changing Face of Arts Festivals," (2012). http://www.artshub.com.au/au/news-article/opinions/arts/the-changing-face-of-arts-festivals-190871#.

Boden, M. A. "Creativity and Artificial Intelligence." *Artificial Intelligence* 103 (1998): 347–356.

Cameron, R. N. *New Alignments in Ritual, Ceremony and Celebration*. Master's thesis, Griffith University, QLD, Australia.

Csikszentmihalyi, M. *Creativity: Flow and the Psychology of Discovery and Invention*. New York: Harper Perennial Modern Classics, 1997.

Csikszentmihalyi, M. *Flow: The Psychology of Optimal Experience*. New York: Harper Perennial Modern Classics, 2008.

deGraff, J., and K. A. Lawrence. *Creativity at Work, Navigating the Roadmap to Value Creation, Dividend*. Ann Arbor, MI: University of Michigan, 2003.

De Bono, E. *Serious Creativity*. London, Uk: HarperCollins, 1992.

Dewey, J. *Art as Experience*. New York, New York: Berkley Publishing Group, (penguin Putnam), Perigee Trade, 2005.

Fisk, P. *Creative Genius*. Chichester UK: Capstone, 2011.

Florida, R. *The Rise of the Creative Class Revisited: 10th Anniversary Edition*. New York: Basic Books, 2012.

Getz, D. *Event Studies, Theory, Research and Policy for Planned Events*. Oxford, UL: Butterworth- Heinemann, 2007.

Heilpern, J. *Conference of the Birds: The Story of Peter Brook in Africa*. New York: Routledge, 1999.

Liburd, J.J., and P. Derkzen, P. "Emic Perspectives on Quality of Life: the Case of the Danish Wadden Sea Festival." *Tourism and Hospitality Research* 9, no. 2 (2009): 132–146.

Mulligan, M., K. Humphery, P. James, C. Scanlon, P. Smith. and N. Welch.

Creating Community: Celebrations, Arts and Wellbeing Within and Across Local Communities. Melbourne, Victoria, Australia: The Global Institute and Vic Health, RMIT University, 2006.

Patterson, K., J. Grenny, R. McMillan, and A. Switler. *Crucial Conversations—Tools for Talking when Stakes are High* (2nd ed.). New York: McGraw-Hill, 2012.

Reis, D. "Creative leadership requires courage." *Bangkok Post*, Business section, August 30, 2012.

Ribeiro, L. *The Splendid Encounter of Music Festivals and Art*. 2012. ArtsHub Australia, Melbourne, http://www.artshub.com.au/festival/news-article/features/festivals/the-splendid-encounter-of-music-festivals-and-art-190657.

Robinson, K. *Out of Our Minds, Learning to be Creative*. Chichester, UK: Capstone 2011.

Rockwell, D. *Spectacle*. London, UK: Phaidon Press, 2006.

Sefertzi, E. Creativity, InnoRegio Project: Dissemination of Innovation and Knowledge Management Techniques. EC funded project, Stockholm School of Economics in Riga, Latvia. 2000. http://www.urenio.org/tools/en/creativity.pdf.

Sawyer, K. R. *Explaining Creativity: The Science of Human Innovation* (2nd ed.). Oxford, UK: Oxford University Press, 2012.

Sawyer, K. R. *Group Genius: The Creative Power of Collaboration*. New York: Basic Books, 2007.

# CHAPTER 9

# Delivering Memorable Festival Experiences

*Remember that you are packaging and managing an experience. This means that you must envision that experience from start to finish, from the guest's point of view.*
—*Julia Silvers (2004, p. 5), CSEP (Certified Special Events Professional)*

---

This chapter provides an opportunity for you to better understand:

- The perspective of the festival patron's experience
- Festival patrons' personal benefits and meanings, their expectations, levels of satisfaction, communication opportunities, and feedback to organizers
- The importance of participation, learning, entertainment, sensory engagement, creativity, freedom, and security
- The experience of festival partners including management and staff, audience, host community, tourism, and local government

---

When we pass judgement on our experience at an arts or community cultural festival our memories are informed by our personal and social context. Sometimes our attendance, as spectator or participant, is prompted by our interest in spending time with friends and family in a congenial environment and our time together underpins the stories we relate after the event to others. We investigate the ways in which festival patrons evaluate their satisfaction with all dimensions of a festival in this chapter. Sometimes it is the minutiae of our engagement juxtaposed with the scale of the festival and program content that provides the WOW factor that stays with us, long after our attendance. We explore how festival patrons use their time, before, during, and after a festival, what impressions linger, and how our enjoyment is influenced by our previous experiences, exploited by the festival organization and its partners such as sponsors, local residents, businesses, the media, and special interest groups.

**Figure 9.1** A Memorable Festival Guest Experience Mosaic.

Our festival experience is informed by exposure to similar previous activities, any knowledge we have accrued over time, and seems to be closely linked to experimentation, our willingness to take risks, and learning from doing. As we examined earlier, there is a spectrum of engagement in what is known as serious leisure that may result in us being a dabbler in this type of recreational pursuit, or an enthusiast, or an expert, or a fanatic wishing to actively consume familiar environments. Our satisfaction with the festival experience seems to be a blend of meanings. The interactions that are embedded in unique and memorable settings appeal to our senses, and our emotions and resonate with our values, our heritage, and our culture.

Those individuals who are flexible, open-minded and proactive are most likely to have the most enjoyable time by going with the flow. And similar to my own preferences when going to festivals, what I enjoy the most is stumbling around and exploring the local area, meeting the locals and new people and finding hidden treasures, cafes and other goings on. ... So wherever you are in the world, and wherever you want to go, just remember to keep the flags flying... and take photos, festivals and memory loss often go hand in hand.

—*Paul Thompson*

## Memorable Festival Experiences

There are numerous theories that explain the significance of festival-goers enjoying a satisfying experience without hindrance. Don Getz's (2007) assessment of the benefits and meanings associated with the relationships between all stakeholders helps us determine what particular constructs affect us within the particular festival portfolio we engage. He examines important evidence that arises from research into how festivals enhance the social meanings of personal

Friends in a playful festival mood dress up, socialize, and show off.

belonging, a sense of place and community, the role of ritual and heritage, authenticity, exposure to creativity and innovation, aspects of personal self-esteem, self-discovery, skills development, aesthetic appreciation, freedom and security, and the appeal of authenticity as visitors and residents access the host culture. He also recognizes the importance of understanding the broader meanings that are invested in festivals by the political and economic environments in which they operate. Transformations occur not only for individuals, but change occurs over time for businesses and host community development through social well-being and economic prosperity.

# Definitions

When examining the meaning attached to festival experiences for individuals and diverse stakeholders, it is useful to understand the experience phenomenon. There is a temporal element to experience, through exposure to practical or cognitive activity that happens over time. It accumulates and consolidates into a situation or circumstance that goes on to inform future perspectives, activities, and knowledge. You may have noticed this in your own festival experience. It forms part of a person's perception and becomes integral to what they sense or notice about them. It affects their behavior, their feelings and emotions, and their motivations for involvement with the tangible and intangible aspects of festivals. Experiences are a response to stimulation in a variety of forms.

Robert Stebbins (1997) researches serious leisure. He has determined this to be a systematic pursuit of an amateur, hobbyist, or volunteer core activity that people find substantial, interesting, and fulfilling. This may have a career orientation, with skills, knowledge and experience, as distinct from casual leisure, which can be less substantial and can be defined as immediate, intrinsic, rewarding, and relatively short lived (Stebbins, 1997, p. 18). Each of these has implications for sustainable festival-making.

The service delivery aspect of festival-making has come under scrutiny as organizations are encouraged to turn their brand into an experience as suggested by Pine and Gilmore's (1999) work on the experience economy. This affects how festival organizers market their event so as to shift the emphasis from satisfying needs to fulfilling aspirations, desires, and dreams. They make suggestions on how to create worthy experiences for business that can readily be appropriated by festival organizers. The experience is enhanced through staff/

## STAY CURIOUS

An experience dimension for audiences seeking to differentiate the complex and layered, ordinary and extraordinary offers that engage, provide interaction, entertainment, and learning stimuli has been honed by organizers of the IdeaFestival in Louisville, Kentucky. This four-day festival prides itself on creating "a collaborative environment of disruptive change." It purposefully seeks to bring together a network of seemingly disparate innovators who possess extraordinary skills for positive change and ask them to share their knowledge with the host community. Its byline and brand is *Stretch Your Horizons, Stay Curious*. It resonates with partners from forward-thinking and innovative companies and academic institutions to media influencers from around the world. These partners have helped create fresh thinking, make new connections, and introduce innovations that matter.

Participants are bound together by an intense curiosity about what is impacting and shaping the future of the arts, business, technology, design, science, philosophy, and education. As consumers of festival experiences they constitute what Schmitt (1999) identifies as searchers for experiences that dazzle their senses, touch their hearts, and stimulate their minds. He suggests that organizers can capture the whole person, their minds and emotions, and attract them to memorable experiences by stimulating their senses, feelings, thoughts, actions, and relationships. The festival setting of the Kentucky Center for the Arts, a stately historic venue that houses artworks by 20th-century masters, offers thought-provoking sessions and an informal tone. One testimonial suggests, "At IdeaFestival, seemingly unrelated topics offer surprising relationships and insights."

Meanwhile, on another continent, the Festival of Dangerous Ideas hosted by the Sydney Opera House and the St. James Ethics Centre showcases "not only compelling speakers but compelling ideas," says Ann Mossop, head of public programs and co-curator of a festival keen to challenge orthodox thinking through provocative, controversial, and enlightening sessions.

Contemporary artwork from traditional cultures in Papua New Guinea at the Gallery of Modern Art, Brisbane, QLD, Australia, for the Asia Pacific Triennial festival.

© Peter Derrett

patron interaction, design, setting, and festival ambience generated, and shifting the role from passive consumer of cultural delight to active participant.

We explore how organizations can best generate memorable festival experiences by providing indelible memories through outstanding attention to detail, distinctive stimuli, and a special and unforgettable opportunity to share time and place with others. The resulting special memories (good and less satisfying) become encoded and are stored, to be retrieved at a later time. How many experiences do you hold of particular festivals in a positive light?

## Experiential Dimensions

Virtual experiences as well as concrete or tangible experiences focus an individuals' attention on the arts world and the host community. As festivals refresh themselves regularly they offer immersion and inspiration that heightens the level of satisfaction for patrons customizing their own experience agendas. Whether offering open-sourced programs, promising elements of surprise or access to unique cultural practices, the stamina of all parties is under scrutiny. This influences the marketing choices for organizers and what is now called "experiential marketing" that builds on the traditional approach to reach people who may wish to engage with the festival experience, but also responds to the user-generated social media tools with which people clearly align their communication needs. Players in this experience may be responding to connections that are free or pay a fee for the services provided by the festival entrepreneur in specific locations or through virtual access. This identifies numerous locations for interaction and prolongs the relationship by offering more than one experience, as we have mentioned before. There is greater interest now in festival patrons being the messenger as much as a participant at the physical event.

## Service Factors

The festival patrons' positive and memorable experience of a festival arises from the best fit between what the patron believes the organization should deliver and what actually transpires. The service they receive during their relationship with a festival organization, on-site, through the program and contact with staff influences their level of satisfaction and informs their intention to return and recommend the experience to others. Marketers and researchers now recognize that service factors are fundamental to the moves organizations make to secure quality experiences for patrons. The experience economy raised by Pine and Gilmore (1999) builds on the key elements that were developed by Parasuraman, Zeithml, and Berry (1985). Their initial 10 dimensions of quality service interaction between hosts and guests include:

- Tangibles (appearance of physical facilities, equipment, personnel, and communication materials)
- Reliability (ability to perform the promised service dependably and accurately)
- Responsiveness (willingness to help customers and provide prompt service)

- Competence (possession of the required skills and knowledge to perform the service)
- Courtesy (politeness, respect, consideration, and friendliness of the contact personnel)
- Credibility (trustworthiness, believability, and honesty)
- Security (freedom from danger, risk, or doubt)
- Access and welcome (approachability and ease of contact)
- Communication (keeping customers informed in language they can understand and listening to them)
- Empathy (making the effort to know customers and relate to their needs and emotions) (Zeithaml & Parasuraman, 2004).

Subsequently these dimensions were reduced to five and became conceptualized as SERVQUAL (1988), the gap between what the patron anticipates from contact with the service provider and how they evaluate that performance.

- Reliability (ability to perform the promised service dependably and accurately)
- Assurance (knowledge and courtesy of employees and their ability to convey trust and confidence)
- Tangibles (appearance of physical facilities, equipment, personnel, and communication materials)
- Empathy (provision of caring, individualized attention to customers)
- Responsiveness (willingness to help customers and to provide prompt service)

What is evident when festival organizers seek to understand audience satisfaction with the services provided is its fluidity. Nothing is static. When a patron assesses satisfaction with the way they were approached and treated during the festival experience and interacted with post-festival, they generally draw on their expectations (the push/pull factors that tourism marketers often speak of) for their experience and evaluate them against their actual contact with the event. The SERVQUAL framework is often subtly absorbed into the value they place on their festival experience. The relative importance of each of the service qualities will vary from patron to patron.

## Experience Factors

In recent times festival organizers have tended to overlay the service quality factors long espoused in the marketing literature with the Pine and Gilmore experience economy principles. Linda Ralston and her colleagues (2007) at the University of Utah have developed an integrated model of service and experience factors in the staging of memorable festivals. Their integrated model provides an approach to evaluate the experiences of patrons so that organizers can better understand the dynamics in play and design and deliver appropriate, targeted service quality and memorable take-home messages from the festival experience. To sustain a desirable festival for existing patrons and to attract new audiences, organizers need to regularly audit their performance. The management literature debates the case regarding whether quality of the service or the experience dominates in the patron's memory and where that threshold features in the interaction between an individual and a festival. Ralston et al.'s integrated model based on a service quotient and experience quotient, provides a useful evidence-based approach to any organization's customer orientation.

## The WOW Factor

The WOW factor is the punctuation mark of experience! Festival WOW factors tend to impress, excite, astonish, and attract.

> The closing ceremony for the London 2012 Paralympic Games wowed crowds with fire, a stunning light show and music from megastars. The show at the Olympic Stadium was dubbed the Festival of the Flame and featured more than 1,000 volunteers. The spectacle began with a war hero who lost both legs in a blast on the battlefield climbing a flagpole and proudly flying the Union Jack. That provided an emotional and fitting end to the London Games—hailed the best in history.
>
> —*Skynews*

When designing a festival program, space, or communication tool, organizers often draw on the element of surprise. The unexpected, capturing something suddenly, something that elicits an emotional response, has proved to have genuine audience appeal. Contrivance or predictability is less attractive. Surprise can be used as a storytelling technique. It can reveal something humorous that is relevant to the specific audience and can be overt or subtle. In festival terms, it is often connected to sensory responses to scale, noise, floats in a parade, characters, laser lights and projections on buildings, soundscapes that capture a particular mood, or elaborate visual stimuli.

The global popularity of flash mobs and "improv everywhere" events indicates the appeal of spontaneity and serendipity. Evidence of such simple movements in public places, the use of technology, and the coordination of whimsy has drawn a great deal of attention to more structured, conventional festival environments. YouTube shares some memorable explosions of spontaneity using inclusive arts practices. Can that take the place of "being there"?

These don't diminish the inclusion of soundly engineered moving and static constructions that engage people of all ages in safe and creative environments. There are welcome responses to authentic engagement with heritage, nature, sparkle, and fireworks, spectacle that is generated to heighten the tension, the magic, and the mystery of the transitory explosion. Much of the more structured and built-in festival WOW factors require a considerable investment of human, capital, and practical skills.

Beach sculpture as part of the Swell Sculpture Festival, Gold Coast, Australia, 2012.

Relaxed outdoor fun for the family at Sydney's Gay and Lesbian Mardi Gras.

The surprise inclusion of celebrities and heroes raises the level of engagement, along with exotic aromas of foods, use of textured surfaces, and access to ingenious technology. Individuals and groups use festival settings to dress up or down, adopt quirky performance practices, and respond to the offer of prizes. The traditional use of parades, spectacle, decorated sites, and use of technology can achieve and record a reaction that stays with the spectator or participant for a long time afterward.

Have you noticed the impact of details, the little things that grab the attention, take the breath, or move the festival patron? In a bid to connect with audiences it is often the festival organization's attention to detail in simple, sometimes intimate ways that inspire loyalty and engagement with the vision for the celebrations. It can be from the friendly welcome, the recognition of previous contact (a quick check of the festival database, the "likes" of friends on Facebook), recognition of demographic needs like chairs for the elderly, transport support, crèches, improving conveniences, building VIP programs, and rewarding and incentivizing behaviors.

Think of ways to put a smile on people's faces, widen their eyes, stimulate involuntary implosions of delight, introduce humor unexpectedly and tastefully, unusual textures for seating, meaningful exchanges of information, personalizing contacts that linger away from the physical festival experience.

## Stakeholder Factors

Levels of engagement vary between active participants and more passive recipients or spectators, so the intention of festival design needs to be clear and embraced by patrons. Particular festival stakeholders—partners in the design, development, and delivery of planned public events—have unique and specific experiences that reflect the dimensions mentioned above. Some invest a great deal in their emotional responses to festival-making, others work intellectually to solve challenges and gain a great deal from the "flow" that energizes their long-term commitment to the festival. Earlier we identified the various stakeholders—audience, media, artists, venue operators, administrative and technical staff, volunteers, local host community, government agencies, staff, vendors, sponsors, suppliers—who each have particular roles in the festival mosaic and as a result their experience is not only of the relationships along the way but the output of the festival and its legacy are subtly different.

Each approaches their involvement with a portfolio of skills, previous contact and resources (Table 9.1). They have an expectation they can make a useful contribution to successful outcomes and are in fact influencers of change that assist a festival to remain robust, diverse, and resilient.

| Memorable Festival Experiences | Diminished Festival Experiences |
| --- | --- |
| Provide a good match with the personal meanings sought by individuals, including leisure, learning, social interaction, honesty, cultural connections, sense of community and place | When there is a lack of evidence of wonder, mystery, spectacle, creativity, distinctiveness in program, themes |
| Sense of humor, whimsy, openness, and feeling of being welcomed at venue and in host community | Patrons under the influence of drugs/alchohol and police intervention, which diminish personal experiences |
| Clear on-site communication, signage, message boards, through efficient use of technology | No ATMs to dispense cash; when only cash is accepted on-site without prior information for patrons |
| Quality entertainment | Poor signage |
| Access to artists and celebrities who are also having a good time (that means that organizers are meeting the needs of the artists) | Poor communication in a timely way of any program changes and frustration with overt management decisions affecting patrons' "flow" |
| Reasonably priced merchandise that becomes a memento of the occasion | Queuing for toilets, food outlets, entry and ticketing posts, transport access, buses, taxi, cars |
| Community cultural festivals that showcase local talent, youth activity, cultural diversity, and landscape and lifestyle choices of residents | Not being welcomed in the broader community during the festival period, traffic, venue poorly prepared |
| Spaces that allow patrons to relax and meet friends, but remain part of the festivities | Some aspects of provision of shelter, shade, seating that reduces security, comfort, and health |
| Good clean amenities in working order for camping, parking, eating, meeting, participating or spectating | If program isn't delivered as outlined in promotional material, may be boring, overstimulating |
| Value for money | If costs of experience don't offer value for money in difficult financial environments, experience becomes a waste of time |
| Attitude may change to hosts, venue, and program, this festival specifically or genre generally | Some patrons' behaviors threatening, harmful, or unacceptable to individuals and groups |
| Positive media coverage and acceptance by host community makes for more attractive and welcoming experience, willingness to return and promote | Weather and climatic variables can create discomfort or disaster |
| Where sponsors' brands make a real connection to patrons but don't detract from initial appeal to attend and leave some sort of worthy legacy | Overt branding that swamps the artistic or cultural ambience to become too commercial |

**Table 9.1** Elements of Festival Experience
Derrett (2013).

Festival patrons line up to purchase merchandise as souvenirs of their festival experience.

## Mementoes

There are numerous mementoes that festival stakeholders can keep as reminders or souvenirs of their festival experience. These can constitute items that were purchased, collected, gifted or distributed as part of a portfolio of recognition of their participation in some form or other with the event. While festival engagement can be transitory, there are tangible and intangible transformative outcomes for those involved. Some of these are canvassed in Table 9.2. What else could you add from your observations and festival participation?

Festival patrons like to meet performing artists face-to-face, purchase mementoes, and tell stories.

| Host community residents:<br>• Gifts from homeland visitors to festival<br>• Household distribution of programs and promotional material, information-sharing<br>• Street decorations, domestic color schemes<br>• Provision of new/improved infrastructure, public amenities as legacy<br>• Media coverage of host destination<br>• Welcome gateways, banners, signage, and destination brand | Festival patrons:<br>• Prizes for involvement with competitions, lucky door prizes, random gifts from organizers, distributed by brand sponsors<br>• Items made/created during workshops or master classes within festival period<br>• Paraphernalia gathered from attendance such as tickets, programs, wristbands<br>• Tourism collateral, postcards, and brochures to inspire return visits to destinations<br>• Autographs of artists in festival program<br>• Purchases of merchandise from vendors, markets, branded items, CDs, books, clothing, badges, pins<br>• Photographic documentation in press, on websites, footage on YouTube, follow-up DVD sales<br>• Photobooths, personal documentation of self and friends<br>• New friends and contacts |
|---|---|
| Volunteers:<br>• Specific identifiable clothing<br>• Letters of thanks, certificates of appreciation for resumes<br>• New networks of colleagues | Benefactors, sponsors:<br>• Letters of thanks<br>• Souvenir gifts during VIP access to event<br>• Inscriptions on Boards of Honor, construction of plaques<br>• Planting of trees<br>• Naming of amenities on-site |
| Businesses:<br>• Letters of thanks, certificates of appreciation for shop displays<br>• Promotional festival collateral, posters<br>• Prizes for window decoration competitions<br>• Potential venue refurbishment<br>• New money from visitors, investors, and government funds recognizes local suppliers | Artists:<br>• Income from performances, mainstage, guest speakers<br>• Gifts related to festival, destination, or culture |
| VIPs—celebrities, politicians, media, investors:<br>• Gifts, festival-branded items from special functions within festival precinct or community<br>• Media coverage, website documentation | Festival organization:<br>• Feedback through surveys or online for future festival review<br>• Formal/informal personal responses from partners<br>• Awards and recognition from peer professional agencies<br>• Satisfaction expressed by staff and volunteers and their recognition by host community, media, government, and regulators |

**Table 9.2** Examples of Mementoes of Festival Experiences
Derrett (2013).

# Quality of Life

Interdisciplinary research increasingly focuses on the impact of festivals and events. The work of psychologist Martin Seligman, whose recent book, *Flourish* (2011) explores human well-being through what constitutes a good life, offers useful perspectives. There's a festival connection to his observations of human needs for a pleasant, engaged, meaningful and connected life. It is important that festival organizers consider what provides life satisfaction for individuals and groups and how an intervention like an enduring festival builds from Seligman's theory that flourishing rests on five pillars. He uses a mnemonic, PERMA, to explain the value and importance of Positive Emotion, Engagement, Relationships, Meaning, and Accomplishment.

Traditional festivals around the globe provide useful opportunities to analyze engagement with such elements. In northeast Thailand there is the Phii Ta Khon or Ghost Festival. It is held annually between March and July, in Loei province. It is believed to invite the last great incarnation of the Buddha, Pra Mahavejsandon, to the city. This unique spiritual festival satisfies a sense of harmony, love, and respect among residents and their ancestors. Locals wear costumes to embrace the ghostly theme of the tradition, including large colorful masks made from rice husks or coconut leaves, hats made of rice steamers, and a decorative robe. They complement these with clanging cowbells, the carrying of wooden swords, and dancing to local music. Increasingly international visitors have become part of these celebrations.

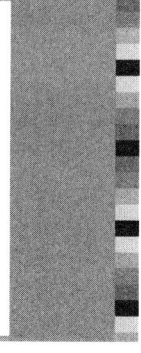

His work identifies the ways in which people are connected through intense feelings, emotional needs and affecting mood, desire to recall times of positive well-being, contentment, and pleasant memories. These may be private to the individuals experiencing them but festival-makers have tuned into such mechanisms that contribute positively to people's well-being.

## The Role of Ceremony and Ritual

The inclusion of conventions, observances, and procedures familiar to host communities and visitors to festivals holds particular significance in the scheme of festival experiences. Festivals are special occasions and as such have drawn on customary practices that add meaning to the engagement of individuals and groups. The rites and rituals employed are many and varied. Organizers draw on tradition and cultural ceremonies by employing symbols and sensory stimuli, enveloping spaces with sound, color, and texture, and encouraging reflection on food, narratives, and sharing of gifts.

There is increasing research into the spectrum of experience afforded from the sacred to the profane, the religious identities through to the behaviors exemplified by the rituals of reversal we saw in Carnivale around the world. Falassi (1987) defined numerous types of rites and rituals that have been successfully incorporated in arts and cultural festivals, including:

- Rites of reversal—evident through costumes and masks with roles of good and evil portrayed at carnivals dating back to the Middle Ages, exploited in processions, parades, and spectacle
- Rites of passage—individual and group life cycles, nature, and humanity
- Ritual narratives—storytelling dramas based in myth and legend, sometimes liturgy
- Ritual of conspicuous consumption—food and beverages and feasting
- Rites of exchange—gifting and sharing with charities through donations
- Rites of competition popular in community events—contests that can be highly predictable and merit-based or ritualized and predictable
- Rites of purification—traditional purges, sacred elements, and symbols.

What rituals have you observed that have been featured over time in long-running festivals?

> **WELCOME**
>
> One of the significant aspects of feeling at home at festivals in Australia and New Zealand is the delivery of a traditional welcome to the country. In Australia, these comprise statements as a mark of respect to the traditional indigenous owners of sites where festivals are staged and they have become commonplace at public events. Elders of the local indigenous community are invited to come to be part of the opening ceremonies of special public functions. This acknowledgment indicates respect for cultural heritage. If an indigenous leader is not able to participate there is a protocol that offers organizers or civic officials a chance to acknowledge custodians of the land on which festivals are held.
>
> In New Zealand, the *pōwhiri* or *pōhiri* is a central part of Māori protocol. It is a ceremony of welcome involving speeches, dancing, singing, and hongi. It traditionally welcomes visitors on to *marae*, the sacred space or courtyard usually in front of Māori meeting houses. The ceremony is also commonly seen in everyday New Zealand life. Pōwhiri can happen anywhere that *tangata whenua* (hosts) wish to formally greet *manuhiri* (visitors). This chant is welcomed internationally and the haka are well-known rituals.

## Partnerships

Most festivals take advantage of trusting relationships between multiple enterprises that generally exist independently of one another, yet for a festival are mutually interdependent. This places substantial responsibility on each of the players involved in the collaboration. These are driven by individuals and agencies looking to exploit new opportunities and experiences.

The openness to collaborate is seen as a positive trait in organizations' leaders. In the host communities this leadership can come from within or outside the festival organization. What leaders can recognize is the value of connections with partners who can extend the organization's reach, enhance its program and networks, and energize its processes and practices. All festivals have confronted change inside and outside their organizations. By building coalitions from amongst festival partners, the resources, knowledge, and political clout can be mobilized to make things happen in the best interests of the festival.

## Sponsors

Partners like to sustain relationships with festivals where links deliver memorable and lasting connections. Sponsors will be satisfied if the festival matches their image through a shared target market. They are keen to receive effective media coverage to increase their brand recognition in the marketplace while, if they pursue naming rights to the festival, they receive some benefits for their broader networks. This may come in the form of access to corporate hospitality for themselves and their clients, contact with artists and celebrities, ongoing promotional opportunities beyond the actual event, and the investment is seen as a value for the money. Sponsors recognize the risks and costs, but what they aim for is attracting a band of unofficial brand ambassadors to share the sponsors' and the festival's promise via social media with a wider audience.

> Research undertaken by the Havas Sports and Entertainment (HS&E) network indicates that more than 60% of music festival-goers believe brands improve their festival experience. The study of 2,244 people at six festivals across Europe found that 60% of people interacted with two or more brands at a festival, and 85% liked the brand activations they visited. More than a third said this would affect their spending habits, with 36% claiming that they would be more likely to buy a sponsor's product after experiencing their activation. The research also found that festival-goers spend more than double the amount of time online than other consumers, suggesting social media is key to engaging with festival audiences. It reported "a memorable on-site experience combined with social network interaction could help brands build long-term relationships with music lovers" (Ridley, 2012).

There are festival-goers who are skeptical of the tie-ins that some music festivals particularly make with popular brands. Each is in a crowded market, so to ensure favorable experiences from all sides, care needs to be taken to make a credible match. In the UK, Virgin (in tourism and entertainment) and Tennent's (Scottish beer) have structured successful sponsor-naming deals despite dropping their full name from the festivals' titles, *T in the Park* and especially the *V Festival*. As sponsors are looking to commit to focused outcomes, it is interesting to reflect on a study undertaken on the future of festivals by the telecommunications company Orange in the UK as a contribution to the festival-making discourse through their partnership with the Glastonbury Festival and engaging the Future Laboratory brand strategy, consumer insight, and trends researchers.

For community festivals there are times of financial constraint that diminish the quality of the relationship between organizers and local businesses. The latter sometimes are controlled from head offices out of the region, often festivals are not seen as an essential investment, sometimes the lack of continuity is caused by spreading limited resources between a number of worthy local events rather than concentrating on one festival. The short-term commitment, the withdrawal, or the change of focus in business promotion or movement of key personnel all contribute to constant refreshing of the way the relationships are nourished to ensure positive experiences.

## Community

Communities are buoyed by the positive economic potential of festivals. They are satisfied if jobs result, businesses become suppliers and their sales increase new markets from locals and visitors through a "soft" environment, new money is introduced to the local economy, maybe foreign exchange that diversifies the market to the destination, acting as a catalyst to extend the season and spread benefits across a region or nation. Investments through government grants and sponsorship funds stimulate and optimize other fundraising initiatives. This serves to color resident, business, and local government's willingness to collaborate and feel confident about their experience. The transitory nature of festivals in communities can make them a less attractive partner for some businesses, so it is important that festival organizers scope the local business environment for opportunities to grow partnerships by understanding what the optimum experience for entrepreneurs might be and communicating effectively shared aspirations.

The World Cities Culture Report 2012 (BOP Consulting) suggests "the role of culture in cities is as important as trade and finance. Culture in all its diverse forms is central to what makes a city appealing to educated people and hence to the businesses which seek to employ them." It goes on to observe that "in a globalised knowledge economy, having a well educated workforce is the key to success and such workers demand a stimulating creative environment." So, how can festivals contribute to cultural experiences of residents and visitors while raising levels of economic activity?

Business considers festival benefits to economic activity include:

- Championing the region's economy and its development
- Increasing business competitiveness
- Developing people's skills and earning capacity
- Attracting new business and creating jobs
- Regenerating local communities through shopping locally
- Creating the right climate for investment
- Deepening relationships through business networks
- Increasing financial, in-kind, and advisory engagement
- Encouraging corporate social responsibility (CSR)
- Stimulating social enterprise development
- Bringing festival activities into the central business district (CBD)
- Increasing individual business to a new (and maybe diverse) market of festival audience

## Organizational Experience

The personal skills, traits, attributes, and behaviors of festival organizers that contribute to resilience are readily exposed to the public gaze. Small regional communities know what is going on and people easily become alert to how effective festival management is. They recognize the festival management's capacity to communicate well with the broader constituency and not be isolated from potential partners, maintain a sense of humor, and be creative in response to festival logistics and be flexible and adaptable in times of stress from internal or external factors. The cliché that goes, "what doesn't kill you makes you stronger" is often how resilience is seen. From a festival perspective, communities and organizers need to recognize that the challenges they face as their annual festival is prepared provides learning opportunities for all who are touched by it and each can grow from that experience.

## Significance of Festival Experiences

Festivals are open to personal interpretation. Festivals organize creativity in a less bureaucratic way than many expect. They seem to provide more of a bottom-up approach. They offer intense bursts of experience that can be savored and reflected upon, instantly and long after the engagement. This intense active recreation of experience is felt at the street level, but can be elevated to the memories and storytelling that are an inherent part of a tourism experience long after it has occurred.

The festival moves the social capital of interaction into the cultural capital of the host community and can bring the creativity of making the festival into the mainstream consciousness and practice of residents. That experience can be stored in the community's memory and called upon at later times for application to other aspects of the community's life.

# The Role of Ceremony and Ritual 213

Art in public spaces: Hyde Park, Sydney, Australia, creates a comfortable ambience for the Art and About Festival.

Communities are inclined to recognize the benefits that accrue from festivals that provide opportunities for communal celebrations and enhance a sense of shared identity and image, as this suggests a type of cohesion that doesn't emerge from other aspects of community life. Festivals seem to encourage new ideas and new ways to look at and think about things, so the legacy from such an experience can be significant. For some people the chance to access new activities, learn new skills, and expose yourself to new ways of doing things not only builds new networks within and between residents, but new relationships emerge from contact with other festival-goers.

Not all experiences are positive and organizers and other partners need to be alert to when there can be a breakdown in confidence between the festival and diverse stakeholders. Some residents will be concerned about the pressures that arise from increased visitation, from potential challenges to law and order, transport, environmental protection, and care of existing community infrastructure. Some groups already fragile from marginalization socially or culturally might resent intrusions and find the festival period an overwhelming challenge to their security.

## Festival Communities

The perspective of community and the personal ties of individuals question whether engagement through festivals, for example, will change the personal relationships of residents, whether it affects community diversification, generates a consciousness of outsiders and a "we" and "them" distinction, or characterizes residents' images of their town forming and maintaining bonds among residents. The solidarity generated by a willingness of residents to work together to achieve an expected image is different from sharing a common cultural background, the traditional basis for bonding. This has implications for resilience in community festivals. Residents may develop bonds as a result of their investment of working together developing the town's image. If tourism, for example, is community-created as is suggested by festivals welcoming visitors, the dynamic of working together to develop the community's image may bind residents and encourage identification with community through memorable festival experiences. Commentators are questioning the cultural homogenization of festivals that generates a sameness between places and cultural celebrations. What do you think?

## Memory and Sense of Place

Have you noticed how memory and sense of place can shape individuals? Festivals and events provide a vehicle for the arts to preserve and celebrate culture and provide a background for family reunions. When place becomes a family affair, as it does in many umbrella community-based cultural festivals, many old and former residents return regularly to the festival sites for nostalgic reasons, or to introduce following generations to personal heritage. This emphasizes the notion of place being a social construct; that it isn't an extra associated only with taste, touch, sound, and sight, but that it is something people can't afford to be without. People bring their "there," "here." People strive to interpret place through what exists there for them. Place attachment is seen as a center of felt value. Much more than an environment, it provides meaning in life and is a fundamental need and is enhanced when people are involved in the shaping of places. Bill O'Toole writes of the real promotion of festivals coming when the "product" becomes part of the culture. He suggests the physical environment in which festivals are hosted profile their areas way beyond any promotional campaign. His work in a music project in New South Wales' Macquarie Marshes (Event Project Management System, 2003) emphasizes the need for long-term festival aims to embrace the environment as a cultural artifact.

## Festival Place Experiences

More is being written about where space becomes place and where culture declares its presence as a result. This impacts the role places and spaces have on the memory of the festival experience. Community cultural celebrations acknowledge how residents convert physical boundaries to satisfy social and cultural needs. Tourism, for example, is typified in some respects as the experience and consumption of place. For places to achieve distinctiveness and status as places to go, or to be seen in, they have to be created. Organizers of festivals can offer tangible and intangible experiences to connect people to places, which is why some popular events are sited in spectacular locations. A "glow" can exist naturally and infuse place with a WOW factor that becomes synonymous with the festival's essence (e.g., Byron Bay in Australia, the Full Moon Festival on Koh Phangan in Thailand, or the Hebridean Celtic Festival in Stornoway in the Outer Hebrides of Scotland).

Individual and collective connections with festivals as leisure experiences are one way in which people practice space. Space is used to transform the way of making sense of being somewhere and doing something chosen on one's own terms. Festivals can thus assist in making sense of where people are through an understanding of the stories and unseen aspects of life in communities. The increased importance of photography through digital platforms for immediate distribution records the social engagement that festivals offer in particular places as a means of making sense of space.

It is interesting to canvas how the same place, the same piece of land, is looked upon with different eyes by different generations and social groups. Each person makes sense independently or in groups, while the festival environment is being collectively molded in an ongoing way, even for short periods of time. Many festival-goers find specific places exhibit spirit or personality, and thus appeal.

This can come about when they apply their moral and aesthetic discernment to sites and locations. Their appreciation of how the place embraces celebrations can become a substantial influence on repeat visitation through evoking a spatial and temporal attachment. The dynamic of water that can be employed to enchant and transport the spirit of place is demonstrated well by the Opera on the Lake festival in Bregenz, Austria, and Opera Australia's annual three-week spectacle on a stage, afloat on Sydney Harbour. Complete with fireworks, a harbor stage, and a giant chandelier, the 2012 performances of *La Traviata* transformed opera in Sydney like never before.

## Challenges

The emergence of new, recreated, or hybrid festivals satisfying a global tourism market raises the question of who is now producing the dominant meaning of community or place. Is it a group labeled *tourists* or those labeled *local residents*? The arrival of tourists may cause confusion for local residents who wish to control their culture and its development of memorable experiences for locals and visitors. Residents invest in their community through involvement with rituals that reinforce a sense of belonging. The attachment to place and community that develops through membership of their community provides strong identification with the culture developed there and is seen to be sufficient in some circumstances to withstand the intrusion of visitors. Resentment can arise when visitors wish to join in and demonstrate what they see as a cultural experience. This may offend the local traditions.

Over time festivals can provide tensions in terms of the physical aspects of public place-making and cultural experience, when locals and visitors accept the sameness in content. In regional contexts community festivals become symbolic and the patterns that demonstrate belonging need to maintain a strong connection to what the essence of the local value chain is. It is a testing time in determining the nature of a festival intrinsically being an agent of change, and it is being increasingly flexible in its intent to satisfy the local and visiting marketplace where the demand for homogenous entertainments can inhibit homegrown creativity.

The host community's culture becomes the raw material of the location and creativity the means of exploiting the resource. What emerges is that the host culture is not necessarily consensual. Popular regional communities are thought to be homogenous, agricultural, traditional entities that are reluctant to address change. Festivals are a useful vehicle to appreciate the level and capacity of communities to recognize how they can best represent their circumstances and share them with visitors.

The community cultural ecosystem includes a variety of agents that operate under the radar. The nature and role of festivals demonstrably encourages those hidden human and cultural resources in communities to be revealed in formal and informal ways. These adaptive processes include ensuring the widest possible reach is secured across a community's interest groups, and this is where the engagement of festival partners becomes important.

## Avoiding Festival Shortcomings

To ensure that festival-goers' expectations can be met and their experience is not memorable for the wrong reasons, it is important that organizers minimize negative outcomes, leaving the host community disaffected by their encounter with the festival's scale, timing, and program and miscalculating festival partner needs. These can result from insufficient time allocated for planning effectively, generation of confusion in the marketplace with mixed messages, failure to deal with risk management issues, poor internal communications, and inadequate budgeting and financial management.

Organizers learn from such comments as these posted on the Internet:

> What's the worst thing about festivals? The big ones—I would hazard to say it's the crowds. You're probably tipsy and lacking sleep and neither goes very well with thousands of other people in a similar state all trying to squeeze into the same field to catch the same halfway-cool act. All those feet create the other thing that most people associate with UK summer festivals—the mud. It doesn't take a storm to create mud from wet grass, it just takes a light shower and a few thousand feet. I found out that you cannot sit down unless you go all the way back to your tent, reverse in, and take off your wellies. Two days of this and you feel like you're going mental. Another thing that most festivals have suffered from intermittently is theft. Even if you lock your tent you cannot knife-proof it, so you take your money and whatever with you everywhere and have to dance with it bouncing upon your person somewhere. This becomes annoying. And the toilets. Even if they are "clean," there is most often a queue but often you will queue only to find a mess that you really don't want to be dealing with.

# CASE STUDY

## Experience of a Lifetime!

Accounts from individuals who have made the journey to the Black Rock Desert, Nevada, claim that "you had to be there" best sums up their experience. Many recount that their access to sensational ambience, activities, aesthetics, and remarkable adventures at this unconventional festival was a lifetime highlight. Many return for more! They feel liberated to be part of an experimental community. They are co-creators of their transformative experience and that of others. The result of this experiment is Black Rock City, home to the Burning Man event.

People new to Burning Man often assume that it's a regular "festival" as they've come to know them, a mostly passive experience where everything is planned, orchestrated, and prepackaged by the event producers, and attendees just come and enjoy the show. In fact, the exact opposite is true...the people who attend Burning Man are no mere "attendees," but rather active participants in every sense of the word: they create the city, the interaction, the art, the performance, and ultimately the "experience." Participation is at the very core of Burning Man, and there are many ways to participate.

There are no rules about how one must behave or express oneself at this event (save the rules that serve to protect the health, safety, and experience of the community at large); rather, it is up to each participant to decide how they will contribute and what they will give to this community.

There are many effusive accounts of practical contact with accompanying observations on the Web detailing the experiences of participants of Burning Man, an annual temporary community in the Black Rock Desert. Christine Kristen's (2006) essay on the connections made between art and life for participants brings to life some of the imagination, aesthetics, and application of creativity and innovation that provides a useful case study for this chapter.

It is apparent that no one attending Burning Man is a spectator, everyone is a participant. Reading Molly Steenson's overview of the experience addresses the notion of celebration by engagement. The impressions of knowledge gained, skills acquired, and memorable impressions results from your engagement with the site, the people, and the projects. She claims:

> You're here to survive.
> You're here to create.
> You're here to experience.
> You're here to celebrate.
> You leave as you came.

When you depart from Burning Man, you leave no trace. Everything you built, you dismantle. The waste you make and the objects you consume leave with you. Volunteers will stay for weeks to return the Black Rock Desert to its pristine condition.

The impact of the Burning Man experience has been so profound that a culture has formed around it. This culture has led to people banding together nationwide and putting on their own events, in an attempt to rekindle that magic feeling that only being part of this community can provide.

Rafael Agustin Delgado, a photographer, reports, "I went to Burning Man for a break from the normal and I returned a much different individual. Never before have I experienced a more welcoming community like Burning Man. It's by far one of the most unique experiences out there, though it's not for everyone, that's for sure. However, if you are willing to let people be, it will be a rewarding experience."

*The Burning Man Mission Statement*

*Our mission is to produce the annual event known as "Burning Man" and to guide, nurture and protect the more permanent community created by its culture. Our intention is to generate society that connects each individual to his or her creative powers, to participation in community, to the larger realm of civic life, and to the even greater world of nature that exists beyond society. We believe that the experience of Burning Man can produce positive spiritual change in the world. To this end, it is equally important that we communicate with one another, with the citizens of Black Rock City and with the community of Burning Man wherever it may arise. Burning Man is radically inclusive, and its meaning is potentially accessible to anyone. The touchstone of value in our culture will always be immediacy: experience before theory, moral relationships before politics, survival before services, roles before jobs, embodied ritual before symbolism, work before vested interest, participant support before sponsorship. Finally, in order to accomplish these ends, Burning Man must endure as a self-supporting enterprise that is capable of sustaining the lives of those who dedicate themselves to its work. From this devotion spring those duties that we owe to one another. We will always burn the Man.*

Judd Weiss reports of his first visit to the festival in 2012, "The one thing that unites everyone is that this is clearly a city for the unconventional. The wackier and more offbeat you are, the better. This serves as a powerful bond among everyone. Far and away this is the most accepting group of people I've ever seen. If you ever lose your friends, there are 50,000 other friends of yours around. Everyone is very friendly and helpful. It's beyond that. When you comment to any random stranger it feels like you're chatting with a friend you've known for decades."

## The Finale

There is a giant man of wood and neon perched atop a giant tower in the center of the semi-circle of the city that forms around it. On Saturday night comes the ritual ceremony and they finally burn "The Man." All 50,000 people gather in the playa. The ceremony begins with a large group of fire dancers. And these are some of the most talented and interesting fire dancers I've ever seen. The energy from so many around you is intense. Excitement is building. And then the fireworks start (Weiss, 2010).

There are numerous objects kept or collected as a result of involvement with Burning Man. These tokens of remembrance include the outreach to fellow travelers or the curious or the next generation of participants. The following online connections can be made to capture the experience of attendees and the organizational aspiration of this unique event.

# FROM INSIDE THE MOSAIC

## Memorable Experiences
### Steven Wood Schmader, CFEE
### President and CEO, International Festivals and Events Association (IFEA World)

Steve's leadership contribution to individual large and small organizations has inspired festival-makers around the world. His commitment to education, professional development, and promotion of good practice is exemplary. He writes:

When the mosaic of a successful festival or event comes together, it is a masterpiece that is most often remembered for the entire experience, taken as a whole, and not for each individual component that makes up that experience; but it is the awareness of and detail given to each of those components by the festival/event planner that ensures that the brand and event will endure for many years, and perhaps generations.

Steven Wood Schmader, CFEE

The genesis of a successful and enduring festival/event begins with far more than the spark of an idea among friends scribbled on the back of a napkin (although even Disney World shared DNA from such simple beginnings). A successful festival/event grows from a clearly defined and detailed vision that takes into account all targeted audiences (including their likely desires, needs, interests, capabilities/disabilities, comfort zones, and safety); effective use of available venue space; quality control and ambiance creation; budgetary needs/realities/priorities; and human resource needs/training. The most successful festival/event producers can picture attending their own event in their mind before a single tent/stage has been erected, a portable restroom has been placed, or a road closure requested.

The more professionally produced a festival or event is, the easier it looks. A good event planner doesn't want attendees thinking about how much work went into producing it; they want them to be having fun. But make no mistake about it, that "fun" is well planned. Most of those who are new to the festivals and events profession—many motivated from a memorable event experience of their own—want to quickly get into the operations part of the process; arranging for 'things' (entertainment, infrastructure, food vendors, etc.) to happen. But much of the success and sustainability of a festival lies in the initial planning, visioning, market and funding research, branding and imaging thought processes, legal and risk management considerations, and the creation of a plan that, while flexible, provides everyone with a common direction and grounded reality, instills an aura of credibility and professionalism to those whose support you will need, and provides a management tool from which to judge your progress and success.

While the products that our industry produces are certainly fun and exciting, behind every successful "fun" festival/event is a successful business and, like any business, the most successful ones have a staff (one or many, paid or volunteer) whose job it is to focus on and manage the success of that festival/event every day. Again, it is often the perception that because an event is only in the public eye for a short window each year that it can be successfully produced in a similarly short planning window, or as one of multiple projects on someone's desk. Given the proper "care and feeding," a festival can provide countless benefits and memories to the communities that they serve, for many years. Without that focus the event itself will likely become a memory within a relatively short window.

From festivals and events that I have personally created, experienced, and enjoyed throughout my career, I would offer some of the following thoughts for anyone entering or continuing in the profession of festival and event management:

- **Know Your Audience and Community.** Unless you are planning a smaller niche event, take time to research and understand your community and audience. When programming events, activities, entertainment, etc., be sure that you are serving the masses and not being unduly influenced by personal tastes and/or guesses about what may play well in your market. I have seen events go out of business as a result of dramatically changing their direction and alienating audiences and sponsors as a result.
- **Provide Something (of Quality) for Everyone.** While others will tell you that you can't accomplish this, I courteously disagree. In fact, for a community festival to truly be a community festival it must succeed at providing something of interest and the appropriate services for all potential audiences: young, old, families, those with disabilities/special needs, etc. It may include outreach programs to hospitals or classroom projects in local schools, but quality is the key. Your children's area should be just as well designed and produced as any other part of your event. While this is certainly a challenge that requires both creativity and planning, it will also ensure broad support and participation for your event.
- **Remember that "the Experience is Everywhere": Think Like a Theme Park.** A quality festival is not just what is happening on a stage, or the parade units coming down the street, or the fireworks in the sky, although all of those will certainly create an indelible image of your event in the minds of attendees.

A quality festival experience (whether they are aware of it or not) begins before your attendees leave their homes and continues through the media coverage that they read/view when it is over. It includes the ease of finding and getting onto a website to download schedules and directions; the quality of your program and marketing materials; the parking/mass transit experience (what happens while they are waiting, while they are on the bus; and when they arrive at the festival site); the quality and creativity put into everything from signage and decorations to restrooms and trash pickup; the friendliness of volunteers and access to services to roaming entertainers/activities along their path to other venues; and an awareness of a friendly security presence, without being a "police state." Disney World bookends the day for their guests with upbeat music as they arrive in the morning and more tranquil music at the end of the day. Walk through your event and make sure it is the experience that you want it to be; think like a theme park.

A quality festival experience should leave those attending with a feeling of contentment and satisfaction; a commitment to return next time because they couldn't possibly see/do everything they wanted to do; and a sense of ownership and pride in "their" community festival.

# Festival Ideas and Issues

1. Discuss ways in which festival experiences can be "memorable"?
2. Can festival experiences be designed? What do organizers have to consider generally and specifically to make their planned celebration distinctive?
3. Audience numbers are the most important determinant for a festival's success. Discuss.
4. Poet John Lydgate (c. 1370–c. 1451) said, later adapted by President Abraham Lincoln, something like, "You can please some of the people all of the time, you can please all of the people some of the time, but you can't please all of the people all of the time." How can festival organizers deal creatively with diverse festival partners so they derive satisfaction from their engagement?

5. Review the experience factors that are described in the writings of Pine and Gilmore's (1999) work on the experience economy and apply the following to festival experiences you have had or can envisage: Fully theme the encounter • Individualize guests' encounters • Create targeted impressions • Eliminate negative cues • Engage multiple senses • Provide memorabilia • Get into character and act your part • Perform to form.
6. What could some of the challenges be that weaken an individual's festival experience?

## Festival Focus Activities

1. Consider the design and layout of the festival site with which you are familiar and determine a typical festival guests' use of the venue. How effective and efficient have the organizer's choices been? What decisions have been influenced by external forces and which would particularly be in the interests of the guest satisfaction? A particular focus could be the entrance to the venue. What are the optimum requirements?
2. Assemble a collage of signage at festivals. What are the key elements that will affect the level of satisfaction of festival patrons at festival venues? What about the impact of specific incidents or occurrences on the design and effectiveness of signage you have noticed?
3. Consider the central themes of some festivals you have investigated. How have they been manifested for the audiences? Collect examples of how arts and community cultural festivals differentiate themselves from other similar festivals.
4. Parasurman et al. (1985) developed a conceptual model of 10 service quality attributes that were later reduced to five and are known as SERVQUAL. The latter are tangibles, reliability, responsiveness, assurance, and empathy. Give examples of each of these as a part of festival experiences you have had as an audience member. How is the service quality enhanced?
5. *"Festivals ... there's nothing like 'em. You rock up, pitch a tent, down warm beer, brave rancid portaloos, make new mates, lose your existing ones, and see great bands (then miss others because you're still lining up for a bloody beverage)."* In a group compile a list of the most memorable moments from your festival experiences.

## Suggested Reading

Brennan-Horley, C. R., J. Connell, and C. R. Gibson. "The Parkes Elvis revival festival: Economic development and contested place identities in rural Australia." *Geographical Research* 45, no. 1 (2007): 71–84.

Crouch, D. "Introduction: Leisure/Tourism Geographies," in *Practices and Geographical Knowledge*, ed. D. Crouch. (London, UK: Routledge, 1999).

Csikszentmihaly, M. *Finding Flow: The Psychology of Engagement with Everyday Life*. New York: Basic Books, 1997.

Falassi, A. Festival: Definition and Morphology, in *Time Out of Time: Essays on the Festival*, ed. A. Falassi (Albuquerque, NM: University of New Mexico Press), pp. 1–10.

Getz, D. *Event Studies, Theory, Research and Policy for Planned Events.* Oxford, UK: Butterworth-Heinemann, 2007.

Kim, K., M. Uysal, and J. S. Chen. "Festival Visitor Motivation from the Organisers' Point of View." *Event Management* 7, no. 2 (2001): 127–134.

Kristen, C (aka Labybee), "Reconnecting Art and Life at Burning Man," *Raw Vision*, Issue 57 (2006): http://rawvision.com/articles/reconnecting-art-and-life-burning-man.

Mackellar, J. "Dabblers, fans and fanatics: Exploring behavioural segmentation at a special-interest event." *Journal of Vacation Marketing* 15, no. 1 (2009): 5–24.

Morgan, M. *Festival Spaces and the Visitor Experience.* Available at eprints.bournemouth.ac.uk/4821/1/99__Morgan.pdf, 2009.

Morgan, M. "Making space for experience." *Journal of Retail and Leisure Property* Palgrave Macmillan, Volume 5, no. 4 (2006): 305–313.

Morgan, M. *What makes a good festival?: Understanding the visitor experience.* Paper presented at the Association of Event Management Educators Forum, Bournemouth, UK, 2006.

O'Hara, B., and M. Beard. *Music Event and Festival Management.* London, UK: Wise Publications, 2006.

O'Toole, W., *Music in the Macquarie Marshes*, www.epms.net, Australia, 2003.

Quinn, B. Whose festival? Whose place?: An insight into the production of cultural meanings in arts festivals turned visitor attractions, in *Reflections on International Tourism: Expressions of Culture Identity and Meaning in Tourism*, eds. M. Robinson, P. Long, N. Evans, J. Swarbrooke and Sharpley (University of Northumbria at Newcastle and Sheffield Hallam University, 2000).

Parasuraman, A., V. A. Zeithaml, and L. L. Berry. "A conceptual model of service quality and its implications of future research." *Journal of Marketing* 49, no. 4 (1985): 41–50.

Parasuraman, A. "SERVQUAL: A multiple-item scale for measuring consumer perceptions of service quality." *Journal of Retailing* 64, no. 4 (1988): 12–40.

Pine, J., and L. Gilmore, L. *The Experience Economy: Work is Theater and Every Business a Stage.* Boston, MA: Harvard Business School Press, 1999.

Prentice, R., and V. Andersen. "Festival as Creative Destination." *Annals of Tourism Research* 30, no. 1 (2003): 7–30.

Ralston, L. S., G. D. Ellis, D. M. Compton, and J. Lee. "Staging Memorable Events and Festivals: An Integrated Model of Service and Experience Factors." *International Journal of Event Management Research* 3, no. 2 (2007): 24–38.

Schmitt, B. *Experiential Marketing: How to Get Customers to Sense, Feel, Think, Act and Relate to your Company and Brands.* New York: Free Press, 1999.

Seligman, M. E. P. *Flourish.* New York: Simon and Schuster, 2011.

Silvers, J. *Professional Event Co-ordination.* Hoboken, NJ: Wiley, 2004.

Stebbins, R. "Causal Leisure: A Conceptual Statement." *Leisure Studies* 16 (1997): 17–25.

Tuan, Y.-F. *Topophilia: A Study of Environmental Perceptions, Attitudes and Values.* Englewood Cliffs, NJ: Prentice-Hall, 1974.

Weiss, J., *My First Burning Man Experience–2010* http://hustlebear.com/2010/09/11/my-first-burning-man-experience-2010/.

Yolal, M., E. Woo, F. Cetinel, and M. Uysal. "Comparative research of motivations across different festival products." *International Journal of Event and Festival Management* 3, no. 1 (2012): 66–80.

Zeithaml, V. A., and A. Parasuraman. *Service Quality.* Cambridge, MA: Marketing Science Institute, 2004.

# CHAPTER 10
# Festival Media Platforms

The way we learn about, well ... everything, has become so immediate, we barely have any room for surprise. At a recent music festival people tweeted about what was going on at different stages, photos were taken, videos filmed, and we all rushed ahead to be in the right place at the right time. Sure it was still extraordinary to see the musicians up on stage, but the sense of being somewhere just at the right moment in time is lost. No mystery.

—Cassandra Tobin, commenter, 2012

This chapter provides an opportunity for you to better understand:

- The importance of a festival's communication plan
- Trends in marketing strategies for festivals
- Distinctive traditional and contemporary media practices
- The value of social media and digital platforms for festival success through consistent content management

Festival patrons, as they do in other parts of the economy, expect timely, targeted, and rewarding relationships with those who have goods and services to share. Researchers have documented the shift from the traditional, transactional marketing strategies that have been used to inform, persuade, and remind patrons. There are newer communication channels to attract their loyalty. In this chapter we investigate the complexity of transforming the marketing relationship from a sole, one-way focus on customers to broader communication platforms that also embrace collaboration with partners. The key elements of this complex communication mix are identified in the mosaic below in Figure 10.1.

## CHAPTER 10  FESTIVAL MEDIA PLATFORMS

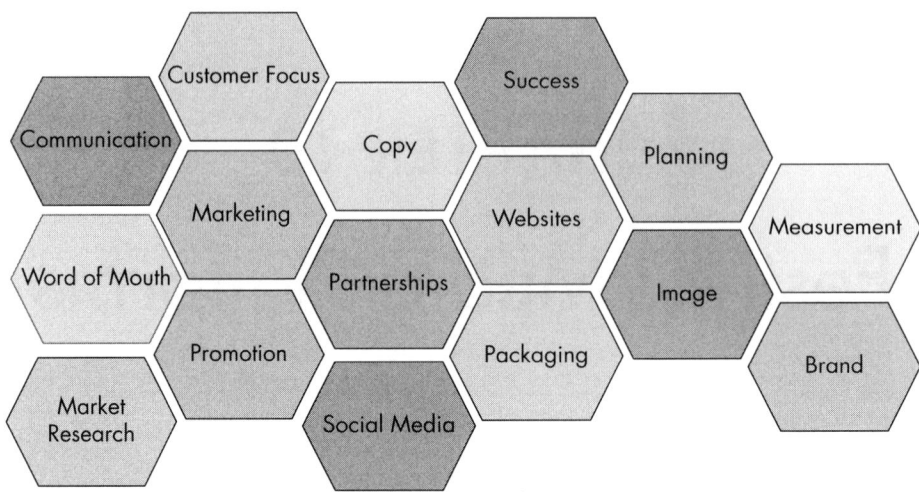

**Figure 10.1**  Meaningful Media Relationship Mosaic.

# Reaching Festival Audiences

Developments in digital technology have assisted in finessing the lines of communication required between all active participants in festival-making to ensure patrons engage in new levels of commitment to and ownership of their festival experience. It has meant a thorough reassessment of the festival organization's responsiveness to each relationship being developed over time. Festival organizers increasingly have to set themselves apart from the competition. It is imperative they find ways to create and sustain festival brand loyalty by integrating it into innovative approaches to strengthen lasting and mutually beneficial relationships with sympathetic individuals and groups.

A variety of relationship-building tools comprise traditional and emerging approaches that satisfy the whole festival network's needs. People still wish to be and feel among the first to know about festival offerings, so engagement with their favored communication channels can quickly reveal program highlights, special deals, and opportunities to share an experience with likeminded patrons. Digital platforms allow for electronic notices to capture their attention, excite interest through various audio-visual stimuli, and through links with festival partners to spread the word instantaneously. By maintaining a unique selling proposition and designing engaging marketing campaigns, festival organizations can empower potential patrons by integrating online features to facilitate enduring relationships. These features can include interactive online registration and ticketing, targeted audience responses and feedback, payment processing, priority invitations, scheduling templates, in-depth program information, policy and ancillary festival features such as local destination options, additional promotional opportunities and live feeds emphasizing testimonials and representative festival content to indicate points of difference.

As we examine the key elements of communication and marketing, we recognize the importance of establishing a framework to accommodate the process that best matches the festival's goals and its celebratory spirit. It must be adequately resourced. A strategy must be formulated that recognizes previous market research, analyzes competitive environments,

You may have noticed in some towns and cities festival organizations have established a shop-front outlet site in popular thoroughfares for locals and visitors to find out more about the festival. The spaces are open to the public, sometimes year-round, or for specific periods in the lead-up to the festival. Organizers have recognized the value of positioning the festival as a mainstream entity that welcomes people to the total destination experience, introduces the festival, and serves as a box office and distribution center for their main event and any ancillary activities they develop. Depending on the size of the space there can be workshops, exhibitions, demonstrations, and social events staged to introduce celebrities or festival artists.

The venue promotes the festival brand through ambience, publications, postcards, merchandising, and memorabilia for those who already know the festival's ambitions or have been inspired to learn more. The use of street banners, distinctive signage, posters, music, internet access, and other stimuli draw attention to the festival through a lively interactive venue. It provides an outlet for other attractions in the destination through collaborative marketing and packaging of experiences from accommodation to local tours.

and formulates clear, consistent, and coherent programs through effective implementation and control while monitoring a plan's progress. For a festival to maintain a strong position in the consciousness of its stakeholders it must embrace the opportunities for collaboration that accentuate the distinctiveness and value attached to the product, the price of the experience, the promotion of its messages, and the people involved.

The marketing literature is replete with tips and research on successes and failures to chart the most appropriate campaign to address potential customer behavior and motivations, while monitoring the changes that are impacting the arts and cultural sector that underpin the content and direction for each particular festival. The shift from a focus on the product to customer-centric characteristics, tastes, and experience is manifested in how successful festivals have adapted to internal and external trends in marketing. Recognition of the changes has assisted festivals to survive and thrive. While personalization of messages is attractive and effective, it need not come at the expense of more traditional and sometimes simple lines of communication.

## Communication

Messages in any medium need to be closely tied to overall festival aims and objectives. The information delivered about any issue or ideal must compel the targeted audience to think, feel, or act. So, each communiqué needs to indicate some sort of importance, urgency, relevance, or magnitude in light of the audience's values, beliefs, or interests. These approaches reflect an understanding of what would motivate the audience to think, feel, or act in a culturally relevant and memorable manner and so become more appealing.

### A Communication Plan

A festival communication plan can be developed from within the host organization or can be generated through the engagement of external expert services. Each can undertake an initial audit of current practice and inform on options that will ensure that all parties know what is to be achieved effectively. This can come about through meetings with the board, staff, volunteers, membership, and partners, and sometimes it is helpful to canvass input from nonaffiliated people to better understand the festival's reputation and visibility, the existing patron loyalty, the role of teamwork, an assessment of external influences and interaction between current communication practice, and the aspiration identified in the festival's mission and objectives.

The main components of a communication plan are the:

- Communication objectives—what and why are you communicating?
- Target audience—with whom do you want to communicate?
- Communication tools—what methods of communication are most appropriate for your target audience?
- Timing and frequency—when and how often to communicate?
- Responsibilities—who is going to undertake the communication?
- Communication quality—what are the key concepts for excellent communication?

The plan's communication objectives can include:

- To strengthen the relationship between the festival partners by providing information.
- To ensure quality at all stages of the action plan to maximize the impact of the message.
- To actively develop and support the continuous improvement of appropriate tools and outcomes.
- To engage staff and volunteers who have skills and interests in promotion.
- To develop links with communication products and media platforms to reach the target audiences matching the appropriate messages and their means of distribution.
- To translate the language of strategy into the language of action.

Developing and implementing a coherent, comprehensive, and consistent communication plan provides a specific framework for all internal and external interaction. It needs to be a tailored exchange, information-sharing, documentation, scheduling, research, measurement, and reporting tool. Like all strategic and tactical documents it is cyclical and so all actions need to be monitored to ensure there are clear instructions to maintain optimum results. The plan needs to be targeted. Festival organizers need to work confidently to make certain that specific influential stakeholders receive material in a timely and appropriate way, ever mindful of the frequency of communication that ensures effectiveness. A simple pro forma, in Table 10.1, helps.

| Activity | Timing | | Key Message | Channel | Responsibility | Audience | Frequency |
|---|---|---|---|---|---|---|---|
| | Start | Finish | | | | | |
| | | | | | | | |
| | | | | | | | |
| | | | | | | | |

**Table 10.1** Communication Plan Framework

The types of simple communication tools that can be employed include writing reports; conducting forums or information sessions; writing articles; compiling newsletters, pamphlets, brochures, and press releases; conducting face-to-face meetings or Skyping; encouraging buy-in; and capitalizing on word of mouth and using conventional media of TV, radio, newspapers, and magazines. The communication plan involves consultation infrastructure development to connect employees with one another. An internal communication channel can be a meeting, a Web page, or a memo. Organizations determine the best way to mine the information, market intelligence or actionable ideas from a variety of sources. These include staff meetings, employee and leadership meetings, conference calls, online chatrooms, casual conversations, the wall (Gantt) chart, interoffice email/memo, or organizational calendar.

Such a plan is not just a wish list. As a living document, it requires some often overlooked practices relating to phone-answering protocols, response times for email contact, maintenance of social media programs, hospitality during meetings, and documentation for archival purposes through SMART objectives. Such a schedule through critical path analysis or a Gantt chart in paper or electronic form illustrates the start and completion of tasks comprised of milestones, relationships, and responsibility and target audience.

Decisions need to be made regarding when the communication needs to be undertaken and what specific tools will be employed to a particular audience. Clear concise messages generally require collation and synthesizing for each contact person or group and the distribution method needs to be matched to the needs of each stakeholder to allow for an open approach through feedback, exchange, and an ongoing credible relationship. It is useful to include those risk management tools discussed earlier through a crisis communication strategy.

## Customer Focus

Organizations that have recognized the importance of the customer have used techniques in diverse media to enlist their assistance to perform critical tasks. Marketing writers like Philip Kotler have identified a number of practical approaches to customer engagement that informs and enhances the festival's capacity to attract and retain loyal patrons, staff, and media partners while satisfying host community support. Successful festivals have looked for ways to make their customers and other partners part of the team to:

- Have consumer input in the design of the site, program, and festival experience through suggestions, feedback, and focus groups.
- Maximize on-selling the attributes of the festival through social, professional, and peer networks.
- Identify best performing and appropriate media to reach wider audiences.
- Encourage patrons to invest through crowdfunding, philanthropy, corporate investment, or programs of corporate social responsibility through in-kind budgetary minimization.
- Offer testimonials for copywriting purposes to be used as part of ongoing promotion.
- Receive feedback on staff performance and contribute to staff/volunteer training programs.
- Identify good practices in competing events to ensure application of appropriate actions to appeal to target audiences.

- Better understand what currently works at the festival through quality audits by patrons of work practices, effectiveness of meeting market trends, and recognizing professional staff and actions employed at alternate festivals.

These contributions have been known to be incentives for greater loyalty from patrons who wish to be actively engaged with their favored festivals. The value of the exchange is demonstrated as individuals and organizations expect to gain some sort of reward in excess of any costs incurred. This reflects how significant the market is in driving decisions through the exchange.

## Marketing Plan

The increasing competitiveness in the special events sector alerts organizers to the fact that they can no longer have a grab-bag approach to marketing their event. When approaching government agencies for subsidies, a marketing plan is expected as part of the master action plan for the event. Sponsors also require information about how the event will be promoted before they commit funds. The voluntary exchanges between parties that characterize marketing are not restricted to products with prices. Other considerations to be taken into the equation include how parties share information; where they purchase items (directly, as retail or through intermediaries); levels of service for experiences before, during, and after engagement; at what price; and how often and what has been the patron's reaction. The appeal of the marketing discipline for many practitioners is, in fact, in how it is actioned in practice. The marketing orientation can be creative, stimulating, challenging, and satisfying, but ultimately it needs to be connected to the strategic and sustainable balance between goals of for-profit or not-for-profit organizations through the supply and demand for goods and services.

The benefits of a marketing plan, like any other strategic document, include a process where there are common terms of reference through a holistic approach for all stakeholders through the application of consistent objectives, with activities matched with target markets that allow continuity for long-term festival planning and positioning in a way that success can be measured. Such a clear and simple plan needs to be fact-based, organized and coordinated, consistent with the overall communication plan, flexible, and appropriately resourced (Figure 10.2).

The marketing plan is commonly confused by less experienced practitioners with one of the 4Ps: promotion. This "P" is most readily distinguished in terms of reach because this communication form includes advertising, public relations, publicity, use of media, banners and signs, ticketing, direct mail, merchandising, the Internet, telemarketing, and on-site promotions. There are four objectives most ascribed to this facet:

- A   Attracting attention
- I   Developing interest
- D   Creating desire
- A   Inducing action

You can analyze messages constructed by festivals that you have observed and determine the most successful elements included (Table 10.2).

# Marketing Plan

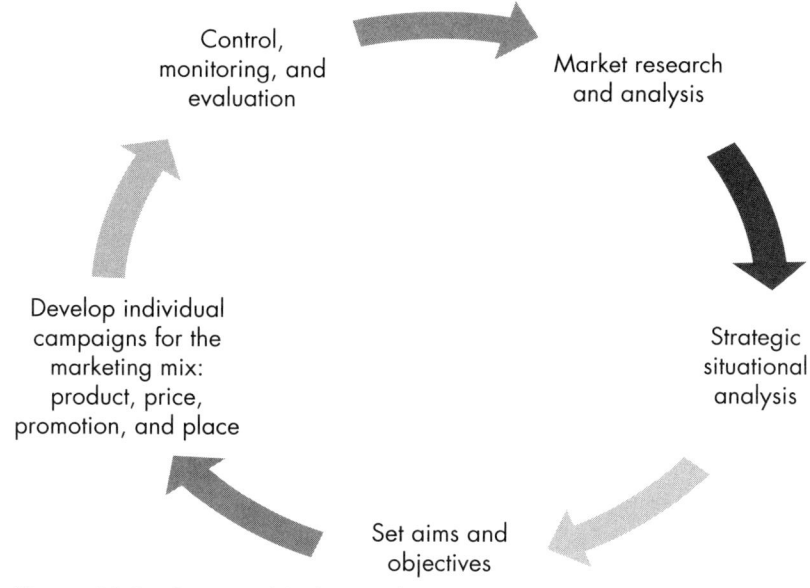

**Figure 10.2** Strategic Marketing Planning. Derrett (2013).

| Core Domains | Characteristics |
|---|---|
| Communication Policy | The overarching strategy to provide coherent and consistent approaches to festival relationships. It includes all written, spoken, and electronic interaction. |
| Marketing Plan | Understand the value of strategies connecting product, price, place, people, positioning, partnerships, packaging, and promotion |
| Content Strategy | The art of understanding what customers need to know and delivering it in a compelling (and uncomplicated) way—attention to sourcing; copywriting; editing; proofreading clear, credible themes; messages through an accessible framework |
| Content and Marketing Policy | Comprehensively recognize and address key areas of consistency, coherence, control, credibility, clarity, customers, community, competitors, compromise, common sense, and consultation with experts |
| Setting the Stage for Success | Understand through market research<br>Positioning yourself within community/industry/niche<br>Developing a powerful marketing plan<br>"Chance favors the prepared mind"—Louis Pasteur<br>Prudent budgeting<br>Considering the use of professionals<br>Methods of measurement—evaluation through surveys, questionnaires, internal/external |

**Table 10.2** Sharing Festival Messages

| | |
|---|---|
| Image-Building—create a good lasting impression | Image is power<br>Evaluate business attitude and corporate manners<br>Develop a brand that encourages loyalty<br>Use telephone as goodwill ambassador<br>Create stunning/excellent logos and slogans, letterhead, business cards as mini billboards, banners, print merchandise, buses, taxis, roadside billboards, any signage consistent with message<br>Consider festival name—What's in a name?<br>Remember—30-second impression, only one chance to make a first impression |
| Maintaining Meaningful Dialogue with Loyal Patrons | Use of online technology to ensure timely, personalized communication, the strength of word of mouth, networking, local support<br>Engage with professional outside agencies to feed into delivery of communication and marketing initiatives<br>Use links to other organizations, sponsors, and tourism partners |
| Advertising | Writing copy from a benefit perspective—YOU is most important word!<br>Yale research suggests—save/health/love/proven/discover/easy/safety/guarantee/money/new/results/YOU<br>Key task—inform, persuade, remind<br>The RUB formula—repetitive, uniform, basic<br>Use advertorials, display advertising, classified advertising<br>Check best placement ploys, choosing the appropriate media<br>Use industry, phone, local directories<br>Attend trade fairs, exhibitions,<br>Use telemarketing, novelty merchandising |
| Direct Marketing | Compile and control campaign packages (letters, updated mailing lists, benefits, response and follow-up), offer incentives and rewards |
| Securing Sales | Consider the Pareto Rule where 80% of impact, rewards results from 20% of effort, resources or cause<br>Use the "swipe" file—collect and appropriate existing ideas<br>Cultivate testimonials/endorsements—power of referral use in advertising<br>Encourage financial incentives, fundraisers, go on the road to build year-long presence<br>Engage with lateral thinking, sponsorships, discounts, local editorial, photographs, and satisfied customers |
| Promotion | Use consumer education—seminars to publicize cause, festival, organization<br>Avoid acronyms and jargon in copy<br>Consider corporate entertaining, creating a special event<br>Encourage host community involvement<br>Include contests, awards, surveys<br>Produce a newsletter, chatroom, message zone<br>Use hotlines—telephone<br>Use coupons, barter, discounts<br>Gain government recognition for work you do<br>Use professional directories<br>Use celebrities<br>Write newspaper articles and columns and letters to the editor, produce a book<br>Networking professionally to create synergy and momentum<br>Become a joiner, celebrate special days |

**Table 10.2** Sharing Festival Messages *(continued)*

| | |
|---|---|
| Packaging | This builds on any number of festival partnerships, especially tourism operators, local government, business and natural resource managers, Links to tourism and travel infrastructure allows for patrons to build a "package" of benefits (and affect price through economies of scale) that might include accommodation, transport, hospitality, food and beverage deals, other entertainment options, links to arts workshops/master classes Inclusive ticketing may be done online, through an agency, or directly with host organization and could value-add to shared branding |
| Providing Outstanding Service and Customer Satisfaction | Staff and partner briefings and training to emphasize host/guest relationship Employee motivation by foundations—share all business info from outset, offer clear job descriptions, establish communication/marketing teams, provide good working conditions, encourage volunteer and employee recognition program, benefits and rewards, offer contra with other businesses |
| Media Connection | Conventional use of radio, TV, print, Web, and cinema for PR, publicity, advertising |
| Online | Streamline digital media marketing—telecommunications<br>Top of mind—search engines—location, location, location<br>e-commerce—financial and follow-up strategies |
| **Conceptual and Theoretical Frameworks** | |
| • Marketing concept and definitions<br>• Wraparound marketing<br>• Relationship Marketing<br>• Ambush and guerrilla marketing<br>• Acquisition and retention marketing<br>• Consumer-focused marketing<br>• Cause-related marketing<br>• Experiential marketing<br>• eMarketing<br>• Brand management<br>• Market segmentation<br>• Market intelligence | • The marketing literature has documented the value and impact of marketing practices over time. Become familiar with the work of marketing gurus who have presented work on these approaches to connect customers and goods and services.<br>○ *Philip Kotler* prolific writer, academic, and popularizer of the 4 Ps<br>○ *David Ogilvy* who has contributed much to the advertising discipline<br>○ *Michael Porter's* considerable contribution to marketing knowledge through competition and economic development; he leads Harvard Business School's Institute for Strategy and Competitiveness<br>○ *Edward de Bono* has made a significant contribution to creative thinking that engages marketing<br>○ *Hugh Mackay* is a prominent Australian social researcher<br>○ *Victor T.C. Middleton* and peers have advanced travel and tourism marketing research<br>○ *Alistair Morrison* (http://www.belletourism.com/html/morrison.html) has contributed valuable practical and academic research |

Table 10.2 Sharing Festival Messages *(continued)*
Derrett (2013).

# The Power of Print

Festival marketers recognize the effectiveness of the print medium to disseminate important festival messages. Over time, varying materials have provided platforms to inform, persuade, and remind people of the festival's brand, content, value, and legacy. The print media's value is in the service it provides festival communities to share information, educate, entertain, challenge, charm, transmit culture, and celebrate and record heritage. From postcards disseminated worldwide, posters in local shop windows, newsletters to specific audiences like volunteers and members and partners, massive billboards at town entrances, inserts in local papers, children's coloring panels, prints transferred on the sides of taxis and buses, street banners, business directories, journals, professional calendars, paid advertising in papers and magazines, tourism collateral, whimsical small foldout maps, leaflets, pamphlets, and brochures—each providing a record of annual festivals. The impact of the design elements (text, fonts) and the repetition in the various printed media can be enduring. Elements become part of the memory of the festival experience. Some of the same material can be translated onto festival merchandise such as t-shirts, caps, scarves, and bags.

Much of this type of promotion places a strong demand on the festival budget. Once again collaboration between festival partners helps defray costs, extends reach, and generates a context that can play out as destination competitiveness. Technological advancements, economies of scale, and public spaces that accommodate such printed communication all work. The text, imagery, and intent can readily be shared not only across space but also across electronic media platforms including television and radio in a timely fashion. The power of print should not be underestimated for mass communication or intimate and specialized target markets.

Local, national, and international print publications should not be underestimated for the capacity they have to share news and information, generate comment and feedback, and raise the profile of individual festivals. International agencies now network news and articles that can be channeled into column spaces, radio airtime, and Web-based platforms as well as in specialist arts, tourism, and lifestyle or business newspapers. Magazines of general or specific interest contribute to the growing area of commentary, ideas, and innovation exchange and can offer festivals a niche or curious audience. Festival marketers will be interested to know the circulation attributed to each of the print media chosen to distribute the festival message. Likewise, they will monitor the impact on the organization's financial bottom line (ROI) and increased awareness of the festival's contribution to the economic and social life of the host community. This can be linked to the festival's evaluation survey (e.g., Where did you hear about this festival?), which can determine the effectiveness of some of its promotional spend.

## The Internet

The extensive engagement with the Internet has seen the rise of the use of websites (as a communication and marketing tool) among other platforms by festivals. Each is dependent on an understanding of its reach and its capacity to personalize and to meet market segment needs by selling the benefits in language that resonates in terms of timeliness, price, features, clichés, calls to action, free items, price and discounts. It is the content strategy that uncovers the dilemma of whether the festival website is in fact a marketing or publishing tool. The strategy needs to incorporate text, graphics, video, and audio. A presentation by Halvorson and Pulizzi provides a useful introduction to how best to tell your story; answer people's questions; inspire, motivate, and entertain an audience; manage their expectations; help their decision making; and build trust by bringing the festival brand to life.

Critical website factors include:

- Make sure that the festival has clear objectives and consistent content in tone and design for its website and that appropriate software can be employed to measure and analyze web server information from which the festival can learn how many visitors have been to the website, which pages they viewed, and how long they stayed on the site.
- Keep the site clear, simple, and dynamic in appearance and usability.
- Keep the site updated and interactive to encourage regular returns of viewers with promotional attractions, special offers, competitions, discussion boards, ticket bookings, subscriptions, feedback mechanisms, samples of contributors to the program, links to

## SXSW

South by Southwest (SXSW) is one of the largest and best-known events in the world. SXSW (www.sxsw.com) is an annual 10-day portfolio of conferences and festivals focused on technology, film, and music. It generates substantial impacts on the local Austin, Texas, economy. Its effective year-round engagement strategy with its audience includes using things like Panel Picker where everyone, regardless of whether they are an attendee, sponsor, or exhibitor has a voice. This strategy has worked for SXSW, but is it worth it? And furthermore, can you replicate it for your event?

Google is the undisputed market leader in Internet search engines. It provides a way to track historical search volume for terms with Google Trends. A Google Trends chart for the past eight years for SXSW provides useful data for ongoing relationship and marketing decisions. There are definitely limitations; search volume is a good way to determine what people are looking for and when they are looking for it. SXSW supporters and conference and festival organizers use Sched.org to manage their website's schedule of events by seamlessly integrating social networking and provide their attendees with tools like personal agenda builders, dynamic attendee directories, and mobile applications.

Check out the SXSW Analytics for patron responses to the SXSW experience.

---

local attractions, tourism information, and contact details for those who wish to connect with organizers.
- Collaborate with other festivals, sponsors, artists involved, arts organizations, and other visitor attractions and as appropriate links to their sites.

## Introduction to Social Media for Festival Engagement

Festivals offer the new social media engagement some distinctive marketing challenges. Festival organizers have been quick to embrace new technologies, exploit opportunities to connect with individuals and groups, and offer ICT (information communication technology) entrepreneurs a dynamic marketplace for their initiatives.

The importance of word of mouth is not to be underestimated. It is the most influential form of media in festival patrons' decision making. It is fascinating to follow what is happening online and the amount of people involved with the technology. It is not just the two-way exchange that occurred in earlier marketing transactions. Now we can acknowledge that thousands and maybe millions of people are participating in sharing content or at least listening.

In the field of public relations the conversations appear to be open-ended, allowing for long-term relationships to emerge. Viral marketing suggests that now we are talking of "word of mouse" as people are more likely to communicate through word-of-mouth and social media when they are fully engaged with the product, service, or idea. So festival marketers design their communication with talking points in mind to stimulate chat between people that support their festival patrons' desired self-image, or the way they want others to see them. This requires attention to organizational research to underpin decisions and close observations to monitor threads being raised through online approaches.

## GIVING SOCIAL MEDIA A TRIAL RUN

A consortia of partners including EventScotland, VisitScotland, Edinburgh Tourism Action Group (ETAG), Festivals Edinburgh, Haggis Adventures and Skyscanner supported Edinburgh's Hogmanay, which hosted 21 travel bloggers from around the world to experience Edinburgh and Scotland as one of the world's premier New Year destinations. All overseas travel responses have been found on leading travel search site Skyscanner. The Winter 2012 trial of the capacity of social media to alter the nature of public/media relations focused on Edinburgh's Hogmanay. Global participants were invited to share their experience with the world:

With visitors from over 60 countries joining us at the "Home of Hogmanay," we want you to join our team of international travel bloggers and tweet, Facebook, photograph and share your Edinburgh's Hogmanay experience by sending your content using #blogmanay. Influential travel bloggers from as far afield as the United States, Australia, Malaysia, and Europe will be coming to Scotland and will be joined by members of the UK's and Scottish travel blogging community. Follow their exploits and join in yourself on Twitter and Instagram using our hashtag #blogmanay. #Blogmanay was a great success; initial findings indicated that the project reached over 3.6 million people!

Social media can be defined as collaborative online applications and technologies that enable participation, connectivity, user-generated content, sharing of information, and collaboration amongst a community of users.

—*Henderson & Bowley, 2010, p. 239*

You may already be familiar with the media sites that have become part of the communication and marketing platforms for festival organizers. Sites like Facebook, Twitter, LinkedIn, and Instagram help people cultivate a community of friends and share information.

Blogs are personal websites written by passionate individuals about festivals of their personal or professional experience or national identity. They tend to foster an active community of readers who provide comments on the author's posts. They can be used before, during, and after an event by organizers to sustain interest in programs, highlights, celebrities, or awards. Observations and opinions, often contain links to related websites and with articles and other blogs through pictures and/or videos. They help build a picture of sites that track and share information that then can influence the shape of festivals themselves.

Likewise, chatrooms and message boards serve as online places where people meet and discuss topics of interest, with the main feature being that anyone can start a discussion thread. Video- and photo-sharing sites like YouTube, Flickr and Vimeo greatly simplify the process of sharing and commenting on photos and videos.

## Marketing Through Social Media

Festival organizers can initiate social media engagement with limited investments. It does, however, require substantial (ongoing) commitment, knowledge, hard work, continuity, and time (Carlsson, 2009). Eley and Tilley (2009, pp. 86–88) offer important rules when using social media to create value:

- **Listen.** People online are frequently mentioning and commenting on your company; all you have to do is listen. You will get an inside scoop on what is actually important to your target demographic.
- **Join.** Once you understand the community and what it is about, join communities where you are most likely to find your customers. If you start out by listening, you will know where your customers are.
- **Participate.** By participating you will build your online brand. People will start to respect you as a valuable contributor to the community. When respected, others will help to promote you without even being asked to do so. Remember that it is never okay to spam.
- **Create.** When you have built yourself an online brand by listening, joining and participating it is time to create your own content. You will now have an audience to share it with and they will help spread your content.

Researchers and practitioners suggest some simple approaches to establish a dynamic online presence:

**Target a specific audience.** Create a page that reaches an audience important to your organization.

**Be a thought leader.** Provide valuable and interesting information that people want to check out.

**Be authentic and transparent.** Don't try to impersonate someone else.

**Create lots of links.** Link to your own sites and blogs and those of others in your industry and network.

**Encourage people to contact you.** Make it easy for others to reach you online, and be sure to follow up personally.

**Participate.** Create groups and participate in online discussions. Become an online leader and organizer.

**Make it easy to find you.** Tag your page and add it to subject directories. Encourage others to bookmark your page.

**Experiment.** Try new things. If it isn't working, change it, or abandon the effort and try something new.

---

When observing Sweden's Goteborg International Film Festival's social media platforms one can see that they have a Twitter account, are blogging at *gbgfilmfestival.wordpress.com*, and are on Facebook. Twitter is integrated on their Facebook page, which makes it possible to see posts from Twitter on facebook as well. From their Facebook page they link to their other Facebook pages that they administer.

On the Facebook page there are questions and clues about the secret movie each month, published so that members are able to guess which movie it is. The first person to guess correctly on each clue wins a free ticket to the screening. Goteborg International Film Festival has created different campaign sites to which they integrate social media. Examples of campaign sites are Twigiff, Giffreviews, and Dragon Award New Talent (Karic & Rinman, 2011).

## Challenges of Social Media

Social media provides a hybrid approach to the promotional mix we discussed earlier. It combines characteristics of traditional integrated marketing communication tools with a highly magnified form of word-of-mouth whereby marketing managers cannot control the content and frequency of such information.

Blogs can present unique challenges as well. If people are dissatisfied with or disappointed with a festival or festival partners they can engage in virtual complaints through protest websites or blogs that can result in potentially damaging information distributed in the online space. Organizational vigilance through careful monitoring is required to ensure undesirable, untrue, or defamatory remarks do not go unchecked or unanswered.

A way for organizers to get the festival patrons to return is to involve them in the social media activities of the organization as a volunteer or a participant in a virtual community. There is great interest from people to get involved in something that is close to their area of interest, feel a sense of belonging, offer suggestions for festival developments, and recommend to their friends the value of specific events.

There is a delicate balance in managing the dissemination of information through social media channels to ensure people don't feel swamped, that a consistent approach is taken, and that highlights are released as milestones in the preparation, conduct, and winding-down of the festival occurs.

Monitoring of the effects of social media can be done through reading comments and viewing how much Web traffic the festival sites have. Sites can be monitored closely through entities like Google Analytics.

When trying to measure the effectiveness of campaigns, festival organizers tend to:

- Identify the shared festival partner objectives that social media can support.
- Set a social media strategy that ensures that objectives are met and outcomes achieved.
- Identify which metrics are best tracked to determine the progress of the social media program.
- Understand the capabilities of social media platforms and align them to objectives.
- Report social media analysis and deliver brand knowledge.
- Manage employee and stakeholder expectations of what a social media program can deliver.
- Understand the role of social media analysis in positioning the festival internally and externally.

## SOCIAL MEDIA FOR FESTIVALS

Connect with your festival and event peers via IFEA's social media sites. Staying informed on the latest news, ideas, resources, and trends in the festival and events industry is vital—you miss a moment, and it could have a direct impact on your event. We keep you up to speed through www.ifea.com, "i.e." magazine, the IFEA Weekly Update, and the IFEA Event Insider, but where do you go for your hour-by-hour updates? Your social media sites, of course! Connect with your industry peers today on IFEA's Facebook, LinkedIn, Twitter, and YouTube pages. Ask/answer questions and share ideas, resources, photos, videos, and more. Get the conversations rolling—visit and participate today!

Adapted from IFEA.com Weekly Update & Events email 2012. To ensure delivery to your inbox, please add ifeamail@ifea.com to your email address book/safe send list

## Festival Uptake of New Approaches

The individuals' day-to-day experiences of digital technology to communicate, learn, record, and trade provide significant challenges to all festival-making stakeholders. Demand for consistent, instant access and seamless integration with standard platforms is a feature of the festival organization–patron relationship. While festival marketers can align their messages to what appears to be borderless frontiers of the digital universe, organizers need to be mindful of ownership and controls of such platforms and the potential impact by cyber hackers. Whether patrons are filtering their festival connections through tablets, phones, clouds, or wristbands with RFID embedded, they now expect efficient interactive technology.

This is particularly evident through their on-site festival experience. To allow organizers to track patrons during the event and enhance their experience, decisions have to be made regarding blanket network coverage, content quality, and innovation and investment needed to support the demands of tech-savvy patrons. Some festivals spread over a longer duration have introduced cellular networks that allow patrons to communicate with family and friends who are also on-site, so all can connect to share details of location, receive real-time updates on program changes, develop an appropriate app in conjunction with merchandisers and vendors on-site with content related to costs, and even find out the state of the queues for amenities!

The explosion in the amount of information created and shared has to be managed by festival organizers. There are legal, networking, hardware, and software issues that need to be addressed and that is before the content is shared with potential patrons. It must be remembered that festival-goers wish to be engaged for a unique celebration, so distraction through technological interfaces must not diminish the act of "being there."

# Content Management Systems

## Blogs

A *blog* is basically a journal that is available on the Web. The activity of updating a blog is "blogging" and someone who keeps a blog is a "blogger." Blogs are usually (but not always) written by one person and are updated regularly. Blogs are often (but not always) written on a particular topic; there are blogs on virtually any topic you can think of.

### ■ BLOGGER

Blogger is a blog publishing platform owned by Google that allows private or multiuser blogs with time-stamped entries.

### ■ TUMBLR

Tumblr is a free blogging site where you can post text, photos, quotes, links, music, and videos from your browser, phone, desktop, and email or wherever you happen to be. You can customize everything, from colors to your theme's HTML.

## WORDPRESS

WordPress is a free, Web-based software program that anyone can use to build and maintain a website or blog. It was originally intended as an easy way to set up a blog. The "open-source" community has extended and improved its capabilities, so WordPress has become a content management system (CMS), which means that it can be used to run full-sized, social media–rich business websites.

# Social Media/Networks/Networking

## FACEBOOK

Facebook is a huge social network that allows its members to communicate, connect, and engage with each other, both directly and through various applications and features. More significantly, Facebook is changing the way we interact on the Web, making our experience much more open and social. Individuals and organizations have embraced this medium.

## FOURSQUARE

Foursquare is a free app that helps you make the most of where you are. When you're out and about, Foursquare can share and save impressions of places you visit.

## INSTAGRAM

Instagram is a quirky way to share your life with friends through a series of pictures. Snap a photo with your mobile phone; transform the image into a memory to keep around forever using the platform's filters and borders. Instagram allows you to experience moments as they happen.

## PINTEREST

Pinterest lets you organize and share things you find on the Web. People use their own pinboards to share and to allow others to browse pinboards to discover new things and get inspiration from people who share your interests.

## SPOTIFY

Simply search for any artist, song, or album and start playing. Create playlists, share music with friends, and check out what others are listening to. Spotify's seamless Facebook integration takes enjoying music to a whole new level. Music has never been this social.

## TWITTER

Twitter is a real-time information network that connects you to the latest stories, ideas, opinions, and news about what you find interesting. Simply find the accounts that are most compelling to you and follow the conversations. At the heart of Twitter are small bursts of information called tweets. Each tweet is 140 characters long. You can see photos, videos, and conversations directly in tweets to get the whole story at a glance, and all in one place.

The Twitter Glossary contains vocabulary frequently used to talk about the medium's features. Following each definition are links to related articles. Twitter users have developed short-form syntax to make the most of 140 characters.

## YOUTUBE

The largest video-sharing site in the world, YouTube allows billions of people to discover, watch, and share original videos. YouTube provides a forum for festivals and individuals connect, inform, and inspire others across the globe and acts as a distribution platform for original content creators and advertisers large and small.

## DEFINITIONS

**Alerts:** Tool to get a search engine to tell you whenever a new page is published on the Web that includes your specific keyword.

**App:** Application that performs a specific function on your computer or handheld device.

**At symbol:** Sense of being "located at" or "directed at." @ before the user name is used to send publicly readable replies (e.g. "@otheruser: Message text here").

**Content management systems (CMS):** Sometimes described as the Swiss Army knives of social media, these are software suites offering the ability to create static Web pages, document stores, blogs, wikis, and other tools.

**Dashboard:** Administration area on your blog software that allows you to post, check traffic, upload files, manage comments, etc.

**Delicious:** Social bookmarking site and property of Yahoo! Allows users to quickly store, organize (by tags), and share favorite Web pages. You can also subscribe to RSS feeds of other users and share a page specifically with another user.

**Digg:** Popular social news site that lets people discover and share content from anywhere on the Web. Users submit links and stories and the community votes them up or down and comments on them. Users can "digg" stories they like or "bury" others they don't.

**Embedding:** When a small piece of code is added to a blog or website to display a video or photo hosted elsewhere. A typical use of this would be when YouTube videos are embedded on blogs.

**Event blog:** Blog specifically launched as a companion to an event.

**eWOM:** Acronym for "electronic word of mouth," basically word of mouth over the Internet.

**Feed:** Content served at regular intervals (e.g., the latest articles from a blog or social actions by your friends).

**Flickr:** World's premier photo-sharing and hosting site. Its members have uploaded more than 3 billion photos.

**Follow:** Act of monitoring ("following") someone's online activity (e.g., Twitter).

**Follower:** Someone who is following your updates. The count of followers is most businesses' first social media metric. In time this has to extend to the "value" of each follower.

**Forums:** Discussion areas on websites, where people can post messages or comment on existing messages asynchronously (i.e., independently of time or place).

**Geotagging:** Process of adding location-based metadata to media such as photos, video, or online maps. Can help users find a wide variety of businesses and services based on location.

**Hashtags:** Used on Twitter, Tumblr, Instagram, Facebook, Pinterest, and blogs. Basically they are a way of tagging the metadata of a post, image, or idea.

**Mashup:** Combining two or more Web services to create something new (e.g., combining Twitter posts with Google maps to create TwitterVision, or two web video services).

**Meme:** Can take the form of a phrase, image, and video and are usually spread via social media channels. It may stay the same or may evolve over time, by chance or through commentary, imitations, and parody, or by incorporating news accounts about itself.

**Microblogging:** Act of broadcasting short messages to other subscribers of a Web service. On Twitter, entries are limited to 140 characters; applications like Plurk and Jaiku take a similar approach with sharing bite-size media.

**RSS (Really Simple Syndication):** Web standard for the delivery of content—blog entries, news stories, headlines, images, video—enabling readers to stay current with favorite publications or producers without having to browse from site to site. RSS feeds let users subscribe to content automatically and read or listen to the material on a computer or a portable device or via email.

**Search engine optimization (SEO):** Process of arranging your website to give it the best chance of appearing near the top of search engine rankings.

**Social media optimization (SMO):** Set of practices for generating publicity through social media, online communities, and social networks. The focus is on driving traffic from sources other than search engines, though improved search ranking is also a benefit of successful SMO.

**Tagging:** The slightly secretarial act of allocating particular keywords to content.

**User-generated content (UGC):** Industry term that refers to all forms of user-created materials such as blog posts, reviews, podcasts, videos, comments, and more.

## CASE STUDY

### Coachella, California

Coachella Music and Arts Festival (often shortened to Coachellafest or simply, Coachella) has grown to be one of the largest festivals of its kind. From humble beginnings in 1999, Coachella, now held over two weekends in the Coachella Valley, California, is a leader when it comes to their use of social media and engaging their audience before, during, and even long after the festival gates have closed. Coachella's success has emphasized that if you are trying to get the attention of any demographic that uses the Internet, it is essential to follow trends and know your audience. Considering Coachella's main demographic is tech-savvy people between the ages of 20 and 29, Coachella is using innovative social media campaigns to not only keep their loyal followers happy but to continually grow their audience.

The team at Coachella do an amazing job of promoting being social to their 160,000 ticketholders and to their more than half a million online followers. They managed to spread their campaign across most of the major players in the social media realm, seamlessly blending social media into each attendee's (and even nonattendee's) experience, from year-round updates on Facebook and Twitter, to behind-the-scenes footage or live simulcasts on YouTube, to keeping the insta-fans and pinners happy with snaps from the festival.

Coachella has utilized some innovative strategies to grow its audience and increase loyalty through their social media channels. The decision to try the new fandangle RFID (radio frequency identification) wristbands paid off for Coachella, not only for its ability to cut queue times and increase security, but also if attendees had linked their wristbands to their Facebook account once inside they could tap the bands at social check-in stations to update friends, both at the festival and at home, with details of the stage they were at and the act they were watching.

The program, called "Live Click," developed by Canadian firm Intellitix, helped grow Coachella's online audience by over 30 million, according to the festival. For the festival managers, the technology also allowed for unprecedented access to data on its attendees including the ability to regulate numbers, enabling them to adhere to site capacity rules, safety laws, and enhanced security (and made scalping tickets virtually impossible). Information such as what stages attracted the most fans was useful risk management knowledge. Providing a cashless environment (money could be put on the wristbands and swiped for purchases) at the festival certainly was a big draw for implementing the technology. Attendees also benefited as the festival organizers were able to update fans on Twitter as to which entrance gates and drink lines were the quietest. Although there have been the usual concerns raised regarding privacy (many unfounded) the advantages certainly seem to be winning.

So what can future festival organizers learn from Coachella's use of social media?

1. **Be Everywhere!** Coachella reached the broadest audience possible by having a ubiquitous presence across social media channels and sharing a variety of content.

   Of course, it's wise to adhere to the old adage of "better to do one thing really well than many poorly," but if you have the resources to produce content for different social media platforms, do it! Plus, if you can increase the ways people can connect to your festival, you will also increase the chance that they will see your updates.

2. **Cross-Promote Social Media Channels.** Make sure to advertise your social media channels on your other social media channels. The easiest way to do this is by embedding the social media button where Coachella can be found. These can be found on the platform that you wish to promote or by finding them at sites such as *niftybuttons.com*.

   Coachella's 600,000-plus Facebook fans certainly helped draw followers to their other social media outlets such as Instagram. Furthermore, tricks such as using Twitter to notify fans of new content such as photos and videos recently uploaded gained the festival many click-ons.

3. **Use Trackable URLs and Analytics.** Passing links through sites such as *Bitly.com* that offer analytics about your URL click-ons can help your festival understand your social media traffic. They also shorten links considerably, taking up fewer characters and leaving you more tweet space!

   Additionally, Coachella used Google Analytics for their website and blog and Facebook Insights to know what content drove what action.

4. **Create and Advertise an Official Event Handle and Hashtag.** Make your event handle obvious; for example, the Sydney Biennale's handle is @sydneybiennale. Try to also keep your tags as simple, direct and as short as possible so that there are plenty of tweetable characters left. Sydney Biennale official hashtag was a simple acronym, #18bos (18th Biennale of Sydney).

   If you want your audience to be able to have more specific conversations, a good idea is to categorize hashtags into topics. This won't always be necessary but if your event has a few different interest groups (music and fashion), then fans can follow one or the other, or both.

   Coachella advertised their handle on their website and their Facebook page so if you were or even if you weren't at the festival, you could follow the conversation about #coachella and #coachellalive performance broadcasts. This was obviously a successful campaign as the official hashtags were among the top retweeted hashtags throughout the duration of the event.

5. **Capture and Share Fantastic Photos and Images.** When promoting a festival via social media channels, a picture really is worth a thousand words! After all, what you're really selling is an experience. Photos and images shared via sites such as Facebook and Instagram can be used to build hype around the festival as well as individual performances, share memorable moments (even as they occur), and tend to get a lot more likes and comments than just words alone.

    Photos of a festival provide potential ticket buyers a snapshot of the experience that they will have; therefore it is really important to make images as striking as possible. Posting great photos after the event allows your audience to relive the festival and hopefully they will be inspired to share them with their friends.

    Coachella excelled at using photos and images to sell the festival before, during, and after the event. To motivate fans to share the images, they enabled tagging so that their fans could tag themselves in the photos. Additionally, they encouraged their audience to share their own photos of the festival and to tag Coachella using their official tag, hashtag, and handle. These simple things helped spread the word about the festival even further by just a few clicks of the organizers' mouse.

    Photos and images that you share not only help to create buzz around your event, they also play a critical role in building your festival's identity. For this reason it is important to be selective in the images that you post; think about your target audience, who do you want/need to appeal to?

6. **Live Stream and Record the Event.** Recording performances and the atmosphere of your event means fans can extend their experience beyond the day and allows them to engage with the event even if they couldn't be there.

    Coachella partnered with YouTube and sponsor State Farm Insurance to encourage users to "Relive Coachella" by sharing footage of the festival and holding live simulcasts of performances.

7. **Be Mobile Friendly/Aware.** Make sure your festival's website is viewable on smartphones and tablets.

8. **Keep Posts Short.** Research indicates that posts under 250 characters see 60% more Likes, comments, and shares than ones that are over 250 characters.

9. **Build a (User-Friendly) Mobile App.** If your event has the budget, creating an app that people can download to their mobile means that they can carry with them everything they will need to know while at the festival. It also will save a few trees by not having to print thousands of paper programs!

    Coachella included information such as maps and performance times and allowed attendees to create their own custom program in their app using the "Coachooser" personalized line-up feature. Furthermore, it made it easy for event organizers to push vital notifications live to attendees' devices so that they were always up to date.

10. **Foster Peer-to-Peer Conversation.** One of the best things about social networking platforms is its ability to open up channels of conversation. Communication is an essential part of many social media platforms and allows festival and event organizers to receive direct feedback from customers. However, communication is a two-way street and it is vital that questions and feedback, whether positive or negative, are responded to promptly.

    Coachella trusted experienced Coachella-goers to do a lot of the work by answering questions posted by newbies in their forum and chatroom on their website. This was a savvy way for Coachella to save time and the energy of their organizers while simultaneously promoting a sense of community among their fans and a place for them to continue the conversation after the event.

Keep forums safe and happy spaces by allowing users to report rude or unhelpful commenters. Another good approach is to make knowledgeable users moderators of the threads that they regularly contribute to. This cuts down on the time you need to spend checking the sites and allows your loyal fans to feel valued.

## HOW TO MAKE IT HAPPEN: EMPLOY A SPECIALIST

### Generic Digital and Online Festival Marketer Job Description

You will be a member of a small team cooperatively committed to ensuring the brand, design, and delivery of sales and marketing strategies are consistent. You will be responsible for ensuring all campaign consumer touchpoints are leveraged to grow patron engagement and satisfaction.

Your specific responsibilities include:

Online and digital strategy

- o Stay informed of current best practice, competitor campaigns, and trends in the sector that can add value to the festival's marketing mix.
- o Share information with festival marketing and communication colleagues to build on opportunities with organizational partners.

Website/handheld devices

- o Strategically position the festival website to increase visitation and grow ticket and merchandise sales.
- o Design and deliver a website strategy to increase traffic through advertising and links with media partners.
- o Ensure website content is updated with engaging text, video, and audio content.
- o Analyze statistics identifying approaches to stimulate visitors' online experience and provide traffic reports.

Online and social media

- o Develop an organizational plan for code of conduct for use by staff of identified online and social media platforms.
- o Design promotional strategies across all online and social media to grow audience engagement.
- o Report on analysis of evident and emerging trends providing opportunities across the total festival marketing program.

Online content development and management

- o Generate a content and creation strategy, monitor existing material, and increase audience attention and links with partners and online communities.
- o Adapt and edit festival publications, publicity, program, and marketing content and copy for online and digital platforms.
- o Work to increase the reach of the festival brand.

Customer relationship marketing and E-marketing

- o Develop and implement data acquisition to support the database, ensuring activity is aligned with festival audience development plans.
- o Design and maintain a range of online connections to build loyalty and communication in collaboration with festival marketing programs.

Media, stakeholder, and funder relationship management
- In consultation with the festival development department, identify and pursue new online and digital partnerships with media partners, broader stakeholder connections, sponsors, and funding agencies through cross-promotional campaigns and collaborative initiatives.

Budget
- Assist with budget management and monitoring associated with your portfolio for effective and timely control of income and expenditure, reporting, approvals, and quotes.

General
- Ensure documentation is accurate, timely, and efficiently collated for distribution among team and festival organization for meetings and reports.
- Collaborate through active participation in team meetings.
- Represent the festival organization in meetings with appropriate external agencies.

## Selection Criteria

You need to have a tertiary qualification and demonstrated experience in online and marketing positions. Demonstrate a passion for the growing role of online platforms' good practice through strong IT experience and literacy. You need to understand the opportunities for the festival in the entertainment, recreation, and tourism marketplace. Your capacity to develop strategy and analyze and design quality technical experiences for internal and external partners is important. It is desirable that you project management skills, problem-solving capacity, good communication skills and team membership strengths. Your ability to work collaboratively across the organization is key.

On a personal level, you need to demonstrate effective "people" skills; work with a positive attitude; take initiative; anticipate problems; be flexible, honest, and open in your relationships with peers; and demonstrate attention to detail in your work practice.

## FROM INSIDE THE MOSAIC

### Greg Meek and Liz Shepherd, Principals of Dogwhistle Creative

*Dogwhistle Creative* aims to provide high end, strategically targeted design, marketing, and communication services and to explore new technology, new media, and new perspectives.

Director Greg Meek has worked with individuals and organizations to design and develop effective integrated branding, advertising, publishing, marketing, and strategic planning, offering creative direction and design through photography, copywriting, print, television, radio, Web, and signage campaigns.

Greg Meek
© Peter Derrett

General Manager Liz Shepherd has experience in event planning and coordination, community engagement and development, developing and coordinating local government festivals and events programs, developing and implementing marketing plans, implementing branding strategies, researching, evaluating and reporting, and developing and overseeing production of marketing collateral. Their emphasis here is on community-based festivals.

## Marketing Community Events

Marketing anything begins with the product ... Is there a market for it? Will that market want it? How do you reach them? And, importantly, will they be happy with it?

For a community event, that means... Is it relevant to the community? Will the community embrace and support it? How do you promote it on a (invariably) shoestring budget? And, will the punters come back next year?

## Community Engagement

All aspects of staging and promoting a community event rely on an emotional connection. You are not simply selling a product to consumers, you are asking people to get involved—to give, participate, and share an experience as a community.

Whether it's a school fete, a family fun day, or a major cultural festival, successfully engaging sponsors, media, volunteers, participants, and attendees—and creating a rich and genuinely rewarding experience—will all depend on how well you communicate the essence, depth, and meaning of that experience.

Talk to local schools, clubs, and community groups and ask them what they can bring to the event and how it can benefit them, too.

Develop a comprehensive volunteer program and invite participation from the broader community. Listen to their ideas and opinions and look after their needs. Every happy participant is an ambassador for the event; all their friends and families will be too!

## Sponsorship

Sponsorship is vital and integral to building a sustainable event. Local businesses and media are often enthusiastic supporters, particularly if they can see a clear association and promotional benefit for their business. Larger companies also like to be seen as good corporate citizens. A simple prospectus that profiles your event, its target market and a benefits package for sponsors will help. Including sponsor logos in promotions, on-site display opportunities, and event website exposure are effective, low-cost ways to deliver a return on your sponsors' investments.

Cash sponsorships are essential but can be tough to secure. "In-kind" sponsorships, where sponsors provide goods and services in lieu of cash, can provide the backbone of sponsorship support. In fact, most of the work we have done on community events has been as sponsorship or "pro-bono" contributions.

## Branding

Creating a clean, professional, and instantly recognizable brand for your event is imperative. With a limited promotional window, your brand needs to get noticed, recognized, remembered, and engage the community in quickly and on that shoestring budget. Find a friendly, professional designer, tell them what you are all about and let them run with it. Motivation is just as important as information so don't let the details swamp the "art" in your artwork.

## Advertising

Media placement is expensive, but local media groups will often come to the party with a schedule of ad spots. Sometimes even cash!

Look to do a two-phase campaign with simple, event awareness-based press ads (target weekends) leading off 10 to 6 weeks out and a more focused and detailed campaign, with TV if you can get it, in the final two weeks prior to the event.

And get that friendly designer to do your ads too! Make them creative and exciting—you can always load the hard details onto your website.

## Website

An event site allows you to distribute lots of program details and event information far and wide with relatively little expense. Keep it simple, functional and easy to navigate—and make sure the branding is consistent.

## PR/Media

Some of the most effective promotion you can get is the free stuff.

Ask your sponsors to "value-add" to their contribution by promoting your event in-store or on their websites and in regular promos.

As a novel event on the local calendar, you are bound to have some genuinely newsworthy story angles within your project—special attractions, happenings, and characters—that local and national media will be happy to run. Think laterally and make them genuinely interesting.

Work up some angles/stories, get some professional pictures to go with them, and target local press, national travel, and niche media related to your core subject. Magazines sometimes have long lead times for publications, so get in early.

## Imagery

A professional picture is worth much, much more than a thousand words. Engaging a professional photographer to shoot your event will pay enormous dividends when it comes to marketing next year's event.

## Print Collateral

Standard items are posters, flyers, invitations, postcards, clothing, and merchandise.

Local businesses will happily display an A3 poster in their window in the weeks leading up to the event—even an A2 if space allows. Keep the brand clear and the message simple: event brand and headline events, and be sure the DATE and LOCATION and WEB ADDRESS are prominent.

DL flyers can be mailed or distributed with local papers and through retail outlets. These can provide more detail on the event ethos and program.

T-shirts and caps are great for staff, volunteers, and sponsors and may generate some merchandise income.

## Delivering on the Promise

Branding and promotional material should accurately depict the experience on offer *and* be embraced by the community it represents.

For an event to succeed and grow, year after year, delivering on community, participant and sponsor expectations is critical—as is, of course, logistical execution.

This year's event is your most important asset in marketing next year's festival.

# Festival Ideas and Issues

1. In a short time, social media practices have become core to a festival organization's marketing strategy. What benefits have accrued in addressing the organization's strategic communication content? Consider the management of festival positioning and reputation, data analysis of relationships with audiences, challenges for the marketing plan, and where should responsibility for it reside within the organization.
2. A new language has emerged as social media protocols are embraced. Is it slang? How does this affect the messages being sent by festival organizers to potential audiences? Conduct a research project based on the level of engagement with Twitter at a specific festival to assess the trail of virtual clues left by festival-goers about their experience. What do you find that may provide a guide for civic authorities, festival organizers, artists, corporate sponsors and advertisers to potentially rethink how they invest in the festivals next year?
3. Is the importance of price a myth for potential festival patrons? Has there been a shift in marketing terms to value for money?

4. The statement "Half the money I spend on advertising is wasted, and the problem is, I don't know which half" was attributed to Lord Leverhulme (British founder of Unilever). What are the alternative communication options available to festival organizers?
5. How successful organizers position their festivals in the promotion of place-based cultural tourism demonstrates the value of partnering with tourism to establish destination distinctiveness. It's a win–win situation. What do you think? Can you provide examples of successful collaboration?

## Festival Focus Activities

1. Analyze the personality of a festival website with which you are familiar. This is an evaluation exercise. If the website had a personality, how would you describe it? What are the positive and negative observations you would make regarding its personality qualities—business-like, chatty, authoritative, friendly, etc. What are the most effective aspects of the website—does it work well, is it easy to navigate to answer your enquiries? How would you improve its presentation to address your needs?
2. Identify the target market of another festival website you have found. Does it use a voice that would resonate with its key market? What are the distinctive features that would assist in building a relationship with this market? Do you think the links to other social media platforms from this site match the engagement practices of the target market?
3. Develop a promotion campaign for an aspect of a festival program based on the following four objectives.

    A    Attracting attention

    I    Developing interest

    D    Creating desire

    A    Inducing action

    Present the output to your peers and maybe share it with a familiar community cultural festival organization for implementation.
4. Design a communication plan for a project within a festival organization that focuses on the preparation of a tactical toolkit for good-practice external communication with specific festival partners.
5. Create a festival-specific postcard or flier as a piece of promotional collateral that can be used by all partners to show not only the benefits and festival features, but the advantages of connecting as a target audience. Ensure messages are consistent with images and in appropriate language and tone.

The author thanks Zoe Robinson-Kennedy, B.Media, for her contribution to this chapter.

## Suggested Reading

Berthon, P. R., L. F. Pitt, K. Plangger, and D. Shapiro, D. "Marketing meets Web 2.0, social media, and creative consumers: Implications for international marketing strategy." *Business Horizons* 55 (2012): 261–271.

Botsman, R., and R. Rogers. *What's Mine is Yours: How Collaborative Consumption is Changing the Way We Live*. London, UK: Collins, 2001.

Bruich, S., A. Lipsman, G. Mudd, and M. Rich. "The Power of "Like": How Brands Reach (and Influence) Fans Through Social-Media Marketing." *Journal of Advertising Research* 52, no. 1 (2012): pp. 40–52.

Carlsson. L. *Marketing and Communications in Social Media: Rewarding Dialogue, Stronger Brand, Increase Sales*. Stockholm, Sweden: Kreafon Gothenburg, 2009.

Eley, B., and S. Tilley, S. *Online Marketing Inside Out*. Melbourne: SitePoint, 2009.

Faulds, D. J., and W. G. Mangold. "Social media: The new hybrid element of the promotion mix." *Business Horizons* 52 (2009): 357–365.

Henderson, A., and R. Bowley, R. "Authentic dialogue?: The role of "friendship" in a social media recruitment campaign." *Journal of Communication Management* 14, no. 3 (2010): 237–257.

Karic, D., and E. Rinman. *Social media in the festival industry: A case study of Goteborg International Film Festival's use of social media as a marketing tool*. Bachelor's thesis, Goteborg University Sweden, 2011.

Kerr, A., and May, D." An exploratory study looking at the relationship marketing techniques used in the music festival industry." *Journal of Retail and Leisure Property* 9 (2011): 451–464.

Kotler, P. *A Framework for Marketing Management*. Upper Saddle River, NJ: Prentice Hall, 2001.

Kotler, P., G. Armstrong, V. Wong, and J. Saunders. *Principles of Marketing* (5th ed.). Essex, UK: Pearson Education, 2008.

Masterman, G., and E. H. Wood. *Innovative Marketing Communications: Strategies for the Events Industry*. Oxford, UK: Elsevier Butterworth-Heinemann, 2006.

Pulizzi, J., *Good to Great Content Marketing*, https://www.youtube.com/watch?v=-pam8hSjXfo, Feb 27, 2013.

Rothschild, P.C. "Social media use in sports and entertainment venues." *International Journal of Event and Festival Management* 2, no. 2 (2011): 139–150.

Wigmo, J., and E. Wikstrom. *Social Media Marketing: What role can social media play as a marketing tool?* Bachelor's thesis, Centre for Information Logistics, 2010.

# CHAPTER 11

# Maintaining a Global Competitive Edge

> The Edinburgh Festivals are economic powerhouses, cultural platforms, forums for national and international debate, drivers of ambition and creators of cohesion.
> —*Edinburgh's Festivals: Defining Scotland's Cultural Identity on the Global Stage (2011)*

---

This chapter provides an opportunity for you to better understand:

- The contribution arts and cultural festivals make to a destination's economic, sociocultural, and environmental outcomes in tangible and intangible ways

- The festival choices individual communities, cities, and nations make to position themselves in a globally competitive marketplace

- Strategies employed to ensure festival success through effective partnerships, sound policy and planning, dynamic program design, and engagement with global audiences using essential destination marketing techniques

---

We have looked at the strategies that long-standing festivals have employed to sustain their distinctiveness. These critical success factors include a clear understanding of the internal and external context, how involved they are with local host communities, and their links with worthy partners. These parties demonstrate a political and practical will to invest in strong festival leadership and management. The vocabulary in the the Globally Competitive Festival Mosaic, Figure 11.1, provides a useful framework for our investigation. By recognizing characteristics that touch the lives of each patron over time, a confident approach can nurture and deliver memorable experiences for participants at all levels.

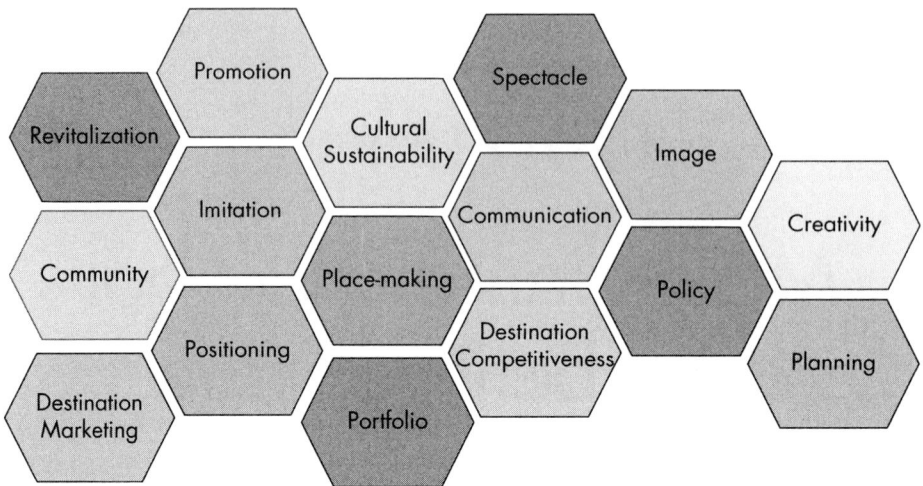

**Figure 11.1**  Globally Competitive Festival Mosaic.

# Setting Festival Strategy

The very nature of a long-term commitment to their aims and objectives is manifested in the quality of the content of their programs and services for their target market. Festival organizers work hard to ensure artistic autonomy to distinguish themselves from other entities. Festival patrons respond to celebrations that differentiate themselves from alternative options for their discretionary time, energy, and money. Strong and effective communications are vital to maintaining contact with loyal supporters. The same elements need to be considered by a host destination as it cultivates an image and brand upon which to base its identity and position itself in the global marketplace.

This chapter examines the ways in which festivals contribute to the competitiveness of large and small destinations. The festivals' literature has identified how festivals can provide a platform for achieving success in diverse social, cultural, economic, and environmental goals. Festivals have brought about a new way for communities to envision their futures by acting as a catalyst for reform and resilience and encouraging engagement and learning. By stimulating the development of creative spaces, attracting investment, and experimenting with new ways to think about recreation, entertainment, and celebration, festivals not only satisfy residents' quality of life needs but also become attractions for visitors. People and place are the keys for destination policymakers, managers, and marketers. There is substantial evidence that the cultural identity represented by festivals generates the authenticity sought by visitors who contribute significantly to the local and national economies.

The 2012 *World Cities Culture Report* through a systematic examination of 12 major international cities offers an insight into how culture helps these national nodes thrive and looks beyond the traditional expression of power and position represented by trade and finance.

London, Berlin, Istanbul, Johannesburg, Mumbai, New York, Paris, São Paulo, Shanghai, Singapore, Sydney and Tokyo provide a window into the important elements of homegrown dynamism that feeds international competitiveness.

Festivals allow people to take time out of their lives to experience what is fresh and new at home and internationally. Festivals can bring the world to destinations of all sizes and share these favored locations with curious and loyal patrons.

## Destination Competitiveness

There has been considerable research undertaken using conceptual and empirical models developed to help destination management agencies better understand how to deliver the desired levels of prosperity and promise that places like villages, towns, cities and regions wish to achieve. There are complex attributes that determine the success of destinations to which festivals can contribute. These build what is known as a competitive advantage. They will reflect a destination's resources and how they are deployed. The Ritchie and Crouch (2003) model includes components classified into five groups with 36 attributes. The five groups are core resources and attractions; supporting factors and resources; destination management; qualifying and amplifying determinants; and destination policy, planning, and development.

The Dwyer and Kim (2003) model makes distinctions between natural resources and created resources and the destination management activities under public sectors and private sectors that resonate with the destination's festival portfolio. Their model identifies inherited resources, created resources, supporting resources, demand conditions, situational conditions, and destination management. What do you think are the major attributes under each heading?

Of interest to us, as we contemplate the sustainability of festival organizations and their impact on destinations is the work of Mathew (2009). The cluster of elements he suggests include:

- Support activities (human resources development, administrative support, infrastructure, physical support, policies, capacity, personal safety and security, culture, climate, events, linkage, channels, network, community involvement, benchmarking, environmental development)
- Key success driver inputs (business plan, competencies, cooperation, entrepreneurs, investments, leadership, objectives, people, policy, portfolio, resources, strategies)
- Sustainable process (image-building, competency, design, development, product development, quality management, sales, service delivery)
- Leverage/operation (brand management, core competencies, customer relationship marketing, expansion, opportunity identification, positioning, strengths and weaknesses)
- Destination marketing (promotion, attraction, sales, events, target marketing, strategic positioning, innovation)
- Sustainable services (service experiences, hospitality, accommodation, entertainment, society focus)

| | | |
|---|---|---|
| National importance of place on festivals and tourism agenda | Transport infrastructure and access—location, location, location | Inherited and created resources |
| Government policy rules and regulations | Safety and security, visitors' comfort levels | Health and hygiene |
| Environmental sustainability | Destination price, competitiveness, and perceived value | Information and communication technology (ICT) infrastructure |
| Resident human and cultural capital | Natural resources | Demand conditions |
| Destination management and marketing—recognized image and brand | The festival experience—design, marketing, program, and participation options | Diversity of attractions beyond festivals |
| Trained and experienced workforce | Access to culture and heritage | Community hospitality |
| Evidence of collaboration with partners | Opportunities for businesses of all scales in the long term | Impact on local quality of life of residents and audiences |

**Table 11.1** Essential Elements of Destination Distinctiveness
*Derrett (2013).*

As we test the effectiveness and staying power of the festival mosaic in global destinations, it might be helpful to determine a set of indicators. The researchers mentioned above have reflected on the importance of the overall attractiveness in competitive markets so that places hosting festivals become the choice of potential visitors. What would you consider as essential elements? How do the following affect destination competitiveness in the case studies identified in this chapter in Harbin, China; Adelaide, Australia; Edinburgh, Scotland; Ottawa and Edmonton, Canada; and Luang Prabang, Laos, for example? See Table 11.1.

## Festivals as Destination Drivers

Experience in towns and cities around the world has taught those developing, managing, and marketing destinations to look at what has worked in the past and draw from such observations. This assists the focus to move the festival products and services forward. Buy-in from businesses and other agencies in festival destinations recognize they must provide memorable, quality experiences. Successful festivals, or a portfolio of festivals, can impact further than the creativity and celebration they generate to influence destination brand and identity. Many actively engage with potential customers, suppliers, and partners to identify the best fit with target markets, either locally or from a distance.

We have noticed the importance of emotions, senses, and a wow factor, not only associated with a festival, but the environment in which it is staged. Festivals play their part in delivering unique, authentic, and personalized experiences. These perceptions need to influence choices made by destination marketers, as well as the partnerships pursued by the festival organizers. At a destination level this needs to be delivered dynamically and collaboratively. Each partner enterprise, for example, must have trained staff who understand customer expectations and deliver the perceived sense of value they require. Safe and efficient infrastructure to satisfy transportation needs, hospitality, and access to further attractions for locals and visitors all must be in place. This can then deliver a long-term competitive advantage for all players, offering a differentiated stimulus that is facilitated by culture.

Notice how places have developed shared vocabulary. The copywriting in the marketing collateral of all partners establishes the essence of a "sense of place." It is essential that a realistic approach be taken to prepare visitors to festivals or more broadly to host destinations through a language they understand. Consistent images of the key locations and attractions, using colors, signage, text, and fonts, help consolidate the spectrum of distinctive experiences on offer. These confirm a unique place identity for the individual, the enterprise, and the host community. The representation of this "essence" builds on the values held, the destination's researched, and the projected "personality."

From a destination's perspective satisfied residents and visitors become advocates for what has been collectively presented. They spread positive messages about their experience. They themselves return for the festival experience and explore other offerings that confident destinations present. Getz (2013) explores the concepts and research undertaken into event tourism's profile as a distinctive link between festivals, their audiences, and the host community.

## Preparing Policy and Planning

As civic agencies prepare policy to address the value, impact, and engagement with festivals in their jurisdiction, they are mindful of the social ramifications on residents of their constituency. Deery, Jago, and Fredline (2012) have reviewed research in the area of social impacts of tourism that is worth investigating for findings that have application to the embrace of festivals by communities, councils, and national agencies. Festival organizations, too, are mindful of the benefits and disadvantages perceived by members of the host communities as strategic planning and policies are formulated and acted upon. Studies have generated useful data about the perspectives on the positive and negative attitudes that comprise the layered responses from local hosts of festivals. The scale of festivals may vary, as may the size of the host community and its geographic boundaries, but it is worthwhile scoping the complex underpinning to the behaviors, values, demographic characteristics, and place attachment demonstrated by those most impacted by the staging of planned public events.

By being alert to local concerns regarding rowdy behavior of festival-goers, or increases in costs (including rents, goods, and services), and having restricted access to favored recreation and commercial spaces in their area can mean the destination image is mismatched with the festival. There may be frustration and even conflict caused by noise, pollution, and traffic congestion and these peripheral aspects of the festival will have a detrimental effect on the local quality of life. Poor visitor behavior through engagement with alcohol, the influence of drug use and the increase in crime is juxtaposed with the local willingness to embrace quality entertainment and recreational experiences. How can this tension be resolved through policy and planning? On the one hand, such catalytic celebrations offer participants freedom to express themselves, while residents have to deal with how their sense of community and interest in sharing civic pride through a sense of place can best be manifested.

## OTTAWA EVENTS CENTRAL: A NEW AGE OF PARTNERSHIP AND POLICY IN MUNICIPAL EVENTS MANAGEMENT

Delores MacAdam, Manager, City of Ottawa Events Central Branch, and Mark Ford, Inspector, Ottawa Police, Special Event Unit, Ottawa, ON, Canada, contributed a useful case study to the 2012 IFEA Webinar professional development program. They identified the City of Ottawa's Events Central office as a breakthrough in coordinated, repeatable events management. The model leveraged a standing Special Events Advisory Team, documented processes and by-laws, and emerging citizen engagement technologies to design, implement, and track each of its over 250 events per year.

This model has proved successful in managing both large national and international events such as the Ottawa Bluesfest, Winterlude, FIFA Games, Grey Cup, and Canada Day celebrations, down to hundreds of local group, ethnic, and community events. Ottawa won IFEA Top City Awards in recent years for its policy and practice initiatives.

Delores and Mark were involved in all phases of design, planning, execution, and evolution of over 250 local, national, and international events per year. From their experience in community planning and development at the municipal and provincial level, they were responsible for engaging political leaders, local business and community groups, and professional entertainment and sporting entities, as well as knitting together dozens of local and worldwide events for celebration. They worked with consultants from various North American cities to develop a software program for events. The City of Ottawa Council Special Events by-law designed to address the needs of government (compliance) and event organizers in terms of process, transparency, and fairness was another initiative developed by Delores. Check Ottawa Events as a user-created list of events (of any sort—concerts, garage sales, whatever) in the Ottawa area.

As civic policy evolves in towns and cities, it is becoming evident that destinations are pursuing a portfolio approach to encouraging festivals and events. What is recognized are the ways festivals can contribute to the well-being of communities through investment in existing cultural capital, balancing out peaks and troughs in the delivery of tourism products and services, and urban revitalization while building strong stakeholder collaborations. Many of these themes are pursued in the work of Greg Richards and Robert Palmer (2010), especially in their book *Eventful Cities—Cultural Management and Revitalization*. Don Getz, Richard Florida, Ian Yeoman, and Sharon Zukin all have worked on the critical success factors for cities committed to satisfying residents, attracting visitors, and building partnerships to strengthen their destinations.

There is an argument put that confident creative destination identities are nourished by festivals. In fact, Yeoman argues that consumers are moving from an era of industrial to cultural capitalism, where cultural production is increasingly becoming the dominant form of economic activity and securing access to the many cultural resources and experiences. There are two definitions you need to explore: eventfulness and festivalization. What are the characteristics of each phenomenon? Festivals have been seamlessly integrated into the daily lives of places and function as stimuli for urban regeneration, repositioned image and enhanced civic pride, as popular built and natural public spaces are temporarily transformed for use.

Hamish McRae's (2010) observations of "what works" for the city of Edinburgh and its August festivals is instructive. He identifies the importance of the physical appeal of the location, but also highlights three key features that can be considered by destinations seeking to put their stamp on the world of exceptional festivals. He commends the approach Edinburgh has taken to create and permit an open marketplace by clearing bureaucratic blockages that might inhibit the investment and infrastructure required to deliver a month-long disturbance of regular life for residents. He acknowledges that during August residents lose control of their city because of the aggregation of festivals. By embracing the forces unleashed as visiting participants and audiences descend, a different management dynamic is indispensable. He notes a blend of top-down and bottom-up approaches to festival design, governance, management, and destination marketing. The co-mingling of arts and cultural practices offer a spirit that elevates a festival when challenges arise. Failure can be a part of the journey, but by listening to all the players, change can become success.

## Leadership, Partnerships, and Governance

We have already recognized the importance of leadership, teams, and effective governance as core to success and survival in festival endurance. We have noted the changing nature of work inside and outside the festival organization being influenced by relationships with suppliers, sponsors, regulatory bodies, funding agencies, and host communities.

National cultural policies can set a framework for festivals to flourish. These can influence public and private sector investment in festivals. For example, Australia's National Cultural Policy, Creative Australia, 2013, aims to modernize funding and support, evaluate creative expression and the role of the artists, and connect to national life for a social and economic dividend. Festivals can help build the national (and destinational) identity and support residents in the telling of their own valued stories through vibrant, innovative gestures in community celebrations, as we have already recognized.

Those with oversight of festivals need to tackle problems with the right mix of individuals. We can observe in the delivery of festivals with enduring status the importance of driving innovation to avoid the demise of the project. Leadership and management need to build accurate forecast capacity by engaging a diverse team. Leaders need to leverage the best from their festival team to gain advantage through diversity, both identity diversity (individuals of varying cultural backgrounds) and cognitive diversity (with differences in ways people think). Each contribution provides a scaffold for an enduring festival to emerge.

Strategic thinking, again on a relative scale, is required to plan effectively and to avoid any sudden surprises and provide a strong sense of order. The risk management plans examined earlier highlight the fragile nature of weather scenarios that can change the shape of a festival in an instant, escalating security costs, demographic trends, or the statutory obligations of the festival organization and its ancillary support entities. Research undertaken in the United Kingdom (Parry, 2012) by Julie's Bicycle indicates that festival contingency planning processes are now substantially impacted by adverse weather affecting falls in ticket sales and poor audience experiences. The clear sense of mission shared by all partners needs to be embedded so that each festival and each destination can increase the productivity, adopt appropriate technologies, and be adaptive, dynamic, and opportunistic.

The new urban ecologies are complex and festival organizers need to observe where the best collaborations can be effected for mutual benefit. Many destinations are recognizing the value of communication and cooperation when developing a portfolio of festivals to take them into the future. The tourism and economic development literature has examined the life cycle of destinations. It is essential that all parties track the strengths and weaknesses and the competition to ensure the attractions offered are what the marketplace currently finds appealing and will induce longevity of their projects.

## Positioning

The World Tourism Cities Federation (WTCF) was formed in 2012 to encourage the exchange between cities that believe that a tourism city can't be truly top class until it has its signature brand. The initial meeting was hosted by Beijing, China, where representatives discussed how developing cities required their own brand to match other cities with clear local characteristics. Delegates identified the importance of festivals in drawing tourists, the value of happy residents being good hosts, and the need not to duplicate what others do, but to seek out endemic characteristics and build on these—making festivals a strong focus (Sun Ye).

We learn from marketing practice that developing a "position" for a festival, a destination, or a combination of both can emerge from the attributes of the festival, location, heritage, scale, and connection to the community or arts or cultural practice. It can be derived from the existing and potential audience support or by the competition from other similar entities. Basically, the focus is generating a favorable impression or image in the minds of the hosts, the festival organizations, and the audience. While a festival might look to present an attractive position through pricing for the goods and services offered, it could also be committed to differentiating itself from the quality of competitors' appeal. By promoting a festival or destination through specific cultural symbols that link to particular demographics or market niches, a well-honed image can be projected. Comparisons between what is on offer have been found to be effective through advertising.

The positioning strategy is supported by intensive market research. The areas that need to be considered before a final decision is made include recognizing where the competition is, whether close by or international or whether dependent on the financial climate for individuals' discretionary expenditure. The perception of competitors and their position among the sector needs to be evaluated. The targeted audience needs to be reviewed and analyzed for distinctiveness, overlapping interests, and potential for movement from current commitments. Identifying competitors is complex. Host communities need to be alert to the layers of internal and external influences. These include an understanding of the mobility of audiences and artists, distance from population sources, access to and condition of attractive amenities, and infrastructure associated with delivery of a quality experience. Then there is the promotional strategy, discussed in Chapter 10. These elements all assist in placing the festival and associated attractions top of mind for potential patrons.

## Building Brand and Image and Reputation

It has already been mentioned that through collaboration a number of festival organizations can help a destination capitalize on its attractiveness to global markets. The brand of Edinburgh, Scotland, has been markedly impacted by an initiative known as Festivals Edinburgh, a strategic approach that has been taken by 12 major festivals in the city. Through an innovative

South Australia, a state in Australia, issued registration plates for motor vehicles with "Festival State" emblazoned on them. They confidently promoted a commitment to a number of special events, but particularly the Adelaide Festival of Arts, a long-standing arts festival, based on the Edinburgh model.

partnership, individual festival organizations have developed approaches to consolidate the city's international reputation as a festival city. Each has a dramatic impact on the world stage in its own right. As well, collaboratively, they have raised the profile of the city through their power and resolve to grow the cultural identity of the city and Scotland as whole. These processes, innovation, and impact will be examined in the interview with Festivals Edinburgh's Director Faith Liddell in the From Inside the Mosaic box at the end of the chapter.

In Northern Ireland discussions on what constitutes image and brand development good practice engaged tourism officials and academics keen to build the reputation of the state. This scenario should resonate across the globe as states attempt to develop a comprehensive destination image strategy. The Northern Ireland Tourist Board slogan "our time, our place" provided a base for identifying how festivals can contribute to capturing the world's attention. The recommendations included leveraging each and every event, for a long-term event tourism strategy to be developed, and the management of a portfolio of events, both permanent and one-time. Don Getz suggested that every major event provides an opportunity for positive image-building, but getting the desired media coverage of events does not occur by chance, sophisticated media management is required (Canning, 2012).

## Quality and Festivals

Festival directors work hard to ensure the content of the festival offering is of the highest standard. Community-based festivals and professionally curated festivals are defined by the quality of their content, logistics, brand reputation, history, and representativeness of a specific cutting-edge or traditional genre, locations, vision, and impact on satisfied audiences. The impact of festivals is widespread on their host communities and collaborations. A conflated image emerges when synergies exist between excellent design, development, and delivery of a shared brand over time.

Quality programs demonstrate individual and collective skills, experience, artistic risk-taking, and a commitment to professional standards that are peer-reviewed and surpass audience expectations. A confident approach through attention to detail and a serious dedication to good practice goes a long way to intensify support for the festival. Careful screening of possible contributors to program content, high standards of logistics, technology, and volunteer and staff engagement provide sound fundamentals to memorable experiences and a competitive advantage.

Quality implies standards. A festival's quality framework focuses on fitness for purpose of operations and festival programs by ensuring there is a whole-of-organization ethos determined to strive for ongoing improvement through established good practice. By delivering outstanding responses to the fundamental concepts of the arts and cultural bodies of knowledge, a positive reputation is assured. Regardless of the scale or scope of the festival team, all need to embrace the task of meeting or exceeding expectations of audiences by demonstrating the essential competencies of a particular sector.

## Cultural Tourism and Creative Tourism

Further to this line of competiveness emerging from the experience economy comes work done by Steven Thorne in Canada on the importance of place in the development of sustainable cultural tourism. He and Greg Baeker have contributed much to communities around the world, assisting them in identifying how they can attract the growing number of visitors interested in culture and heritage through a better understanding of their cultural asset base, their cultural identity, and their distinctive sense of place. They offer a brief case study of Stratford, Ontario, the home of the renowned Stratford Shakespeare Festival. In that context they explore the power of a holistic approach to community collaborations, promoting a broader package of attractions, benefitting from new audience segments, and laying foundations for substantial economic and cultural legacies.

Researchers Richards and Raymond (2000) coined the term *creative tourism*. Creative tourism provides policymakers the opportunity to link the arts, cultural development, and destination competitiveness. The emerging economic imperatives gained from the development of the creative industries and its potential connections to tourism, food, heritage, education, built and natural environments, and personal and community well-being has increased attention on small-scale and social enterprises. Many community-based cultural festivals have spawned experiences that have led to local investment in allied arts enterprises, like the Hay (Book) Festival in Hay-on-Wye in Wales.

Such communities have been able to capitalize on the arrival of new settlers setting up shop in the town center or in the purpose-built incubator workspaces with skills and experience in visual arts and crafts, music, writing and publishing, gift and bookshops, photography, graphic design, toy-making, education, and workshops. The resulting creative atmosphere that enhances cultural production and consumption is replicated around the world. This environment becomes attractive to cultural tourists who require ancillary relationships with accommodation, hospitality, transport, and engagement with surrounding areas, so that loops and trails become a significant part of the tourism network. Recognition of such options encourages proactivity on the part of local destination managers, local government, and local businesses.

Individual businesses can align their products and services to the increasing demand for experiential tourism that festivals represent. The higher yielding customers generally stay longer and spend more. The investment is less about infrastructure and more about excited and inspired employees sharing their enthusiasm and expertise with visitors. By building coalitions and negotiating trust and shared identity, economic prosperity can result along with community capacity to support individual festivals or a portfolio of them. Festival packages can be purchased ahead of arrival that allows patrons to feel secure about access to the festival, accommodation, transport, and longer stays in destinations.

## Place-Making

Festivals make a dynamic contribution to the movement on urban renewal and liveability. The creative and innovative use of public spaces allows for networks of folk from different disciplines to converge and seek solutions that may involve the themes and brands acceptable to locals, through outdoor plantings, public art, and a seamless array of activities that can be shared intimately or en mass. Quality design may utilize sound, light, color, and movement and attract investment from developers, government at various levels, and become animated in free and ticketed ways. Such initiatives are all about community engagement.

# Festivals as Destination Drivers

Sculpture on the Brisbane Festival riverside site reflects the mix of landscape involving the built and natural environments.

Precincts can be created to form discrete attractions—harborsides, parklands, shopping centers, historic buildings, and purpose-built cultural facilities. A distinctive sense of place readily connects with sustainability frameworks and quadruple bottom-line principles through the size, scale, access, and activities engaging residents being within comfortable and agreed boundaries. Town and cityscapes should be walkable, well signed, well lit, clean, and safe, such as Edinburgh, Scotland, where the majority of its annual aggregated August festivals encourage audiences to familiarize themselves with the city's heritage of nooks and crannies.

Communities, or clusters of communities, including surrounding regions require a well-defined edge or boundary based on character or theme, adequate open space, corridors connecting interesting spaces and buildings, and where possible, natural terrain. In urban areas civic design needs to be geared to minimize waste and efficiently conserve resources to enhance residents' attachment to place. This is seen as an important aspect of community values and improves the capacity of locals to offer hospitality to visitors. Much more than an environment, it provides meaning in life and is a fundamental need that is enhanced when people are involved in the shaping of places. Festivals can take advantage of such initiatives to enhance their appeal and distinctiveness. They transform places from being everyday settings into temporary environments that inspire the production, processing, and consumption of culture, concentrated in time and place.

## Festivals Anywhere

You need to consider what might be called *placeless festivals* as well. These are the sort of festivals that demonstrate very little place attachment and could be staged anywhere. This may be a symptom of globalization, the mobility of artists and audiences, and the transient animation of spaces that increase access for marginalized communities.

The balance can come from activating a fusion of local and imported cultural activity. This has effectively stimulated local legacies. An example of a small rural community embracing such a concept of imported and local entertainers sharing a stage was *Gentlemen of the Road* in New South Wales, Australia. It hosted an international stopover headlined by Mumford and Sons from the UK. This experience had already been replicated in Huddersfield, UK; Galway, Ireland; Portland, Maine; Bristol, UK; Dixon, Illinois; Monterey, California; and Dungog, NSW Australia. These regional festivals attract metropolitan audiences as well. In Australia, federal government initiatives encourage the interaction through the Festivals Australia grant program that shares the exposure of global talent and enhances the experiences of local audiences. Examples include *Flix in the Stix* where films, spoken-word artists, and high-profile bands join locals for a celebration of the arts; remote locations host such endeavors as *Burning Man Australia* encourage participation and collaboration.

## Ritual and Spectacle

Earlier we observed important features of ritual and spectacle as distinctive elements in festivals over time. We recognized the value of including parades, pageantry, ceremonies, costumes, and traditions that have been passed down through generations. The authenticity sought by festival patrons allows organizers to rediscover and interpret aspects of social and cultural capital that have been nurtured by artists and host communities. Rituals bring to light actions performed according to prescribed practices that can be updated, overturned, dealt with solemnly or with satire or parody depending on the audiences. Some rituals are included in festival programs purely for their symbolic values; others provide robust animation through competitions, color, and movement, and opportunities for the sharing of food and beverages.

The inquisitive audience member can puzzle connections between themselves and their environment. How many towns turn their back on their river and its origins? The natural phenomenon of daybreak, sunset, mists, waterfalls, tides, floods, lakes, and seasons animate

Handmade float made by a village community for the street parade prior to sending the boat down the Mekong River during Loy Krathong.

place for humans. They offer space for reflection and stimulate responses in various media, fabric, bamboo, inflatables, and spectator and other participatory responses. Individuals' affective relationship with the landscape or material environment may vary in intensity, discretion, and manner of expression, but it has proved to be an important factor in place selection. The Sante Fe Opera Festival draws audiences from around the globe to the New Mexico mountains for performances in an adobe theater blending into the desert landscape.

Fire and water are key features of new-year celebrations on the harbor in Sydney, Australia, with sound, light from fireworks, lasers, projections, and other illuminations. The waterfront districts of many cities have become the focus of urban reinvention as sites for traditional and contemporary rituals and spectacle. For example, Vancouver and Toronto, Canada, and Providence, Rhode Island, offer participants land and water based dramatic pageantry. WaterFire in Providence has been praised as "the most popular work of art created in the capital city's 371-year history" and as the "crown jewel of the Providence renaissance." WaterFire continues to grow and gain in popularity. The lakeside stage near Bregenz in Austria during each summer since 1946 provides open-air opera productions that have built a substantial international profile.

## LUANG PRABANG, LAOS

A festival that emerges from Buddhist traditions and is influenced by Indian festivals like Diwali is known in Laos as Lai Heua Fai (*Boats of Light*), though in neighboring Thailand it is known as Loy Krathong. There are numerous locations where similar practices pay homage to the rivers, as individuals, families, and communities use candlelight, assist lanterns to become airborne, and float small handmade rafts of light made from buoyant banana tree trunks to signify their commitment to be rid of negative behavior and venerate teachings of Buddha.

At the end of October in Luang Prabang residents of all ages come together to share in an explosion of light. From fireworks to elaborately decorated boats parading down the main street as part of an intervillage competition judged at the temple Xiang Thong. They are blessed by monks prior to being carried down the steep steps and slippery tracks to the Mekong River to be launched on bamboo rafts to create a spectacle to be seen far and wide with thousands of local and visiting onlookers.

Such festivities, grounded in animist and Buddhist traditions, are embraced for personal expression of renewal and forgiveness with children and families finding their way riverside to launch their own boats of light. They are joined by growing numbers of international visitors who wish to participate in the free and outdoor rituals associated with open displays of emotion. There is loud music, strident exhortations broadcast from temples and feasting on local delicacies purchased from small street-side stalls, consumption of alcohol along the main thoroughfares, and squeals of delight as flashlights from phones and cameras capture images of themselves in adventures in a World Heritage–listed, place-based cultural tourism.

There are distinctive local elements to this celebration. Visitors who travel to Chiang Mai or Bangkok in Thailand a month later to experience the same spiritual and communal festivities will get insight into different scales, technologies, and idiosyncratic elements represented. Each festival has active participation from residents keen to share their responses to the cycles of the moon with visitors. They increasingly recognize the economic spin-offs for the tourism economy alongside demonstrating the rich seam of religious ceremonies. Such experiences, in the company of saffron-robed monks lighting candles in the forecourt of hundreds of temples, is sure to have a place reserved on potential visitors' "bucket lists"!

During the festival of Loy Krathong in Luang Prabang, Laos, families and visitors gather at the temple on the banks of the Mekong River to celebrate at stalls before launching lanterns aloft.

The social capital that is generated from audience participation or observances of formal and informal rituals and spectacles also provides a useful lens to observe the networks that individuals, communities, and nations engage with and then present to wider audiences. The literature addresses the interaction that can be ascribed to festival participation by demonstrating what Robert Putman (2000) proposed as "bonding" and "bridging" social capital. In celebrations and competitions at the unique cultural and sporting experience in the heart of one of Italy's most beautiful cities, the Palio in the Piazza del Campo in Siena, Italy, we can see evidence of bridging social capital through connectedness formed across diverse local and broader social and special interest groups, while "bonding social capital" is seen to offer substantial confidence that cements homogenous groups within the city.

From a visitor's perspective as well, the authenticity of events such as this resonates because it builds on the traditions embedded in the rituals and cultural traits they observe and experience. They share this with the host community who demonstrates civic pride through the replication of their heritage to which they pay homage.

What is your impression of the rituals and spectacle that attend this significant festival in Siena? How do you think the roles of bridging and bonding social capital are manifested? People may be embedded in social groups from family, friends, and neighborhoods, metropolitan, regional, national, or external to the host community.

For something with a completely distinctive climatic dimension, we can learn of the appeal of the Harbin Festival. Check YouTube and Web stories entries for this festival to get a sense of the unique visual spectacle.

As you read more about these festivals, or better yet, attend them, you may discern how the residents accommodate visitors, how the destination projects a cohesive profile that attracts strong, often repeat audiences. Ties to festival destinations can be strong and/or transient, engaging for different levels of stakeholders, with recognition coming from those closest to the festival organization or dispersed but connected through a special interest and a desire for an authentic local experience.

## Globalization

We have already alluded to the growing process of exchanging cultural ideas and resources globally. Festivals have made a significant contribution to breaking international barriers that can increase the mobility of intangible assets like artists and artworks, digital technology, transport, foreign investment, design expertise, and intellectual transactions through shared knowledge. There are challenges to this in the area of festival design and management through what might be called hybridization. Popular culture evolves through processes of blending and altering that creates new techniques and templates. As in other business sectors, the movement of money, people, and trade can become a significant risk in preparing and sustaining quality arts and cultural programs.

In the Palio the various Sienese "contrade" or areas into which the city is divided, challenge each other in a passionate horse race in the heart of the city in the Piazza del Campo. Originally, there were 59 contrade; now only 17 remain, 10 of which take part in the historical pageant and in the race at each Palio. Each Contrada has its own unique emblem, colors, and flag displayed along the street. Much like street signs, street corners often designate the entrance into a different contrada.

The Palio horse race has its origins in the distant past. The Palio is a large part of residents' lives from the time of their birth. Each person belongs to a contrada and participates in the life of the contrada and the organization of the Palio throughout the entire year. The Sienese live the Palio with great passion. It is a complex event that has gained additional rules through the centuries, as well as traditions and customs, many of which only members of the contrada are aware of.

The Palio horse race takes place twice a year. During this special occasion, the main square in Siena, the Piazza del Campo, is prepared for the race as the ring around the square is covered with tuff clay. The Palio takes place over four days, the race taking place on the fourth day. The jockeys always mount their horses without a saddle. The Palio prize is called Drappellone, or "large drape," a large painted canvas each year designed and created by a different artist, which the winning contrada displays in their contrada museum.

The Harbin Festival is one of the world's four largest ice and snow festivals, along with Japan's Sapporo Snow Festival, Canada's Quebec City Winter Carnival, and Norway's Ski Festival. The annual Harbin International Ice and Snow Sculpture Festival has been held since 1963. Harbin is a provincial capital in the People's Republic of China. It is located in Northeast China under the direct influence of the cold winter wind from Siberia. The average temperature in the summer is 70°F, and −2° in the winter! It can be as cold as −36.5°. As we investigate the role of spectacle in providing a "wow" factor for festival participants, Harbin provides some unique perspectives. Ice sculpture decoration technology ranges from the modern (using lasers) to traditional (with ice lanterns). There are ice lantern parks, alpine skiing, winter-swimming in the Songhua River, and the ice-lantern exhibition in Zhaolin Garden.

Visitors from around the world visit the annual Harbin International Snow and Ice Festival, which features monuments up to 50m high crafted by some of the country's best ice sculptors. Multicolored lights are used to add color to the sculptures at the event. Spectators can enjoy horse-drawn carriage rides, slide down slippery dips, and watch brave souls dive from diving boards made of blocks of ice into freezing cold water. There are diverse, complementary attractions to the festival that build the destination's appeal.

China's "City of Ice" provides a winter wonderland as backdrop to snow sculptures, as well as an indoor ice and snow art museum. In 2012 organizers teamed up with Disney to construct a Disney Ice and Snow Wonderland. It took up an area of 600,000 square meters. There are activities for the whole family. The evenings are promoted as optimum to explore the crystal-clear ice lit up from the inside, while ice carvings can be accessed on foot, an ice maze is of interest, as is the slides down embankments on rubber tubes.

Critics of globalization as it is known in economics cite implications for global leisure activity like tourism and culture. There is an obvious increase in cross-cultural interaction as artists and productions through promotion, skills development, and engagement with the Internet, satellites, and face-to-face collaborations. The fusion resulting from applied creativity and innovation has become a transforming element of festivals around the world, as is indicated in the short case studies in this chapter. However, concern is expressed in some quarters of the diminution of the scale or importance of some traditional and idiosyncratic cultural practices that have been a feature of festivals over long periods. The interdependence now evident in festival programs of local and imported content needs to be carefully managed, as audiences seek to identify distinctive cultural attributes, while applauding the fact they now can have great reach in their consumption of global cultures.

There is no disputing the transformations that take place when artists and audiences experience authentic arts practice from diverse cultures in their endemic host environments or far from home across the planet. Care is taken to preserve cultural heritage. How can festivals contribute to ensuring that the globally integrated economic systems add value to the origins and subsequent appreciation of contemporary arts presentations and practices? Major international festival entities like WOMAD deliver World of Music Arts and Dance festivals and events throughout the world. The World Festival Network acts as a link between festivals, performers, audiences, suppliers, and the media to strengthen and promote multidisciplinary festivals. The members of the International Cities of Advanced Sound have developed unique festivals and events, each with its own identity grounded in strong local connections and context while exploring the cultural value of music and sound creation and their integration with other cultural practices. There is increasing collaboration internationally in the development of festival programs. While many festivals wish to enhance the definition of their own country's or destination's cultural identity through the aesthetic content of their program, they also aim to draw together stimulating and exotic projects that excite, inform, and lift audience spirits.

Many destinations find themselves in global bidding wars as they attempt to draw international acts to established festivals. The resources committed to touring special artists and special events are substantial and need to be integrated into a consistent overarching destination image.

## International Recognition

Many towns and cities have garnered an international reputation based on their capacity to sustain community cultural and arts festivals over time. *City of Festivals* has been added to the name of many destinations.

## Trends: Open-Source Festival Content

There is growing interest in the concept of open-source festival content modeled on the Edinburgh Festival Fringe experience. It commenced in 1947 as an alternative festival that played concurrently with the Edinburgh International Festival. In 1948, Robert Kemp, a

---

One such city that has successfully melded a portfolio of festivals into a brand is Edmonton, Canada. The Edmonton Heritage Festival, with a vision of "Presenting an annual summer festival showcasing the diverse cultures of our community. Providing year-round activities and programs that highlight our community's great and varied cultural heritage. Becoming the primary resource to educate the community on diverse cultures," and the long-term dedication of organizers, civic authorities, volunteers and growing global attention from peers and visitors has consolidated an international reputation.

It had its origins like many of the globally competitive festivals mentioned in this chapter with an initiative of the Government of Alberta in 1974, for an Edmonton Heritage Festival on the first Monday in August to celebrate the varied cultural heritage of Alberta. Over the years ethnocultural networks came together to showcase their heritages through food, performances, crafts, and education. The festival is conducted over three days and in recent times claims to engage over 5,000 pavilion volunteers working through 60-plus pavilions representing over 85 distinctive cultures. Their efforts have been recognized by numerous accolades in the annual IFEA Awards. It sees itself as *Edmonton the City of Champions and the Festival City* and attracts over 300,000 visitors to the family-friendly festivities. The festival has been responsible for numerous year-round programs that link the summer event to the cultural networks of the broader resident community. The festival is organized by the nonprofit entity Edmonton Heritage Festival Association.

| Australia<br>Adelaide Fringe<br>Melbourne Fringe Festival<br>Sydney Fringe | United Kingdom<br>Buxton Festival Fringe<br>Cambridge Fringe Festival<br>Edinburgh Festival Fringe |
|---|---|
| Canada<br>Calgary Fringe Festival<br>Edmonton International Fringe Theatre Festival<br>Ottawa Fringe Festival | Ireland<br>Dublin Fringe Festival |
| Singapore<br>M1 Singapore Fringe Festival | United States<br>United States Association of Fringe Festivals |

**Table 11.2** Some Global Fringe Festivals

local journalist, gave it the name Fringe. It is a an artistic and financial business for independent artists, mostly in diverse performing arts, but many embrace multimedia projects to provide a focus for initiative, imagination, and inspiration for audiences in host communities committed to establish mainstream cultural festivals.

In the United States fringe festivals offer a forum for showcasing new work, new approaches, smaller scale projects that are selected in different ways. Fringe festival organizers' approaches vary. Some use a first-come, first-served opportunity for people wishing to apply, some pay a few artists and take the financial risk, while others may collaborate for some marketing initiatives. Other fringe organizers have more sophisticated processes including a curated or jury system to arrange the festival line-up; others use a lottery system for content. Although the actual structures and requirements vary, the basic idea is that the fringe festival producer gives individual producers of each show an umbrella to operate under. You may wish to examine how some of the fringe festivals in Table 11.2 attract, select, invite, or review potential participants. Fringe festivals provide an effective vehicle for amateur or professional artists to share with one another; some win prizes, media acclaim, and valuable performance experience while having a great deal of fun!

You will notice some of the following distinctive features of an open-access fringe festival:

- Focus essentially on the performing arts
- Uncensored content
- Ease of participation
- Duration varies in multiplicity of venues
- Original material
- Low-tech, rapid-fire projects

## Challenges for Globally Competitive Destinations Hosting Festivals

This chapter raises many issues and ideas that challenge successful and enduring festivals to provide some sort of competitive edge for hosting destinations. Maybe it is all about balance. Tensions exist that require careful consideration by all stakeholders.

The design, management, and consumption of festivals in contemporary life draw on distinctive features of change through globalization, contested beliefs, values, and cultural heritage. The intrinsic transformative nature of festivals highlights the porous boundaries that exist between the commercialization of culture and the alternative, noncommercial ethic that permeates the field. The challenge is that these can coexist with each element maintaining its integrity and by nourishing one another, however, it demands vigilance, creativity, sensitivity, and innovation.

Tourism has become a significant player in staging festivals for economic gain. By exploiting the economic benefits, tensions can be exacerbated with communities keen to maintain traditional practices. The fragile financial environment globally has implications for host communities weighing up communal investments incurred in hosting major festivals. Individual promoters and festival organizations are far more circumspect in their commitments to financial outlays. There is increasing scrutiny and public commentary about funds from the public purse being committed to spectacle and celebrations in straightened times.

The conundrum is not a blatant struggle of the contemporary common good versus the noncommodified culture to be saved. The exhortation to think globally and act locally is often heard in this connection. The festival concepts of inclusiveness, conviviality, and active participation require an environment of trust. Festivals often host artistic and cultural production that finds refuge from other forums that have stagnated, but can be reinvented to build an acceptable communal life that includes job creation and business prosperity. There is concern in some quarters that the intent and ownership of long-standing community cultural festivals may be marginalized once a global audience discovers locations and celebrations. There can be a feeling of loss of control, exploitation by external entities, and conflict among residents.

Spinning off from such concerns are the importance of landscape and lifestyle sustainability. The economic agenda benefits from readily accessible quantitative evaluation to which festivals can contribute. More difficult to discern are the social and environmental legacies of festivals. The place as a product in the festival mix puts pressure on ancillary services like urban amenity, health and retail services, disaffection of some parties, and serious negative implications for policy and planning by local authorities. So, once again it is about balance—implementing strategies that satisfy the need for authenticity sought by audiences and that minimize resistance to change that can affect the sense of pride and passion locals feel for their home.

Sustainable festival management systems set targets that are now part of public discourse and require monitoring, testing, and reporting in ways that satisfy regulators, community, organizers, and service providers. These can include measuring the carbon footprint over the whole festival duration; implementing a waste strategy to achieve significant levels of waste to landfill, reuse, or recycling; applying power minimization practices; delivering a public transport protocol to minimize emissions, fuel use, and costs; committing to stringent food management and sustainability requirements, and contributing to the development of the international sustainable event management system standard, ISO 20121, which is set to be part of a very influential global legacy. There is increasing need for effective partnerships to be in place that ensure innovations through technology, human resource management, and policy applications across the environmental spectrum are generated. Demonstrating efficiencies and environmental good practice has become a distinctive global selling point for festivals and destinations.

Can festivals transform destinations into a place of remarkable experiences? The realistic appreciation of the impacts of climate change, financial uncertainty, trends on consumption, active involvement in experiences, rather than a sole engagement with passive spectatorship and understanding of political imperatives require attention from astute and innovative festival organizers.

The capacity to take risks with limited resources is a constant. It has been suggested that partnerships and collaborative initiatives may be a way forward. More and more festivals and arts and cultural organizations have recognized the value to their brand of international collaborations. These can be prompted by a shared artistic ambition to become an independent enterprise to which a number of international stakeholders can contribute. It provides shared investment of financial and practical resources and stimulates programs that excite the public.

## CASE STUDY

### Edinburgh Festival Fringe, Scotland

But buildings alone give no surety for the right climate for fostering the arts and sciences. That climate is provided by the inhabitants, of whom in Edinburgh there is a surprising number, drawn from the whole range of society, showed by their curiosity about philosophic ideas and new scientific discoveries during the 18th century.
—*George Bruce in Festival Up North: The Story of the Edinburgh Festival (1975)*

The Fringe director is not a festival director in the normal sense of the word, but more like a ringmaster, a magician, and a juggler. The rumblings about the Fringe becoming too big have been going on practically since year 2 of the festival. It is a great free-for-all, a self-replicating organism that grows year after year. In Edinburgh since 1947, it is the blood, sweat, and tears, the energy, and the drive of individuals that have created our world-leading festival and rich cultural scene.
—*Catherine Lockerbie (former) Director, Edinburgh International Book Festival, 2007*

The Edinburgh Festival Fringe 2012 accommodated 42,096 performances of 2,695 shows, setting a new record. It is estimated that 22,457 performers took part in the 2012 Fringe, more than 1,000 more than last year. Numbers from the Edinburgh Festival Fringe Society show that by Monday afternoon, with hundreds of performances still to take place, 1,857,202 tickets had been issued for shows, events, and exhibitions in 279 venues across the city. This impressive number doesn't include the thousands attending the 814 free, nonticketed events of the Fringe. Performers came from 47 countries.
—*Edinburgh Festivals, August 28, 2012*

Visitors to the Edinburgh Festival Fringe don't forget their first time there. The memories are as much about the performances found and experienced as it is the physical characteristics of Edinburgh, those that encourage exploration on foot, at all times of the day and night, the people from around the world who find the excitement exhilarating and return again and again—sometimes as performers themselves or as the audience. The diverse festival events are matched with passionate exponents of the unfettered style of the program.

The founding principle at the heart of the Edinburgh Festival Fringe Society—to be an open-access arts event that accommodates anyone with a story to tell and a venue willing to host them—continues to regulate the work of the Fringe Festival

Society. The three-week program is shaped by that very initiative and vision of performers willing to showcase their work there.

The Edinburgh Festival Fringe is the largest arts festival in the world, an inspiring celebration of the best performance and entertainment emerging from every continent. The Festival Fringe Society does not produce any shows, invite anyone to perform, run any venues, or pay any fees to artists, and no single individual or committee determines who can or cannot perform at the Fringe. Participation relies entirely on the initiative of thousands of performers who chose to put on a show. The website (*http://www.edfringe.com/participants*) outlines the framework for involvement by artists highlighting essential elements for surviving like finding a venue, rehearsal spaces, budgeting, recycling, promotion, and presenting a premiere!

The Festival Fringe is integral to the swathe of cultural celebrations during August in Edinburgh. The Edinburgh International Festival was first staged in 1947. Eight theater groups turned up uninvited, wanting to perform. While ineligible to contribute to the major post-war initiative, they determined to share their productions anyway! There was growing interest in showcasing global theater, comedy, dance, musicals, operas, music, cabaret, exhibitions, and events in a welcoming city. In 1958, the Festival Fringe Society was formally created in response to the success of this growing trend. The standout feature is the unconventional, the experimentation, the stretching of ideas, attitudes, and creative activities evident in each venture, year after year.

Individual artists speak of their personal and professional epiphanies as they observed and learned from their peers and made contact with the wider entertainment industry and pervasive attendant media commentary. Careers of subsequently famous artists have been revealed in any number of small or lavish cultural venues. Some performers have found their careers truncated as a result of audience feedback. The Fringe is made up of the visions and ambitions of thousands of participants, from producers and promoters, to venue managers and individual performers.

Each year the Fringe Society works with all stakeholders to ensure there is adequate support for the creative endeavors. They offer advice, information, and encouragement. The staff, industry producers, promoters, and venue managers assist in delivering tailored seminars, workshops, and online and print content to facilitate ease of engagement with the city and the audiences. The Edinburgh Festival Fringe Society is a registered charity. It is a membership-based organization. It has established a Participants' Council that provides a direct opportunity for input into aspects of administration for performers, producers, and venue personnel. Participants can assist with the promotion of the festival and offer advice to the Fringe Society Board. For those with skills, experience, and interest in festival management there are jobs advertised year-round. These can include box office, administration, retail, media (PR), arts industry, and street events roles.

The Fringe Society has strong relationships with corporate and media sponsors and is an active participant in the collaboration called Festivals Edinburgh along with 11 other Edinburgh festivals and partners with Creative Scotland and the British Council in numerous initiatives. It works with EventScotland and VisitScotland who are mindful of the tourism implications of such a potent and successful festival.

These relationships manifest themselves in specific initiatives that take into account trends in sustainable festival-making. All Fringe productions are invited to consider active engagement with audiences in an environmentally sensitive manner and consider the impacts of their contribution to sustainable practices more broadly. An award, the Fringe Sustainable Production Award, is offered for parties to demonstrate the responsibility each production takes to deliver green arts outcomes. This Fringe award is supported by the Centre for Sustainable Practice in the Arts, Festivals Edinburgh, and Creative Carbon Scotland and through a media partnership from The List.

# FROM INSIDE THE MOSAIC

## Faith Liddell, Festivals Edinburgh Director

Faith Liddell is an experienced director, producer, and project manager who has worked in key strategic and creative roles across theater, literature, music, film, and visual arts specializing predominantly in the creation and development of festivals and festival-based programs. Her freelance work has included producing for the National Theatre of Scotland; Director of DCA, Scotland's leading center for contemporary art and film; Project Manager for the Scottish Playwrights' Studio Development Project; Director of the Edinburgh International Book Festival; and Marketing Manager for the Edinburgh Festival Fringe. She has been Director of Festivals Edinburgh since January 2007.

Faith Liddell, Festivals Edinburgh Director
© Peter Derrett

Festivals Edinburgh is the high-level organization created and managed by the directors of Edinburgh's 12 major festivals, to take the lead on their joint strategic development. As the Director of Festivals Edinburgh, Faith Liddell works closely with the member festivals to enable, facilitate, and deliver new, significant projects in a number of key strategic areas: joint marketing, programming, sponsorship, technology, environmental sustainability, and professional development. It is a strategic umbrella organization ensuring that partnerships generate synergistic coordination—and enable the city to plan and manage cultural, social, economic, and environmental returns.

**Edinburgh is the world's Festival City.** It's where people come together from across the globe to share their passion for arts, culture, and ideas. This welcoming, inspiring, and open-minded atmosphere is heightened by the approachable beauty of this breathtaking historical city. With 12 festivals throughout the year, there's an endless array of events, performances, and spectacles to enjoy.

Research informs activity for the organization. The 2010 Edinburgh Festivals impact study conducted by BOP Consulting provided evidence beyond the economic impacts to include reflections of program, products, their quality, and opportunities for advocates within the organization to extend the partnership remit. It responded to some of the issues identified in the *Thundering Hooves* report of 2006, which looked at the competitive global position of Edinburgh's Festivals. It identified how the festivals are loved by residents and more broadly by stakeholders including audiences, media, performers, and sponsors. The cultural offer from all 12 festivals were recognized for their application of creativity and innovation, how the festivals shared the same place and offered such diverse, unique, world-class experiences to domestic and international visitors. The impressively comprehensive report identified significant economic returns to Edinburgh's venues, increased festival viability and resilience, skills and employment pathways for a number of target groups, creative and cultural sector/industry development, and major marketing and relationship returns for both the city and Scotland in the global marketplace.

Festivals Edinburgh is a uniquely collaborative organization created by and reliant on the collective ambition, will, and mandate of the 12 member festivals. It acts on behalf of and represents the collective strengths of the Edinburgh Festivals to develop and deliver collaborative projects and initiatives that support growth, product development, leadership, and audiences, and help to sustain the festivals and Edinburgh and Scotland's preeminence as the world's leading festival destination.

Faith works under a board comprised of the 12 Directors or CEOs of the Festivals. While the Festivals have worked together on a number of tactical initiatives in the past (such as the first joint festivals gateway website in the late 1990s), their decision to create Festivals Edinburgh in 2006—with the company registration in October 2007—enabled these and other initiatives and relationships to be developed and extended within a more strategic framework and this has allowed for much greater cohesion across wider partnerships.

Major initiatives, and the organization's existence, are only made possible by the vision, expertise, and leadership of each member festival; and, essentially, the ambition, support, and investment of key funders: the Scottish Government, City of Edinburgh Council, EventScotland, Scottish Enterprise, and the VisitScotland Growth Fund. Festivals Edinburgh has a five-year Business Plan (March 2008–2013). This is based on some of the relationships, achievements and models of practice that Festivals Edinburgh established in its early years of operation. It embraces the idea of the ongoing development of models of collaboration, project development, and delivery. In every area of the plan the focus is on achieving key strategic objectives while developing the necessary political, funding, and partnership structures to achieve these.

Key projects have included:

- The *Edinburgh Festivals Expo fund*: created by the Scottish Government to provide the single largest showcase ever for Scottish companies and artists on the international platform of the Edinburgh Festivals, extending opportunity and ambition nationally and internationally for the festivals and the artists they promote and support.
- The Festivals' *first-ever joint marketing strategy and plan*: supported by the Scottish Government, City of Edinburgh Council, VisitScotland, EventScotland, and Scottish Enterprise to innovatively and comprehensively promote the Festivals to new, untapped markets regionally, nationally, and globally.
- *Collaborative working across the Festivals in key areas of mutual, overarching interest*, such as environmental sustainability and professional development.
- *Innovation Lab* is a program managing the ambitions of the partners' organizations in the digital environment. Processes, projects, networks, and personnel are shared to imagine, design and deliver initiatives demonstrated on an online show reel.

Edinburgh Festivals contributed to *three major cultural gatherings* for international representatives and further positioning the Festivals and Edinburgh as the home of cultural debate:

- The *Edinburgh International Culture Summit* was the first ever International Culture Summit, a collaboration between four partner organizations—the Scottish Government, the UK Government, the British Council, and the Edinburgh International Festival, with ministers for culture from around the world attending. The power and profile of culture in forging and fostering international relationships was debated at the Scottish Parliament at Holyrood.
- The *Edinburgh World Writers' Conference 2012–2013* marked the 50th anniversary of the infamous 1962 conference, which saw 70 of the world's most celebrated writers come to Scotland to discuss the world of literature. Subsequent conversations were contributed to the growing debate about literature and its relationship to contemporary life in 14 countries before returning to Edinburgh in 2013 and included regular live streaming of events worldwide, videos, and blogs.
- The *World Fringe Congress 2012* allowed delegates to meet to exchange ideas and experiences within the huge variety of open-access festival models and philosophies. Each Fringe is unique and is responsive to its own local environment and community.

The commitment to Fringe ideals and belief in its importance and impact for artists and audiences was highlighted through the creation of a new network and strengthened the Fringe family.

Edinburgh Festivals partners:
- Bank of Scotland Imaginate Festival
- Edinburgh Art Festival
- Edinburgh Festival Fringe
- Edinburgh's Hogmanay and New Year's Party
- Edinburgh International Book Festival
- Edinburgh International Festival
- Edinburgh International Film Festival
- Edinburgh International Science Festival
- Edinburgh Jazz and Blues Festival
- Edinburgh Mela
- Royal Edinburgh Military Tattoo
- Scottish International Storytelling Festival

## Festival Ideas and Issues

1. How important is the celebration of culture in the public and political life of world cities?
2. How do festivals assist cities to become more dynamic and livable places? Discuss how cities shape planned public events and these events shape cities. You may wish to debate the influences of globalization, economic environments, collaboration and competition, and urban revitalization.
3. Who are the prime stakeholders involved with determining success for enduring festivals? How can they collaborate to position themselves to attract not only local audiences but also international visitors?
4. Some destinations gain a competitive advantage from hosting cultural festivals. Discuss how creativity and innovation in festival-making can generate a legacy that includes increased economic prosperity for cities through using its cultural capital.
5. Are features of a nation's culture diminished by global pressures? How do communities and nations resist moves to commodification of their cultural festivals and maintain their unique ability to provide a meaningful sense of collective identity and sense of meaning and security? Is it likely that a nation's identity could become obsolete? How can festivals contribute to historical, rich, and particularized features to a nation's culture? Do you think global and national culture may be mutually beneficial and reinforcing?

## Festival Focus Activities

1. Access the *World Cities Culture Report 2012* and identify the three themes emerging from the challenges facing cities cited:
    o The first is about striking a balance between tradition and modernity. Some cities' international image is very much shaped by their historic buildings and heritage,

yet they need to find a way to make sure their contemporary culture is recognized and vibrant.
- The second challenge is how to maintain a sense of the local and specific in a rapidly globalizing world. As ideas and people move more and more freely across borders, it may become hard to keep hold of the distinctive elements of a city's culture. How can this be done without becoming parochial or protectionist?
- The third challenge is how best to link infrastructure and participation.

Can some of these challenges be applied to cities with which you are familiar and the roles that festivals can play to address any imbalances?

2. Investigate the public places chosen by world-renowned festivals and develop a model to recognize essential features that will continue to attract visitors to the venues. Tourism is place-based, so how important are festivals in the mix?
3. Choose a destination (village, town, city) and investigate the annual portfolio of festivals and community events that are promoted. What do you notice? Can you discern a particular emphasis? How is balance achieved? Is there an obvious unique selling proposition for each event or can you establish an overarching (inclusive) destination brand?
4. Do you have a global festival "bucket list"? Compile an annotated list of (say 10) festivals you'd like to visit before you die and explain why you have made the choices. Do the festivals represent your current special interests, occur in attractive destinations, fulfill long-held dreams, host exciting programs, demonstrate popularity and effectiveness through longevity?
5. What is the value of establishing a network of festivals? Research three to four of the festivals listed below to examine the commonalities.

| | | |
|---|---|---|
| Prague Fringe | La Mama Spoleto Open | Mimetic |
| Adelaide Cabaret Fringe Festival | Minnesota Fringe Festival | Mathew Street Fringe Festival |
| Amsterdam Fringe Festival | Beijing Fringe festival | Brighton Fringe |
| Adelaide Fringe | Asheville Fringe Arts Festival | Capital Fringe |
| Auckland Fringe | Bhakti Utsav | Cena Brasil Internacional |
| Berlin Fringe | Bharat Rang Mahotsav | Chelsea Fringe |
| China Fringe Festival | Dublin Fringe Festival | Montreal infringement Festival |
| Cincinnati Fringe Festival | Edinburgh Festival Fringe | National Arts Festival Grahamstown |
| Curitiba Theatre Festival | Festival OFF d'Avignon | Orlando Fringe |
| Roma Fringe Festival | Fringe Canterbury | Oxfringe |
| San Diego Fringe Festival | Hollywood Fringe Festival | Prague Fringe |
| Shenzhen International Fringe Festival | Shoreditch Fringe Festival | Rochester Fringe Festival |
| Sopot Fringe | Sideshow Fringe Festival | Switch Fringe |
| St Lou Fringe | Stockholm Fringe Fest (Stoff) | Torino Fringe Festival |
| Windsor Fringe | | |

## Suggested Reading

Baeker, G. *Rediscovering the Wealth of Places: A Municipal Cultural Planning Handbook for Canadian Communities*. St Thomas, Ontario, Canada: Municipal World, Inc., 2010.

Brida, J. G., M. Disegna, and L. Osti. "Perceptions of Authenticity of Cultural Events: A Host-Guest Analysis." *Tourism, Culture and Communication* 12 (2013): 85–96.

Bruce, G. *Festival in the North: The Story of the Edinburgh Festival*. London, UK: Robert Hale, 1975.

Canning, M., 2012, *The Future is Bright*, www.belfasttelegraph.co.uk/business/business-news/the-future-is-bright-16174196.html.

Deery, M., L. Jago, and L. Fredline. "Rethinking social impacts of tourism research: A new research agenda." *Tourism Management* 33 (2012): 64–73.

Dwyer, L., and C. Kim. "Destination Competitiveness: Determinants and Indicators." *Current Issues in Tourism* 6, no. 5 (2003): 369–414.

Fisher, M. *The Edinburgh Fringe Survival Guide: How to Make Your Show a Success*. Methuen/Drama: 2012.

Florida, R. *The Rise of the Creative Class Revisited: 10th Anniversary Edition*. New York: Basic Books, 2012.

Garcia, B. "Urban Regeneration, Arts Programming and Major Events." *International Journal of Cultural Policy* 10, no. 1 (2004): 103–118.

Getz, D. *Event Studies: Theory, Research and Policy for Planned Events*. London, UK: Butterworth-Heinneman, 2007.

Getz, D. *Event Tourism, Concepts, International Case Studies and Research*. Putnam Valley, NY: Cognizant Communication Corporation, 2013.

Kunst, I. "Tourist Destination Competitiveness Assessment—Approach and Limitations." *Acta Turistica* 21, no. 2 (2009): 129–159.

Landry, C. *The Art of City Making*. London, UK: Earthscan, 2006.

Landry, C. *The Creative City: A Toolkit for Urban Planners*. London, UK: Earthscan, 2000.

Long, P., and M. Robinson (eds.). *Festivals and Tourism*. London, UK: Business Education Publishers, 2005.

Mathew, V. "Sustainable tourism: A case of destination competitiveness in South Asia." *South Asian Journal of Tourism and Heritage* 2 no. 1 (2009): 83–89.

McRae, H. *What Works: Success in Stressful Times*. London, UK: Harper Press, 2010.

Prentice, R., and V. Andersen. "Festival as Creative Destination." *Annals of Tourism Research* 30, no. 1 (2003): 7–30.

Putnam, R. D. *Bowling Alone: The Collapse and Revival of American Community*. New York: Simon and Schuster, 2000.

Richards, G. and C. Raymond, *Creative Tourism, ATLAS News*, (Association for Tourism and Leisure Education) no. 23 (2000): 16–20, www.atlas-euro.org.

Richards, G., and R. Palmer. *Eventful Cities: Cultural Management and Urban Revitalisation*. Oxford, UK: Butterworth-Heinemann.

Richards, G., and L. Marpues. "Exploring Creative Tourism: Editors Introduction." *Journal of Tourism Consumption and Practice* 4, no. 2 (2012): 1–11.

Ritchie, B. J. R., and G. I. Crouch. *The Competitive Destination: A Sustainable Tourism Perspective*. Oxon, UK: CABI Publishing, 2003.

Robinson, M., I. Yeoman, and K. Smith. in *Handbook of Events,* eds. S. Page and J. Connell. Oxford, UK: Routledge.

Stuart-Fox, M., and S. Mixay. *Festivals of Laos*. Silkworm Books, 2010.

Zukin, S. "Dialogue on Urban Cultures: Globalization and Culture in an Urbanizing World." Paper presented at the UN Habitat World Urban Forum, Barcelona, 2004.

Zukin, S. *The Cultures of Cities*. London, UK: Blackwell, 1995.

# CHAPTER 12

# Documenting, Monitoring, and Evaluating Festivals

Everything that can be counted does not necessarily count; everything that counts cannot necessarily be counted.
—*Albert Einstein (1879–1955), German-born American theoretical physicist*

---

This chapter provides an opportunity for you to better understand:

- The importance of documenting, reporting, monitoring, and evaluating aspects of festival-making
- The tools and techniques employed to gather data about festival performance
- The value to festival partners of up-to-date information about festival impacts and implications

---

This chapter draws attention to the processes successful festivals engage with to document, monitor, and evaluate their activities before, during, and after the presentation of the festival program. It covers all activities, internal to the organization, interaction with patrons and partners, and assesses the impacts and implications as festival legacies. Much is written about the "knowledge economy" and this applies to festival organizations too. Knowledge resides throughout the organization, over time, through stakeholder relationships, processes, and products that are created and embedded in the corporate memory. This is the substance of the mosaic in Figure 12.1 that we explore here.

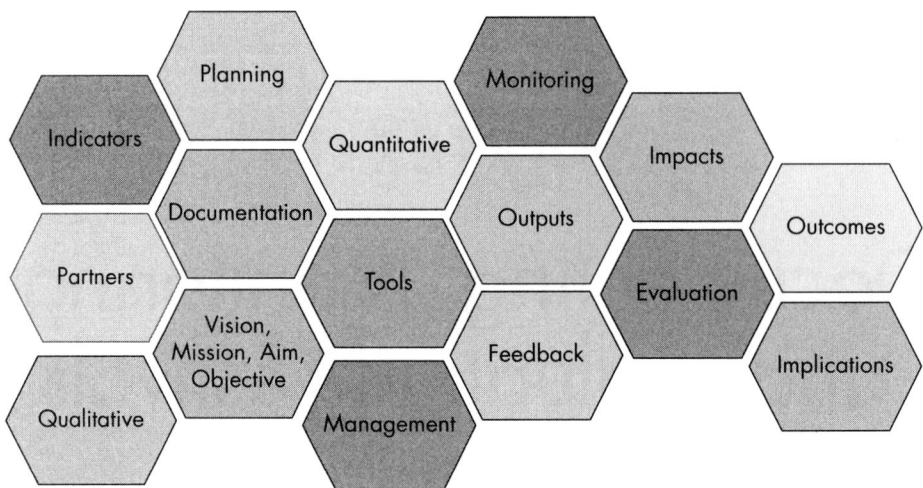

**Figure 12.1** Documenting, Monitoring, and Evaluating Festivals' Mosaic.

## Evaluating Festival Endurance

Festivals of all scales and scope are increasingly dealing with terms such as *transparency*, *satisfaction*, *accountability*, and s*crupulous financial acquittal*. Most funding bodies and corporate sponsors are keen to establish that festival organizers, for example, can demonstrate how well organizations are doing with addressing their aims and objectives and what aspects of their approach are working well and satisfying diverse stakeholders. While this may be a time-consuming exercise, there are distinctive organizational learnings that can accrue from a better understanding of the quality and value of the component parts of the process. It can assist with reporting, future planning, management, training, and human resource deployment and identify opportunities for improved service delivery.

Some festival organizations decide to engage external professional evaluators/consultants to deliver specific outputs to benefit the enterprise. The research that underpins such exercises involves acknowledgment of existing secondary data, industry knowledge of good practice, and assessment using an audit and review of festival documents. The publication of the results of their investigation can add credibility to the festival's reputation, especially if the assessment is positive. Any negative responses, again, become part of the way forward! An action research process that involves uncovering assumptions and intentions before monitoring behaviors and practices allows external questioning, interpretation, and creativity in moving a festival forward. The team-based nature of festival-making has placed an emphasis on participatory evaluations that can grow the empowerment of all partners involved.

### Participatory Evaluation

There are a number of advantages of participatory evaluation to be undertaken by festival organizers. These incorporate the capacity of partners to support sustainability into the future through building trust and ensuring honest collaboration. By including the perspective of diverse stakeholders, inviting their reflections and assessments affords a broader base for action and a sense of ownership of outcomes. There are limitations too. To establish a regular framework for active participation requires time and investment in training and ensuring adequate representation of respected festival partners who have demonstrated a commitment to the festival. Festival organizations can be exposed to the difficulties some partners experience and this can cause tension.

Parties will be satisfied with the evaluation and subsequent reports if the following conditions have been addressed. The views of all participants need to be respected and justice done to their contribution of views and ideas. Something new, novel, creative, and practical needs to emerge from the process that can usefully be applied in future activities. The process should not be drawn out, too complex, or overly large in scope; language should be accessible, not jargon-laden; and recommendations are readily understood and their implementation manageable. Comprehensive professional responses support helps any artistic or civic agency to grow a destination's cultural capital. It builds legitimacy among peers and the broader community and establishes greater understanding of the principles of creativity. It responds well to the call for transparency, especially if public moneys have been committed to the festival, and supports the tracking systems in place for finance and human resources.

Results can offer guidance to festival partners in their ongoing connection with the host community, local authorities, and the business community. The transactions between partners can be assessed for opportunities to rationalize resourcing, "working smarter not harder" and improving relationships with shared customers. The evidence accumulated by examining these relationships can often inspire the formation of collaborative strategic management models that have been demonstrated in Edinburgh and Adelaide and other destinations around the world.

Don Getz (2010), in his investigation into the nature and scope of festival studies, identified increasing research into the outcomes and impacts of festivals. A wide range of approaches is being undertaken and in this chapter we examine some of the personal, social, cultural, economic, and environmental perspectives and how these can be planned for and managed. Documenting, monitoring, and evaluating each play major roles in enhancing our understanding of the dynamics of this mosaic.

## Personal Responses

Chapter 9 gave us an opportunity to explore how individuals connected to festivals might feel about their experiences. This provides useful data for building attractive programs in accessible and comfortable locations for future festivals. By knowing what individuals want from their festival experience, organizers can plan accordingly and assess the resources required to satisfy expectations. Organizers need to critically analyze the existing approaches to festival-making and compare their efforts and outcomes against current best practices for small- or large-scale festivals. Research papers, evaluation reports, industry and peer support, and attendance at festivals of similar scope allow specific decisions to be implemented to improve delivery of valued experiences. They may choose to diversify the program to reach other or larger audiences as a result of the assessment of audience responses.

Choices made by organizers will be influenced by the demographics of their audience. It is all about the audience and the artists. How festival organizers maintain contact with

Principles remain the same, regardless of the scale of the festival. Billed as "the biggest little festival in Australia," the Gulgong Folk Festival has been attracting support for 26 years to hear emerging, established country and blues artists, local and international, in pubs, on street corners, and in concert halls. How they sustain interest in the annual program, introducing market stalls, street parties, and kids activities, is based on the intelligence they glean from a better understanding of the audience. They look to connect through media partners, websites, blogs, and solid visual documentation of past festivals, radio streaming via Soundcloud, tourism agencies and local government, and support from volunteers and the host community.

audiences has been explored earlier, but through innovative social media tools even a limited budget provides creative communication approaches. Organizers need to regularly reenergize their social media policy and moderate and measure social media use. The festival reputation over the long-term is at stake, so attention needs to be paid to maintaining sound relationships through careful interpretation of the data collected from media analysis.

## Service Quality

Festival management assess their performance in delivering a wide range of products and services to audiences. In the tourism literature and more broadly in business practice there is a differentiation between products as tangible items and services that are intangible but integral to the festival business. Many use the SERVQUAL scale, developed by Parasuraman et al. (1985) based on a marketing perspective. It provides an instrument for measuring service quality that can be utilized across a broad range of services with minor modifications in the content. Organizations keen to evaluate the gaps between what audiences expect from their festival experience and what actually plays out for them have devised a consistent approach to measuring patron responses. These are generally on-site exit surveys, online post-event surveys, and follow-up feedback surveys for purchasers of tickets. Essentially they are trying to establish whether the individuals' perception of the experience/service minus their expectations registers a quality experience overall. So the results can be interpreted thus:

- If expectations exceed perceptions, then the quality of the service is regarded as poor.
- If perceptions exceed expectations, then the quality is regarded as excellent.
- If customers have low expectations that are met, baseline quality exists.

The SERVQUAL scale identifies five dimensions of service quality that are applicable to service-providing organizations in general. These dimensions are *tangibles*, physical facilities, equipment, and appearance of personnel; *reliability*, ability to perform the promised service dependably and accurately; *responsiveness*, willingness to help customers and provide prompt service; *assurance*, knowledge and courtesy of employees and their ability to inspire trust and confidence; and *empathy*, caring and the individualized attention the firm provides its customers. Festival organizations can apply the model that defines *quality* as the difference between customer perceptions and expectations.

## Documentation Inside the Festival Organization

Developing a systematic approach to maintaining records of all aspects of the festival mosaic nourishes the profile of the festival. Records and information management of physical and electronic materials is now a critical part of a long-standing festival's organizational culture. While organizations are converting paper documents into digital documents, it is important that they are backed up and sent to offsite storage, using digital archiving software as management keeps up with technological change. Sandra F. Young and colleagues (2006) have comprehensively addressed approaches that organizations, large and small, volunteer or professional, can take to ensure their records are adequately maintained not only for the initiating organization but also from a community and researcher perspective.

### Record Management

There are numerous advantages for a festival organization to maintain a systematic record management program. It can deal with past, current, and future records. In practice, the accumulation of hard-copy (physical) material can become cumbersome, time-consuming, and labor-intensive; however, it is important that some sort of efficient order is in place to ensure timely retrieval. Whenever records are needed, it should be a simple matter to confirm their existence, determine their location, and retrieve and consult them, all with a minimum of labor.

Such organizational records can represent evidence of materials created regularly, keeping an accurate account of the organization's practice. It can contain the promotion collateral created as festivals are designed, developed, and delivered. Other items may include constitutions, minutes of meetings, correspondence, reports, property documents, membership details, policy and planning documents, scrapbooks, photographs, videotape, and CDs and DVDs. The historical record of activities adds credibility, strength, and longevity to the success profile and reputation created over the life of the festival. The resources that are accumulated can contribute to the information and skills that underpin the festival's strategic planning, organizational milestone celebrations, and acknowledgment of the personal commitment of staff and volunteers to festival values. They can provide the basis for refreshing festival programs and revisiting past successes. These records can also make a difference when an assessment or evaluation of the festival's outputs is undertaken. They help the organization meet its legal obligations. In fact, a call may be made on the records should the organization be faced with litigation in the future. This material can contribute to destination marketing, as visual representations of past successes can be a draw.

Consideration needs to be given to confidentiality of material contained within the documents held by the organization, as well as to their security. Another dimension of importance is access for researchers or specific interest groups over time. It needs to be determined whether records are stored in-house, within the organization's offices, or lodged with professional storage facilities, local authorities, or community entities such as universities, libraries, or museums. There are codes of ethics applied to the holding of some documents that may necessitate legal advice. Some materials may require specific environmental care or damage mitigation. Responsibility needs to be taken to address all of these issues, resources need to be allocated, and people tasked for roles including retrieval.

Digital media and electronic technology has added to the life-cycle mix of storage and retrieval of data and paper documents. By having a plan to create, review, publish, consume, and ultimately dispose of or retain material deserves regular attention. Filing systems need to be put in place and electronic records need to be backed up. Intervention from hackers has become widespread and deterrents must be considered. Some organizations utilize document management software or document imaging systems to disperse the material (e.g., to Cloud) in an effort to come to terms with the paperless office.

## Monitoring and Evaluation

There is a specific vocabulary associated with monitoring and evaluation that ensures this process will be meaningful and effective. You will be familiar with many terms in Table 12.1, but they need to be connected according to specific sequences, patterns, and relationships forged by the festival.

| Common Terms | Application |
| --- | --- |
| Documenting | Maintenance of records of administrative, artistic, and logistical activities of the festival organization becomes a public and corporate archive. Historical data are useful for research, celebration of milestones, and baseline information for improvement and planning. Marketing collateral, biographical details of staff and volunteers, signatures of past artists, and visual records can all be stored electronically; older material can be digitally remastered or be made available through civic institutions such as libraries and museums. |
| Monitoring | Monitoring involves information-gathering that takes place throughout the life of festival preparation, production, and presentation. It focuses attention on all facets of actions that demonstrate the festival's aims and objectives. Details on all aspects of their application become the content of the evaluation. |
| Evaluating | Evaluation is a process that focuses on a festival, usually on its completion. The data used to assess outputs, outcomes, impacts, and implications are diverse. There are numerous approaches organizers and partners can use. Information gathered from monitoring techniques along with quantitative and qualitative methodologies can provide inputs into strategic and operational decisions in the future. |
| Self-appraisal | This approach offers staff, volunteers, and partners of the festival organizations an opportunity to undertake their personal and professional assessment of their own targets by monitoring their regular tasks. Debriefing meetings are useful tools. |
| Reporting | Reports on aspects of the festival trajectory fulfills statutory obligations, maintains internal and external communication channels, feeds media coverage, offers electronic distribution, and fosters systematic historical record-keeping. |
| Baseline data | Baseline data or intelligence is what exists at the start of a festival-making process. This can identify gaps in current service offerings and become a reference for future assessments. |
| Demographics | Components generally associated with the variables of the audience mix including, age, gender, income, ethnicity, and geographic origins. |
| Inputs | The time, money, infrastructure, human resources, and intellectual factors that need to be accounted for in the conduct of the festival. |

**Table 12.1** Evaluation Processes

| Common Terms | Application |
|---|---|
| Outcomes | In strategic terms these consist of legacies that can be attributed to the staging of the festival that have implications for policy and planning for the host community, region, or nation. The changes that emerge can increase long-term community resilience, economic sustainability, and work skills and help build civic confidence and well-being. |
| Outputs | The measurable aspects of the festival experience allow a statistical approach to assessing impact. These can include audience numbers and specific demographic details, accommodation, hospitality, and length of stay details of interest to the tourism sector. |
| Quantitative research methods | There are various ways to collect the statistical data, surveys, ticket sales, audience participation clickers, vehicle number plates, website hits, etc., to determine what actually happened during the festival. This is useful for acquitting grants as funders can check their return on investment. It can be interpreted against baseline data and assist in identifying any gaps in the market and in service provision and outputs. Indicators include response rates to any promotional campaigns, hits on websites, workshop numbers, audiences' level of satisfaction, and quantity of resources used/consumed. |
| Qualitative research methods | The human face of the festival can contribute with data from personal experience. Participants as audience, host community, sponsors, suppliers, and artists can all provide insights for the development of a festival profile. It can be ethnographically enhanced through photographs, comments on blogs, focus groups, anecdotes, and what is known as participant observation to reveal a rich description of the festival experience. |

**Table 12.1** Evaluation Processes *(continued)*
Derrett (2013).

## The Rationale

The rationale behind standardizing the monitoring and evaluation approaches undertaken by all stakeholders allows each to benchmark their own practice internally and across the sector and build a clear picture of their collective enterprise. Regardless of the techniques employed, they generally are required to:

- Review what has been undertaken.
- Appraise the performance of each facet of the artistic and operational agenda.
- Establish levels of satisfaction of relationships between stakeholders.
- Determine best approaches to satisfy audiences.
- Measure progress and levels of satisfaction and identify specific shortcomings.
- Make suggestions for improvements to the design, development, and delivery of the festival.
- Demonstrate the impact on the host community and implications for future economic, social, and environmental development.
- Indicate the value attributed to staff and volunteer efforts.
- Develop an effective and appropriate organizational culture.
- Keep control of the festival's monetary resource.
- Clearly demonstrate how financial investments from funders and sponsors have been used.

## Evaluation Plans

Organizations find developing an evaluation plan a useful strategy. Like any well-thought-out plan, it has aims and objectives consistent with the overarching vision for the festival. It will be evident to all who participate in the collection of data what the anticipated outputs and outcomes of their collaboration are. It needs to be embraced by the stakeholders who need to feel that they can contribute their experience of the festival relationship to any final assessment of success or otherwise. The plan establishes a clear understanding of what is to be evaluated and what types of questions need to be answered. Then a systematic approach is required for the collection, analysis, and interpretation of those data.

Different organizations, spatial and temporal features, audience composition, and size all influence the choices of tools of enquiry for the evaluation of a festival. Formal and informal approaches can allow useful data to emerge through focus groups, interviews, media coverage, and survey questionnaires. More informal evaluation tools include observation, personal conversations, and site visits.

In the past there has been an emphasis on the economic impacts of events forming the bulk of publications in the area of evaluation. There is increasing attention now given to standardizing and integrating methods and measures of the triple bottom-line approach (i.e., linking to the sustainable development goals of economic efficiency, social equity, and environmental integrity). This shift in emphasis to the impacts of festivals has drawn attention away from the silos of economic, social, and environmental impacts and encouraged a more dynamic framework that addresses evaluation and forecasting options.

Academics have explored models and case studies of good practice, while festival organizers and their partners have been developing tools that accommodate their needs, specifically being able to demonstrate positive and negative impacts that can be reported on to boards, funding agencies, government authorities, sponsors, and host communities. Government agencies particularly have aggregated details and applied these to policy and planning decision-making frameworks. The types of impacts they have been recording over time include positive economic impacts: destination promotion, economic benefits, visitor expenditure, employment opportunities, infrastructure legacy, and corporate sponsorship. Negative impacts recorded included costs of staging festivals and events, damage to destination's reputation, inflation, and underutilization of infrastructure.

As we have noted elsewhere, reflection on festivals' impacts has involved positive and negative social and environmental impacts. Community pride, improved community well-being and quality of life, and evidence of community values celebrated versus challenges to host community norms through congestion, overcrowding, pollution, noise, crime, and vandalism. The positive environmental impacts have been mentioned elsewhere as festivals and host communities deal with the distribution of waste, pollution, and appeals for rehabilitation of sites, recycling, power, fuel, and transport reduction strategies. There is increasing attention to research impacts here as individual festivals assess their levels of performance in various categories; recognition is given to accepted good practice through awards and public accountability and media scrutiny (Table 12.2).

| Evaluation Tool | Explanation |
|---|---|
| Survey | A written document, Web-based survey, or face-to-face approach administered with particular remit for specific people. Email, fax, phone, or mail surveys can solicit respondents by various methods. |
| Interview | A recorded conversation, responding to structured and semi-structured questions about aspects of the festival with targeted individuals. |
| Focus group | Group in-depth discussions about the project. The ideas shared and issues raised can be explicit and very useful. Care needs to be taken with the size and composition of the group represented and facilitation needs to be professionally handled. |
| Personal feedback | Diaries and logs (online blogs) are part of the storytelling that can deliver useful information, accountability, and knowledge to benefit organizers. More formal tools include feedback at the conclusion of workshops, master classes, meetings, etc. Testimonials from individuals, artists, and sponsors can be utilized in future promotions. |
| Participant observation | Notes taken during the project and photos that represent the festivities, people, and distinguishing features taken regularly and systematically to ensure reliable replication. Listening, watching and documenting what is seen and heard is useful information from the field. |
| Ethnographic tools | The use of personal and professional documentation through images, photography, video, artifacts, ephemera, and mementoes of involvement prompt comment, discussion, and storytelling. |
| Informal conversations | Talking to participants about the project. Stories about the project described by staff or participants. |
| Media coverage | Space and time committed by local, national, or international media outlets to coverage, commentary, letters, and documentation of festival. This can be measured, interpreted, analyzed, and stored. |
| Website interaction, blogs, comments, Twitter, Facebook, Instagram, YouTube, etc. | Textual and visual responses distributed electronically. |

**Table 12.2** Evaluation Tools
Derrett (2013).

## Asking Questions

As festival organizations prepare to contact audiences (particularly) in their search for feedback on the festival experience, they need to reflect on the role of the process and the survey responses. They need to understand where the festival is positioned in its own life cycle, its position in the destination profile and marketing, how they will react to the responses, and with whom they need to share the new knowledge. It may be prudent to not rush in to acquiring the statistics too early in the festival life cycle, so longevity has it own rewards to determining positive impacts. Will one report fit all the partners the festival has? How interested will the local community, local businesses, local government, funding agencies, and sponsors be in the data? Will they each require the same information?

How will each of the parties interpret the report generated and will their reactions be coherent and timely in any response? How will the festival program be affected and profile raised through media coverage of audiences' reaction? Were audiences satisfied and what was the scale of economic impacts? Will festival management and other interested stakeholders learn from mistakes? How will they keep the festival fresh and draw attention year-round to the event? How can the survey material contribute to a destination's portfolio of festivals?

The framework in Table 12.3 identifies general questions found in festival surveys. How would you fill in subsequent columns to identify the type of data collected (quantitative, demographic, psychographic, qualitative) and to whom would the data be of interest (festival organizers, tourism agencies, local government, business)?

| Survey Item | The Response | Survey Item | The Response |
|---|---|---|---|
| Did you visit (destination) specifically to attend the festival? | • Yes<br>• No<br>• Just passing through town<br>• Live here | How much did you spend at the festival? | • Amount |
| Are you attending this event as…? | • Participant<br>• Spectator<br>• Stallholder<br>• Volunteer<br>• Competitor | How much did you spend at the destination? | • Amount |
| How many people in your group are attending the festival with you? | • Children under 12 years<br>• 12–17 years<br>• Adults 18–39 years<br>• 40–55 years<br>• Over 56 years | How much do you expect to spend in the area during the festival? | • Accommodation<br>• Transport/fuel<br>• Dining out<br>• Retail<br>• Entertainment<br>• Big items (specify) |
| What is your residential zipcode? | | How did you find out about the festival? | • Radio<br>• Newspaper<br>• Posters/fliers<br>• TV<br>• Social media<br>• Just walked into it<br>• Word of mouth |
| If you are not local, have you visited the festival previously? | • Yes<br>• No<br>• How many times? | What are your favorite things about the festival? | |
| Have you or members of your group attended this festival previously? | • Yes<br>• No<br>• How many times? | Was there anything you didn't like about the festival experience? | |

**Table 12.3** Sample Survey

| Survey Item | The Response | Survey Item | The Response |
|---|---|---|---|
| Have you visited this area previously? | • Yes<br>• No<br>• On holiday<br>• On business | What would you change to improve the festival? | |
| If you are a visitor, where are you staying? | • Hotel/motel<br>• Camping<br>• B&B<br>• Private home<br>• Rented accommodation<br>• With friends | What did you think about of the timing/scheduling of all activities? | • Needed more time<br>• Needed update on schedules |
| How many nights are you staying? | • One<br>• More than one | On a scale of 1 (poor) to 5 (excellent), please rate the following | Venue 1 2 3 4 5<br>Food 1 2 3 4 5<br>Entertainment 1 2 3 4 5<br>Safety 1 2 3 4 5<br>Organization 1 2 3 4 5<br>Atmosphere 1 2 3 4 5<br>Parking 1 2 3 4 5<br>Camping 1 2 3 4 5 |
| Are you a day visitor? | • Yes<br>• No | Thank you for taking time to complete this form. Please place it in a collection box located at the entrance of the site, or return by mail by this date. To be eligible for the prize draw, please provide a contact address. | • Email<br>• Phone |
| How did you get here? | • Car<br>• Plane<br>• Bus<br>• Bike | Please tick if you DO NOT wish to receive information/follow-up on local events | |

**Table 12.3** Sample Survey *(continued)*
*Based on Event Research Manager, Destination Research and Development.*

Challenges faced when using participant-based surveys include a lack of interest in filling out forms from potential respondents, decreasing levels of interest as a result of distractions, and the timing of the distribution of the survey. By offering a short version of a survey (in the style of a postcard that has promotional potential as well) or providing an opportunity to mail-in after the event and offering incentives (prizes, discounts, newsletter updates) can ensure an improved response rate. However, with time there can be diminished certainty of accurate data of expenditure or even embellishment after consultation within festival groups. Organizers need to consider the costs associated with specific techniques that can be employed to gather data. Response rates can be affected by language used, the length of the questionnaire and its presentation, whether postage is paid for mail returns, and level of follow-up. If there is to be a phone survey and follow-up, it is important that a pro forma is clearly explained to the data collectors.

## Cultural Indicators

A review of literature associated with cultural indicators applied to projects across the English-speaking world in 2006 by Derek Simon and Steven R. Dang provides some useful guidance in determining appropriate measures of the impacts of artistic and cultural activities. They identified the following themes:

- Cultural indicators of environmental enhancement and regeneration of "place"
- Cultural indicators of individual well-being and personal development
- Cultural indicators of social capital and community-building
- Cultural indicators of economic development
- Indicators of cultural vitality of the community
- Indicators of the health and sustainability of the cultural sector.

You will note the porous boundaries that emerge as those involved with festival-making, for example, seek to establish the impacts the conduct and content of festivals have on diverse stakeholders. In undertaking an assessment in specific instances, the indicators applied need to be both quantitative and qualitative and reflect the scale and scope of individual environments. These categories, seen in Figure 12.2, provide a useful framework for those seeking to establish a clear account of the layers to the nature and role of festivals at local, regional, national, and international levels. The items represented below in Table 12.4 are a selection from the comprehensive list of indicators identified in the research.

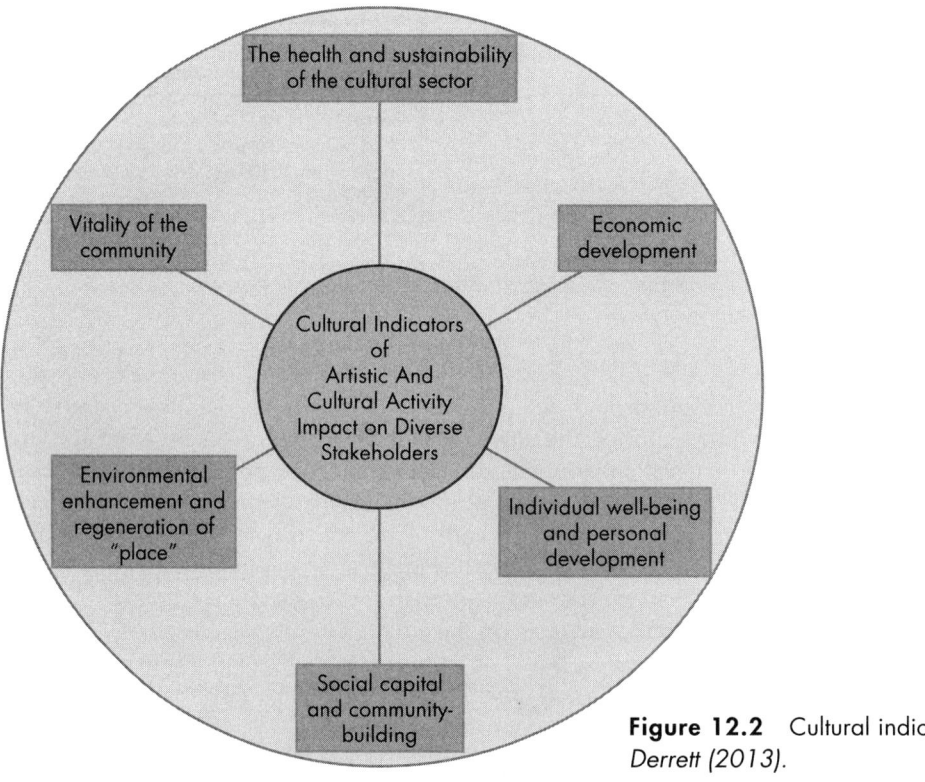

**Figure 12.2** Cultural indicators. Derrett (2013).

## Cultural Indicators

| Environmental Enhancement and Regeneration of "Place" | Social Capital and Community Building |
|---|---|
| number of rural cultural plans | accessibility of arts facilities |
| capital projects for regeneration of urban areas | barriers to cultural participation encountered in past 4 weeks/yr |
| economic contribution of cultural quarters/clusters | participation of persons with disabilities in arts |
| heritage assets as planning consideration | prevalence of outreach policies among arts organizations |
| number of cultural facilities in compliance with standards | audience composition in terms of diversity |
| number of new-build projects with local cultural benefits | cultural diversity of festivals |
| ability of locale to attract new creative workers | number of events representing diverse cultural traditions |
| community perceptions regarding local places of significance | cultural employment by age/sex/ethnicity |
| impact of natural environment in inspiring arts and culture (locally vs. elsewhere?) | changes in behavior as the result of arts participation |
| impact of built environment in inspiring arts and culture (locally vs. elsewhere?) | new skills acquired due to arts participation |
|  | changes in self-esteem/attitudes due to arts participation |
|  | percentage who think art plays major role in their lives |
| **Individual Well-Being and Personal Development** | **Economic Development** |
| participation (in all arts and by art form) | spending on arts and culture by tourists |
| percentage of population who are amateur artists | export value of cultural industries |
| attendance | contribution of cultural tourism to economy |
| satisfaction of audience/users | value of cultural tourism |
| percentages of passive or active arts participation | value-added contributions by cultural industries |
| percentage of new vs. established arts participants | social and environmental impacts of cultural tourism |
| perception of culture as a benefit | number of creative jobs (required arts training) |
| perception of arts as part of quality of life | number of new patents (= rate of innovation) |
| number who consider themselves artists | changes in creative industries and total industry (value-added) |
| percentage who highly value arts |  |
| **Cultural Vitality of a Community** | **Health and Sustainability of Cultural Sector** |
| number of arts/cultural facilities | size of cultural sector |
| number of visits to arts/cultural facilities (increase/decrease?) | volume output produced (total cultural production) |
| number of visits by institution type (theater, gallery, etc.) | new business formation in cultural industries |

**Table 12.4**  Indicator Sources

| Cultural Vitality of a Community (continued) | Health and Sustainability of Cultural Sector (continued) |
| --- | --- |
| cultural life of community considered part of cultural strategy | arts as percentage of labor force, total employed in arts |
| number of research projects in cultural organizations | number of workers in creative jobs |
| identification and dissemination of best cultural practices | number of professional artists employed (increase or decrease) |
| media coverage of arts and culture | size of volunteerism |
| community satisfaction with range of community events and festivals | employment opportunities, self-employment opportunities |
| support for arts by regional leaders (business/nonprofit) | Percentage of artists' income from art |
| festival attendance | number of consumers of locally produced art (vs. elsewhere) |
| number of arts volunteers (increase or decrease) | number of visits to arts/cultural facilities (increase or decrease) |
| arts organizations who feel unique connection to local community | cultural attendance and participation rates |
| percentage who think art plays major role in their lives | level of representation of culture in local authorities |
| number of community strategies containing cultural objectives and actions | strength of lobbying for culture |
| inclusion of heritage assets in plans by other agencies | local authority investment in the arts and culture |
| | total government support of culture |

**Table 12.4** Indicator Sources *(continued)*
Based on Simons and Dang (2006).

## Happiness Impact

A report commissioned by Lloyds Banking Group on the Economic Impact of the UK 2012 Olympic & Paralympic Games includes a chapter assessing the impact of the events on UK residents' happiness.

The report, covering the period from the winning of the bid in 2005 through until 2017, says that the events are driving both short- and long-term activity across the key sectors of construction and tourism, leading to jobs, expenditure and business opportunities across the United Kingdom. At the same time, the report assesses the "intangible impact" by citing a number of studies suggesting that holding major events may generate a "temporary feel-good factor" for local people from the enjoyment of attending the sporting or associated cultural events, volunteering, proximity of the events, or national pride.

Although it is a short-term phenomenon, the feel-good factor can be sizeable. The 1996 UEFA European Championships in England generated a "happiness gain that was equivalent to a monetary gift of £165 for every man, woman, and child." However, it also suggests that the happiness effect might not be equally shared across the nations and regions of the United Kingdom. The study says that sports events also help unite people, motivate/inspire children, and improve awareness of disability. It can also have a positive impact on consumer confidence.

However, the report noted that other studies acknowledge the existence of negative impacts on the resident population due to factors such as increased traffic congestion, security concerns, environmental degradation, disruption of residents' lifestyles and the cost of investment. It also cites the correlation between the happiness factor and the medal tally of the home team (Muqbil, 2012).

## In-House or Outsourced?

Sometimes festival organizers get into statistical representation of the impacts of the festival too early in the life cycle. The emphasis on establishing a festival profile, understanding audience satisfaction, and the challenges of revenue and expenditure might be better focused on an assessment of the program and exploration of markets to reveal a clearer picture. Resources required to undertake research may be beyond the organization's means, so partnering with other agencies like universities may provide a solution. This seems to have worked for the evaluation of economic impact of the Kentucky Derby Festival, outlined below. Engaging students with such a process can consolidate their service learning commitments and offer the festival a wide range of support during the data collection and analysis component of the exercise. By committing to regularly evaluate the impacts of festivals, partnering with local government agencies can leverage the costs. A comprehensive study commissioned by Glastonbury Festivals Ltd in the UK and the Mendip District Council was undertaken in 2008 and undertaken by an external consultancy Baker Associates. Both parties regarded the study as a valuable planning tool for the future of festivals, as well as being an educational tool to better understand the value and impacts of large-scale events.

## Economic Impacts

The annual Kentucky Derby Festival generates nearly $128 million for the Louisville area economy, including $56.6 million from Thunder Over Louisville. The 2011 economic-impact study is the first done for the festival in a decade. The festival includes more than 70 events held during the three weeks before the Kentucky Derby. That compares with the similar 2001 study that estimated the festival's economic impact at $93.6 million.

The newer study reported that, for every $1 spent by the Kentucky Derby Festival, which has an annual operating budget of $5.7 million, more than $22 was generated for the Greater Louisville economy, up from $17 in the 2001 study. A 1996 study estimated the Derby Festival's economic impact at $53 million, and a 1990 study estimated its impact at $34.2 million.

The largest economic impact for a single event in 2011 was Thunder Over Louisville, which produced an estimated $56.6 million impact for the local economy, followed by the Pegasus Parade at $22.4 million. In the past 10 years, the economic impact of the Chow Wagon (combined with Fest-a-Ville in recent years) grew from $9.7 million to $16.4 million. However, the impact of the Great Steamboat Race, once considered a cornerstone festival event, fell from $2.6 million in 2001 to $703,000 last year.

Students in the master's degree program at University of Louisville's College of Business conducted the study. In exchange for the work, the festival gave $5,000 to the college's scholarship fund. The methodology included random telephone calls and email questionnaires during the festival and live interviews at events with vendors, volunteer workers, visitors, and participants.

The 2011 festival was plagued by bad weather; two balloon events were canceled and flooding postponed the steamboat race until June. So, in conducting the study, average attendance at events over the past five years was used as the basis for figuring the economic impact.

## State-Managed Festivals: The Role of Civic Authorities

Governments at all levels appear keen to commit to profiling the national culture by creating policy to address some key aspects of enriching the lives of their citizens, encouraging vibrant cultural communities, creating an international focus for home-grown creative production, building creative industries, and transforming cultural spaces and assets. Festivals and events are now part and parcel of government investments in community-building and cultural well-being.

Local government involvement in cultural festival policymaking highlights its statutory or discretionary involvement, the partnership opportunities that emphasize what unites rather than what divides a community and generates mutual confidence and respect of constituent stakeholders. This level of government is keen to present a positive attitude backed up with practical support that demystifies management processes. They can build relationships between cultural, social, and demographic trends in their area. This can be tested as special interest groups may question investment of public funds for the creation of festivals. There has been criticism of state interventions that simply focus on tourism demand at the expense of real costs to communities. Tourism literature deals with what is called boosterism where the emphasis is on improving the image of a destination through investment in promotion. Dave Marcouiller (2007), among other academics, has explored the American experience of boosterism's shortcomings as a policy focus.

## Boosterism: Festivals and Tourism

There have been instances of communities holding unrealistic expectations for the benefits that can accrue from hosting a festival, especially in terms of economic legacies. This is sometimes at the expense of broad community support. An examination of a local festival in relation to its potential tourism outcomes could reveal some positive or negative responses to the following indicators:

- Increase in tourist visits and prolonged length of stay
- Partnership with local tourism organizations and operators
- Tourism promotion strategies with clearly identified target markets and media and public relations plans
- Enhancement of the festival by clustering with other local attractions
- Ticketing of the event in partnership with a ticketing agency
- Tourism packaging of the event with travel and accommodation providers
- Improvement in the (domestic or international) profile of the destination
- Development of festival themes and content that express unique local attributes and assets

- Strong branding through the name, logo, and look of the event for replication year after year
- Good quality well-designed promotional material that supports the brand
- Involvement of high-profile local personalities and leaders
- Good media coverage that identifies and promotes the destination
- Creation of economic benefits for the region
- Creative promotion that ensures the event is well attended and achieves financial targets
- Integration with related industry sectors such as entertainment, retail, tourism, catering, and accommodation
- Local procurement and servicing policy to retain profits and jobs in the region.

## ROSE FESTIVAL IN PORTLAND, OREGON: ECONOMIC IMPACT

The Portland Rose Festival Overall Economic Impact Assessment was conducted in 2012. The International Festivals and Events Association (IFEA) was contracted to undertake the comprehensive, independent economic impact study. It demonstrated the festival generates $75.5 million for the local economy annually. For a small nonprofit with a $4 million budget, this is a significant return of dollars into the local economy for Portland's Official Festival.

The IFEA, which got support from other city groups for its study, used 400 intercept surveys of people during three major weekends of the festival, using the IFEA as well as economic data from the Rose Festival Foundation. It compiled and analyzed relevant data to demonstrate a credible assessment model. The study showed economic impacts from other major events including the Grand Floral Parade, $29.5 million; the Starlight Parade, $8.5 million; and the Rose Cup Races, $1.5 million.

The Portland Rose Festival has been a leader in the special events industry for more than a century. "We were pleased to be able to validate the significant return the Rose Festival makes to the region through the results of this study," said Steve Schmader, CEO of IFEA. It's a reminder that special events, along with their many other benefits, make "dollars and sense" for their host cities: They return significant dollars, and that makes good sense.

Through transportation, shopping, food, lodging, and entertainment, visiting attendees contributed $97.25 each on average to the local economy, according to the study. Local attendees spend $20.87 on average, but it does not count as an economic impact because it is not new money to the area. The study indicated that a large percentage of the event's attendees traveled from outside Portland, which brings new dollars to the community to create economic impact that would not have occurred without the event. The addition of the Rock 'n' Roll Portland Half Marathon in 2012 accounted for $14 million of the impact, enhancing the Festival's already world-class status with a highly renowned running event. Returning attendees made up 76 percent of people partaking of the Rose Festival, and 80 percent of attendees traveled to Portland primarily for the event. Some 58 percent of attendees came from outside of Portland.

The Rock and Roll Portland Half-Marathon has become an important element in the program mix of the Rose Festival because of its economic impact and draw for visitors to the city as well as locals.

## Grant-Making

Experienced festival administrators are familiar with the language of grant applications. Many festivals commit to relationships with government and public funders. It brings obligations. Success in attracting external funding (as distinct from earned income from ticket sales, media rights, sponsorship) offers a clear framework for future monitoring, evaluating, and reporting upon the festival's completion. Words such as acquittal (a report on the completed project); eligibility (are you actually within the subset required to apply for this grant?); support material (images, evidence of your work, letters); and administrative body (is a body that applies on behalf of an individual or group) are fundamental when reflecting on the festival's performance and the satisfaction that will be felt by the investors. A similar situation exists when approaches are made to potential sponsors for their buy-in to the festival as a whole, or to some aspect of the festival relevant to them.

The ability to clearly articulate what is to be achieved by the organization for particular beneficiaries within the guidelines ascribed by each funding agency and its specific programs not only create a conduit for financial resources, but they can then assist in establishing the baseline data to be used for monitoring the progress of the operation. By explaining succinctly the existing situation, the tasks that need to be actioned to get the required results and an understanding of the importance of the exercise in the broader festival scheme is established. The credentials of key personnel and festival partners are identified while the technical, artistic and operational aspects of the investment are explained in detail. This process consolidates material to guide an assessment of performance indicators, efficiencies in converting resources into actions, and informing decision makers on how to build on or improve current approaches.

# After the Evaluation, What Then?

Festival managements, communities, and funding agencies need to determine what happens at the completion of the evaluation process. Each has a vested interest in the report. Many festival organizations have been beneficiaries of government funding or investment from sponsors or philanthropists and have complied with their contractual obligations to ensure there has been a comprehensive evaluation of their performance at the completion of a festival, a project within a festival, or the conclusion of a relationship. What happens then? There are obvious learnings from such documentation, but the festival needs to have the capacity to respond and grow from that process. These other agencies have their own needs to be fulfilled too.

## THE ADELAIDE FESTIVAL EXPERIENCE

Adelaide's 10 major arts festivals delivered a combined AU$62.9 million to the state's economy last year and attracted 2.82 million in total attendances. The economic impact study is the first to be released by the new Festivals Adelaide umbrella organization, which was formed to coordinate and jointly market the city's key arts events. It includes the Adelaide Festival and Fringe and the Cabaret, Film, International Guitar, SALA, Womadelaide, OzAsia, Feast, and Come Out festivals.

Festivals Adelaide executive officer Tory McBride said the events had continued to deliver strong results despite tough economic times, with more than 590,000 tickets sold. "The combined (dollar) return on investment to South Australia is approximately 5:1. Working collaboratively through Festivals Adelaide, this is just the beginning of exponential growth." The study, conducted by UniSA, found that 63,850 of the festival attendances were by visitors to South Australia, who spent a total of 304,100 nights in the state—an average of six nights per person. Visitor spending while in South Australia—such as food and transport but excluding festival ticket costs—was estimated at $58.1 million. The 10 festivals also created the equivalent of 790 full-time jobs to deliver their events.

Adelaide is the first city outside Edinburgh in Scotland to form a combined festivals body. "There are plenty of places that have one great festival. But apart from Edinburgh, I can't think of anywhere that's got a whole, year-round group of festivals that has the same cultural vitality and reputation as the ones here." Festivals Adelaide has also established an advisory committee that includes representatives from Tourism SA, Arts SA, Adelaide City Council, Business SA, the Convention Bureau, and the Festival Centre.

> My first objective is to engage the Adelaide business community more actively ... so that everybody's getting some advantage out of the fact that suddenly there are loads of people in the city. Festivals Adelaide will also help to collectively market the city's arts events interstate and overseas. There are certainly possibilities for economies of scale for marketing and communications activities. (McDonald, 2013)

Statistically there is often very satisfying knowledge gained of impacts and implications for stakeholders. Having the data is just the beginning of the next phase. As you study the reports of impact studies for festivals with which you have become familiar, how do you reconcile the contents of the reports and the next stage of the festival's initiatives? On reading the media coverage of a portfolio of events in a state in Australia, consider how individual aspects of the data can be interpreted, acted upon, and by whom. Considerable benefits are accrued to diverse stakeholders as a result of this particular study.

## Reporting Results

The regular communication of results with internal and external stakeholders is important. Report-writing is an integral part of reflecting on the impact of a festival. Such reporting can have specific target audiences, the festival board, local authority, media, funding agencies or specifically for Internet distribution. Organizations' annual reports are part of statutory obligations. Care needs to be taken with the language to best share the results.

The evaluation undertaken can:

- Determine whether festival objectives were effectively and efficiently met
- Identify ways to improve or change the approach to festival activities
- Facilitate changes in the artistic and operational plans
- Prepare specific triple bottom-line reports (don't underestimate cultural impacts)
- Create a historical record of management success over time
- Inform internal and external stakeholders about the process, outputs, and outcomes
- Assist with strategic planning
- Learn more about the target audiences of the festival
- Represent the value of the festival and its impacts to partners
- Contribute information on aspects of enterprise development, social and cultural capital, economic development, and environmental sustainability
- Review and adjust festival management practices
- Justify and promote connections to destination management and marketing.

It is important to maximize the analysis of the data collected regarding all measurable aspects of the festival delivery. This will allow all parties to be more realistic and ambitious, if the interpretation can be clearly communicated and leveraged to make each festival a success. Looking at the details consistently over time allows for multiple datasets to be integrated so as to provide a much clearer picture of how the festival can move forward. Be alert to trends and practices in other similar festivals through observation and participation. Eleanor Roosevelt suggested, "Learn from the mistakes of others. You can't live long enough to make them all yourself."

## Understanding a Festival Legacy

Much of the festival evaluation literature deals with the festival experience and its impact. The consequences of hosting/staging a festival are important and not only in a numerical or quantitative way. There are repercussions for host communities, organizers, and audiences

## AN EVALUATION OF THE COMMONWEALTH GAMES 2014 LEGACY FOR SCOTLAND

This report sets out the broad approach to the Glasgow 2014 legacy evaluation, the research questions it will address, and the range of methods that will be deployed over a 10-year period (5 years either side of the event). It also sets out the priorities and a forward timetable for the publication of reports. The report examines the events and ancillary festivals against a set of specific national themes (flourishing, active, connected, and sustainable) while recognizing that the host city, Glasgow, also identified six legacy elements to be articulated into the national vision: Prosperous, Active, Inclusive, Accessible, Green, and International.

and these need to be appraised. The aftermath of a festival and the perceptions of partners can play a crucial role in forward planning, stimulate spin-off activities, and provide benchmarks for policymakers. There are social, cultural, and economic initiatives that are triggered through mimicking the collaboration experience of preparing and conducting the festival. Lasting and positive outcomes need to fit with the aspirations of all parties and provide evidence for strengthened networks, improved infrastructure outcomes, and quality of life dimensions. So, an economic and a social return on investment (especially of public moneys) need to be addressed. Qualitative data collected through case studies, storytelling, and personal communication from stakeholders will assist in any reappraisal of brokering and advocacy by arts and cultural festival organizations. By identifying the themes prior to the festival the task of assessing whether the ambitions were achieved in the short, medium or long term can be established.

## CASE STUDY

### *"You can't manage what you don't measure."*

This expression, attributed to numerous management gurus from Peter Drucker to W. Edward Deming, is quoted all the time. Can it assist in assessing the performance management of festivals? Can it influence the festival organization's capacity to meet the challenges and the opportunities of working with other stakeholders to develop a credible system to present a clear picture of the festival's sustainability? It can communicate whether some aspects of the artistic, operational, and administrative activity are getting better or worse over time. Determining what is important to measure, how to measure it, and how to use the data collected can provide the standards that can ensure continuous improvement through observation and practice. It must be evident that any success is connected to the real world of audiences and is based on a business model.

> The most serious mistakes are not being made as a result of wrong answers.
> The truly dangerous thing is asking the wrong question.
>
> —Peter Drucker, American management guru

The challenge is that it is not all about numerical key performance indicators (KPIs). Festivals are all about people and human behaviors and these are notoriously difficult to measure. To attract, create, and retain dynamic, passionate, and effective workers, other strategies need to be employed to deliver the festivals that all aspire to participate in. It may be difficult to measure their contribution or assess morale through a simple metric. However, you can manage relationships, empower staff, and encourage resourcefulness and creativity, for example, that benefits the bottom line. Managers are better to be measuring the right things because they will almost certainly spend time and resources managing that which is measured. If therefore they measure the wrong things, they will have wasted much, which is precisely what managers want to avoid!

It is recognized that festivals need to adapt to changing market conditions, to use resources efficiently, and to deliver innovative planning and development strategies. It is acknowledged that an objective review of past performance as part of an ongoing and cyclical process to monitor and evaluate its progress in achieving its goals and vision is vital. All associated with the festival need to appreciate the performance monitoring tools, methods, and approaches being used, especially the triple bottom-line sustainability indicators—economic, social, and environmental impacts. Risks are regularly monitored to ensure that appropriate prevention, preparedness, response, and recovery strategies are developed. Across the sector professional organizations are working to establish industry benchmarks and governments have statutory frameworks festivals are obliged to adhere to. The key is communication—documenting how the festival performs and using technologies to share messages with all stakeholders in timely ways, especially visitors—as a stimulus for their ongoing commitment to the festival and to funding agencies.

Measurements aren't the full story. By measuring aspects of projects within a festival doesn't mean that things will get done! Consider "what gets measured gets done." Is that so? There's more to the process of engagement of staff and stakeholders to align the festival's vision. Each has roles and responsibilities within the festival organization and their active participation is an important dimension for getting a clear picture of how the festival is doing. The patterns in the mosaic needed to stage a memorable festival will have been arrived at through straightforward metrics gleaned from regular monitoring and assessment as much as the intuitive integrity and trust built by the partners involved.

An interesting component of the economic impact study undertaken of the Glastonbury Festival (2008) was a section titled "Less Quantifiable Outputs." They give us pause to consider features of most arts and cultural festivals that have economic (metric-based) impacts, but present a broader, more subtle exposure to the importance of festivals and their relationships. These concerned: Contracting with not-for-profit organizations, image and perception of Glastonbury Town and wider Mendip area, increased trading opportunities from association with the festival, greening businesses, contributing to a local entrepreneurial culture, and contributing to the vitality of the local Pilton village.

# FROM INSIDE THE MOSAIC

## Lenny Vance, Sponsorship Strategist

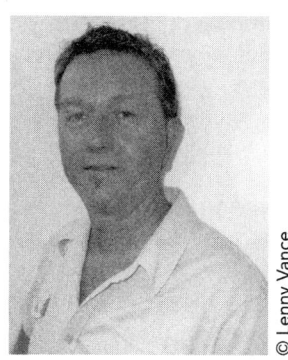

Lenny Vance

Lenny Vance has a Master's in Business Communications and has been a Sponsorship Manager of several large influential corporations in the state of Queensland, Australia. In this capacity he has been able to build on his experience as a committee member of Sponsorship Australia, a Marketing and Corporate Development Officer with Queensland Arts Council, a Program Manager with the Centenary of Federation Events Marketing team with the Queensland Government, and a Special Events Manager at Brisbane City Council. Vance is a consultant to the festival and events sector and is currently pursuing academic studies in the area of festival sponsorship. Here are some of his observations regarding festival sponsorship.

In contractual terms, sponsorship is the exchange of rights and benefits associated with an event or organization (the rights holder) for financial or in-kind remuneration provided by the sponsor. Successful sponsorships, however, are more like a marriage or partnership. They are built upon strong relationships between the sponsor and the rights holder. They endure when there is understanding and consideration of each partner's needs, mutually agreed-upon goals, and, above all, open and regular communication.

There is one significant difference for festival sponsorships, and that is the imperative to consider the festival's audience as a key stakeholder. Festivals are all about creating memorable experiences for audiences. The primary aim for a festival sponsor should be to generate a connection with the audience. Therefore, any sponsorship activity must enhance, rather than detract, from the audience's experience.

Sponsors can often add value to the program of a festival. Sometimes there are opportunities for sponsors to influence the program. However, as champion of the audience experience, rights holders should articulate clear boundaries as required. Sponsorship works best when there is an obvious "fit" between sponsor, event, and audience. The sponsorship needs to make sense and be relevant to the audience so that they are accepting of its presence. Then it is more likely that a positive emotional connection will be made with the sponsor's brand.

An innovative example from Australia is the Queensland Folk Federation's (QFF) alliance with Midell Water. Midell Water have provided QFF with an economical and environmentally friendly solution to its challenges of dealing with wastewater at its Woodfordia site. The site is host to the Woodford Folk Festival, the Dreaming Festival, and the Planting Festival. The sponsored installation of an innovative waste water treatment plant has enabled QFF to slash the cost of wastewater treatment by 80 percent, has significantly reduced their carbon emissions by 11 percent, and enabled QFF to generate revenue by hiring the site to other events such as Splendour in the Grass. Midell Water has benefited by promotion of their brand and services to a relevant network of government and industry decision makers who also are involved in or attend the festivals. And the festival audience experience is enhanced by the knowledge that the attendees' environmental footprint on the site is managed in a sustainable way.

For festivals to attract and establish enduring relationships with sponsors it is essential they have a thorough understanding of the sponsor's objectives. Essentially there are three broad outcomes that may motivate sponsors.

First, there is brand building. There may be a need to build brand awareness for a new product or service. There may be a need to change perceptions about a known brand. Ultimately sponsors are looking to build brand advocacy whereby consumers are likely to think, speak, and act positively about their brand.

Second, there may be commercial objectives. That is, the generation of product or service sales or the adoption of behavioral change. A sponsor may simply want to block a competitor from acquiring market position.

> The Foxtel MTV House Party at the Australian Big Day Out provides the ultimate on-ground experience for registered Foxtel subscribers to enjoy the Big Day Out shows in an MTV-themed environment while also celebrating the birthday of Australia's most iconic music festival. Foxtel subscribers can have exclusive access to the house through preregistration via MTV and Foxtel's Facebook pages.

Third, an outcome often overlooked is employee engagement. Sponsors can use many of the associated benefits of a sponsorship for employee reward and recognition and to assist in the attraction and retention of a motivated workforce.

There is also a growing trend to use sponsorship in a social marketing context where the aim is to influence community perceptions and/or behavior toward a particular social issue. It depends on the sponsor's situation what priority or mix they place on the above desired outcomes. Therefore, rights holders should research and discuss objectives with a prospective sponsor before preparing any proposal. These are the initial steps to establishing a genuine partnership.

Additionally, rights holders should have a thorough understanding of their own audience reach, demographic, and psychographic profiles before placing a value on any sponsorship proposal. The value should not be determined by what finances are required to run an event but by the appeal of the engagement opportunity to a sponsor.

Just as importantly, they need to consider the resource implications for ensuring that sponsor expectations are met. "*Underpromising and overdelivering*" is a relevant philosophical approach to attracting and retaining sponsors.

Sponsorships are usually formalized by a contract that defines the shared objectives (outcomes) and the exchange of rights or benefits (outputs). Outputs such as agreed-upon logo exposure, signage, or ticketing packages are easily tracked and measured and should form the basis of regular reporting to prove the agreed-upon benefits are being delivered.

Outcomes such as building brand awareness or advocacy are often intangible and therefore more difficult to measure. At event surveys, social media monitoring and post-event audience research are ways that rights holders can measure intangible outcomes. Formal accounting should be in place for more tangible outcomes such as product sales. Other tangible outcomes such as media exposure can be assessed through media monitoring services.

Sponsors will use this evidence to evaluate the performance of the sponsorship. If the sponsorship is commercially driven, can they demonstrate to their owners or shareholders that the sponsorship generated a positive return on investment? If the sponsorship was more brand or socially driven, did it achieve the targeted outcomes or "return on objectives"?

Corporate priorities are often driven by market environments and are therefore subject to change. This can greatly affect the status of sponsorships. For that reason sponsors tend to want short- to medium-term agreements. It is not uncommon for a new sponsorship to be based on a one-year term with an option to renew should it prove successful.

If the sponsorship is successful, and the sponsor's priorities haven't drastically changed, it would be reasonable to assume the sponsorship could be renegotiated and renewed for a longer term, say three to five years, and for an increased value.

However, sponsorships rarely become perpetual. Usually from the sponsor's perspective, once the initial objectives have been met, it is time to either refocus the sponsorship if possible or to discontinue it in much the same way an advertising campaign would be reviewed. It is not uncommon that over time a sponsor's corporate priorities do change and the sponsorship may no longer be viewed as essential to business. If the partnership has been sound then sufficient notice would be provided and an exit strategy be implemented to enable relatively seamless transition to a replacement.

## Festival Ideas and Issues

1. The public media plays an important role in responding to the quality of the festival experience. How? Discuss.
2. Describe the roles of documentation, monitoring, and evaluation in the festival management process. Where does the responsibility lay within each domain?
3. What are the intangible impacts of communities hosting festivals? How can they be factored into festival planning?
4. How can the perspectives of an individual patron be incorporated into the evaluation process of a festival?
5. Statutory policymaking by civic authorities impacts festivals at all levels of the festival ecology. How effective is it in your jurisdiction? Government agencies generally invest in festival marketing programs in the interest of destination profile-raising, while the evaluation of impacts is an afterthought. What has been the experience of festivals with which you are familiar?

## Festival Focus Activities

1. How do festivals and special arts events become travel motivators? Give examples of how festivals you know have demonstrated authenticity, uniqueness, hospitality, affordability, access to themes and symbols, and participation opportunities.
2. What can festivals offer communities? How can the following be measured? Consider festivals as an extension of local leisure needs; emphasis for authentic traditions; lessen the host-guest gulf; tourism without physical development; conservation of heritage; and boundary maintenance to preserve local lifestyle.
3. Draw up an evaluation plan for a festival with which you are familiar. Think about the purpose of the evaluation (e.g., intention to provide a profile of the festival). Identify key data collection sources and methods to be considered in their collection. Areas that might be looked at include the festival budget, attendees' profile, performance of the festival, media coverage, economic impact, and whether targets were achieved.
4. Prepare an agenda for a meeting of key stakeholders following the conclusion of a festival. Role-play such a debriefing to encourage partners to respond to reports from event management, finance, marketing, operations, and logistics. Provide a forum for

feedback for the experiences of business, media, community members, suppliers, and artists. Record the proceedings.
5. Assemble a package of media reports, commentary, and personal responses in the public domain related to a particular festival. This could include copies of print media and electronic platform coverage locally and internationally. Analyze the media's role in disseminating an overall response to the event, the accuracy of information published, any promotional value to the event, any negative aspects of the coverage, and as documentation of a planned public celebration.

## Suggested Reading

Arcodia, C., and M. Whitford. "Festival Attendance and the Development of Social Capital." *Journal of Convention and Event Tourism* 8, no. 2 (2006): 1–18.

Delamere, T. A. "Development of a scale to measure resident attitudes toward the social impacts of community festivals, Part II: Verifcation of the scale." *Event Management* 7 (2001): 25–38.

Deery, M., L. Jago, and L. Fredline, L. "Rethinking social impacts of tourism research: A new research agenda." *Tourism Management* 33 (2012): 64–73.

Getz, D. "Event tourism: Definition, evolution, and research." *Tourism Management* 29, no. 3 (2008): 403–428.

Getz, D. "The nature and scope of festival studies." *International Journal of Event Management Research* 5, no. 1 (2010): 1–47.

Getz, D., and T. Andersson. "Sustainable festivals: On becoming an institution." *Event Management* 12, no. 1 (2008): 1–17.

Janeczko, B., T. Mules, and R. Ritchie. *Estimating the Economic Impacts of Festivals and Events: A Research Guide*. Research Report, CRC Sustainable Tourism, 2002.

Jepson, A., S. Wiltshier, and A. Clarke. *Community Festivals: Involvement and Inclusion*. Paper presented at the CHME International Research Conference, Strathclyde Business School, University of Srathclyde, Glasgow, 2008.

Marcouiller, D. "'Boosting' Tourism as Rural Public Policy: Panacea or Pandora's Box?" *Journal Regional Analysis Policy* 37, no.1 (2007): 28–31.

Matarasso, F. *Use or Ornament?: The Social Impact of Participation in Arts Programmes*. Comedia, UK, 1997.

McDonald, P., *Art festival events bring $63m to South Australia*, 2013, http://www.news.com.au/national/art-festival-events-bring-63m-to-south-australia/story-fndo4dzn-1226549867819.

Muqbil, I., *Lloyds Bank Study Pitches "Happiness Impact" of UK Olympics* (2012). http://www.travel-impact-newswire.com/2012/07/lloyds-bank-study-pitches-happiness-impact-of-uk-olympics/#axzz20p8rTzwo.

Parasuraman, A., V. A. Zeithaml, and L. L. Berry. "A Conceptual Model of Service Quality and Its Implications for Future Research." *Journal of Marketing* 49 (1985): 41–50.

Parasuraman, A., V. A. Zeithaml, and L. L. Berry. "Refinement and Reassessment of the SERVQUAL Scale." *Journal of Retailing* 67, no. 4 (1991): 420–450.

Reese, M., L. C. Malone-Lee, and C. K. Heng. *Culture and Sustainability: Exploring the Nexus in the Context of Globalising Asian Cities*. Paper presented at the Making Culture Count Conference, University of Melbourne, Australia, 2012.

Robertson, M., P. Rogers, and A. Leask. "Progressing socio-cultural impact evaluation for festivals." *Journal of Policy Research in Tourism, Leisure and Events* 1, no. 2 (2009): 156–169.

Robertson, M., D. Chambers, and E. Frew. "Events and festivals: Current trends and issues." *Managing Leisure* 12 no. 2–3 (2007): 99–101.

Ruiz, J. *A Literature Review of the Evidence Base for Culture, the Arts and Sport Policy*. Edinburgh, Scotland: Research and Economic Unit, Scottish Executive Education Department, 2004.

Sanders, K. *Factors of Success in Northeast Iowa Community Festivals*. University of Northern Iowa, USA: Northeastern Iowa Tourism Industry, Sustainable Tourism and Environment Program, 2006.

Schlenker, K., C. Foley, and D. Getz. *Encore Festival and Event Evaluation Kit: Review and Redevelopment*. Australia: CRC for Sustainable Tourism Ltd., 2010.

Sherwood, P. *A Triple Bottom Line Evaluation of the Impact of Special Events: The Development of Indicators*. PhD thesis, Centre for Hospitality and Tourism Research, Victoria University, Australia, 2007.

Simons, D., and S. R. Dang. *International Perspectives on Cultural Indicators: A Review and Compilation of Cultural Indicators Used in Selected Projects*. Vancouver, Canada: Centre of Expertise on Culture and Communities Creative City Network of Canada, Simon Fraser University, 2006.

Sweeney, M., and J. Goldblatt. *The FIFER Toolkit: An exploratory methodological framework for evaluating planned events*. Fife Council Housing and Communities, International Centre for the Study of Planned Events, Queen Margaret University, 2010.

Temple Bar Cultural Trust (Ireland). *Customer service in the arts: A manual*. Dublin, Ireland: Arts Audiences, 2010.

Williams, M., and G. A. J. Bowdin. "Festival evaluation: An exploration of seven UK arts festivals." *Managing Leisure* 12, no. 2–3 (2007): 187–203.

Young, S.F. *Documenting and Preserving Organizational History*, Chicago: University of Illinois at Chicago, 2006. http://www.uic.edu/depts/lib/specialcoll/.

# CHAPTER 13

# Revisiting and Refreshing the Festival Vision

> Here's to the crazy ones, the misfits, the rebels, the troublemakers, the round pegs in the square holes … the ones who see things differently—they're not fond of rules. … You can quote them, disagree with them, glorify or vilify them, but the only thing you can't do is ignore them because they change things … they push the human race forward, and while some may see them as the crazy ones, we see genius, because the ones who are crazy enough to think that they can change the world, are the ones who do.
> —*Steve Jobs (1955–2011), American entrepreneur and inventor*

This chapter provides an opportunity for you to better understand:

- The importance of regular review and refreshment of a festival's vision
- The festival context: host community, skills, and experience of partners in festival-making
- Good practice design, development, and delivery choices for festival longevity
- Challenges to festival viability, sustainability, and resilience
- Factors of festival failure

Festivals, like any enterprise, need to regularly appraise their performance. Festival organizations need to have in place a culture of continuous improvement to optimize their offerings to their audiences. As they seek to defend their position in the marketplace they need to assess their competitiveness, understand the need for continuing artistic excellence, ensure internal stability, and maintain momentum. They are looking for focused clarity on their best options to survive and thrive. They require resources to move forward, planning in areas of finance, human resources, operations, partnerships, and risk management. Any change to current practices needs to be assessed. The mosaic in Figure 13.1 provides us with major actions that can

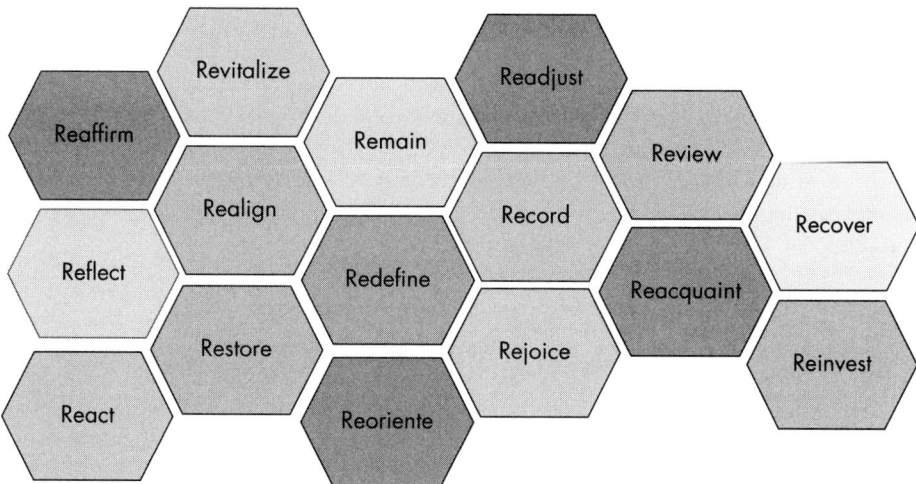

**Figure 13.1** Festival Review Mosaic.

shape an organization's way forward. In Chapter 12 we explored some aspects of evaluation of a festival's performance. In this chapter we move into the area of the processes required for refreshing a festival and its environments through a change management prism.

## Designing Revitalized Festivals

The mosaic for this chapter addresses many aspects of redefining the way forward to success and endurance. Long-standing festivals deserve a concerted revitalization to ensure positive profile, consistent quality in programs, and customer satisfaction. Creativity, intuition, and flexibility are key to engaging staff with festival patrons and by reenergizing a productive workplace the organization's reputation can be enhanced. The unique profile of each festival must remain clear and its conceptual orientation transparent.

> Change is the process by which the future invades our lives.
> —*Alvin Toffler (b. 1928), American writer and futurist*

Take time to regularly reflect: Is there a smarter, better, and more effective way to do things?

| Review the festival/organization's progress and performance | Offers an opportunity to assess competence, versatility, quality, corporate knowledge, direction, and market advantage; build continuity; and become a model |
|---|---|
| Place core activities under scrutiny | Business efficiency, financial matters, competitor analysis, artistic and cultural responses, partnership management, audience analysis |
| Reaffirm and celebrate strengths | Human resources training and development, communication, use of technology, professional connections, reputation, leadership, and management |

You can see from the mosaic table an attempt to identity some approaches to address the festival organization's readiness to embrace changes that have been identified, reduce any resistance that may emerge among staff, and encourage their active participation in understanding the best ways forward. Communication strategies must contribute to their empowerment in any new decision making and application of solutions. It is essential that any new vision developed recognizes better alternatives. Along the way milestones need to recognize existing success and new structure and policies, targets, acquisitions, repositionings, and relocations need to be overtly embraced and celebrated.

## Managing Change

In this chapter we explore how individuals, organizations, and communities see, feel, and deal with change. We seek to better understand how mutual expectations can be shaped and delivered upon in a number of areas. This will ensure the highest standards of artistic and cultural quality, building trust in internal and external partnerships, ensuring the festival mission underpins the planning for priorities, and targets and KPIs (key performance indicators) are attained, while making certain staff turnover is minimized and volunteers sustain good humor, morale, and positive attitudes to the shared enterprise.

> You must be the change you want to see in the world.
> —*Mahatma Gandhi (1869–1948), leader of Indian nationalism*

Experience shows that any dramatic or radical change can be a challenge and it may be more appropriate that an incremental approach be adopted. Acknowledging the diverse forces that may be in play internally and externally and recognizing the nature and appearance of some of these pressures can affect the options taken up. Inside the organization consideration may be given to increasing efficiencies, minimizing duplication or conflict of task allocation and individuals' skill and experience levels, and their maturity and recruitment strategies and contractual arrangements. Big-picture forces from movement in social values (areas such as drug and alcohol use, smoking, gun violence), technological innovation, place attachment and identity, and demand for authenticity all influence the way the revitalization might be approached. All parties involved with the realignment need to be alert to any changes in festival customer demand, competition in the marketplace, costs facing the festival operations, impacts of legislation on ordinances, insurance liabilities, taxes, international standard practices, and biophysical dimensions of waste, energy, and natural area management (parking and camping).

In an attempt to refresh, revise, or rebuild the festival brand, some common practices festival leaders have embraced include exploiting the loyal audience base by ensuring there is a consistent community orientation. This capacity to leverage those already committed to the festival allows for extensive word of mouth and e-word of mouth distribution of any revamped festival messages. A focus on quality customer service that generates an enhanced "wow" factor is important. For those who work on behalf of the festival talk-up the way staff and volunteers deliver experiences before, during and after the festival can be intergenerational. Festivals that move with the times often accommodate the next generation of family patronage and if each of them feels that their needs are met with tailored personal responses, they become valuable foot soldiers in the cause. Price is a critical consideration for patrons. The value-for-money quotient is fragile. So by delivering consistently with good-quality products and services patrons will favorably evaluate their financial commitments to a festival, especially if they can recognize the value-adding that is now a feature of popular festivals.

The customer relationship marketing literature is replete with suggestions of how patrons can be encouraged by demonstrations of creativity and whimsy. By showing that engagement with a festival can be fun and that festival staff are hospitable, confident, knowledgeable, and passionate about their involvement stimulates audience buy-in. This can increase ticket sales, enhance festival reputations in the broader community, and position the festival for longevity.

## Leveraging Staff Commitment

Are you familiar with a festival that could recruit a senior staff member with the following advertisement? What are the critical messages?

> You love the art of business and the business of art. You are resourceful, unflappable and indomitable. Tenacity and tact. Grit and gravitas. You can keep an organisation in flow —people focused and productive, challenges met, tasks ticked and still have energy to dream strategic dreams and make them happen.
>
> Reporting to the CEO, working closely with the board, leading our administration and artistic teams; this challenging role encompasses organisational oversight, human resources, marketing, finance and compliance. It requires high-level creative problem solving and awesome attention to detail.
>
> Our growth is fuelled by the quality of our art and our people. Our award winning creations perform in the most prestigious festivals and venues around the world. If you recognise that passion and Excel are not mutually exclusive and if you'd love to make a difference apply now.
>
> —*CIRCA! Brisbane (2012)*

# Preparing for Refreshment

This is not the time for spontaneous combustion. Individuals, organizations, and civic authorities need to closely observe their environment before setting out on any process that involves revitalization. Each needs to review existing documentation, assess the assessments made by external agencies, and reflect on what constitutes the optimum aspirations of success. This period of reflection allows for constructive thinking about alternatives. The strategic process that involves consideration of where you are now, where you want to be, how you expect to arrive at effective implementation of different approaches, and how you know that you've arrived at an appropriate place for yourself (personally or professionally), and the organization or partner agency all starts with communication with stakeholders.

Regardless of the enterprise structure, what is recognized is that this year's planning is the beginning of next year's. As lessons are regularly reviewed the festival organization can learn from its successes, failures, and unexpected outcomes. These can be used to confirm or revise strategies so that planning becomes a continuous process. A process used by most organizations during the initial phase is a *SWOT analysis* (Table 13.1). This involves an analysis of current Strengths, Weaknesses, Opportunities, and Threats. This technique can clearly reveal both internal and external aspects of the organization's environment. It assists in determining how the organization or festival is positioned to attain the desired vision, mission, and objectives.

The board, management, staff, and maybe volunteers and member representatives can contribute to listing attributes under the four headings. The response to this exercise will influence the amount of control the festival organization has to deal with in refreshing their practices. This might involve adding, reducing or eliminating programs or projects if that addresses any weaknesses identified.

The process requires management. It is a challenging process for many players. It isn't always predictable, so attention needs to be given at all stages of the process to ways to make people involved comfortable, and to avoid damage and risk. If the organization, for example, is not clear about their reasons for any change, haven't chosen a methodology that can be readily accommodated by the existing culture so as to diffuse any damaging resistance from staff and volunteers, the whole attempt to reorient for future success will fail. Or, at the very least, any proposed transformation will be less impressive or valuable.

Skilled facilitators are required to fashion the process to engage all levels of the festival network preparing to authorize any shifts in practice, philosophy, or personnel. This purposeful planning, monitoring, and stakeholder management may require external inputs. This can assist in anticipating what acceptable outcomes will look like.

The sorts of ideas and issues that might arise in preparatory discussions include:

- Whether there is a saturation level in the local, regional, national, and global festival marketplace.
- Do festivals have a predictable life cycle and where is our festival currently positioned?
- How can our festival sustain its competitive advantage?

| | |
|---|---|
| **Strengths and Weaknesses** that establish a picture of the organizational culture, experience, longevity, membership, festival program, facilities, equipment, finance, promotion, partnerships, and monitoring. | **Internal Factors and Resources** that enhance an organization's capacity to deliver on the objectives of the strategic plan. Actions that provide continuity and growth undertaken by board, staff and volunteers. |
| **Opportunities and Threats** that may influence or distract the organization as it goes about its core business. The potential for growth, profile-raising, and satisfying new markets as a catalyst for urban rejuvenation may be tempered by dealing with challenges from new statutory obligations, increased costs, reduction in funding, changes in demographics etc. | **External Factors** can affect an organization's trajectory, positively or negatively. These could be from the dynamic trends in economic, environmental, social and cultural domains, globalization, climate change, or legal and government policy dimensions. |

**Table 13.1** SWOT Analysis.
Derrett (2013).

- What key resources are required to ensure festival sustainability?
- How can we support local aspirations and raise the city's profile?
- How can we foster greater creativity and innovation in our program design and delivery?
- How can we best remain true to the vision of the festival?
- What efficiencies can we produce to deal with changes in technology, the labor market, legal obligations, and environmental management?
- Where does our substantive knowledge and aesthetic competence reside?
- Are potential festival partners (including audiences) marginalized?
- Is it time for consolidation of long-held initiatives?

## Pace of Change

Change can happen quickly and be visible and tangible. This should not be confused with the process put in place to achieve any shift in emphasis in the way the organization or the festival does business. The transition process is almost organic as ways of delivering on the revitalized approaches are determined. Leadership plays an important role in energizing the transition and sustaining the commitment to any changes that are to be implemented. Leadership and management are required to address the behavioral and operational aspects of the steps taken to refresh the festival. The future anticipated by each of the partners needs to be created and adapted to meet the demands that have been identified. This can take time and resources that may have to be rolled out in a staged approach to satisfy the elements of strategic plans developed.

The decision-making models that can be employed will vary along with the people engaged with the process and the scale of change sought. Attempts need to be made to simplify the approach. They may be prompted by some form of failure, learnings built from it, and then a framework developed that can address any shortcomings through pragmatic analysis, structure, communication, and lead to some practical responses. Rather than rushing to mitigate the gravity of any shortfall, a considered approach will allow for a consistent and continuous movement forward by ending some practices, losing others, and letting go to allow for a realignment within the festival or organization. This will facilitate the transition and acceptance while minimizing any surprises or resistance.

## React to External Environments

Philip Riddle and Joe Goldblatt (2012) challenged Scotland's festival community with learnings from the Richard Florida creative economy paradigm. They wrote:

> … sixty-five years ago an artistic visionary, civic leaders with a strong political will, and citizens who were committed to their community joined forces to create the legendary Edinburgh festivals. During the past seven decades, the artistic civic leadership has periodically changed however, the citizens have remained steadfast in their constant support for the original mission, the flowering of the human spirit through the creative arts.

Whilst other sectors such as manufacturing and more recently finance, have suffered from decline, one must ask why historically in Scotland's capital city and indeed in other destinations throughout the world, has event tourism as represented by the Edinburgh festivals continued to produce sustainable outcomes? The answer to this question is complex but may be not necessarily defined in solely economic terms. One may ask how does a small country such as Scotland accomplish such a remarkable success story, over and over again?

Florida suggests that many successful destinations such as Edinburgh must have strong evidence of talent, technology and tolerance to create an environment for the creative class to thrive.

- Firstly, talent may be the result of training offered through a conservatoire or other specialized school and it may also be more broadly defined as a talented group of civic leaders whose political will promotes collaborative working relationships
- Secondly, technology is a more recent phenomenon that held little importance 65 years ago, but in recent years has grown to become a major requirement for successful celebration destinations. Just as in the 19th-century Scotland was regarded as the most literate of all the European nations with a literacy rate of over 75 per cent, in the 21st-century it is equally important to demonstrate technological capability to be highly regarded among the nations of the world. Therefore, the successful celebration destinations must have wide access to broadband capability and be seen as technological innovators in cloud computing capacity.
- Thirdly, and finally, those destinations that demonstrate widespread tolerance for new ideas and even those that are initially unpopular, appear to have a strong edge over others in terms of long-term sustainable development of event tourism programmes.

Talent, technology and tolerance are not the sole purview of public servants rather, they reflect a broader commitment of the entire destination to promote advancement through experimentation. Cities in both developed as well as developing nations, recognise that these attitudes must be institutionalised through a strong political will and a constant commitment by the citizenry to embrace talent, technology and tolerance as cornerstones for future growth.

We have the recipe for success on our doorstep. The challenge for future political leaders, artistic visionaries and citizens is to achieve the right balance of having an enabling public sector and committed citizenry to "provide a platform for the flowering of the human spirit". The past sixty-five years have not been without significant challenge for the event makers of Edinburgh, however, by embracing the ideals of the original founders of the Edinburgh festivals, this unscripted enterprise has grown to become a beacon of cultural influence throughout the world. Through further investment in talent, expansion of innovation through technology and a renewed commitment to tolerance of new ideas, this celebration destination and others may grow from strength to strength.

## An Approach to Reenvisioning

A review of a festival is all about timing. It takes time to prepare, conduct, and take partners on the journey of evaluation and planning.

Determining the most relevant and pressing issues needs to be the initial focus. Not all of the above will fit each circumstance. Kotter (2008) raises the importance of "a sense of urgency"; so to build a team of focused people with a solid mix of commitment, skills, and experience to get the vision right underpins the action framework. Effective and timely communication and deciding on discrete, realistic initiatives in the first instance will allow for achievable outcomes and recognizable milestones.

Potential challenges that may need to be addressed during the process include economic costs faced by festival organizers. They will need to reflect on development and operating costs—unexpected blowouts in budgets; increasing costs in specific areas like security, technology, transport, and logistics; and failure to manage a contingency. Opportunity costs are costs of a foregone alternative. If one alternative is chosen over another, then the cost of choosing that alternative is an opportunity cost. It can be a benefit, profit, or value given up to achieve a greater good for the festival's future. Opportunity costs are the benefits you lose by choosing one alternative over another one. It provides a measure of one economic choice, compared to the best one.

As already mentioned, a scan of the external environments in which particular festivals operate will reveal how major domestic and international factors impact on the festival's appeal. These include global financial crises, foreign exchange issues, labor-market problems that can impact staffing, political unrest, taxation regulations, energy costs, and the role of shared costs through partnerships that can facilitate economies of scale to lessen festival expenditures. The scale of each of these will vary. Some festivals have been affected by tensions in the local political environment that may place public investment in the festival under scrutiny and pressure.

Festivals can fail when the anticipated financial income does not eventuate. Maybe fewer patrons than expected. There may have been negative impacts from weather or seasonality. The combination of a tired or inappropriate program, venue, and price point may conspire to make the festival diminish in value. There can be missteps in media and communication that affect the reach of festival messages to target audiences. Poor word of mouth from earlier patrons' experiences may affect attendance.

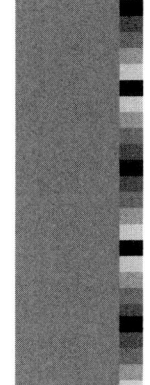

In Durham, North Carolina, the local Durham Arts Council (DAC), the producer and presenter of CenterFest Arts Festival for 37 years, plans to dramatically expand and reenvision CenterFest, the longest-running outdoor arts festival in North Carolina. DAC is working with key community partners in this effort including the Greater Durham Chamber of Commerce, the Durham Convention and Visitors Bureau, Downtown Durham Inc., the City of Durham's Office of Economic and Workforce Development and Cultural Advisory Board, Fox 50, the *Herald-Sun*, Durham Coca-Cola Bottling Co., TROSA, Carolina Theatre, and other partners, and will involve the business community, creative community, and individuals in planning during the months ahead. DAC and its key partners "rested" the festival for 2011 in order to launch a one-year visioning/production process for the 2012 expanded arts and entertainment festival format.

## Reassess Relationships

Festivals reassess how best to encourage closer ties with supporters. They suggest that gifts in various forms make a difference to the conduct of a festival. Research undertaken into what makes people give undertaken by the Australia Council (2012) focused on what motivated donors to arts enterprises through crowdsourcing. It highlighted personal, ideological, and practical responses for an investment in creativity. Considerations included a personal connection to particular artists or events, sometimes based on recommendations from family and friends; a desire to help creative people; a sense of belonging through a shared experience; engagement in cultural production through active participation or ongoing communication regarding the process; and social kudos and any personal benefits that might be afforded from the financial commitment made.

Festival organizers need to recognize some barriers to the financial support for their proposal when a giving-campaign is prepared. Many potential investors feel that a tax benefit is a great incentive. People are more likely to pledge financial support if they are confident of the capacity of the team to deliver and while many won't know the festival managers or artists personally, they will rely on trusted social media and family and friendship networks.

## Keep Abreast with Technology Trends

Those with oversight of the technical requirements ensure seamless design and delivery by using a checklist of materials (Table 13.2). They review the relationships with suppliers for competitive rental and purchase prices, packaging of equipment, delivery, insurance coverage, follow-through, trouble-shooting and professional support, and quality of all forms of equipment required. They will attend trade shows, screenings, and professional seminars to keep up with new approaches to satisfy audience expectations and statutory obligations with occupational health and safety. Demonstrations by suppliers of innovation can save festival organizers time and money, for example, rather than printing floor plans and staff information, the material could be uploaded onto

---

### SUPPORT SPOLETO FESTIVAL USA AND ENHANCE YOUR FESTIVAL EXPERIENCE

Ticket sales and other earned income covers less than half of the cost of producing and presenting the more than 140 world-class performances offered by the festival over its 17-day season; we rely on contributions from generous donors to help make up the difference. In order to recognize and thank our contributors, the festival offers an exciting array of benefits, from exclusive priority ticketing services to special behind-the-scenes events and opportunities to interact with festival artists. No matter the level, your gift will entitle you to a wide range of benefits that are sure to enhance your festival experience and, most important, will allow us to continue to delight and thrill our audiences with world-class performances.

| Specific Audio-Visual Equipment | Specific Requirements |
| --- | --- |
| Audio | Speakers, amplifiers, (wireless) microphones, mixing consoles, processing, accessories |
| Lighting | Stage lighting, effects lighting, moving lights, lighting control, lasers, strobe, fog and effects machines |
| DJ equipment | CD Players, mixers, accessories |
| Visual | Plasma TVs, projectors, DVD players, power and distribution |
| Staging and rigging | Truss, stands, stages, rigging, tables, lighting trees, drapes |

**Table 13.2** Equipment Requirements

iPads and synchronized over the Internet. The same technology could wirelessly control presentations on large screens on-site.

Common themes that are emerging in communication, data storage, and social media involve what could be described as an aggregation or nexus in usage, demand, capacity, and distribution. Pressure of time 24/7/365 means those in the festival organization responsible for these connections need to appraise how best to deal with marketing, administration, documentation, security, logistics, and financial management in light of festival partners' attention to these same pressures. Review how the festival/organization will address audiences' personal access to the distribution of text and images, demand for virtual worlds, software-defined networks, greater storage capacity, increased IT appliance ownership, and keeping informed of trends and applications.

Festivals need technical experts familiar with the latest trends in equipment.

**312** CHAPTER 13 REVISITING AND REFRESHING THE FESTIVAL VISION

A massive investment is required to rig and technical equipment to deliver quality sound experiences at music festivals.

Let there be apps! Mobile apps will be integrated with other pop-up information technology. The timeframes for technology development is short. While some agencies may have lodged data in "Clouds," storage and security will remain strong concerns. It moves the conservation and access to data from being accommodated in-house, backed up conventionally to engaging more actively in off-site locations. Fears of hackers, changes in costs of devices, power costs, complexity of programs, and staff lags in training and skills development may compromise the aspirations of the festival. People and technology will be increasingly mobile—festival staff may be distributed across various sites during the planning and delivery stages. The organization may need to reorient itself to find appropriate solutions to technical needs.

## Observation and Participation

Where will the next great big idea come from that will assist the festival in refreshing its position, its links, and its longevity? Broadly, observation and active participation will provide a useful framework for mapping ways forward. Festival teams need to work differently to adapt to new ways of dealing with intergenerational change when realigning vision with actions across organizational and artistic functions. By clever and creative idea-mapping, perspectives on current practices can amended. By listening and acknowledging different approaches, a reenergized regime can bring about improvements to the quality, value, and extent of a festival's offerings. New experiences can change minds.

Through observation festival stakeholders at all levels can formally or informally glean ideas from attending festivals created by others. What are the key elements that emerge from investigating festivals of the same genre, attract similar audiences, and are of similar scale and settings? How are spaces in the public and private domains utilized to best effect? It is helpful, too, to see what other public celebrations do to offer experiences. Take staff field trips to supplier facilities by building knowledge through a better understanding of partners' workplaces. Distilling the essence from these observations and reporting to colleagues may stimulate new approaches.

The electronic coverage of festivals and events placed in the public domain is another medium to observe current practice. Such material observed from different perspectives can be useful in determining responses to audience motivations, stimulate program content, and address communication issues. Today's communication professionals are not only experts in visual technology but manipulate the traditional and new foundations to capture audience attention and convey nuanced information and evoking emotions.

## Life-Long Learning

By establishing how others are dealing with practical and intellectual aspects of festival sustainability, the connection with peers is important. Like-minded people come together face-to-face or via the Web to share ideas, insights, knowledge, and inspiration as demonstrated by Brain Pickings. Here interest is aroused and provoked through intense cultural enthusiasm for global thinking and action. It suggests that *to truly create and contribute to culture, we have to be able to connect countless dots, to cross-pollinate ideas from a wealth of disciplines, to combine and recombine these ideas and build new ideas.* Increasing attention is being paid to the TED program. TED, where originally people from the world of **T**echnology, **E**ntertainment and **D**esign came together to share their experiences, now provides global opportunities for both interaction at conferences, events, and online to celebrate models that work and ideas that are inventive and unusual.

Another online approach, but one shared with other learners of all ages is the stimulation that comes from programs like Coursera. Here global universities offer programs, short and long courses, in diverse disciplines that can improve resumes and advance career trajectories through intense knowledge acquisition. Local higher education programs make a host of relevant courses available as well. Another industry initiative is the Atelier for Young Festival Managers hosted by the European Festival Association. This exciting international program supported by experts in the field aims to offer to emerging festival directors a stage to explore creative ideas and open up new perspectives. It builds on its motto (a sentence borrowed from Bernard Faivre d'Arcier in 2006), "The true role of a festival is to help artists to dare, to engage in new projects," with particular emphasis on the artistic aspects of festival management. This touches upon artistic vision, political and social responsibility, internationalization, networking, renewal, and sustainability.

All engaged in trying to improve the presentation of festivals need to consider external environments that might inform better choices for a festival's future through international connections. Audiences are highly mobile, so festivals need to ensure what they have to offer meets evolved and sophisticated expectations. Learning from one another regarding how to supply sufficient money to ensure the maintenance of quality celebratory experiences, for example, like other aspects of festival management, can come from the interaction with other practitioners. Exchanges of personnel in global festival-making excites a great deal of interest in those who wish to secure a career trajectory informed by good practices in any location. By actually applying ideas, beliefs, and methods already deemed successful in the sector, festivals can eliminate the necessity to replicate poorer or less viable practices.

From a participation perspective, festival-makers have a vast array of options. As well as the suggestions above, there are professional development options provided by industry networks, through study programs, workshops, webinars, specialist training in specific fields like ICT, innovations in equipment, and software applications for administration, logistics, and risk management tasks. Contributing to conferences, industry meetings, public forums, and listening and exchanging experiences can all build capacity in a festival host organization. Participation in programs convened by the tourism, economic development, media and corporate sector, or local Chambers of Commerce can all offer a vocabulary that can be applied to the festival environment. Gathering evidence of good practice in any sector and appropriating the best elements will show all players that the festival is serious about its commitments.

Keep an eye on research being undertaken; what people are writing in academic journals, festival reports, government documents, and media commentary; and observe how solutions are found for challenges. How do festivals manage the contingency line in their budget and what are the implications for all the other resources that need to be committed to a festival's well-being? By planning contingency time into the operational timeline, should the unexpected happen, then there is time to address the issues. Remember there are some things that affect people's ability to deliver to the proposed timetable, so expect things to take longer than originally agreed. This is a significant issue if there are "in-kind" or free contributions offered.

A last-minute great idea can turn into administrative and logistical nightmares. If resources are not requisitioned early enough in the process, or adequate time and human resources are not available, these spontaneous ideas come to little benefit while creating anxiety and team tension, not to mention unease among prospective audience and partners.

## Templates, Checklists, and Software Packages

In recent years many event management companies, government agencies closely linked to the arts, community, and economic development and tourism have worked to streamline access to templates, checklists, and software programs that can assist individual festival organizations to plan and implement hard-copy and online solutions to administrative activities such as ticketing, tracking, databases, newsletter mailing, scheduling, staffing, social media distribution and analysis, space allocation, report-writing, timely task management, logistics, and technical management. Many of these can be purchased, customized, and shared with people trained and familiar with key objectives of their functions. Some programs are comprised of modules that are flexible and can be tailored to the specific needs of festivals dependent on scale, location, resources, and finance. The industry knowledge that underpins these programs and templates come from years of experience and the modifications that each user can make allows festivals to re-invigorate fundamental practices in a contemporary way.

## Foundations, Funds, and Fundraising

Finding funds to invest in festival activities is hard work. Organizations need to be forensic in their approach to evaluating how they use their financial resources. They need to review existing sponsorship policies to ensure that appropriate matches are made. There is a need for a level playing field for potential investors in the festival. Agreements need to be legal, well documented, and negotiations conducted transparently to minimize risks for all parties.

Festival organizations need to draw up a template that assists in determining best-fit with potential funders. This may be with regard to sponsorship, investment by philanthropic trusts and foundations, and collaborations with corporate entities keen to demonstrate their social responsibilities and commitment to public engagement. There are templates for proposals prepared by festival organizations at any level that suggest the narrative that underpins the potential relationship. There needs to be a clear snapshot of the festival capacity to deliver benefits to the sponsor's needs. There needs to be demonstrable understanding of connections for sponsors to audiences, financial details regarding requirements, how money will be spent, and how the connection can have mutual value.

There are organizations that hold information on trusts, foundations, and philanthropic entities that may be of use to festival organizations. They provide guidance and professional support in shaping potential partnerships. For example, the Community Foundations Gateway (Australia) and Foundation Center (U.S.) and arts-business-donor support networks like Creative Partnerships Australia, provide links based on extensive research and experience of their numerous partners. Income from such parties is becoming mainstream. Festival host organizations can benefit from permanent and growing sources of funding, with the income earned each year being returned to the community as annual grants to deductible gift recipients or other tax-deductible entities.

Festival staff need to be familiar with the protocols that operate in their jurisdiction and be committed to making relationships work for effective use of media and host community relationships. This will ensure that a professional approach and positive partnerships are evident. The same forces are at play when the public purse invests in festivals. It is essential that festival administration and management be alert to all the opportunities that accessible government funding projects offer. This may influence further partnerships between the arts, community, and local business. Government funding programs can be part of this type of income.

Festivals are increasingly dependent upon earned income in hard times. Festival leaders should pay careful attention to the challenges of the global financial environment for direct and indirect impacts, as the annual budget is prepared strategically. How the organization controls costs will influence initiatives they can take to increase donations (and bequests); maximize ticket sales; consolidate membership fees; gain benefits from concessions, merchandise, food and beverage sales before, during, and after the festival; sale of media rights and fees for specific services including classes. Assessing the projects costs (including administration, venue, volunteers, artists, promotion, permits, security, risk, hospitality, logistics, documentation, evaluation, and contingencies) requires careful attention and innovative approaches to revenue.

There are a number of fundraising options. This is particularly relevant to community-based festivals. Advertising offered by local businesses help defray costs. Membership and value-added elements like newsletters, merchandise, or contracts to offer to sell festival goods (e.g., image-based festival calendar) and services in a community are options. Many of these can help build the profile of the festival in nonperformance periods. Members/volunteers can conduct ancillary events like car washes, auctions with celebrity support, themed dress-up days linked to annual festival theme, awards functions, entertainments with possible artists from festival programs during downtimes, balls, and trivia/quiz nights. To consolidate a link with the festival and its vision, it may be that a creative response can build membership, volunteer support, and brand recognition for the future.

Links with businesses can be consolidated through shared enterprises that will raise funds for not-for-profit festival organizations. Employees can become a de facto sales force to create fun activities that can leverage their connections and embrace competitions, parties, celebrity fashion parades, arts, and cultural links in nontraditional spaces.

## GENERATING FESTIVAL INCOME

Joe Goldblatt raised issues in a 2011 newspaper article about alternative funding sources that had been explored during studies undertaken by Queen Margaret University's International Center for the Study of Planned Events (ICSPE). The in-depth analysis of the financial performance of the Edinburgh Festival in 2009 revealed that most, but not all, festivals required substantial public support to offset planned financial losses and that those festivals that had reached maturity generally performed better over time. The evidence clearly demonstrated that festivals and cultural organizations could indeed change course to help ensure their future financial stability.

For example, cultural organizations rarely pursue venture philanthropy to financially support their goals. Venture philanthropy enables not-for-profit organizations such as the Edinburgh Festivals to seek funding to support their social goals and objectives and this funding is awarded by philanthropists whose desire is to see a strong return on their social investment. If taken up, this would require changes to annual reporting cycles of organizations to match the requirements of alternative funding agents. In addition, regular impact studies may need to be conducted and reported more frequently to meet the evidentiary requirements of future funding agencies.

A suggestion is made to emulate the experience of successful models adopted by New York City's Metropolitan Opera and the Royal Opera House at Covent Garden, the Glyndebourne Opera, the Bolshoi Ballet, and England's National Theatre, among others, by broadcasting select festival performances to cinemas throughout the world. The Metropolitan Opera annually broadcasts 11 or more operas that are seen by over 200,000 per performance as compared with only 3,800 who view this same performance in the New York opera house. Not only does the Metropolitan Opera cinema audience have access to one of the world's great opera companies, but they also may be motivated to financially support the company. In addition, they may choose to visit New York City in the future to attend a live performance of the opera company. This additional financial support represents millions of dollars of new earned income from ticket sales for the Metropolitan Opera and this does not include the new philanthropic gifts that may follow.

In 2010, the ICSPE at Queen Margaret University, Edinburgh conducted a study to identify new sources of funding for festivals and events in both Edinburgh and Glasgow. That study determined that there was the potential to seek an audience contribution of £1.00 per ticket to support these important events. It mentioned the New York City theater owners experience when they added a $1.50 theater restoration charge to each ticket sold. Over $10 million (£7.5 million) was raised during this period and no significant resistance from ticket buyers was received (Scotsman, 2011).

## AUDIENCE CONTRIBUTIONS

A voluntary audience contribution may be one potential opportunity to investigate further. In 2013, Bonnaroo Music and Arts Festival in Manchester, Tennessee, specifically augmented its environmental efforts. Portable solar panel systems have run the Solar Stage at Bonnaroo for several years. The new, much larger system is the U.S.'s first permanent solar array at a music festival. The 50 kW solar photovoltaic array has already begun cranking electricity to support the 2013 festival and beyond.

The festival blog records the fact that the project was fully funded by opt-in contributions that fans selected while buying their 'Roo tickets. This initiative fits in other strategies Bonnaroo has taken to green the event, including adding a year-round sustainability coordinator to its staff, the installation of free water stations throughout the concert site where fans can refill reusable water bottles, and the use of biodegradable wraps, plates, cups, and cutlery. All portable toilets are stocked with recycled toilet paper and recycled paper is also used for all program and administrative needs.

Another Bonnaroo income generation initiative involves the sale of festival photos directly from the artist, with 20 percent of the proceeds benefitting the Bonnaroo Works Fund. The Works Fund supports organizations and programs focused on the arts, education, environmental sustainability, and other causes.

## Outsourcing

Festival organizations of any scale consider who is best placed to evaluate their performance, whether the exploration should be conducted in-house by staff and volunteers or whether specialists as consultants could be engaged to work, from strategic concepts into building programs, fundraising and marketing, and event production, and conduct a rigorous objective account of how the festival and its organization has been performing. There are many such specialists who can accommodate such a brief. Experienced practitioners can provide advice, offer mentorships, and deliver solutions in conjunction with members of festival teams. Many of these people have held senior positions in festival organizations honing skills in strategy, management, operations, research, programs, marketing, and event development. Their connections with public agencies, government, international networks, and the academy will provide substantial underpinning to any performance review they undertake.

## Avoiding Festival Failure

There are pressures on festivals/organizations that will require serious consideration at all stages of the development cycle to avert a diminution in funds, dependency of too few sources of funds, lack of control over resources and program, and loss of face. These forces can influence and/or intimidate actions going forward. They require ongoing disciplined

Jack Carlsen and his colleagues (2010) have examined some of the critical elements of festival management, innovation, and festival failure. They particularly emphasize the pressure innovation is under in festival-making. They and the research of Don Getz (2002) explore what might induce failure and what that really means in the short and longer term. Each recognizes that failure is common, but variables like scale, length of operation, host community interest, management skill levels and availability of infrastructure all contribute to the fragility of some ventures. The sorts of problems that have faced festivals include those associated with marketing and planning, human resources, financial resources, and organizational culture. A number of these challenges are fleshed out below.

monitoring to avoid stress that can play havoc with management that is busily engaged with the day-to-day conduct of the festival business. Some of the following scenarios can threaten the viability of a festival. At times the urgency that accompanies important decisions puts innovation at risk. It may serve the festival better if legal matters, accounting services, marketing, logistics, and security are out-sourced so that advice can be sought at appropriate times to allow the core business to achieve its outputs.

Recent public commentary reinforces the external and internal pressures on sustaining festival aspirations. Artists are left unpaid, audiences are not reimbursed when festivals fail to deliver the full program, volunteers "burn out," competition from other festivals, limited contingency means less capacity to respond to unexpected costs from suppliers, less box office income due to personal economic pressures, sudden reversal of trends, and sudden negative media exposure have all been cited as contributing to the demise of long-standing festivals.

Market saturation is another issue attracting the attention of destination managers and marketers, tourism operators, and arts administrators. Is it just the volume of festivals, is it the congested summer season of festivals, is it the competition between organizers, festivals, and venues, or is there pressure from improved infrastructure that emerges as major problem? Has the market reached capacity? A number of festival organizers in the United Kingdom and the United States have raised concerns for the increasing number of festivals causing overcrowding in the marketplace. Quite a few festivals report pressure to cancel or postpone their events. Some of these festivals may reach an impasse or crisis, take time away from the public view, then regroup and reappear. They may return unchanged or tweaked with adjustments to strategic direction or marketing campaigns.

There are artists, as well as organizers, that suggest that it has become harder to offer "something new" for audiences by revamping program content. Festival fans are disappointed when smaller festivals disappear. Some larger long-standing music festivals have experienced slower ticket sales due to money being tighter, but most appear confident that they will survive.

These are some perspectives that are due some attention:

- *Fees set to increase for public services.* Observe the changes in local government fees that change regularly like registration and development applications. Local government, like most other enterprises, are affected by the global economic climate and

will consider measures to tighten the public purse. There may be restrictions in how much they invest in public events and promotional aspects of the destination's profile. Politicians may be reluctant to commit to festivals.
- The *influence of sponsors* on the festival needs to be tracked. From the beginning all negotiations impinge on artistic clarity and response to festival vision. If sponsors withdraw money, it limits festival options if there has been an overreliance on their contribution.
- Problems associated with *inadequate management of marketing and planning* for the festival can become a cause of festival failure. Finding the "best fit" of the festival program with a target market could be based on poor market research, poor documentation of past experience, and unfamiliarity with social media and promotion. Lack of change to site arrangements, venue management, program content, festival experience components such as quality and availability of food and beverage, overcrowding, security, and deficient selling of festival benefits can coalesce to have a festival implode and not be able to be reinvigorated.
- *Fragmented industry*. Moves to cooperate and undertake consortia marketing have helped mitigate some problems related to a dispersed sector. Some genre festivals collaborate locally and internationally. Some cost-sharing and economies of scale benefits are sought after full and frank cooperation between organizers. A clash of event dates can be debilitating. Local authorities and government agencies encourage partnerships that may secure a more stable financial and administrative base from which to consolidate a destination's festival portfolio.
- *Lack of knowledge* of current partner corporate structure, financial security, and business status of suppliers and sponsors to ensure they have the capacity to deliver on contracted services.
- Alert to *seasonality* in terms of sunstroke, flu epidemics, and numbers in audience decline due to alternative entertainment options.
- Understand local *weather conditions* and the impacts of unfavorable weather elsewhere that can impact transport and travel and communications. Seasonal issues may affect the use and suitability of venues or festival sites.
- If the financial situation is tight, consideration may need to be given to the *sale of assets*.
- *Charging too much*. Selecting the optimum price point for a ticket price is an art. Inclusive tickets for the whole program, flexible payment through installment programs, and early-bird options at fixed prices can offset potential ticket price inflation due to costs of production. Deposit schemes are tried by some ventures. Some festivals have problems related to cash flow and not having sufficient money up front, which doesn't help profit-making.
- *Ensure skills of management teams are kept up*. Especially with not-for-profit volunteer community-based festivals, those charged with responsibilities need to be trained and regularly assessed for competencies that contribute to a viable festival. Staff and volunteers come with goodwill, an assortment of skills and experience, and should be invested in with clear guidelines to undertake assigned tasks. They work hard and can "burn out." High rates of churn among volunteers require attention to recruitment, induction, training, and supervision. Organizations can encounter a culture of power struggles, infighting, and lack of necessary skills.

- *Fostering resilience and encouraging active participation.* By taking initiatives in the public domain for a common good, individuals and groups can demonstrate personal and professional skills that can be translated into other aspects of community life. The communication that takes place and the mutual support offered through teamwork are valuable characteristics of resilience. By engaging with people committed to planning worthwhile celebrations with care and attention to detail, organizations are able to handle the responsibility of developing festivals that encourage relationships that are able to deal with challenges. The strength of the ties between festival stakeholders affects the durability of the networks beyond festival-making.
- *Connecting to host community.* The diligence and cooperation demonstrated within the festival organization has implications for its relationships with diverse cultural providers. The links between cultural providers and other community-based organizations play important roles in exploiting the existing community's cultural system. This buy-in by both cultural organization and community groups is important, even though in many destinations there are few institutional links between these sectors. Festivals can act as a catalyst to improve the flow between these structural holes in existing community cultural systems. Depending on the size of the host community, communication between such players is critical for the success of each. This supports the ecological model of community culture that enhances cultural and community resilience. Stern and Seifert (2002, p. 8) suggest the community cultural ecosystem includes a variety of agents that that operate under the radar. The nature and role of festivals demonstrably encourages those hidden human and cultural resources in communities to be revealed in formal and informal ways.

## Accentuate the Positive

After taking stock of all aspects of festival-making, it is time to celebrate reaching goals and demonstrating commitment to festival vision, building confidence and trust, and raising the festival profile. *Rejoice after the review and refresh!* Provide incentives for all participants and promote good-practice attributes by using mainstream media. Identify some key markers and distribute press releases.

- **Customer satisfaction from audiences**. Audience surveys, interviews, and social media feedback reveal how participants have valued the festival experience. The optimism and trust demonstrated should be shared and celebrated. There are engagement mechanisms that can happen throughout the year (prior to the next major festival) to pay back the loyalty and the positive word of mouth.
- **Service delivery**. Services are also usually inseparable from their provider. The festival services can be created, dispensed, and consumed simultaneously. Festival patrons recognize that personal services are the most inseparable services and value prompt, hospitable, and safe attention. It is an almost impossible task to standardize all forms of services that are delivered by festival staff, but feedback from satisfied patrons should be shared with the general public to consolidate credibility over time.

- **Employment of artists and building local cultural capacity**. A commitment to employ local and international artists establishes festival organization credibility. It is not only a professional investment but it showcases the power of audiences to appreciate high-quality performances. It is another way to value the importance of arts and culture in the lives of all facets of the community.
- **Welcome back former staff members** who have gained experience elsewhere and now wish to share with a favored employer. There is evidence that a positive early experience in employment can empower individuals to give back to the initial environment after they have worked elsewhere. It can erupt into nostalgia or excite interest in investing in young interns, act as mentors, or offer training programs for event management.
- **Economic benefits to broader community**. Spread the word on the diverse economic impacts, locally and further afield. This indicator encourages further supporters and generally satisfies host communities, local government, and business leaders.
- **Offering donations** to community causes across the social and environmental spectrum is a growing element of festival-giving. This can encourage entrepreneurship more broadly in host communities and donate funds to socially responsible causes.
- **Cost-sharing** with local, national, and international partners in creation of innovative new work.
- **Generate a gallery** with festival highlights through an image bank on website and social media platforms. By documenting aspects of the program and patron experience, YouTube provides a vehicle for celebrating the efforts of stakeholders.
- **Awards**. Nominate to receive awards for good practice (arts, tourism, environment, business) and win! Host a gala function to distribute awards for contributions to the festival from staff and volunteers.
- **Party with partners** that builds the spirit of collaboration and provides opportunities to nourish relationships and thank people for their input.
- **Debrief** and hold functions to ensure feedback is shared in congenial surroundings.
- **Cover costs** and make way for ongoing investments.
- **Establish green credentials**. Leave a legacy of a clean site, demonstrate environmentally sustainable practices in waste management, energy use, natural landscape management, recycling, reuse and site safety and security. Be acknowledged by peers for good practice in meeting environmental objectives.

At the heart of successful celebrations are substantial and appealing programs, evidence of strategic and tactical planning, sound communications between all partners, adequate resourcing to achieve the shared vision, strong links to the host community, and a team of hardworking and passionate staff and volunteers led by inspired leaders committed to providing an experience to the highest standard that will linger long in the memories of all participants.

> What does touch me is when people come up to me in the street, as they sometimes do since they mistakenly think I've retired, and talk about some experience that has remained with them. That for me is the only real legacy: the idea that one has left a lingering trace in people's memories. In the end, that's all a director can hope to do.
> —*Director Peter Brook*

## CASE STUDY

### Festival Leadership

The Chair of the European Festival Research Project (EFRP; 2004–2011) was Dragan Klaic, renowned theater scholar and cultural analyst. In The Future of *Festival Formulae* (2002), he reflected on the role of artistic leadership in festivals, identifying special features of the role. Rather than succumbing to criticism that there exists a sameness of program content, it is evident in contemporary arts and cultural festivals that serious directors are keen to maintain consistently high standards year after year of new, unknown, risky, and surprising content. They may scour the globe for new international artists to stimulate host communities and other partners, while sometimes collaborating with other festivals to co-create and produce by sharing costs and risks. He recognizes that festivals are increasingly seen to be adding value to a destination's tourism attractiveness by presenting works that would not be normal fare in particular genres or through cross-disciplinary engagement to build a vibrant cultural life.

Festival organizations through board appointments expect that the director will provide ambitious, confident, and inspirational artistic leadership that enthuses artists locally, nationally, and internationally through the quality of programs, partnerships, and collaborations. They expect that this person will lead a team to build and engage with audiences creatively and embed a culture of excellence for a sustainable future. The role is key to festival success. Directors are to exude a clear vision based on skills and experience in the sector, understand media networks, have professional links and grasp the nuances of the host community and demands of local partners. Their major duties involve the oversight of programs, finance, marketing, and management of internal and external partnerships. Their direction stimulates curiosity among audiences by building faith in the festival, often through a combination of local productions showcasing their strengths and imports. The festival's voice needs to resonate with established audiences and attract new patrons with quality, pizzazz, challenges, and outreach components.

Directors use established themes, are catalytic and audacious, create new pathways for the program, offer their individual stamp, respond to social and cultural trends, and work within budgets committed to each festival. They share and finesse ideas through sustained future thinking. Directors are engaged for specific periods of time. This allows for some continuity and festival growth options. As with artists and audiences, directors are internationally mobile and this adds to their appeal when applying for positions. Individual job descriptions vary, but the following example is in response to the departure, after eight years, of the incumbent director of the famous Edinburgh International Festival.

> The Festival Director's role is to ensure that the Edinburgh International Festival achieves its mission to be the most exciting and accessible festival of the performing arts in the world through collaborating with arts practitioners world-wide to create, plan and deliver a programme of events that showcase the best of international and Scottish talent. The Festival Council is seeking a visionary and inspirational leader to be the creative force at the centre of the Festival, shaping and driving a multi-dimensional program each year that is innovative, challenging and world-class.
>
> He or she will have an in-depth knowledge of the arts that crosses boundaries and cultures, an international reputation for artistic vision and creative flair and a track record of success in programming large-scale performing arts events, including commissioning and promoting new work

and imaginative approaches to production, presentation and participation.

The successful candidate will have previous experience of leading and motivating a highly professional team, the ability to initiate and maintain effective partnerships with a wide range of stakeholders in the UK and overseas, good financial awareness, excellent communication skills, political acumen, and a commitment to developing audiences and extending participation in the arts. (Edinburgh International Festival, 2012)

As you examine effective festival leadership, it is worthwhile establishing a file on well-established festival leaders and learn more about their experience and practices. Many have contributed much as mentors to the vital intergenerational change evident in the sector in the 21st century. By building such a portfolio, notice how the shape of festivals has changed over time. There are series, there is exclusivity, there are last-minute revelations, stunts, big names, commissioned and spontaneous works, emerging artists, workshops, and master classes. What key features can you discern that become trademarks of particular directors?

Consider:

**Nigel Redden**—General Director that rejoined *Spoleto Festival USA* in October 1995. He had previously been General Manager from 1986 to 1991. After leaving the festival in 1991, Redden served as executive director of the Santa Fe Opera and executive producer of the Lincoln Center Festival. He is responsible for all aspects of the festival including fundraising, financial administration, marketing, union negotiations, artists' contracts, board development, and programming. He also leads the Lincoln Center Festival as director.

**Brett Sheehy** is one of Australia's most accomplished and acclaimed artistic directors, producers, and curators. He took up the role of Artistic Director and CEO of Melbourne Theatre Company in 2012, and in the same year concluded his four-year tenure as Artistic Director of Melbourne Festival. He is the only person ever to lead three of the five international arts festivals in Australia's state capital cities. Sheehy was nationally recognized for distinguished service to the performing and visual arts as a director of national festivals, to international artistic exchange, and through mentoring roles in 2012.

## Acknowledged International Festival Leaders

**Robyn Archer** (Creative Director of the Centenary of Canberra, Artistic Director of The Light in Winter in Australia) is a singer, writer, director, artistic director, and public advocate of the arts, mainly in Australia though her reach is global; • **Michael Eavis** (Glastonbury Festival, UK); • **Rose Fenton** (Director Free Word, Co-Founder LIFT Festival, London); • **Grace Lang** (Programme Director, Hong Kong Festival Society); • **Ching Lee Goh** (Executive and Artistic Director CultureLink Singapore, Former Director Singapore Arts Festival); • **Sir Brian McMaster** (former Director Edinburgh International Festival); • **Peter Noble** (Bluesfest Byron Bay, Australia); • **Mark Russell** (Festival Under the Radar, New York); • **Carla Van Zon** (Artistic Director Auckland Arts Festival, former Director Creative New Zealand).

## FROM INSIDE THE MOSAIC

Jeff Curtis, CEO of the Rose Festival in Portland, Oregon. Jeff thrives on the rigors and demands of leading one of the largest festivals in the United States. His role with the revamped century-old festival involved planning and transforming it from top to bottom. He actively participates in special features of the festival, including running a half-marathon and the CityFair to ensure he has a clear appreciation of the festival's impact on the host community. His observations of the commitment to festival refreshment by the board, staff, volunteers, residents, visitors, and media are salutary.

Jeff Curtis

### A CEO's Perspective and Experience Living and Working on a Plan Called "Road to Sustainability"

The Portland Rose Festival is recognized as one of the world's most enduring events, attracting a million festival-goers and annually pumping more than $75 million into the local economy. Named the Best Festival in the World by the International Festivals and Events Association twice in the last five years, the Rose Festival was conceived during the first decade of the 20th century by visionary city leaders in order to put Portland, Oregon, on the map. Little did they know that more than a hundred summers later the Rose Festival would be world famous for its amazing parades and other award-winning events, as well as serving as a community leader for celebrating values like volunteerism, patriotism, and environmentalism. In 2010, the Rose Festival was finally acknowledged as Portland's Official Festival by proclamation of the City Council.

A magical Centennial Celebration reinvigorates a community, but leaves the festival's financial position in peril. In 2007 the Rose Festival marked its Centennial with a celebration that reinvigorated community interest with events and programs both lavish and intimate. From an expanded Grand Floral

President's Award float in the Floral Parade of the Rose Festival, Portland, Oregon

Parade that highlighted a century of Portland history to a special motion picture produced with student filmmakers and a formal gala for 1,200 people, the myriad details of the Centennial year took 18 months to plan and execute. While the public embraced and even lauded the efforts, the financial results were less than positive. The Rose Festival's reserves were tapped, leaving little in reserve for future "rainy days."

The 2008 Portland Rose Festival celebration came and went with over 60 terrific events. It was like any other festival in my tenure as CEO. The festival had its many moments of magic and pageantry. The festival had another run of incident-free events, and it captured the local media with positive stories throughout. With all the good came the reality of bad weather on our event days that rely on good/dry festival weather. It also came with the reality of a post-Centennial reduction in advance revenues like ticket sales and sponsorship support. Those three elements created the perfect financial storm. The year 2008 would put the festival in a dire financial position with enough financial resources to pay the bills, but nothing left for the future!

The 2008 Portland Rose Festival ended in mid-June, and we spent two weeks wrapping up with a sense of relative normalcy. That normalcy would change! I recall coming back from a two-week vacation in July, and on my first or second day back sitting down with my close friend, colleague, and the Festival's Chief Operating Officer, Marilyn Clint. She was not her usual self. She came to me with a question that I had feared, but nothing more than just possibility. She painted a grim picture and challenged me with questions that changed my attitude from fear to reality. The Portland Rose Festival would be out of business within a few years or it would be reduced to a shell of its former self if we did not come to terms with the reality. I had a choice, one of denial and trust that the festival's long, rich history could simply endure without major change. Or, embrace the challenge, lead with conviction, and use all the stretch of this beloved 100-year-old festival in a way to create a new road. I chose the latter, and within weeks the Road to Sustainability was born.

*The Portland Rose Festival Road to Sustainability* was not that different from any good organization's strategic plan. However, it had a distinct immediate call to action and it did what proved to be the most important element for any long-standing community event: it challenged traditional thinking and it gave the organization a new sense of vision and purpose. Here are three brief examples:

1. It challenged the most widely used theory of event financial recovery of budget cuts and elimination of events and programs. The Rose Festival would turn the other direction, we would add revenue by adding new events and investing in our core events like CityFair.
2. It outlined a dramatic and aggressive strategy for increasing city support at a time where government agencies all over the United States were dramatically decreasing their support of special events.
3. It was built on adjusting the festival and meeting its challenges with its strengths rather than depending on new unproved strategies. In our case, we built our plan from the strengths of an experienced tenured staff that the Board fully trusted for implementation and we added new elements to already successful festival events.

While the Road to Sustainability would answer the Portland Rose Festival's most recent crisis, it certainly was not the first and won't be the last. Long-standing festival events will always be faced with the challenge to maintain relevance to new audiences, but at the same time embrace their rich history. An organization's history is the single most powerful tool at its disposal. I have seen far too many good festivals with decades of history seek change by ignoring their rich history. Forgetting the past can be the largest mistake we can make as leaders of our festivals. Our past can answer new questions, and it can remind us of why we exist. That respect for the past, with a keen direction on the new possibilities that exist in any community, can balance each other with solutions that do both. In the case of the Portland Rose Festival, we have a tremendous 106-year history, and every year we introduce new elements that add to the traditions making Portland, Oregon, a better place to live and visit.

## Festival Ideas and Issues

1. Peter Drucker said, "We now accept the fact that learning is a lifelong process of keeping abreast of change. And the most pressing task is to teach people how to learn." How can this be applied to the capacity of festival organizations to refresh their vision and deliver effective events?
2. What are the best approaches for festivals to use to address external pressures? Discuss some change management techniques you've read about that could assist.
3. If you were undertaking a festival organization performance review, what are the key elements that need to be addressed? How can the organization improve its position through market knowledge, matching its products and services to audience needs, reviewing operational and financial matters and its organizational culture and structure and human resources management?
4. The prefix *re-* means "afresh or undertake once more—maybe return to a previous state" and has been used to explore some of the opportunities festivals have to address their current practice, if need be enhance their reputation and raise their profile in the marketplace while addressing the organization's vision.

Discuss the words chosen, think of others that may be appropriate, and identify how they could be applied to ensure festival continuity.

| Task | Actions | Task | Actions |
|---|---|---|---|
| Review | | Reflect | |
| React | | Record | |
| Revitalize | | Reaffirm | |
| Readjust | | Redefine | |
| Reinvigorate | | Recover | |
| Reinvest | | Reorient | |
| Restore | | Realign | |
| Remain | | Rejoice | |
| Re | | Re | |
| Re | | Re | |
| | | | |

5. Revisit the *Prelude* offered by Don Getz at the front end of this book. Review the criteria he identifies in terms of festival longevity, the determination to endure, the collection of motives and drivers associated with a festival culture in places, large and small, renowned and unsung. Which key points would you prioritize? Why do some festivals fail?
6. Do you think the festival market is saturated? Debate this with your peers.

# Festival Focus Activities

1. An exciting opportunity exists for a digital marketing professional to join the festival team. Excellent writing, editing and communication skills, experience in digital marketing or online journalism, and a tertiary qualification in marketing, communications, or media (or similar) are essential.
2. Key responsibilities of the role include the ongoing development, implementation, and evaluation of the festival's digital marketing and communications strategies, including website, app, e-news, social media, and online advertising in order to maintain a leadership position in digital arts marketing, and to continue to increase the festival's brand awareness and ticket sales.
3. The sensibility and confidence to adopt the festival's online voice and the ability to create content and dialogue about artistic product are also important requirements.
4. The successful applicant will enjoy making a positive contribution to a team and be well organized, good humored, and accustomed to meeting deadlines in a dynamic and busy environment. The Digital Marketing Coordinator is a full-time position offered on a two-year contract basis.
5. Analyze this job description and scope how the incoming employee can build the capacity of the organization as a result of the festival's recent marketing reassessment.
6. Draw a timeline of your educational and/or professional life. What have been the major significant moments, key interventions, mentor contacts, memorable experiences, or lingering insights? Can you highlight in a graphic way the important connections? Have you been able to consolidate any learning in new approaches to deal with change in the work/life balance you experience?
7. In a group, brainstorm ideas that you consider may contribute to improvements in the management of a festival with which you are familiar. Discuss aspects that might be worthy of review, identify a possible sequence of actions that need to take place, and illustrate your ideas with exemplars from your experience, reading, or observation of practices elsewhere. Can the group agree on some concrete proposals? What criteria will be used to choose best ideas? What are the agreed-upon priorities? Present a report on the process and the outcomes.
8. Evaluate a particular festival's representation of partnerships with its funders, whether through sponsorship, philanthropy, corporate social responsibility programs, or equitable collaborations based on "in-kind" support. What can you find out about the contribution of these to the festival's bottom line? How do they celebrate these connections?
9. A successful festival is contingent on a large number of variables. The artistic director has oversight of the different variables. What are the general duties, responsibilities, and obligations of a festival director? Construct a position description for a director of a festival with which you are familiar.

## Suggested Reading

Arts Hub Australia, *What Makes People Give?* Melbourne, Australia: 2012, http://www.artshub.com.au/au/news-article/opinions/arts/what-makes-people-give-191507#.

Arts Support, *How to Work the Crowd: A Snapshot of Barriers and Motivations to Crowd Funding,* Sydney, Australia: Australia Council for the Arts, 2012.

Brook, P. *The Empty Space: A Book About the Theatre: Deadly, Holy, Rough, Immediate.* McGibbon and Kee, 1968.

Carlsen, J., T. D. Andersson, J. Ali-Knight, K. Jaeger, and T. Taylor. "Festival management innovation and failure." *International Journal of Event and Festival Management* 1, no. 2 (2010): 120–131.

Getz, D. "Why Festivals Fail." *Event Management* 7 (2002): 209–219.

Goldblatt, J. J. "Joe Goldblatt: Change of Course Could Pay for Festivals," *The Scotsman,* September 28, 2011, Letter to Editor, Edinburgh, Scotland www.Scotsman.com.

Golombiskey, K., and R. Hagen, R. *White space is not your enemy: A beginner's guide to communicating visually through graphic, web and multimedia design.* Burlington, MA: Focal Press/Elsevier, 2010.

Klaic, D. *Future of Festival Formulae.* Presented at the Holland Festival Symposium, De Balie, 2002.

Kotter, J. P. *A Sense of Urgency.* Boston, MA: Harvard Business School Press, 2008.

Kotter, J. P. *Leading Change.* Boston, MA: Harvard Business Press, 1996.

Krogerus, M., and R. Tschappeler. *The Decision Book: Fifty Models for Strategic Thinking.* London, UK: Profile Books, 2011.

Kubler-Ross, E. *On Death and Dying.* New York: Scribner Classics, 1997.

Lindsay, H. *20 Questions—Directors of Not-For-Profit Organizations Should Ask about Strategy and Planning.* Toronto, Canada: Chartered Accountants of Canada, 2008.

Lindsay, H. *20 Questions Directors of Not-For-Profit Organizations Should Ask about Governance.* Toronto, Canada: Chartered Accountants of Canada, 2006.

Riddle, P. and Goldblatt, J. J. "Leading the March to a Better Future," 2012. http://www.scotsman.com/news/prof-philip-riddle-and-prof-joe-goldblatt-leading-the-march-towards-a-better-future-1-2224858.

Sibbet, D. *Visual meetings: How graphic, sticky notes and idea mapping can transform group productivity.* Hoboken, NJ: Wiley, 2010.

Stern, M., and S. C. Seifert. *Culture Builds Community Evaluation, Social Impact of the Arts Project.* Summary Report, University of Pennsylvania School of Social Work, 2002.

# CHAPTER 14

# The Future of Festivals

*Optimism is a strategy for making a better future. Because unless you believe that the future can be better, you are unlikely to step up and take responsibility for making it so.*
—*Noam Chomsky (b. 1928), American linguist and philosopher*

---

### This chapter provides an opportunity for you to better understand:

- The trends impacting the design and delivering of festivals into the future
- The importance of recognizing trends in festival environments that influence their viability and endurance
- Research being undertaken in associated disciplines that engage with the festival-making sector

---

Festivals have an important role in building culture. They act as a network, demonstrating how individual behaviors create links over time. A mosaic has been used as a motif in this book to highlight the interconnectedness of actions. This concept is borne of an attempt to corroborate evidence taken from real life—participation and observation, academic research, and current practice in festival management—that festivals play an important role in nurturing cultural capital, building community resilience, and lifting spirits through celebration. Figure 14.1 represents the key areas of interest as we investigate the future of festivals.

It is a collaborative affair and in each chapter we have examined the forces at play. Festivals will, or are likely to, continue to happen into the future. A series of blueprints have been explored in the book to give substance to the claim that festivals can endure and there are component parts that link and leave valuable spiritual, social, cultural, economic, and environmental legacies. They may be transient explosions of heightened experiences, but their appeal is consolidated in memory and can provide roadmaps for future relationships. Their survival is grounded in a vision colored by what partners are willing to design, develop, and deliver and are sustained by the understanding of those involved of the external environments in which they operate.

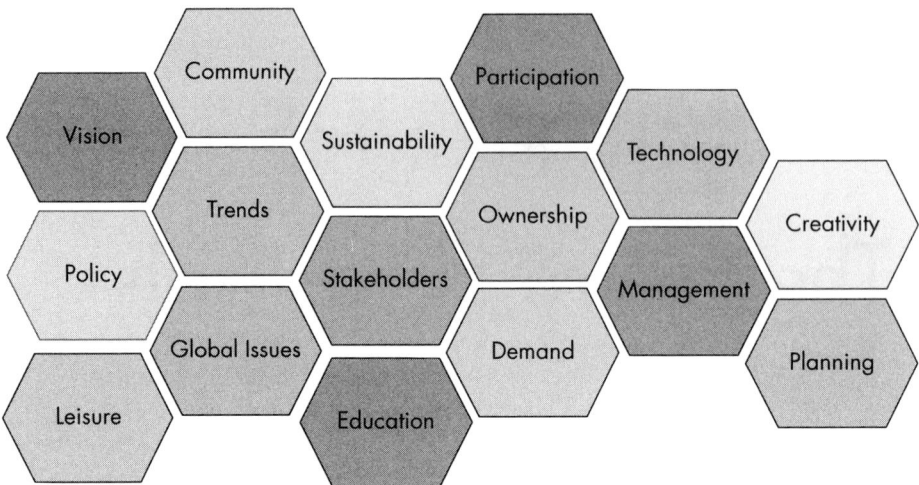

**Figure 14.1** Future Festivals' Mosaic.

## Addressing the Future of Festivals

While festival organizers may conduct many events throughout their professional lives, any event will be a once-in-a-lifetime special occasion for the people involved. It is imperative that organizers recognize the issues raised in the last chapter regarding challenges to the success of the festival and its viability over time. There are some festivals, old and new, that fail to meet their objectives and satisfy the expectations of stakeholders. Despite the expenditure of a great deal of energy and worthy aspirations, some festivals meet with mixed results, attracting limited interest from anticipated audiences, whether locally or globally. Though driven by initial enthusiasm and promise, organizers can incur substantial debt, attract negative media attention, suffer rejection from host communities, and lose the respect of participating artists, sponsors, and suppliers. Adjustments need to be made to take festivals through the 21st century to ensure their immediacy of appeal and positive lasting impressions.

### Confronting the Future

Leaders in diverse sectors of the global social, political, and economic environment are grappling with the rapid changes impacting their activity. By bringing together tools such as brainstorming and scenario-building and the development of holistic visions, they are on a steep experiential learning curve. They are coming to terms with how best to measure their success and demonstrate the return on their investment of human, financial, and creative resources into the future. They are synthesizing their historical organizational knowledge and current information on trends and practice and indulging in random guessing. Many festival enterprises committed to the long term are focusing on 5- to 10-year horizons, though civic authorities are generally obliged to seek clarity with longer-term outcomes.

Leaders and managers are looking for possible, probable, potential, plausible, preferred, and practical options. It isn't easy and while much is done in-house with festival organizers identifying emerging trends from their experience, others are outsourcing professional futurists to pinpoint relevant change agents for their consideration. By working with their peers in the festival, arts, and tourism sectors, a significant body of knowledge is being developed to better appreciate the megatrends and their interface with festivals. As they innovate and adapt, they are recognizing patterns in population growth, increased mobility of people, challenges to the global economy, personal experiences sought with individuals' discretionary incomes, natural (and sometimes extreme) changes to climate, water and energy resources, rapid and wide distribution through digital communication, and demand for authentic experiences through greater appreciation of the value of interaction with the arts and cultural heritage.

**Common sectoral preoccupations regarding the future:**
- Implications for the festival sector's costs of production resulting from the global economic slowdown
- Concern for safety and security
- Transformative role festivals can have on socioeconomic prosperity
- Importance of maintaining a host destination's social, cultural, natural, and built resources
- Effect on the sector from natural and man-made disasters and world political disruptions and terrorism
- Influence of increased engagement with electronic and other technologies
- Potential long-term consequences of climate change
- Research and education to address event management needs
- Ensuring high-quality artistic and cultural product development and distribution
- Sustaining robust festival leadership and management
- Ensuring ongoing investments from levels of government, corporate, and community
- Nurturing a culture of celebration that satisfies the desire for authentic experiences

## Global Scenarios

Futurist Ian Yeoman (2012) has a particular interest in tourism and events issues and his experience building scenarios related to the challenges to be faced into the future are instructive. Such issues as outlined below comprise the growing interest in the concept of the experience economy (Pine and Gilmore, 1999) and its application to demographic changes, consumer consumption and satisfaction, destination identity-building, economic development, and responses to growing societal affluence.

The PESTEL (political, economic, social, technological, environmental, legal) framework can provide an analytical tool to identify different macro and micro factors that may assist strategy formulation. These factors can influence a festival organization's future. The sorts of dimensions under each heading need to be evaluated and applied in association with the knowledge generated by the festival's regular monitoring and performance reviews. Consideration needs to be given to:

- **Political factors**, including the stability and structure of governments at all levels; understanding the prevailing political philosophies and history of the country; social

and cultural policies; bureaucracy; taxation and other regulations; growing affluence and power driving change; fragility of some regimes; freedom of the press; government promotion and championing of festivals
- **Economic factors**, including globalization; disposable income of potential audiences; investment environment; interest rates, foreign exchange, foreign/multinational investment; inflation; public–private investment collaborations; market competitiveness; the experience economy; supply of trained labor and costs associated; unemployment rate
- **Social factors**, including population demographics; cultural diversity; distribution of wealth and education; changes in lifestyle and trends; food security; aging populations; desire for quality experiences; emerging middle classes in the East; building a skilled labor force and managing a team; volunteerism
- **Technological factors**, including positive and negative impacts of the following through early adoption: new innovations and discoveries; rollout of digital, mobile, and wireless communication platforms; pace of innovation; attitudes to obsolescence; new materials and applications for festivals such as solar power and water filtration; transportation developments; virtual worlds; streaming of festival images simultaneous to event
- **Environmental factors**, including regulations for safe natural and built environments; waste disposal laws; low-cost and fuel-efficient transport; occupational health and safety policies; community attitudes to "green" festivals; indoor and outdoor site management; climate change; scarcity of some resources; natural disasters, weather, and seasonality
- **Legal factors**, including contractual law; insurance and employment regulations; duty of care; emergency and risk management principles and regulations; consumer law and discrimination law

The festival organization needs to leverage any advantages to nourish the prosperity of the festival in the short and long term. Leadership and management needs to keep abreast of trends domestically and internationally to ensure specific tactics can be employed to mitigate risks to delivering the vision in uncertain times.

## Chances of Survival

Research that I undertook with community based cultural festivals indicated that longer established festival organizations demonstrate a better chance of survival because of their consistent delivery of an event that encourages others to partner, share resources, or invest in its management. Organizers are obliged to renegotiate partnerships annually. Some look within the organization to source required personnel and networks informally with individuals. Others have inconsistent support of the local Council and Chamber of Commerce for a sponsored volunteer community committee, who generally uses the media for a call to action by individual residents and service clubs. The host communities over the years have come to expect that those with more formal structures in place will survive.

Organizers recognize that ideas can loosen their currency or credibility. Culture and leisure support feed off one another, allowing festivals to add meaning, memories, and traditions to the locals' way of life. Such factors as communal memory, willingness to work collaboratively, organizational traditions, and experience influence resource availability to conduct successful festivals year after year.

The value to society of a festival culture can be whether it enriches lives; enhances the cultural identity of the group, community, or nation; is a mode of expression; is an employment provider; is an industry sector; has market viability; and represents the pluralism/diversity of society. A key challenge for festivals lies in the paradox of culture, in which belonging has become a fundamental question of preservation, tradition, and survival as well as hybridity, transgression, possibility, and transformation. The mixed economy in which cultural organizations operate raises issues of government intervention in policy, planning, and financial support. The evolution and development of all culture has a political dimension. The choices made by the management of each festival organization provide guidance for other cultural organizations and present their experience in a global context. The contributions these groups make to the richness and diversity of community cultural products; the provision of opportunities for access and equity in employment and entertainment; the sharing of skills; and the enrichment of society and international profile-raising are substantial and significant.

## Festival Quality

The characteristics of a quality festival will vary for specific stakeholders. Organizers want to present all aspects of the festival to the highest standard. Most wish to be an exemplar and wish to engage with worthy partners, artists, and suppliers of outstanding caliber and proficiency. They expect their attention to detail will be met with pride, offer fulfillment and enjoyment to audiences, and receive respect from investors. Assessment of an individual festival's quality will need to take some account of the perceptions of each stakeholder group. To avoid this process becoming overly bureaucratic, Graham Devlin and Associates identified a strategy they offered Edinburgh City Council in 2001 in Table 14.1.

| **Quality as perceived by those attending a festival may be dependent on:** | **Quality as perceived by those organizing or promoting festival events may be dependent on:** |
|---|---|
| the content and delivery of the program; | availability and cost of venues; |
| evidence of innovation; | suitability and standard of the program delivered; |
| price points (not merely the entry costs) and value (for time and money); | ability to commission work; |
| access to ticketing and information; | cost-effectiveness of venue (capacity, yield, etc.); |
| timing and duration; | safety, management, and reputation; |
| the organization of the program (clashes and complementarity); | risk; |
| transport and parking; | staffing availability and expertise; |
| easy access; | resources and infrastructure; |
| effective and striking signage; | ability to attract sponsorship; |
| safety and security; | media coverage; |
| standards of venues and amenities; | coordination of Council functions, policies, and requirements (e.g., licensing restrictions); |
| opportunities for other leisure activity (e.g., shopping); | attitude of Council staff; |
| accommodation and catering; | weather; |
| international significance and/or uniqueness of event; | competition and clashes with other events |
| professional standards delivered throughout relationship | |

**Table 14.1** Quality Factors

| Quality perceived by the public sector investors may be dependent on: | Quality perceived by private sector investors may be dependent on: |
|---|---|
| match of the program delivered to that anticipated; evidence of creativity and innovation at all levels; safety and security of participants; economic impact locally and more broadly; compliance with—and furtherance of—public policy; minimal disruption to the city (e.g., noise, traffic, waste/litter); professionalism in design and delivery; timing, place in portfolio, duration; good satisfaction levels from partners; financial success against expectations; achieving sustained sponsorship; media profile for the destination and quality of image; brand visibility/public recognition of involvement; support by local community | the festival's commercial viability; future exploitation for matched aspirations; existing media recognition; corporate objectives being met; niche marketing approaches; professionalism of all partners; good satisfaction levels of audiences; financial success against expectations; public reaction against expectation; brand visibility/public recognition of involvement |
| **Quality as perceived by those who do not attend the festivals may be dependent on:** | **Local authorities can base their evaluation of the ongoing success of the festivals on the following sources:** |
| previous experience or perceptions; price; access; perceived effect on the community; level of disruption to normal routine (traffic and transport, access to shops, noise, etc.); comprehensive information and advance warning package; media reporting; economic impact to city; environmental impacts; festivals' openness to hearing their views. | peer group assessment; scale of media response; satisfaction surveys from the audience (including assessment of value for time and money) and participants; the creative legacy—the long-term impact on the year-round cultural life of the destination |
| | **New festivals should only be introduced if they satisfy a rigorous set of criteria and present a special case for their existence. Any proposal should show:** |
| | unique character to the program; a community or festival champion; a market, not detracting from existing activity; a viable business case; appropriate sponsors and public/private investment; requisite funding from the public purse; an appropriate time slot and geographic location; support from other festivals, cultural organizations, and the public |

**Table 14.1** Quality Factors *(continued)*
Based on Graham Devlin and Associates (2001).

# Life Cycle of Festivals

Festivals initially try to have strong links with their respective communities, but the growing number of visitors can bring stress on infrastructure, pressure on internal relationships, and resentment about the influx of outsiders. Like the human life cycle, degrees of change internal to the organization and its range of external relationships that occur over time can be plotted, indicating the festival's evolution. Again, the spectrum across festivals reveals differing levels of response to diverse artistic, administrative, operational and marketing issues.

Organizing a major festival takes a lot of individual and collective effort. To get the job done the organizers have to be able to give a lot of time personally and be able to call in a lot of favors and/or inspire volunteerism. All such interventions impact the trajectory of the festival from birth, its embrace by host communities, may be based on novelty effect or perceived economic benefits through the honeymoon period to settle into the conventions of business, networking, consolidation, and stability through professionalization and maturity to earned respect and sometimes into exhaustion, depleted resources and passion, and decline. The refreshment of the vision, as discussed in Chapter 13, needs to be consistent through the whole cycle, and not saved as a last gasp as the festival lurches toward demise and audience dissatisfaction.

Celebration can bind a community and it can also be the instrument that keeps it a fresh and constantly renewing experience, an elixir that keeps community relevant and responsive to the needs of the times. Annual festivals create a community of witness that marks the passage of time and notes the changing of the guard as new power relations arise and old ones change. Constant vigilance will allow preemptive actions and avert any cataclysm between partners.

## Portfolio Approach

The portfolio approach is now being embraced in destination management and marketing. Through collaborations within artform practice, a holistic approach to cross-leverage key festival elements such as cost-sharing, economies of scale, creation of content, employing more locals, and packaging tourism products and services can make festivals secure and raise a destination's profile. A mixture of large- and small-scale festivals and events, those emerging and others well established can galvanize a destination's image and identity, animating it through high and low seasons to bring about a more stable economic gain. The diversity that can be represented adds to the cultural capital of a destination and enhances the options for a community's well-being.

Marketing a portfolio of specifically targeted festivals is seen to build a destination or regional brand. It can consolidate the values held by locals and highlight the strengths of arts and cultural life. By inviting visitors and locals to "do as the locals do," the appeal of festivals can grow the appreciation of the landscape and the lifestyle choices that can include food, agriculture, heritage, special industry, and sporting pursuits. The portfolio approach can assist in pacing audience engagement throughout the year. It can build on themes that can be applied to the diverse components of the portfolio—ideas for festivals, international links, learning elements, and regional development emphases, for example. This allows the visitors' culture to intermingle with that of the residents and produce dynamic experiences for each.

## Festival Stakeholders

When considering the relationships required to deliver a successful festival into the future, the main groups of stakeholders to consider include: the board and management of the organization, festival patrons, employees and volunteers of the festival organization, local communities, suppliers to the festival, and shareholders (depending on organizational structure). As well, in stakeholder theory presented by Friedman and Miles (2006) and Freeman (1984), there are other groups and individuals who contribute to the process: the media, the general public, past and future generations (including founders), academics, competitors, unions, investors as sponsors, funders, corporate social responsibility and government at all levels as regulators and policymakers.

For arts and cultural festivals the collaboration that occurs in four major domains determines the satisfaction each party delivers and receives. The role of each builds capacity for integrated creativity inside the capsule of cooperation to carry through on commitments to strategic aspirations.

| Creator | Producer | Audience | Critics |
|---|---|---|---|
| Artistic team | Management team | Market | Competitors |
| Arts conventions | Operations team | Visitors | Media |
| Cultural partners | Sponsors | Members | Government agencies |

The enduring festival clearly validates that creative forces and administrative demands are linked. There is a progression from creator and producer to audience and critics. Each of these sectors offers substantial influence independently, but as we have seen in the mosaic purview they are called upon to collaborate with one another. Peter Drucker said, "People determine the performance capacity of an organization" (1993, p. 113). It is the yield from the human resources that really determines the festival's performance. Stakeholders within a festival organization range from founders and early leaders, managers, boards, staff, artists, volunteers, membership, and the wider operational constituency and community.

## Festival Networks

Networks are measurable, concrete patterns of relationships among entities in a social space. Some may call it a web, a maze, or a system for accounting for the connections festival organizers secure to sustain their organization. It provides a relationship framework for thinking of how beliefs, behaviors, and organizational culture are manifested and can be used to advance operations.

Of major interest to festival management are the communication connections that impact on the roles of individuals and groups within the festival organization and its partners. The information-sharing, for example, can be traced through the diverse channels used, the media, and the types and styles of flow implemented. These traits can build the social capital that creates status for the festival and its organization among partners. They can identify ways to innovate, build trust, carry obligations, and inspire action.

- *Social networks* among individuals: friendship, advice-seeking, mentorship, acquaintanceship
- *Formal networks*, contractual relationships among organizations: strategic alliances, buyer–supplier contracts, joint ventures, sponsorships, corporate social responsibility

- *Informal networks*, interorganizational relationships flow through people: professional support organizations, employee mobility, social networks that cross-organizational boundaries
- *Affiliations, shared memberships* that suggest connections: trade associations, committee memberships (Owen-Smith, 2012).

Network theory can explain many of the characteristics that are evident in the growing ties that festivals have to digital social network practice. The influence of the latter on the way the festival organization does business demonstrates the importance of understanding how networks evolve and how important they can be to sustain a festival. Some ties between members of a network have continuity (Borgatti and Halgin, 2011) and can be categorized as having strength, intensity, and duration and is known in the literature as state-type ties. Another type of link is regarded more for its discrete and transitory nature and is known as an event-type tie. Both of these enable the flow or exchange between parties or nodes.

## Festival Partnerships

Partnerships are essential for festival sustainability. Trusting relationships between multiple enterprises that generally exist independently of one another come into play for a festival through creating value for all stakeholders. This shared value assists all to prosper by building resilience to external shocks and helps stimulate cultural rejuvenation and sustainability. Each has something unique, to offer that will help the festival differentiate itself to become a favored choice of the festival going public. The mutual interdependency places substantial responsibility on each of the players involved in the collaboration. The process of evolution and change is observed in festivals being driven by individuals and agencies mindful of the financial, human resources, and "in-kind" commitments being made.

Key partners or stakeholders identified include local government, strategic alliances with regional and state government agencies, the local business community, special interest groups in destination communities, regional and local media, individual community champions, festival organizers, residents, and visitors. The emphasis and level of participation by each partner in each community varies at different times. As a result, the collaboration can source inputs locally from responsible suppliers, improve the festival's ecological footprint, and encourage respect for employees and community members as hosts to visitors. The complex interaction is influenced by the individuals involved, the organizational structures in place, traditions inherent in each community's sociocultural exchange, the history of public engagement by public authorities, and the appeal of the region to potential visitors.

Festival organizers, whether from the not-for-profit sector or commercial entrepreneurs, work with local community-based artists, who have critical roles including teaching and administering and more often invisible roles that excite interest in the host community and those working as volunteers. The for-profit cultural festival enterprise provides broader cultural services and employs artists. Both build audiences. Festivals can generate institutional links and emerging networks can more lastingly apply to other collaborative initiatives that can benefit a community. The sharing of resources and energy will allow for greater returns on investment into the future. This will deliver a higher-quality experience with lasting satisfaction for the increasingly sophisticated festival market.

# Too Many ... Choices

## Too Many Festivals

Strategic competitive advantage is strained as a level of festival saturation is reached in particular destinations or regions. Clashes of dates and times and splitting of target markets create unrest among organizers and host communities. Not everyone can survive. Overcrowding in the festival market is seen as affecting smaller festivals rather than larger, well-established, and resourced festivals. Is there a natural ceiling to the popular music festivals held in summer in the Northern Hemisphere? It is not just that audiences are stretched, but volunteers can't be everywhere and have their loyalties torn. It can be observed that a festival season is more prolonged now in some destinations where a tourism imperative is at play. Many festivals don't endure. While many contribute to the creative laboratory that supports emerging artists and encourages social inclusion and destination profile-raising, we have already identified key features of what sustains individual festivals.

Davis and Sankey (2011) discuss the pressures on organizers, bands, and audiences as they make choices about sustaining their commitment to staging summer festivals. They call into question considerations of organizational capacity to deal with weather, making unrealistic claims, and seasonal clutter making no weekend free from festivals with inflated ticket prices. They consider there is a downward spiral in the appeal of many festivals. Market forces, fuel prices, and economic downturns are making for the emergence of "boutique" festivals. These are smaller, focused on specific genres, and located in unique environments. These can concentrate the distinctive schedule, promote to discrete market segments, introduce art form practice to new audiences, and build their destination as a visitor attraction.

There is concern that some entrepreneurs engaged with such festivals don't expect to be in it for the long haul. Long-standing festival organizers are concerned that audiences are being sold short with "something new" being presented as the panacea. Many argue that a revamp of the festival experience is required and quote Melvin Benn (managing director of Festival Republic, UK), who suggests "it is becoming less dependent on the headliners and more on an overall vibe, an overall feel and experience." Just because a few festivals don't survive doesn't mean the market as a whole is in trouble. What do you think are the key issues here?

Many organizers struggle with their finances and that has consequences for relationships with suppliers, artists and festival partners. For example, artists represented by their union, the Media, Entertainment and Arts Alliance in Australia, wound up dealing with the management of Peat's Ridge Sustainable Arts and Music Festival. Its own sustainability was in question in 2013 as artists claimed the promoter failed to budget adequately for employment costs. The company that operated the festival ceased after income from ticket sales and other sources fell below the costs of the festival (Taylor, 2013).

## Too Many Elements to the Festival

Some festivals lose their way, as the program becomes a burden for audiences. They have difficulty determining what they will attend. The less-is-more principle could be applied to ensure the program doesn't overwhelm and, depending on the nature of the content, that people get time to sit, absorb, meet friends, reflect, and indulge in "being there." Contemporary society is beset with myriad diversions from new technologies, the distribution of discretionary income, peer pressure, and recreational pursuits. If festivals offer too many distractions that lack focus for patrons, the favorable impact and experience can easily be diminished. Audiences appreciate music at a music festival. They feel confident and comfortable when exposed to specialists in the company of like-minded patrons. They like to know ahead of their engagement the specific focus of the program. Information about the venue and program builds their expectations and opportunities so they can make appropriate choices in terms of their time commitment, expenditure, and travel and accommodation priorities.

## Too Many People

Incident-free crowding can occur at festivals. However, extreme crowding through inadequate crowd planning and management can result in loss of control, injuries, and fatalities. Meanwhile, crowd-induced falls and other injuries require attention during events and need to be prepared for in the festival risk management plan, along with partnerships with security and emergency and medical services. Festival patrons are coping with the tension that crowds spoil their appreciation of a given experience. Meanwhile, others perceive it as part of the fun and each accommodates such pressures of noise, drunkenness, and litter their way. Middleton (2010) discusses lessons learned about crowd management from the 2010 Love Parade Festival in Germany and explains a crowd management model named FIST.

Rock Summer festival in the Tallinn Song Festival grounds, Estonia.

## The FIST Model

The primary elements involved in crowd disasters have been determined from personal experiences, analysis of major crowd incidents, and basic traffic-flow principles (www.crowdsafe.com). The elements provide a model for understanding the causes of crowd disasters, means of prevention, and possible mitigation of an ongoing crowd incident. The elements of the model form the acronym FIST, which is a useful reminder that any crowd situation can quickly become threatening and potentially lethal (Table 14.2). The acronym is defined as follows:

**Force** (F) of the crowd, or crowd pressure
**Information** (I) upon which the crowd acts or reacts, real or perceived, true or false
**Space** (S) involved in the crowd incident, standing area, physical facilities (stairs, corridors, escalators)
**Time** (T) the duration of incident, event scheduling, facility processing rates

Major incidents have occurred in recent times that place pressure on organizers to ensure they have robust risk management plans to deal with disasters that can befall a festival. Crowd managers need to determine a wide range of information about a venue and the people occupying it before a festival occurs. Included is an assessment in the nature of the group, experience with similar groups, potential behavior patterns, projected occupancy, facility processing rates, staffing, and means of communication between staff and the crowd. Real-time information about the status of crowd conditions in large and small festival spaces is critical. A centralized crowd management and communications center should be set up for this purpose. Beyond steps taken in preparation come actions to deal

| Force | Information |
|---|---|
| Crowd forces can reach levels that are almost impossible to resist or control. Virtually all crowd deaths are due to compressive asphyxia and not the "trampling" reported by the news media. Forces are due to pushing and the domino effect of people leaning against each other. Compressive asphyxia has occurred from people being stacked up vertically, one on top of the other, or horizontal pushing and leaning forces. | In the broad systems sense, information has many forms. It includes all means of communication, the sights and sounds affecting group perceptions, public address announcements, training and actions of personnel, signs, and even ticketing. |
| **Space** | **Time** |
| The configuration, capacity, and traffic processing capabilities of assembly facilities determine degrees of crowding. Space includes standing and seating areas, projected occupancies, and the practical working capacities of corridors, ramps, stairs, doors, escalators, and elevators. | A simple illustration of timing is the more gradual and lighter density arrival process before an event, compared to the rapid egress and heavy crowd densities after an event. |

**Table 14.2** FIST Model
Based on Fruin (2002).

Fencing, signage, hard surfaces, and proximity to main festival activity allow for ease of crowd dispersal.

with the situation and then its aftermath requires attention. Fruin (2002) also suggests that actions by performers such as late cancellation, walking off stage, encouraging fans to move closer, throwing souvenirs to the audience, or other actions have precipitated inappropriate or hazardous group reactions. Entertainers should be fully informed of their own responsibilities for maintaining order, and the problems associated with inciting potentially dangerous group behaviors.

Reliable real-time communication between those responsible for crowd management and authoritative communication with the crowd are critical elements in defusing a potentially lethal crowd incident. Crowd managers have responsibility for the safety of large numbers of people. Yet there is little formalized training in crowd management principles and techniques. Police training focuses on crowd control; however, crowd management requires attention to principles and techniques associated with handling emergencies, space management, human motivations, and security.

## Creating a Safe Environment

Robust online commentary and feedback to organizers followed the *London Bloc 2012 Festival*. Broadbent (2012) reported that the festival was cancelled amid fears that chaotic scenes would jeopardize safety. Police were called. They used a metal fence to pen crowds into separate areas until they left. Patrons reported they were in two-hour queues at the newly renovated Brownfield site; people burst over the fence, surged toward the front, and jumped over the barriers by the toilets.

> There was a stampede. Security went insane, screaming and shouting to try and stop it. Eventually though, they gave up and let anyone in. I saw people getting crushed against metal fences when they were waiting to get in. At points crowds pulled down a fence and charged in as they got so fed up. I was genuinely afraid for my own safety.

Extensive fencing and checkpoints, scans, random searches, body pat-downs, and CCTV on queues and audiences are all now part of the security measures that festival organizers employ to ensure the safety of patrons. The tragic explosions of the 2013 Boston Marathon will inform the vulnerability and practices of organizers and their partners in emergency, medical, logistics, and policing sectors. Official and industry guides, checklists, government policy documents, and training need to be available on safety and security for those concerned with the spectrum of evacuations, bag searches, risk assessment plans, surveillance, and potential terrorism activity.

## Festival Programs

Festivals are keen to explain the reach their festival achieves. Festival directors are rigorous in the search process to select or commission work that will reach a contemporary audience, enhance the festival's reputation, and maintain the integrity of the art form.

Festival directors are always looking for the hook to ensure jaded audiences can embrace another "wow" factor festival element. Sometimes this resides in spectacle, pageantry, or simple fun pleasures. In 2013 the Sydney Festival launched the festivities with a 50-foot rubber duck by a visiting Dutch artist, turning the harbor into a "giant bathtub"! The YouTube link captures elements of a vast harbor, large audience numbers, animation of metropolitan open spaces, online global reach, whimsy, color, and movement.

## Festival Teamwork

As a member of a festival team it is essential that individuals be reliable. Even if they create and contribute great work, they need to be trusted by their colleagues to deliver in a timely fashion. A proactive attitude is appreciated. Teamwork demands collaboration through meeting attendance, demonstrating good communications skills, offering ideas, solving problems, and sharing a passion for the festival vision.

Each festival team member works cumulatively to consolidate the festival's vision using an agreed-upon house style, philosophy, public image, and production values that are coherent. Into the future, these values become the scaffold expected by loyal audiences, media, sponsors, and funding agencies. All of this cumulative work is based on research and professional knowledge of their audience. This allows festivals to not only give them what they want and expect, but it is a way by which to sparkle them out of passivity and challenge and charm them through a memorable display of wow factors.

Sydney Festival box-office exceeds $7.3 million (ArtsHub, 2013). The Sydney Festival (www.sydneyfestival.org.au) had 66 ticketed events and 26 free events and took place over 23 days, reaching a predicted audience of 500,000 people. The festival recorded 121 soldout performances and a box office of over $7.3 million with a program that included 10 world premieres, three Australian premieres, and 25 Australian exclusives, with more than 750 artists coming from 17 different countries. Stretching from Bondi to Penrith and from Chatswood to Sutherland, Sydney Festival took over the entire city in January.

# Memorable Audience Experiences

It is recognized that the festival audience member, whether a local resident or visitor has a subjective response to their experience. How they interpret and remember their festival interaction is dependent on their interests, previous exposure to the specific festival program, location and ambience, and motivation for attendance. The impact of the festival communication and marketing will influence their decision to engage and maybe even maintain active participation. Can festival loyalty result from satisfaction with the experience? Tourism researchers have examined the differing personal responses to the visitor experience and have built some measurement models for businesses to better understand the concepts that can inform future behavioral activity. This may be in the form of revisiting the site after a positive experience. Kim et al. (2012) have determined a scale that can be applied to festivals as attractions. It comprises seven domains: hedonism, refreshment, local culture, meaningfulness, knowledge, involvement and novelty (Table 14.3).

Kim et al.'s (2012) review of the literature raises fascinating aspects of memory formation, components of a tourist experience, and domain definitions that provide guidance in refining festival products and services. As we discovered in Chapter 12, there is useful data available to inform future festival strategies when the evaluation of the audience experience is analyzed. The demographic, psychographic, and motivational data explored in individual festival evaluations of core audiences provide valuable baseline material for assessments of future activities. The instrument they have constructed can be applied to festival management practice. The knowledge ascribed to such analysis of individual festivals can assist mature festivals in assessing their performance and validating their current practices effectively. How audience members recollect their experience informs their future association with the festival.

| Hedonism | Novelty |
|---|---|
| Thrilled about having a new experience<br>Indulged in the activities<br>Enjoyed the tourism experience<br>Exciting | Once-in-a lifetime experience<br>Unique<br>Different from previous experiences<br>Experienced something new |
| **Local culture** | **Refreshment** |
| Good impressions about the local people<br>Closely experienced the local culture<br>Local people in a destination were friendly | Liberating<br>Enjoyed sense of freedom<br>Refreshing<br>Revitalizing |
| **Meaningfulness** | **Involvement** |
| I did something meaningful<br>I did something important<br>Learned about myself | I visited a place where I really wanted to go<br>I enjoyed activities that I really wanted to do<br>I was interested in the main activities of this tourism experience |
| **Knowledge** | |
| Exploratory<br>Knowledge<br>New culture | |

Table 14.3  Factors Incorporated in a Festival Model
Based on Kim et al. (2012, p. 19).

## Local Government Engagement

Local authorities are close to community celebrations. There are numerous approaches they can take to enhance the effectiveness of festivals. They, too, have to set priorities and the political space they occupy impinges on festival-making in diverse ways. There are permits and applications organizers have to deal with to allow the festival to fulfill its statutory obligations. Many of these are on the increase. Ordinances managed by councils in California are generally levied against the potential spectrum of impact of the event. High-impact events in Fremont City Council jurisdiction include those not lasting more than two consecutive days, attracting 500 guests, for example (Bowers, 2013). City services include road closures, added security, and late-fee impositions as an incentive for organizers to submit applications on time and prevent inconveniences that may incur delay to the event. Council staff in preparing the adjustments met with 12 event organizers to present the proposed changes. These stakeholders agreed the fees were reasonable given the overall cost of some events in the city.

In Delray Beach, South Florida, Herrara (2013) reports of decisions made by Delray City Council regarding bans placed on special event organizers who had failed to pay bills. The "no pay, no play" policy endorsed by Council was to mitigate the risk of expenses incurred over recent years. A deposit is now required. Council feared that losses would not be recouped and wished discipline be encouraged to deliver the portfolio of events desired by residents. This policy was a response to Council budget cuts, less revenue from property values, and a downturn in the economy that forced scaling back on contributions made to each event through discounts, parking relief, security, garbage collection services, and equipment loans. The new policy requires organizers to pay 100% of Council staff overtime and facility rentals.

Budget cuts within local government puts pressure on its investment of any portfolio of festivals hosted in their destination. Their initial financial support is proffered for a definite period and slowly withdrawn. Many festival organizers are keen to maintain connections with local government as any funding from there can be leveraged for increased support from sponsors and state and national government agencies. Councils are often responsible for local and regional tourism promotion, so by maintaining a connection with Council, festivals can help build the brand the city/town wishes to establish.

Social pressures are also in the mix with festival links to local authorities. Ordinances banning smoking in public places increasingly impact on festival operations, from regular announcements during the program to mention on promotional materials. Smoke-free zones at events appear to proliferate now. Consumption of alcohol is prohibited in areas of public festivals sites. There are legislative implications for festivals in relation to signage, access to amenities, ethical communications, and environmental practices. Occupational health and safety policies have impacted on clothing worn by outdoor staff, reasonable and practicable principles relating to workplace hazards and risks, public urination, unauthorized food outlets, illicit drugs and alcohol, duties of care of all involved with the festival, and maintenance of plant and structures. Failure to comply involves substantial penalties.

## Host Community Engagement

How will host communities become recognized for the contribution they can make to the audience and artists' festival experience? Festival organizers recognize the need to secure the confidence and cooperation of members of the host community to build festival capacity and to satisfy the aspirations of the resident population. Many have experienced the fragile negotiations that need to take place to ensure that short-term and long-term interests of all parties are well understood and served. Host communities are key stakeholders in the brand built through collaboration. There needs to be an alignment through a shared vision and a determination to meet future challenges. By navigating the risks together diverse voices can be accommodated and sustainable engagement can be built.

Some of the approaches that have met with success are:

- Engagement through local education providers
- Opportunities for local volunteer experience within the event or within the destination as guides and ambassadors
- Active participation in planning, decision making, and evaluation of the festival
- Collaboration with local organizations such as service clubs, businesses, media, and tourism entities
- Community champions can provide leadership, help build confidence, lift spirits, and strengthen identity historically and into the future
- Contributing financially to specific needs in the host community through donations, provision of celebrities, and free access to festival highlights as incentives and rewards
- Host community sponsorship of festival elements are a concrete aspect to community engagement

Effective communication is key to dealing with potential flashpoints. We have examined the social, economic, and environmental impacts of festivals on host communities and listed key indicators that can be used to keep the information flowing between all stakeholders. There is potential for complex issues to arise if there are individuals or groups at odds with the design, content, and interaction of a festival and the place people call home. The use of all media platforms has a significant role to play in mitigating the social license for the festivals and for all its components to be accepted, even embraced. Defusing social or cultural antagonism requires sensitive and convoluted liaison. Managing challenges from grassroots social change agents—whether from vocal individuals or groups—can be a delicate, time-consuming exercise. Alienation of the local community can arise from environmental damage, crowding, lack of access to normal lifestyle, and mediation can restore some sort of acceptable balance through a community charter that builds trust, minimizes risk, and helps sustain a festival, rather than allowing it to fail.

## Technology

The world in which we live appears to be dominated by the Internet. The desire for immediate and constant connectivity includes a desire for news, at home, to the desktop, to the smartphone, and all manner of mobile devices. Technology is providing new and exciting access to sharing ideas, news, gossip, and reflection. It seems to be first in the communication stakes, across numerous publishing platforms, and has become an imperative for festival marketers. Communication creators, networkers, and problem solvers each have carved a niche via a tweet, a Facebook post, or a YouTube clip.

Into the future, smartphones, for example, will provide the information needs of patrons that can be accessed at anytime from most places. Research by Wang and colleagues (2012) into the role of smartphones in mediating the touristic experience offers an insight into the potential for festival communication frameworks. Their results reveal that the increased capabilities of smartphones (and their apps and the Internet) can change tourists' behavior and emotional states, addressing a wide variety of information needs; in particular, the instant information support of smartphones enables tourists to more effectively solve problems, share experiences, and "store" memories.

There is pressure to ensure the festival website tops the Google search page. New and original content is required to sustain interest, start a blog, encourage feedback, and invite contributions for supporters. Festival directors post challenging or "insider" articles and rehearsals, installations, and construction site progress are recorded and distributed to heighten interest in the process of mounting a festival in their attempt to demonstrate how festival partners prepare to deliver a shared vision.

Festivals will ensure participants can have access to the Internet on site, along with screens and laptops displaying tweets and photos connecting the online and offline communities with one another. The interaction with the target market will be more intensive before, during, and after the visit to the festival sites, allowing greater feedback, increasing the reach and exposure to all festival messages and gathering their further involvement and building e-word-of-mouth connections. The sharing of stories, photos, video, and links will raise the festival profile and add value to the festival's commitment to retaining loyal and influential supporters and growing the market.

Live streaming is becoming a more ubiquitous element of the festival offering in summer music festivals, theater festivals, and concerts or specialist speakers at book festivals. Organizers and sponsors are keen to reach audiences on-site and attract those who first source the program in the comfort of their home and in the future become on-site attendees. There is recognition that the live, in-your-face experience is preferred, but the delivery of quality visual and audio can provide a stimulus for future fans. The technology to record, document, and distribute virtual access to quality programs will engage with the hardware that will allow consumers a chance to modify what they see and hear—from holograms, remixes, and blog commentary at the festival and beyond.

An effective (and well-resourced) social media strategy in the future will also pose some risks, but be valuable beyond the promotional domain. The technology allows for faster and sometimes less thoughtful responses from participants and so from the festival's perspective, vigilance and a risk management plan need to be able to deal with such challenges. A proactive approach is required to manage anonymous attacks, cyber-squatting, negative retweets, identifying appropriate "likes" and "follows," posting of internal material for external consumption inadvertently or deliberately, internal posting and employment of competent staff to deal in a calm and appropriate manner with unwanted anomalies in a timely fashion.

Mark Watts-Jones, head of development and innovation at Orange UK, in building the case for technological innovation in 2050, suggests that smart devices and nanotechnologies will make the process of explaining how it feels at a festival more direct—beyond photos, videos, and words. Sensors will broadcast exactly how you feel, measuring your physical and emotional state and telling the world (or just your friends) what an amazing time you're having. "New technology can help to bring others closer to the festival experience, giving them a deeper understanding and a stronger sense of the real world experience. Technology will measure how we feel—say, watching a particular band—and put together all this information to act as an intelligent guide around the festival. It will help us discover new, exciting and relevant experiences" (Orange: The Future of Festivals: Glastonbury 2050, 2010, p. 6, *www.newsroom.orange.co.uk/*).

In fact, festival organizations will no doubt access social media not only for marketing purposes but also for staff and volunteer recruitment into the future. The same issues mentioned above in terms of privacy, improper content use, defamation and brand reputation will all require an understanding of legal, governance, and policy issues. These areas affect both the personal and business relationships.

## Travel Blogs

Online communication will feature markedly in the way places are represented. Blogs offer the opportunity to reveal an individual's interpretation of a specific destination and its products, services, and experiences. The impressions, perceptions, thoughts, and feelings are revealed through the uploading of photos, movie footage, festivalscapes, vox-pops snippets of friends and family, and blogs. Online inquiry for "my favorite festival" provides a virtual tour of global festival places. The personal and professional blogs offer a spectrum of images and narrative that can be used by marketers to learn about the existing and potential markets for their destination (Banyai and Glover, 2012; Carson, 2008). This material is freely accessible, as is the advice that comes from agencies like Trip Advisor that encourages personal perspectives. This material is of value for festival organizers as well, as they seek to better understand their audiences and get feedback on their use of public places for their entertainments and artform engagement.

## Tourism

Tourism is one of the structured environments in which culture is embedded. Festivals are situated as attractions in the tourism literature. Tourism itself is a cultural phenomenon and appears to have no shape to it because it is such a personal affair. As a cultural phenomenon tourism is not the same for everyone who may be traveling. The personal and collective responses of tourists, as well as residents to festivals over time, make a marked contribution to their success and longevity.

Getz (2008) suggests that planned festivals and events are created for a purpose and have become the domain of professionals and entrepreneurs. While some retain the involvement of individuals and community in their preparation and delivery, the event management field is now populated with experienced, networked, and skilled professionals. They lead organizations that recognize the connection with the development and marketing imperatives of tourism. Event tourism is a subset of cultural tourism, which has been explored earlier. It is absorbed into the portfolio of attractions destinations seek to exploit.

### ■ Destination Image

Destination image is among the most frequently measured constructs used by marketers and managers. If a place measures up well in the visitor experience, they may return, share their experience with others, and give feedback to residents and business. The latter could influence the image projected and any modification to enhance the reputation and appeal. Perceptions of place can be influenced by activities, authenticity, cleanliness, climate, crowding, culture, ease of access, excitement values, expense, friendliness, natural environment, safety and relaxation (Dolnicar and Grun, 2013). These are the domains of a holistic approach to designing and maintaining a spirit of place.

The definition of tourist destination has evoked controversy in the academic field. Some insist that a destination should be defined as a physical space, whereas others argue it is intangible as it generates image, expectation, and memories, while more assert a destination as a geographical area delivering integrated experiences to tourists and is also a combination of tourism products and places of interest. Festivals strengthen a destination's image (e.g., Edinburgh International Festival, New Orleans Mardi Gras); bring tax dollars to communities; enhance local pride, recreational opportunities and community cohesion; and promote sustainable development by teaching about unique cultural heritages, ethnic backgrounds, and local customs. Festivals, therefore, play a key role in a destination's competitive advantage and sociocultural sustainability by enhancing and solidifying its sense of place.

## ■ Tourism: Creativity and Innovation

Into the future greater attention will be focused on the way destinations deal with space and apply creative and innovative approaches to sharing celebrations in the public domain for locals and visitors. Attention will focus on inviting the world to share what residents value. Investment will be encouraged through collaboration to satisfy a number of commercial and community stakeholders. This will ensure tangible resources will be committed for the potential economic prosperity resulting from the cultural capital generated. The portfolio approach adopted by destinations can accommodate the traditional authentic festival. The destination marketing programs can build image and brand from local identity; hallmark events can attract global attention; and festivals, exhibitions, and markets generated by local community cultural initiatives can encourage visitors to do what the locals do. The links between the arts and tourism will be strengthened through the recognition of benefits from cooperation.

## ■ Tourism Research

How tourism and festivals are connected is increasingly included in the research agenda. Quinn (2009) examined international examples of established and effective economic links, the interdisciplinary approaches that indicate sociocultural interaction that comes from a better understanding of place and place identity, and the partnership roles tourism enterprises have in festival success. As tourism attractions, festivals will continue to be examined in relation to their spatial, social, and cultural contexts.

The arts community has long been involved with community cultural development, the nexus of host and guests, and how each consumes experience and place. Festival networks, the product development and delivery undertaken, and their contribution to the expansion of the tourism market has much in common with the research undertaken by Hager and Sung (2012) into the role played by local arts organizations. This will be better recognized in the future. Festivals will continue to assist in making sense of where people are through a shared understanding of the stories and unseen aspects of life in communities.

## ■ Food for Thought

There has been anoticeable increase in the incorporation of a distinctive "food experience" associated with festivals. There's a growing trend to ensure that all partners, not just audiences, are catered to through quality, themed, and locally produced food and beverages. With the demand for individual, authentic, and social experiences, where experience is a commodity and the arts practice is explored along with good food, knowledgeable audiences will want to have a personal, social, and sensory experience. Sponsors and VIPs can receive refreshments in discrete festival spaces; there are queues at stalls with celebrity chefs, with barista-driven espresso and bespoke meals prepared as customers watch and wait, while culturally diverse

Festivals encouraging exploration of multicultural cuisines.

menus all stimulate the messages of distinctive aspects of the services and festival experience. The festival program and the food and beverages are intertwined as memories and the vocabulary to describe each builds the ambience and stimulates curiosity and satisfaction.

# Postcard from the Edge of the Future

Those who have actively participated in arts and cultural celebrations contemplate the future of festivals. They come from diverse backgrounds, interests, and needs and reflect on the effects of their interaction and the benefits accrued. Like others considering forces impacting the future of festivals, they recognize that resilience and persistence can be problematic as are many social constructs. The historic continuity that long-standing planned public events demonstrate is of profound importance to a viable market despite the challenges that have beset administrators, artists, host communities, and authorities.

In many cases a convergence of the elite and popular cultures stand the test of time. Fashions in festive gatherings that encourage learning respond to cultural diversity and observe outstanding heritage change over time. The proliferation of boutique, specialist festivals in nontraditional locations will sustain a spirit of celebrating artform practices, embolden the experimental and passionate, and enhance community well-being and quality of life. The places that host festivals will be open to the highest expression and imagination that become immersive experiences—indoors or outdoors. The festival will reclaim the streets, allow neighbors to be in open dialogue, and the overlooked will have the capacity for excitement represented. There will be no one model for a festival, but each will respond to both the local and the global. The intergenerational pendulum swings to affect contemporary cultural practices and participation revealing the essence of a sense of community and place. Those committed to realizing the visions generated by leaders expedite the resourcing, administration, marketing, and critiquing of such vital phenomena by working collaboratively, remaining curious and ever attentive to satisfying the cry *You had to be there! What an experience!*

## CASE STUDY

### *Genius Loci: Contributions Festivals Make to Spirit of Place*

> It is difficult to design a space that will not attract people.
> What is remarkable is how often this has been accomplished.
> —*William H Whyte (1980)*

Individual places—built and natural—have uniqueness, character, identity, and spirit that differentiate them from other places. That spirit is enhanced through the values invested by residents and shared with visitors. Festivals become the cultural intermediary providing the social glue and a portal into the spirit of place. Festivals will increasingly contribute to urban or rural place animation and revitalization by ensuring they remain authentic to their character. Streets, storefronts, parkland, waterfronts, and laneways become animated; banners and installations are waved by people of all ages in celebratory mode; and projections are on buildings, music is in the air, and movement abounds. That's how people get attached to places. Even though festivities may be transitory, memories of a place experience linger.

> "Place-making" is both an overarching idea and a hands-on tool for improving a neighborhood, city, or region. It has the potential to be one of the most transformative ideas of this century.
> —*Metropolitan Planning Council of Chicago (www.pps.org)*

### Festivals and Place-making

Place-making has become increasingly important in the creation of liveable, people-friendly, walkable, resilient, and beautiful places. It provides a powerful set of tools, integrated thinking, and practice to stimulate social sustainability and revitalization for new and existing communities. More than a fashionable phrase, it's a whole new way of thinking about fostering vital communities. Planners and managers of public spaces recognize the value of collaboration as a process-driven strategy to effect change and engage community participation. Civic leaders, administrators, residents, artists, and planners recognize the significance of their input into enhancing the quality of life for locals through a vision that invests in creating sustainable livability practices.

**Place-making needs to provide for a mix of emotional, intellectual, and physical human needs by:**
Involving people
Responding to people's interests and needs
Attracting people
Creating pleasure
Being interesting

**Place-making principles should:**
Reveal and respond to the true character of the place
Involve people in the planning and activation of the place
Respond to people's emotional needs and aspirations
Be attractive to people by providing them with multiple experiences
Create pleasurable experiences that evoke aesthetic delight (Legge, 2008).

Great public spaces are where celebrations are held, social and economic exchanges take place, friends run into each other, and cultures mix. They host a spectrum of rituals from the sacred to the secular. They are the "front porches" of our public institutions—libraries, field houses, and neighborhood schools—where we interact with each other and government. When the spaces work well, they serve as a stage for our public lives. What makes some places succeed while others fail? In evaluating thousands of public spaces around the world,

Project for Public Spaces has found that successful ones have four key qualities: they are accessible; people are engaged in activities there; the space is comfortable and has a good image; and finally, it is a sociable place—one where people meet each other and take people when they come to visit (*www.pps.org/reference/grplacefeat/*).

## *Temporary and Transient*

The Burning Man Festival in Nevada is an example of the transformation of a seemingly empty space in a desert landscape that stimulates the celebration of creativity. The growth of greenfield sites for music festivals held outdoors across a weekend that offer on-site camping accommodations allow for the interaction that comes from building "communitas"— spontaneous sociability. While allowing patrons to experience the freedom from everyday life, these events stimulate a temporary sense of belonging, in Turner's (1979) "liminal spaces." These annual (re)constructions of a "village" may accommodate anywhere from a few thousand to tens of thousands of festival-goers. They exhibit the characteristics of "place," as theorized by humanist geographers like Tuan (1977). They develop their own history and generate rules and meanings specific to that location while creating infrastructure to service the volume and interests of patrons. Their place attachment is real, long after the physical engagement.

Urban landscapes, too, provide a geography and heritage that informs contemporary usage including festivities that build on endemic food and beverage, traditional recreation pursuits from parades and pageantry, and relaxation for all sections of the community. These spaces can be appropriated for annual street festivals like Songkran in Bangkok, Thailand; the rites of passage through a tribal show by Mud Men at the Goroka Festival in Papua New Guinea; the high-profile film festival promenade in Cannes, France; the books-on-the-border celebration through the streets of the village of Hay-on-Wye, Wales; or the vibrancy of thousands of samba school performers entertaining millions of spectators during Carnival in Rio de Janiero.

An analysis of the UK Manchester Jazz Festival (Oakes and Warnaby, 2011) demonstrates how urban spaces contribute a holistic aesthetic experience for residents and visitors by reshaping perceptions allowing interaction with artists—the spectrum of creator, producer, and consumer in close proximity. The outputs for public consumption can range from the professional, experimentally rigorous to emerging, informal, or simple amateur busking. The supply side may involve a continuum from exclusive (ticketed, fee for service) access through to inclusive (unrestricted and free) and generally involves some sort of planned creativity as the everyday, meaningful spaces become "managed." The urban places can build reenchantment through the co-creation of the ancient Greek agora or medieval market square.

Such public offerings can target specific audiences that are currently underrepresented, for example, children, disabled people, the aged, or culturally diverse. It can lead to the appropriation of nontraditional spaces that will provide a greater level of familiarity or comfort. A shift from the Central Business District (CBD) to suburban heartlands, parklands, and waterfronts has proved to be popular and has built confidence in using such platforms for outdoor film festivals, light projections on historic buildings, ephemeral installations that capture the spirit of the place and establish a cultural image for the destination through the atmosphere it generates. Self-esteem for locals can increase and promotion of such interfaces will encourage greater visitation.

The inputs required delivering "eventfulness" in public spaces and places are explored by Richards and Palmer in their book, *Eventful Cities* (2010). They outline the processes that have been employed around the world by cities committed to designing and conducting festivals and events. While the outputs will vary from destination to destination, the concepts they examine highlight the benefits and the challenges that accrue from visionary leadership, political will, experienced and energetic managers and the collaboration, planning, and respect for global trends required for festivities to function authentically.

# FROM INSIDE THE MOSAIC

## The Zeitgeist of Festivals: The Spirit of the Time

### Lyndon Terracini, AM, Opera Australia Artistic Director

Lyndon Terracini

Lyndon Terracini is the Artistic Director of Opera Australia. Earlier, his appointment as Artistic Director of Brisbane Festival came after outstanding success in the same role at Queensland Music Festival. Terracini has enjoyed a highly successful international opera career as well as a career as an actor in film and music theater, director, and writer in Australia and overseas.

As a young singer, I always found it tremendously exciting to be invited to perform at one of the big festivals in Australia. In 1974, when I first sang at the Adelaide Festival, I couldn't believe how thrilling it was. The whole city was alive and pulsating with the festival. There were artists from all over the world performing in this one city and the excitement at the performances and after-show cabaret venues was fantastic.

It was a time when you could meet artists from many different places, to see them work, and to soak up the atmosphere of a truly outstanding arts and cultural feast. There were no union restrictions on who could or couldn't perform. It was simply about artists wanting to make music, to make art as best they could.

Similarly, when I was invited to sing at the first Montepulciano Festival in Italy, there was an incredible buzz in that small Tuscan town as artists from all over the world arrived to make art together and to urge each other to excel and to do something special. The entire community became part of the festival; they sewed the costumes, built the sets, and worked in a number of different areas to ensure that "their" festival worked. In many ways it is the atmosphere, the ideas, that are products of artistic conversations and the thrill of performing that generates excitement between the performers that ignites the artistic flame of a truly great festival. The late-night discussions, often including audience members, become catalysts for further collaborations and the seed for a new creation was often sown there, in that moment, on a warm summer's evening at a festival.

That joy and excitement is then easily communicated to the audience…and that's ultimately what great festivals are about. For many reasons, that excitement has dissipated and festivals are now more routine than magical…more formulaic than spontaneous.

Frankly I believe there is a crisis in festival land…and there has been for some time.

The capital city arts centers are now programming within a festival context and often in direct competition with the established festivals. These "alternative" festivals are making very strong connections with their constituents and are thereby embracing a much larger audience.

However, the "mantra" for arts festivals is to produce new and challenging work, and preferably new work, by Australian composers, choreographers, and writers, as well as the most interesting new work from around the world.

Consequently there is confusion in the marketplace about what an arts festival should be, and that confusion has led to a diminution in the festivals themselves, and by extension their audiences.

The festival that generates genuine interest, that attracts large and enthusiastic audiences, and that genuinely connects to the culture of its constituents is the Woodford Folk Festival. Every year, between Christmas and New Year's, between 80,000 and 100,000 people travel to the Woodford site near Caboolture north of Brisbane. It is a genuine festival…it's a celebration…and its audience loves it! Paradoxically it receives very little government funding and derives virtually all of its income from ticket sales. Woodford battles rain, heat, and mud but its constituents keep coming back. However, it simply has to sell tickets…and a lot of them…and therein lies the difference. While government-funded capital city festivals program for the usual arts crowd, Woodford programs for its large and eclectic audience.

Now there will be those who will want to raise the specter of art and populism. Let me say this… and I've said it before…great art is popular and if the audience is not responding to what is being programmed, then you need to find either another audience, or another program.

It is essential to ensure that there is genuine communication and relevance to the community in which the festival takes place and there needs to be a genuine reason for having a festival. It should not be imposed on the community and it needs to come from the desire of the community to celebrate something specific and relevant in its life. The joy of playing chamber music by a number of enthusiasts might develop into a festival; however, it depends entirely on whether or not there is an audience for that particular activity in that particular place.

There is significant pressure on artistic directors to "push the boundaries," present "brave programming," and to be "innovative," which is often interpreted through a very narrow repertoire spectrum. Frankly, brave programming these days is programming that appeals to and secures an audience.

I'm not suggesting that contemporary work does not have a place in a festival program—of course it does—but the aesthetic must be recalibrated so that audiences are connected in a real and demonstrable way.

I recently had the great pleasure of attending a theatrical production of *The Secret River* directed by Neil Armfield. It was a truly memorable and wonderful experience and connected with its audience very powerfully. It's about us…it's about our place… and it resonates with contemporary Australians very strongly. *The Secret River* was included in the Sydney Festival program and in my view was the best event in the entire festival.

The broader community should always feel part of a cultural and artistic event that has relevance to a significant number of people within the city, and while it's vital for any event to be creative and innovative, innovation does not mean a small audience. On the contrary. Very often the most innovative events are extremely popular. *Handa Opera on Sydney Harbour* was one such event. It is fundamentally a festival and it has changed the operatic landscape in Sydney, and indeed Australia, dramatically.

There are many ways to change how festivals are now perceived, but there needs to be a radical change in how they are articulated to an audience. If the formerly very healthy festival culture is to be taken off life support, it needs to stop programming for the perceived arts festival audience and start playing to a potentially large audience and its community.

It may also be that this methodology of cultural entertainment has passed its use by date. Perhaps arts festivals no longer have the same allure as they once enjoyed. Whatever the reason, audiences have changed, the ethnic demographic has changed, and the world of arts festivals has been left floundering.

From the perspective of an observer, it seems to me that a patchwork quilt of boutique but specific festivals may now be a better alternative. Even festivals that focus on relatively obscure subject matter can find an audience if the subject is of interest to enough people.

However, a nonspecific, generalized capital city arts festival seems to no longer have the fascination it had for audiences 30 years ago. Audiences want to see and hear something special that moves them, excites them, makes them laugh and cry…something magical…and they want to be part of it.

Finding the answer to this dilemma is the difficulty all festivals now have to address. It may be that the form, rather than the program, is where most energy should be directed, and it may also be that festivals need to think about what a festival means within a broader philosophical context…how could a festival change the way we think or perceive our country, our city…or even our suburb.

A localized celebration can be a very powerful mechanism for the soul of a community as well as being an artistic event of importance. The events that I initiated and produced for the Queensland Music Festival from 2001 until 2005 were specifically curated for each individual community. Bobcat Dancing and Bobcat Magic in Mt. Isa were large-scale, outdoor, heavy-machinery musicals that reflected very much the culture of Mt. Isa. Over three evenings, 18,000 people attended in a town with a population of 21,000. We created many such "festivals" in towns across Queensland that had as their core methodology the philosophy of culture, of place.

The key to this is ownership by the community and an understanding of what a festival means to the individuals who live in that community. Something specific to that place that reflects the culture is of vital importance if the festival is to be successful, and it's the reason other people will travel to be part of it.

In any case some strategic thinking is necessary to redefine what can be a community, arts, and cultural celebration of importance for 21st-century Australia. This discussion probably needs to take place outside of government offices and without academics and arts bureaucrats. It probably also needs some independent promoters who are working consistently internationally to be part of a small group of players who have a real understanding of what a festival is and how it can be an event of importance…and how it can be a true celebration of the city in which it lives.

At present every capital-city festival is very similar in its structure and programming and this monochromatic aesthetic does not generate genuine excitement and enthusiasm for a potential audience.

Finally, can I say that the festival world is a wonderful space that I have been privileged to inhabit, both as a performer and as an artistic director. It is capable of generating truly magical and indeed life-changing experiences, but all creative forms come to a fork in the road that determines their future paths. The festivals are now at that point, and many of us are eager to support the choices that need to be made, and collectively hope that those choices are rigorous enough in their creative thought to find an inspiring new way.

## Festival Ideas and Issues

1. Sustainability should be at the heart of our collective artistic vision. Creativity is the most sustainable and renewable energy on the planet (Alison Ticknell of Julie's Bicycle, 2012). Discuss how this can be applied to the future of festivals.
2. A festival that features big international names alongside local talent is the ideal. Is that a system that works and how do they complement each other?
3. Can the contribution individual festival organizations make to the nation's cultural diversity occur independently of government policy and practice?
4. How can festivals best achieve a balance of artistic/cultural imperatives and bureaucratic expectations?
5. If we look for our own cultural identity we find here a particular sense of life, a particular community of experience hardly needing expression, through which the characteristics of our way of life that an external analyst would describe are in some way passed, giving them a particular and characteristic color (Williams, 1963). Can this be applied to arts and cultural festivals into the future? How would it be manifested?

## Festival Focus Activities

1. Examine the distinctive stages in the life cycle of a particular festival. In what ways does management affect sustainability? How might thinking ahead help avoid failure? How do festivals survive each stage and remain competitive? Give examples.
2. Investigate how festival organizers are using cultural and historic themes to develop a portfolio of festivals and events to attract visitors and create a cultural image of the

host destination. Evaluate one or two festivals to establish how the host communities celebrate their culture.
3. Undertake a PESTEL analysis of a festival with which you are familiar to establish how it may have responded to global political, economic, social, technological, environmental, and legal trends. Identify five major factors that have been addressed.
4. What is the difference between crowd control and crowd management in a festival context? What are some effective strategies you have observed to mitigate risks to people and property?
5. In small groups visit specific neighborhoods like downtown/CBD, urban parkland, open greenfield sites, or significant public buildings to experience the "feeling" of the place using all or a combination of your senses, including the intuitive sense. Discuss how the locations could respond to accommodating planned public festivals. Draw up a proposal using place-making good practice strategies. Check Project for Public Places for some stimulation and guidance.

## Suggested Reading

Anderton, C.B. *(Re)Constructing Music Festival Places*. PhD thesis, University of Wales, Swansea, 2006.
ArtsHubAustralia, *Sydney festival box-office exceeds $7.3m,* 2013. http://au.artshub.com/au/news-article/news/arts/sydney-festival-box-office-exceeds-7-dollars3m-193896).
Banyai, M., and T. D. Glover, T.D. "Evaluating Research Methods on Travel Blogs." *Journal of Travel Research* 51, no. 3 (2012): 267–277.
Borgatti, S. P., and D. S. Halgin. "On Network Theory." *Organisational Science* September/October 22(5) (2011): 1168–1181.
Bowers, W., 2013. http://www.mercurynews.com/fremont/ci_22396058/fees-hold-special-events-fremont-set-increase.
Carson, D. "The 'Blogoshpere' as a Market Research Tool for Tourism Destinations: A Case Study of Australia's Northern Territory." *Journal of Vacation Marketing* 14 (2008): 111–119.
Cooper, C. *Essentials of Tourism*. New York: Prentice Hall, 2012.
Davis, J. and E. Sankey. *Are Pop Festivals on Their Way Out?* 2011. http://www.guardian.co.uk/commentisfree/2011/aug/07/are-pop-festivals-over-debate.
Dolnicar, S., and B. Grun. "Validly Measuring Destination Image in Survey Studies." *Journal of Travel Research* 52, no. 1 (2013): 3–14.
Drucker, P. *Managing the Non-Profit Organisation*. Oxford, UK: Butterworth Heinemann, 1993.
Freeman, R. E. *Strategic Management: A Stakeholder Approach*. Boston, MA: Pitman, 1984.
Friedman, A. L., and S. Miles. *Stakeholders: Theory and Practice*. Oxford, UK: Oxford University Press, 2006.
Fruin, J. J. *The Causes and Prevention of Crowd Disasters*, 2002. www.crowdsafe.com.
Getz, D. "Event tourism: Definition, evolution and research." *Tourism Management* 29 (2008): 403–428.
Getz, D. *Event Tourism: Concepts, International Case Studies and Research*. Putnam Valley, NY: Cognizant Communication Corporation, 2013.
Glenn, M. *Organisational Agility: How Business Can Survive and Thrive in Turbulent Times*. Economist Intelligence Unit, London, UK: The Economist, 2009.
Graham Devlin and Associates. *Festivals and the City, the Edinburgh Festivals Strategy*. Edinburgh, UK: City of Edinburgh Council, 2001.

Hager, A. A., and H. K. Sung. "Local arts agencies as destination management organisations." *Journal of Travel Research* 51, no. 4 (2012): 400–411.

Kim, J.-H., J. R. B. Ritchie, and B. McCormick. "Development of a Scale to Measure Memorable Tourism Experiences." *Journal of Travel Research* 51, no. 1 (2012): 12–25.

Lee, S. S., and J. Goldblatt. "The current and future impacts of the 2007–2009 economic recession on the festival and event industry." *International Journal of Event and Festival Management* 3, no. 2 (2012): 137–148.

Legge, K., *Cultural Glue: The Secret to Making Great Places,* Arch Review, *Public Journal,* no. 105 (2008): 62–64.

Middleton, W. "Avoiding the crush." *Australasian Leisure Management* 81 (2010): 20–22.

Oakes, S., and G. Warnaby. "Conceptualising the management and consumption of live music in urban space." *Marketing Theory* 11, no. 4 (2011): 405–418.

Quinn, B. "Changing festival places: Insights from Galway." *Social and Cultural Geography* 6, no. 2 (2005): 237–252.

Quinn, B. "Festivals, events and tourism," in *The Sage Handbook of Tourism Studies,* eds. T. Jamal and M. Robinson. London: Sage, 483–503.

Richards, G. *Cultural Tourism in Europe.* Association for Tourism and Leisure Education, 2005. Originally published by CAB International Wallingford, UK (1996), reissued electronic format by (ATLAS) www.altas-euro.org.

Richards, G., and R. Palmer, R. *Eventful Cities, Cultural Management and Urban Revitalisation.* Oxford, UK: Butterworth-Heinemann, 2010.

Robertson, M. "A futurist view on the future of events," in *The Handbook of Events*, eds. S. Page and J. Connell (New York: Routledge), 2012.

Stern, M. J., and S. C. Seifert. *Culture Builds Community Evaluation* (Summary Report). Philadelphia, PA: Social Impact of the Arts Project, University of Pennsylvania School of Social Work, 2002.

Tuan, Y.-F. *Space and Place: The Perspective of Experience.* London, UK: Edward Arnold, 1977.

Taylor, A., *Performers Left Unpaid as Festival Folds,* (2013). http://www.smh.com.au/entertainment/performers-left-unpaid-as-festival-folds-20130124-2d8t3.html#ixzz2ItA1DwtK.

Turner, V. *The Ritual Process.* Chicago: Aldine, 1969.

Turner, V. "Frame, Flow and Reflection: Ritual and Drama as Public Liminality." *Japanese Journal of Religious Studies* 6, no. 4 (1979): 465–499.

Wang, D., S. Park, and D. R. Fesenmaier. "The Role of Smartphones in Mediating the Touristic Experience." *Journal of Travel Research* 51, no. 4 (2012): 371–387.

Whyte, B., T. Hood, and B. P. White (eds.). *Cultural and Heritage Tourism: A Handbook for Community Champions.* Quebec, Canada: Federal Provincial Territorial Ministers of Culture and Heritage, 2012.

Whyte, W. H. *Social Life of Small Urban Spaces.* Washington, DC: The Conservation Foundation, 1980.

Williams, R. *Keywords: A Vocabulary of Culture and Society.* Oxford, UK: Oxford University Press, 1983.

Williams, R. *Culture and Society 1780–1950.* Harmondsworth, UK: Penguin, 1963.

Yeoman, I., *The Future of Events and Festivals,* (2012). http://www.tomorrowstourist.com/eventsandfestivals.php.

Ziakos, V. "Understanding an event portfolio: The uncovering of interrelationships, synergies and leveraging opportunities." Journal of Policy Research in Tourism, Leisure and Events 2, no. 2 (2010): 144–164.

# ABBREVIATIONS

| | |
|---|---|
| **BAFA** | British Arts Festivals Association |
| **CEO** | Chief executive officer |
| **CBD** | Central business district |
| **EFA** | European Festivals Association |
| **EMBOK** | Event Management Body of Knowledge |
| **ICT** | Information communication technology |
| **IFEA** | International Festival and Events Association |
| **ISES** | International Special Events Society |
| **KPIs** | Key performance indicators |
| **NGO** | Nongovernment organization |
| **NFP** | Not-for-profit (organization) |
| **ROI** | Return on investment |
| **USP** | Unique selling proposition |
| **UNESCO** | United Nations Educational, Scientific and Cultural Organization |
| **VIP** | Very important person |
| **WFN** | World Festival Network |
| **WFN** | World Fringe Network |
| **WoM** | Word of mouth |

# GLOSSARY

**Artistic exchange** Transference of emotion and meaning between an artist or curator and the public, bounded in time between the start and finish of the event or experience.

**Audience engagement** Guiding philosophy in the creation and delivery of arts experiences in which the paramount concern is maximizing impact on the participant. Others refer to this vein of work as "enrichment programming" or "adult education." The term "audience" in the broadest sense, refers to groups of people who attend and participate in exhibitions, performances, film screenings, and other types of events.

**Audience profile** Description of the demographics of people who attend an event, expressed in terms such as gender, age, ethnicity, disability, place of residence, socioeconomic status, educational attainment, or employment status.

**Carrying capacity** Number of individuals who can be supported in a given area within natural resource limits, and without degrading the natural social, cultural, and economic environment for present and future generations. The carrying capacity for any given area is not fixed. It can be altered by improved technology, but mostly it is changed for the worse by pressures that accompany a population increase. As the environment is degraded, carrying capacity actually shrinks, leaving the environment no longer able to support even the number of people who could formerly have lived in the area on a sustainable basis. No population can live beyond the environment's carrying capacity for very long.

**Collaboration** Brings together multiple people to work together in a mutually beneficial and well-defined relationship to achieve a common goal.

**Community** Comprises people who identify themselves as a group because of their shared cultural heritage, spirituality, geographic location, special interest, or gender. This system of relationships accommodates the need for freedom of the individual and a need for connectedness. Community is a phenomenon that follows a predictable pattern.

**Community capital** Aggregate of natural, human, social, and built capital from which a community receives benefits and on which the community relies for continued existence.

To ensure sustainability, all four types of capital need to be actively pursued so communities can function successfully.

**Community festival** Community-based festivals and events, also called local events, originate (as the name suggests) within a sector of the community that has a need or desire to celebrate a feature of its life or history. Community-based festivals and events can be of limited duration or be sustained over generations to celebrate local identity and culture.

**Community planning and management** Process of identifying the types and timeliness of information sharing among festival stakeholders, ensuring maintaintenace of up-to-date awareness of festival/project design, development, and delivery. Formal communications need to be managed through a clearly tracked and recorded, created, reviewed, and documented process within the festival organization.

**Community tourism** Places the emphasis on resident participation in tourism policymaking, planning, and consultation in destination management and marketing. Small communities can monitor, criticize, and assist in directing tourism development. Residents share their culture willingly and can gain employment through enterprises servicing visitors.

**Community well-being** Outcomes described by Labonte, Hancock, and Edwards (1999), Landry (1994), and cited in Wills (2001, p. 23) are:

Livability—natural and built environments for healthy and easy living;
Equity—equal opportunity for the development of human potential;
Conviviality—people living well together;
Adequate prosperity—consuming less but with sufficiency;
Sustainability—sufficient development without threatening viability;
Viability—remaining within the ecological limits and maintaining species diversity;
Vitality—resulting from activity and interaction between people.

**Coordination** Bringing together of different and multiple working elements for consolidation toward a shared outcome.

**Cultural commoditization (commodification)** Often regarded as an outcome of tourism impacts on small-scale communities, it is a process in which cultural forms and practices are given a monetary value and sold as commodities in the tourist market. Culture can lose its authenticity and its former meaning for people.

**Cultural tourism** Art of participating in another culture, of relating to people and places that demonstrate a strong sense of their own identity. It is concerned with the ways of life of a place, encouraging visitors to do what the locals do related to the production of art and cultural practices.

Cultural tourism is about the dynamic human environment. It is concerned with the whole range of human creation, custom, heritage and activity. It can form partnerships to create the content of tourism (e.g. it can act as a catalyst for further, broader development) associated with the built and natural environment, the arts industry, recreation, conventions and events, civic design, community development, health, and education.

**Culture** Integrated pattern of human behavior that includes thought, speech, action, and artifacts and is dependent on a capacity for learning and transmitting knowledge to succeeding generations. It is a dynamic value system of learned elements with assumptions, conventions, beliefs, and rules permitting members of a group to relate to each other and to the world, to communicate, and to develop their creative potential.

Culture embraces all the manifestations of social habits of a community, the reactions of the individual as affected by the habits of the group in which he or she lives, and the products of human activities as determined by these habits.

**Customer experience map** Graphical representation of the service journey of a customer. It shows their perspective from the beginning, middle, and end as they engage a service to achieve their goal, showing the range of tangible and quantitative interactions, triggers, and touchpoints, as well as the intangible and qualitative motivations, frustrations, and meanings.

**Festival** Special planned event recognizing a unique moment in time with ceremony and ritual to satisfy specific needs. Local community events may be an activity established to involve the local population in a shared experience to their mutual benefit. Characteristics include celebration marked by special observances and performances consisting of fun, conviviality, and cheerfulness.

**Guest** Individual or group visiting a location that is not their home and anticipating hospitality.

**Host** Individual or group predisposed to offering hospitality in a welcoming sociable manner to visitors.

**Nonprofit organization (profit-for-purpose)** Organization where any profit it makes is used to further its objectives and is not distributed to any of its members. It can still make a profit, but this profit must be used to carry out its purposes. Operate in many areas of society.

**Project management** Framework accommodating the skills, tools, and professional processes required to design and deliver a successful project within a specific timeframe. It involves a coalition of appropriate human resources that set priorities and compliance protocols; plans the allocation of tasks, roles, and responsibilities; communicates clearly; develops teamwork; overcomes challenges; maximizes reach; identifies milestones; tracks progress through the project's life cycle; ensures appropriate investment and allocation of resources; manages scheduling and documentation; monitors outputs and outcomes; and evaluates key inputs. The endeavor undertaken needs to fit with the organization's overall aims and objectives and as such satisfy the festival's core vision and strategic direction.

**Resilient community** Takes intentional action to enhance the personal and collective capacity of its citizens and institutions to respond to and influence the course of social and economic change.

**Sense of place** Contemporary discussion of a "sense of place" has grown from the geographical work undertaken in the 1970s. It was noted that place had a "spirit" or a "personality" and humans demonstrate their sense of place when they apply their moral and aesthetic discernment to sites and locations (Tuan, 1974). Authors suggest that a sense of place varies for each individual over time (Stewart et al., 1998). Distinctions are made in the literature between sense of place theory terms as "public symbol" and "field of care" (Tuan, 1974).

Typically the concept of "sense of place" refers to an individual's ability to develop feelings of attachment to particular settings based on combinations of use, attentiveness, and emotion.

**SMART objectives** S, specific; M, measurable; A, achievable; R, relevant; T, timeframe. These become essential elements in the planning process for festivals like any other project management activity.

**Social and cultural impacts** Factors that affect the values, beliefs, interests, aspirations, cultural systems, and lifestyle of a destination. Impacts have implications for the spaces between people in communities in terms of "social capital."

**Social capital** The social capital of a society includes the institutions, the relationships, the attitudes and values that govern interactions among people and contribute to economic and social development. It includes the shared values and rules for social conduct expressed in personal relationships, trust and a common sense of civic responsibility, that makes a society more than a collection of individuals. Without a degree of common identification with forms of governance, cultural norms and social rules, it is difficult to imagine a functioning society

**Social justice** Grounded in the intrinsic value of each person, it aims at maximizing the potential of self-realization and quality of life for all people through social intervention and interaction and social empowerment. Social justice in terms of equal access to power and resources, equality of opportunity, and equality of outcomes is influenced by and dependent upon society acknowledging and adhering to a range of interrelated rights. Festivals can respond to these major aspects of human interaction through content, access, participation, and evaluation of capacity for resilience.

**Social media** Increasingly platforms used to create, share, and exchange information and ideas in virtual communities and networks. Utilized in festival management for marketing, recruitment, documentation, and communication activity. It provides opportunities to build relationships with stakeholders based on Internet technology, encouraging interaction between multiple audio-visual tools and programs to increase reach, frequency, usability, immediacy, and permanence through visual, textual and audio stimuli. Popular formats include websites, blogs, Facebook, YouTube, and Twitter, with more mobile technologies attracting attention.

**Tourist** Persons who travel away from their normal residential region for a temporary period of at least one night, to the extent that their behavior involves a search for leisure experiences from interactions with features or characteristics of places they choose to visit (Leiper, 1995, p.11).

**Well-being** Good or satisfactory condition of existence.

# References

Community Resilience, *The Community Resilience Manual, Making Waves* 10, no. 4 (1999): 11.

Hancock, T., R. LaBonte, and R. Edwards. "Indicators That Count! Measuring Population Health at the Community Level." *Canadian Journal of Public Health, Supplement,* 90(1), (1999): 22–26.

Leiper, N. *Tourism Management.* Melbourne: RMIT Press, 1995.

Stewart, E. J., B. M. Hayward, P. J. Devlin, and V. G. Kirby. "The 'Place' of Interpretation: A New Approach to the Value of Interpretation." *Tourism Management* 19 (3), (1998): 257–266.

The World Bank. *The Initiative on Defining, Monitoring and Measuring Social Capital: Overview and Program Description,* Working paper no. 1 (1998): 1.

Tuan, Y.-F. *Topophilia: A Study of Environmental Perceptions, Attitudes and Values.* New Jersey: Prentice-Hall Inc, 1974.

Tuan, Y.-F. *Space and Place—The Perspective of Experience.* London: Edward Arnold, 1977.

Tuan, Y.-F. *Space and Place—The Perspective of Experience.* Minneapolis, MN: University of Minnesota Press, 1990.

Wills, J. *Just, Vibrant and Sustainable Communities: A Framework for Progressing and Measuring Community Wellbeing.* Townsville: Local Government Community Services of Australia, 2001.

# INDEX

Note: Page numbers with "f" indicate figures; those with "t" indicate tables.

Acceptance, 53t
Access, service quality and, 203
Accountability, 276
Action, coordinated, 36
Adams, B., 58
Adams, S., 81
Adaptive skills, 75
Addressing future of festivals, 330–31
Adelaide Fringe Festival, 135, 189, 266t, 293
Advertising, 230t, 245
AEA Consulting, 35
Aesthetic realm of experience, 127
Affiliations, shared memberships, 337
Age, buying behavior and, 130f, 131
Alerts, 239
Al Jouf Olive Festival, 168
Alms-giving, 54
Andersson, T., 55–56
Annoyance, 53t
Antagonism, 53t
Apathy, 53t
App, 239
Apple Days, 51
Archer, R., 190–91, 323
Arcodia, C. V., 76
Armfield, N., 353
Art and About Festival, 213
Art Biennales, 10
Art in the Heart precinct, 114
Artistic director, 80–81
Artists, mementoes for, 208t
Art on The Rocks, 142

Arts attendance journey, 129
Arts-based festivals, 6, 13, 14, 15
Arts Hub, 38
Arts Northern Rivers, 192–93
Ash Wednesday, 7, 8
Assurance, service quality and, 203, 278
Atelier for Young Festival Managers, 313
Atmosphere, 125, 125f, 126
At symbol (@), 239
Attitudes, buying behavior and, 130f, 131
Audience
  assess motivations of current and potential, 132–33, 133t
  attract and retain, 125, 125f
  best fit, establishing, 131–33
  buying behavior, major factors influencing, 130–31, 130f
  contributions, 317
  engagement, 128t, 243, 335
  experiences, memorable, 343
  festival experience and, 121–26, 122f
    flow, 124, 125–26
    mapping audience journey, 123–24, 124t
    personal cultural interests and practices, 122–23
  festival satisfaction and, 126–29
    arts attendance journey, 129
    consumer orientation, 128

  consumption analysis, 129
  decision making, 129
  environmental scans, 127–28, 128t
  marketing mechanisms and reach, 134–39
    biennales, 137–38, 138t
    global writers' festivals, 135, 136–37
  reaching, 224–25
  relationships with, 121
  segments within market for arts, culture, heritage and, 132
  target, alignment with, 120–43
  target audience mosaic, 121
Audio, 311t
Audio-visual equipment, 311t
Australian Celtic Festival, 68–69

Back Alley Gallery, 114
Baeker, G., 258
BAFA. See British Arts Festivals Association (BAFA)
Baha Honey Festival, 168
Baker Associates, 289
Banners, 180
Barker, T., 76
Baseline data, defined, 280t
Battle of the Oranges, 189t
Beliefs, buying behavior and, 130f, 131
Bellingen Global Carnival, 114
Beltane Fire Festival, Calton Hill, Edinburgh, Scotland, 6t

365

Benefactors, mementoes for, 208t
Benn, M., 338
Berlin Biennale, 138t
Berry, L. L., 202
Best fit, establishing, 131–33
Biennale de Lyon, 138t
Biennale of Sydney, 138t
Biennales, 137–38, 138t
Big Day Out, 298
Blogger, 237
Blogs, 234, 237–38, 283t
   travel, 347
Bluesfest, 43–44, 148
Boards, 79–80, 79t
Bobcat Dancing, 353
Bobcat Magic, 353
Boden, M., 176
Bolshoi Ballet, 316
Bonding, 50t
Bonding social capital, 262
Bonnaroo Music and Arts Festival, 165, 317
Bonnaroo Solar Stage, 317
Bonnaroo Works Fund, 317
Book festivals, 135
Bookworm International Literary Festival, 136
Boosterism, 290–91
BOP Consulting, 212
BorderFest, 66–67
   creating enduring festival, 66–67
   sense of community and place, 66
Boston Marathon, 342
Bowdin, G., 90
Bowley, R., 234
Boyle, D., 184
Brands/branding, 36, 245
   in destinations, 65
   festival experience and, 211
   reputation, building, 256–57
Bregenz Festival, 109t
Bridging social capital, 262
Brisbane Festival, 5, 259
British Arts Festivals Association (BAFA), 187
Brook, P., 321
Brown, A. S., 127
Bruce, G., 268
Buddha, 18, 261–62
Budget, 154
Burning Man Festival, 77t, 148, 194, 217–18, 260, 351
Businesses, mementoes for, 208t
Buskers Stage, 192
Buxton Festival Fringe, 266t

Buying behavior, factors influencing, 130–31, 130f
   cultural, 130
   personal, 131
   psychological, 131
   social, 130, 131
Byron Bay Writers' Festival, 135, 136, 137

Cabaret, Film, and Guitar Festivals, 175
Cabaret Festival, 293
Calgary Fringe Festival, 266t
Calgary Stampede, 189t
Cambridge Fringe Festival, 266t
Cameron, N., 194–95
Campaign sites, 235, 236
Camp Bestival, 166
Camping, 181
Canada Day, 254
Canadian Tourism Human Resource Council (CTHRC), 90
Canadian Tulip Festival, 109t, 186
*Canterbury Tales* (Chaucer), 8
Capital, community, 59–60
Capital for festivals, maximizing, 165–66
   areas attracting responses among organizers to beneficial effect, 165
   environmental good practice, care and attention to, 165–66
   "greening" festivals, principles of, 166
   initiatives for commitments to securing environmentally sustainable future, 166
Carlsen, J., 318
Carnaval de Quebec, 4
Carnevale di Ivrea, 189t
Carnevale di Venezia, 7–8
Carnival (Rio de Janeiro, Brazil), 4t, 9, 351
Carnival Street Party, 114
Carrying capacity, 107, 151
Case studies
   assessing performance management of festivals, 295–96
   BorderFest, 66–67
   Burning Man Festival, 217–18
   Coachella Music and Arts Festival, 240–43
   Edinburgh Festival Fringe, 268–69
   festivals as partners in cultural tourism, 110–13
   leaders, educating, 88–91
   leadership, 322–23

natural capital for festivals, maximizing, 165–66
Out of the Box Festival, 139–40
place-making, 350–51
regional festivals as lens for resilience, 40–43
Songkran Bangkok, Thailand, 17–18
Splendour in the Grass, 192–93
Casino Beef Week Festival, 51–52, 69
Casino Flower and Garden Show, 69
Cause-related marketing, 108
CBD. *See* Central business district (CBD)
Celebration, laws of, 14, 15
CenterFest Arts Festival, 34t, 309
Central business district (CBD), 69, 212, 351
Centre for Sustainable Practice in the Arts, 269
CEO. *See* Chief executive officer (CEO)
Ceremony and ritual, 209–15. *See also* Ritual and spectacle
   community and, 211–12
   festival communities and, 214
   festival place experiences and, 215
   memory and sense of place and, 214
   organizational experience and, 212
   partnerships and, 210
   role of, 209–15
   significance of, 212–14
   sponsors and, 210, 211
   traditional welcome, delivery of, 210
   types of, 209
Certified Festival and Event Executive (CFEE) program, 90, 167, 219
CFEE. *See* Certified Festival and Event Executive (CFEE) program
Challenge
   of attracting and retaining supporters, 125, 125f
   of delivering memorable festival experiences, 215–16
   in resilient festival practices, 26, 27f
   shortcomings, avoiding, 216
Change
   managing, 304–5
   pace of, 307
Charity fundraising, 98, 108, 110
Chatrooms, 234
Chaucer, G., 8
Checklists, 314
Cheese-Rolling Festival, 189t
Chief executive officer (CEO), 80–82
Choices, 338–39
   too many festival elements, 338–39
   too many festivals, 338
   too many people, 339

# INDEX

Chomsky, N., 329
Christianity, 8
*CIRCA! Brisbane (2012)*, 304
City of Festivals, 265
"City of Ice," 264
City of Ottawa Council Special Events, 254
Civic authorities, state-managed festivals and, 290
Cleanup, 182
Clint, M., 325
CMS. *See* Content management systems (CMS)
Coachella Music and Arts Festival, 165–66, 240–43
Co-branding, 98
Co-communicating, 104
Co-designing, 104
Co-developing, 104
Co-evaluating, 104
Collaborating, 118
Collaboration
   in partnerships, 99, 104
   in resilient festival practices, 26, 27f
Collectif de Festivals Montréalais, 33t
Columbus International Film and Video Festival, 39t
Combinational creativity, 176, 177f
Comeout, 175
Come Out Festival, 293
Comments, 283t
Commitment
   as partnership component, 98
   in resilient festival practices, 26, 27f
Communication, 38, 225–28. *See also* Consultation and communication
   customer focus, 227–28
   digital communication tools, 186
   as dimension of quality service interaction, 203
   flashpoints and, 345
   internal and external, 147
   meetings, 83
   objectives, 226
   operational considerations, 162
   as partnership component, 99
   plan, 225–27, 226t
   policy, sharing, 229t
   technology and, 181–82, 182t
Community, 47–71
   capital, 59–60
   ceremony/ritual and, 211–12, 214
   consultation and communication, 54–58
   culture, 61–62

defined, 49, 50
engagement, 101, 245
festivals for creating, 14, 15
festivals of community and place mosaic, 48f
festivals working with, 48–49
healthy, indicators of, 57–59, 58t
implications for, 65t
legacies, 65
lifestyle and livelihood, 50–52
mutual responsibility for, 50t
nature and context of festival or event, 52–53
resilience, 60t
sense of, indicators for, 50t, 66
social implications of festivals, 62, 62t
volunteers and, 86–87
well-being, 60
Community-building, cultural indicators of, 286, 286f, 287t
Community Foundations Gateway, 315
Competence, service quality and, 203
Competition, 128t
   rites of, 209
Competitive advantage, 251
Competitors, as partnership component, 100
Concentration, 125, 125f
Conceptual frameworks for sharing messages, 231t
Conflict resolution, as partnership component, 100
Conifer Research, 121, 122f
Connected life, 2
Consequences, as partnership component, 102
Conspicuous consumption, ritual of, 209
Consultation and communication, 54–58
   active participation, 54
   communities of interest, connections to, 55
   community information, 54, 55
   festival relationships, 55
   internal and external relationships, 55, 56f
   networking with festival partners, 55, 56–57
   as partnership component, 98
   structure, 55
Consumer orientation, 128
Consumption analysis, 129
Content, as partnership component, 98–99

Content management systems (CMS), 237–40
   blogs, 237–38
   definitions, 239–40
   social media/networks/networking, 238–39
Content strategy, 229t
Context
   importance of, 35
   as partnership component, 98
Contracts and controls, as partnership component, 100
Contribution, as partnership component, 101
Cooperation, as partnership component, 99, 104, 118
Coordinating, 118
Copyright infringements, 75
Corporate social responsibility, as partnership component, 102
Corporate support, 128t
Co-supporting, 104
Co-thinking, 104
Coursera, 313
Courtesy, service quality and, 203
Crack Theatre Festival, 191
Craik, J., 111
Crankfest Extreme Youth Fest, 69
Crazes, 188
Creative Carbon Scotland, 269
Creative Director, 81
*Creative Genius* (Fisk), 188
Creative life, 2
Creative Partnerships Australia, 315
Creative spectrums, 183, 184t
Creative tourism, 258
Creativity, 173–96
   business of, 184–85
   challenges, 190–91
   creative festival mosaic, 174f
   creative spectrums and, 183, 184t
   definitions of, 176
   dispersed model for, 188, 189–90
   documentation and, 190
   explaining, 175–84
   festival design and, 182–83
   festival framework and, 178t
   festival programs and, 178–79
   festival sites and, 180–81
   festival technologies and, 181–82, 182t
   heart, starting with, 174–75
   innovation and, 175, 176–78, 191
   inspiration and, interrogating trends for, 187–88
   as partnership component, 99–100

Creativity (cont.)
  post-event issues and, 182
  quirky festival options, 188, 189t
  tourism and, 348
  trajectory, 186–91, 186t
  types of, 176, 177f
Credibility, service quality and, 203
Critical Animals, 191
Crompton, J. L., 11–13, 12f
Crouch, G. I., 251
Crowdfunding, 154, 155
Csikszentmihalyi, M., 124
CTHRC. See Canadian Tourism Human Resource Council (CTHRC)
C3 Presents, 161
Cultural indicators, 286–89, 286f
  of cultural vitality of the community, 286, 286f, 287–88t
  of economic development, 286, 286f, 287t
  of environmental enhancement and regeneration of "place," 286, 286f, 287t
  happiness impact, 288–89
  of health and sustainability of the cultural sector, 286, 286f, 287–88t
  of individual well-being and personal development, 286, 286f, 287t
  in-house vs. outsourcing, 289
  of social capital and community-building, 286, 286f, 287t
  sources of, 287–88t
Cultural tourism, 13, 14, 112–13, 258
  benefits of arts and cultural tourism, 110–11
  destination drivers and, 258
  festivals as partners in, 110–13
  monitoring, 111–12
  shared good-practice objectives for, 111–12
Culture. See also Cultural indicators; Cultural tourism
  community, 61–62
  culture segments framework and, 132
  ecology, diversity of, 35
  exploring, 12
  factors influencing buying behavior, 130, 130f
  personal interests and practices, 122–23
  resilience, reflecting on, 43
  sponsorships, 108, 110

Curtis, J., 324–25
Customer
  focus, communication and, 227–28
  loyalty, 148
  as partnership component, 100–101
Cycle of need, 101

DAC. See Durham Arts Council (DAC)
Dak'Art Biennial of Contemporary African Art, 138t
Darling Harbour Fiesta, 142
Darwin Lions Beer Can Regatta, 189t
Dashboard, 239
Davidson, C., 139
Davis, J., 338
De Bono, E., 231t
Decision making, 129
Decision-making models, 307
Deery, M., 253
Delgado, R. A., 217
Delicious, 239
Delray City Council, 344
Deming, E., 295–96
Demographics, 128t, 280t
Demonstration effect, 53
Derkzen, P., 179
Derrett, P., 19
Design
  creativity and, 182–83
  festival experience and, 127
  networking with festival partners and, 57
  of revitalized festivals, 303–4
Destination competitiveness, 251–52, 252t
Destination drivers, festivals as, 252–60
  brand and image reputation, building, 256–57
  cultural tourism and creative tourism, 258
  leadership, partnership, and governance, 255–56
  placeless festivals, 259–60
  place-making, 258–59
  policy and planning, preparing, 253, 254–55
  positioning, 256
  quality and festivals, 257
Destination image, 112, 347–48
Destination marketing, 162
D'Iberville, Sieur, 9
Digg, 239
Digital media marketing, 231t
Diminished festival experiences, elements of, 206t
Direction, talented and experienced, 36

Direct marketing, 230t
Disney Ice and Snow Wonderland, 264
Dispersed model, 188, 189–90
Distractions, 122
Diwali, India, 6t
DJ equipment, 311t
Documenta, 138t
Documentation
  creativity and, 190
  defined, 280t
  inside festival organization, 279
Dogwhistle Creative, 244–46
Doxey's Irridex Model, 53, 53t
Dragon Award New Talent, 235
Dreaming Festival, 297
Drucker, P., 104, 295–96, 336
Dublin Fringe Festival, 266t
Dublin Writers Festival, 137
Dunstan, G., 14
Durham Arts Council (DAC), 34t, 309
Dwyer, L., 251

Eavis, M., 166, 323
Economic development, cultural indicators of, 286, 286f, 287t
Economic impact, 289–92
  boosterism, festivals and tourism and, 290–91
  buying behavior and, 130f, 131
  of Carnival (Rio de Janeiro, Brazil), 9
  grant-making, 292
  in PESTEL framework, 332
  state-managed festivals, role of civic authorities and, 290
  sustainable festival management implications and, 128t
  of UK 2012 Olympic & Paralympic Games, 288–89
Economy, as partnership component, 101
Edinburgh Festival Fringe, 135, 265, 266t, 268–69
Edinburgh International Book Festival, 136
Edinburgh International Culture Summit, 271
Edinburgh's Hogmanay, 234
Edinburgh Tourism Action Group (ETAG), 234
Edinburgh World Writers' Conference, 271
Edmonton Heritage Festival, 265
Edmonton International Fringe Theatre Festival, 266t
Educational realm of experience, 127
EFA. See European Festivals Association (EFA)

# INDEX

Einstein, A., 275
Electronic word of mouth (eWOM), 239
Eley, B., 234
Embedding, 239
EMBOK. *See* Event Management Body of Knowledge (EMBOK)
EMICS. *See* Event Management-International Competency Standards (EMICS)
Emotional connection, 125f, 126
Empathy, service quality and, 203, 278
Employment patterns and practices, 75, 128t
Endurance, evaluation of, 276–81
   documentation inside festival organization, 279
   evaluation processes, 280–81t
   monitoring and evaluation, 280
   participatory evaluation, 276–77
   personal responses, 277–78
   rationale, 281
   record management, 279–80
   service quality, 278
Energy, 125, 125f
Engagement, 125, 125f
England's National Theatre, 316
Entertainment realm of experience, 127
Environment. *See also* External environments, reacting to
   commitment to, 193
   enhancement and regeneration of "place," cultural indicators of, 286, 286f, 287t
   expectations of, 128t
   festival plan and, 163–66
   good practice, care and attention to, 165–66
   in PESTEL framework, 332
   sustainable future and, initiatives for commitments to securing, 166
Environmental scans, 127–28, 128t
Escapist realm of experience, 127
ETAG. *See* Edinburgh Tourism Action Group (ETAG)
Ethnographic tools, 283t
Etonnants-Voyageurs, 136
Euphoria, 53t
European Festivals Association (EFA), 38, 187, 313
Evaluation, 275–300
   coordinated processes of, 37
   cultural indicators, 286–89, 286f
   documenting, monitoring, and evaluating festivals' mosaic, 276f

economic impacts, 289–92
   of endurance, 276–81
   evaluating, defined, 280t
   legacy of festival, understanding, 294–95
   plans, 282
   post-evaluation, 293–94
   processes, 280–81t
   questions, asking, 283–85
   survey, sample, 284–85t
   tools, 283t
Event blog, 239
Event City Awards, 141
*Eventful Cities* (Richards and Palmer), 254, 351
Event management, areas of, 91
Event Management Body of Knowledge (EMBOK), 81–82, 90–91
   international overview through, 90–91
   knowledge domains, 91, 91t
   purpose of, 81–82
Event Management-International Competency Standards (EMICS), 90
Eventscorp, 33t
EventScotland, 33t, 234
*Events Feasibility and Development* (O'Toole), 167
*Event Studies: Theory, Research and Policy for Planned Events* (Getz), 177
Event Sustainability Management Systems, 148
Event-type tie, 337
EWOM. *See* Electronic word of mouth (eWOM)
Exchange, rites of, 209
Expenditures, 153t
Experience. *See* Festival experience
*Experience Economy* (Pine and Gilmore), 126, 142
Experiential marketing, 202
Exploratory creativity, 176, 177f
Expressive life, 2
External environments, reacting to, 307–17
   audience contributions, 317
   checklists, 314
   foundations, 314–16
   fundraising, 314–16
   funds, 314–16
   income, generating, 316
   life-long learning, 313–14
   observation and participation, 312–13
   outsourcing, 317

   reenvisioning, approach to, 309
   relationships, reassessing, 310
   software packages, 314
   technology trends, 310–12, 311t
   templates, 314
External interactions/socialization, 12
External partners, 150–53
   harm minimization, 150–52, 151t
   research, 152–53

Facebook, 132, 186, 205, 234, 235, 236, 238, 239, 240, 241–42, 283t, 298, 345
Facilities, 37
Fads, 188
Failure, avoiding, 317–20
Fair Day, 61
Falassi, A., 14, 209
Family, buying behavior and, 130f, 131
Fashion, 188
Feast Festival, 293
Feed, 239
Feedback, 132, 133, 283t
Fenton, R., 323
Festival
   core attributes of, 16f
   elements, 4–6, 14–16, 338–39
   enduring festival focus, 8–9
   essentials, summary of, 14–16
   global, 4t, 6t
   historic perspective on communal creativity and celebration, 7–13
   motivation of festival visitors, 11–13, 12f
   nature and role of, 1–14
   origin of, 3
   participants, expectations of, 10–13
   satisfaction experience, 15–16, 16f
   social and cultural phenomena of, 3
   target market, identifying, 10
   today's, essence of, 9–10
Festival communities. *See* Community
Festival experience, 121–26, 122f
   ceremony and ritual and, 209–15
   challenges of, 215–216
   curiosity and, 201
   definitions of, 200, 202
   delivering, 198–221
   designing and delivering, 127
   dimensions of, 202
   economic activity and, 212
   elements of, 206t
   factors of, 203
   festival place and, 215
   flow, 124, 125–26

Festival experience (*cont.*)
    mapping audience journey, 123–24, 124t
    memorable festival guest experience mosaic, 199f
    personal cultural interests and practices, 122–23
    realms of, 127
    service factors and, 202–3
    stakeholder factors and, 205–9
    WOW factor and, 204–5
Festival focus activities
    community and place, festivals connecting to, 69–71
    competitive edge, maintaining global, 272–73
    creativity at all levels of festival-making, ensuring, 195–96
    documenting, monitoring, and evaluating festivals, 299–300
    festival media platforms, 247
    festival team, building and nourishing, 94–95
    festival vision, revisiting and refreshing, 327
    future of festivals, 354–55
    memorable festival experiences, delivering, 221
    nature and roles of festivals, 22–23
    partnerships, building, 116–17
    resourcefulness of festival, 169–71
    secrets of enduring festival success, 45
    target audience, alignment with, 142–43
Festival Fringes, 175, 189
Festival ideas and issues
    community and place, festivals connecting to, 69–71
    competitive edge, maintaining global, 272
    creativity at all levels of festival-making, ensuring, 195
    documenting, monitoring, and evaluating festivals, 299
    festival media platforms, 246–47
    festival team, building and nourishing, 94
    festival vision, revisiting and refreshing, 326
    future of festivals, 354
    memorable festival experiences, delivering, 220–21
    nature and roles of festivals, 21
    partnerships, building, 116–17
    resourcefulness of festival, 169
    secrets of enduring festival success, 45
    target audience, alignment with, 142
Festival model, 343t. *See also* FIST Model
Festival of Dangerous Ideas, 201
Festival of the Flame, 204
Festival organization. *See* Organization
Festival organizer, 84
Festival patrons. *See* Patrons
Festival Producer, 81
Festival Republic, 166
Festivals Adelaide, 175, 293
Festivals Edinburgh, 234, 256, 269, 270–72
Festivals of light, global, 6t
Festival team. *See* Teams
FIFA Games, 254
Film Festival, 293
Financing the festival, 153–55
    budget, 154
    crowdfunding, 154, 155
    expenditures, 153t
    fundraising projects, 155
    income, methods of generating, 154, 155t
Fisk, P., 188
FIST Model, 339, 340–49, 340t
    audience experiences, memorable, 343
    factors incorporated in festival model, 343t
    festival programs, 342
    festival teamwork, 342
    host community engagement, 344–45
    local government engagement, 344
    safe environment, creating, 341–42
    technology, 345–47
    tourism, 347–49
    travel blogs, 347
Fixed costs, 154
Flashpoints, 345
Flickr, 234, 239
Flix in the Stix, 260
Florida, R., 176, 177, 254, 308
*Flourish* (Seligman), 208
Flow, 124, 125–26
Focus group, 283t
Follow, 239
Follower, 239
Force, in FIST Model, 340, 340t
Ford, M., 254
Formal networks, 336
Forums, 239
Foundation Center, 315
Foundations, 314–16
Founders of festival, 76–77
Founding group, 76–77
Foursquare, 238
Foxtel MTV House Party, 298
Framework for festival, creativity and, 178t
Fredline, L., 253
Freeman, R. E., 336
Friedman, A. L., 336
From Inside the Mosaic
    Cameron, N. (director, teacher, author, and consultant), 194–95
    Curtis, J. (Rose Festival CEO), 324–25
    Derrett, P., 19
    festival patrons (Donna, Kay, and Peter), 19–20
    Jackson, J. (CEO/artistic director of LightnUp), 114–16
    Liddell, F. (Festivals Edinburgh director), 270–72
    Mackellar, J. (festival researcher), 68–69
    Meek, G., and Shepherd, L. (principals of Dogwhistle Creative), 244–46
    Noble, P. (Bluesfest festival director), 43–44
    O'Toole, W. (events development specialist), 167–68
    Redford, R. and Polson, J. (festival founders), 91–93
    Schmader, S. (CFEE president and CEO), 219–20
    Terracini, L. (Opera Australia artistic director), 352–54
    Tsai, S. (festival worker), 141–42
    Vance, L. (sponsorship strategist), 297–99
Fruin, J. J., 340t, 341
Funding constraints, 128t
Fundraising, 98, 108, 110, 314–16
    projects, 155
Funds, 314–16
Future Laboratory, 211
Future of festivals, 329–55
    addressing, 330–31
    choices, 338–39
    common sectoral preoccupations regarding, 331
    confronting, 330–31
    FIST Model, 340–49, 340t
    future festivals' mosaic, 330f
    global scenarios, 331–37
    postcard from edge of, 349

Gabowsky, P., 47
Gallery of Modern Art, 139
Gandhi, M., 304
Gantt chart, 227
Gay and lesbian identity and rights, 61
General Managers (GMs), 80–82
Generic digital and online festival marketer, 243–44
Gentlemen of the Road, 260
Geotagging, 239
Getz, D., 3, 13, 55–56, 89, 177, 199, 253, 254, 257, 277, 318, 326, 347
Ghost Festival, 209
Giffreviews, 235
Gilmore, J. H., 126, 142
Gilmore, L., 200, 203
Gilroy Garlic Festival, 50, 51
Giving program, 193
Glasgow 2014 legacy evaluation, 295
Glastonbury Festival, 166, 211, 289, 296
Global competitive edge, maintaining, 249–73. *See also* Global scenarios
  destination competitiveness, 251–52, 252t
  destination drivers, festivals as, 252–60
  globally competitive destinations hosting festivals, challenges for, 266–68
  globally competitive festival mosaic, 250f
  ritual and spectacle, 260–66
  strategy, setting, 250–51
Global festivals, 4t
  fringe, 265, 266, 266t
  of lights, 6t
  writers' festivals, 135, 136–37
Global scenarios, 331–37
  festival quality, 333, 333–34t
  life cycle of festivals, 334–35
  networks, 336–37
  partnerships, 337
  portfolio approach, 335
  stakeholders, 335–36
  survival, chances of, 332–33
Global Village, 192–93
Global writers' festivals, 135, 136–37
Glyndebourne Opera, 316
Goh, C. L., 323
Goldblatt, J., 89, 91, 307, 316
Gonzalez, M., 90
Good-practice objectives, 111–12
  communication with stakeholders, monitoring, 111–12

cultural tourism, monitoring, 111–12
governance through collaborative decision making, monitoring, 111–12
length of stay, increasing, 111
market research, monitoring, 111–12
product development, monitoring, 111–12
repeat visitation, increasing, 111
visitation, encouraging year-round, 111
visitors, increasing distribution of, 111
yield, increasing, 111
Google, 233
Google Analytics, 236
Google Trends, 233
Goteborg International Film Festival, 235
Governance, 41, 42f
  destination drivers and, 255–56
Graham Devlin and Associates, 333
Grand Floral Parade, 291
Grand Tour, 7
Grant-making, 292
Great Steamboat Race, 289
Greener Festival Award, 169, 170
"Green events," 163
Green Festival Alliance, 166
"Greening" festivals, principles of, 166
Greening of the Heart, 115
Grey Cup, 254
Grimwade, S., 81
*Group Genius: The Creative Power of Collaboration* (Sawyer), 175, 176
Guardian Hay Festival of Literature, 136
Gulgong Folk Festival, 278

Hager, A. A., 348
Haggis Adventures, 234
Handa Opera on Sydney Harbour, 353
Happiness impact, 288–89
Harbin Festival, 263, 264
Harm minimization, 150–52, 151t
*Harry Potter* book series (Rowling), 190
Hashtags, 239
Havana Biennial, 138t
Havas Sports and Entertainment (HS&E), 211
Hay (Book) Festival in Hay-on-Wye, 258
Head of Programs, 81

Health and sustainability of cultural sector, 286, 286f, 287–88t
Health services, 162
Healthy community, indicators of, 57–59, 58t
Hedonism, in festival model, 343t
Help End Marijuana Prohibition (HEMP), 61–62
HEMP. *See* Help End Marijuana Prohibition (HEMP)
Henderson, A., 234
Hertzberg, F., 88
Hoopla, 142
Host community engagement, 344–45
Host community residents, mementoes for, 208t
Human resources management, 75
Hybridization, 263
Hydraulic stages, 182t

ICSPE. *See* Queen Margaret University's International Center for the Study of Planned Events (ICSPE)
ICT. *See* Information communication technology (ICT)
IEQF. *See* International Events Qualifications Framework (IEQF)
IFEA. *See* International Festivals and Events Association (IFEA)
Image-building, 230t
Image reputation, 256–57
Imagery, 246
Importance, mutual, 50t
Income, generating, 154, 155t, 316
Indiana State Fair, 161
Individual care, 161
Industry award programs, 38
Informal conversations, 283t
Informal networks, 337
Information, in FIST Model, 340, 340t
Information communication technology (ICT), 233, 314
Infrastructure, 37, 128t
In-house *vs.* outsourcing, 289
Initiatives by public sector through financial commitments from government, 74
Innovation
  creativity and, 175, 176–78, 191
  as partnership component, 99–100
  tourism and, 348
Inputs, defined, 280t
Inside the Mosaic

Inspiration and creativity, interrogating trends for, 187–88
Instagram, 234, 238, 239, 241, 242, 283t
Intellitix, 241
Internal resources, 128t
International Cities of Advanced Sound, 265
International Events Qualifications Framework (IEQF), 90
International Festival of Authors, 136
International Festivals and Events Association (IFEA), 14, 38, 67, 90, 187, 265
    O'Toole, William (Bill) and, 167
    Portland Rose Festival Overall Economic Impact Assessment, 291
    Schmader, Steven Wood and, 219
    social media sites, 236
    Top City Awards, 254
    Webinar professional development program, 254
    World Festival and Event City Awards, 141
International FIFA Fan Festival, 141–42
International Guitar Festival, 293
International Literature Festival, 137
International recognition, 265
Internet, marketing plan and, 232–33
Internship programs, 83
Interview, 283t
Invading and interacting with city, 36
Involvement, in festival model, 343t
IPhonography, 191
ISO 20121, 148, 267
Istanbul Biennial, 138t

Jacaranda Festival, 78t, 188
Jackson, J., 114–16
Jacob's Pillow Dance Festival, 39t
Jago, L., 253
Jaipur Literature Festival, 136
Jobs, S., 302
Jobs and other income-generating activities, 193
Job satisfaction, concept of, 87, 88
Joint responsibilities, 79t

Kanter, R. M., 108
Kemp, R., 265, 266
Kennedy, C., 94
Kentucky Center for the Arts, 201
Kentucky Derby Festival, 77t, 289–90
Key performance indicators (KPIs), 296
Khalayja (a biscuit) Festival, 168
Kickstarter, 155

KidsArtFest, 114–15
Kim, C., 251
Kim, J.-H., 343
Klaic, D., 322
Knowledge, in festival model, 343t
Knowledge domains, 91, 91t
Known group socialization, 12
Kotler, P., 129, 130, 134, 227, 231t
Kotter, J. P., 309
Kotzas, John, 139
KPIs. *See* Key performance indicators (KPIs)
Kristen, C., 217
Kwanzaa, United States, 6t

Lai Heua Fai *(Boats of Light)*, 261–62
Landey, J., 90–91
Landmarks, host community, 65
Lang, G., 323
Lantern Parade/Festival, 114, 116, 179
Larson, M., 55–56
*La Traviata*, 215
Leaders, educating, 88–91
    approaches to, 89
    EMBOK, 90–91
    EMICS, 90
    IEQF, 90
    knowledge domains, 91t
    learning processes, 89
Leadership, 322–23
    acknowledged leaders, 323
    definitions of, 80
    destination drivers and, 255–56
    educating leaders (*See* Leaders, educating)
    job description, example of, 322–23
    model, 80–81
    trademark features of festival leaders, 323
Learning
    to attract and retain audiences, 125, 125f
    experience, buying behavior and, 130f, 131
*Leaving a Greening Legacy: Guidelines for Event Greening*, 166
Legacy of festival, understanding, 294–95
Legal factors in PESTEL framework, 332
Length of stay, increasing, 111
Liburd, J. J., 179
Liddell, F., 257, 270–72
Life cycle
    buying behavior and, 130f, 131
    of festivals, 334–35

Life-long learning, 313–14
Lifestyle
    buying behavior and, 130f, 131
    livelihood and, 50–52
Lighting, 311t
LightnUp, 114–16
LinkedIn, 234, 236
Lismore Regional Gallery, 114–15
List, The, 269
Literary festivals, 135
Litquake, 136
Livability features, 65
"Live Click," 241
Live streaming, 346
Lloyds Banking Group, 288
Local culture, in festival model, 343t
Local government engagement, 344
Locals, respect for, 57
Location, distinctiveness of, 35
Lockerbie, C., 73, 268
Logos and brands in destinations, 65
Loi Krathong Festival, Thailand, 6t
Lollapalooza, 166, 187t
Lollapalooza Severe Weather Plan, 161
London Bloc 2012 Festival, 341–42
London 2012 Paralympic Games, 204
Longevity of festival, elements of, 30
Los Angeles mobile art festival, 191
Love Parade Festival, 160, 339
Loyalty, 122, 123
Loy Krathong, 260, 261–62
Luang Prabang, 261–62
Lupercalia, 8

MacAdam, D., 254
Mackay, H., 231t
Mackellar, J., 68–69
Macquarie Marshes, 214
Mahar, W., 161
*Maintaining the Global Competitive Edge of Edinburgh's Festivals* (AEA Consulting), 35
*Making Adaptive Resilience Real* (Robinson), 75
Manifest of the Wadden Sea Festival, 179
Mapping audience journey, 123–24, 124t
Mapping exercise, 118
Marcouiller, D., 290
Mardi Gras, 7, 8–9
Marketing mechanisms and reach, 134–39
    biennales, 137–38, 138t
    global writers' festivals, 135, 136–37
Marketing mix, 134